PENGUIN BOOKS

THE NIGHT IS LARGE

Martin Gardner was born in 1914 in Tulsa, Oklahoma. In 1936 he took his BA at the University of Chicago, majoring in philosophy, in which he went on to do some graduate work. He worked as a journalist and publicity writer up to the outbreak of the Second World War, during which he served in the United States Navy. Since then he has been a freelance writer. From 1957 to 1982 he wrote a monthly recreational mathematics column in *Scientific American*, which delighted a world-wide audience comprising mathematicians and dreamers, scientists and schoolchildren, computer programmers and poets. He has also contributed to the *Journal of Philosophy*, *Philosophy of Science*, *Philosophy and Phenomenological Research* and other philosophical journals. He edited and wrote the introduction to *The Moscow Puzzles* by Boris A. Kordemsky. Of his many books Penguin publish *Mathematical Puzzles and Diversions*, *More Mathematical Puzzles and Diversions*, *Mathematical Carnival*, *Mathematical Circus*, *Mathematical Magic Show*, *The Ambidextrous Universe* and *The Night is Large*, as well as *The Annotated Alice* and *The Hunting of the Snark*, of which he is editor. Among his other books are *Fads and Fallacies in the Name of Science*, *The Relativity Explosion*, *Logic Machines and Diagrams*, *The Annotated Ancient Mariner*, *Order and Surprise*, *The New Age*, *Science: Good, Bad and Bogus*, *How Not to Test a Psychic*, *The Whys of a Philosophical Scrivener* and *Gardner's Whys and Wherefores*.

Mr Gardner is married and has two sons. His main hobby is conjuring.

MARTIN GARDNER

THE NIGHT IS LARGE

COLLECTED ESSAYS 1938–1995

PENGUIN BOOKS

PENGUIN BOOKS

Published by the Penguin Group
Penguin Books Ltd, 27 Wrights Lane, London W8 5TZ, England
Penguin Books USA Inc., 375 Hudson Street, New York, New York 10014, USA
Penguin Books Australia Ltd, Ringwood, Victoria, Australia
Penguin Books Canada Ltd, 10 Alcorn Avenue, Toronto, Ontario, Canada M4V 3B2
Penguin Books (NZ) Ltd, 182–190 Wairau Road, Auckland 10, New Zealand

Penguin Books Ltd, Registered Offices: Harmondsworth, Middlesex, England

First published in the USA by St. Martin's Press 1996
Published in Penguin Books 1997
1 3 5 7 9 10 8 6 4 2

Printed in England by Clays Ltd, St Ives plc

CONTENTS

viii   *Contents*

FOR CHARLOTTE

Should the wide world roll away,
Leaving black terror,
Limitless night,
Nor God, nor man, nor place to stand
Would be to me essential,
If thou and thy white arms were there,
And the fall to doom a long way.

—STEPHEN CRANE

ILLUSTRATIONS

Man is a small thing,
and the night is very large
and full of wonders

—LORD DUNSANY,
The Laughter of the Gods

INTRODUCTION

Is there a philosophical thread that binds together the diverse chapters of this book, *The Night Is Large*, into some sort of unity? I think there is. It is expressed in the book's title, taken from a character in one of Lord Dunsany's plays, and made explicit in the book's final essay on surprise.

For as long as I can remember I have been impressed, perhaps overwhelmed is more accurate, by the vastness of the universe and the even greater vastness of the darkness that extends beyond the farthest frontiers of scientific knowledge, beyond what Dunsany liked to call "the fields we know."

Suppose physics soon succeeds, as Stephen Hawking and a few other physicists hope and believe, in reducing physics to a single equation or a small set of equations that will "explain" all of nature's fundamental laws. We can then ask the unanswerable question, "Why *this* set of equations?"

It may be true that the big bang was produced by a random quantum fluctuation of nothing. Of course it cannot be nothing in the full sense because there had to be quantum laws, and the source of those laws would remain impenetrable. Why does the universe, as Hawking has recently phrased it, go to all the bother of existing? Why is there something rather than nothing? Things would be so much simpler if nothing, absolutely nothing, existed, not even a God.

Clearly the superultimate question, as philosopher Paul Edwards calls it in *The Encyclopedia of Philosophy*, is cognitively meaningless. But it is not emotionally meaningless. If you have never experienced before those fortunately fleeting moments during which you are suddenly overpowered by the mystery of Being, arousing an emotion of dread (Sartre's novel *Nausea* is about this kind of metaphysical sickness) then you and I are on different wavelengths. There will be pages in this book you will not even understand.

Consider a moment the ancient argument for God based on design. Evolution, operating with random mutations and natural selection, shattered all the old arguments based on the intricate forms and adaptive behavior of living things. Curiously, the big bang has reintroduced the design argument in a much more powerful way. I don't mean powerful in any logical sense—there *are* no logical proofs of God—but powerful in an emotive sense.

Even the most thoroughgoing materialist has to admit that within the mathematical properties of a possibly finite number of fields and particles, the entire universe, including you and me, were there *in potentia*. Given the mathematical structure of those fields and particles, a spot smaller than a pinhead managed to explode and generate a mammoth universe of galaxies, not only suns and planets, but millions of bizarre life-forms on at least one insignificant planet—organisms which finally evolved into strange featherless bipeds capable of wondering how they got here and what it all means, if anything. Immanuel Kant, who overturned the logical force of all arguments for God, recognized that the design argument had such intense emotional impact that it should be treated with enormous respect. Were he alive today he would surely have found that impact strengthened by evolutionary cosmology.

The human mind, with its curious awareness that it exists, is as mysterious as the universe itself. Kant spoke of the two things that most filled him with awe: the starry heavens above and the human mind with its free will and the weird ability to act for good or evil.

Every now and then a philosopher or scientist tries valiantly to do away with the mystery of mind. The latest example is Daniel Dennett in his best-selling *Consciousness Explained*. As several reviewers have observed, consciousness is the one thing Dennett doesn't explain. His book bristles with fascinating information about recent research by neurobiologists and cognitive psychologists, but it no more explains how that complex little bundle of gray matter inside our skulls could become aware of its existence than did endless books by earlier materialists.

In the eighteenth century, Julien Offray de La Mettrie, a French atheist philosopher and physician, wrote an influential book titled *L'homme machine (Man a Machine)*. On a fundamental level there is nothing in Dennett's book that wasn't said by La Mettrie. How Dennett could have failed to mention his distinguished predecessor or even to list *Man a Machine* in his extensive bibliography beats me. The main difference in how Dennett argues is that we now have electronic computers to model the brain rather than mechanical machines of the sort La Mettrie understood.

Dennett's top opponent at the moment is Roger Penrose, the British mathematical physicist. I have no idea whether Penrose is on to something in suggesting that quantum effects may occur in the brain's microtubules. On this we shall have to wait and see. However, as you will learn from my essay, "Computers near the Threshold?," I share Penrose's conviction that the brain is more than just an organic computer, doing nothing more mysterious than switching electrical impulses here and there, and storing memories.

Please do not suppose that either Penrose or I wish to deny that mind is a function of the brain. That isn't at issue. The question is whether we know enough about quantum mechanics, or about undiscovered laws that may underlie quantum mechanics, to explain consciousness and free will. Dennett thinks it is all very clear and easily explained. Indeed, he believes he has explained it. Penrose and I think otherwise. We belong to a small group that has aptly been called the Mysterians. We believe there are deep mysteries about the brain that neurobiologists are nowhere close to solving.

It is this sense of endless, unfathomable magic that envelops almost everything I have written, and which, I hope, is reflected in the essays that I have selected here. We humans are incredibly tiny things in a universe that is huge and full of wonders.

—MARTIN GARDNER
Hendersonville, North Carolina
December, 1995

PART I

PHYSICAL SCIENCE

When I was in high school my ambition was to become a physicist. I planned to go to the California Institute of Technology, but found they would not take a student until he had completed two years of general education elsewhere. At the University of Chicago, then in its Hutchins-Adler Great Books phase, I knew elementary physics well enough to pass a test that allowed me to skip the physical science survey course entirely, though I did attend some of its lectures by Arthur Holly Compton.

Fortunately or unfortunately I got hooked on philosophy, which became my major. I decided to become a writer, rather than a physicist or teacher, though I have done my best to follow the amazing developments in this most fundamental and rigorous of the sciences.

The essays selected here are tinged with philosophical opinions strongly influenced by the views of Bertrand Russell and Rudolf Carnap.

ONE

FEARFUL SYMMETRY

Symmetry is a hot topic these days, not only in mathematics and science, but also in art, music, and word play. The following review of four books about symmetry ran in The New York Review of Books *(December 3, 1992). For more on the topic see my* New Ambidextrous Universe *(Freeman, 1990), a chapter on "Rotations and Reflections" in my* Unexpected Hanging *(Simon & Schuster, 1969), and* Symmetry: A Unifying Concept *(Shelter, 1994), a beautiful work by chemists Istvan and Magdolna Hargittai.*

> *Tyger Tyger, burning bright,*
> *In the forests of the night;*
> *What immortal hand or eye,*
> *Could frame thy fearful symmetry?*

> —WILLIAM BLAKE,
> *"The Tyger"*

When Blake wrote of the Tyger's "fearful symmetry" he was using the noun as a synonym for beauty. Today the word usually means any kind of regular pattern. Geometers sharpen the definition by making symmetry the property of a figure that stays the same after a given operation is performed. A snow crystal, the Star of David, and patterns in a kaleidoscope, for examples, have hexagonal or six-fold symmetry because they look the same after a rotation through any multiple of sixty degrees. You and the tiger have bilateral or mirror reflection symmetry because you both seem unchanged after a mirror has exchanged left and right sides. A wallpaper pattern has translation symmetry, meaning it is unaltered when shifted in any direction. If every other unit of a periodic pattern is reversed by horizontal reflection, such as R Я R Я R Я R . . . the symmetry is called a glide reflection.

The letter A has bilateral symmetry with respect to its vertical axis. H is richer in symmetry because it also looks the same when turned upside down. The letter O, if shaped like a circle, is the most symmetrical of all. In addition to reflection symmetry it has circular symmetry—it stays the same after an infinity of rotations.

Palindromes, such as "Straw? No, too stupid a fad. I put soot on warts," have reversal symmetry with respect to letters. "You can cage a swallow, can't you, but you can't swallow a cage, can you?" is reversible with respect to words. The following poem, by J. A. Lindon, is reversible with respect to lines:

> As I was passing near the jail
> I met a man, but hurried by.
> His face was ghastly, grimly pale.
> He had a gun. I wondered why
> He had. A gun? I wondered . . . why,
> His face was ghastly! Grimly pale,
> I met a man, but hurried by,
> As I was passing near the jail.

Sentences, even musical scores, can be written that have upside down and/or reflection symmetry. NOW NO SWIMS ON MON, a sign by a swimming pool, is the same inverted. CHOICE QUALITY appears on the side of Camel cigarette packages. Turn the words upside down and view them in a mirror. QUALITY is reversed but CHOICE, having a horizontal axis of reflection symmetry, is not.

All these symmetries involve static forms. Physicists broaden the term to cover properties of dynamic systems and their equations. Electrical charge is symmetrical with respect to an interchange of positive and negative. Magnetic force is symmetrical with respect to an interchange of north and south poles. Protons are the same as neutrons after what physicists call a "rotation"—in this case meaning that the spin directions of their three constituent quarks are reversed.

Emmy Noether, an eminent mathematician forced out of Germany because she was Jewish (she died in the United States in 1935), was the first to show that associated with every symmetry is an algebraic structure called a group. The "elements" of a group are operations. A square, for example, stays the same after rotation in either direction through multiples of right angles. A 360-degree turn is the same as no turn at all. This is called the "identity" operation. Four other operations of the square's group are turning it over or reflecting it with respect to its vertical or horizontal axis, or either diagonal. If combining two operations has the same effect as the identity, they are called "inverses" of each other. For example, turning a square 90 degrees in one direction is the inverse of turning it 270 degrees the other way.

It is impossible to understand modern physics without understanding

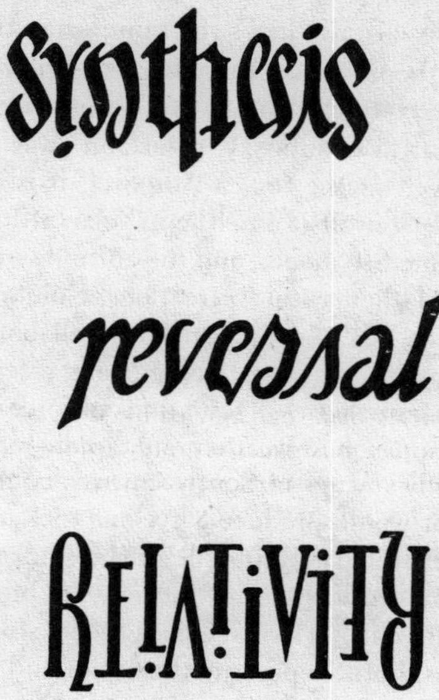

synthesis

reversal

Relativity

Figure 1. Some ambigram inversions by John Langdon

symmetries and groups; above all, without grasping the concept of broken symmetry. Water has spherical symmetry. Like a crystal ball it looks the same no matter how you turn it. But when water freezes, under certain conditions this perfect symmetry shatters to produce the lower but more beautiful hexagonal patterns of snowflakes.

With a bit of glue stick a golf ball to the top of a Mexican sombrero. Viewed from above, the structure has circular symmetry. Without the glue, however, it is unstable. The ball rolls to the brim, breaking circular symmetry but leaving a lower mirror-reflection symmetry. Hold a cork in the center of a bowl of soup and you preserve the system's circular symmetry. Let go. Surface tension breaks the symmetry by floating the cork to one side.

Immediately after the big bang, an unimaginably hot universe had perfect spherical symmetry. As it cooled, this and other symmetries began to vanish. Some of the breaks are fairly well understood, but others remain conjectural. The symmetrical electroweak force, a union of weak and electromagnetic forces, is believed to have been broken into the two forces by what is called the Higgs field, with its quantized Higgs particle. Do Higgs particles exist? Probably, but they are yet to be detected. There are many rival TOEs (Theories of Everything) but all of them place us in a cold universe of broken symmetries.

Several nontechnical books have discussed symmetry, notably Hermann Weyl's classic *Symmetry* (1952), but *Fearful Symmetry: Is God a Geometer?*, by Ian Stewart and Martin Golubitsky, is far and away the most informative and up-to-date book yet on the topic. Moreover, it is entertainingly written and lavishly illustrated. Stewart is a mathematician at England's University of Warwick, author of some fifty books, and the current writer of *Scientific American's* department of Mathematical Recreations. Golubitsky is a University of Houston mathematician. He and Stewart have collaborated on many papers about how symmetry is related to the fast-growing research on chaos theory.

In chaos theory extremely tiny fluctuations in forces that make up a complicated physical system, such as weather, are rapidly magnified. It is said that the flutter of a butterfly's wings in South America could trigger a cascade of causes and effects that would produce a cyclone in Kansas—a storm no meteorologist could have anticipated. In still air the smoke from a cigarette may rise in a straight plume until slight air movements break the symmetry and the plume dissolves into chaotic swirls. Chaos theory studies the ways in which symmetrical structures, both in pure mathematics and in the physical world, can plunge into chaos.

It is one of the great surprises of recent mathematics that seemingly disheveled structures are far from patternless. *Fearful Symmetry* was written after Stewart's popular introduction to chaos, *Does God Play Dice?* (1989). Because symmetry is simpler, and underlies chaos, he regards his new book as a "prequel" to the previous one. On symmetry generally he and Golubitsky write:

> Some symmetries are imposed by human agency. We can *make* a spherical ping-pong ball or a cylindrical coke can. We usually do. Their symmetry is convenient for technological control and development; but we could put fizzy drinks into asymmetric cans if we wanted to. For some reason, we seem to prefer symmetrical things. Aeronautical engineers have done calculations showing that an aircraft with one wing swept back and the other swept forward actually has advantages over the conventional bilaterally symmetric configuration. However, no aircraft manufacturer has yet dared to make a jumbo-jet with a skewed wing: it's unlikely that the public would trust such an ungainly design.
>
> While we may not understand the reasons for this human preference for symmetric objects, it's easy to see how that could lead to their widespread manufacture. Manufacturing processes themselves are conducive to symmetry: it's easier to make lots of copies of the same thing. Human-inspired symmetry isn't such a problem. But symmetries arise in nature, spontaneously, and pose much deeper questions. Raindrops and planets are spherical. Crystals have lattice symmetries. Galaxies are spiral. Waves in the ocean are spaced periodically. The polio virus is an icosahedron. Hornets, hamsters, harriers, herrings, and humans are bilaterally sym-

Figure 2. The symmetry of a splash, from Fearful Symmetry

metric. The methane molecule is a tetrahedron, with a carbon atom at the center and a hydrogen atom at each of the four vertices. A new form of the element carbon, known as "Buckminsterfullerene" after the famous architect, has recently been discovered: it has 60 carbon atoms, arranged at the vertices of a truncated icosahedron. Although designed to human specification, it's proving unusually stable, and is believed to exist naturally in interstellar space.

How does all this symmetry arise?

The common underlying cause seems to be the fact (itself an even deeper mystery) that the universe is "mass-produced"—it's composed of large numbers of identical bits, rolling off the cosmic production line.

The authors introduce broken symmetry by reproducing a classic photograph of the splash produced by a spherical drop of milk falling into a bowl of milk. Because the bowl, drop, and milk all have circular symmetry, the form of the splash is totally unexpected. It is a jeweled crown with twenty-four spikes, each with a tiny bead at its end! As the authors point out, it is something of a paradox that forces of high symmetry can transform a circularly symmetric structure to one of twenty-four-fold symmetry.

Although *Fearful Symmetry* is mainly about symmetry breaking in dynamic systems, many pages are devoted to the static symmetries of the five Platonic (regular) solids and their appearances in nature. The polio virus, for instance, is a tiny 20-faced icosahedron. The methane molecule is a 4-faced tetrahedron. In recent years chemists have created quasicrystals. The authors explain how their remarkable nonperiodic structure is a three-dimensional form of a bizarre tiling, with "almost" five-fold symmetry, discovered by the British mathematical physicist Roger Penrose. More recently chemists have constructed "buckyballs" (buckminsterfullerenes), named after Buckminster Fuller. These molecules have the symmetries of a soccer ball, and who knows what properties?

The book's examples of broken dynamic symmetry are taken from a vast array of both natural and humanmade phenomena. You can learn from *Fearful Symmetry* how to construct, from a disk and elastic bands, a whimsical "catastrophe machine." It has unstable bilateral symmetry which suddenly snaps to asymmetry. You will be introduced to the broken symmetry of plants with helical stalks, the helical patterns of bark on certain trees, and the spiral forms of snail shells. One might expect the dew that glistens along the strands of spider webs to coat each thread smoothly. But no, surface tension breaks the continuity into regular spaced droplets.

Cosmology, as the authors make clear, swarms with broken symmetry. The spherical shapes of stars are demolished by a variety of forces: rotations that bulge equators, vibrations that alter shapes, asymmetrically placed sunspots, and other phenomena. The spiral arms of certain galaxies are broken symmetries probably caused by gravity, though cosmologists are not sure how. Something also not understood has broken the circular symmetry of Saturn's rings into mysterious "spokes." The same planet's north pole is surrounded by a strange hexagonal pattern that slowly rotates. It is called "Godfrey's kinky current," and there is a photograph in the book to prove it exists.

In recent years cosmologists have been shaken by the discovery that the universe is much lumpier than previously suspected. Galaxies clump into enormous bubble-like clusters that surround monstrous voids, and here and there form huge "sheets" or "walls." Exactly what broke the spherical symmetry of the primeval universe into these vast asymmetries is a question now hotly debated.

Once you grasp the concept of symmetry breaking, the authors write, you see it everywhere. In living forms an obvious example is provided by the beautiful symmetry of a freshly laid egg. Its interior is quickly transformed into the complicated bilateral symmetry of a bird or reptile. You and I are broken symmetries of fertilized eggs. Even the bilateral symmetry of animals is broken in hundreds of ways. Examples include the irregular spots on leopards, dogs, and cats, the huge claw of the fiddler crab, flatfish with both eyes on the same side, a bird's crossed bill. Our heart is on the left side.

The authors describe several easily performed experiments in symmetry shattering. Let a hose hang vertically, with water coming from its nozzle. As the flow speed increases, the system's circular symmetry becomes unstable and the hose starts to wobble violently. Rapidly rotating cylinders of water produce surprising patterns of vortices, stripes, and helices. Squashing symmetrical cans and cartons are familiar examples of how our actions can both destroy symmetry and produce new patterns.

A delightful chapter is devoted to time asymmetries in the gaits of horses, elephants, cats, kangaroos, camels, centipedes, and other creatures. A camel's gait has a peculiar way of breaking bilateral time symmetry. Its left legs follow exactly the same movements as its right legs, but half a period out of phase. Most birds flap both wings simultaneously. The authors don't mention it, but the chimney swift flaps them alternately. The chapter is headed by the following stanza:

> A centipede was happy quite,
> Until a frog in fun
> Said, "Pray, which leg comes after which?"
> This raised her mind to such a pitch,
> She lay distracted in a ditch
> Considering how to run.

The highest time symmetry possible is possessed by such steady-state systems as rocks. They may weather over very long time periods, but for shorter periods a rock has greater temporal symmetry than you and I have. However, as the authors confess, we are not inclined to rhapsodize over a stone's "magnificent temporal symmetry."

In their final chapter the authors take up briefly a philosophical question raised by the physicist Eugene Wigner in his often cited paper, "The Unreasonable Effectiveness of Mathematics in the Natural Sciences." How is it that mathematical theorems, obviously invented by human minds, apply so accurately to the outside world? They offer a simple, reasonable, answer: "Mathematics is effective in describing the universe because that's where we got it from." The cosmos, of which we are part, has an astonishingly deep mathematical structure that we only dimly comprehend. "God," declared Plato, "ever geometrizes." Earlier the authors quoted Paul Dirac, one of the great pioneers of quantum mechanics: "One could perhaps describe the situation by saying that God is a mathematician of a very high order, and he used very advanced mathematics in constructing the universe."

In that sense, "Yes," the authors answer the question in their book's subtitle, "God is a geometer." Then they add: "But never forget. She's much better at it than we are."

Four color plates in *Fearful Symmetry* display striking patterns created by computer programs which mix chaos with symmetry. The astonishing fact that out of chaos can emerge beautifully symmetrical patterns is the topic of another impressive book, *Symmetry in Chaos: A Search for Pattern in Mathematics, Art, and Nature*, on which Martin Golubitsky also collaborated. The book's other author, Michael Field, is a mathematician at the University of Sydney. It is an oversize volume with fifty-four full-color plates and more than a hundred illustrations in all. The book overlaps *Fearful Symmetry* in covering basic concepts of symmetry and chaos, but there is greater emphasis on periodic patterns such as wallpaper designs and quilts, and on chaos and fractals.

Fractals are swirling patterns that look the same when portions of them are dilated. Blow up even a very small segment and you will see that it contained the elements of the large one. Chaos and fractals closely intertwine. So many marvelous books have been written about fractals, starting with *The Fractal Geometry of Nature* by Benoit Mandelbrot, the "father of fractal theory," that almost everybody now knows vaguely about them. The authors reproduce a *New Yorker* cartoon by Sidney Harris that shows a living room in which one woman is saying to another, "We did the whole room over in fractals."

Field and Golubitsky are very good in explaining how equations and natural forces can produce stunning chaotic patterns with their "bifurcations" and "strange attractors." The colors, by the way, are arbitrary. Each point or "pixel" on a computer's monitor screen may be visited many times as the pattern evolves in obedience to a program. Colors assigned to the pixels are based on how many times a pixel is visited. For computer buffs, one of the book's appendices gives several programs in BASIC that generate symmetrical chaos patterns.

Symmetry in Chaos begins innocently enough with elementary mathematics, but by the time you get to the end you will have been introduced to nontrivial number theory, group theory, probability theory, and the complex plane. The complex plane is similar to the familiar Cartesian coordinate system except that the horizontal axis represents real numbers, and the vertical axis represents imaginary numbers (products of real numbers and the square root of minus one). Computer pictures of fractals and chaos are generated on the complex plane.

It is almost impossible to write a book about symmetry without reproducing one or more pictures by Maurits Escher, and both books under review are no exceptions. American art critics still ignore Escher, but he has acquired an enormous cult-like following among mathematicians, physicists, and college

Figure 3. M. C. Escher: plane-filling motif with reptiles, 1941

students in general. Scores of prints of his mathematically inspired graphic art are available, and now wrapping paper, T-shirts, scarves, neckties, and even socks feature Escher tesselations.

A dozen books about Escher are in print, but none is as mathematically sophisticated as Doris Schattschneider's *M. C. Escher: Visions of Symmetry*. The author is a mathematician at Moravian College, in Bethlehem, Pennsylvania, and former chief editor of *Mathematics Magazine*. Her book's more than four hundred illustrations, many in color, include almost 180 Escher drawings never before published.

Mrs. Schattschneider devoted fifteen years of research to her book, including trips to the Netherlands to interview friends of the artist. The book was first published in 1990, but I mention it here because it has just been reissued in less expensive paper covers. The author has enlightening comments on individual pictures, and there is an extensive bibliography. It, too, is an excellent introduction to geometrical symmetry.

It may be surprising to learn that a triangle or a quadrilateral of any shape will "tile" the plane periodically—i.e., can be laid edge to edge on a plane, as with tiles on a floor, without overlaps or spaces in between. When polygons have more than four sides, or have curved edges, it is not always easy to decide whether a given shape will tile a surface. There are many fascinating unsolved problems in tiling theory. It is amazing that Escher, who had no formal training in mathematics, would have based his tilings on so many different kinds of planar symmetry, even including technically difficult tesselations of non-Euclidian planes.

On a more recreational level involving wordplay, several oddly talented persons discovered about two decades ago that it is possible to write names and even phrases in such a way that they remain identical when turned upside down or reflected in a mirror. The effect can seem magical. Scott Kim's *Inversions* (1980) was the first book about such hard-to-believe calligraphy. It was followed by Douglas Hofstadter's *Ambigrammi*, published in Italy in 1987, but not yet here. *Wordplay: Ambigrams and Reflections on the Art of Ambigrams*, by John Langdon (for which I wrote a foreword) is the latest collection of this curious symmetry art. They are called ambigrams because they exploit the mind's surprising ability to recognize words even when their letters are distorted in ambiguous ways. The illustrations (see Figure 1) show some of Langdon's constructions. Invert them and try to figure out how they were made.

THE TWIN
PARADOX

It has been said that the best way to learn about a difficult, complex topic is to write a book about it. This was one of my motives when I wrote Relativity for the Million. *Lavishly illustrated by old friend Anthony Ravielli, the book was intended for young readers and for anyone with little or no background in mathematics or physics who wanted to grasp the essentials of Einstein's famous theory. It was originally published by Macmillan in 1962. I revised and updated the book for Vintage, which issued it in a paperback edition in 1976 under the new title* The Relativity Explosion. *I have selected here the chapter on the clock or twin paradox because it has been featured in so many science fiction tales, and because it continues to trouble so many students of relativity theory.*

How did the world's leading scientists and philosophers react when they caught their first glimpse of the strange new world of relativity? The reaction was mixed. Most physicists and astronomers, confused by the violations of common sense and the difficult mathematics of the general theory, maintained a discreet silence. But scientists and philosophers capable of understanding relativity were inclined to accept it with exhilaration. Eddington immediately perceived the greatness of Einstein's achievement. Moritz Schlick, Bertrand Russell, Rudolf Carnap, Ernst Cassirer, Alfred North Whitehead, Hans Reichenbach, and many other eminent philosophers were early enthusiasts who wrote about the theory and tried to clarify its implications. Russell's book *The ABC of Relativity*, first published in 1925, is still one of the best popular accounts of relativity ever written.

Here and there scientists were unable to shake themselves loose from old Newtonian habits of thought. In many ways they resembled the scientists back in the days of Galileo who could not bring themselves to admit that Aristotle might have been mistaken. Michelson himself, a limited mathematician, never accepted relativity, even though his great experiment smoothed the way for the special theory. As late as 1935, when I was an undergraduate at the University of Chicago, I took a course in astronomy from Professor William D. Macmillan, a widely respected scientist. He was openly scornful of relativity.

"We of the present generation are too impatient to wait for anything," Macmillan wrote in 1927. "Within forty years of Michelson's failure to detect the expected motion of the earth with respect to the ether we have wiped out the slate, made a postulate that by no means whatever can the thing be done, and constructed a non-Newtonian mechanics to fit the postulate. The success which has been attained is a marvelous tribute to our intellectual activity and our ingenuity, but I am not so sure with respect to our judgment."[1]

All sorts of objections were raised against relativity. One of the earliest, most persistent objections centered around a paradox that had first been mentioned in 1905 by Einstein himself, in his paper on special relativity. (The word "paradox" is used in the sense of something opposed to common sense, not something logically contradictory.) This paradox is very much in the scientific news today because advances in space flight, coupled with progress in building fantastically accurate timing devices, may soon provide a way to test the paradox in a very direct manner.

The paradox is usually described as a thought experiment involving twins. They synchronize their watches. One twin gets into a spaceship and makes a long trip through space. When he returns, the twins compare watches. According to the special theory of relativity, the traveler's watch will show a slightly earlier time. In other words, time on the spaceship will have gone at a slower rate than time on the earth. So long as the space journey is confined to the solar system, and made at relatively low speeds, this time difference will be negligible. But over long distances, with velocities close to that of light, the "time dilation" (as it is sometimes called) can be large. It is not inconceivable that someday a means will be found by which a spaceship can be slowly accelerated until it reaches a speed only a trifle below that of light. This would make possible visits to other stars in the galaxy, perhaps even trips to other galaxies. So, the twin paradox is more than just a parlor puzzle; someday it may become a common experience of space travelers.

Suppose that the astronaut twin goes a distance of a thousand light-years and returns: a small distance compared with the diameter of our galaxy. Would not the astronaut surely die long before he completes the trip? Would not his trip require, as in so many science-fiction stories, an entire colony of men and women so that generations would live and die while the ship was making its long interstellar voyage?

The answer depends on how fast the ship goes. If it travels just under the limiting speed of light, time within the ship will proceed at a much slower rate. Judged by earth-time, the trip will take more than two thousand years. Judged by the astronaut on the ship, if he travels fast enough, the trip may take only a few decades!

For readers who like specific figures, here is a calculation by Edwin M. McMillan, a nuclear physicist at the University of California in Berkeley. An astronaut travels from the earth to the spiral nebula in Andromeda. Assume that the nebula is 1.5 million light-years from the earth (a conservative estimate; some astronomers believe it is closer to 2 million) and that the ship travels at such speed that the astronaut ages fifty-five years while making the trip there and back. When he returns, he finds that on the earth 3 million years have gone by!

(Note of caution: The reader should regard all references in this book to interstellar or intergalactic space trips, made at speeds close to that of light, as primarily thought experiments intended to clarify aspects of relativity. For a good account of the enormous practical difficulties in obtaining such speeds, see Edward Purcell's contribution to *Interstellar Communication*, edited by A. G. W. Cameron (Benjamin, 1963). "All this stuff about traveling around the universe in space suits," Purcell concludes, "—except for *local* exploration, which I have not discussed—belongs back where it came from, on the cereal box." Perhaps.)

You can see at once that this raises all sorts of fascinating possibilities. A scientist of forty and his teenage laboratory assistant fall in love. They feel that their age difference makes a marriage out of the question. So off he goes on a long space voyage, traveling close to the speed of light. He returns, age forty-one. Meanwhile, on the earth his girl friend has become a woman of thirty-three. Perhaps she could not wait fifteen years for her lover to return; she has married someone else. The scientist cannot bear this. Off he goes on another long trip. Moreover, he is curious to know if a certain theory he has published is going to be confirmed or discarded by later generations. He returns to earth, age forty-two. His former girl friend is long since dead. What is worse, his pet theory has been demolished. Humiliated, he takes an even longer trip, returning at the age of forty-five to see what the world is like a few thousand years hence. Perhaps, like the time traveler in H. G. Wells's story "The Time Machine," he will find that humanity has become obsolete. Now he is stranded. Wells's time machine could go both ways, but our lonely scientist has no means of getting back into the stream of human history where he belongs.

Unusual moral questions would arise if this sort of time travel became possible. Is there anything wrong, for instance, in a girl marrying her own great-great-great-great-great-great-grandson?

Please note: This kind of time travel avoids all the logical traps that plague science fiction, such as dropping into the past to kill your parents before you are born, or whisking into the future and shooting yourself between the eyes. Consider, for example, the plight of Miss Bright in that familiar limerick:

> There was a young lady named Bright,
> Who traveled much faster than light.
> She started one day
> In the relative way,
> And returned on the previous night.[2]

If she returned on the previous night, then she must have encountered a duplicate of herself. Otherwise it would not have been truly the night before. But there could not have been two Miss Brights the night before because the time-traveling Miss Bright left with no memory of having met her duplicate yesterday. So you see, there is a clear-cut contradiction. Time travel of *that* sort is not logically possible unless the existence of parallel worlds running along branching time tracks is assumed. Even with this gimmick, matters become quite complicated.

Note also that Einstein's form of time travel does not confer upon the traveler any genuine immortality, or even longevity. As far as *he* is concerned, he always ages at the normal rate. It is only the earth's "proper time" that for the traveler seems to gallop along at breakneck speed.

Henri Bergson, the famous French philosopher, was the most eminent thinker to cross swords with Einstein over the twin paradox. He wrote about it at some length, poking fun at what he thought were its logical absurdities. Unfortunately, what he wrote only proves that it is possible to be a great philosopher without knowing much about mathematics.[3] In the 1970s the same objections were raised again. Herbert Dingle, an English physicist, refused to believe the paradox. Until his death in 1978 he wrote many witty articles about it and accused other relativity experts of being either obtuse or evasive. The superficial analysis to be given here certainly will not clear up this controversy, which quickly plunges into complicated equations, but it will explain in a general way why there is almost universal agreement among experts that the twin paradox will really carry through in just the manner Einstein described.

Dingle's objection, the strongest that can be made against the paradox, is stated this way. According to the general theory of relativity, there is no absolute motion of any sort, no "preferred" frame of reference. It is always possible to choose a moving object as a fixed frame of reference without doing violence to any natural law. When the earth is chosen as a frame, the astronaut makes the long journey, returns, finds himself younger than his stay-at-home brother. All well and good. But what happens when the spaceship is taken as the frame of reference? Now it must be assumed that the earth makes a long journey away from the ship and back again. In this case it is the twin on the ship who is the stay-at-home. When the earth gets back to the space-ship, will not the earth rider be the younger? If so, the situation is more than a paradoxical affront to common sense; it is a flat logical contradiction. Clearly, each twin cannot be younger than the other.

Dingle stated it this way: Either the assumption must be made that after the trip the twins will be exactly the same age or relativity must be discarded.

Without going into any of the actual computations, it is not hard to understand why the alternatives are not so drastic as Dingle would have us believe. It is true that all motion is relative, but in this case there is one all-important difference between the relative motion of the astronaut and the relative motion of the stay-at-home. *The stay-at-home does not move relative to the universe.*

How does this affect the paradox?

Assume that the astronaut is off to visit Planet X, somewhere in the galaxy. He travels at a constant speed. The stay-at-home's watch is attached to the inertial frame of the earth, on which there is agreement among clocks because they are all relatively motionless with respect to each other. The astronaut's watch is attached to a different inertial frame, the frame of the ship. If the ship just kept on going forever, there would be no paradox because there would be no way to compare the two watches. But the ship has to stop and turn around at Planet X. When it does so, there is a change from an inertial frame moving away from the earth to a new inertial frame moving toward the earth. This shift is accompanied by enormous inertial forces as the ship accelerates during the turnaround. In fact, if the acceleration during the turnaround were too great, the astronaut (and not his twin on the earth) would be killed. These inertial forces arise, of course, because the astronaut is accelerating with respect to the universe. They do not arise on the earth, because the earth is not undergoing similar acceleration.

From one point of view it can be said that the inertial forces produced by this acceleration "cause" a slowing down of the astronaut's watch; from another point of view the acceleration merely indicates a shift of inertial frames. Because of this shift, the world line of the spaceship—its path when plotted on Minkowski's four-dimensional graph of space-time—becomes a path on which the total "proper time" of the round trip is less than the total proper time along the world line of the stay-at-home twin.[4] Although acceleration is involved in the shifting of inertial frames, the actual computation involves nothing more than the equations of the special theory.

Dingle's objection still remains, however, because exactly the same calculations can be made by supposing that the spaceship instead of the earth is the fixed frame of reference. Now it is the earth that moves away, shifts inertial frames, comes back again. Why wouldn't the same calculations, with the same equations, show that earth-time slowed down the same way? They would indeed if it were not for one gigantic fact: when the earth moves away, *the entire universe moves with it.* When the earth executes its turnaround, the universe does also. This accelerating universe generates a powerful gravitational field. As explained earlier, gravity has a slowing effect on clocks. A clock on the sun, for instance, would tick more slowly than the same clock on earth, more slowly on the earth than on the moon. Now, it turns out, when all the proper calculations are made, that the gravitational field generated by the accelerating cosmos slows down the spaceship clocks until they differ from earth clocks by precisely the same amount as before. This gravity field has, of course, no effect on earth clocks. The earth does not move relative to the cosmos; therefore, there is no gravitational field with respect to the earth.

It is instructive to imagine a situation in which the same time difference results, even though no accelerations are involved. Spaceship A passes the earth with uniform speed, on its way to Planet X. As the ship passes the earth it sets its clock at zero time. Ship A continues with uniform velocity to Planet X, where it passes spaceship B, moving with uniform speed in the opposite direction. As the ships pass, A radios to B the amount of time (measured by its own clock) that has elapsed since it passed the earth. Ship B notes this information and continues with uniform speed to the earth. As it passes the earth it radios to the earth the length of time A took to make the trip from the earth to Planet X, together with the length of time it took B (measured by its own clock) to make the trip from Planet X to earth. The total of these two periods of time will be less than the time (measured by earth clocks) that has elapsed between the moment that ship A passed the earth and the moment that ship B passed the earth.

This difference in time can be calculated by the equations of the special theory. No accelerations of any sort are involved. Of course, now there is no twin paradox because there is no astronaut who goes out and comes back. It can be supposed that the traveling twin rides out on ship A, then transfers to ship B and rides back, but there is no way he can do this without transferring from one inertial frame to another. To make the transfer he must undergo incredibly strong inertial forces. These forces indicate his shift of inertial frames. If we wish, we can say that the inertial forces slow down his clock. However, if the whole episode is viewed from the standpoint of the traveling twin, taking him as the fixed frame of reference, then a shifting cosmos that sets up gravitational fields enters the picture. (A major source of confusion in discussing the twin paradox is that the situation can be described in so many different verbal ways.) Regardless of the point of view adopted, the equations of relativity give the same time difference. This difference can be accounted for by the special theory alone. It is only to counter the objection raised by Dingle that the general theory must be brought into the picture.

It cannot be stated too often that it is not correct to ask which situation is "right": Does the traveling twin move out and back or do the stay-at-home and the cosmos move out and back? There is only *one* situation: a relative motion of the twins. There are, however, two different ways of talking about it. In one language, a change of inertial frames on the part of the astronaut, with its resulting inertial forces, accounts for the difference in aging. In the other language, gravitational forces overbalance the effect of a change of inertial frames on the part of the earth. *From either point of view, the stay-at-home and the cosmos do not move relative to one another.* Thus the situation is entirely different for each man, even though the relativity of motion is strictly preserved. The paradoxical difference in aging is accounted for, regardless of which twin is taken to be at rest. There is no need to discard the theory of relativity.

An interesting question can now be asked: What if the cosmos contained nothing except two spaceships, A and B? Ship A turns on its rocket engines, makes a long trip, comes back. Would the previously synchronized clocks on the two ships be the same?

The answer depends on whether you adopt Eddington's view of inertia or the Machian view of Dennis Sciama. In Eddington's view the answer is yes. Ship A accelerates with respect to the metric space-time structure of the cosmos; ship B does not. The situation remains unsymmetrical and the usual difference in aging results. From Sciama's point of view the answer is no. Acceleration is meaningless except with respect to other material bodies. In this case, the only material bodies are the two spaceships. The situation is perfectly symmetrical. In fact, there are no inertial frames to speak of because there is no inertia (except an extremely feeble, negligible inertia resulting from the presence of the two ships). In a cosmos without inertia it is hard to predict what would happen if a ship turned on its rocket motors! As Sciama said with British understatement, "Life would be quite different in such a universe."

Because the slowing of the traveling twin's time can be viewed as a gravitational effect, any experiment that shows a slowing of time by gravity provides a kind of indirect confirmation of the twin paradox. There have been such confirmations by means of a wonderful laboratory tool called the Mössbauer effect.[5] A young German physicist named Rudolf L. Mössbauer discovered, in 1958, how to make a "nuclear clock" that keeps unbelievably accurate time. Imagine one clock ticking five times every second and another clock ticking at so nearly the same rate that after a million million ticks it has lost only one hundredth of a tick. The Mössbauer effect is capable of detecting at once that the second clock is slower than the first! Experiments using the Mössbauer effect have shown that time near the bottom of a building (where gravity is stronger) is a bit slower than time near the top of the same building. "A typist working on the first floor of the Empire State Building," Gamow observed, "will age slower than her twin sister working on the top floor." The difference in aging is, of course, infinitesimal; nevertheless, it is real and can be measured.

Physicists have also discovered, using the Mössbauer effect, that a nuclear clock slows down a bit when placed on the edge of a rapidly rotating disk as small as six inches in diameter. The revolving clock can be viewed as the traveling twin who undergoes constant changes of inertial frames (or alternatively, as the twin affected by a gravitational field if the disk is assumed at rest and the cosmos rotating), so this provides an excellent test of the twin paradox. The twin effect is also evident in the slower aging of muons, making circular trips in magnetic fields, as compared with muons that "stay at home."

A more direct test was made in 1971 by Joseph Hafale and Richard Keating. They carried four atomic clocks around the earth on commercial jetliners, first circling the earth eastward, then making a western round trip. The eastward plane moved faster (relative to the universe) than the westward plane. Compared to a reference clock in Washington, the traveling clocks performed as expected. They lost time on the eastward trip, gained time on the westward trip. *Scientific American* (September 1972) called it the cheapest test ever made of relativity. It cost about $8,000, of which $7,600 was for air fare.

The time is rapidly approaching when an astronaut can make the final, definitive test by carrying a nuclear clock with him on a long space voyage. No physicist doubts anymore that the astronaut's clock, when he returns, will be slightly out of phase with a nuclear clock that stayed at home.

POSTSCRIPT (1995)

Herbert Dingle died in 1978, age eighty-eight, still raging against the physics "establishment" for its conspiracy to silence his incessant attacks on relativity theory. Mendel Sachs, a physicist at State University of New York, at Buffalo, is now almost the sole opponent of the twin paradox. Dingle agreed that relativity theory predicted the paradox, and that this proves relativity to be false. Sachs, on the other hand, in many papers and in his 1993 book Relativity in Our Times, *argues that relativity theory does* not *entail the paradox, and that Einstein blundered when he thought it did.*

For a more detailed account of the paradox see chapter 2 of Paul Davies's 1995 book About Time: Einstein's Unfinished Revolution.

NOTES

1. From Macmillan's contribution to A *Debate on the Theory of Relativity*, by Robert D. Carmichael and others (La Salle, Ill.: Open Court Publishing Company, 1927).

2. This limerick about Miss Bright was written by A. H. Reginald Buller, a professor of botany at the University of Manitoba, and first published in *Punch*. The contradiction that arises from Miss Bright's journey back in time also applies to "tachyons" (conjectured particles that go faster than light) if tachyons can be used for transmitting signals. See my

chapter on time travel in *Time Travel and Other Mathematical Bewilderments* (W. H. Freeman, 1988).

3. Bergson's attack is in his book *Durée et Simultanéité* (3rd ed.; Paris, 1926). In the United States the same naïve arguments were repeated by philosophers William Pepperell Montague and Arthur Oncken Lovejoy. See Montague's "The Einstein Theory and a Possible Alternative," *Philosophical Review*, Vol. 33 (March 1924), pages 143–170. (Montague's alternative is the assumption—physicists now call it the Ritz theory—that light *is* influenced by the motion of its source; his attacks on Einstein reveal an amazing lack of comprehension of relativity theory.) For Lovejoy's attack on the twin paradox, see "The Paradox of the Time-Retarding Journey, Part I," *Philosophical Review*, Vol. 40 (January 1931), pages 48–68; Part II appeared in the March issue, same volume, pages 152–167. Lovejoy concludes that Bergson is right: there are many "fictitious times" but "only one real time." Evander Bradley McGilvary rebuts Lovejoy in the July issue, pages 358–379, but Lovejoy, unconvinced, replies in November, pages 549–567.

4. To see exactly how this works out mathematically, read the excellent article on "The Clock Paradox in Relativity Theory," by Alfred Schild, in *American Mathematical Monthly* (January 1959).

5. See Sergio DeBenedetti, "The Mössbauer Effect," *Scientific American* (March 1960).

THREE

QUANTUM WEIRDNESS

I do not believe that the weirdness of quantum mechanics in any way negates the reality of a universe, mathematically structured, that exists independently of minds. Assume with physicist John Wheeler that intelligent creatures exist nowhere in the universe except here on earth. Assume further that a nuclear war destroys all life on our planet, and that no life flourishes anywhere else. Can anyone seriously believe that the entire cosmos, with its billions upon billions of galaxies, would go out like a blown candle flame?

My defense of realism in the face of quantum weirdness was published in Discover (October 1982). It was illustrated with a painting of an eye observing a tree. The original now hangs above my desk, reminding me that trees exist even when no one is observing them. For this article I had the honor of receiving from the American Institute of Physics and the United States Steel Foundation their annual science writing award of 1983.

Some is balls and some is strikes, but until I calls 'em, they ain't nothin'.
—REMARK ATTRIBUTED TO VARIOUS BIG-LEAGUE UMPIRES

In the early eighteenth century the Anglican bishop George Berkeley (for whom, by the way, Berkeley, California, was named) startled the philosophical world by arguing, with great subtlety, that nothing can exist unless it is perceived by a mind. To be is to be perceived. Why, then, does a tree seem to keep existing when no one looks at it? Monsignor Ronald Knox expressed it this way:

> *There once was a man who said: "God*
> *Must think it exceedingly odd*
> *   If he finds that this tree*
> *   Continues to be*
> *When there's no one about in the Quad."*

The answer was supplied by an anonymous author in an equally famous limerick:

> *Dear Sir, your astonishment's odd.*
> *I am always about in the Quad.*
> > *And that's why the tree*
> > *Will continue to be*
> *Since observed by yours faithfully,* GOD.

Berkeley restored the objective universe, in all its rich variety, by redefining matter as part of the mind of God. Indeed, he thought his philosophy provided a new proof of God's existence. Modern physicists hesitate to make this metaphysical jump, but more recently a number of experts on quantum mechanics, notably the late Nobel Prize–winner Eugene Wigner and John Wheeler of the University of Texas, have defended a point of view curiously close to Berkeley's. Their position, which some physicists have called "quantum solipsism," had a strong influence (much to Wheeler's dismay) on younger physicists and science writers who have dipped into Eastern religions and parapsychology. It has produced a spate of eccentric but popular books such as Fritjof Capra's *The Tao of Physics*, Gary Zukov's *The Dancing Wu Li Masters*, Michael Talbot's *Mysticism and the New Physics*, and (the worst of the lot) *Space-Time and Beyond*, by Bob Toben and Fred Alan Wolf.

Quantum solipsism is a response to the fact that quantum mechanics (QM)—a universally accepted mathematical theory that describes and predicts the properties and behavior of matter—is saturated with dazzling paradoxes that seem to suggest that the external world has no well-defined structure until minds observe it. It was quantum theory that established, for example, the dual nature of light, which can be described either as an energy wave or as a stream of quanta (tiny packets of energy). QM replaced the strict causal determinism of classical physics with statistical laws about events in which randomness is so fundamental that Einstein was forced to protest that he could not believe that God plays dice with the universe. Although the laws of QM have been confirmed with great accuracy, they also display what physicist Heinz Pagels, in his marvelous book, *The Cosmic Code*, called "quantum weirdness." It is a weirdness that springs from the dark mystery of what happens when the wave function of a quantum system is "reduced" or "collapsed" by the act of measurement.

In QM, the wave function is a mathematical expression that describes a particle (an electron or a photon, for example) or a system of particles (a molecule or a tree or a solar system) and how it changes in time. The function gives the probabilities that when the system is measured certain variables— such as position, velocity, momentum, energy, and spin—will acquire certain values. The probabilities are not the same as in, say, flipping a penny; it is only our ignorance of the many forces operating on the penny that makes it impossible to predict heads or tails with better than 50 percent accuracy. In the case of the particle there are no forces in or near the particle, no local "hidden variables," that cause it to acquire definite properties when it is measured. It is as if nature makes no decision about these properties until the instant of measurement, and then the decision is made by pure chance.

Unfortunately, QM also tells us that as soon as a wave function is reduced to definite values by measurement, the entire system, which now includes the measuring apparatus, acquires a new wave function that gives only probabilities for the properties that will be found if the entire system is measured. This leads directly to a notorious thought experiment known as the paradox of Schrödinger's cat (after Erwin Schrödinger, one of the giant architects of QM, who first proposed it).

Imagine a cat inside a closed opaque box. The box contains a radioactive substance that has a 50 percent chance of emitting an electron within a given time interval. The electron will produce a click in a Geiger counter, which in turn will trigger a mechanism that will kill the cat. Because the entire system has a wave function that gives only probabilities until the system is observed, QM seems to say that at the end of the time interval the cat is neither alive nor dead until someone looks into the box. This observation then collapses the wave function, and at that instant the cat acquires the definite property of being dead or alive. Before observation, aliveness and deadness are somehow, in a way nobody understands, fused with equal probability in the wave function that describes the cat-box system.

Suppose the box is opened by a friend of Wigner's, who sees whether the cat is alive or dead. The box, cat, and friend now form a larger quantum system with a more complex wave function in which the state of the cat and the state of the friend's mind are indefinite until observed by Wigner or someone else. Physicists call this the paradox of Wigner's friend. It leads to an infinite regress. If Wigner observes a friend who observes the cat, the total system of box-cat-friend-Wigner remains indefinite (the cat still not alive or dead) until observed by a third person, and so on. The regress is sometimes called the von Neumann catastrophe, because it seems to follow from a classic formalization of QM by the great Hungarian mathematician John von Neumann.

In his collection of essays, *Symmetries and Reflections* (1967), Wigner argues that the regress is *not* infinite. It ends as soon as a conscious mind interrupts the chain of wave-function reductions. Only a mind, so goes his reasoning, has the faculty of introspection that allows it to *know* that "I am in such and such a state." To be "even more painfully precise," Wigner adds, it is "my own consciousness, since I am the only observer, all other people being the object of my observations." A friend who observes the cat will know if the animal is alive or dead, but until Wigner observes his friend, the cat *for Wigner* is still in an indefinite state.

Wigner confesses that he finds even the permanence of such things as trees "profoundly baffling." Because a tree is a quantum system, it too seems to have no definite properties until its wave function is reduced by observation. Since for Wigner his own consciousness is the fundamental reality, objects that seem to be "out there" are little more than useful constructs inferred from the regularities of his experience. He quotes with approval a statement by Schrödinger: "Would it [the world] otherwise [without conscious observers] have remained a play before empty benches, not existing for anybody, thus quite properly not existing?"

Most physicists do not buy this collective solipsism. They believe there are final reductions of wave functions whenever a macro event (an event above the subatomic level) occurs that cannot be time-reversed, such as the death of a cat, the registering of a particle's bubble-chamber track on film, the sound recording of a Geiger-counter click. Although Wigner seldom invokes Berkeley, or any other philosopher who wrestled with similar problems, his views seem to force him to say that a tree has no definite properties, and therefore only a vague existence, until a conscious mind perceives it.

Wheeler, in numerous papers, has taken a similar though less extreme tack. QM does indeed force us to deny, he says, that on the micro (or subatomic) level there is an external world of precise structure, independent of minds. "No elementary phenomenon is a phenomenon until it is an observed phenomenon." In some strange sense the universe is what Wheeler calls a "participatory universe." We are not observing something out there, behind a thick glass wall, Wheeler says. We must shatter the glass and influence the state of what we see.

In Wheeler's stupendous cosmological vision, there is an infinity of oscillating universes continually being born in big bangs and eventually dying in big crunches. Each universe has its own set of physical constants that arise by chance from its fireball. These constants must be finely tuned to allow the formation of suns and planets, and even more carefully tuned to permit life. Indeed, Wheeler believes, life is so unlikely that we are probably the only intelligent life anywhere in the entire cosmos. Moreover, unless a universe is so finely tuned as to allow conscious minds to evolve, it cannot be observed and so is not really real in any strong sense. An unobserved photon has a vague kind of reality, yes; but for Wheeler it is of a "paler and more theoretic hue" than the reality of an observed photon.

The last quotation is from Wheeler's book *Frontiers of Time* (1978). In this book and elsewhere he proposes a fantastic thought experiment known as the delayed-choice test. It is a variation of the famous experiment involving a screen with two slits. A photon comes through one slit (like a particle) if measured by one kind of detector, or through both (like a wave) if measured by another detector—an experiment that demonstrates the dual nature of light. Suppose, says Wheeler, we wait until the photon has gone through the screen, then quickly decide which detector to use. Will not our decision determine which of two events (passage through one or two slits) took place in the past?

There is no alteration of the past, Wheeler makes clear, but rather a bringing of the past into existence. Our choice of measuring instrument determines whether the photon has penetrated the screen like a particle going through one slit or like a wave going through two. But this, says Wheeler, is a misleading way to put it. The photon *has* no precise past until we measure it! Perhaps the entire universe is like a delayed-choice experiment. It starts with the singularity of the Big Bang, then grows larger and more complex until finally it creates a giant eye (our consciousness) by which it observes itself, and in this way "imparts tangible reality to even the earliest days of the universe."

More recently Wheeler has stated his belief that "observation" in QM need not involve a mind. It can be made by instruments, such as a Geiger counter, a bubble chamber, a grain of silver bromide, the retina of an eye, and so on. Records left by such measurements are macro structures as unalterable by minds as rocks and trees. Only on the micro level does an unobserved structure have a reality of paler and more theoretic hue. Like Niels Bohr before him, Wheeler does not push his solipsism to the Wignerian point at which one is puzzled by the persistence of rocks and trees. Nevertheless, on the quantum level, which underlies everything else, reality for both Bohr and Wheeler remains rather formless until it interacts with macro objects that ultimately will be observed by minds.

No physicist denies that a quantum particle is a ghostly thing for which it is impossible to build consistent models using the space-time of classical Einsteinian physics. There is a sense in which an electron does not "exist" until it is measured. Nobody knows if its wave function is linked to waves as real as water or sound waves, or whether the function is as fictitious as the probability function that tells us a die will show any face with equal probability when it is tossed, or whether the function describes some third kind of thing that nobody yet understands. But from the ghostliness of an electron it does not follow, at least for most physicists, that a stone or a tree is equally ghostly.

The notion of both Wheeler and Wigner that a universe without conscious observers cannot be said to exist in a strong sense, on its fundamental level, is surely laced with difficulties. Does a chimpanzee have enough consciousness to give full reality to a universe? And if a chimp does, why not a bird or a fish? As Einstein remarked at one of Wheeler's Princeton seminars, "It is difficult to believe that such a description [QM] is complete. It seems to make the world quite nebulous unless someone, like a mouse, is looking at it."

Suppose the mechanism in Schrödinger's box does not kill the cat but only chops off an ear. Is the cat's consciousness strong enough to cut the chain of wave-function reductions, or is a human mind needed to make definite what happened to the cat? Must we say that the universe was only partly real before life appeared, and is slowly becoming more real as life evolves higher forms of consciousness?

As a result of later experiments, there was a marked revival of interest in another famous paradox of QM. It is known as the EPR paradox, after the initials of Einstein and two younger friends, Boris Podolsky and Nathan Rosen, who collaborated on a paper about it in 1935.

The EPR paradox has many variants. One of the simplest involves two photons that speed off in opposite directions when an electron and its antimatter equivalent, a positron, annihilate each other. No matter how far apart they get—it could be millions of light-years—they remain "correlated" in the sense that certain of their properties have opposite values. If, for example, photon A is measured for its spin and the result is +1, the spin of photon B must be −1. Recall that a particle does not have a definite spin before it is measured. According to QM, the photon's wave function dictates that at the moment of measurement nature decides to give it a plus or minus spin with equal probability. Thus if you measure a stream of photons, you get a sequence of plus and minus spins that are as randomly distributed as the heads-tails sequence obtained by flipping a coin.

Now we are in a terrible predicament. How can measuring photon A collapse the wave function of B (thus giving it a spin opposite that of A's), which may be millions of light-years away and is connected in no known causal way with its twin? Many physicists hoped and believed that the two particles remain correlated because of hidden variables inside or near them, like the correlation between two spinning Frisbees that are simultaneously tossed in opposite directions, one with each hand. Alas, experiments that violate a beautiful but highly complex theorem discovered in 1965 by John Bell have ruled out all hidden variables as an explanation for particle correlation.

Bell's theorem provided a way of testing the EPR paradox in a laboratory, and since 1965 many such tests have confirmed the paradox. One of them was a sophisticated experiment by French scientists reported in the July 30, 1982 issue of *Science*. It is no longer a thought experiment. Somehow one particle "knows" instantly (or almost instantly) the outcome of a measurement of the other particle. In no way does this violate relativity's rule that energy and signals cannot go faster than light. You can no more send a coded message by correlated photons than you can send a message by transmitting a sequence of heads and tails generated by flipping a coin. If there were some way to force a photon to acquire a desired spin when it is measured, it would be easy to use photon correlations to send coded messages faster than light. But QM forbids such forcing because it would destroy the irreducible randomness that is at the heart of quantum theory.

Nevertheless, the EPR paradox does suggest that distant parts of the universe are connected in some peculiar way not yet understood, a way that permits quantum information to travel faster than light. One of the strangest explanations put forth came from Costa de Beauregard, a respected French physicist who shares with Brian Josephson (the Welsh Nobel Prize-winner who abandoned physics many years ago to investigate Transcendental Meditation and the paranormal) the belief that QM is the key to the claimed phenomena of parapsychology. Quantum information, said Beauregard, travels backward in time from photon A, when it is measured, to the instant the two particles were created. Then it goes forward in time to photon B, arriving there at the precise moment it left A!

The EPR paradox disturbed Einstein profoundly. That measuring a particle could collapse the wave function of another particle many miles away seemed to him as absurd as the collapse of a person in Paris when a witch doctor in Haiti stabs a doll. And there were other aspects of QM that troubled him. As a disciple of Spinoza, who believed that every event in nature is completely determined by prior causes, Einstein could not abide the absolute chance at the heart of QM. But most of all he objected to QM because it seems to imply that on its most fundamental level the universe does not have a structure independent of human minds.

During the last decades of Einstein's life, his misgivings about QM isolated him from colleagues, who spoke with sadness about their "lost leader." Today, now that the EPR paradox is being dramatically confirmed around the world, some physicists are beginning to worry about it as much as Einstein did. Is it possible that the old maestro's intuitions were not so foolish after all? At any rate, many young physicists are now working on ingenious theories designed to replace QM with a deeper theory in which QM becomes a limiting case, a kind of first approximation, somewhat as Newton's theory of gravity became a limiting case of general relativity. Newton's laws work well for the ordinary velocities and masses on earth. But they are not accurate enough to account for phenomena that involve massive stars and velocities close to the speed of light.

In several later papers Wheeler likened the measurement problem in QM to a game of Twenty Questions he once played with a group of prankish friends. Unknown to Wheeler, they had agreed to have no word in mind when he began questioning. They answered yes or no at random, but with the proviso each would have at least one word in mind that fitted all the previous answers. Eventually Wheeler and the group narrowed the word down to "cloud." The point is that, in terms of the game, the word did not exist until it was created by Wheeler's interaction with his friends.

It seems to me that the Twenty Questions analogy applies only to properties of particles, not to the reality behind those properties. A particle may indeed have no precise position or momentum until it is measured. It may not even have an exact path in the past. But unless one is an extreme solipsist, one must believe in some kind of structured reality supporting the properties that is as mind-independent as the tree no one observes.

Consider a rainbow. It is as observer-dependent as an electron. Nothing is "out there" that deserves to be called *the* rainbow. Each person sees a different bow, a bow that has no position in space until it is observed. In a sense the bow has no reality apart from its observation. On the other hand, the bow is mind-independent in the sense that it can be photographed. It is a pattern that rests firmly on a structure of relations between falling raindrops, light from the sun, and an eye or a camera lens. Even the green of a leaf depends on a set of relations between leaf, light, and an observer. In no way does this justify a solipsism that insists a leaf has no reality until it is observed, or that quantum waves and particles have no reality until observed.

Here is how Einstein, in an essay on "Physics and Reality," looked at the way scientists choose their words when they play the question game with nature: "The liberty of choice, however, is of a special kind; it is not in any way similar to the liberty of a writer of fiction. Rather, it is similar to that of a man engaged in solving a well designed word puzzle. He may, it is true, propose any word as the solution; but, there is only *one* word which really solves the puzzle in all its forms. It is an outcome of faith that nature—as she is perceptible to our five senses—takes the character of such a well formulated puzzle. The successes reaped up to now by science do, it is true, give a certain encouragement for this faith."

No physicist doubts that the micro level swarms with quantum weirdness. It springs from the fact that the waves of QM are mathematical fictions, abstract waves of probability in multidimensional spaces constructed solely to describe quantum systems. What sort of reality is behind those waves, and how it is structured, nobody knows. But most physicists agree with Pagels that only the micro world is weird. "Once information about the quantum world is irreversibly in the macroscopic world," he writes, "we can safely attribute objective significance to it—it can't slip back into the quantum never-never land."

I count myself among those who are unable to believe, as Einstein could not and most philosophers and physicists today cannot, that the universe, or a stupendous event like the explosion of a supernova, is dependent for its existence on being observed by such paltry creatures as you and me.

POSTSCRIPT

To see how a solipsistic interpretation of QM leads to backward causality, consider the following thought experiment.

Imagine that a counter records whether an electron is emitted by a radioactive substance within a certain time interval. Automatic machinery then withdraws the substance and takes a photograph, A, of the counter reading. Ten minutes later another photograph, B, is taken of the same reading. Picture A is automatically conveyed to one room, B to another. From Wigner's point of view the wave functions of both photographs remain indefinite until a conscious mind observes them. Suppose Wigner looks first at B and sees that an electron has been emitted. A week later Wigner's friend enters the other room and looks at A. Picture A must, of course, show the same reading. Somehow, when Wigner looked at B it collapsed the wave function of A, giving it a definite state even though B did not exist when A was taken!

Among paraphysicists who are basing experiments on the possibility that psychics can influence past events, the most notable is Helmut Schmidt. He uses electronic randomizers (based on radioactive decay) to generate random numbers. A recording is stored without being observed. At a later date, a copy of the original recording is played for a psychic who tries to influence it by PK (psychokinesis). Schmidt reports that significant deviations from chance are then found on both the original recording and the copy (they are, of course, identical). Presumably, if the original had been examined before the PK experiment, it would have shown no deviations from randomness. But because it was not observed, both the original and the copy remain in a vague state, though correlated with one another, until the psychic alters them by his observation.

"The implication seems to be that the effect can work backward in time," Schmidt told the *New York Times* (January 27, 1980), "and that is an outrageous idea from a conventional standpoint. But it may be that some quantum effects not yet understood could account for just such an outcome."

Schmidt works at the Mind Science Foundation, San Antonio, Texas, a foundation funded by Texas oilman William Thomas Slick, Jr. For my views on recent attempts to base psychic forces on QM see "Parapsychology and Quantum Mechanics" in *Science and the Paranormal*, edited by George O. Abell and Barry Singer (Scribner's, 1981).

A word more about the EPR paradox. It is customary for physicists who have little interest in philosophical interpretations of QM to "resolve" the paradox by pointing out that the two correlated particles should be thought of as a single quantum system. Measuring one particle collapses the entire system's wave function (or "rotates its state vector" if one adopts the language of Hilbert Space), thereby providing information about both particles. But this merely restates the paradox. The mystery remains in the sense that only sheer magic seems available to explain how two particles, separated by millions of light-years and not causally connected, can remain entangled as part of a single system.

FOUR

THE COMPUTER
AS SCIENTIST

In Logical Foundations of Probability *and later papers, the philosopher Rudolf Carnap tried to lay the foundations for an inductive logic. Given the total evidence relevant to a theory, both theory and evidence expressed in a precise, formal language, such a logic would enable a scientist to calculate what Carnap called a theory's "degree of confirmation."*

Even if Carnap's dream of an inductive logic is some day realized, it would be of little help, as Carnap was aware, in telling a scientist how to go about inventing a fruitful theory. In recent decades a number of AI (Artificial Intelligence) researchers have been struggling to create computer programs capable of surveying a mass of empirical data, then constructing laws that would explain the evidence and make successful predictions about future observations and experiments. My article on these pioneering efforts appeared in Discover *(June 1983). Since then there has been little progress along such lines.*

If we could climb into a time machine and visit a research center of the far future, is it possible that we would find computers acting like theoretical scientists? Would they be not only recording data and telling robot technicians what to do but also making shrewd guesses about new laws and theories?

Let us fantasize. Robots fitted with sensitive devices for seeing, hearing, touching—perhaps even tasting and smelling—are performing complicated experiments suggested to them by a computer. The results of their sensory readings are transmitted to the computer, where they are systematically searched for patterns that confirm or falsify old conjectures and suggest new ones. On the basis of this analysis, more instructions are issued to the robots. The scientist has become an outsider. His job is to see that the lab operates smoothly and to make sure that its discoveries are promptly reported to other research centers around the world and translated into new technology.

Recent research on what are called computer "induction programs" suggests that this picture may not be as visionary as it seems. But first we must understand an important distinction—the difference between deductive and inductive thinking.

Deduction is the process by which statements in a formal system are obtained by logical inference from other statements in the system. It is entirely a matter of manipulating information or symbols according to prescribed rules. No observations of the outside world are required in deducing, for instance, that if all squirrels are rodents and if all rodents are mammals, then all squirrels are mammals.

Induction requires looking at the world. It is the process by which scientists generalize from observations of individual instances to a universal law. If every electron measured is found to have one unit of electrical charge, it is assumed that all electrons, everywhere in the cosmos and at all times, have the same property. Induction is never absolutely certain. For all we know, there may be some vast cyclic law that will give every electron two units of charge next Tuesday. Nevertheless, evidence for a law may be so overwhelming that belief in its universality will come extremely close to certainty.

Both types of reasoning are used constantly in everyday life. If you assume that your car keys are either in your pocket or in the car and if you find that they are not in your pocket, you deduce that they are in the car. When you add up a restaurant check, you are applying a simple deductive algorithm (procedure) to arrive at the sum. But when you take a sip of wine, your expectation that it will not taste like coffee is an induction, a conjecture based on past experience.

We all know that computers are whizzes at deduction. Even your pocket calculator can deduce in a microsecond the product of two four-digit numbers. The deductive powers of a big computer extend far beyond number twiddling. Give it the posits and rules of any formal system, and it can make deductions with fantastic speed and efficiency.

Chess is a formal system. Computer programs can now deduce chess moves good enough to defeat even a grand master if there is a time limit of a few seconds per move. Some game-playing programs do a certain amount of induction, analyzing patterns and devising strategies on the basis of past experience. This is true also of the so-called "expert systems" that are now proliferating rapidly at centers for artificial-intelligence research. A computer is given information about a specialized field such as medical diagnosis and is programmed to deduce from Mr. Smith's symptoms that he has, say, the measles. Similar programs in geology can tell a company what the chances are of finding oil or copper at a specific spot. Although these systems use induction and give only probable conclusions, they are essentially deductive programs. They are little more than computerized textbooks, with rapid procedures for searching out desired information.

In recent years induction programs of a much more exciting sort have been developed. Like scientists, these programs search systematically through raw empirical data for regularities, then formulate the simplest mathematical laws that can explain the regularities.

In an interview in 1983, Richard Feynman, a Nobel laureate physicist at Cal Tech, likened the scientific method to the game of guessing the rules of another game. Imagine, he said, that a man who knows nothing about chess is allowed occasional glimpses of small portions of boards on which chess games are in progress. It does not take him long to realize that the board is an eight-by-eight array of alternately colored squares. More observations lead him to conclude that each player has one bishop that moves diagonally only on dark squares and another bishop that is similarly confined to white squares. Suddenly comes a surprise. He sees a game in which a player has two bishops on black squares.

Have the rules of chess suddenly altered? No, because sooner or later he observes the curious procedure by which a pawn that reaches the opponent's first row may be exchanged for a bishop. Other seeming violations of rules are explained when he sees such rare phenomena as castling and capturing *en passant*. Because the board, pieces, and rules of chess are finite, eventually he will obtain a complete understanding of the game.

The game played by the universe is not so simple. Indeed, it may be infinitely complex. Already, nuclear physicists are talking about subquark entities that make up quarks that in turn make up protons, neutrons, and other particles. Scientists are never certain that what Einstein called the "secrets of the Old One" are completely understood. They may never be fully understood. Scientists cannot even be sure that the rules will not change in time, as the rules of Western chess have altered over the centuries. Nevertheless, nature seems to play fairly (it may be subtle, said Einstein, but never malicious) and with a fixed strategy based on unalterable laws. No one can deny that science has been fantastically successful in learning some of these laws, especially after it discovered how to extend observations by making complicated experiments and by using ingenious instruments.

Why does induction work so well? How is it that human minds can gaze at tiny patches of nature and formulate laws that have such amazing powers to predict how all of nature will behave? Philosophers give different answers to such questions, arguing interminably over what they call the problem of "justifying" induction. Some philosophers of science, such as Britain's Sir Karl Popper, have abandoned the term induction altogether. But one way or another, science must decide between competing conjectures, and no one, not even Popper, doubts that science works. We know that computers are good at mathematics and chess and lots of other things, but can they be taught to play the science game? The answer is yes. The only debate now is over how well they can learn to play it.

A lot of fascinating computer research is under way on science induction programs. The basic scheme is simple. A computer is fed observational data about the outcome of experiments. It then searches this information for low-level equations that describe how the values of certain variables change with respect to one another. Suppose, for example, that a series of tests determines the intensity of light on a screen as the source of light is placed at different distances. A physicist would plot the results as spots on a graph; then, from the curve formed by the spots, he would guess the simple law: Light intensity varies inversely with the square of the distance. There are now computer programs that, given the same data, will quickly reach the same conclusion.

The most promising of recent programs of this sort are called BACON programs after Francis Bacon, one of the earliest philosophers to look for systematic procedures of inductive inference. These programs were developed in the late 1970s by Patrick Langley of Carnegie-Mellon University, one of the leading centers of artificial-intelligence research. Langley is now expanding and improving the programs along with Herbert Simon, who is best known for his pioneering work in artificial intelligence even though his Nobel Prize (awarded in 1978) was for economics.

The latest of these programs, BACON 4, is the work of Simon, Langley, and Gary Bradshaw, a graduate student at Carnegie-Mellon. When given data about the outcome of experiments, it has rediscovered scores of fundamental laws that were major discoveries in past centuries. It has formulated Archimedes's principle of floating bodies, Kepler's third law of planetary motion, Boyle's law of gases, Snell's law of light refraction, Black's law of specific heat, Ohm's law in electricity, and many others, including some basic laws of chemistry. And there are other induction programs at other research centers, such as meta-DENDRAL, developed by B. G. Buchanan and T. M. Mitchell at Stanford to generate and test hypotheses. There is even an induction program that discovers concepts in mathematics. It is called AM and was written by Douglas Lenat, also at Stanford. (By manipulating numbers and diagrams, mathematicians also experiment when they search for interesting theorems).

It is true that no induction program has yet found a new law and that the programs are not very good at filtering "noise" (errors) out of raw data. Critics of BACON contend that it works only on data that have been "cleaned" for analysis. Nevertheless, no one can see why, as induction programs improve, they will not some day be capable of discovering new laws. It was only a short time ago, remember, that skeptics of artificial intelligence were predicting that computers would never play chess above the tyro level.

Closely related to research on induction is work on programs that play induction games. What is an induction game? Consider the old parlor game that involves handing a pair of scissors around a circle of seated players. Each

B	G			B	
R	Y	B		R	Y
	G	R			G
		B		R	
			Y		
R			G		Y

Figure 1: Problems in inductive thinking
a) Eleusis: These cards were dealt, from top to bottom, according to a rule. Can you discern
and state the Eleusis rule?
b) Patterns: The lettered squares suggest a pattern that would emerge if the grid were filled
in. Can you complete the grid?

time the scissors are transferred, the person offering the scissors must say
either "crossed" or "uncrossed." A moderator, who alone knows the secret
rule, tells whether the player spoke correctly or incorrectly. The object of the
game is to guess the rule. At first, most people suspect it has something to
do with how the scissors are held, and experiments are made to test conjectures. Eventually the secret dawns on a perceptive player. One says "crossed"
if one's legs are crossed and "uncrossed" if otherwise. Guessing the rule is an
induction; the underlying regularity is obtained by generalizing from a set of
observations.

A more sophisticated induction game, which models many aspects of scientific procedure, is Eleusis (after the site of the ancient Greek religious mysteries), a card game invented by Robert Abbott of New York City.

In Eleusis, players try to guess a secret rule that states what kind of card
can be played on another. The rule is invented by the dealer, who, if the
players prefer, can also be called God, Nature, Tao, Brahma, or the Oracle.
Scoring in the game is cleverly designed so that it is to the dealer's advantage
to think of a rule neither too hard nor too easy to guess. Too simple a rule
would be: On every card play a card of opposite color. Of course the complexity of a rule likely to give the dealer a high score depends on how experienced the other players are. For beginners, a typical good rule would be: Play
a black card on all cards with odd values, a red card on all with even values.
How would you fare in playing Eleusis? As an exercise, study the sequence of
played cards shown in Figure 1 to see whether you can guess the simple rule
that governs the sequence. Then check the answer, shown in Figure 2 at the
end of the chapter.

Many computer programs have been written for Eleusis, both to generate rules and to guess rules. It was not until the early 1980s, however, that workers in artificial intelligence created programs better at guessing Eleusis rules than were most human players.

Another induction game, Patterns, is based on visual patterns rather than sequential plays and was invented in the late 1960s by Sidney Sackson of New York City. In Patterns, each player draws a six-by-six grid of squares. One player, called the Designer, secretly creates a pattern by coloring each square of his grid with one of four colors or by using four symbols—such as a square, triangle, circle, and cross and puts his sheet facedown on the table. As in Eleusis, scoring rules ensure that the Designer scores highest with a pattern that is neither too easy nor too hard for the other players to guess.

At any time a player may make an inquiry by putting a small check mark in the corner of one or more squares of his grid. The sheet is passed to the Designer, who must put in those squares the correct color (or symbol) of his secret pattern. Each square filled in by the Designer corresponds to the result of an observation of the facts by the players, who try to guess the pattern as soon as possible. The highest scores go to players who guess the most squares with the fewest inquiries. Low scores go to poor or unlucky guessers, to those who fill in squares too quickly (like scientists who rush into print with poorly confirmed conjectures), or to those so overcautious that they delay forming a hypothesis until others beat them to it.

Several computer programs play Patterns skillfully. Can you? To test your skill, see whether you can guess the pattern of the partly completed grid shown in Figure 1, where the letters stand for colors red, yellow, blue, and green. (The answer appears at the end of the chapter.)

Programs such as BACON and programs for playing induction games are similar to inductive programs that search cipher texts for patterns that may help break a code. There is a strong analogy between scientific induction and the kind of thinking that enables a person to solve a cryptogram or code. (Think, for example, of current work in cracking genetic codes.) And there are sophisticated induction programs now being used to analyze the noise received by radio telescopes, to see whether patterns can be found that would imply an extraterrestrial message. For all these reasons, there is growing confidence that computers some day may indeed be able to discover new scientific laws.

As for scientific *theories*, that is a different ball game. Although no sharp lines divide laws from theories, just as no sharp lines separate facts from laws, the distinctions are obvious and useful. Laws are descriptions, usually mathematical, of how observable quantities are related. The word "observable" is extremely fuzzy, but it usually means a property of nature that can be observed and measured in simple, direct ways: length, volume, mass, velocity, momentum, color, pitch, and so on. Properties observed through special instruments such as microscopes and telescopes are counted as observables be-

B	G	R	Y	B	G
R	Y	B	G	R	Y
B	G	R	Y	B	G
R	Y	B	G	R	Y
B	G	R	Y	B	G
R	Y	B	G	R	Y

Figure 2: Answers to problems in inductive thinking
a) Eleusis: The Eleusis rule is to deal a card that matches the previous card either in color
or in value.
b) Patterns: The completed board above shows one of the possible patterns that can be
induced.

cause the process is so simple that no one doubts that what they see is actually there.

Theories involve "unobservable" concepts such as electrons, neutrinos, quarks, electromagnetic fields, gluons, and a thousand other ghostly things. Can you imagine anything less observable than a gravity field or the wave function of an atom? Yet relativity and quantum mechanics could not do without these concepts. Laws are designed to account for facts. Theories are constructed to explain both laws and facts. There are algorithms for getting laws from facts (otherwise the BACON programs would not work), but there are no known algorithms for getting good theories from facts and laws.

Are algorithms for devising good theories possible in principle, or do they require some mysterious creative ability of the human mind that will be forever beyond the reach of computers? Of course, once a theory is constructed, empirical consequences can usually be deduced, and then observations can confirm or refute the claims. General relativity, for example, with its incredible assertion that gravity and inertia are the same force, was poorly confirmed until recently. Now it is supported by hundreds of tests made possible by atomic clocks. How the hardware and software inside Einstein's skull arrived at the theory remains a mystery.

Philosophers argue fiercely over whether the intuitive leap needed for theory construction can be simulated by a computer. Some think that artificial intelligence will never formulate a good theory. Simon is among the optimists. In his view, theory invention is simply a more complicated level of problem solving, and he points out that in the process of analyzing data and searching for laws, his BACON programs actually introduce new low-level theoretical concepts. Like most of his colleagues in artificial intelligence, Simon believes that there are no good reasons for doubting that computers will eventually be programmed to do any kind of thinking a human mind can do.

We are, of course, now deep into metaphysical questions about the nature of human consciousness and creativity. As to whether Simon is right or not, we shall just have to wait and see—or perhaps wait and not see.

POSTSCRIPT

For detailed rules on how to play Eleusis, see both the chapter on this game in my *Second Scientific American Book of Mathematical Puzzles and Diversions* (1959) and my follow-up chapter on improved versions of the game in *Penrose Tiles to Trapdoor Ciphers* (1989). For the rules of Patterns, see both Sidney Sackson's book *A Gamut of Games* (1969) and the chapter on Patterns in my *Mathematical Circus* (1979).

In 1984 the Fredkin Foundation, established by Edward Fredkin, an artificial-intelligence expert at MIT, announced a prize of $100,000 for the first computer program to make a mathematical discovery. More precisely, the discovery must be a major new theorem based on mathematical ideas not implicit in the program that discovers it. A committee of distinguished mathematicians will rule on the award.

The foundation has an award of the same amount for the first computer program to become the world's chess champion in tournament play with human grand masters. As of now, no one seems even close to winning either prize.

FIVE

WAP, SAP, PAP, AND FAP

As you will see from this review, which ran in The New York Review of Books *(May 8, 1986), I take a dim view of the anthropic principle. For an even dimmer view of Frank Tipler's wild speculations about the future of the universe and the emergence of a God who will resurrect us all, see my essay on Tipler in* On the Wild Side *(Prometheus Books, 1992). Tipler has since written a big book about his bizarre theology,* The Physics of Immortality, *published here by Doubleday after it became a best-seller in, of all places, Germany. I have yet to see a favorable review of what I consider the funniest crank work by a reputable physicist written in this century.*

It has been observed that cosmologists are often wrong but seldom uncertain, and the authors of this long, fascinating, exasperating book, *The Anthropic Cosmological Principle* (Oxford University Press, 1986), are no exceptions. They are John Barrow, astronomer at the University of Sussex, and Frank Tipler, Tulane University mathematical physicist. Physicist John Wheeler provides an enthusiastic foreword. No one can plow through this well-written, painstakingly researched tome without absorbing vast chunks of information about QM (quantum mechanics), the latest cosmic models, and the history of philosophical views that bear on the book's main arguments.

Just what is this "anthropic principle" that has become so fashionable among a minority of cosmologists and is arousing such passionate controversy? As the authors make clear in their introduction, there is not one principle but four. Each is more speculative than the previous one, with the fourth blasting the authors out of science altogether into clouds of metaphysics and fantasy.

The simplest of the four is called (the authors are fond of acronyms)

WAP, the Weak Anthropic Principle. Although it goes back to Protagoras's famous declaration that "man is the measure of all things," its modern cosmological form seems first to have been stated by the physicist Robert Dicke in the late 1950s. As Barrow and Tipler readily admit, it is a trivial tautology, totally noncontroversial. It merely proclaims that because we exist the universe must be so constructed as to allow us to have evolved. The laws of nature clearly must be such as to permit, if not actually force, the formation of CHON (carbon, hydrogen, oxygen, and nitrogen), the four elements essential to life as we know it.

Does this mean that all life must be carbon based? Although the authors believe this, it does not follow from WAP. Even if there is noncarbon life elsewhere in the universe, the fact that *we* are carbon imposes a variety of tight restraints on the universe and its past. For example, the cosmos has to be about fifteen billion years old. Why? Because, the authors argue, elements necessary to organic molecules are cooked inside stars. If the universe were much younger, those elements would not be available and we would not be here. If the universe were much older, all the suns would have burned out, and we would not be here either.

WAP was invoked over and over again in earlier centuries by proponents of the design argument for God. It was WAPish to point out that if the earth were slightly closer to the sun, like Venus, water would boil away and carbon life would be impossible. If the earth were slightly farther from the sun, water would freeze and Earth would have the barren deserts of Mars. Theists liked to note that when water freezes it expands and floats on water and that, otherwise, lakes and rivers would freeze to the bottom in winter and all their life be destroyed. If Earth did not have an ozone atmosphere, animals could not survive ultraviolet radiation. And so on. Hundreds of similar arguments, most of them analyzed by Barrow and Tipler, seem to show that our universe, and especially our planet, were carefully designed to permit us to exist.

The close ties between WAP and the creation hypothesis impel the authors to write almost one hundred pages on traditional proofs of God from design. It is an excellent history, followed by almost as long a section on more recent teleological arguments. There are informative discussions of such post-Darwinian "process" thinkers as Henri Bergson, Samuel Alexander, Alfred Whitehead, and Charles Hartshorne, who see the universe as rolling toward a predetermined goal, as well as of "process theologians," who anchor the goal in God.

If WAP were all there is to the anthropic principle, the book would not have been worth writing. The authors continually stress the triviality of asserting no more than that the universe has a structure that makes carbon life possible. It is easy to caricature such retrograde reasoning. Instead of saying I am here because my parents met, I say that because I am here I know my parents met. How lucky for vacationers that sandy beaches are so near the sea! From the fact that I wear spectacles I can deduce the positions of my ears and nose. If a chess game ends with no queens on the board, I can infer with iron logic that both queens were captured. From the present state of the world one can obviously make all sorts of highly probable, sometimes certain, conjectures about its distant past.

But there is more to the anthropic principle than WAP. The next step is SAP, the Strong Anthropic Principle. Proposed in 1974 by the British cosmologist Brandon Carter, it maintains that life of any sort is impossible unless the basic laws of nature are exactly what they are. Consider gravity. If it were slightly stronger, the cosmos would long ago have stopped expanding, gone the other way, and collapsed into a black hole before galaxies could form. If gravity were slightly weaker, the cosmos would have expanded too rapidly to allow matter to clump into stars. In either case, you and I would not be here.

The strength of gravity is one of a dozen or more constants called dimensionless because they are independent of any measuring system. If one banana is twice as long as another, the number two is the same whether you measure the banana in inches or centimeters. It turns out that these fundamental constants are so finely tuned that if they varied ever so slightly, there could not be any carbon atoms and we would not be here. Instead of saying we are here because the constants are precisely what they are, SAP turns it around. We are here; therefore the constants had to be what they are.

In long chapters on physics, astrophysics, and biochemistry, often dense with technical details and mathematical formulas, Barrow and Tipler defend this reverse way of reasoning. A recurring theme is that SAP puts such narrow constraints on the constants and natural laws that it can lead to falsifiable predictions. Opponents of SAP take a dim view of this claim. The late physicist Heinz Pagels, in a slashing attack on anthropic arguments in his article "A Cozy Cosmology,"[1] dismissed WAP and SAP as pure flimflam. Although they may occasionally suggest testable conjectures, they do so in such obvious ways that nothing is gained by elevating them into new principles.

According to Barrow and Tipler, the first successful anthropic prediction was made by the University of Chicago geologist Thomas Chamberlin. Geological evidence indicates a great age for the solar system. If the sun did not feed on atomic energy, Chamberlin guessed, it would have long ago burned out and we would not be here. Chamberlin guessed right, but did he do anything except apply ordinary reasoning?

Writing just before the Barrow and Tipler book was published, Pagels cites a more recent example. England's Stephen Hawking and Barry Collins once invoked the anthropic principle to explain why the universe is so isotropic—the same in all directions. If it were less so, matter would not condense into galaxies and we would not be here. This, says Pagels, explains nothing. By contrast, the new inflationary models of the Big Bang hypothesis of the origins of the universe actually do provide a plausible mechanism for isotropy.

In old Big Bang models the initial explosion would have produced permanent irregularities. In the inflationary models, immediately after the bang the universe jumps from a trillionth the size of a proton to about the size of a softball. This sudden inflation smoothes out all irregularities, leaving an isotropic cosmos expanding at its present slow rate. In light of such speculations, the anthropic principle seems irrelevant. Surprisingly, Barrow and Tipler agree. They are strongly critical of Hawking and Collins for what they see as a misuse of the principle.

Similar efforts to use SAP as a tool for investigating the constants have been equally feeble, Pagels continues. Meanwhile, the new unified-field theories really are providing significant explanations of why the constants are what they are. WAP and SAP are so needless that they raise a new mystery. "How can such a sterile idea," Pagels asks, "reproduce itself so prolifically?" He suspects it may be because scientists are reluctant to make a leap of faith and say: "The reason the universe seems tailor-made for our existence is that it *was* tailor-made. . . . Faced with questions that do not neatly fit into the framework of science, they are loath to resort to religious explanations; yet their curiosity will not let them leave matters unaddressed. Hence, the anthropic principle. It is the closest that some atheists can get to God."

If one leaves aside the hypothesis of a transcendent Creator or of a Mind that either is the universe or permeates the universe, what alternatives are left? Barrow and Tipler consider several possibilities.

One is the startling view that only one kind of universe is possible—the one we know. This was skillfully defended by the Harvard chemist Lawrence Henderson in two books that were largely ignored until recently: *Fitness of the Environment* (1913, reprinted in 1970 by Harvard University Press) and *The Order of Nature* (1917). Leibniz argued exactly the opposite. He believed an infinity of universes are logically possible and that God selected the one he liked best.[2]

The authors discuss several variations of the many-possible-worlds view. Other universes could have the same laws as ours but entirely different histories depending on different initial conditions before the Big Bang. Parallel worlds could flourish side by side in our familiar three-dimensional space or in higher spaces, but because of limitations on the speed of light, no contacts between them are possible even if they are all in our space. We need not, however, assume infinite space. Alternate worlds could follow one another in some sort of supertime. Each explodes into existence, expands, contracts, and vanishes in the Big Crunch to be followed (whatever that means) by another fireball.

John Wheeler has a stupendous vision in which an infinity of universes pop in and out of existence, each with a randomly determined set of laws. Every logically possible universe appears an infinite number of times. (If an infinity of bridge hands are dealt, every possible distribution of the cards will be dealt an infinite number of times.) Of course only a tiny subset of these possible worlds will have forces and particles that permit life. This naturally emasculates any argument from design to God. It is not surprising we are in a universe that allowed us to evolve. How could it be otherwise?

The wildest of all variants of the infinite-universes theme, designed to counter the standard Copenhagen interpretation of QM (named for the city where Niels Bohr worked), is the many-worlds interpretation. In the Copenhagen view, the central mystery is what happens when a quantum system is measured. Take the case of a single particle. Every particle has associated with it a set of probability waves in an artificially constructed multidimensional space. A single expression, called the wave function, gives the probabilities that a particle will assume each of its possible states when it is measured. Before measurement, all possible states of the particle are said to be mixed in some sort of weird potential sense. Not until the particle is measured does nature "decide," by pure chance, what value to give a variable. At that instant the wave function is said to "collapse" from an indefinite to a definite state.

This notion of wave-function collapse leads to all sorts of paradoxes, of which the EPR paradox (after the initials of Einstein and two associates) has become the most notorious. A particle and its antiparticle can be simultaneously created by an interaction that sends them in opposite directions. Regardless of how far apart they get, perhaps light-years in distance, they remain "correlated." If, for instance, one particle is measured for the direction of its spin, the wave function for the pair instantly collapses and the other particle acquires an opposite spin. Since neither particle has a definite spin until one is measured, and since there is no known causal connection between the pair, how does the other particle "know" what spin to acquire?

Einstein was deeply troubled by what he called the spooky telepathic aspect of this famous thought experiment, which he believed showed that QM is not a complete theory. Niels Bohr strongly disagreed. Most quantum experts still side with Bohr, though a growing number are beginning to suspect that Einstein may have been right after all. The EPR paradox has recently been confirmed by several laboratory tests that could not have been made in Einstein's day. Perhaps this has awakened physicists to a fuller awareness of the paradox's deep implications.

The many-worlds interpretation dissolves the mystery of the EPR and similar paradoxes by denying that wave functions ever collapse. For this simplification, however, a horrendous price is paid. At every instant when a collapse seems to occur, the entire universe is said to split into parallel worlds, each containing one of the possible outcomes of measurement. At every instant billions upon billions of such splits take place. There is no communication between these worlds. We cannot tell that we are constantly splitting into duplicate selves because our consciousness rides smoothly along only one path in the endlessly forking chains. This splitting process is completely deterministic, perhaps guided by one monstrous wave function that keeps expanding but never collapses unless there is a God outside the universe to observe it.

The many-worlds interpretation has been called a beautiful theory that nobody can believe. Nevertheless, a number of eminent physicists, including Wheeler, Hawking, and Murray Gell-Mann have taken it seriously, at least as a way of interpreting QM that removes its thorniest difficulties. Although Wheeler has withdrawn his support of the theory, Barrow and Tipler are defenders. "The wave function collapse postulated by the Copenhagen Interpretation is dynamically ridiculous," they write, "and this interpretation is difficult if not impossible to apply in quantum cosmology. We suggest that the Many-Worlds Interpretation may well eventually replace the Statistical and Copenhagen Interpretations just as the Copernican system replaced the Ptolemaic. . . . Physicists who think in terms of the Copenhagen Interpretation may become handicapped in thinking about quantum cosmology." Poor old Bohr! Too bad he did not think of how to solve the problems of measurement by letting the universe copy him billions of times!

We come now to Wheeler's radical version of SAP, which the authors call PAP, or the Participatory Anthropic Principle. No universe can exist in a strong sense, Wheeler maintains, unless it contains conscious observers. This view rests on the fact that when a wave function collapses, the measuring instrument (a device or a person) becomes part of a larger system. All the potential states remain mixed as before until the larger system is measured.

Erwin Schrödinger, who disliked QM even though he helped get it started, invented a famous cat paradox to ridicule wave-function collapse. The cat is in a closed box with a mechanism that will kill the cat when it is triggered by a quantum event such as a click in a Geiger counter. The click has an equal probability of occurring or not within, say, an hour. At the end of the hour QM seems to say that until the cat is "measured" by someone looking into the box, the cat is neither alive nor dead. The two states remain mixed until an observer collapses the cat's wave function.

The paradox gets worse when you realize that even when an observer looks into the box he at once becomes part of a still larger system in which the cat's two states continue to be mixed until someone observes the observer. This is called the "paradox of Wigner's friend" after Eugene Wigner, a physicist who is troubled by it. It obviously leads to an infinite regress of observers. Wigner avoids the regress by cutting it whenever a chain of events is registered in a conscious mind. This raises more difficulties. Is the cat conscious enough to end the regress if it is not killed? If the mechanism merely chops off a leg? Although the chain ends for Wigner's friend when he opens the box, it does not end for Wigner until he observes his friend, so the regress does not really go away.

These solipsistic speculations have led Wheeler to the view that our universe is a participatory one in which reality is a collusion between minds and whatever is out there, perhaps only a bare mathematical field. For Wheeler the universe does not exist except in a pale mathematical sense unless it contains conscious observers. Here again the continuum of minds in the animal world raises disturbing problems. Einstein said he could not believe the moon's reality depends on being observed by a mouse. If a mouse will do, why not a bee?

Wheeler's view seems to be that a universe becomes real only when it is structured at the Big Bang so that it eventually can observe itself through conscious minds. Or perhaps reality can be thought of as a spectrum. The universe grows more real as life evolves to higher forms. In either case, Wheeler's vision sees conscious life as essential if a universe is to be more than a mathematical abstraction. His vision is close to Bishop Berkeley's "to be is to be perceived," except that Wheeler, unlike the Irish cleric, does not restore the external world by having it observed by God. Not for a moment did Berkeley, as sometimes said, doubt the external world's full reality. He only denied it was material. Indeed, he argued anthropically. Because we and the external world surely exist, there must be a God.

Barrow and Tipler move on from PAP to what they call FAP, the Final Anthropic Principle, but not before a long attempt to show that ETIs (Extraterrestrial Intelligences) do not exist. For many years Tipler has been arguing strenuously in both technical and popular articles that there are compelling grounds to assume that life on a level above microorganisms exists nowhere else in our galaxy, perhaps nowhere else in the universe. This has understandably brought him into sharp conflict with Frank Drake, Philip Morrison, Carl Sagan, and other scientists who strongly support SETI (the Search for Extraterrestrial Intelligence). Tipler is convinced that this search is a foolish waste of money.

Those who agree usually base their reasoning on the fact that long sequences of improbable events appear to be required for life even to get started. First there must be a sun with a planet on which conditions are extremely close to those on Earth. Even if it is assumed that such planets exist, the chance probability that a self-replicating molecule will arise on one of them may be vanishingly small. Finally, even if such a molecule does arise spontaneously, another sequence of improbable events must occur if it is to evolve into anything as intelligent as a fish or a bird.

In *Science Year* (1973) Wheeler had a science-fiction story called "Beyond the Black Hole." In it a character called Audrey, with whose views I assume Wheeler identifies, comes to this conclusion:

> Let's carry what you are saying to the logical extreme, Fred. It takes a very narrow squeak for a cycle of the universe to permit life at all, even at one place. If life had originated in more than one place, that would

have meant that the universe was larger and longer-lived than necessary. The creation of life would be more "expensive" than it needed to be. So the chances are overwhelming that Earth is the sole outpost of life in the universe, and we had no right to expect to find life on Zeta Zeta. Am I wrong in my reasoning?

To such reasoning Tipler has added a curious new argument that goes like this. There are planets in the cosmos millions of years older than Earth. If there is intelligent life on any of them, its technology would be far more advanced than ours. We know from experience that there is an overwhelming desire to explore the universe and that this is possible. It can best be done, Tipler claims, by what he calls von Neumann machines after the mathematician John von Neumann, who first proved that self-replicating robots can be constructed. Superbeings on other planets would surely build such robots and give them an intelligence equal to or surpassing their own. These robots would multiply at an explosive rate. In a short time they would be poking their spaceships into every corner of the galaxy. Because we see no signs of them (the authors have no interest in UFOs), ETIs do not exist.

Sagan is understandably infuriated by this reasoning. "Absence of evidence is not evidence of absence," he and William Newman said in their paper on "The Solipsist Approach to Extraterrestrial Intelligence."[3] In any case, the only way we can know is by searching. "We have an alternative denied to the medieval scholastics; we are able to experiment."

Why has the notion that we are alone in the galaxy been gaining ground? Partly, I suspect, because of the shock of finding no traces of life on Mars, partly because of a revival of theism that seems to be taking place among intellectuals. Whatever the reasons, those who have shared Tipler's unbelief in ETI include many distinguished evolutionists (Alfred Russel Wallace wrote an entire book about it) and such top physicists as Enrico Fermi and Freeman Dyson. "I find that the universe in some sense," wrote Dyson in his autobiography, "must have known that we were coming."

In his collection of essays, *The Flamingo's Smile*, Stephen Jay Gould attacks what he calls the "moth-eaten" arguments of the anthropicists. He accuses Tipler of misinterpreting what evolutionists mean when they speak of improbable events. They mean only that it is highly improbable evolution would take precisely the paths it has taken on Earth. They do not mean that once life starts the steps would not lead to intelligence. No one expects to find animals on another planet that duplicate beasts on Earth, but there are no good reasons for assuming that evolution could not take many paths to other forms of intelligence.

The assumed absence of ETI leads Barrow and Tipler to FAP, their *Final Anthropic Principle*. Although life probably exists only on Earth, now that it has begun FAP says it will be impossible to destroy. Otherwise, the universe would lose all its observers—and by PAP would have demolished itself! In the author's FAP fantasy, life is now taking its first faltering steps toward colonizing the universe. This is likely to be completed by intelligent von Neumann machines. The authors expect about half the universe to be colonized by the time our universe reaches the limit of its expansion and starts the other way. The red shift of stars turns to blue. Colonization goes on until the entire cosmos teems with computer life.

If there is an infinity of other universes, presumably these events will take place in all of them that permit life. Borrowing from Teilhard de Chardin, the Catholic paleontologist, the authors posit an Omega Point that will be the end of Everything. Here are the book's final sentences: "At the instant the Omega Point is reached, life will have gained control of *all* matter and forces not only in a single universe, but in all universes whose existence is logically possible; life will have spread into *all* spatial regions in all universes which could logically exist, and will have stored an infinite amount of information, including *all* bits of knowledge which it is logically possible to know.[123] And this is the end."

Footnote 123 is: "A modern-day theologian might wish to say that the totality of life at the Omega Point is omnipotent, omnipresent, and omniscient!" The God of Moses, Jesus, and Mohammed will finally have come into being. Instead of creating all the universes, however, it is the other way around. The universes got together and created the Almighty. This places the authors within the tradition of Samuel Alexander who, in his masterwork *Space, Time, and Deity* (1920), put forth the notion of a finite God who is slowly developing and growing in perfection as the universe evolves. Their eschatology is even closer to that of several famous science-fiction yarns. In Isaac Asimov's "The Last Question" a supercomputer evolves in hyperspace into a deity who creates a new universe to replace the old one that wore out and died the "heat death" dictated by thermodynamics.

What should one make of this quartet of WAP, SAP, PAP, and FAP? In my not so humble opinion I think the last principle is best called CRAP, the Completely Ridiculous Anthropic Principle.

POSTSCRIPT

Frank Tipler, in a long letter to *The New York Review of Books* (December 4, 1986), accused me (among other things) of misunderstanding the many-worlds interpretation of QM. I replied in two words: "I'm speechless!" For a discussion of how the many-worlds interpretation relates to traveling backward in time and for some comments on Tipler's plan for a possible time machine, see the first chapter of my *Time Travel and Other Mathematical Bewilderments* (W. H. Freeman, 1987).

NOTES

1. *The Sciences* (March/April 1985).
2. Isaac Newton held the same opinion. Here is a famous passage from his *Opticks*: "It may also be allowed that God is able to create particles of matter of several sizes and figures, and in several proportions to space, and perhaps of different densities and forces, and thereby to vary the laws of nature, and make worlds of several sorts in several parts of the universe. At least, I see nothing of contradiction in all this."
3. *Quarterly Journal of the Royal Astronomical Society* (Vol. 24, 1983).

SIX

INFINITY AND
INFORMATION

Rudy Rucker, like the mathematician Eric Temple Bell, has combined two careers: writing popular books about math, and writing science fiction. My review of his Mind Tools, *along with a review of a book by Eli Maor, appeared in* The New York Review of Books (*December 3, 1987*).

> *The world is colors and motion, feelings and thought . . . and what does math have to do with it? Not much, if "math" means being bored in high school, but in truth mathematics is the one universal science. Mathematics is the study of pure pattern and everything in the cosmos is a kind of pattern.*

In the above quotation, the first paragraph of Rudy Rucker's *Mind Tools: The Five Levels of Mathematical Reality* (Houghton-Mifflin, 1987), observe the word *pure*. Mathematical patterns are pure, timeless concepts, uncontaminated by reality. Yet the outside world is so structured that these patterns in the mind apply to it with eerie accuracy. Nothing has more radically altered human history than this uncanny, to some inexplicable, interplay of pure math and the structure of whatever is "out there." The interplay is responsible for all science and technology.

Perhaps it is a dim awareness of the explosive role of mathematics in altering the world, together with the low quality of math teaching in this country, that accounts for the growing number of books intended to teach mathematics to those who hated it in school. The two books here under review are general surveys, in the tradition of such popular classics as Edward Kasner and James Newman's *Mathematics and the Imagination*. Unlike most such surveys, each book is organized around a unifying concept.

For Eli Maor, an Israeli mathematician now at Oakland University in Rochester, Michigan, the unifying concept of *To Infinity and Beyond: A Cultural History of the Infinite* (Birkhäuser, 1987) is infinity. *Finite mathematics,* a term that has come into recent use, is precalculus math in which infinity is avoided as much as possible; yet even in the most elementary math there is no way to escape completely from the concept. As Maor points out, counting numbers go on forever, and straight lines are endless in both directions. Textbooks on finite math have chapters on probability, but what is meant when you say the odds are equal that a flipped coin will fall heads or tails? "We tacitly assume," writes Maor, "that an infinite number of tosses would produce an equal outcome."

Maor begins his admirable survey with the concept of limit. In one of Zeno's notorious paradoxes, a runner can not get from A to B until he first goes half the distance. Now he must run half the remaining distance, then half the still remaining distance, and so on into an infinite regress. Because at any time the number of distances yet to be traversed is infinite, how can he reach B? Worse than that, how can he begin? If the distance is sixteen miles, he must first run eight miles. To go eight he must go four. Again, the halves form an infinite sequence. How does he get started? Of course mathematicians are no longer troubled by such paradoxes of motion, but it is impossible to resolve them without a clear notion of the limits of infinite sequences of magnitudes in both time and space.

Maor's well-chosen examples are wide-ranging. Archimedes determined the value of pi (the ratio of a circle's circumference to its diameter) by calculating the perimeters of inscribed and circumscribed regular polygons. By increasing the number of sides of these nested figures he was able to squeeze the value of pi between inside and outside polygons that came closer and closer to the limit of a circle. In this way he got pi correct for the first time to what today we call two decimal places. In 1986 a Japanese supercomputer calculated pi to more than 134 million digits.

At present no one knows whether certain patterns, say a run of a hundred sevens, occur somewhere in the nonrepeating endless decimals of pi. Are we entitled to say the run is either there (wherever "there" is) or not there? Here the concept of infinity generates a curious split in the philosophy of mathematics. A Platonic realist would answer "of course," the run of sevens is there or not, but there are mathematicians called constructivists who will have none of this. The either/or cannot be asserted, they insist, until such a run is actually found, or until someone proves in a finite number of steps that the run must or cannot "sleep" in pi, as William James once put it. It is, of course, legitimate for a constructivist to say that a run of a hundred sevens does or does not exist in the first billion decimals of pi, because there are algorithms (procedures) for answering this question in a finite number of steps.

Proving whether certain types of numbers belong to finite or infinite sets is a major ongoing task of number theory. Maor gives Euclid's elegant proof that the number of primes is infinite. (A prime is an integer greater than 1, divisible only by itself and 1.) Twin primes are primes that differ by two, such as 3,5 and 11,13. Are they infinite as well? Twins of monstrous size have been found by computers, but whether there is an infinity of them remains unanswered. Maor reports that in 1982 a computer software company offered $25,000 for the first proof of this old conjecture.

The harmonic series, which has so many applications in physics, is 1/1 + 1/2 + 1/3 + 1/4 + . . . , where the ellipsis indicates an infinity of the reciprocals of the counting numbers. (The reciprocal of x is 1/x.) As the number of terms increases, the partial sums become larger. Do these sums converge (approach a limit) or diverge (increase without limit)? Because the terms are increasingly smaller, one suspects the sum converges. Amazingly, it does not though the divergence becomes increasingly sluggish. It takes 12,367 terms to reach a sum that exceeds 10; to exceed 100 the number of terms required has forty-four digits.

Maor provides many curiosities involving this remarkable sequence. If you remove all the terms that contain a specified digit in the denominator, the series converges. For example, if you remove all fractions that contain 9, the sequence converges on a sum slightly less than 23. Suppose you remove all fractions with denominators that are not prime. The series still diverges. On the other hand, the reciprocals of twin primes (assuming they are infinite) have been shown to converge.

Maor's discussion of numbers comes to a climax with chapters on Georg Cantor's revolutionary discovery that it is possible to define "transfinite" numbers that stand for an infinite hierarchy of infinities. The smallest—Cantor called it aleph-null—counts the integers, as well as any infinite subset of the integers. For instance, there are as many primes as there are integers. The proof is simply to put the two sets of numbers into one-to-one correspondence:

$$1,2,3,4,5, \ldots$$
$$2,3,5,7,11, \ldots .$$

Any set of objects that can be put into correspondence with the integers is called countable. Cantor was able to show that the set of all integral fractions is countable but that the set of irrational numbers (numbers such as pi and the square root of 2) that cannot be expressed as integral fractions is not countable. Cantor called the number that counts the real numbers (rational and irrational) aleph-one, or C (for continuum), because, as Maor shows, it counts the number of points on a line segment. Cantor believed that 2 raised to the power of aleph-null is the same as C, and he proved that an endless ladder of alephs can be generated simply by raising 2 to the power of higher and higher alephs.

Turning to geometry, Maor covers a variety of fascinating topics, such as infinitely long "pathological curves" that enclose a finite area, and surfaces of infinite area that surround a finite volume. A section on inversion explains how a circle or sphere can be turned inside out to put all its points into correspondence with all outside points on an infinite plane or in infinite space. There is an old mathematical joke about how to catch a tiger. You invert the space outside an empty cage. This puts the tiger (along with everything else) into the cage.

A chapter on the Dutch artist Maurits Escher reproduces many of his pictures (some in color) that involve infinity, such as his marvelous mosaics of birds and animals that tile the infinite plane. (The plane is said to be tiled if the shapes completely cover it, without gaps or overlaps, like the hexagonal tiles of a bathroom floor.) The jacket of Maor's book has an Escher drawing of a globe covered with loxodromes. These are helical paths followed by ships and planes that travel at a constant angle (not a right angle) to the earth's meridians. The paths spiral around the poles, making an infinity of revolutions until they strangle the poles.

Maor ends his survey by leaving pure math for the disheveled outside world. Discussions of modern cosmology and particle physics raise deep questions about the infinitely large and the infinitely small. Does space-time extend forever, or is it finite but unbounded, as the surface of a sphere would be for flatlanders living on it? Are there other universes out there in some sort of hyper space-time? Does the infinitely small stop with a truly fundamental particle (the latest speculation is that the basic units are infinitesimal strings), or is matter an infinite regress of endlessly smaller entities, like an infinite nest of Oriental wooden dolls?

Rudy Rucker, who holds a doctorate in set theory, is a professor of computer science at San Jose State University in California. He is well known to science-fiction readers for his far-out fantasies, including *White Light*, a novel based on Cantor's alephs. Another novel assumes that as you shrink down into smaller and smaller levels of reality you eventually enter the same universe you started from. Rucker's previous nonfiction books, including *Infinity and the Mind* and *The Fourth Dimension*, mix mathematics with occasional bizarre science-fiction themes. *Mind Tools*, a survey of math organized around the modern concept of information, is a similar blend.

Rucker divides mathematics into what he calls five archetypes or modes of thought: Number, Space, Logic, Infinity, and Information. A section of his book is devoted to each mode, the first four approached from an information perspective. To explain the modes, Rucker considers a human hand.

From the perspective of number, the fingers model the integer 5, but scores of other numbers count such quantities as hairs, wrinkles, cells, lengths of fingers, areas of nails, weight, temperature, blood-flow rate, electrical conductivity, and so on. Viewed as space, the hand is a three-dimensional solid.

Because it lacks holes, it is topologically equivalent to a ball. (Topology studies properties that remain the same when an object is continuously deformed.) The hand's blood vessels branch in a pattern that mathematicians call a tree. Parts of the hand's surface are concave, parts convex. From a logic point of view the hand is a machine about which all sorts of "if, . . . then" statements can be made: if it clenches, knuckles get white; if it touches fire, it jerks away; if it digs in dirt, fingernails get black.

Infinity enters when you consider the hand as an abstract solid with an uncountable infinity of points. As an actual solid, if the nested-dolls conjecture holds, it may have an infinity of components. Viewed as information, the hand grew in accord with detailed instructions coded by the body's DNA. Information about the hand's past is embodied in such traces as scars and freckles. How many questions would someone have to ask about your hand to build a replica? What is the shortest computer program that would give this information?

Rucker likes to substitute familiar words for technical jargon. Instead of saying the world is a mixture of discreteness and continuity, he speaks of spottiness and smoothness. The usual references to the wave/particle duality of quantum mechanics are replaced by talk of lumps and bumps. Sometimes an electron acts like a discrete lump, sometimes like a bump in the shifting patterns of a wave field. Which is more fundamental, a particle or its field? This, says Rucker, is like asking which is more fundamental, a person or society? He invokes Niels Bohr's famous aphorism: "A great truth is a statement whose opposite is also a great truth." Bohr called this the principle of complementarity. He was so intrigued by the Oriental yin-yang symbol of complementarity that he put it on his coat of arms.

Following in the mental steps of his great-great-grandfather, the German philosopher Hegel, Rucker is a monist who believes that in some ultimate sense, like the circle that surrounds the yin and yang, all is One. There is no need, he writes, to distinguish either a particle from its field or a person from society. "Reality is one, and language introduces impossible distinctions that need not be made." Need not be made? To a pluralist—William James for example—the distinctions *have* to be made, not just because language forces them but because that is how the universe is fragmented. I once ran across a couplet by some unknown poet whose name I long ago forgot, though not the lines:

> *If all is One,*
> *Who will win?*

In some transcendent sense, monism may prevail, but the white light of Hegel's Absolute is stained by Shelley's dome of many-colored glass, and without the distinctions we could not think, talk, or live. Indeed, Rucker could not have written his book without thousands of distinctions in pure mathematics. As for the outside world, nothing is perfectly smooth. Everything has lumps.

Such metaphysical animadversions need not hinder a pluralist from enjoying Rucker's lively explorations. His number section tells how to use your fingers as flip-flops for binary counting. This leads to a discussion of logarithms, figurate numbers (numbers modeled by spots in patterned arrays), giant numbers, and the numerology of interesting numbers from 1 to 100. Ninety-one is particularly interesting. It counts the spots in a triangular array of thirteen spots on the side, the spots in a hexagonal array of six spots on the side, and the number of balls in a pyramid with six on the side of its square base. It is the sum of the cubes of 3 and 4, and when you write it in base-9 notation it is 111. Twenty-three is the smallest integer Rucker found relatively boring.

The section on space allows Rucker to introduce tiling theory, with special attention to an extraordinary discovery in 1974 by the British mathematical physicist Roger Penrose. Penrose found a pair of quadrilateral figures, usually called "kites and darts" because of their shapes, that tile the plane in only a nonperiodic way. A periodic tiling is one on which you can outline a region that tiles the plane by translation (shifting without rotating or reflecting), in the manner of the bricks that tile a brick wall. On a nonperiodic tiling, no such region can be outlined. It is of course possible to tile the plane nonperiodically with replications of a single shape as simple as a triangle or square, but such shapes also tile periodically. Whether there exists a single shape that will tile *only* nonperiodically is one of the major unsolved problems of tiling theory.

The amazing thing about Penrose's kites and darts is that the only way they will cover the plane, without gaps or overlaps, is nonperiodically. Mathematicians—notably John Conway, now at Princeton University—at once began finding all sorts of astonishing properties of Penrose tiling, when a few years ago a wholly unexpected event took place. Crystals were constructed with atoms arranged in a nonperiodic pattern based on a three-dimensional analog of Penrose tiles! Hundreds of papers have since appeared about these strange "quasicrystals." It is a superb instance of how a discovery in what can be called pure recreational mathematics suddenly found a totally unexpected application to the shaggy world "out there."[1]

The same Conway invented the most profound of all computer recreations, the cellular-automaton game of Life. A cellular automaton is a structure of cells, each of which can assume a certain number of states. At each "tick" of time, the states simultaneously alter according to "transition rules" that govern the passage of information to a cell from a specified set of "neighbors." Cellular-automata theory is now a hot topic on the fringes of math, with many applications to robot theory and artificial intelligence. Edward Fredkin, at

MIT, has conjectured that the universe itself may be one vast cellular automaton. As Rucker points out, this vision is similar to Leibniz's dream of a cosmos composed of isolated monads that "have no windows," and are incessantly changing in obedience to transition rules decreed by God. Viewed this way, the universe is playing a computer game so awesomely complex that the fastest way anyone will ever be able to predict its future states is just to let the game go on and see what happens.[2]

Discussions of classical curves (including some with such splendid names as Pearls of Sluze and the Nephroid of Freeth) lead Rucker into the exciting new field of fractals, a remarkable kind of irregular pattern that Benoit Mandelbrot was the first to investigate in depth. A fractal is an infinitely long curve or infinitely complex pattern that always looks the same if you keep enlarging portions of it. Mandelbrot called them fractals because he found an ingenious way to assign them fractional space dimensions. During the last ten years, following Mandelbrot's brilliant leads, fractals have found hundreds of applications in science and aesthetics.[3] A coastline, the surfaces of mountains, and the surface of the moon are familiar approximations of fractals. As a camera gets closer to the moon, photographing smaller and smaller craters, the surface still looks the same. Computer programs are now generating fractal music and fantastic fractal landscapes for science-fiction films. The topic propels Rucker into one of his wild conjectures, but you will have to consult his chapter "Life is a Fractal in Hilbert Space" to get the details.

Rucker's next section, on logic, begins with Aristotle's syllogisms, followed by the propositional calculus and the predicate calculus, the two lowest levels of symbolic logic. Next comes a stimulating discussion of Kurt Gödel's famous undecidability proof that in any formal system complicated enough to include arithmetic, true theorems can be stated that can not be proved within the system. For instance, Goldbach's conjecture—that every even number is the sum of two primes—could, in the light of Gödel's theorem, be undecidable. If so, mathematicians may be doomed never either to find a counterexample or to prove the conjecture true.

Rucker examines Gödel's theorem from his five perspectives; he ties the discussion into the theory of Turing machines (idealized computers), and a theorem of Alonzo Church's that says that no algorithm (step-by-step procedure) exists that will in a finite time tell whether an arbitrary statement in a complex formal system (one more complex than the propositional calculus) is true. The section ends with musings on how dull life would be if Gödel's and Church's theorems did not hold. "Our world is endlessly more complicated than any finite program or any finite set of rules. You're free, and you're really alive, and there's no telling what you'll think of next."

The section on information carries Rucker into questions about infinity. Cantor's alephs are explained; then, going the other way, the infinitesimally small numbers of a modern approach to calculus called nonstandard analysis are explained. Bishop George Berkeley ridiculed the infinitesimal magnitudes in the calculus of Newton and Leibniz, but now, thanks to the labors of Abraham Robinson, infinitely small quantities are as respectable as Cantor's alephs. The section leads into subtle information theorems recently established by Gregory Chaitin and his colleague Charles Bennett. Rucker paraphrases their theorems in a characteristically cryptic way:

> Speaking more loosely, Chaitin showed that we can't prove that the world has no simple explanation. Bennett showed that the world may indeed have a simple explanation, but that the world may be so logically deep that it takes an impossibly long time to turn the explanation into actual predictions about phenomena.
>
> To make it even simpler: Chaitin shows that we can't disprove the existence of a simple Secret of Life, but Bennett shows that, even if someone tells you the Secret of Life, turning it into usable knowledge may prove incredibly hard. The Secret of Life may not be worth knowing.

Hegel had a compulsion to group ideas into triads of thesis, antithesis, and synthesis. His great-great-great grandson's book ends not with a triad but a pentad:

> My purpose in writing *Mind Tools* has been to see what follows if one believes that everything is information. I have reached the following (debatable) conclusions.
>
> 1) The world can be resolved into digital bits, with each bit made of smaller bits.
> 2) These bits form a fractal pattern in fact-space.
> 3) The pattern behaves like a cellular automaton.
> 4) The pattern is inconceivably large in size and in dimensions.
> 5) Although the world started very simply, its computation is irreducibly complex.

So what is reality, one more time? An incompressible computation by a fractal CA [cellular automaton] of inconceivable dimensions. And where is this huge computation taking place? Everywhere; it's what we're made of.

NOTES

1. You can find out more about Penrose tiling in chapter 10 of *Tilings and Patterns*, a beautiful book by Branko Grünbaum and G. C. Shephard (W. H. Freeman, 1986), and in my *Penrose Tiles to Trapdoor Ciphers* (W. H. Freeman, 1989).

2. Even the ridiculously simple transition rules of Life, concerning cells with only two states and eight neighbors, create patterns impossible to predict. An entire book about Life and its philosophical implications is William Poundstone's *The Recursive Universe* (Morrow, 1984).

3. On fractals, see Benoit Mandelbrot's masterpiece, *The Fractal Geometry of Nature* (W. H. Freeman, 1982), and *The Beauty of Fractals*, by H. O. Pietgen and P. H. Richter (Springer-Verlag, 1986).

SEVEN

CAN TIME STOP?
THE PAST CHANGE?

I hope that this essay, which ran in Scientific American *(March 1979) will arouse a sense of awe about the mystery of time. I am among those who believe that time, like space, is an ultimate mystery that must be accepted as given—something that cannot be explained by science or philosophy now or in the future. There is no way to define time without introducing time into the definition. To say time is change is to say nothing because you can't define change without assuming time. Time, physicist John Wheeler likes to say, is what keeps everything from happening at once.*

It is impossible to imagine oneself existing without existing in time. To be conscious is, at the minimum, to have thoughts in a serial order, which implies time. I am convinced that the mystery of free will is interlocked with the mystery of time. Is God in or outside of time? Did time start with the Big Bang or was there a time before the bang? I do not know the answers to such questions, and neither do you.

"It is impossible to meditate on time and the mystery of the creative passage of nature without an overwhelming emotion at the limitations of human intelligence."

—ALFRED NORTH WHITEHEAD,
The Concept of Nature

There has been a great deal of interest among physicists of late in whether or not there are events on the elementary-particle level that cannot be time-reversed, that is, events for which imagining a reversal in the direction of motion of all the particles involved is imagining an event that cannot happen in nature. Richard Feynman has suggested an

approach to quantum mechanics in which antiparticles are viewed as particles
momentarily traveling backward in time. Cosmologists have speculated about
two universes for which all the events in one are reversed relative to the
direction of time in the other: in each universe intelligent organisms would
live normally from past to future, but if the organisms in one universe could
in some way observe events in the other (which many physicists consider an
impossibility), they would find those events going in the opposite direction.
It has even been conjectured that if our universe stops expanding and starts
to contract, there will be a time reversal, but it is far from clear what that
would mean. Most of the speculations of this kind are quite recent, and interested readers will find many of them examined in four chapters of my *New
Ambidextrous Universe*.

In this essay I shall consider two bizarre questions about time that are
not discussed in the book. Indeed, these questions are of so little concern to
scientists that only philosophers and writers of fantasy and science fiction have
had much to say about them: Is it meaningful to speak of time stopping? Is
it meaningful to speak of altering the past?

Neither question should be confused with the familiar subject of time's
relativity. Newton believed the universe was pervaded by a single absolute
time that could be symbolized by an imaginary clock off somewhere in space
(perhaps outside the cosmos). By means of this clock the rates of all the events
in the universe could be measured. The notion works well within a single
inertial frame of reference such as the surface of the earth, but it does not
work for inertial systems moving in relation to each other at high speeds.
According to the theory of relativity, if a spaceship were to travel from our
solar system to another solar system with a velocity close to that of light,
events would proceed much slower on the spaceship than they would on the
earth. In a sense, then, such a spaceship is traveling through time into the
future. Passengers on the spaceship might experience a round-trip voyage as
taking only a few years, but they would return to find that centuries of earth-
years had elapsed.

The notion that different parts of the universe can change at different
rates of time is much older than the theory of relativity. In the Scholastic
theology of the Middle Ages angels were considered to be nonmaterial intelligences living by a time different from that of earthly creatures; God himself
was thought to be entirely outside of time. In the first act of Lord Byron's
play, *Cain, A Mystery*, the fallen angel Lucifer says:

> With us acts are exempt from time,
>   and we
> Can crowd eternity into an hour
> Or stretch an hour into eternity.

*We breathe not by a mortal
measurement—
But that's a mystery.*

In the 20th century hundreds of science-fiction stories have played with the relativity of time in different inertial systems, but the view that time can speed up or slow down in different parts of our universe is central to many older tales. A popular medieval legend tells of a monk who is entranced for a minute or two by the song of a magical bird. When the bird stops singing, the monk discovers that several hundred years have passed. In a Moslem legend Mohammed is carried by a mare into the seventh heaven. After a long visit the prophet returns to the earth just in time to catch a jar of water the horse had kicked over before starting its ascent.

Washington Irving's "Rip Van Winkle" is this country's best-known story about someone who sleeps for what seems to him to be a normal time while two decades of earth-years rush by. King Arthur's daughter Gyneth slept for 500 years under a spell cast by Merlin. Every culture has similar sleeper legends. H. G. Wells used the device in *When the Sleeper Wakes,* and it is a common practice in science fiction to put astronauts into a cryogenic sleep so they can survive interstellar voyages that are longer than their normal life span. In Wells's short story "The New Accelerator" a scientist discovers a way to speed up a person's biological time so that the world seems to come almost to a halt. This device too is frequently encountered in later science fiction.

The issue under consideration here, however, is not how time can vary but whether time can be said to stop entirely. It is clearly meaningful to speak of all motion ceasing in one part of the universe, whether or not such a part exists. In the theory of relativity the speed of light is an unattainable limit for any object with mass. If a spaceship could attain the speed of light (which the theory of relativity rules out because the mass of the ship would increase to infinity), then time on the spaceship would stop in the sense that all change on it would cease. In earth time it might take 100 years for the spaceship to reach a destination, but to astronauts on the spaceship the destination would be reached instantaneously. One can also imagine a piece of matter or even a human being reduced to such a low temperature (by some as yet unknown means) that even all subatomic motions would be halted. For that piece of matter, then, one could say that time had stopped. Actually it is hard to understand why the piece of matter would not vanish.

The idea of time stopping creates no problems for writers of fantasy, who are not constrained by the real world. For example, in L. Frank Baum's "The Capture of Father Time," one of the stories in his *American Fairy Tales* (now back in print in a Dover facsimile edition), a small boy lassoes Time, and for a while everything except the movements of the boy and Father Time stops completely. In Chapter 22 of James Branch Cabell's *Jurgen: A Comedy of Justice*, outside time sleeps while Jurgen enjoys a pleasurable stay in Cocaigne with Queen Anaïtis. Later in the novel Jurgen stares into the eyes of the God of his grandmother and is absolutely motionless for 37 days. In Jorge Luis Borges's story "The Secret Miracle" a writer is executed by a firing squad. Between the command to fire and the writer's death God stops all time outside the writer's brain, giving him a year to complete his masterpiece.

Many similar examples from legend and literature show that the notion of time stopping in some part of the universe is not logically inconsistent. But what about the idea of time stopping throughout the universe? Does the notion that everything stops moving for a while and then starts again have any meaning?

If it is assumed that there is an outside observer—perhaps a god—watching the universe from a region of hypertime, then of course the notion of time stopping does have meaning, just as imagining a god in hyperspace gives meaning to the notion of everything in the universe turning upside down. The history of our universe may be like a three-dimensional motion picture a god is enjoying. When the god turns off the projector to do something else, a few millenniums may go by before he comes back and turns it on again. (After all, what are a few millenniums to a god?) For all we can know a billion centuries of hypertime may have elapsed between my typing the first and the second word of this sentence.

Suppose, however, all outside observers are ruled out and "universe" is taken to mean "everything there is." Is there still a way to give a meaning to the idea of all change stopping for a while? Although most philosophers and scientists would say there is not, a few have argued for the other side. For example, in "Time without Change" Sydney S. Shoemaker, now a philosopher at Cornell University, makes an unusual argument in support of the possibility of change stopping.

Shoemaker is concerned not with the real world but with possible worlds designed to prove that the notion of time stopping everywhere can be given a reasonable meaning. He proposes several worlds of this kind, all of them based on the same idea. I shall describe only one such world here, in a slightly dramatized form.

Imagine a universe divided into regions A, B, and C. In normal times inhabitants of each region can observe the inhabitants of the other two and communicate with them. Every now and then, however, a mysterious purple glow permeates one of the regions. The glow always lasts for a week and is invariably followed by a year in which all change in the region ceases. In other words, for one year absolutely nothing happens there. Shoemaker calls the phenomenon a local freeze. Since no events take place, light cannot leave the region, and so the region seems to vanish for a year. When it returns to view, its inhabitants are unaware of any passage of time, but they learn from their neighbors that a year, as measured by clocks in the other two regions, has elapsed. To the inhabitants of the region that experienced the local freeze it seems that instantaneous changes have taken place in the other two regions. As Shoemaker puts it: "People and objects will appear to have moved in a discontinuous manner or to have vanished into thin air or to have materialized out of thin air; saplings will appear to have grown instantaneously into mature trees, and so on."

In the history of each of the three regions local freezes, invariably preceded by a week of purple light, have happened thousands of times. Now suppose that suddenly, for the first time in history, purple light appears simultaneously in regions A, B, and C and lasts for a week. Would it not be reasonable, Shoemaker asks, for scientists in the three regions to conclude that change had ceased for a year throughout the entire universe even though no minds were aware of it?

Shoemaker considers several objections to his thesis and counters all of them ingeniously. Interested readers can consult his paper and then read a technical analysis of it in the fifth chapter of G. Schlesinger's *Confirmation and Confirmability*. Schlesinger agrees with Shoemaker that an empirical, logically consistent meaning can be found for the sentence "A period of time *t* has passed during which absolutely nothing happened." Note that similar arguments about possible worlds can provide meanings for such notions as everything in a universe turning upside down, mirror-reversing, doubling in size and so on.

The question of whether the past can be changed is even stranger than that of whether time can stop. Writers have often speculated about what might have happened if the past had taken a different turn. J. B. Priestley's play *Dangerous Corner* dealt with this question, and there have been innumerable "what if" stories in both science fiction and other kinds of literature. In all time-travel stories where someone enters the past, the past is necessarily altered. The only way the logical contradictions created by such a premise can be resolved is by positing a universe that splits into separate branches the instant the past is entered. In other words, while time in the old branch "gurgles on" (a phrase from Emily Dickinson) time in the new branch gurgles on in a different way toward a different future. When I speak of altering the past, however, I mean altering it throughout a single universe with no forking time paths. (Pseudoalterations of the past, such as the rewriting of history satirized by George Orwell in *1984*, obviously do not qualify.) Given this context, can an event, once it has happened, ever be made not to have happened?

The question is older than Aristotle, who in his *Ethics* (Book 6) writes: "It is to be noted that nothing that is past is an object of choice, for example, no one chooses to have sacked Troy; for no one *deliberates* about the past, but about what is future and capable of being otherwise, while what is past is not capable of not having taken place; hence Agathon is right in saying: 'For this alone is lacking even to God, to make undone things that have once been done.' "

Thomas Aquinas believed God to be outside of time and thus capable of seeing all his creation's past and future in one blinding instant. (Even though human beings have genuine power of choice, God knows how each one will choose; it is in this way that Aquinas sought to harmonize predestination and free will.) For Aquinas it was not possible for God to do absolutely impossible things, namely those that involve logical contradiction. For example, God could not make a creature that was both a human being and a horse (that is, a complete human being and a complete horse, rather than a mythical combination of parts such as a centaur), because that would involve the contradiction of assuming a creature to be simultaneously rational and nonrational.

Similarly, God cannot alter the past. That would be the same as asserting that the sack of Troy both took place and did not take place. Aquinas agreed with Aristotle that the past must forever be what it was, and it was this view that became the official position of medieval Scholasticism. It is not so much that God's omnipotence is limited by the law of contradiction but rather that the law is part of God's nature. "It is best to say," Aquinas wrote, "that what involves contradiction cannot be done rather than that God cannot do it." Modern philosophers would say it this way. God can't make a four-sided triangle, not because he can't make objects with four sides but because a triangle is *defined* as a three-sided polygon. The phrase "four-sided triangle" is therefore a nonsense phrase, one without meaning.

Edwyn Bevan, in a discussion of time in his book *Symbolism and Belief*, finds it odd that Aquinas would deny God the ability to alter the past and at the same time allow God to alter the future. In the 10th question of *Summa Theologica* (Ia. 10, article 5.3), Aquinas wrote: "God can cause an angel not to exist in the future, even if he cannot cause it not to exist while it exists, or not to have existed when it already has." For Aquinas to have suggested that for God the past is unalterable and the future is not unalterable, Bevan reasons, is surely to place God in some kind of time, thus contradicting the assertion that God is outside of time.

I know of no scientist or secular philosopher who has seriously believed the past could be altered, but a small minority of theologians have maintained that it could be. The greatest of them was Peter Damian, the zealous Italian reformer of the Roman Catholic church in the 11th century. In *On Divine Omnipotence*, his most controversial treatise, Damian argued that God is in no way bound by the law of contradiction, that his omnipotence gives him the power to do all contradictory things including changing the past. Although Damian, who started out as a hermit monk, argued his extreme views skillfully, he regarded all reasoning as superfluous, useful only for supporting revealed theology. It appears that he, like Lewis Carroll's White Queen, would have defended everyone's right to believe six impossible things before breakfast. (Damian was also a great promoter of self-flagellation as a form of penance, a practice that became such a fad during his lifetime that some monks flogged themselves to death.)

One of my favorite Lord Dunsany stories is the best example I know of from the literature of fantasy that illustrates Damian's belief in the possibility of altering the past. It is titled "The King That Was Not," and you will find it in Dunsany's early book of wonder tales *Time and the Gods*. It begins as follows: "The land of Runazar hath no King nor ever had one; and this is the law of the land of Runazar that, seeing that it hath never had a King, it shall not have one for ever. Therefore in Runazar the priests hold sway, who tell the people that never in Runazar hath there been a King."

The start of the second paragraph is surprising: "Althazar, King of Runazar. . . ." The story goes on to recount how Althazar ordered his sculptors to carve marble statues of the gods. His command was obeyed, but when the great statues were undraped, their faces were very much like the face of the king. Althazar was pleased and rewarded his sculptors handsomely with gold, but up in Pegāna (Dunsany's Mount Olympus) the gods were outraged. One of them, Mung, leaned forward to make his sign against Althazar, but the other gods stopped him: "Slay him not, for it is not enough that Althazar shall die, who hath made the faces of the gods to be like the faces of men, but he must not even have ever been."

> *"Spake we of Althazar, a King?"*
>   *asked one of the gods.*
> *"Nay, we spake not."*
> *"Dreamed we of one Althazar?"*
> *"Nay, we dreamed not."*

Below Pegāna, in the royal palace, Althazar suddenly passed out of the memory of the gods and so "became no longer a thing that was or had ever been." When the priests and the people entered the throne room, they found only a robe and a crown. "The gods have cast away the fragment of a garment," said the priests, "and lo! from the fingers of the gods hath slipped one little ring."

POSTSCRIPT

When I wrote about time stopping I was using a colloquial expression to mean that change ceases. If there are no moving "clocks" of any sort for measuring time, one can say in a loose sense that time stops. Of course time does not move or stop any more than length can extend or not extend. It is the universe that moves. You can refute the notion that time "flows" like a river simply by asking: "At what rate does it flow?" Shoemaker wanted to show in his paper not that time stops, then starts again, but that all change can stop and some sort of transcendental hypertime still persists. Change requires time, but perhaps, Shoemaker argued, time does not require change in our universe.

Harold A. Segal, in a letter in *The New York Times* (January 11, 1987) quoted a marvelous passage from Shakespeare's *As You Like It* (Act III, Scene 2) in which Rosalind explains how time can amble, trot, gallop, or stand still for different persons in different circumstances. It trots for the "young maid" between her engagement and marriage. It ambles for a priest who knows no Latin because he is free from the burden of "wasteful learning." It ambles for the rich man in good health who "lives merrily because he feels no pain." It gallops for the thief who awaits his hanging. For whom does it stand still? "With lawyers in the vacation; for they sleep between term and term, and then they perceive not how Time moves."

Isaac Asimov, in an editorial in *Asimov's Science-Fiction Magazine* (June 1986) explained why it would not be possible for a person to walk about and observe a world in which all change had stopped. To move, she would have to push aside molecules, and this would inject time into the outside world. She would be as frozen as the universe, even though dancing atoms in her brain might continue to let her think. Asimov could have added that she would not even be able to *see* the world because sight depends on photons speeding from the world into one's eyes.

Two readers, Edward Adams and Henry Lambert, independently wrote to say that the god Koschei, in *Jurgen*, could alter the past. At the end of the novel he eliminates all of Jurgen's adventures as never having happened. However, Jurgen recalls that Horvendile (the name Cabell often used for himself) once told him that he (Horvendile) and Koschei were one and the same!

Edward Fredkin is a computer scientist who likes to think of the universe as a vast cellular automaton run by an inconceivably complex algorithm that tells the universe how to jump constantly from one state to the next. Whoever or whatever is running the program could, of course, shut it down at any time, then later start it running again. We who are part of the program would have no awareness of such gaps in time.

On the unalterability of the past, readers reminded me of the stanza in Omar's *Rubaiyat* about the moving finger that having writ moves on, and all our piety and wit cannot call it back to cancel half a line. Or as Ogden Nash once put it:

> One thing about the past.
> It's likely to last.

I touched only briefly on the many science-fiction stories and novels that deal with time slowing down or halting. For references on some of the major tales see the section "When time stands still" on page 153 of *The Visual Encyclopedia of Science Fiction.* The most startling possibility, now seriously advanced by some physicists, is that the universe comes to a complete stop billions of times every microsecond, then starts up again. Like a cellular automaton it jumps from state to state. Between the jumps, nothing changes. The universe simply does not exist. Time is quantized. An electron doesn't move smoothly from here to there. It moves in tiny jumps, occupying no space in between.

The fundamental unit of quantized time has been called the "chronon." Between chronons one can imagine one or more parallel universes operating within our space, but totally unknown to us. Think of a film with two unrelated motion pictures running on alternate frames. Between the frames of our universe, who knows what other exotic worlds are unrolling in the intervals between our chronons? Both motion pictures and cellular automata are deterministic, but in this vision of parallel universes running in the same space, there is no need to assume determinism. Chance and free will could still play creative roles in making the future of each universe unpredictable in principle.

EIGHT

WERNER HEISENBERG

Uncertainty: The Life and Science of Werner Heisenberg, *by David C. Cassidy, is a work of 669 pages, published in 1992 by W. H. Freeman and Company. When Howard Schneider, an editor of* Dimensions, *a journal of holocaust studies published by the Anti-Defamation League, asked me to review this book, I eagerly agreed. The review appeared in Volume 7, Number 1, 1993.*

Werner Karl Heisenberg's eminence in the history of physics is assured. His paper on the uncertainty principle, written in 1927 when he was 26, marked the beginning of quantum mechanics, the most profound revolution in science since relativity theory. But it is not Heisenberg's monumental contribution to physics that has placed him at the center of intense, continuing controversy. As the title of David Cassidy's massive and admirable biography implies, it is uncertainty about the man's moral character.

Dr. Cassidy, who calls himself a "physicist turned historian of science," now teaches at Hofstra University, on Long Island. Although his book expertly covers the history of quantum theory, I shall have little to say about this technical portion of the book beyond a few paragraphs. In 1927, when Heisenberg's famous paper was published, Niels Bohr in Copenhagen, and Arnold Sommerfeld in Germany, regarded the atom as a miniature solar system. Around its central nucleus electrons orbited like tiny planets. Heisenberg changed this conception. Electrons became ghostly, pointlike concentrations of energy in mathematical fields. They had a distressing habit of not even existing until they were measured. Moreover, if you knew where an electron was, you couldn't exactly determine its momentum. And if you knew its momentum, its position became "smeared." A particle obviously can go from A to B, but between measurements of the two locations it has no precise path.

Electrons go wherever they like. The best one can do is determine the probability they will be found at certain spots.

Heisenberg based his theory on matrix algebra, a discrete approach in which space is divided into little cells like rooms in a hotel. As so often is the case with prodigies in physics, he invented the algebra without knowing it had been familiar to mathematicians for a century. A year later Erwin Schrödinger, another German, approached quantum theory from a different perspective, basing it on continuous waves which he believed to be as "real" as sound or water waves. Each man was at first repelled by the other's theory. Schrödinger soon proved that the two approaches were mathematically equivalent. They were just different languages for saying the same thing.

The next giant step was taken by Germany's Max Born. He showed that Schrödinger's waves were no more than useful fictions, waves of probability in artificial spaces that simplified calculations. No one ever explained this better than the British astronomer Sir James Jeans. In *The New Background of Science* (1938) he wrote:

> As this is one of the most difficult parts of the new quantum theory, let us try to illustrate it by a very prosaic illustration. Suppose I am anxious to meet my relative John Smith, who is owing me a sum of money, and that all I know of him for certain is that he left his home in London three days ago for an unspecified destination. My knowledge as to the whereabouts of John Smith is represented by a fog which extends over all those parts of the earth's surface which are within three days' travel of London. I next find that a passenger named John Smith sailed on the *Majestic* three days ago for New York, and the fog becomes particularly dense in mid-Atlantic, three days out from land. I hurry to a cable office to communicate with the *Majestic* in the hope of getting a reply which will inform me, with the speed of light, whether my relative is in mid-Atlantic or not. But, on my way, I run into John Smith himself. This simple act not only concentrates all the fog into one spot in space, namely that at which my relative is standing; it also abolishes the fog in the Atlantic, and does this far more promptly than a wireless message, travelling with the speed of light, could do. It can do this because the fog is not a material fog, such as delays shipping; it consists of knowledge—knowledge about John Smith.

In quantum mechanics the deterministic causal laws of classical physics, both Newtonian and relativistic, were replaced by a beautiful haphazardry. The position of a quantum particle, and many other of its properties, could be predicted in advance of measurement only with varying degrees of probability. The fundamental laws of physics became statistical. This fuzziness is not caused, as in classical physics, by the imperfections of measuring instruments. It is built into the very heart of things. Not even in principle can one escape quantum uncertainty. An electron does not have a precise position until you measure it. The scanning beam of your television screen works because it contains billions of electrons; therefore it is highly probable that most of them will strike the screen's correct pixel.

Werner Heisenberg was born in Duisberg in 1901. In his teens he was an enthusiastic supporter of the German youth movement, serving as *führer* (leader) of a group in the New German Pathfinders. At the University of Munich he was Arnold Sommerfeld's star pupil. He became a professor at the University of Leipzig in 1927, won a Nobel Prize in 1932, and married Elisabeth Schumacher in 1937. They had seven children. Early in life he played the cello. Later he became an accomplished pianist. Next to physics, his family, and the Fatherland, his great love was classical music.

Heisenberg never joined the Nazi party, as did so many of his friends and colleagues. He had no respect for Hitler, but Germany he loved with the passion of a patriot who defends his country "right or wrong." It was impossible for him to consider leaving. When, in 1938, Germany's Otto Hahn and others showed that atomic fission was possible, it was inevitable that Heisenberg, the nation's top physicist, would be asked by certain Nazi officials to head a laboratory to explore the feasibility of obtaining fission and making atomic weapons. Unable to refuse, he became Germany's J. Robert Oppenheimer. Five other laboratories in Germany were also assigned work on fission, but Heisenberg's work in Berlin was the most important.

Jewish scientists, such as Einstein and scores of others, were quick to leave Germany and Italy as soon as they realized that Hitler and Mussolini were tyrants destined to inflict untold horrors on the world. Heisenberg had every opportunity to emigrate. He was repeatedly offered lucrative posts at non-German universities, including Columbia University in the United States. He turned them all down.

Ironically, even though Heisenberg was not Jewish, it was not easy for him to obtain clearance for his war research. He had straw-colored hair and Nordic blue eyes, but his acceptance of relativity theory, formulated by a despised Jew, made him deeply suspect. Nazi scientists called him a "white Jew." For a while he was subjected to humiliating interviews, and his relatives and friends were secretly investigated. The Gestapo bugged his home. His mail was surely opened and read. Insinuations were raised, totally unfounded, of early gay behavior. Eventually and grudgingly, the Nazis finally accepted him. Cassidy quotes from a letter of Himmler's: "I believe that Heisenberg is decent, and we could not afford to lose or to silence this man who is relatively young and can educate a new generation." Himmler graciously allowed Heisenberg to use and teach relativity theory, provided, of course, he would never mention Einstein.

Heisenberg thanked Himmler profusely. From then on he worked tirelessly on atomic fission. Whatever misgivings he had about Hitler were craftily concealed. He and his wife talked politics only on the street, fearing their house was still bugged. Heisenberg routinely gave the Nazi salute. He ended his official correspondence with "Heil Hitler." Earlier, in 1935, he had signed a civil service order pledging allegiance to Hitler. For several months he was in army uniform and almost sent to war. Cassidy believes that at this time he must have signed the usual army pledge of willingness to die for the Führer.

An indispensable reference on Heisenberg's cooperation with the Nazis is the 1947 book *ALSOS* by Samuel Goudsmit,[1] a Dutch physicist who was codiscoverer of a property of particles called "spin." The circumstances leading up to the writing of the book are as follows. Goudsmit's aged Jewish father and his blind Jewish mother died in the gas chambers of Auschwitz. Goudsmit had earlier sought Heisenberg's aid in getting them out of Germany, but Heisenberg's efforts were feeble. Stronger efforts could have cost him his job, maybe even his life.

As the war drew to a close, Goudsmit was appointed the science supervisor of a secret U.S. mission with the code name Alsos, a Greek word derived from "grove." The name refers to the last name of General Leslie Groves, who was in charge of the Manhattan Project program to make an atom bomb. American physicists, knowing Heisenberg's competence, were deeply fearful that German science would produce the atomic bomb before they did. The objective of the Alsos team was to follow Allied troops into Germany in 1945, arrest Heisenberg and his assistants, and confiscate their records.

Written by a man with a droll sense of humor, *ALSOS* is a saga of high comedy, detailing huge expenditures of funds and all sorts of cloak-and-dagger shenanigans. The outcome of the mission was a total surprise: To the vast amazement of everyone involved, Heisenberg's laboratory was nowhere close to making an atomic bomb. The researchers had not even obtained a chain reaction. The frontispiece of *ALSOS* is a picture captioned "Germany's Oak Ridge." It shows a building not much larger than a big outhouse.

When Goudsmit first entered Heisenberg's laboratory, an accompanying army general was startled to see a photograph of Goudsmit and Heisenberg standing side by side. The general was unaware that great physicists know one another and tend to be friends. Heisenberg had fled the laboratory on his bicycle, after hiding research documents in a can that had been lowered into an assistant's home privy. Goudsmit assigned a lieutenant the disagreeable chore of retrieving this can. His revenge, Goudsmit writes, was leaving the can under an open window of the room where Goudsmit slept.

When Heisenberg was finally captured, he at once offered to share all his secrets with Goudsmit, and spoke with great pride about how much he had accomplished. Goudsmit listened patiently, unable to tell his former friend how trivial it all was. "Why don't you come with me to America?" Goudsmit asked. Heisenberg refused. "Germany needs me," was his answer.

Heisenberg and nine other physicists, including Otto Hahn, soon found themselves imprisoned in Farm Hall, a comfortable country mansion near Cambridge, England. Their conversation was secretly recorded. It is amusing to learn that when someone suggested to Heisenberg that their remarks might be recorded, he laughed and said this was not possible because the Americans were too "old-fashioned" to be familiar with Gestapo methods. Transcripts of the recordings were not made available to the public until early in 1992. (The complete transcripts were published in 1993.) The best account up to now of what they contain is Jeremy Bernstein's article, "The Farm Hall Transcripts," in *The New York Review of Books* (August 13, 1992).

When news of the destruction of Hiroshima reached Farm Hall, the ten physicists could not believe that Americans had succeeded where their great German science had failed. Heisenberg strongly doubted that the bomb was atomic. He believed the Americans were bluffing, and that it was an ordinary "high-pressure bomb" which had "nothing to do with uranium." Cassidy quotes Hahn as saying: "If the Americans have a uranium bomb, then you're all second-raters. Poor old Heisenberg!"

Otto Hahn, who was soon to receive a Nobel Prize for his discovery of fission, was the most staggered by the news. He repeatedly said he felt morally responsible for a discovery that made possible the killing of hundreds of thousands of civilian Japanese. He even contemplated suicide. Heisenberg, finally convinced that the bombs dropped on Japan were genuine atom bombs, complained bitterly that Goudsmit had lied to him by not telling him how far the American project had advanced. As Bernstein comments, "That Heisenberg thinks Goudsmit was obliged to tell him anything seems astonishing."

Among the physicists at Farm Hall, a series of excuses for their failure to make a bomb slowly began to take shape. Richard von Weizsäcker, Heisenberg's assistant and friend, said he believed the reason was that "all the physicists [in Germany] didn't want to do it on principle. If we had all wanted Germany to win the war, we would have succeeded." To which Hahn replied, "I don't believe that but I'm thankful we didn't succeed."

When Walther Gerlach broke into sobs, and talked of shooting himself, Hahn asked: "Are you upset because we did not make the uranium bomb . . . or are you depressed because the Americans could do it better than we could?" As Bernstein points out, the "Americans" were mostly Europeans, "along with a small army of lesser-known refugees from Hitler's Europe. This fact seems never to have occurred to any of the Germans."

On many occasions in the past, Heisenberg had said he hoped Germany would win the war. He naively thought that if Germany lost, hatred of the Fatherland would be so intense that the Allies would destroy Germany the way Rome destroyed Carthage. He was convinced that if Germany won, "good Germans" would soon take over and get rid of Hitler and his stupid Nazis. However, after the war, he insisted that he and his associates were concerned, while working for the Third Reich, entirely with developing fission as a post-war source of energy.

His chief aim during the war years, Heisenberg later claimed, was to preserve at all costs the continuity of German physics. Had he left Germany, who else could have done this? With deep revulsion against the bomb, he had actually done his best to sabotage the work he and his friends were doing! True, he had worked very hard to obtain a controlled chain reaction that would have made the bomb possible. He even told a horrified Nazi group that such a bomb, as small as a pineapple, could destroy a city the size of London. However, said Heisenberg later, funds for the project had been limited; given the resources at his disposal, so much smaller than those of the Manhattan Project, there was no way his laboratory could have built such a ghastly weapon in time to make a difference in the war. Even if they had the time and technology, he maintained, they would not have tried to make the bomb. Their only goal was to encourage Germany's peaceful use of atomic energy after the war.

Did Heisenberg really believe all the above or was he lying? It is this uncertainty that is the most significant aspect of Cassidy's biography. The book is not only the first full-scale portrayal of a brilliant and controversial scientist, but it is the most detailed exploration yet of the controversy that still rages over Heisenberg's motives.

Bohr made much of what he called "complementarity," the fact that seemingly contradictory aspects of quantum theory must each be accepted as true. In certain experiments, for instance, an electron behaves like a particle. In other experiments, it just as clearly acts like a wave. Which is correct? Most physicists accept Bohr's so-called Copenhagen interpretation. An electron is something more complicated than either a wave or a particle, but its exact nature is not yet understood. A great truth, Bohr liked to say, is a truth whose opposite is also a great truth. Perhaps this is how Heisenberg's contradictory behavior will ultimately be evaluated. As he often said to his wife, "You have to be able to stand living with the tensions of opposites."

Heisenberg's yin—his many justifications of why he did not emigrate—is echoed in Elisabeth Heisenberg's *Inner Exile* (1980), a book of recollections about her husband. She describes him as a man of great wisdom and courage who risked his life to remain in Germany in secret exile from a political system which he took great care not to offend. She pictures him as walking a swaying tightrope to preserve his life in order to save German science. He tried his best not to fabricate a weapon of mass destruction. Had he, after September 1939, openly voiced his opposition to Hitler, or abandoned his post, it would have cost him dearly. As Cassidy puts it, he did not stay in Germany to be a martyr.

The same yin is defended by the German science writer Robert Jungk in his popular but flawed history *Brighter Than a Thousand Suns*, first published in Germany in 1958. Waldemar Kaempffert, then the *New York Times*'s science writer, completely bought Jungk's line. German physicists, Kaempffert maintained, for moral reasons tried not to build atomic bombs. American physicists, for immoral reasons, actually built them and urged that they be used.

Goudsmit, in *ALSOS*, blamed the failure of Germany to build a bomb, not on lack of trying, but on incompetence. Heisenberg violently disagreed. The two men exchanged bitter letters in *The New York Times* and elsewhere. Kaempffert, after personally interviewing Heisenberg, described him as a man who spoke "with an objectivity that is convincing." Goudsmit accused Heisenberg of lying when he denied he was working on a bomb. "Liars do not win Nobel Prizes," was one of Kaempffert's most absurd statements. When Einstein was asked for his opinion, he sensibly replied that Nobel winners may indeed lie when under the pressure of circumstances.

To his death, his pride deeply wounded, Heisenberg insisted that his work on atomic fission, given his limited funding, had been a huge success. Goudsmit never wavered from his view that the German effort was mediocre for a variety of reasons, not the least being the "stifling atmosphere of a dictatorship." Hitler managed to drive the best scientists from Germany, leaving science in the hands of bureaucratic Nazi bunglers. Goudsmit confessed that his book contained some blunders, notably a false accusation that Heisenberg thought the only feasible atom bomb would be the dropping of a massive atomic pile. Moreover, Cassidy tells us, by the time Heisenberg died in 1976, Goudsmit's hatred of Heisenberg had considerably softened. He saw him more as a victim of Hitler than a supporter. But his fundamental objection to Heisenberg's behavior remained. Here is how Cassidy sums it up:

> Again and again Goudsmit made the same point to Heisenberg and his emissaries: what he really wanted to see from Heisenberg, Hahn, and other leading scientists was articles about the frustration of scientific progress under a totalitarian system of government. He insisted that they should stop extolling the greatness of German science and acknowledge its decimation by the Nazis—a demand that they were hardly in a position to fulfill. In fact, their position was almost impossible to maintain under any circumstances: trying to distance themselves from the Nazi regime while at the same time claiming that they had done great but harmless work under it. That Heisenberg would even attempt to defend the pursuit of decent science under the Nazi regime, or believe such were possible, seemed outrageous to many American scientists. Goudsmit had already declared of Heisenberg: "He fought the Nazis not because they were bad, but because they were bad for Germany, or at least for German science."

If Heisenberg had truly wanted Germany not to build an atomic bomb, say those on the yang side of the controversy, why did he not leave Germany?

Perhaps the real reason Heisenberg failed to ascertain how to construct an atomic bomb was not for lack of effort but because Hitler, in his vast ignorance of science, was never sold on the bomb's possibilities. His notions of warfare, Cassidy writes, were based on memories of the First World War— a war won by tanks, airplanes, submarines, and conventional artillery. Rockets to carry bombs he could understand. After all, the loyal Wernher von Braun had proved their usefulness against England. A pineapple-sized bomb capable of destroying all of London struck Hitler as sheer fantasy.

(When Hitler was willing to entertain the possibility that the atom bomb might be a viable weapon, there were other problems. Hitler's architect Albert Speer, in his memoirs, says that Heisenberg once warned Hitler that an atom bomb's explosion might cause a chain reaction that would engulf the entire planet. "Hitler was plainly not delighted," Cassidy quotes Speer as saying, "with the possibility that the earth under his rule might be transformed into a glowing star.")

Fortunately for the rest of the world Hitler did not mind in the least when the greatest German scientists and mathematicians, almost all of them Jewish, abandoned the Fatherland. It was good riddance. Heisenberg, Cassidy tells us, was especially angry with Schrödinger for leaving because, as Heisenberg put it, "he was neither Jewish nor otherwise endangered."

Nazi attacks on "Jewish science" accelerated under Hitler to unbelievable heights. Philipp Lenard, a good enough physicist to win a Nobel Prize in 1905 for his work on cathode rays, went to insane lengths to promote "Aryan science." He was a rabid Nazi and anti-Semite. Einstein's relativity theory was constantly denounced by Lenard and other Nazis as a prime example of the "Jewification" of German science. (Lenard, at least, was consistent: he had attacked relativity theory in a pamphlet published in 1920, when every physicist outside Germany already knew that relativity was indispensable to modern physics. There is a photograph in Cassidy's book of the pamphlet to prove that a Nobel winner could actually write such nonsense.) Of course, even the working of an atom bomb rested on Einstein's famous $E = mc^2$. Cassidy quotes Lenard's declaration that "science, like everything else that mankind produces, is conditioned by race, by blood." Lenard's magnum opus was a four-volume work modestly titled *German Science*.

German physicists who did not emigrate knew, of course, that physics could not be taught without relativity theory. How did they manage such teaching without being sent to a concentration camp? It is hard to believe, but in paper after paper they argued that Einstein really had little to do with relativity. Aryans in Germany and France had thought of it first. Dull-witted Einstein merely scribbled a few trivial details and falsely got credit for the theory!

Suppose Hitler had possessed the foresight of Franklin Roosevelt and been persuaded that atomic weapons could be built? Hitler would, of course, have given top priority to working on such weapons. If funds comparable to the Manhattan Project's had been available, would Heisenberg have refused to work on such a crash program? Everything suggests that he would have been obedient to his beloved Germany, right or wrong, and done his best to make the dreaded bomb.

It strains credulity to suppose, in light of the German physicists' enthusiasm for making rockets to kill British civilians, that those working on an atomic bomb would have sabotaged their own efforts out of moral scruples. Indeed, transcripts of conversations at Farm Hall make clear that although the ten physicists had all sorts of explanations for their failure to build a bomb, or even to obtain fission, only Weizsäcker gave as a reason that they secretly wanted Germany to lose the war. The American physicist Philip Morrison summed things up crisply in a review of ALSOS in The Bulletin of Atomic Scientists (Volume 3, 1947), from which Cassidy quotes:

> No different from their Allied counterparts, the German scientists worked for the military as best their circumstances allowed. But the difference, which will be never possible to forgive, is that they worked for the cause of Himmler and Auschwitz, for the burners of books and the takers of hostages.

Although Heisenberg and his wife did indeed view Hitler with contempt, and were shocked when they learned the details of the Holocaust, there is no evidence known to me that he ever regarded Hitler and his pals as more than temporary flies to be swatted after Germany won the war. It is worth noting that he made contingency plans to emigrate to the United States if the Soviets took over Germany. He could live under Hitler. He could not live under Communism! It took a curious kind of courage to remain in Germany in what his wife called "inner exile," but he lacked the greater courage to live outside Germany.

New publications concerning the secretly recorded conversations at Farm Hall have not settled the yin-yang debate. Writer Thomas Powers, in Heisenberg's War, published in 1993 by Knopf, argues the yin side—that the transcripts support Heisenberg's claim that moral scruples inhibited his research work during the war. Another of Powers's arguments is based on a mysterious trip Heisenberg made during the war to German-occupied Copenhagen, where he drew for Bohr a sketch of an atomic reactor. Powers thinks that Heisenberg, knowing Bohr would pass this information on to the Allies, was trying to alert the world to the fact that Germany was working on an atomic bomb. To put it plainly, Powers believes that in going to see Bohr, Heisenberg was engaged in what can only be called treason. Physicists less eager to defend Heisenberg think he made the trip to find out if Bohr knew what Allied physicists were working on.

No one doubts that Heisenberg was a great physicist, a loving husband and father, charming in person, and liked by his friends. Perhaps he came to believe all his rationalizations for not having achieved atomic fission. There is, however, something both he and his wife lacked. It was a profound moral revulsion against Hitler and everything Hitler wanted. Although Elisabeth Heisenberg wrote her book of memories as late as 1980, you will not find in it a single mention of the Final Solution.

NOTES

1. *ALSOS* was first published in 1947. A revised edition (Tomash Publishers, 1983) has an informative introduction by R. V. Jones, a former British intelligence officer.

NINE

SUPERSTRINGS

Superstring theory is the latest, most promising candidate for a "theory of everything." It developed too late to be covered in my Ambidextrous Universe *(Basic Books, 1964), but when I revised, corrected, and updated that book for* The New Ambidextrous Universe *(W. H. Freeman, 1990), I was able to discuss superstrings in a final chapter, here reprinted. Even if this theory turns out to be viable, I cannot believe it will be the end of understanding the mathematical structure of matter. There is, of course, no way a scientist can answer the superultimate question of why, as Stephen Hawking recently put it, the universe bothers to exist.*

One of the greatest lessons that can be learned from the history of science is one of humility. Science may indeed be steadily learning more about the structure of the world, but surely what is known is exceedingly small in relation to what is unknown. There is no scientific theory today, not even a law, that may not be modified or discarded tomorrow. "The great invariant principles of nature," wrote Philip Morrison in "The Overthrow of Parity" (*Scientific American*, April 1957), "may be relied upon within the domains of their application, but they are not *a priori* self-evident or necessarily of universal application. It is worthwhile to test to higher and higher precision the great fundamental principles. . . . We have entered an exhilarating time."

One of the most exhilarating prospects at the moment, which many physicists believe is almost upon us, is the construction of a deep theory of particles that will explain, in some elegant mathematical way, why all the particles are what they are. Abraham Pais, in an article titled "Particles" (*Physics Today*, May 1968), described particle physics as in a state "not unlike the one in a symphony hall a while before the start of the concert. On the podium one will see some but not yet all of the musicians. They are tuning up. Short brilliant passages are heard on some instruments; improvisations elsewhere; some wrong notes too. There is a sense of anticipation for the moment when the symphony starts."

If we could now hear a few strains of the great new symphony, the music might well strike us as insane. Freeman Dyson, in his article "Innovation in Physics," (*Scientific American*, September 1958), recalled that in 1958 Werner Heisenberg and Wolfgang Pauli put forward an unorthodox theory of particles that would explain the violations of parity in weak interactions. Pauli was lecturing in New York on these new ideas to a group of scientists that included Niels Bohr. In the discussion that followed the talk, younger scientists were sharply critical of Pauli.

Bohr rose to speak. "We are all agreed," he said to Pauli, "that your theory is crazy. The question which divides us is whether it is crazy enough to have a chance of being correct. My own feeling is that it is not crazy enough."

Dyson commented in his article:

"The objection that they are not crazy enough applies to all the attempts which have so far been launched at a radically new theory of elementary particles. It applies especially to crackpots. Most of the crackpot papers which are submitted to *The Physical Review* are rejected, not because it is impossible to understand them, but because it is possible. Those which are impossible to understand are usually published. When the great innovation appears, it will almost certainly be in a muddled, incomplete and confusing form. To the discoverer himself it will be only half-understood; to everybody else it will be a mystery. For any speculation which does not at first glance look crazy, there is no hope."

The physicist Jeremy Bernstein was in the audience at Columbia University when Pauli lectured on the strange theory he and Heisenberg had cooked up to explain everything in particle physics by way of a single equation. Details are fleshed out in Bernstein's delightful autobiography, *The Life It Brings* (Ticknor & Fields, 1987). Bernstein describes what happened when Bohr was asked to comment:

There then occurred one of the most unusual, and in its unearthly way most moving, demonstrations I have ever witnessed. . . . These two monumental figures in modern physics began moving in a conjoined circular orbit around the long lecture table. Whenever Bohr faced the audience from the front of the table, he repeated that the theory was not crazy enough, and whenever Pauli faced the group, he would say it was. I recall wondering what anyone from the other world—the non-physicists' world—would make of this. Dyson was asked to comment and refused. Afterward he remarked to me that it was like watching the "death of a noble animal." He was prescient. Pauli died not many months later, in 1958, at the age of fifty-eight, of a previously undetected cancer. Before

that, he had renounced "Heisenberg's theory," as he now referred to it,
in the most acidulous manner. One could only wonder whether Pauli's
brief love affair with it was a sign that he was already ill.

Among the many crazy speculations that continue to proliferate, the two
taken the most seriously at the moment are the twistor theory of Roger Penrose, and the newer and far more fashionable theory of superstrings. Twistors
may some day provide a geometrical foundation for superstrings. They are
abstract geometrical objects, closely related to spinors, modeled in a complex
space that Penrose puts below the level of ordinary space-time. Not the least
startling aspect of twistor theory is that it regards the universe, on its most
fundamental level, as asymmetric with respect to left and right.

Superstring theory is just as "crazy." Some of the brightest minds in particle physics are now working furiously on it, with dozens of papers appearing
every month that are usually out of date by the time the ink dries. If either
theory, or a blend of the two, turns out to be on the right track, it will generate
a paradigm shift of colossal magnitude.

Relativity theory was essentially the product of one man. Einstein started
with the bold conjecture that the universe does not permit absolute measurements of lengths, time intervals, or motions relative to a fixed framework.
At first his theory, called the *special theory of relativity*, applied only to uniform
motion. Then, by an incredible feat of creative imagination, Einstein generalized the theory to accelerated motion. This required a new theory of gravity,
and the seemingly insane notion—Einstein called it the *principle of equivalence*—that gravity and inertia are the same. The final result, the *principle of
covariance*, says that regardless of the motion of an observer, all the laws of
nature can be expressed by the same equations. Einstein himself once said
that *invariant theory* would have been a better name for his achievement than
relativity.

Superstring theory does not rest yet on any such grand scheme. Its history
is more like the patchwork progress of quantum mechanics. In Dyson's prophetic words, it has started in a muddled, incomplete, partly understood form.
There still are no broad ideas behind it comparable to Einstein's covariance
or principle of equivalence, or to the wave-particle duality or the uncertainty
principle of quantum mechanics. In spite of its achievements, superstring
theory continues to resemble a snarl of many strands of twine, ad hoc tangles
of string that lack any unified vision. Indeed, the search for such a vision is
one of the main objectives of current superstring speculation.

The basic posit of string theory is that the so-called pointlike particles,
the fermions and quarks, only seem pointlike from our macroscopic perspective. On what is called the *Planck scale*, these particles are modeled by inconceivably tiny one-dimensional line segments, or *strings*. At first it was assumed
that the strings could be either open with two free ends, or closed into loops

like rubber bands. Now the most promising approach is to regard all of them as permanently closed. The analogy with Lord Kelvin's vortex rings is inescapable. Of course string theory is vastly more sophisticated, combined with relativity and quantum mechanics, and drawing on the advanced topology of surfaces and on a vast amount of data not available to Lord Kelvin.

The diameter of a loop of string is estimated at the Planck length of 10^{-33} cm, a fraction of 1 over 1 followed by 33 zeros. Some idea of how small this is can be gleaned from the frequent assertion that a string is as much smaller than an atom as the atom is smaller than the solar system. It is 100 billion billion times as small as a proton. You must not think of these strings as "made" of anything smaller, any more than you should think of a field as made of something more fundamental. It may turn out that geometrical objects such as twistors underlie strings, but at the moment the strings are irreducible mathematical abstractions. As we have seen, atoms and molecules, once regarded as "unreal" mathematical entities, eventually became "observables." Whether this will ever happen to strings is something no one can say. As of now there is no conceivable way to "observe" them. It is possible there never will be.

Yoichiro Nambu, about 1970, was the first to suggest that open-ended strings might provide useful models for hadrons, the strongly interacting particles such as neutrons and protons. Almost no one took this seriously, but during the 1970s efforts were made here and there to extend Nambu's idea to all particles. For a time quarks were taken to be the ends of open strings, a quark at one end of a hadron string and an antiquark at the other. The notion seemed to explain why quarks were never observed in isolation. You can't detach the end of a string. Break a string in half and you produce two new quarks at the two new ends. Join the ends—two quarks disappear. The notion faded when it became necessary to model baryons with quark triplets that would require strings with three ends.

John Schwarz, at Cal Tech, and Joel Scherk, a brilliant young French physicist who later killed himself (he was severely diabetic and depression-prone), thought of combining strings with supersymmetry theory—hence the name *superstrings*. Their superstring was open, massless, and with enormous tensile strength. It moved and rotated in ordinary space, but also vibrated in other space dimensions. The vibrations produced energy, and (as Einstein taught us) energy has mass. The mass and other properties of particles were explained by the different harmonic frequencies of a vibrating superstring, like the harmonics of a twanging piano or guitar string. How did other physicists react to this new version of string theory? As Michio Kaku puts it in his popular book *Beyond Einstein*, it "flopped like a lead balloon." One reason for the flop was that the theory bristled with inconsistencies, and implied such unwelcome nonsense entities as "ghost" particles with negative probabilities, and tachyons that go faster than light.

It also was riddled with infinities. There is always something radically wrong when an equation in physics leads to an infinite value for a variable. The equations of relativity, for instance, do not permit objects to move as fast as light, because as light's speed is approached the mass of an object "blows up," as physicists like to say, to infinity. The most awful aspect of a black hole, if relativity holds all the way down, is a singularity where density and the curvature of space go to infinity. Purging a theory of infinities has been one of the most agonizing of tasks in quantum mechanics. Usually it is done by a tricky technique called *renormalization*, in which infinities are made to cancel one another. The technique is so ad hoc and ugly that many experts, notably Paul Dirac, always considered it a form of cheating that eventually would have to be abandoned.

In 1984 string theory experienced a dramatic rebirth. That was the year when Schwarz, working with Michael Green, of London's Queen Mary College, managed to eliminate from superstring theory all the difficulties and inconsistencies that had earlier plagued it. Almost overnight the theory rose from the ashes, like the fabled Phoenix, to become today's leading contender for a TOE (Theory of Everything). Infinities, ghost particles, and tachyons vanished from the theory like magic. Most significant of all, it was the first TOE to require gravity as an essential aspect. Other TOEs dropped gravity into the scheme by hand, so to speak, simply because it couldn't be left out. But in the new superstring theory of Green and Schwarz, Einstein's theory of gravity, with its equivalence principle, is implied by superstring theory. The graviton (a conjectured carrier particle for gravity) *has* to be there. Indeed, it is the simplest mode of vibration a string can have.

The first theory proposed by Green and Schwarz, called type 1, involved both closed and open strings that shimmered in a space-time of 10 dimensions. Type 2 theory, formulated a year later, was confined to closed strings or loops, and based on a group known as SO(32). The little loops twist, spin, vibrate, and can even become knotted.

When I introduced the Kaluza-Klein theory in the *Ambidextrous Universe* (1954), I considered it no more than a whimsical curiosity. It seemed a clever but thoroughly improbable way to unify gravity and electromagnetism, and to account for positive and negative electric charge with helices of opposite handedness as gravity waves that spiraled around a compacted fifth dimension. Before writing the book I had opportunities to ask several experts on quantum mechanics what they thought of the theory. None had even heard of it. You can imagine my astonishment, 20 years later, when physicists rediscovered the theory and generalized it to more than one compacted dimension. These generalized KK theories were incorporated in the early GUTs (Grand Unification Theories) and TOEs, and are also essential to superstring theories.

In the type 2 theory of Green and Schwarz, the compacted space has six dimensions that are curled up and attached to every point in space-time.

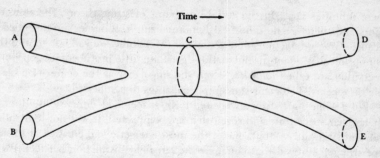

Figure 1. A two-trousers string version of a Feynman diagram. Loops A and B join to form loop C, then separate to form loops D and E. The "world sheet"—the surface traced by the moving loops—has minimal area

Loops of string rotate and move about in ordinary space, but they also vibrate in directions perpendicular to our three familiar space coordinates, in invisible compacted dimensions that we cannot even visualize. The different harmonics of these vibes are responsible for all the properties of particles.

What kind of topological shape do the six hidden dimensions assume? This is a question of intense dispute. It is the same as asking for the topological structure of the universe's so-called vacuum state. There are literally thousands of topologically distinct forms the compacted space can take, ranging from hypertoruses, with one or more holes, to more bizarre forms. If the compacted space is a manifold (a continuum with no singularities) it is called a *Calabi-Yau manifold* after Eugenio Calabi and Shing-Tung Yau. If the structure has singularities, it is called an *orbifold*.

Different vibration modes of the loops determine the kind of particles they are. Interactions take two forms: loops can join to make one large loop, or a loop can have a portion pinch off to form two or more loops. In relativity theory a moving point-particle traces a geodesic in space-time called a *world line*. It is the simplest, straightest possible path between two points in space-time. In superstring theory a loop moving in our space-time traces a two-dimensional surface called a *world sheet*.

The movement of an open string generates a surface topologically the same as a piece of paper. If it is closed, the loop moves in a direction perpendicular to the plane of the loop, tracing a tubelike surface. If a loop pinches off to form two loops, the moving loops generate a world sheet that resembles a pair of pants. The same "pants" surface is produced when two loops merge to make one large loop. Figure 1 shows two loops that join, then separate, forming a surface with trousers at both ends. In a beautiful analogy with world lines, world sheets have a minimal area between two positions of a moving loop.

In Feynman diagrams—graphs of particle interactions—there are points where infinities arise. In the surface diagrams of string theory, there are no points and therefore no infinities! Renormalizing techniques are not needed because string interactions don't blow up! (Mercifully, we will not go into the assumption that quantum fluctuations generate little protuberances on world sheets that are called *tadpoles*.) Even the singularity at the center of a black hole disappears. The giant star simply collapses to a superstring!

For a while superstringers favored a KK space of 11 dimensions—four of our familiar space-time and seven that are compacted. It was not long, however, until Edward Witten, one of the most energetic and creative of today's superstringers, proved that chirality (the left-right distinction between particles and antiparticles) could be maintained only in space-times with an even number of dimensions (one of time, and an odd number of space dimensions). The proof rests on the fact that if you reflect a mirror-symmetric object an even number of times the final result is superposable on the original object. For example, if you reflect your right ear an even number of times the final reflection is a right ear. If you reflect it an odd number of times, it turns into a left ear. The Kaluza-Klein space now favored by superstringers is one of 10 dimensions. In 1989 Witten announced a new quantum field theory for superstrings that is intimately tied to developments in knot theory. How this tack relates to his interest in twistors, if at all, is not clear.

The latest, most popular version of superstring theory is *heterotic* string theory. The word is intended to suggest a hybrid combination of two earlier theories. This new approach was advanced by a group of four Princeton physicists—David Gross, Jeffrey Harvey, Emil Martinec, and Ryan Rohm. They are known as the Princeton String Quartet. It is hard to imagine a more bizarre theory of particles. Ripples in a loop can travel around it in two directions. Those whose frequencies produce left-handed fermions go clockwise and vibrate inside six compacted dimensions. The right-handed bosons (carrier particles) go counterclockwise around the loop, their vibrations penetrating 22 compacted dimensions. Bosons and fermions simultaneously circle the loop in the two directions without interfering with each other. The 10 dimensions (including time) in which fermions "live" are considered "real." The bosons live in a space of 26 dimensions (including time) of which 6 are the compacted "real" dimensions, 4 are the dimensions of ordinary space-time, and the other 16 are deemed "interior spaces"—mathematical artifacts constructed to make everything work out right. If we stretch the meaning of *soliton* we can regard the ripples as topological solitons—waves permanently trapped inside their topological "houses."

At this point I would like to have added a page or two on how heterotic string theory explains the chirality of particles, as well as plus and minus charges. If electrons and positrons go around the loop in the same direction, are they distinguished by helices of opposite handedness? Is there a chiral basis for opposite charges of various sorts, or does the theory say no more than that opposite-charge quantum numbers are somehow smeared along the string? On these questions the books on superstrings become too opaque for me to follow, nor have I been able to contact an expert able or willing to discuss such matters in ways I can comprehend. Please—will someone who is knowledgeable write a popular article for, say, *Scientific American* on the precise role of reflection symmetry in superstring theory?

A magic number, 496, keeps turning up in string theory. In open-string theory, Green and Schwarz found 496 combinations of 16 charges attached to string ends. In heterotic closed-string theory the same 16 charges produce 496 bosons. All but a few are assumed to be too massive to be detected at the low energy levels of today's particle colliders. The number derives from the fact that both the SO(32) group (the basis of open-string theory) and the $E_8 \times E_8$ (the basis of heterotic string theory) have 496 generators.

I asked my numerologist friend Dr. Irving Joshua Matrix about this mysterious 496. He reminded me that it is a triangular number and the third perfect number. It equals $31 \times 4 \times 4$, and if you multiply it by another 4 you get $31 \times 4 \times 4 \times 4 = 1984$, the very year that Green and Schwarz first discovered the significance of 496! Moreover, it was August 1984, and August is the eighth month, or 2×4. Dr. Matrix sketched the following curious equation on my notepad:

$$496 = 1 + 2 + 4 + 8 + 16 + 31 + 62 + 124 + 248$$

Observe the curious anomaly, he said, where the sequence breaks the first doubling series by jumping from 16 to 31, then continues in a new doubling series.

One of the strangest aspects of heterotic theory is that it raises the possibility of what is called *shadow matter*. It seems that at the big bang, which caused the six dimensions to curl up (or was it the curling that produced the big bang?), a parallel universe may have been created. We saw in chapter 32 how Boscovich toyed with the idea of two interpenetrating universes, each unable to interact with the other. It is a common science-fiction theme. Heterotic string theory now suggests that such a parallel world may actually exist. The shadow universe would be totally invisible to us, but could be complete with suns, planets, and even people. However, because its mass would interact with ours, it could be detected: Perhaps shadow matter explains the missing mass which astronomers believe necessary to account for the formation of galaxies and other cosmological riddles.

A shadow sun near ours would have a perturbing influence on our solar system. There is some indication of such perturbation, and astrophysicists have conjectured that it is caused by a companion star they have named

Nemesis. Is it possible that Nemesis is an invisible shadow sun? More likely, shadow matter is floating around the universe and forming distant invisible stars, perhaps some of it sinking to the centers of our planets. It has been suggested that when the two worlds split, the shadow world may have broken into an entirely different set of fields, particles, and laws. "Who knows what secrets lurk in the heart of the universe?" Dietrich Thomsen asked in an article on shadow matter (*Science News*, May 11, 1985). "The Shadow knows," he answered. "Shadow matter, that is." I must add that not many physicists take the shadow world seriously.

Are superstrings here to stay, or will they dissipate in the winds of future science like Lord Kelvin's smoke rings? Experts are divided. Witten has called superstring theory "beautiful, wonderful, majestic—and strange." He predicts that the next 50 years will be devoted to working out its details and implications. It is a discovery he considers comparable in scope to quantum mechanics.

Steven Weinberg is another enthusiastic superstringer. "Superstring theory is our only hope of understanding physics at the scale where gravity is important," he has said. "Furthermore, it is beautiful. I have the same reaction to it that Einstein and Eddington had to general relativity." The great Murray Gell-Mann has given superstrings his blessing as the only big TOE in town.

Here is how Michio Kaku opens his book *Beyond Einstein*: "A thundering revolution is rocking the foundations of modern physics. A fresh, brilliant theory is rapidly overturning cherished obsolete notions about what our universe is, and replacing them with new mathematics of breathtaking beauty and elegance."

There are dissenting voices, not just among physicists in general, but among those who are highly respected. The late Richard Feynman was deeply skeptical. Gerard t'Hooft, in Holland, compared superstring theory to television commercials—a lot of fanfare but no substance. "It is not a theory in the usual sense," declared Julian Schwinger, "but an aesthetic and emotional glow about how things would work if only we could compute them."

Howard Georgi calls string theory "recreational mathematical theology." Robert Crease and Charles Mann, in their marvelous history *The Second Generation* (Macmillan, 1986), tell of an occasion when Weinberg was lecturing on strings at Harvard. Before he spoke, Georgi chalked on the blackboard:

> *Steve Weinberg, returning from Texas,*
> *Brings dimensions galore to perplex us.*
> *But the extra ones all*
> *Are rolled up in a ball*
> *So tiny it never affects us.*

Sheldon Glashow, a principal player in the unification of electromagnetism and the weak force, has been the most outspoken critic. His animadversions appear in many places, but most notably in the last chapter of his autobiography, *Interactions* (Warner, 1988), written with Ben Bova; in *Superstring: A Theory of Everything?*, edited by Paul C. W. Davies & Julian Brown; and in "Tangled in Superstrings," an article in *The Sciences* (May–June 1988). What are his main objections?

1. The theory is running too far ahead of empirical evidence. It is true that many successful theories have been formulated before they could be tested—general relativity, for instance. But Einstein at least proposed ways his theory could be tested, and it was not long until such tests began to confirm the theory. The trouble with superstrings, in Glashow's opinion, is that the theory does not even suggest how it could be tested. As he put it, "There is not yet even one teeny-tiny experimental prediction."

Barring unforeseen luck, the energies needed for testing string theory are far beyond the power of foreseeable particle smashers. Physicists talk of a "desert" of energy stretching between the coming accelerators and the level at which string theory could be tested. Glashow does not expect this stretch to be deserted. He thinks it likely to bloom with exotic flowers. He believes new supercolliders will reveal surprises that will chop off many a TOE, perhaps even the TOE of superstrings.

Glashow likes to distinguish between the upward path from empirical evidence to theory, and the downward path from theory to evidence. The second path starts high up with a grand theory of everything, then works its way down "to the mundane, silly little effects seen in accelerators or on the earth." Glashow prefers the "low road"—the road that begins with experimental results and then slowly climbs up to theory.

2. "The superstring theory does not follow as a logical consequence of some appealing and elegant set of hypotheses about nature." An important ingredient of elegance is simplicity, but is superstring theory really simple? In some ways yes, in other ways no. It is certainly simple to have just one basic particle, the loop, and to reduce all interactions to the joining and separating of loops. But when it comes to explaining the properties of particles, string theory—this applies also to twistor theory—is a tissue of complicated, conflicting guesses. It does not explain why particles have the masses they have. It does not explain their lifetimes, or the strengths of their interactions. It has no clear explanation of the various charges. How, for example, is the unit of negative electric charge smeared over a superstring loop? In principle these magnitudes should be calculable from the theory, but in practice they can't be made. Beauty is in the beholder's eyes. Superstringers are dazzled by what Abdus Salam has called the theory's "incandescent beauty." Skeptics are put off by its unlovely loose ends.

3. Superstring theory does not explain why six spatial dimensions curled up at the moment of the big bang. Nor can it explain why the curled-up dimensions remain stable while the other three expand and time marches on.

4. Superstringers cannot agree on the topological structure of the compacted dimensions. As we have seen, it can take thousands of forms.

Superstring's one great, undisputed achievement is that for the first time it has provided a quantum theory of gravity. "I've got to give superstring theory a brownie point for this," Glashow admits. But in other respects he sees it as a movement of main interest to sociologists of science who can study it as an example of how physicists like to leap on bandwagons. "String theory may be more appropriate to departments of mathematics or even schools of divinity. How many angels can dance on the head of a pin? How many dimensions are there in a compacted manifold thirty powers of ten smaller than a pinhead? Here's a riddle: Name two grand designs that are incredibly complex, require decades of research to develop, and may never work in the real world. Star Wars and superstring theory." Will all the young Ph.D.s, after wasting years on string theory, Glashow asks, "be employable when the string snaps?"

Glashow has this to say in his contribution to the Davies and Brown anthology:

I'm very happy that so many of my colleagues are working on string theories, because it really keeps them effectively out of my hair. I know that they are not going to say anything about the physical world that I know and I love. Mainly that's the reason that I don't like these theories. I have the greatest respect for the people in Britain and the States who do work on them. At the same time I do everything I can in my power to keep this contagious disease—I should say far more contagious than AIDS—out of Harvard, but so far I've not been very successful. Nonetheless, some of us at Harvard are still trying to follow the upward path, to go from experiment to theory, rather than pursuing the superstring vision, which requires the highest inaccessible dream-like energies to build a theory that deals with the down-to-earth world under our feet.

"Only a continued influx of experimental ideas and data," wrote Glashow and Paul Ginsparg in "Desperately Seeking Superstrings?" (*Physics Today*, May 1986), "can allow paths from top and bottom to meet. The theory of everything may come in its time, but not until we are certain that Nature has exhausted her bag of performable tricks." They quote, with reference to superstrings, a famous remark that Wolfgang Pauli once made about a theory. It was so far out, said Pauli, it was "not even wrong."

In the proceedings of the Seventh Workshop on Grand Unification (WOGU), held in Toyama, Japan, in 1986, Glashow summarized the conference in the following couplets:

> Let us honor the forces of unification
> Believing in things such as nu oscillation

And mourn not the monojet that couldn't be deader
For Carlo[1] is coming with something much better.
The Seventh WOGU we have held in Toyama
While waiting for word of the death of all matta.
We must pity the student in his deep dark hole
Whose thesis depends on that one monopole,
Or on solar neutrinos that wriggle about
Unless they are saying our sun has gone out.
Some of us wonder how all things came to be
Leaving nary a clue but for old gravity,
And just seventeen particles, some of them quarks.
Maybe seventeen more and some of them squarks.
Something happened, they say, out in Cygnus the Swan,
Don't bother to look 'cause now it's all gone.
The Universe from Harvard looks like suds in the sink,
So crash your computers and take time to think.
The Theory of Everything, if you dare to be bold,
Might be something more than a string orbifold.
While some of your leaders have got old and sclerotic,
Not to be trusted alone with things heterotic,
Please heed our advice that you too are not smitten—
The Book is not finished, the last word is not Witten.

Superstring theory is in a fantastic fever of ferment. From one point of view there are only about half a dozen viable theories, but if you consider all the variants, there are thousands. Some superstringers think that the theory can finally be expressed entirely in the four dimensions of ordinary space-time. Compacted dimensions and internal spaces will prove to be nothing more than temporarily useful artifacts. Others think that the hidden dimensions are just as real as the three we know. Some expect that even the strings themselves will turn out to be mere abstractions. Others expect them, like seventeenth-century atoms, eventually to glide over that vague boundary into what can be "observed" by relatively direct means.

Suggestions have been made for generalizing strings to two-dimensional membranes, but the mathematics is so horrendous and ugly that few are following this up. Astronomers have been speculating about what they call "cosmic strings"—enormously long and massive filaments that may be weaving here and there across the universe. If such strings exist—and there is no evidence that they do—could they be superstrings stretched into light-year lengths by the universe's expansion after the primeval explosion?

The hope, of course, is that string theory will slowly evolve toward a single theory as variants and rival theories self-destruct. "My high school buddy Steve Weinberg leads the Texas contingent on the string wagon," writes Glashow, "while keeping one foot firmly on the low road. He feels that string theory will be tested in the laboratory in the near future so that it may either be adopted or abandoned. I pray that he is right."

Where does all this leave us with respect to what I called the Ozma problem? (The Ozma project, named after the ruler of Oz, was the title of an early search for extraterrestrial life signals.) As far as our universe is concerned, it has been solved. Right and left can certainly be communicated by pulsed codes to sentient creatures in any galaxy. All three neutrinos in our universe are permanently left-handed. To convey the meaning of left to minds in another galaxy we have only to describe a parity-violating experiment.

There is an old joke about someone who said, "I'd give my right arm to be ambidextrous." For some reason many physicists seem willing to give their right arm to make the universe ambidextrous. As we have seen, this can be done in two essentially different ways. One is to start the universe off as ambidextrous and then introduce handedness by later symmetry breaking. The other way is to imagine an ensemble of other universes, somewhere out there, where half are right-handed and half are left-handed. Unfortunately, as Charles Peirce once observed, universes are not as plentiful as blackberries. Because we know only one, it may be that questions like these will be forever unanswerable.

Why is it necessary, Penrose has asked, to assume that God, or Nature if you prefer, is ambidextrous? Why must the fundamental ground of being have more symmetry than, say, Michelangelo's "Pietà"? We know that Michelangelo could have carved his "Pietà" so that everything went the other way. We can even see what the other way would look like by viewing the statue in a mirror. Would it not seem just as beautiful? Why should we be dismayed because the "Pietà's" enantiomorph doesn't exist? What is wrong with Mother Nature having a beauty spot on one cheek? Could it be that perfect left-right symmetry, and other kinds of symmetry as well, strike the Old One as more ugly and more boring than asymmetry?

As we have seen, asymmetric forms like the swastika can be made to go the other way simply by turning them over. We can read TUO as OUT by walking to the other side of a glass door. Perhaps our universe, and all other universes, have a handedness only for observers trapped in their space-time. The Old One, inhabiting a higher space-time, can look at any asymmetric universe from another perspective and see it go the other way.

As for the universe we know and love, is it possible, as Stephen Hawking and others claim, that physics is rapidly approaching the end of its string—a day when all the fundamental laws of physics will be known, unified by one elegant set of equations? Perhaps. However, eminent physicists have made such predictions before only to have new discoveries open trapdoors that lead to vast unexplored basements.

"In ultimate analysis everything is incomprehensible," wrote Thomas Huxley (in *Darwiniana*, 1893), "and the whole object of science is simply to reduce the fundamental incomprehensibilities to the smallest possible number." The trouble is that new discoveries keep increasing the number of incomprehensibilities.

I find my intuitions vibrating in sympathy with Glashow's. After a crazy theory has been corrected and polished until it no longer seems crazy, but simple and almost inevitable, and the present disorder of the particles has given way to a beautiful order, I believe that the very success of such a theory will lead to deeper levels of dishevelment. God may not be malicious, as Einstein remarked, but is the Old One's subtlety on such a low level that we, with brains only a trifle better than those of monkeys, are capable of understanding all its mysteries?

I do not belong to that school of thought which believes science will someday discover everything. Such a view strikes me as an expression of simpleminded arrogance, and I am at a loss to know how to converse with anyone who holds it. Surely, to vary a well-known metaphor of William James, there are truths about existence as far beyond the range of our minds as Dublin is beyond the mind of a fish in the river Liffey.

"A man is a small thing," remarks King Karnos, in Lord Dunsany's play *The Laughter of the Gods*, "and the night is very large and full of wonders."

POSTSCRIPT (1995)

Interest in superstrings cooled down a bit for a few years. There seemed no way to decide which of some ten thousand different structures of the curled-up spaces, structures now called Calabi-Yau spaces, was the one Nature chose. And there continued to be no known way to test the theory.

In 1995 superstrings got an unexpected shot in the arm from recent speculations about black holes. It has been conjectured that black holes eventually collapse into what are called "extremal black holes." These are holes that lose entirely their volume and mass, and turn into superstrings! In brief, massless black holes are the same as the basic particles!

The theory is enormously controversial, but its defenders hope it can lead to a choice of a particular Calabi-Yau structure that in turn will provide a single, correct theory of superstrings. See Gary Taubes's "How Black Holes May Get Superstring Theory Out of a Bind," in Science *(June 23, 1995), and "Strings and Webs," by Ivars Peterson, in* Science News *(August 26, 1995).*

NOTES

1. Carlo Rubbia, the famous Italian experimental physicist whose group discovered the electroweak gauge bosons $W^\pm$ and Z^0.

TEN

THE ULTIMATE TURTLE

Charles Krauthammer opened an editorial in The Washington Post *(December 2, 1988) this way:*

> *There are two great mysteries in this world. First, how did the universe begin? Second, how does a book that attempts to answer that question—a book about muons and gluons, about thermodynamic arrows and space-time singularities, about quantum gravity and superstrings, a book that argues convincingly against the existence of Einstein's cosmological constant—become the No. 1 best-seller for 20 weeks in a row? Having now twice read Stephen Hawking's* A Brief History of Time, *a smash popularization of modern physics, I am preoccupied with the second question and no closer to an answer for the first than I was when I started.*

Krauthammer's answer to the second question is that people simply don't read inscrutable books about science. "They only want to own them. Not out of snobbery, I think, but out of a kind of reverence. Not many people read their Bibles, either. But they like having them around."

My review of Hawking's best-seller, A Brief History of Time: From the Big Bang to Black Holes *(Bantam, 1988), appeared in the* New York Review of Books *(June 16, 1988).*

> *"My goal is simple. It is complete understanding of the universe, why it is as it is and why it exists at all."*
>
> —STEPHEN HAWKING, *1981*

Stephen Hawking opens his new book with a marvelous old anecdote. A famous astronomer, after a lecture, was told by an elderly lady, who was perhaps under the influence of Hinduism, that his cosmology was all wrong. The world, she said, rests on the back of a giant tortoise. When the astronomer asked what the tortoise stands on, she replied: "You're very clever, young man, very clever. But it's turtles all the way down."

Most people, Hawkings writes, would find this cosmology ridiculous, but if we take the turtles as symbols of more and more fundamental laws, the tower is not so absurd. There are two ways to view it. Either a single turtle is at the bottom, standing on nothing, or it's turtles all the way down. Both views are held by leading physicists. David Bohm and Freeman Dyson, to mention two, favor the infinite regress—wheels within wheels, boxes inside boxes, but never a final box.[1] Hawking is on the other side. He believes that physics is finally closing in on the ultimate turtle. But before discussing his stimulating book, which climaxes with this amazing prediction, I shall say something about the book's even more extraordinary author.

Hawking is the Lucasian Professor of Mathematics at Cambridge University, a chair held by Isaac Newton and Paul Dirac. Few living physicists could occupy this chair more deservedly, even though, as many by now know, Hawking has for several decades been confined to a wheelchair. He is already a legend, not just because of his brilliant contributions to theoretical physics, but also for his courage, optimism, and humor in the face of a crippling illness. Lou Gehrig's disease may be gnawing away at his body, but it has left his mind intact. Hawking actually sees himself as fortunate. He has chosen a profession in which he can work entirely inside his head, and his disability has freed him from numerous academic chores.

A tracheostomy made necessary by a pneumonia attack in 1985 has silenced his voice. He speaks by way of a computer and speech synthesizer attached to his wheelchair. Because the synthesizer was made in California, he apologizes to strangers for his American accent. He has a devoted wife and three children. He has visited the United States some thirty times, Moscow seven times, and flown around the world. At a Chicago discotheque he once wheeled onto the floor and spun his chair in time to the music.

A *Brief History of Time* is Hawking's first popularly written book. Warned that every equation would cut sales in half, he has left out all formulas except Einstein's famous $E = mc^2$, which he hopes will not frighten half his readers. Hawking's prose is as informal as his topics are profound. Work that he accomplished during what he calls his early "classical" phase—by "classical" he means work in relativity theory—is summed up in *The Large Scale Structure of Spacetime*, a book written with South African cosmologist George Ellis. Avoid it, Hawking advises; it is so technical as to be "quite unreadable." His "quantum phase," begun in 1974, supplies the subject matter for his *Brief History of Time*.

The book's first chapter is a quick survey of changing models of the universe, starting with Aristotle's concentric spheres that rotated about a round earth. Its elaboration by Ptolemy held sway in the Western world until Copernicus moved the sun to the center in one of the greatest paradigm shifts in the history of science. Medieval thinkers continually debated two big questions:

Did time begin with creation? Did God create matter out of nothing or out of pre-existing primal matter? Hawking does not mention Aquinas, who argued that God could easily have made a universe with an eternal past, but we know better because Genesis says so. Hawking does mention Augustine's earlier argument that time had no meaning until God, who is outside of time, created the heavens and the earth. What was God doing before then? Here is how Augustine replies in his *Confessions*:

> I answer not, as a certain person is reported to have done facetiously (avoiding the pressure of the question), "He was preparing hell," saith he, "for those who pry into mysteries." It is one thing to perceive, another to laugh,—these things I answer not. For more willingly would I have answered, "I know not what I know not," than that I should make him a laughing-stock who asketh deep things, and gain praise as one who answereth false things. But I say that Thou, our God, art the Creator of every creature; and if by the term "heaven and earth" every creature is understood, I boldly say, "That before God made heaven and earth, He made not anything. For if He did, what did He make unless the creature?"

An even more familiar passage occurs a few paragraphs later:

> At no time, therefore, hadst Thou not made anything, because Thou hadst made time itself. And no times are co-eternal with Thee, because Thou remainest for ever; but should these continue, they would not be times. For what is time? Who can easily and briefly explain it? Who even in thought can comprehend it, even to the pronouncing of a word concerning it? But what in speaking do we refer to more familiarly and knowingly than time? And certainly we understand when we speak of it; we understand also when we hear it spoken of by another. What, then, is time? If no one ask of me, I know; if I wish to explain to him who asks, I know not.

Einstein's model of the universe, the first to be based on relativity theory, is best understood as a three-dimensional analogue of the surface of a sphere. The sphere's surface is finite but unbounded. A plane flying in the straightest possible line across the earth's surface never reaches an edge, but eventually returns to where it started. In Einstein's model space is the curved three-dimensional surface of a four-dimensional sphere, analogous to the two-dimensional surface of a three-dimensional sphere. The cosmos is finite in volume but unbounded. A spaceship traveling the straightest possible path would eventually circle the cosmos. To prevent gravity from collapsing his model, Einstein imagined a repulsive force that would keep the universe stable, but it was soon shown that stability would be impossible. His universe would have to be either expanding or contracting.

After overwhelming evidence was found that the universe is expanding, two influential models were proposed. The physicist George Gamow claimed that the universe started with what the astronomer Fred Hoyle derisively called the "big bang." Hoyle and his friends countered with a "steady state" universe, infinite in both space and time, that has always looked the same as it does now, and is destined to look the same forever. To maintain the overall structure, it is necessary to assume that hydrogen atoms are continually forming in space to provide the matter that keeps coalescing into stars.

The steady-state model was shot down by the discovery of background radiation that could only be explained as a remnant of a primeval fireball. Gamow's big bang became the standard model. For a while, cosmologists toyed with the notion of "oscillating" models in which the universe expands, reaches a limit, contracts to a small size, then starts over again with another explosion. Recent theoretical work, Hawking writes, makes such "bouncing" models extremely unlikely.

Before describing his new model of the universe, Hawking provides an artfully condensed overview of relativity theory and quantum mechanics. In Newton's cosmology, motion is "absolute" in the sense that it can be measured relative to a fixed, motionless space that nineteenth-century physicists called the "stagnant ether." Newton's time is also absolute in the sense that one unvarying time pervades the universe. Einstein abandoned both notions. Space and time were fused into a single structure. Light became the only nonrelative motion, its velocity impossible to exceed, and never changing regardless of an observer's motion. Gravity and inertia became a single phenomenon, not a "force" but merely the tendency of objects to take the simplest possible paths through a space-time distorted by the presence of large masses of matter such as stars and planets.

There is a curious mistake in Hawking's discussion of Newton's cosmology. We are told that Newton believed in absolute time but not in absolute space, and for this was sharply criticized by Bishop Berkeley. It was the other way around. Newton defended absolute space against the "relational" view of his archrival Leibniz, who argued that space is no more than the relative positions of objects. Inertial phenomena, such as the centrifugal force that turns the surface of water concave in a bucket rotating rapidly around its vertical axis, makes it necessary, Newton insisted, to view motion as relative to a fixed space. Berkeley argued that no body could move or rotate except in relation to other bodies—a striking anticipation of relativity theory.

Hawking also misleadingly attributes to Berkeley the belief that "all ma-

terial objects . . . are an illusion." The Irish bishop did not think objects were
illusions in any ordinary sense of the word. No one argued more cogently than
he that the outside world is not dependent on human observations. For Berkeley, the structure of a tree or stone is maintained by the mind of God. He
would have been delighted by quantum mechanics in which "matter" dissolves into mathematics. All material objects are made of molecules, but molecules are made of atoms, and atoms in turn are made of electrons, protons,
and neutrons. And what are subatomic particles made of? They are quantized
aspects of fields that are pure mathematical structures, made of nothing else.
Applied to a field or its particle, the word "matter" loses all meaning. Nevertheless, for both Berkeley and a particle physicist, rocks are as nonillusory
as they were for Samuel Johnson, who naively supposed he refuted Berkeley
by kicking a large stone.

Hawking's chapter on the expanding universe centers on a famous paper he
wrote with Roger Penrose, now at Oxford University. Penrose had been the
first to show that if a massive star collapses into a black hole, a region of
space-time from which light cannot escape, it must (if the laws of relativity
hold "all the way down") produce a space-time singularity—a geometrical
point of zero extension. At that point gravity would produce an infinite density
and an infinite spatial curvature. When the variables of a law acquire infinite
values, the law becomes meaningless. In plain language, physicists have no
idea what happens at black hole singularities, if indeed they exist.

Hawking devotes two chapters to black holes. Although there is yet no
decisive evidence that black holes exist, most cosmologists now are convinced
that they do. (The best candidate for a black hole is the invisible part of a
binary star system in the constellation of Cygnus, the swan.) Hawking's major
contribution to black hole theory was showing that as a star's matter falls into
a black hole, quantum interactions must occur and particles escape in what
is known as "Hawking radiation." As the title of a chapter indicates, "black
holes ain't so black." Mini-black holes are tiny structures that may have
formed in great numbers after the big bang. Hawking showed that if they
exist, radiation will cause them to evaporate and ultimately explode. When
Hawking delivered his classic paper on this in 1974, the conference chairman,
John Taylor, called the paper rubbish. Dennis Sciama, a British cosmologist,
had an opposite reaction. He called the paper one of "the most beautiful in
the history of physics."

A chapter called "The Origin and Fate of the Universe" is the book's
centerpiece. About 1981 Hawking and Penrose became more and more impressed by the possibility that relativity ceases to apply on the quantum level.
Just before the universe exploded there would be no singularity because quantum mechanics completely dominated the scene. Nor would there be a sin-

gularity if the universe contracted to the big crunch. These thoughts led Hawking to an elegant new model of the universe that he constructed with Jim Hartle, at the University of California, Santa Barbara.

It is hopeless to explain the new model in any detail here because it makes use of a special kind of time called "imaginary time," which plays a role in calculating the most probable paths of particles. It is called imaginary because it is measured by complex numbers—numbers of the form $a + b \sqrt{-1}$, where a and b are real numbers and $\sqrt{-1}$ is imaginary.[2] Like Einstein's model, the new model is finite in volume but unlike Einstein's model it has boundaries in both space and time. Unlike Einstein's model, time is treated in exactly the same way as a space coordinate. Einstein's three space coordinates were closed in a circle, but his time was open at both ends. In Hawking's model, "real time" is replaced by a circular (closed) imaginary time.

Hawking makes no attempt to explain his model except by a vague analogy. The universe is likened to a tiny region at the earth's North Pole. Think of the earth's axis as an imaginary time axis. The universe explodes and expands until it reaches its maximum size at the equator, then contracts to a tiny region at the South Pole. The two end spots are "singular" in the ordinary sense of being unique, but not in the technical sense of unextended points where the laws of science break down. Because the time axis is imaginary, it is not necessary to assume that the universe had a beginning or will have an end. The two spots are regions where disorder is total, the arrow of real time vanishes, and quantum events fluctuate aimlessly and forever in imaginary time.

From the standpoint of real time, the universe looks as if time began with the initial explosion and will cease after the big squeeze, but in imaginary time there are no singularities where time starts and stops. The universe emerged from a chaos that always was, and will go back to a chaos that will never cease. As Hawking puts it, the universe is eternal, "completely self-contained and not affected by anything outside itself. It would neither be created nor destroyed. It would just BE."

It is not clear whether Hawking is a determinist who thinks history has to be the way it is, or whether chance and free will intervene, although early in his book he raises a curious paradox. If determinism reigns it would impose the outcome of our search for universal laws, but "why should it determine that we come to the right conclusions from the evidence? Might it not equally well determine that we draw the wrong conclusions? Or no conclusion at all?" Because the search has so far proved increasingly successful, Hawking sees no reason to abandon Einstein's faith that the Old One may be subtle, but not malicious.

Space coordinates are symmetrical in the sense that they are the same in both directions and you can travel along them either way. But time is like a one-way street, with an arrow that points in only one direction. Hawking considers three foundations for the arrow: psychological, cosmological, and thermodynamic. The psychological basis is memory of the past. The cosmological basis is the expansion of the universe. The thermodynamic basis is the second law of thermodynamics, which says that events move in the direction of increasing entropy or disorder. Our psychological arrow points the same way as the thermodynamic arrow, Hawking reasons, because our minds are parts of the physical world. We remember events in the order in which disorder increases. "This makes the second law of thermodynamics almost trivial. Disorder increases with time because we measure time in the direction in which disorder increases. You can't have a safer bet than that!"

Will the cosmological arrow ever reverse? That depends on the amount of mass in the universe. If it is below a certain ratio to the volume of the cosmos, the universe will expand forever and eventually die of the cold. If it is above the critical ratio, gravity will slow down the expansion and eventually reverse it. Early in his career Hawking defended the bizarre view that in a contracting universe time's other two arrows would turn around and human beings (if any still existed) would live backward like a motion picture run in reverse. It is impossible to reconcile this with consciousness and free will, but in any case Hawking now admits that this was a youthful blunder. His new model allows disorder to continue increasing throughout the contracting phase, although disorder would be too extreme to permit life. Of his earlier view he writes:

> What should you do when you find you have made a mistake like that? Some people never admit that they are wrong and continue to find new, and often mutually inconsistent, arguments to support their case—as Eddington did in opposing black hole theory. Others claim to have never really supported the incorrect view in the first place or, if they did, it was only to show that it was inconsistent. It seems to me much better and less confusing if you admit in print that you were wrong. A good example of this was Einstein, who called the cosmological constant, which he introduced when he was trying to make a static model of the universe, the biggest mistake of his life.

Chapter ten sketches some of the grand unification theories (GUTs) now being proposed to explain all the known forces in nature in relation to one another, including the latest theory of superstrings. In superstring theory, pointlike particles (electrons, for example) are replaced by inconceivably tiny strings, closed like rubber bands. Their vibrations in different modes determine the properties of all the particles. The strings vibrate in a space-time of ten dimensions; one is time, three are the spatial ones we know, and the other six are curled into tiny little hyperspheres as much smaller than an atom as the atom is smaller than the universe.

Superstrings solve so many problems about why the different particles have the properties they have that some physicists are euphoric over the possibility that they are about to discover a TOE—a theory of everything. Hawking is aware of similar overconfidence in the past. He quotes a notorious 1928 prediction by the physicist Max Born: "Physics, as we know it, will be over in six months." Only two particles were then known: the electron and the proton. In spite of such failed prophecies, Hawking actually believes that physicists are nearing the end of their quest for all the fundamental laws of the universe.

One of the big mysteries that remain is why after the big bang all but three space dimensions "compacted" into the tiny hyperspheres. On this question Hawking invokes familiar arguments that we could not exist in a universe with fewer or more than three dimensions. He includes a drawing of a two-dimensional dog showing how food digestion would be impossible because a tube from mouth to anus would split the flat dog in half. Evidently Hawking has not looked into A.K. Dewdney's fantastic book *The Planiverse* (Poseidon, 1984), in which methods of digestion in flatland are carefully worked out. As for dimensions above three, Hawking is quite right in saying that solar systems and atoms would be impossible, but the catch is that they are impossible only if based on laws we know. In my opinion Dewdney's book provides strong grounds for not ruling out the notion that universes could operate efficiently with laws we don't know.

"Even if there is only one possible unified theory," Hawking writes in his last chapter,

> it is just a set of rules and equations. What is it that breathes fire into the equations and makes a universe for them to describe? The usual approach of science of constructing a mathematical model cannot answer the questions of why there should be a universe for the model to describe. Why does the universe go to all the bother of existing? Is the unified theory so compelling that it brings about its own existence? Or does it need a creator, and, if so, does he have any other effect on the universe? And who created him?

Hawking wisely does not try to answer these questions. He does, however, say that if the ultimate theory exists it should eventually be understandable by everybody. We will then be able to get on with the superultimate question of why we and the universe bother to exist. "If we find the answer to that," writes Hawking in his book's final sentence (except for three idiosyncratic appendixes that capsule the lives of Galileo, Newton, and Einstein), "it would be the ultimate triumph of human reason—for then we would know the mind of God."

To me, a philosophical theist, there is not a chance of such a triumph. Even entertaining such a possibility strikes me as total folly. I firmly believe that it is not possible for science to discover any fact, or confirm any theory, that has the slightest bearing on why the universe bothers existing. As for time, I am among those who, like Augustine and Miguel de Unamuno, consider it the most terrible of mysteries. It is something given. You cannot even define it without smuggling time into your definition. The physicist John Wheeler is fond of saying that time is what keeps everything from happening at once. True, but this throws not a glimmer of light into the darkness. I have written elsewhere about why I believe time is bound up with other impenetrable mysteries such as free will and the foresight of God. I can imagine a possible world without time—just think of the universe as frozen to a halt—but I cannot conceive of you and me "existing" in such a world.

As Carl Sagan recognizes in his perceptive introduction, Hawking's book is almost as much about God as it is about time and the universe,

> . . . or perhaps about the absence of God. The word God fills these pages. Hawking embarks on a quest to answer Einstein's famous question about whether God had any choice in creating the universe. Hawking is attempting, as he explicitly states, to understand the mind of God. And this makes all the more unexpected the conclusion of the effort, at least so far: a universe with no edge in space, no beginning or end in time, and nothing for a Creator to do.

POSTSCRIPT (1995)

Not many (if any) physicists or cosmologists buy Hawking's trick of introducing imaginary time to argue that with it the universe is infinite in both directions, but has a beginning and end if you assume "real" or ordinary time.

Physicists have long used imaginary numbers for the time coordinate, but have always regarded this as a "dodge" (the term used by Eddington) to do nothing more than simplify calculations about space-time. Hawking's incredible suggestion is that imaginary time may be more than just a dodge, perhaps even more "real" than ordinary time. Here is how he puts it:

This might suggest that the so-called imaginary time is really the real time, and that what we call real time is just a figment of our imaginations. In real time, the universe has a beginning and an end at singularities that form a boundary to space-time and at which the laws of science break down. But in imaginary time, there are no singularities or boundaries. So maybe what we call imaginary time is really more basic, and what we call real is just an idea that we invent to help us describe what we think the universe is like.

I agree with Roger Penrose that this is as preposterous and unbelievable as the many-world's interpretation of quantum mechanics, which Hawking also espouses.

Somewhat similar sleight-of-math was devised by the Oxford University astronomer Edward Milne. Early in the century Milne distinguished between two kinds of time for his bizarre, now abandoned rival to Einstein's relativity theory. In one time the universe is infinite in age and size, and not expanding. In the other time the universe is finite in size, has a beginning, and is in a steady state. It is only a matter of convenience, Milne maintained, which time you choose.

In 1991 Hawking and his wife Jane Wild, after 26 years of marriage and three children, were divorced. Hawking had earlier left Jane to move in with Elaine Mason, one of his nurses and former wife of the man who designed his voice synthesizer. They were married in 1995.

Jane does not appear in the movie based on Hawking's book because by the time it was made she and Stephen had separated. One reason for their marital conflicts was Hawking's total disinterest in religion. Jane is a devout Anglican. Bryan Appleyard interviewed her in 1988 for his article "A Master of the Universe: Will Stephen Hawking Live to Find the Secret?," in London's Sunday Times Magazine (June 19, 1988, pp. 26–30).

Jane's puzzlement over what her husband believed about God reminded me of Watson's puzzlement, after rooming with Sherlock Holmes for many weeks, over what Holmes's profession was. He didn't think it proper to ask! Here is what Jane said to Appleyard:

There is one aspect of his thought that I find increasingly upsetting and difficult to live with. It's the feeling that, because everything is reduced to a rational mathematical formula, that must be the truth . . . You can't actually get an answer out of Stephen regarding philosophy beyond the realms of science. He is now postulating a theory in which the universe is . . . with no beginning and no end and no need for God at all. What I can't understand is whether—and this is something in the whole 22 years of being married to him that I haven't been able to understand—he is working within the bounds of maths and science and saying: "This is what the theory predicts; if you have other interpretations that's up to you." Or whether he is saying: "This is the only concrete evidence we have of anything." I can never get an answer, I find it very upsetting.

Since then Hawking has unequivocally stated that he is an atheist.

NOTES

1. Dyson's new book, *Infinite in All Directions* (Harper and Row, 1988), is, as the title suggests, a hymn to the inexhaustible diversity of nature toward both the large and small. He writes: "I hope that the notion of a final statement of the laws of physics will prove as illusory as the notion of a formal decision process for all of mathematics. If it should turn out that the whole of physical reality can be described by a finite set of equations, I would be disappointed. I would feel that the Creator had been uncharacteristically lacking in imagination."

2. The clearest explanations of imaginary time I know of for nonspecialists are in the late Richard Feynman's book *Q.E.D.*, which stands for quantum electrodynamics (Princeton University Press, 1985), and in Paul Davies's *About Time* (Simon and Schuster, 1995).

PART II

SOCIAL SCIENCE

The so-called behavioral sciences differ from the physical sciences in an obvious way. They involve the unpredictable behavior of sentient creatures with free wills. We humans have the curious ability to choose between goals that cannot in principle be justified by logic or science. A social science can describe human behavior. It cannot tell us how we should behave without specifying goals based on the needs of a common human nature. I have in mind such posits as that it is better to be alive than dead, better to be healthy than sick, and better to be happy than miserable. On the basis of such assumptions it is possible, I believe, along with John Dewey, Bertrand Russell, and many other thinkers, to construct a naturalistic ethics that avoids the absurdities of extreme cultural relativism.

When we turn from such assumptions that it is wrong to murder or steal to questions such as what is the most rational economy, or the ideal form of government, we enter a thicket of complex, difficult questions for which there are no clear-cut answers. The essays that follow are tainted by more personal prejudices than others in this anthology.

ELEVEN

WHY I AM NOT
A SMITHIAN

The following chapter, from Whys of a Philosophical Scrivener *(Morrow, 1983) explains why I prefer to call myself a democratic socialist. I could, of course, just as well call myself a liberal or a conservative, depending on suitable definitions of those vague words. For Milton Friedman, the United States has become a democratic socialist nation, and on this point I agree. Indeed, as I use the word, all the world's democracies are democratic socialisms in their mix of free markets with government controls, but some are more socialist than others.*

Although I wrote this chapter in 1982, it could almost have been written yesterday. Our Republican-controlled Congress, having learned nothing from the fate of supply-side Reaganomics, is now struggling to move us even further back to the days of Coolidge and Hoover.

It has been well said: "If Milton Friedman had never existed, it would have been necessary to invent him."

—PAUL SAMUELSON

To avoid business depressions, to stimulate economic growth, John Maynard Keynes stressed government efforts to maintain an adequate consumer demand. Today's supply-side economists, who in 1980 captured the mind and heart of Ronald Reagan, turn this around. The United States and other democratic countries, they believe, have gone much too far in the direction of socialism and welfarism. The only way to revive the stagflating American dream is to stimulate the economy's supply side. Lower taxes on corporations and the wealthy, abolish minimum-wage laws, reduce welfare handouts, and get the government off the backs of business. Not until after-tax profits are sufficiently high, as they were in the golden past, will entrepreneurs find it worthwhile to take those risks so essential to a vigorous, expanding technology.

To dramatize the importance of lowering taxes, the supply-siders draw the "Laffer curve," a curve said to have been sketched on a cocktail napkin by California's economist Arthur B. Laffer when he explained his supply-side views to an official of the Ford administration. If federal taxes are zero, obviously the government gets no money at all. If taxes are 100 percent, it is just as obvious that nobody will work (the country would revert to a secret barter economy), and again the government would get nothing. So you draw a mysterious bell-shaped curve, the Laffer curve, that plots tax rates against government revenue; then you find on it the point E where revenues are maximized.

There is a big catch. Nobody knows what a Laffer curve looks like. George Gilder, whose rousing defense of supply-side theory, *Wealth and Poverty*, sold so well in 1981 that he began to look for tax shelters, has a Norwegian elkhound named Laffer. Gilder calls the dog's tail a Laffer curve. It is not a bad model. The curve may symbolize the ancient and incontrovertible fact that when taxes are too high they are counterproductive, but otherwise it is about as much use to economists as an elkhound's tail.

There is another catch. Even if we knew what a Laffer curve looked like, we wouldn't know where along it to put the economy. Irving Kristol, defending supply-side in *Commentary* (April, 1981) admits he can't prove it, but he agrees with Laffer that we are "too far up" on the Laffer curve. He applauds Reagan's plan to slide down the curve by across-the-board tax cuts, arguing that if the rich were taxed less they would abandon unproductive tax-evasion schemes, and the government would get more money than it does now. In the long run, as Gilder exclaims, "Regressive taxes help the poor!" Talk about the Laffer curve sounds impressive until you realize that it is just a trivial application of Aristotle's golden mean. Taxes are best when neither too low nor too high.

But when are they neither too low nor too high? This is not easy to answer. Will lowering marginal tax rates on corporations increase employment enough to justify Reagan's welfare cuts? Maybe big corporations will use their tax savings for research and development, but maybe not. Maybe they will just use the money to buy other corporations, or to expand overseas where labor is cheap. Will lowering marginal taxes on the rich and middle class really cause them to save and invest more, or will they just spend more on conspicuous waste? Will broad tax cuts cause people to work harder, or will they work less because they can afford more leisure? As Galbraith has observed, the assumption that executives will experience a burst of creative energy if they have less taxes to pay implies widespread malingering on their part which simply is not supported by any evidence.

Even if Reagan's program stimulates production, will it hold inflation to an acceptable rate once the economy starts growing again? The phenomenon of stagflation is enormously complex and poorly understood. Surely it is obvious that big firms and big unions are not going to hold prices and wages down voluntarily, no matter how passionately a president jawbones, unless the country is near to collapse. A corporation or a union has too much to gain by disobeying, especially if some others obey. It could be that the only way to quench inflation without simultaneously increasing unemployment is by carefully applied federal controls on selected industries and unions. This, of course, is creeping socialism still so abhorrent to the American pysche that such controls may not be politically possible except in extreme emergencies.

To many ill-informed citizens, the notion of wage and price controls raises a specter of a mammoth bureaucracy to determine and enforce them, and the rise of criminal black markets. This, of course, is rubbish. Advocates of wage and price controls have in mind only controls on big corporations, big labor, and big farming, sectors where prices already are controlled, and where federal standards can easily be enforced. Nobody is suggesting price controls on the retail level where good old-fashioned Smithian competition still flourishes.

The sad truth is that economists don't know the best way to halt inflation. Empirical evidence is too thin. Few economists predicted stagflation, which today afflicts most of the world's mixed economies, and there is no consensus on either the causes of inflation or ways to cure it without producing social misery.

As to how Reagonomics will fare in the years ahead, economists can only guess. I am writing this soon after Reagan, with the help of his enemies in Congress and to the vast dismay of his conservative friends, has pushed through tax increases to partly offset the earlier cuts. But Reagan's economic program continues to be the same jumble of supply-side theory, monetarism, industry deregulation, and strange mumblings about the gold standard, a flat tax, a constitutional amendment requiring a balanced budget, and other fantasies. It is still what Kevin Phillips describes in *Post-Conservative America* (1982) as a Rube Goldberg machine in which each triggering step has to work perfectly or the contraption fails. It is still an effort, based on dream theory, to move America back to the days of Calvin Coolidge.

If Reaganomics has not worked by 1984, you can be sure that not a single supply-sider will blame supply-side theory, just as no monetarist will blame monetary theory. The failure will be blamed on such things as past administrations, Congress, David Stockman, Milton Friedman, unforeseen events, the liberal media, Reagan's unwillingness or inability to avoid compromises, insufficient time for tax cuts to stimulate growth, and other parameters.

Shortly before Reagan's election, Laffer was asked how it was possible for cuts in taxes to have an instantaneous explosive effect on the economy. Would it not take at least three years for the incentives to work? Laffer replied: "How long does it take you to reach over and pick up a fifty-dollar bill in a crowd?" After the economy had responded to Reagan's tax cuts by moving into a recession, Laffer told *The Wall Street Journal* that he really meant the incentive would *start* to act at once, but that the cuts would not pay for themselves until two to four years later. In a long interview in *Barron's* (December 21, 1981), Laffer blamed the recession on the postponement of tax cuts, which he in turn blamed on David Stockman, the budget director. "Once we are in '83 and '84," he predicted, "we are going to be in a great economy. . . . There is no question of that in my mind. I couldn't be more certain of a proposition than I am of that." Asked what he saw as the greatest threat to this prophecy, he replied with one word: "Stockman." The two had been good friends before Stockman broke the faith.

Monetarist Beryl Sprinkel, the Treasury Undersecretary, is equally optimistic. On *Wall Street Week* (November 5, 1982) he spoke with pride about how the Dow was rising, inflation steadying at 5 percent, interest rates plunging to single digits, and so on. The unfortunate but necessary recession, he said, had ended. The economy would soon be booming, and by the end of 1983 everybody would agree that Reaganomics had been a whopping success.

From my perspective, Reagan's attempt to free America from its bondage to big government resembles nothing so much as the plan devised by Tom Sawyer, at the close of *Huckleberry Finn*, to free Jim from slavery. Huck's commonsense advice was much too dull for Tom's romantic impulses. Here is how Tom reacted to Huck's plan:

> "*Work?* Why, cert'nly it would work, like rats a-fighting. But it's too blame' simple; there ain't nothing *to* it. What's the good of a plan that ain't no more trouble than that? It's as mild as goose-milk. Why, Huck, it wouldn't make no more talk than breaking into a soap factory."
>
> I never said nothing, because I warn't expecting nothing different; but I knowed mighty well that whenever he got *his* plan ready it wouldn't have none of them objections to it.
>
> And it didn't. He told me what it was, and I see in a minute it was worth fifteen of mine for style, and would make Jim just as free a man as mine would, and maybe get us all killed besides. So I was satisfied, and said we would waltz in on it. I needn't tell what it was here, because I knowed it wouldn't stay the way it was. I knowed he would be changing it around every which way as we went along, and heaving in new bullinesses wherever he got a chance. And that is what he done.

For me it is as difficult to believe in the present powers of Smith's invisible hand as to believe in the magic of Glinda. Lacking today's federal controls, our economy periodically got so out of kilter that in the thirties, had the government not intervened with massive welfare programs, there would have been suffering and chaos of the sort that often leads to tyranny. It is easy to forget that before the crash of 1929, few economists believed that government had any responsibility at all for managing the economy. The concept of the gross national product was then unknown. Had it been known, economists would not have known how to compute it. (Even today they don't agree on how to compute the GNP.) The most a government can do about depressions, said Herbert Hoover, is let them "blow themselves out."

Milton Friedman's views are not that extreme, but almost. He thinks the government should cushion depressions, but only by manipulating the money supply. The Big Depression of the thirties, he is persuaded, can in no way be blamed on a failure of free-market capitalism. It occurred because the Fed failed to regulate money properly. Only a sound monetary policy, he is convinced, can prevent depressions and hold down inflation.

You might suppose that the supply-siders, who share Friedman's enthusiasm for Adam Smith, would be sympathetic to Friedman's monetary views— essentially a demand for a slow, steady, predictable growth of the money supply, keyed to a growth of GNP. This is not the case. Jude Wanniski, in his popular defense of Lafferism modestly titled *The Way the World Works*, (1978), has as low an opinion of Friedman as he has of Marx and Keynes. None of the leading economic models, Wanniski believes, is accurate enough to explain the crash of 1929. He reminds us that Irving Fischer, the godfather of monetarism, issued almost daily statements in late October 1929 telling investors the economy was sound and to keep buying. "Stock prices have reached what looks like a permanently high plateau," Fischer declared just before losing about $9 million of his own money. Wanniski blames the monetarists for making the Depression worse than it would have been if the Fed had not listened to them.

What *did* cause the crash? Every economist who has written a book on this question is wrong. Wanniski, all by himself, has found the answer. "The stock market Crash of 1929 and the Great Depression ensued because of"— so help me, I quote verbatim from chapter 7—"the passage of the Smoot-Hawley Tariff Act of 1929."

Jack Kemp, a former quarterback for the Buffalo Bills who is now the most vocal Lafferite in Congress, assures us (in his book, *An American Renaissance*) that Wanniski has "demonstrated beyond any reasonable doubt" the truth of his remarkable discovery. (This statement is less surprising when you learn that Wanniski helped Kemp write his book.) Irving Kristol, who should know better, has hailed Wanniski's volume as "the greatest economic primer since Adam Smith." Laffer, on whose screwball theories the book is based, is less restrained. "In all honesty," he is quoted on the cover of the paperback edition, "I believe it is the best book on economics ever written."

Some Smithians, like some monetarists, believe that the best way to lower inflation is by letting a severe recession blow prices down. This is exactly what has happened under Reagan, whether intended or not, and it remains to be seen how far the administration will allow unemployment to increase before it tells the Fed to loosen the money supply. Kristol is to be applauded for taking a dim view of such a cure. A government might get away with it in pre-welfare days, he argues in his *Commentary* article, but no party can expect to stay in power if it permits a long, deep recession. We shall soon see if Margaret Thatcher, England's Iron Lady, can survive the social costs of having taken this road. We shall soon see how Reagan and his party will fare if unemployment continues to be high in 1984.

Though he calls himself a neoconservative, Kristol's acceptance of federal controls to prevent needless suffering—welfarism but not paternalism is how Kristol likes to put it (yes, Virginia and North Carolina, this means that A meets with B to decide what C gives to D)—brings him so near to the kind of democratic socialism favored by his friend Daniel Bell that a strong shove could conceivably (though not likely) propel Kristol back into a neosocialist camp. This is even more true of Paul Samuelson, who describes himself as a "post-Keynesian eclectic." When Samuelson speaks of "structural changes" in the economy that are necessary to ease inflation, he may mean such an increase in government planning (preserving of course the welfare state and traditional liberties) that one could call him a closet socialist. Like Galbraith he sees the democratic mixed economies of the world as adopting the same basic strategies regardless of whether they are called socialist or capitalist. Both words, as I have said, are becoming so fuzzy as to be almost useless. There are countries in which groups calling themselves "radical socialists" actually want less government tinkering with the economy than some American political leaders who, under no circumstances, would call themselves socialists.

We who openly call ourselves democratic socialists, for want of a better phrase, believe as much as any Smithian in an untrammeled free market in every area where untrammelism actually works. We, too, oppose government overloads, if by this is meant attempts by the state to do more than it can do adequately. We socialists—perhaps now I should speak only for myself— recognize that citizens have the mysterious power of free will. (Economists seldom use such a metaphysical term; they prefer to hide it under such euphemisms as "capriciousness of expectations" and "mood management.") We, too, are aware of the impossibility in principle of transforming economics into a science with the predictive power of physics. Atoms, planets, and bees obey unalterable laws. Human societies don't.

That much we share with Smithians. But unlike most Smithians we are overwhelmed by a modern phenomenon which Smith could only dimly foresee. For Smith, a factory could consist of no more than a dozen people. Since his time, capitalism has seen the inexorable rise, as Marx correctly predicted, of mammoth corporations and multinationals that employ hundreds of thousands, and that behave like independent nondemocratic socialist states more powerful than small nations. In the United States, if you add the assets of Exxon and AT&T they just about equal the total assets of firms owned by single persons. About 80 percent of all sales are made by the five hundred largest firms. "General Motors," remarked Ralph Nader, "could buy Delaware if Du Pont would sell it." Free of government regulations, oligopolies have the power to administer prices in ways that have little respect for the short-run fluctuations of a free market. What should an ideal state do about these behemoths?

Suppose a giant oil company, one of the Seven Sisters, gobbles up a dozen small independent producers. Is not competition drastically curtailed? The Seven Sisters, as we all know, collaborate for their mutual benefit by sharing pipelines, agreeing on prices, and in many other ways. Let us admit at once that the exploration, production, refining, transporting, and marketing of oil and gas is much more efficient if only one company, or a small number of companies, dominates the scene. Nothing is more wasteful than fifty companies extracting oil from one large pool as rapidly as they can, unshackled by laws regulating the spacing of wells and the speed with which they pump. The oil industry is a natural monopoly. The bigger the companies, the smaller their number, the less waste.

What policy should Smithians take toward such giant firms? Should the government try to break them up to restore competition and market-set prices, ignoring the waste that would result? Should it regulate the Seven Sisters to prevent abuses of their power, or take them over? Are the evils of private ownership of big oil less or greater than the evils of government ownership? If state ownership of natural monopolies and oligopolies is ultimately best, then attempts to break them up, even if possible, would not be desirable. Leave them alone, some socialists have argued (and many conservatives have feared!) to make the eventual paper transfers easier! After Mitterand nationalized France's strongly controlled banks and big industries, were there any visible differences in the way the managers behaved? It is a great irony that some conservatives who plead for a federal "hands off" policy toward mega-corporations may actually be hastening the day when a strong government will take them over.

You will look in vain through Robert Nozick's *Anarchy, State, and Utopia* for light on these thorny questions. We are told that a state should not prohibit "capitalist acts between consenting adults." A clever phrase, but what does it mean? Does it mean that the state should not prohibit the formation of companies so powerful that they interfere with free markets? Nozick's book is not so much a defense of specific economic programs as it is a book offering no economic programs. With his central theme—that an ideal state should not be too small to do what it ought to do, or so large that it does what it ought not to do—who could disagree? It is as vapid as the statement that taxes should not be too high or too low, or the declaration of the German social democrats that government interference with competition should be neither too much nor too little. Evil is a bad thing.

On the practical level at which Friedman argues with Samuelson, and Samuelson argues with Galbraith, and Galbraith argues with Friedman, Nozick's pronouncements are either too lofty or too extreme to be relevant. His book is fun to read, filled as it is with amusing asides and bizarre arguments based on game theory, but it comes straight out of Oz. Behind its fantasy is a "me generation" approach to economics that differs little from Ayn Rand's. Leave me alone! Don't take any of *my* money. Don't trouble my conscience about corpses on the roadsides of Africa, or the unemployed, or the aged, or the sick who live where the only doctors are chiropractors and veterinarians. Don't worry over the possibility that if the poor get too miserable and too numerous they might burn down Boston, and Harvard Yard along with it. The poor will be taken care of, in the sweet by-and-by, by the prestidigitation of Smith's nimble fingers.

Although today's Smithians are more sophisticated than the early anarchist dreamers, they share with those dreamers a fervent hatred of big government, and for this reason their writings often reflect more sympathy for anarchism than for democratic socialism. Pierre Proudhon called his French anarchist periodical *La Liberté*, and in America, Benjamin Tucker called his similar magazine *Liberty*. Liberty has always been the top buzzword for both anarchism and libertarianism. It is not surprising to find Nozick quoting Proudhon's famous tirade against the state, to learn that Friedman's son David, an economist at the University of California, Los Angeles, is an anarchist whose book, *The Machinery of Freedom: Guide to a Radical Capitalism* is much admired by his father. It is not surprising to find libertarians getting misty-eyed when they write about the Wobblies.

Capitalism versus socialism! The conflict, it seems to me, is almost obsolete. The burning question is not one of either/or. It is over the most desirable blend of free enterprise and state controls. In my view this is an open question involving both technical knowledge and moral assumptions. There may not even be a best mix, just as there may be no best system of voting or best city or best house or best spouse. The best mix may be so interwoven with cultural habits as to make it impossible to compare, say, Japan's best mix with ours. Variety itself can be a good. A world in which all economies were alike could be as dull and undesirable as a world in which all cities were alike, or a city in which all houses were alike.

To underscore the room here for legitimate debate, let me dredge up some memories of the time when I was an undergraduate at the University of Chicago, and Frank H. Knight and Jacob Viner were leaders of the "Chicago School" of economics. One of Knight's disciples and colleagues was a troubled young man named Henry C. Simons. His monetary views would later have a strong influence on Friedman, the man destined to become Simons's most eminent student. At that time the campus hangout was a bar on Fifty-fifth Street called Hanley's. It stayed open illegally after closing hours, and could be entered only by walking through an adjoining all-night restaurant, knocking on a back door, and being inspected through a small window. If you looked like a student or a faculty member, you were let in. Every night Professor Simons, who suffered from insomnia, would be there, sitting at a back table and mulling over the bulldog edition of the *Chicago Tribune*. In 1946, aged forty-six and in ill health, Simons died from an overdose of sleeping pills.

In 1934 the University of Chicago Press published a pamphlet by Simons entitled *A Positive Program for Laissez-Faire*. It blew up a storm in academic circles, and is still cited as a basic reference on the Chicago School. When the pamphlet came out, I bought a copy and read it with mounting bewilderment. Simons, like Adam Smith, did not like monopolies. They were "malignant cancers," said Simons, to be "stamped out" as soon as possible. He recognized that they were inevitable in areas where competition would be wasteful, but since they provide no support for laissez-faire, and because it would damage the economy to break them up, he believed the state should own them outright rather than try to muzzle them. Accordingly, his pamphlet recommended that the government gradually take over such key industries as the railroads, public utilities, and "all other industries in which it is impossible to maintain effectively competitive conditions." Where free markets are possible, Simons wanted competition to be encouraged and enforced by regulations of the most extreme sort.

I could hardly believe it. Here was Simons, hailed as the prophet of a new laissez-faire, urging a policy of socialization so radical that Norman Thomas considered it premature! Thomas used to say that one of his recurring nightmares was dreaming that the government had seized the railroads. (Today, railroad passenger service has in effect been nationalized by a whopping federal subsidy to Amtrak, and a good portion of freight service has been nationalized under Conrail, not to mention the less visible subsidies to airlines and buses.) Thomas believed that a long period of education, and improvement in federal skills and morality, should precede such an extreme move. Otherwise would not a corrupt bureaucracy mismanage the railroads even more than their private owners? Not only did Simons recommend federal ownership of natural monopolies, he also favored extending government welfare services and tightening federal controls over advertising. After all, he argued, how can a consumer make a free and rational choice if he or she is brainwashed by Madison Avenue?

Can anyone except Milton Friedman and employees of advertising agencies seriously believe that the millions spent every year on huckstering cars, soap, cigarettes, beer, aspirin, deodorants, stomach-relief pills, hemorrhoid preparations, and so on, operate for the benefit of the consumers? Or the billion dollars that was spent in 1981 on non-product advertising by big companies just to improve their public image? ITT and sixteen other firms spent $10 million each. ITT's main concern was to combat a poll's finding that 60 percent of the public thought they were AT&T.

Simons's views on monopoly may be embarrassing to today's Smithians; nevertheless there is as much disagreement among them over the structure of the best mix for an economy as there is among democratic socialists. Most native conservatives favor a variety of welfare programs as well as strong police forces and a large military establishment. Some—Kristol for instance—would like to see laws against pornography. Their disagreements, like those of the democratic socialists, are mostly over questions of degree and timing. What controls should be added, what dropped, what altered, and when is the best time to make a change? The line between democratic socialism and managed capitalism is not easy to draw. To me this gray "best mix" question is largely empirical. In the absence of a better phrase, I call myself a democratic socialist because, adding up the pluses and minuses, I believe our government should move circumspectly, always preserving democratic freedoms, toward a mixed economy in which there is more and better central planning than we have now.

As for the business community, how can it possibly agree on what government controls are best when the controls desirable for one company are undesirable for another? If a regulation helps A and injures B, obviously the managers of A will favor it and managers of B will oppose it. Have you ever met a businessman (or labor leader) capable of saying: "I know that federal law x will decrease my company's (union's) profits but I support it nonetheless because x is good for the nation"? Or a business manager (or labor leader) capable of saying: "Law x would greatly benefit my firm (union) but I oppose it on the grounds that it would be bad for my country"?

Eugene V. Rostow, the eminent Yale professor and frequent government official, is a highly paid consultant to AT&T. In 1980 Ma Bell gave him $180,000. Is it thinkable that Rostow would favor antitrust action against AT&T? In 1975 he wrote an article for The New York Times titled "Keeping Ma Bell in One Piece." The belief that what is good for company B is good for the country is a universal syndrome among those who work for B, whether it be Ma Bell, Bell's hardware store, or Dr. Bell, a dentist who has incorporated to save taxes.

Can you imagine an executive of Chrysler or Braniff, even though an admirer of Friedman, opposing government aid to his firm because he believes that when a big firm goes broke in a free economy it should be allowed to disappear? The fact is, some of the most regulated industries in the United States want to be regulated. It all depends, naturally, on whether the regulations help or hurt.

At the time I write, certain car manufacturers would like to see federal action stem the flow of cars from Japan because the flow decreases their sales. But General Motors and Chrysler, which import cars, have a contrary view. Big banks want to be deregulated; small banks need regulations to survive. Big truckers and the Teamsters union want trucking regulated; small truckers don't. Big booze stores would like deregulation; mom-and-pop liquor stores fear it. Big TV stations deplore controls that hamper their freedom, but they want controls that discourage new stations and cable systems. Big gas wants federal help because without it Alaska's natural-gas pipeline could not be completed. The big airlines wanted deregulation until they found themselves in a destructive price war. Now they would like some regulations back. We are the only nation on earth that permits its airlines to be privately owned.

Jesse Helms, North Carolina's extreme rightist senator, is gung ho for unfettered free markets except when it comes to federal support of the tobacco and peanut growers of North Carolina. Tennessee senator Howard Baker is eager to get government off the backs of business except when it comes to federal aid for Tennessee's Clinch River breeder reactor. Have you ever heard of a congressman, Democrat or Republican, who breathed a word against federal subsidies and helpful regulations on the back of any major industry in his or her home state?

My father was a small independent oil producer, sometimes called a wildcatter, in Tulsa. One of our neighbors was a vice-president of Gulf. Both men were ultraconservative. When I was a child listening to them talk, it was apparent that my father heartily favored all federal regulations that helped the independents, and objected to all regulations that helped Gulf. Our neighbor had the reverse opinion. On these questions the gulf between Gulf and Gardner was unbridgeable.

"Get the government off the back of the oil industry" is a vacuous demand unless you specify which part of the industry you mean, and exactly what controls you want lifted. Take away all controls from the finding and production of oil and what happens? Does the hand of Smith take over? It does not. The hands of the Seven Sisters take over. And it is much the same with other major industries. Remove certain federal controls and the oligopolies grow fatter, the small competitive firms (and hence the free market) grow weaker. Remove other controls and it works the other way.

In 1981 the FCC lifted old regulations on AT&T, allowing it to enter the exploding market for computer data processing. AT&T is naturally delighted by this deregulation, but IBM, GTE, Xerox, and a hundred smaller firms who will be hurt by Ma Bell's power to eliminate competition, through its monopoly on long-distance telephone lines and its ownership of Western Electric, would much prefer to have the old regulations back. Is the free market served by the FCC's action? The answer depends on what business manager you ask.

Most economists and journalists who call themselves conservative are understandably vague on what to do about ways in which the megacorporations hinder competition. Sometimes they pretend that the giant firms are not there. At other times they pretend that they are just large versions of small businesses; in Galbraith's words, "Mobil is just the corner store grown up." Because the big corporations are not going to vanish—what they do can be done only by big corporations—what should the government do about them? Leave them alone and let them get bigger? Take them over? Try to regulate them so as to maximize competition? If the last option is chosen, the option favored by Kristol, then the task is not to abandon controls but to improve them. Here there are no simple guidelines for either Smithians or socialists because the issues are too snarled and technical.

If all the world's economists were stretched end to end—so goes a one-liner usually attributed to George Bernard Shaw—they still would not reach a conclusion. In 1980, on Larry King's radio talk show, I heard King ask Friedman why he and his colleagues so often quarreled. This, said Friedman, is a myth. Economics is a science. Economists agree on all basic issues. You mean, said the surprised King, that you and Galbraith have no fundamental differences? "Oh," said Friedman, "I thought you asked me about economists."

Sidney Weintraub, coeditor of *The Journal of Post Keynesian Economics*, described Friedman's recommendations in 1980 to the government as a "sure-fire recipe for disastrous stagflation." This, as we all know, is just what happened when Margaret Thatcher tried to follow Friedman's monetary strategy in England, but Friedman is predictably (and correctly) complaining that the lady failed to follow his advice. No doubt Friedman considers Weintraub not an economist. In mid-1982 Friedman began to complain (again correctly) that Reagan was not following his advice when he agreed to compromise with Congress on raising taxes. In his latest book, *Free to Choose*, Friedman not only never mentions Galbraith, he also never mentions Samuelson. Maybe he considers Samuelson also not an economist.

On November 1, 1981, I heard Friedman and Walter Heller interviewed on television by Louis Rukeyser. Friedman gave Reagan "high marks" for his tax cuts, budget cuts, and deregulations. (The tax cuts are welcomed by Friedman mainly because they force budget cuts.) His advice to Reagan was to hold firmly on course, and never, under any circumstances, at any time, agree to tax increases. Heller disagreed. He compared the conflict between Friedman monetarism and Laffer supply-side to "two scorpions in a bottle," and urged Reagan to boost taxes as soon as feasible to avert disaster. The following month Herbert Stein declared: "If the captain of the ship sets out from New York Harbor with a plan of sailing north to Miami, 'Steady as you go!' will not be a sustainable policy, and that will be clear before the icebergs are sighted." I assume that Friedman doesn't think Heller or Stein are economists.

At least Uncle Miltie is candid and consistent, and as invulnerable in debate as a fundamentalist preacher. Instead of shouting like Herbert Armstrong, "Wake up, America, and blow the dust off your Bible!" Friedman is shouting, "Wake up, America, and blow the dust off *The Wealth of Nations!*" Some of his views are anathema to business leaders and opposed even by many economists who call themselves conservative. He is for unrestricted free trade, and believes that a unilateral lifting of all tariffs would do more to combat administered prices by corporations than any kind of trust busting. If the Japanese can make better and cheaper cars than we can, we should all buy Japanese. Not a penny should go to Chrysler, or to Lockheed or Braniff or any other company that stumbles in the marketplace. He wants to replace all welfare programs by a negative income tax—a novel plan also favored, by the way, by such liberals as Samuelson and James Tobin, and advocated by the three Presidents who preceded Reagan. (It has about as much chance of becoming law as the "flat tax" now being touted.) He recommends a voucher system that would give parents the freedom to choose between public and private schools.

Most of Friedman's opinions spring from an intense devotion to Smith's invisible hand, and a firm conviction that almost all efforts by government to improve the economy or aid the poor, here or anywhere else, are less effective in the long run than doing nothing. In the eleventh revised edition of his celebrated textbook *Economics*, Samuelson suggests that before you read one of Friedman's persuasive books you should ask yourself if it is possible today for a professional economist to be against the following:

1. Social security
2. Flood relief
3. Farm legislation
4. Pure food and drug regulation
5. Compulsory licensing and qualifying of doctors
6. Compulsory licensing and qualifying of car drivers
7. Foreign aid
8. Public utility and SEC regulation
9. Post office monopoly
10. Minimum wage
11. Peacetime drafts
12. Wage and price controls
13. Anticyclical fiscal and monetary policies
14. Auto-safety standards
15. Compulsory and free public schools
16. Prohibition of heroin sales
17. Stricter federal and state standards for migrant workers
18. Minimum interest-rate ceilings on usurious lenders
19. Truth-in-lending laws
20. Government planning
21. Pope Paul VI's encyclical naming central economic planning the key to economic growth

Go through Friedman's books and his *Newsweek* columns, Samuelson comments, and you will find him opposing every one of the above features of our mixed economy. Although you may agree with some of these negations, Samuelson adds, you must admit that to argue relentlessly for all of them is a startling indication of how far Friedman pushes his Smithism.

Friedman is as down on the American Medical Association as he is on the Pure Food and Drug Administration. Both block the freedom of Americans to choose their own doctors, even if they are quacks, and the freedom to choose their own remedies, even if they are worthless or harmful. Better an occasional thalidomide tragedy, better to have worthless drugs on the market (and greater profits to the drug hucksters), than to have an agency which, in Friedman's opinion, blocks the introduction of new medicines in its zeal to protect consumers. The FDA, he declares flatly, "has done more harm by retarding progress in the production and distribution of valuable drugs than it has done good by preventing the distribution of harmful or ineffective drugs." Friedman would like to abolish the FDA totally, not reform it. Naturally he is opposed to all forms of socialized medicine.

On some issues I find myself more in agreement with Friedman than with his antagonists. In the absence of a public sufficiently informed and motivated to support democratic socialism, political compromises and halfway measures that involve federal tinkering with the economy can indeed be worse than doing nothing, or doing something so trivial that it allows free markets to solve a problem better than bureaucrats can solve it. (There is a wise old chess adage: When in doubt, push a pawn.) Our health system is a case in point. No other industrialized democracy has such a shoddy way of meeting the health needs of its citizens. As Michael Harrington has put it, "The American system combines the worst of capitalism with the worst of socialism." On the whole, however, I see Friedman as a witty and doctrinaire radical who is fighting for a mystical vision that had much to recommend it in the days of Herbert Spencer, but today is as simplistic as, say, Say's law, or Laffer's curve, or Von Thünen's marvelous square-root formula for the wage every worker ought to get.

Friedman is one of those economists—he has his doubles in all economic schools—who seems to me similar in many ways to a chiropractor. Suppose you suffer from a lower-back pain. You go to a reputable M.D. and what happens? He is too busy to listen to all your complaints, and seems to have no precise idea of just what is wrong. Instead of a diagnosis, he proposes numerous laboratory tests, all costly and time-consuming. But if you go to a chiropractor, he will diagnose your trouble in ten minutes. It is a subluxation of a certain vertebra, and he assures you it will clear up after a few inexpensive spinal rubs. He listens patiently to all your troubles, and replies with unbounded confidence and authority. Indeed, he talks more like a doctor than a real doctor. Of course the reason the real doctor is vague is because he knows too much. He knows that a lower-back pain can have a hundred different causes, and that he would be a fool to commit himself until he has sufficient facts. Given the current state of affairs in medical science and practice, and the public's medical ignorance, if chiropractors didn't exist, our society would have to invent them.

I once heard Norman Thomas deliver a ringing sermon in the University of Chicago Chapel, where his old friend Charles Gilkey was the dean. At the finish the congregation did something unprecedented. It stood up and applauded. The sermon's theme couldn't have been simpler or more fundamental. It was on the right of children and older people not to die by the millions from lack of food in a world capable of eliminating hunger.

It is a sobering thought that with all our vaunted science and technology we are still far from refuting the dismal prophecies of the Reverend Thomas Malthus, though for reasons Malthus did not anticipate. An agricultural technology for feeding a world population many times its present size is already here; only social and political barriers keep the food from getting to the starving.

I know that accurate statistics about world hunger are unavailable. I am aware that estimates of world population can be off by hundreds of millions, and that malnutrition is the fuzziest of concepts. From my perspective, both the optimists and doomsdayists who write popular books about world hunger have a distressing lack of humility in extrapolating to the future on the basis of shaky information, imprecise terminology, complex parameters, and vast uncertainties about social and political change.

The point I wish to make, however, is as undeniable as it is depressing. Even though there may be grounds for long-range optimism, the short-range problem of hunger remains a terrible reminder of how far social progress lags behind the progress of science. "Gigantic inevitable famine," as Malthus called it—"the last, the most dreadful resource of nature" for checking population growth when it outruns food supply—still stalks the world. The number of hungry people around the globe is certainly increasing in absolute numbers, and may even be increasing at the moment (because of inflation) as a percentage. It takes a lot of blind faith, and a peculiar insensitivity to suffering, to believe that Smith's hand is the best way to give millions of starving children the right to live.

Norman Thomas may have been weak in his knowledge of philosophy and economic theory but he was strong in love and compassion. Consider one small instance. During World War II our government herded 110,000 persons of Japanese ancestry (75,000 of them American citizens, all but 5,000 citizens by birth) into ten concentration camps where they were kept for three to four years. They had commited no crimes. It is no good to say that this monstrous violation of civil liberties was necessary to prevent sabotage or spying, or to preserve their safety. No comparable program was even suggested for Americans of German or Italian descent. No Japanese were interned in Hawaii.

Who protested? Not the communists or their lobotomized fellow-travelers. After all, one must show no mercy to possible enemies of the Soviet Union! Not the conservatives or the liberals. Except for some ineffective church groups and a few independent thinkers such as Eugene Rostow, they were all caught up in a racism bred by war hysteria. President Roosevelt ordered the internment; Congress approved; the Supreme Court validated.

Earl Warren actively supported the evacuation, as did other liberals: Francis Biddle, William Douglas, Tom Clark, Carey McWilliams, Walter Lippmann, Hugo Black, Henry Stimson, Abe Fortas . . . the list is endless. (Some of them later regretted their words and actions.) No college students demonstrated. Even the national office of the American Civil Liberties Union, in spite of divided opinion among members, remained officially silent. Only one notable American cried shame: Norman Thomas. From left, right, and center, the only vigorous protests came from Thomas and his democratic socialists. Here is how Thomas expressed himself in "Dark Day for Liberty," *Christian Century* (July 29, 1942):

> In an experience of nearly three decades I have never found it harder to arouse the American public on any important issue than on this. Men and women who know nothing of the facts (except possibly the rose-colored version which appears in the public press) hotly deny that there are concentration camps. Apparently that is a term to be used only if the guards speak German and carry a whip as well as a rifle.

American liberals still feel twinges of guilt about the Red "witch hunt" that came later. Comic and reprehensible though it was, it was trivial beside the suffering inflicted so senselessly upon, and endured so patiently by, our Japanese minority. Yes, their suffering was mild compared to that of the millions of Jews murdered by Hitler, and the even larger number of victims killed by Stalin without regard to race, color, or creed. I am also aware that the incarcerated Japanese were eventually compensated in part for financial losses.

As for the victims of Hitler and Stalin, it is good to remember that American liberal and conservative leaders were as quiet about these crimes as they were about our Japanese concentration camps. Thomas's efforts to persuade Roosevelt to open America to German Jews fell on uncomprehending ears. When Thomas, John Dewey, Sidney Hook, and other democratic socialists spoke out about the Russian purges and death camps, they were roundly denounced by fellow-travelers and ill-informed liberals as reactionary, red-baiting, pro-fascists, as little to be trusted as the editorials and stories about Russian famines that were appearing in the Hearst papers, and which happened, by the way, to be true.

Few liberals read or cared to read the 800-page report, *Not Guilty*, issued in 1938 by a committee chaired by Dewey that was formed to investigate the Moscow trials. Corliss Lamont, than whom no fellow-traveler ever more consistently fellow-traveled, regarded Dewey and his friends as "completely discredited enacters, conscious or unconscious, of Hitler's well recognized strategy of sowing misunderstanding, suspicion and hostility between Russia and Western democracies ... you are all ... simply an ignominious spot of mud whirling down the great sewer hole of history." From Lamont's letter to Sidney Hook in *Free Inquiry* (Winter 1981–82).

A depressing anthology ought to be assembled some day of quotations from leading liberals and intellectuals of England, America, and Europe who steadfastly refused to listen to what leaders on the non-communist left tried to tell them about Stalin. To me the incident that best highlights this sordid tale was Vice-President Henry Wallace's visit to Magadan in 1944. Magadan was the capital of the Kolyma slave-labor system in the gold-mining area of northern Siberia. Although it was well known to be one of the most notorious of the labor camps, Wallace toured the region without once suspecting that Magadan was anything but a happy, thriving pioneer town!

Elinor Lipper, who was there as a prisoner, has a chapter about Wallace's visit in her book *Eleven Years in a Soviet Prison Camp*. The scene was high comedy. Wallace and his party, which included Owen Lattimore, were easily gulled by taking down all the guard towers, keeping the prisoners out of sight, and dressing pretty office girls as swineherds. The ladies had difficulty with some of Wallace's knowledgeable questions about pigs (asked through John Hazard, his interpreter), but poor Wallace suspected nothing. He described Magadan in glowing terms in his book *Soviet Asia Mission*, and Lattimore did the same in an article in *National Geographic* (December 1944). "There has probably never been a more orderly phase of pioneering than the opening up of Russia's Far North under the Soviet," wrote Lattimore. To which Elinor Lipper replied: "This is absolutely true. What other government would send hundreds of thousands of its own citizens every year to forced labor in new territories?"

When Lipper's chapter on the Wallace visit ran in the *New York Post* (June 11, 1951), Wallace sent the *Post* an incredible letter which it published on June 20. "It was not until long afterward," said Wallace, "that I knew that slave labor camps existed. The testimony of those who have escaped from the camps indicates that Communist Russia treats political dissidents in much the same way as czarist Russia but on the whole less humanely."

This prompted me to make a comment which the *Post* ran on June 24. I listed six excellent books in English about the labor camps, all published before 1943, and pointed out that under the czars the number of prisoners never exceeded 50,000. Only a small fraction of this number were political prisoners. That a man of Wallace's stature could have written a book about

Russia without bothering to read anything critical of Stalinism is now hard to believe, yet such was the temper of the times. I recall lending a copy of David Dallin's *Forced Labor in Soviet Russia* to a liberal friend, only to have him return it unread on the grounds that Dallin had been a Menshevik and therefore couldn't be trusted. In France, Albert Camus tried to convince his former friend Jean Paul Sartre about the horrors of Russian slave labor, only to be held up to ridicule in Simone de Beauvoir's novel *The Mandarins*.

Wallace was sufficiently enlightened by 1952 to call the Soviet system "something utterly evil," but it took him a long time to learn what Norman Thomas and his friends had tried to teach him for twenty years. In 1948, when Wallace ran for President as a Progressive, the American Communist Party, which then controlled the Progressive Party, bamboozled Wallace with as little difficulty as did the fake lady hog-farmers in Magadan. I agree with Dwight McDonald's characterization of Wallace (in his book *Henry Wallace: The Man and the Myth*) as the "most boring and humorless egomaniac on the American political scene since William Jennings Bryan."

Much as I deplored the know-nothing antics of Senator Joseph McCarthy and his friends, who, as Thomas once said, didn't know the difference between communism, socialism, and rheumatism, it must be admitted that the blindness of American liberals and intellectuals to the evils of the Soviet system was a major cause of the slow swing to the right that is still with us. If you think *blindness* is too strong a word, I recommend the following painful experiment: Go to a large library and read the accounts of Stalin's purge trials in *The New Republic*, *The Nation*, and in Walter Duranty's dispatches to *The New York Times*.

I know of no political leader in American history, other than Thomas, who so consistently raised a booming voice of indignation whenever and wherever injustice was being done. Who knows when we shall see his like again? On Park Avenue, in Manhattan, there is a Norman Thomas High School. I would be surprised if any high school were named after Milton Friedman or any other contemporary Smithian. I doubt if anyone will ever refer to Friedman, or to Buckley or Kristol or President Reagan, as the "conscience of America."

POSTSCRIPT

Although Reagan believed the supply-side arguments, his understanding of economics is not much above the level of his understanding of the physical and biological sciences, and it is now recognized that Reaganomics is a weird mixture of incompatible ideas. James Tobin (interviewed by *U.S. News & World Report*, February 1, 1982) compared Reaganomics with a train at New

Haven that has a locomotive at both ends. "The stationmaster announces that the train will leave for both Boston and New York. But, under the circumstances, it's doubtful the train will reach either destination."

At the time I write (1982), Reagan's popularity continues to be high, mainly because the public still perceives him as a conservative—upright, patriotic, a good Christian (even though he believes in astrology), friendly, smiling, skilled at telling jokes, brave in the face of danger, and (not least) an actor with a glamorous Hollywood background. Voters have not yet realized that Reagan is not so much a practical, flexible politician, like his four predecessors in office, as a hard-nosed radical of the right who is doing his best to turn the country around 180 degrees from the direction given to it by Roosevelt. Of course Reagan has for thirty years been declaring this intention, but most Americans either weren't listening or they didn't take him seriously until they woke up one morning to find that the old showman had conned his way into the White House.

For a sympathetic account of Reagan's attempted rollback, see *The Reagan Revolution* (1981) by Rowland Evans and Robert Novak. For a slashing attack by an economist and democratic socialist, see *Greed Is Not Enough: Reaganomics* (1982) by Robert Lekachman. Here is Lekachman's crisp summary of the Reagan program:

> The Reagan manner clothes a political initiative unique in our national
> history: a quite deliberate redirection of income and wealth from the poor
> to the rich; blacks and Hispanics to whites; women to men; the elderly
> to the young; old, declining regions to booming Sun Belt cities; and social
> services to the Pentagon.

Like his friend Jude Wanniski, George Gilder is both a journalist and a disenchanted liberal. In fact, at one time Gilder even edited *The New Leader*, a democratic socialist journal. In 1973 he got himself into a bind with the feminists when his book *Sexual Suicide* explained how women "socialize" men by persuading them to marry and support them. The book was followed by *Naked Nomads: Unmarried Men in America* (1974). David Stockman, Reagan's blabbermouth budget director, found Gilder's *Wealth and Poverty* "Promethean in its intellectual power and insights. It shatters once and for all the Keynesian and welfare state illusions that burden the failed conventional wisdom of our era." That was before Stockman became a turncoat who advocated increasing taxes and cutting defense spending.

Gilder made another lurch to the right in 1980 by giving a speech in which he announced that although he owed much to the neoconservatives, especially to Midge Decter, who edited two of his books for Basic Books, he now must abandon them for being too evasive. All their insights, said Gilder, add up to less than you can find in William Buckley's first book, *God and*

Man at Yale. For one thing, neoconservatives ignore God. Phyllis Schlafly, said Gilder, knows more about foreign policy than Pat Moynihan, Anita Bryant knows more about gays than the American Association of Psychiatrists, and the Moral Majority is more responsible than the Democratic Party.

Gilder reiterates his central dogma: Capitalism is not based on greed, as Adam Smith perversely assumed, but on altruism and old-fashioned moral values. It must be combined with religious faith, although Gilder doesn't specify which kind. Buckley reprinted this adolescent speech in *The National Review*, March 5, 1982, with a response by Ben Wattenberg, a neoconservative, and a rebuttal by Gilder. For reader comments see the April 2, 1982 issue, pages 360–361.

In *The New York Times* business section (Sunday, July 26, 1981) Wanniski's attack on Friedman was vitriolic. Although Friedman is "barely five feet tall," said Wanniski, he weighs so much that he is now a "deadweight burden" on the backs of Menachem Begin, Margaret Thatcher, Ronald Reagan, and the entire U.S. economy.

Interviewed by Louis Rukeyser on his TV show *Wall Street Week* (November 13, 1981), Wanniski called Friedman a demand-sider, and said he agreed with Galbraith that Reagan's big mistake was trying to walk in two directions at once. One direction is toward supply-side tax cutting, the other is toward Friedman's monetary policy which hopes to stop inflation by permitting a deep recession. The only way to stabilize the dollar, according to Wanniski, is by returning to the gold standard. He declared this to be inevitable, and predicted it would occur before the end of Reagan's first term. "I don't expect that a gold standard would last more than a hundred years," said Wanniski, "but I'm willing to take even fifty."

Friedman has a low opinion of the views of supply-side goldbugs: Laffer, Wanniski, Gilder, Jack Kemp, and starry-eyed former Reagan aide Jeffrey Bell, to name five. It is customary to call this group the radical supply-siders to distinguish them from conservative supply-siders with less extreme views. The radicals actually were convinced that Reagan's tax cuts would increase government revenue so rapidly that budget cutting, especially defense cutting, would not be necessary!

Simons's pamphlet defending laissez-faire is reprinted in his posthumous collection of papers, *Economic Policy in a Free Society* (1948). Although an opponent of Keynes, Simons favored vigorous government action to eliminate all private monopoly, including labor unions. He also favored monetary and tax reforms, and the elimination of all tariffs, but it was his extreme opposition to monopoly that led to his being labeled a "radical conservative." Wage and price controls, even antitrust policies, are no more than stopgap measures, Simons believed, that accomplish little and are easily corrupted by bureaucracies. Only when monopolies are eliminated altogether can the free market function as it should.

Another University of Chicago economist widely hailed as a conservative is the Nobel Prize–winner (1982) George Stigler. Conservative journalists like to praise Stigler's attacks on government efforts to regulate big business, but they seldom tell you why he opposes such efforts. It is because he believes that the regulations are usually in the interests of the regulated; indeed, are often requested by the regulated. They benefit not consumers but the megacorporations.

In the fifties Stigler was as down on oligopoly as Simons. In "The Case Against Big Business" (*Fortune*, May 1952) he argued that oligopolies compete only in superficial and socially undesirable ways (for example, the competition among the big four tobacco companies). Moreover, they stimulate the growth of big government and big labor, both of which Stigler deplores. Instead of taking over the giants or trying to control them, Stigler then wanted the government to dissolve them, leaving the field to genuine competition among smaller firms. It was the only way, he was convinced, that private enterprise can counter the drift toward socialism. Stigler wanted stronger antitrust action, a weakening of patent laws that stifle competition, and the elimination of all restrictive tariffs. "The obvious and economical solution . . . is to break up the giant companies. This . . . is the minimum program and it is essentially a conservative program." Conservative? Two decades later Stigler decided that megacorporations compete more than he formerly thought, and administer prices less than he thought. His present views seem to be that government should leave big business alone.

Simons's most famous student, Milton Friedman, has never looked kindly on federal takeovers, federal regulations, or trust busting. It is not big business that causes big labor and big government, he has declared, but the other way around. Big government causes big business and big labor! (See Lekachman's book cited earlier). Presumably, if government power can be reduced, so will the power of megacorporations to interfere with free markets.

U.S. News & World Report (January 31, 1983) asked six American Nobel Prize economists what they believed the government should do to promote recovery. Their lack of agreement is monumental. Friedman, as usual, writes as if all the other Nobel winners are crazy except for his old friend Stigler, and he is not too sure about Stigler. Stigler in turn makes what I consider the most vacuous statement ever uncorked by a top economist. "The human race existed for several million years," he said, "without governmental rules; now we suddenly need so many of them. That's a little paradoxical to me."

Because economists are always annoyed by the allegation that when ten economists are asked to solve a problem, they produce eleven solutions, it is worthwhile to consider what they mean when they deny this. They mean that, given the same data, they will usually agree on the nature of the problem and what the immediate outcome will be if certain measures are adopted. But there are so many complex parameters that economists, like weathermen, are poor at long-range forecasting. Moreover, they disagree profoundly on moral and political questions; that is, over what the economy *should* be. Since all important economic questions involve long-range forecasts joined to what ought to be, the claim that economists are in substantial agreement reduces to the tautology that they agree on just those trivial technical questions about which it is possible for them to agree.

There is a joke going around about a group of people who survived a shipwreck and found themselves on a deserted island. Lots of canned goods had washed ashore, but without a can opener how could they get to the food? No one had a pocket knife, and the island was devoid of rocks that could be used for smashing. One of the survivors was an economist of the Chicago School. After hours of frustration and debate he suddenly announced that he had solved the problem. "Let's *assume*," he said, "that we have a can opener."

The exact number of innocent people executed by Stalin or sent to die in slave labor camps is not known, because the massive data gathered in the inquiry initiated by Khrushchev and Mikoyan is still buried in Soviet archives or has been destroyed. The most authoritative figures can be found in *The Time of Stalin* (1981) by Anton Antonov-Ovseyenko, who had partial access to this data. He estimates that 19 million died in the purges of the thirties. Nine million more were executed after the Second World War. If to these deaths you add those resulting from the civil war that followed the Bolshevik appropriation of the Menshevik revolution, deaths from famine that inevitably followed harsh measures for collectivizing the farms, deaths from the enforcement of other government policies, and needless deaths in World War II that were the direct result of Stalin's blundering, barbaric orders (over 30 million Soviets died in that war, of which the Germans were responsible for about half), you get a total of some 80 million souls who were murdered by Soviet leaders. No tyranny in history has thrown away so many of its own people.

TWELVE

THE LAFFER CURVE

I would have expected supply-side theory to die a slow death after Ronald Reagan's failed promise to balance the budget by cutting taxes, emasculating the federal government (but without touching social security), and increasing military spending. Alas, it is still alive and well. As I write (1995), many Republican leaders are promising to balance the budget by cutting taxes (especially on the rich), emasculating the federal government (but without touching social security), and increasing military spending.

My spoof on the Laffer curve ran in Scientific American *(December 1981).*

The Kettle-Griffith-Moynihan Scheme for a New Electricity Supply, Traveling in the Olden Times, American Lake Poetry, the Strangest Dream that was ever Halfdreamt.

    I've lost the place, where was I?

    Something happened that time I was asleep, torn letters or was there snow?

—JAMES JOYCE,
Finnegans Wake

Economists love to draw curves. In the early decades of modern capitalism, classical economists were fond of explaining prices by constructing supply and demand graphs such as the one shown in Figure 1. If the price of a commodity is on the level indicated by the broken line *a*, it is easy to see from where this line crosses the curves that people will buy less of the product. Since the seller will have an oversupply, he will lower its price to get rid of it. If the prices are on the lower level of the broken line *b*, increased demand will bid up the product's price and the seller will produce more.

These up and down forces stabilize the price at *E*, the equilibrium point

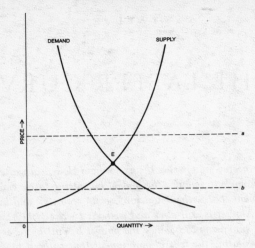

Figure 1. Classical supply and demand curves

where the amounts demanded and supplied are equal. At this point, according to early classical theory, the seller maximizes profit. If there is a general increase in demand, with supply constant, the demand curve shifts to the right and E rises. If there is a general increase in supply, with demand constant, the supply curve shifts to the right and E falls. If both curves move to the left or the right the same distance, E stays at the same level.

These curves are still indispensable because supply and demand play basic roles in any economy, even one without free markets; but these days economists refer to them less, because in a mixed economy such as ours hundreds of variables play havoc with the curves. The government, by innumerable stratagems, keeps many prices far above or below what they would be in a free market. Organized labor pushes up wages, and companies pass the increases along to prices, in what Arthur M. Okun of the Brookings Institution calls "the invisible handshake." Oligopolists find subtle ways of getting together to avoid market fluctuations, something they must do to remain efficient.

In the 1960's, when Keynesian economics was still carrying all before it ("We are all Keynesians now," said Richard Nixon), many economists were impressed by the Phillips curve. This curve was first proposed in 1958 by the London economist Alban William Housego Phillips and applied to the U.S. economy in 1960 by neo-Keynesians Paul A. Samuelson and Robert M. Solow. As you can see in Figure 2, a typical Phillips curve plots the inverse relation between unemployment and inflation. By taking into account the ability of labor and business to administer prices, the Phillips curve indicates that the double goals of full employment and price stability are not compatible in a mixed economy. Full employment (F) is attainable only at the cost of steady

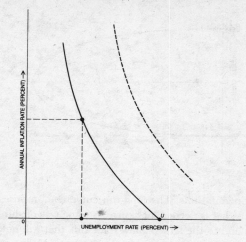

Figure 2. The Phillips curve

inflation. Stable prices (zero inflation) are impossible without high unemployment (U).

What to do? The best we can hope for, implies the curve, is to find a reasonable trade-off that does the minimum amount of harm. If prices rise too high, let a recession pull them down. If too many people are out of work, let inflation restore their jobs. With luck a government may find a point on the curve where "normal" unemployment will combine with an acceptable mild inflation of, say, 4 or 5 percent per year.

While economists were arguing about the "cruel dilemma" posed by the Phillips curve—the difficulty of finding a trade-off that would not lead to either a deep recession or a galloping inflation—a funny thing happened. During the late 1950's and early 1960's the economy got itself into the mysterious state of "stagflation" where, contrary to the curve, unemployment and inflation began to rise simultaneously. The Phillips curve started to disintegrate.

Keynesians struggled to rescue the curve. It was soon obvious that there is no such thing as a Phillips curve that is stable in the short run. The curve can be drawn dozens of ways, depending on what variables (including psychological expectations) are taken into account, and it varies widely from time to time and place to place. Is there a Phillips curve that is stable in the long run? Some say yes, some say no. Even if there is, economists disagree on how to apply it. Should the government try somehow to slide up and down the curve, with inflation and unemployment fluctuating like a seesaw? Should it try "looping" around the curve in various risky ways?

According to Keynesians, a force called demand-pull tries to twist the curve into a vertical straight line, while another force called cost-push tries to

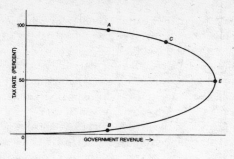

Figure 3. The Laffer curve

twist it into a horizontal line. The long-run curve compromises with a steep downward slope. What is needed, of course, is some way of shifting the entire curve back down and to the left to allow trade-offs that will not lead to social chaos. Some economists, for example John Kenneth Galbraith, believe this can be done only by combining fiscal and monetary policies with wage and price controls. Nothing could be worse says Milton Friedman. In Friedman's monetarist view the long-run Phillips curve is a vertical line at the "natural rate" of unemployment, and any trade-off effort to reduce unemployment below that line will set off an explosive inflation.

The Phillips curve, Daniel Bell wrote in 1980 (summarizing earlier remarks by Solow), "provided more employment for economists . . . than any public-works program since the construction of the Erie Canal." If unemployment is plotted against inflation for the 1960s, the result is a reasonably smooth curve. But if the same chronological plotting is done for the 1970s, as the U.S. economy drifted deeper into stagflation, the result is what the Wonna-cotts, in their textbook *Economics*, call a "mess." Today the Phillips curve has become little more than an out-of-focus symbol of the fact that inflation and unemployment are not independent evils but are functionally linked in com-plex ways that nobody is yet able to understand.

Now, as a result of the upsurge of interest in "supply-side" economics, the curve of the hour is a brand-new one called, with strangely resonant overtones, the Laffer curve. Arthur B. Laffer was a professor of business at the University of Southern California. The curve was named and first publicized by Jude Wan-niski, a former writer for *The Wall Street Journal,* in his bible of supply-side the-ory, confidently titled *The Way the World Works.* Figure 3 shows how Wanniski orients the Laffer curve at the beginning of his chapter 6.

Is it not a thing of beauty bare? As any child can see from inspecting the curve's lower end, if the government drops its tax rate to nothing it gets nothing. And if it raises its tax rate to 100 percent, it also gets nothing. Why? Because in that case nobody will work for wages. If all income went to the state, people would revert to a barter economy in which a painter paints a dentist's house only if the dentist caps one of the painter's teeth.

The Laffer curve gets more interesting when we slide along its arm toward the center. At point A, where taxes are not quite 100 percent, people will find it to their benefit to take some of their income in taxable wages. At point B the economy hums along with unfettered high production, but because tax rates are low the government gets the same small amount it would get if taxes were at A.

Now look at point E at the extreme right of the curve. That is where the tax rate maximizes government revenue. If taxes fall below E, that may stimulate production, but it obviously diminishes government revenue. Because E, by definition, is the point of maximum revenue, the government also must get less if taxes rise above E. The supply-siders stress many reasons for this being so. Some rich people find it unprofitable to work as productively as before. Some escape from excessive tax burdens by finding unproductive "shelters." Some even move to another country where taxes are low. If the government is relying on high taxes for welfare programs, millions of people are encouraged not to work at all. Why work if you can get almost the same income from welfare? Big corporations spend less on research and development. Entrepreneurs, the backbone of dynamic growth, are less willing to take risks. As a result of these factors and others, the economy becomes sluggish and tax revenues decline.

It is important to understand, Wanniski tells us, that E is not necessarily at the 50 percent level, although it could be. The shape of the Laffer curve obviously changes with circumstances. Thus, in time of war, when people and business are persuaded that a sacrificial effort is essential, they are willing to accept a high tax rate while they keep production booming. In peacetime they are less altruistic.

Now, the heart of the supply-side argument is the conviction that our current economy is somewhere near C, far too high on the Laffer curve. Lowering taxes (which some supply-siders believe calls for huge cuts in welfare spending) will give the supply side of the economy such a shot in the arm that the U.S. will slide down the Laffer curve to point E, perhaps not right away but soon. Tax revenues eventually will rise enough to take care of increased funding of the military, stagflation will end, dynamic growth will begin, the budget will be balanced by 1984 and the American dream will regain its luster.

Of course, supply and demand are always intertwined, but the supply-siders call themselves supply-siders in order to emphasize how they differ from neo-Keynesians. John Maynard Keynes stressed the importance of maintaining demand by minimum-wage laws and welfare payments. The Lafferites turn this around and stress the importance of stimulating supply. With the government off the back of business, production will soar, new inventions

will be made, more people will be employed and real wages will rise. Everyone benefits, particularly the poor, as prosperity trickles down from the
heights.

The second book to gild the virtues of Lafferism is George Gilder's
Wealth and Poverty. The title intentionally plays on the title of Henry George's best-seller *Progress and Poverty*, which created a stir late in the 19th
century by recommending the abolition of all taxes except a single tax on
land. Gilder's book is more impassioned than Wanniski's. "Regressive taxes
help the poor!" Gilder exclaims on page 188. William Safire once described
capitalism as the "good that can come from greed." Gilder is furious when
people talk like that; he finds capitalism motivated by the good that comes
from "giving." By this he means that the best way to give the poor what
they want, particularly the unemployed young men and women of minority
groups, is to leave the free market alone so that the economy will start
growing again.

The trouble with the Laffer curve is that, like the Phillips curve, it is
too simple to be of any service except as the symbol of a concept. In the
case of the Laffer curve the concept is both ancient and trivially true—
namely that when taxes are too high they are counterproductive. The problem is how to define "too high." No economist has the foggiest notion of
what a Laffer curve really looks like except in the neighborhood of its end
points. Even if economists did know, they would not know where to put the
economy on it. Neoconservative Irving Kristol, defending supply-side economics in *Commentary*, writes that he cannot say where we are on the Laffer curve, but he is sure we are "too far up." President Reagan's
across-the-board tax cuts are, he says, just what we need in order to slide
the economy toward point *E*.

To bring Laffer's curve more into line with the complexities of a mixed
economy dominated by what Galbraith likes to call the "technostructure,"
and also with other variables that distort the curve, I have devised what I call
the neo-Laffer (NL) curve. The NL curve is shown in Figure 4. Observe that
near its end points this lovely curve closely resembles the old Laffer curve,
proving that it was not a totally worthless first approximation. As the curve
moves into the complexities of the real world, however, it enters what I call
the "technosnarl." In this region I have based the curve on a sophisticated
statistical analysis (provided by Persi Diaconis, a statistician at Stanford University) of the best available data for the U.S. economy over the past 50 years.
Since the data are represented on the graph by a swarm of densely packed
points, the actual shape of the curve is somewhat arbitrary. Nevertheless, it
dramatizes a number of significant insights.

Consider any value *r* on the revenue axis within the segment directly
below the technosnarl. A vertical line through *r* intersects the snarl at multiple
points. These points represent values on the tax-rate axis that are most likely

to produce revenue *r*. Note that this also applies to the maximum value of *r*, producing multiple points *E* on the technosnarl. In brief, more than one tax rate can maximize government revenue.

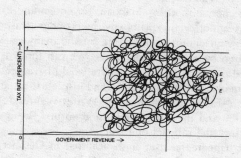

Figure 4. The neo-Laffer (NL) curve

Consider any value *t* on the tax-rate axis within the segment directly to the left of the technosnarl. A horizontal line through *t* also intersects the snarl at multiple points. These points represent values on the revenue axis that are most likely to result from tax rate *t*.

Note that at some intersection points lowering taxes from a given tax rate will lower revenue, and that at other points for the same tax rate it will raise revenue. Even if we could determine at which point to put the economy, it is not clear from the snarl just what fiscal and monetary policies would move the economy fastest along the curve to the nearest point *E*.

Like the old Laffer curve, the new one is also metaphorical, though clearly a better model of the real world. Since it is a statistical reflection of human behavior, its shape constantly changes, like the Phillips curve, in unpredictable ways. Hence the curve is best represented by a motion picture that captures its protean character. Because it takes so long to gather data and even longer to analyze all the shift parameters, by the time an NL curve is drawn it is out of date and not very useful. I have been told in confidence, however, that the Smith Richardson Foundation has secretly funded a multimillion-dollar project at Stanford Research International to study ways of improving the construction of NL curves. It is possible that with better software, using the fast Cray computer at the Lawrence Livermore Laboratory, one will be able to assign current probability values to the multiple intersection points. If one can do so, the NL curve could become a valuable forecasting tool for rational Federal decisions.

The Lafferites combine supreme self-confidence with a supremely low opinion of their detractors. Of the 18 economists who have won Nobel prizes, only two, Milton Friedman and Gunnar Myrdal, appear in the index of *The*

Way the World Works. Not even Alan Greenspan, now of the abandoned "old right," gets a mention. You might suppose that, since Friedman and Wanniski are both mentors to conservatives, Wanniski would have a high opinion of Friedman. Not so. Wanniski goes to great lengths in his book to explain why three famous economic models—Marxian, Keynesian and Friedmanian—are all wrong. They cannot even explain why the economy crashed in 1929.

There is now an enormous literature on the many causes of the crash, much of it written by eminent economists. We can throw it all away. Wanniski has figured out the real reason. There would have been nothing wrong with the stock market if Herbert Hoover had just left it alone. Instead he and Congress made a stupid political blunder. Writes Wanniski: "The stock market Crash of 1929 and the Great Depression ensued because of the passage of the Smoot-Hawley Tariff Act of 1930."

How did it happen that the crash occurred in October of the previous year? It is simple. The stock market, says Wanniski, anticipated the dire consequences of the coming restraints on free trade. Not all supply-siders agree. Jack Kemp, the New York congressman who coauthored the Kemp-Roth tax bill (which paved the way for Reagan's fiscal program), is one who does. In Kemp's rousing book *An American Renaissance,* he assures us that Wanniski has "demonstrated beyond any reasonable doubt" the truth of his remarkable discovery.

What do professional economists make of radical supply-side theory? Most of them, including the most conservative, regard it in much the same way as astronomers regard the theories of Immanuel Velikovsky. To Galbraith it is "a relatively sophisticated form of fraud." Walter W. Heller has likened it to laetrile, and Solow terms it "snake oil." Vice-President Bush has called it "voodoo economics." Herbert Stein labeled it "punk economics" (as in "punk rock"), and Martin Feldstein described it as "excess rhetorical baggage." Nevertheless, the books by Wanniski, Gilder, and Kemp are said to have much influence in the current administration.

Lafferites enjoy heaping praise on one another. Laffer, the hero of Wanniski's book, is quoted on the back of the paperbound edition as saying: "In all honesty, I believe it is the best book on economics ever written." Kristol, on the front cover, is more restrained. He thinks it is "the best economic primer since Adam Smith." Gilder asserts Wanniski "has achieved an overnight influence of nearly Keynesian proportions." Gilder has been greeted with similar euphoria. David Stockman, President Reagan's budget director, has hailed *Wealth and Poverty* as "Promethean in its intellectual power and insight. It shatters once and for all the Keynesian and welfare-state illusions that burden the failed conventional wisdom of our era."

How puzzled the president must be by the violent clash between his old friend Friedman and his Lafferite advisers! (The clash is not only over Friedman's monetary views but also over his distaste for the supply-side "gold bugs" who are urging an immediate return to the gold standard.) In the business section of *The New York Times*, Wanniski's attack on Friedman was vitriolic. The burden of it was that although Friedman is "barely five feet tall," he "weighs" so much that he is now an enormous "deadweight burden" on the backs of Menachem Begin, Margaret Thatcher, Ronald Reagan, and the U.S. economy.

Will the Lafferism of the Administration succeed, or will it, as many economists fear, eventually plunge the nation into higher inflation and higher unemployment? Economists cannot know. The technosnarl is too snarly. The idle rich might not invest their tax savings, as Lafferites predict, but might spend it on increased conspicuous consumption. The hardworking poor and middle class might decide to work less productively, not more. Big corporations and conglomerates might do little with their tax savings except acquire other companies.

Of course, ideologues of all persuasions think they know exactly how the economy will respond to the Administration's strange mixture of Lafferism and monetarism. Indeed, their self-confidence is so vast, and their ability to rationalize so crafty, that one cannot imagine any scenario for the next few years, that they would regard as falsifying their dogma. The failure of any prediction can always be blamed on quirky political decisions or unforeseen historical events. It is inconceivable, for example, that Friedman would consider the triple-digit inflation in Israel or the recent riots in Britain or high U.S. stagflation in 1983 as suggesting the slightest blemish on his monetarist views even though he enthusiastically supported Begin, Thatcher, and Reagan, and all three have in turn been strongly influenced by Friedman's brand of monetarism.

As for the Lafferities, they have all kinds of outs in case Reagan's policies lead to disaster. Some will blame it on Friedman. Others may follow an escape plan mapped out by William F. Buckley. Although the administration's tax and budget cuts have been called the biggest in American history, Buckley thinks both cuts are not big enough. "The trouble with the Reagan tax cuts," he wrote in *National Review* (July 24, 1981), "is (*a*) they are insufficient, and insufficiently targeted; and (*b*) the cuts in the budget are equally insufficient. . . . You cannot make long-range, significant cuts by concentrating on only a single one-third of the budget. It is the equivalent of saying you are going to lose weight by exercising only your right leg."

One can hope that President Reagan will not try to reconcile these conflicting conservative views by resorting to astrology. This possibility is not quite as remote as one might think. In an interview with Angela Fox Dunn the President said he followed the daily advice for his sign in the syndicated horoscope of Carroll Righter. Born on February 6, Reagan is an Aquarian. "I believe you'll find," he told Dunn, "that 80 percent of the people in New York's Hall of Fame are Aquarians."

President Reagan and his wife Nancy were for many years personal friends of both Righter (who advised Gloria Swanson and other Hollywood figures) and the astrologer Jeane Dixon, who lives in Washington. "I'm not considered one of his advisers," Dixon cryptically told newspaper columnist Warren Hinckle, "but I advise him." Joyce Jillson, who writes a syndicated astrology column for *The Chicago Tribune* and has among her clients several Hollywood studios and multinational corporations, says that in 1980 Reagan aides paid her $1,200 for horoscopes on eight prospective vice-presidential candidates. The White House communications director has, however, called her a liar. Michael Kramer wrote in *New York Magazine:* "Ronald Reagan, says Ronald Reagan, is a nice, well-intentioned man who loves his family, likes to consult his horoscope before making major decisions, and cries when he watches *Little House on the Prairie.*"

Will the president seek help from the zodiac in trying to decide whether to follow Friedman or Laffer or someone else? One may never know. As the Yale economist William Nordhaus put it (*The New York Times*, August 9, 1981): "We can only hope that supply-side economics turns out to be laetrile rather than thalidomide."

POSTSCRIPT

It may be hard to believe today, but the extreme supply-siders convinced Reagan that if he lowered taxes it would give the economy such a shove that defense spending could be increased, the entitlement programs preserved, and the budget balanced by 1984 with a healthy surplus. At least that's what Reagan told the voters. There is now some evidence that he and his advisors anticipated a large deficit but kept this secret because they were convinced that only such a deficit would persuade Congress to dismantle welfare. In any case, everybody except a few diehard supply-siders such as Arthur Laffer, Jack Kemp and his writer friends, the economist Paul Craig Roberts and, of course, the president himself now realizes that the 1980 campaign promises were fantasy. The one big achievement of the Reagan administration was lowering the inflation rate—but at what a cost!

It's no economic mystery that inflation can be checked if you pay the Keynesian price of a severe recession and a monstrous deficit. Indeed, one of the many ironies of Reagan's career is that although he began his first term as a radical rightist—it's not easy to pin the label "conservative" on him—he ended the term by reviving a moribund Keynes. Economists now generally agree that the recession was caused by the Fed's tight money policy (plus other things), and it ended only when the Fed abruptly eased the money supply in 1983, again aided by other factors. These other factors included rising government spending on defense, increased purchasing power created by tax cuts, and the sheer fact that depressions are cyclical. Whatever the multiple reasons, Reagan was lucky. The depression ended just before his 1984 campaign. The point, however, is this: Everything happened according to classical Keynesian doctrine.

"Reagan became the ultimate Keynesian," was how Lester Thurow put it (see Karen Arenson's article, "Heroes of the Economic Recovery," *New York Times*, Sunday, January 19, 1984). "Regardless of what he said he was doing, it was simply the old Keynesian medicine at work, stop and go economics. It got us out of the worst recession since the depression, and we're now in the go phase. But the problem is that we will eventually stop."

At the time I am typing this (late 1985), Reaganism is falling apart, and it is impossible to predict how Congress will eventually handle the deficit catastrophe without cutting defense, chipping away at entitlements, raising taxes, or some combination of the three. One thing, though, is clear. The Laffer curve is a joke.

The big stumbling blocks are Reagan's persistent hope for an economic miracle, and his declaration that he would never raise taxes or trim defense spending and Social Security. When he was governor of California, he similarly did his best to reduce taxes and chop welfare. "The entire graduated income tax structure was created by Karl Marx," Reagan said in 1966. He wanted to declare war on Vietnam ("We could pave the whole country and put parking stripes on it, and still be home for Christmas"). He described welfare recipients as "a faceless mass waiting for a handout." Yet when the state budget jumped up 122 percent, Reagan approved the largest tax increase in the history of California. By the end of his second term we will know if he is capable of approving a tax increase for the nation even though he promised in 1984 that this would be done "over my dead body." Reagan knows, of course, that the Democrats will never stop recalling Walter Mondale's campaign prediction that the administration would be forced to raise taxes to prevent the deficit from wrecking the economy.

Reagan wants to go down in history as the far-sighted president who reversed what he sees as evil drifts toward socialism, toward accommodation with the godless Soviet Union, and toward a general decay of morality and Christian faith. He wants to be remembered as the David who slew the Goliath of Big Government, unraveled the welfare state and put a free market back at the center of the economy. More likely he will be seen by future historians as another Herbert Hoover. ("We should soon, with the help of God, be in sight of the day when poverty will be banished from the nation," said Hoover just before the Big Crash of 1929). Conservative writer William Safire (in an August 1985 column) described Reagan's present strategy as the "masterly inactivity" of a leader too stubborn to go back on his "demogogic pre-election promises," standing on the bridge of the ship of state "smiling into the fog, as we head toward his trillion-dollar iceberg."

My neo-Laffer curve produced a flood of letters, many from indignant readers who actually took the curve seriously. Some conservative economists congratulated me for saying what they had avoided saying out of respect for a newly elected, enormously popular president. David Warsh, of the *Boston Globe*, wrote a feature article about my curve ("No Laffing in D.C. This Week," December 15, 1981). I was taken to task by several economists for implying that the Laffer curve was something the profession considered significant, when in fact it was the product of media hype. Three letters, two blasting me and one defending me, were published in *Scientific American* (March, 1982).

Neither supply-siders not monetarists buy the old Phillips curve. Indeed, as we have seen, they apparently sold Reagan on the dream that inflation could be checked without either wage and price controls or a recession. In some cases their understanding of economic realities behind the curve was on a primitive level. Leonard Silk, describing the 1982 economic summit conference at Versailles (*New York Times*, June 11, 1982) reported a briefing of reporters by supply-sider Donald Regan, then Secretary of the Treasury. "If you recall the Phillips curve," said Regan, "that's where the more you have of inflation, the more unemployment you'll have—and the less inflation, the less unemployment."

Of course, Regan had it exactly wrong. The curve shows inflation and unemployment moving in *opposite* directions. Regan, Silk reminded his readers, had been an English major at Harvard. There was sharp disagreement at the conference over whether the Phillips curve could be made to go away, though everybody agreed it would be great if it would. Meanwhile, added Silk, "The president is still clinging to the Laffer curve, with its claimed relationship between lower taxes, and higher production, national income, and tax revenues."

Jude Wanniski has been almost as subdued lately as Milton Friedman, but Laffer and Gilder continue to bubble over with supply-side enthusiasm. In the *Washington Post* (August 20, 1985) Laffer maintained that the drop in inflation was not the result of tight money; it resulted from an increase in the supply of goods. "The size of our national debt is not a crisis situation," he said a few days later (*Sacramento Bee*, August 29, 1985). "It is by no means a reason to overturn Reaganomics. It's far better to keep tax rates low and run temporary deficits than it is to raise tax rates and destroy economic growth." Congress, according to Laffer, is solely to blame for the big deficit because it refused to cut nondefense spending enough.

Gilder's latest work, *The Spirit of Enterprise* (1984) is another breathless hymn to the invisible hand of Adam Smith. "No one understands the entrepreneurial spirit and the entrepreneurial basis of economic growth better than

George Gilder," said his friend Irving Kristol, who seems unable to curb hyperbole whenever he is asked to supply a jacket blurb for a book by a supply-sider.

Keynesian economists naturally see Gilder's book in a different light. "Only someone with a sense of humor could survive reading this book," commented Robert Solow (*New Republic*, October 22, 1984). "And no one with any trace of a sense of humor could have written it. . . . the prose is mind numbing. . . . if he wrote a chapter in praise of lettuce, it could turn you against green leafy vegetables forever."

Here is how Solow said what I tried to convey with my neo-Laffer curve:

> The truth is that the tradeoff between incentive and equity in taxation is a complicated and tough issue of public policy. Our tax system probably does a terrible job. It is riddled with loopholes that tend to direct energy into unproductive activities. It does not achieve much real equity (and even less nowadays). If we had the will to reform it—which we do not—we might gain on both the equity and incentive sides. But it is neither clever nor honorable to do as Gilder does and submerge the equity issues in undocumented claims and claptrap. It irresistibly reminds one of what Bernard Shaw is supposed to have said to Samuel Goldwyn as they negotiated over the royalties for a film version of one of Shaw's plays: "Mr. Goldwyn, you seem to be interested only in art, while I care only about money."

David Stockman, as we all know, resigned in 1985 as budget director after another outburst of harsh and honest words about Reaganomics. Incidentally, it has been reported that Stockman used to baby-sit for Daniel Patrick Moynihan. Contrary to James Joyce's prophecy (see the epigraph of this chapter), Moynihan never bought his baby-sitter's supply-side mythology. Exactly where Stockman stands today on the "promethean" intellects of Wanniski and Gilder is not clear. Perhaps he will tell us in the memoirs he is writing, for which Harper and Row paid him more than $2 million. To quote Joyce again: "Stockins of Winning's Folly Merryfalls. . . . Godamedy, you're a delville of a tolkar!"

THIRTEEN

H. G. WELLS IN RUSSIA

When David Madden was preparing an anthology titled Rediscoveries: Non-fiction, *he asked for a contribution. I responded with an essay on Wells's long forgotten book* Russia in the Shadows. *After Madden's anthology failed to find a publisher, I was able to place my essay in* The Freeman *(May 1995). An editor removed some final paragraphs about Wells's Russian mistress, partly for space restrictions and partly because he thought them irrelevant. I have restored them here.*

A much earlier piece on Wells and Marxism, "H. G. Wells: 'Premature' Anticommunist," appeared in the New Leader *(October 7, 1950), and can be found in my* Order and Surprise *(Prometheus, 1983).*

Today's college students, preoccupied with everything except a liberal education, have only the dimmest awareness of how many famous writers, artists, and thinkers around the world were once under the magic spell of Communism. They have no conception of how many bright, attractive young people in American universities during the 1930s called each other "comrade," exulting in the delusion that they were part of a vast, inevitable Revolution destined to overthrow an evil capitalism.

The Soviet Empire has now crumbled, communist parties are dissolving, the old tricolor Russian flag has replaced the hammer and sickle, statues of Lenin have been toppled, and Marxist ideology is dead except in the atrophied brains of a few elderly die-hards around the globe. As history takes this unexpected turn, it is good to remember that from the beginning—not just among conservatives but among democratic socialists—there were many who saw clearly that Marxism was a weird mystique set forth by an egotistical crank.

In 1920, three years after the Bolsheviks seized power, two of England's most influential writers, Bertrand Russell and H. G. Wells, made trips to Moscow to converse with Lenin. Each recorded his negative impressions in a book. Russell's *Practice and Theory of Bolshevism* is the more perceptive of the two books, and it is still in print and widely known. Here I shall focus on the book by Wells, *Russia in the Shadows*, because it has been almost totally forgotten. It deserves to be read today for three reasons: its vivid account of Russian chaos following the first world war, its portrait of Lenin, and its insights into Wells's early opinions of Marx and the future of Russia.

Wells made three visits to Russia. The first, accompanied by Maurice Baring, was in 1914, just before the outbreak of war, to see his old friend Maxim Gorky. Gorky's secretary and mistress was then the Countess Benckendorff, formerly Moura Zakrevskaya. She had been planted on Gorky as a government spy. But Moura had told Gorky this. Admiring her straightforwardness, Gorky did not seem to mind.

In 1920, when Wells returned to Russia, Gorky, a personal friend of Lenin, arranged for Moura to be Wells's guide and interpreter. Although there is no hint of it in Wells's book, he fell passionately in love with her. The full story of this beautiful and witty woman has yet to be told, although Anthony West, Wells's illegitimate son by Rebecca West, devotes many pages to her in his biography of Wells. "My father could not reason himself out of his intoxication with her, and however little future his passion might seem to have, he went home with it burning in him."

Wells's account of his 1920 trip first ran as a series of articles in London's *Sunday Express*, instantly boosting that paper's circulation by 80,000. The English publisher Hodder and Stoughton brought the series out as a book in 1920, the same year that Russell's book appeared.

Wells went first to St. Petersburg (later renamed Petrograd, then Leningrad, now back to St. Petersburg) to renew his friendship with Gorky. Since 1914 Moura had been imprisoned several times by the Bolsheviks, and was now forbidden to leave Petersburg to return to her children in nearby Estonia.

Petersburg, Russia's second largest city, was in a state of almost total ruin. The old Czarist order had collapsed because of what Wells called its "inherent rottenness." The Bolsheviks had snatched power from the democratic but indecisive Mensheviks. There had been much killing to establish order and there was a crude rationing system for food and goods. Everywhere there was evidence of a "vast irreparable breakdown." Shops were closed, clothes were shabby, roads were terrible, houses had been torn down for firewood. A black market flourished, though occasionally a profiteer was caught and shot. Men were unshaven only because they had no razor blades. Hospitals had broken down. Medicines were unavailable. Everybody looked sick and sad. People stood for hours in long queues to get bread. Wherever Wells looked, and he was allowed to roam freely, he saw nothing but decay and desolation.

Over and over again, Wells insists that this decay was not the product of Bolshevism but the cause. "It was not communism which built up these great, impossible cities, but capitalism. It was not communism that plunged this huge, creaking, bankrupt empire into six years of exhausting war. It was European imperialism. Nor is it communism that has pestered this suffering and perhaps dying Russia with a series of subsidized raids, invasions and insurrections, and inflicted upon it an atrocious blockade. The vindictive French creditor, the journalistic British oaf, are far more responsible for these deathbed miseries than any communist."

The Communist Party, Wells stressed, was at the moment the only possible government for Russia. Small in number, the Bolsheviks had been able to take over during the confusion that followed six years of war because they were the only party with a clear vision. Its leaders, Wells believed, were fanatical but honest. He acknowledged their brutalities, but suspected that a Red Terror, inspired by hate, was the only way order could have been restored.

Russell, whose visit to Russia preceded Wells's, found Gorky "dying along with Russian culture." Wells chides Russell for this. Russell had simply caught Gorky with a bad cold, then his imagination led him into a "dark and purple passage." Although Gorky was a great admirer of Lenin, Wells found him bitter toward the Communist Party, and strong in his respect for western science and literature. Now, thanks to Bolshevik efforts to prevent counter-revolutionary forces, Russian art, literature, and science had almost disappeared. Eminent scientists were without funds or access to western journals. "The crude Marxist philosophy," Wells wrote, "which divides all men into bourgeoisie and proletariat, which sees all social life as a stupidly simple 'class war,' had no knowledge of the conditions necessary for the collective mental life."

Amazingly, only in plays and operas did pockets of the old culture persist. "When one faced the stage, it was as if nothing had changed." Another hopeful sign was the government subsidy for a vast encyclopedia, though how would it be distributed? Wells granted that the Bolsheviks were basically honest, but they were also naive and simple-minded. Astonished to find themselves in power, they were without plans or ideas. "Marx the Prophet and his Sacred Book" provided no leads. Although Marx had given a good factual account of the evils of unfettered capitalism, he offered no blueprints for what would replace it. All he did was intimate vaguely about the new paradise that would eventually result after a temporary socialist phase had withered away. Communism, wrote Wells, was like a magician who had lost his rabbit and could produce nothing from his hat.

In a chapter titled "The Quintessence of Bolshevism" Wells slashed away at Marxist ideology in two memorable paragraphs:

> It will be best if I write about Marx without any hypocritical deference. I have always regarded him as a Bore of the extremest sort. His vast unfinished work, *Das Kapital*, a cadence of wearisome volumes about such phantom unrealities as the *bourgeoisie* and the *proletariat*, a book

for ever maundering away into tedious secondary discussions, impresses me as a monument of pretentious pedantry. But before I went to Russia on this last occasion I had no active hostility to Marx. I avoided his works, and when I encountered Marxists I disposed of them by asking them to tell me exactly what people constituted the proletariat. None of them knew. No Marxist knows. In Gorky's flat I listened with attention while Bokaiev discussed with Shalyapin the fine question of whether in Russia there was a proletariat at all, distinguishable from the peasants. As Bokaiev has been head of the Extraordinary Commission of the Dictatorship of the Proletariat in Petersburg, it was interesting to note the fine difficulties of the argument. The "proletarian" in the Marxist jargon is like the "producer" in the jargon of some political economists, who is supposed to be a creature absolutely distinct and different from the "consumer." So the proletarian is a figure put into flat opposition to something called capital. I find in large type outside the current number of the *Plebs*, "The working class and the employing class have nothing in common." Apply this to a works foreman who is being taken in a train by an engine-driver to see how the house he is having built for him by a building society is getting on. To which of these immiscibles does he belong, employer or employed? The stuff is sheer nonsense.

In Russia I must confess my passive objection to Marx has changed to a very active hostility. Wherever we went we encountered busts, portraits, and statues of Marx. About two-thirds of the face of Marx is beard, a vast solemn woolly uneventful beard that must have made all normal exercise impossible. It is not the sort of beard that happens to a man, it is a beard cultivated, cherished, and thrust patriarchally upon the world. It is exactly like *Das Kapital* in its inane abundance, and the human part of the face looks over it owlishly as if it looked to see how the growth impressed mankind. I found the omnipresent images of that beard more and more irritating. A gnawing desire grew upon me to see Karl Marx shaved. Some day, if I am spared, I will take up shears and a razor against *Das Kapital*; I will write *The Shaving of Karl Marx*.

Marxism, Wells wrote, was a cult that appealed to energetic young men and women, who were aware of capitalism's excesses and who longed for a new order. They would have become Marxists if Marx had never lived. Wells recalls his own youth. Denied an education, he had worked long hours in a detestable shop which he would have gladly burned down if he had not assumed it was over-insured. Marxism spread like fire around the world not because Marx was wise but because capitalism was "stupid, selfish, wasteful, and anarchistic."

Marx saw a "great conspiracy against human happiness concocted by a mysterious body of wicked men called capitalists." Wells saw these tycoons as "no more than a scrambling disorder of mean-spirited and short-sighted men." Marxism, with its conspiracy mania and revolutionary ardor offered an illusory hope for a quick fix. Unfortunately, the Bolsheviks had no experience

in running a giant nation. Wells found their incompetence amazing, their
ignorance profound. Repeatedly he was asked, "When is the social revolution
going to happen in England?"

Every intelligent Bolshevik, wrote Wells, is bothered by the fact that the
revolution happened first in Russia. According to Marx, it was to occur in
advanced capitalist countries—first in England, then France and Germany,
and finally in America. Instead, it happened in Russia where there was no
specialized working class at all. Russian factories were worked by peasants who
came and went from villages. There was no proletariat, in Marx's sense, to
unite with the workers of the world. Slowly dawning on the minds of Bolsheviks was the "chill suspicion" that what happened in Russia was not a Marxist
revolution at all, but only the capture of a derelict ship.

Wells tried to convince Russian leaders that in England there were at
least 200 different classes, and the only class-conscious proletarians he knew
were a small band of Scotch workers under the leadership of a gentleman
named MacManus. Wells was amused by the repeated scoldings that came
by wireless to British labor leaders because they refused to behave like Marx
said they would. They ought to be Red. They were just yellow.

In Wells's eyes "never was there so amateurish a government." Their
preposterous ideology was doing irreparable damage to science and art. The
teaching of chemistry was actually forbidden unless it was Marxist chemistry.
Art and literature were suppressed if not politically correct.

Wells visited a school selected by the government. When children were
asked what western writers they liked best, Wells's name dominated! "Such
comparatively trivial figures as Milton, Dickens, Shakespeare ran about inter-
mittently between the feet of that literary colossus." Wells was furious. The
next day he visited a school of his own choice and found it far superior. There
were no Wells books in its library. None of the children had ever heard of
him.

At a meeting of Petersburg leaders he heard himself repeatedly praised.
They urged him to write fairly about Russia; not to emulate Russell who had
accepted their hospitality then gone home to write harsh criticism. To avoid
mistranslations, Wells wrote down his speech and had it carefully translated
before he gave it. He was not a Marxist, he told his listeners. He was a "col-
lectivist." He wished Russia well, but assured them that in England any movement toward socialism would be peaceful, the product of education, not class
hatred. The speech was reported fairly in *Pravda*. The meeting ended with
everyone singing the *Internationale*. Wells realized that in no way was the
meeting democratic. It simply rubber-stamped what it had been told. It was
like "a big bagful of miscellaneous wheels" compared to an "old-fashioned
and inaccurate but still going clock."

The sixth chapter of Wells's book, titled "The Dreamer in the Kremlin,"
describes Wells's chat with Lenin. He found Moscow in less disrepair than

Petersburg. Its churches were open. Ten thousand crosses glittered in the sunlight, and kissing icons was still a flourishing industry. A sign outside one church said, "Religion is the opiate of the people." It had little effect, Wells observed, because most of the people in the street could not read.

After a long irritating wait, Wells was ushered through a labyrinth of passageways and guards to Lenin's sanctum. Wells was surprised at how small Lenin was. He had expected to find a doctrinaire Marxist, but found him nothing of the sort. He had a pleasant, quick-changing, brownish face, lively smile, and a habit of screwing up one side of his face because of defective vision in one eye. Speaking excellent English, Lenin asked the inevitable question. Why is there no social revolution in England?

Wells in turn wanted to know what Lenin planned to do with the mammoth country he found on his hands. There were huge plans. The cities would become smaller, all Russia would be electrified, agriculture would be seized by the state and modernized. "Come back," he said, "and see what we have done in ten years." Wells was favorably impressed. In spite of Lenin's cumbersome Marxist baggage, Wells believed that "this amazing little man" might actually succeed in revitalizing Russia.

Wells stressed his faith in evolutionary socialism. Lenin disagreed. Capitalism was incurable. It had to be totally overturned. Their argument ended indecisively, but they parted warmly. Wells and his Russian-speaking biologist son G. P. ("Gip") who had accompanied him on the trip returned to Petersburg, then went on to Revel to catch a ship home. Wells left convinced that western nations should do all they could to provide aid, especially food to prevent a looming famine during the coming winter. If Russia were to collapse again, Bolshevism might be replaced by a new ideology and a dictatorship worse than Lenin's. Such a collapse, Wells feared, could spread westward, and "possibly all modern civilization may tumble in."

Leon Trotsky, in his biography of Lenin, wrote that several years after Wells's visit Lenin had said of Wells, "Ugh! What a narrow petty bourgeoise he is! He is a philistine! Ugh! What a philistine!" Anthony West, in his biography of his father, says that he thinks Trotsky fabricated Lenin's remark out of whole cloth.

Although *Russia in the Shadows* sold well in England, it was bitterly denounced by Communists for its attacks on Marx, and by conservatives for its tolerance of the Russian experiment and for its admiration of Lenin. Winston Churchill, who correctly perceived Communism as a growing cancer, blasted Wells's book in *The Daily Express* (December 5, 1920), followed by Wells's reply. Churchill and Wells had long been at odds. Wells would later caricature him as Rupert Catskill in his science fantasy *Men Like Gods* (1923). Archconservative Henry Arthur Jones was so enraged that he barraged Wells with abusive letters which he later published as a book, *My Dear Wells* (1921).

Who today can fault Wells for seeing clearly through the shams of Marx, and for his fears that Bolshevik fanaticism would stifle Russian science and culture? But there are three glaring defects in his book.

Wells was curiously unimpressed by the absence of democracy in the new Russia. Not once did he ask Lenin if there were plans for free elections and secret ballots. Wells had never been keen on allowing uneducated people to vote, preferring instead a state governed by an appointed elite of scientists and technicians. Perhaps he bought the Bolshevik notion that a democracy of sorts operated in Russia as decisions made by low-level party cells filtered upward to the Kremlin. There is no excuse for Wells not realizing that without a vigorous democracy, and a press free to criticize, there could be no guarantee that a tyrant would not gain total control, as indeed one did.

Nor did Wells show an awareness that a free-market economy, combined with private property, is a far more efficient way to produce food and goods than a command economy that stifles initiatives and regulates with a clumsy, easily corrupted bureaucracy. As a democratic (of sorts) socialist, Wells shared Marx's indictment of unrestrained capitalism, but he did not understand, as even democratic socialists do today, that a modern economy must be a mixture of free markets and wise government controls.

Finally, as an atheist himself, Wells was not appalled by Lenin's efforts to eliminate Christianity from Russian culture and establish atheism as a state "religion." Wells should have realized that efforts to stamp out religious faith, especially in a culture as deeply pious as Russia, would only alienate the masses and increase their hostility toward the government. As we now see, the Russian people are as hungry as ever for the right to worship God, and are flocking back by the millions to their newly opened churches. Some Russian leaders are even daring to end their speeches with "God bless you"!

Our review of *Russia in the Shadows* would be incomplete without saying more about the remarkable Moura. She was born in 1892 as Moura Zakrevskaya. Her first husband, H. von Benckendorff, was the Russian ambassador to England. The Bolsheviks shot him during the Revolution. Moura then married Baron Budberg. She divorced him, it was said, because of his addiction to gambling, although she permanently kept the name of Moura Budberg. After her last prison term in Moscow, she was released in the custody of Bruce Lockhart, a secret British spy who became her lover. (He writes about their relationship in his book *British Agent*.) Moura, who spoke five languages (Russian, English, German, French, and Italian) supported herself by translating books by Thomas Mann and others.

After the brief affair with Moura during his 1920 trip to Russia, Wells longed to see her again. About 1930 she began making annual trips to London, having broken with Gorky who by then had become a slavish Stalinist. In 1934, after Wells's third visit to Russia to interview Stalin, he spent a month with Moura in Estonia. He was then 68, she 42. Wells had wanted her to join him in Moscow, but she insisted they could not meet there because she feared she would be arrested and shot. Wells later learned that not only had she been making repeated trips to Moscow, but that she was still serving the government as a secret agent!

Did Moura's deceptions break up their romance? Incredibly, they did not. Moura played on Wells the same clever ruse she had played on Gorky. She freely admitted everything. She was, she said, only trying to stay alive as best she could. Why should Wells worry about her checkered past?

Now an old man, Wells was too smitten by Moura not to accept this. In 1935 she moved permanently to London, and from then until Wells's death in 1946 she was his mistress. Wells wanted to marry, but she refused. They kept separate homes, though as Wells put it in a letter, "We live in open sin." This new situation destroyed Wells's relationship with Odette, his previous mistress whom he kept in a house in France. Moura Budberg, said Odette, should be called Moura Bedbug.) Moura survived Wells by almost thirty years, dying in London in 1974, at age 82. The funeral was held in a Russian Orthodox cathedral. *The New York Times* covered it in an obituary on November 2, 1974. In 1976 a film about her life was made for the BBC.

This is not the place to cover the history of Wells's growing realization that nothing good would ever come from the Russian experiment, and that universal suffrage was essential for the health of any nation. In 1934, during his three-hour conversation with Stalin, Wells tried to persuade Stalin that Roosevelt's New Deal was the beginning in America of a movement toward socialism, and that the world's two great superpowers should seize the chance to work together for a world socialist state. Stalin countered, as had Lenin, with the usual Marxist bromides. American capitalists were simply making a few trivial concessions to stay in power. They would never give up without a worker's revolt that would totally overthrow them.

Wells's last full-length novel, *Babes in the Darkling Wood* (1940) was about the disenchantment of two young Stalinists, a change of heart triggered by Stalin's invasion of Finland. Hard as it is to believe, Wells still clung to his view that Stalin was a sincere, essentially decent fellow who was caught in the coils of a worthless ideology. By 1940 many books had accurately described Stalin's terror—the millions of innocents he had shot or sent to die in the Gulag—but Wells either had not read them or he knew about them and did not believe them. His last great outburst of anger, *Crux Ansata* (1943) was directed not against the crimes of Stalin, but against what he considered the crimes of Roman Catholicism. When Wells died in 1946, soon after the first atom bomb fell on Japan, he had given up hope that humanity could save itself from wars that would plunge it back to barbarism.

Many of Wells's prophecies were eerily accurate. As early as 1914, in his science-fiction novel *The World Set Free*, he described a second world war beginning in the forties in which "atom bombs" were dropped from planes. The one great event he totally failed to see was the abrupt collapse in the U.S.S.R. of its entire Marxist-Engels-Leninist-Stalinist heritage.

As I write, Russia is back in shadows strangely similar to those Wells encountered in 1920. Its economy is in chaos, famine is again a threat, and help from the west is desperately needed. As in 1920, its leaders have only the vaguest plans for restructuring a shattered empire along democratic and free-market lines. It is one of the magnificent and ironic surprises of history that this great culture, after 74 years of brutal Communist dictatorship, is now eager to construct a political and economic system of the very sort that Marx regarded as so malevolent that it had to be destroyed utterly by workers of the world who had nothing to lose but their chains.

FOURTEEN

BEYOND CULTURAL RELATIVISM

If "cultural relativism" means nothing more than a respect and tolerance for the morals and customs of all cultures, and an attempt to understand them, then of course we should all be cultural relativists. In the past, however, the term meant much more than that. It meant that there was no rational basis for making value judgments that crossed cultural boundaries. It meant that no anthropologist had a right to say that culture A was more successful in meeting the needs of its members than culture B. The job of the anthropolgist was solely descriptive. One could describe, say, the culture of Nazi Germany which resulted in the Holocaust, but to condemn German anti-Semitism as evil would be to make a verboten value judgment.

My earliest attack on this extreme form of cultural relativism, which dominated anthropology in the days of Boas, Benedict, and Mead, appeared in Ethics *(October 1930). For a later essay on this topic see chapter 5 of* The Whys of a Philosophical Scrivener *(Morrow, 1983).*

Some of the Ethiopians tattoo their children, but we do not; and while the Persians think it seemly to wear a brightly dyed dress reaching to the feet, we think it unseemly; and whereas the Indians have intercourse with their women in public, most other races regard this as shameful. . . .

T he sentences above are not from a modern textbook on cultural anthropology. They are from the writings of Sextus Empiricus, the ancient Greek skeptic who flourished in the second and third centuries of the Christian Era. Sextus was one of the earliest, though by no means the first, of the apologists for the point of view anthropologists call "cultural relativism"—the view that there are no standards of "good" and "bad" other than the laws and customs of a given culture.

By numerous examples Sextus made clear that the laws and customs of the ancient world varied widely from one society to another. Since there are no universal standards to which one can appeal, he reasoned, it is impossible to decide which is "best" among conflicting customs. "No more"—a phrase meaning that one point of view is "no more" true than another—was the central axiom of the Greek skeptics. What course of action, then, should the wise man follow? Sextus Empiricus gave a clear and simple answer: Suspend judgment on ethical matters and conform to the customs of your country.

Since the time of Sextus a distinguished number of thinkers have shared his ethical views. In this paper, however, we shall be concerned only with the growth of "no more" in the social sciences, particularly in recent anthropology. The question will be raised of whether this growth, so necessary and healthy at the outset, has not reached such bizarre extremes that it obscures from the cultural anthropologist what may well be his major scientific task.

In the late nineteenth century, under the influence of Darwin, sociologists and anthropologists were convinced that cultures followed an orderly development from low, brutelike forms to the refinements of modern civilization. Primitive societies were investigated, not to determine objectively what they were like, but to uncover facts that would fit previously conceived patterns of progress. The savage in Spencer's *Principles of Sociology* is only slightly above the gorilla in mental and moral attainments. At the opposite end of Spencer's scale, exemplifying the highest type of culture, was, of course, British middle-class society.

It was against this "genetic" approach that twentieth-century social scientists rebelled. As methods for investigating primitive societies grew more efficient and less biased, it soon became apparent that the savage was not nearly so stupid and immoral as Spencer had supposed. He was capable of quite complex reflection on practical problems posed by his environment, and he was caught in a matrix of moral restrictions fully as elaborate as those of Victorian England.

Of course it was true that if you went back far enough you could find a rough evolutionary development of man, marked by such discoveries as fire and iron; but, in the period of, say, the last ten thousand years, investigations disclosed only a bewildering and changing pattern of cultural traits that were impossible to force into schemes of orderly upward movement. To avoid the ethnocentrism of his predecessors, the modern cultural anthropologist leaned over backward to refrain from expressing a "value judgment" concerning any aspect of his data. To be rigidly objective, all expressions of "good" and "bad" dropped out of his vocabulary. His work became purely "descriptive." Different cultures were regarded as "incommensurable" because no external yardstick existed by which they could be compared.

In 1907 a Yale sociologist, William Graham Sumner, published his famous *Folkways*. The book was a somewhat haphazard compilation of variations in social customs, designed—like Sextus Empiricus's compilations of seventeen centuries previous—to impress the reader with the diversity of human behavior and the tendency of every culture to suppose its customs superior to all others. It was this book that introduced the word *mores* into the social sciences. "Folkways" was Sumner's generic term for all customs; "mores" are folkways that have acquired ethical value, so that violation of them is considered evil or immoral. A woman who went about Manhattan with her hair dyed green would be violating the folkways. She would be regarded as eccentric but not immoral. If, however, she walked up Broadway in the nude, this would violate the mores, and she would be promptly arrested.

Like Sextus, Sumner recognized the wisdom of conformity. He wrote:

> It is vain to imagine that a "scientific man" can divest himself of prejudice or previous opinion, and put himself in an attitude of independence toward the mores. He might as well try to get out of gravity or the pressure of the atmosphere. The most learned scholar reveals all the philistinism and prejudice of the man-on-the-curbstone when mores are in discussion.

Sumner himself was an outstanding example of scholarly prejudice. He accepted without question, as did Spencer, the mores of the conservative businessman, devoting a good part of his energies to public agitation against trade-unions, child-labor laws, the eight-hour day, and all government measures that interrupted the "natural laws" of supply and demand. One of his essays was titled, significantly enough, "The Absurd Attempt to Make the World Over." Even his phrase "the forgotten man," which Franklin Roosevelt appropriated in 1932 for a different purpose, had reference to the forgotten citizen who Sumner believed was being injured by government welfare services and swollen union wages.

Impossible though it may be to escape the mores in daily life, it is not impossible to evade them in the practice of cultural anthropology. Stimulated by the extraordinary progress of twentieth-century investigations and still in reaction against the naïve moralizing of Victorian schools, modern anthropologists (with the exception of the Russians, who are still in the evolutionary phase) have come to regard a "value judgment" as the cardinal sin of their profession. Any expression of "better" or "worse" is looked upon with horror as a gross violation of scientific objectivity.

A moment's reflection and you will see that *as a scientist* the anthropologist holding this point of view cannot be concerned with progress. For progress assumes that, after a culture pattern has changed, the new is somehow superior to the old. But to admit this is to make a moral judgment in terms of standards outside the process of change. An "unscientific" group within the culture might propose a change, and the anthropologist could advise how to achieve it; but he cannot, as a scientist, suggest the change. Of course he may slip occasionally and make a passionate plea for some type of reform (for example, to eliminate racial prejudice). The following section from Ruth Benedict's well-known *Patterns of Culture* is typical:

> Like the behavior of Puritan divines, their [American business tycoons] courses of action are often more asocial than those of the inmates of penitentiaries. In terms of the suffering and frustration that they spread about them there is probably no comparison. There is very possibly at least as great a degree of mental warping. Yet they are entrusted with positions of great influence and importance and are as a rule fathers of families. Their impress both upon their own children and upon the structure of our society is indelible. They are not described in our manuals of psychiatry because they are supported by every tenet of our civilization. They are sure of themselves in real life in a way that is possible only to those who are oriented to the points of the compass laid down in their own culture. Nevertheless a future psychiatry may well ransack our novels and letters and public records for illumination upon a type of abnormality to which it would not otherwise give credence.

This is excellent rhetoric, but one wonders how Dr. Benedict harmonized such emotions with the theme of her book, namely, that cultures cannot be compared on ethical grounds but must be viewed simply as different, but equally valid, patterns of life. Of course a future society may regard the American business tycoon as abnormal. But on what basis can we expect this judgment to be superior to the judgment of our own society, in which the getting of wealth and power is venerated?

In *Man and His Works: The Science of Cultural Anthropology*, Melville J. Herskovits writes: "Cultural relativism is a philosophy which, in recognizing the values set up by every society to guide its own life, lays stress on the dignity inherent in every body of custom, and on the need for tolerance." But, as a shrewd reviewer pointed out, "dignity" and "tolerance" are by no means universally recognized values even within our own culture. Herskovits concludes his 650-page book with the statement that cultural relativism is anthropology's "greatest contribution" and that it "puts man yet another step on his quest for what ought to be"—apparently oblivious to the patent fact that, if man "ought to be" anything other than he is, there must be standards of value with their loci outside individual cultures.

Since the time of Sumner, every aspect of human life has tumbled into the anthropologist's bag of folkways. Aesthetics was one of the first to go. No anthropologist would dare assert that the art or music of one tribe was better or worse than that of another. Of course it may be more "complex," but that is a different matter. Frazer's *Golden Bough* and the science of "comparative religion" long ago relegated sacred "projective systems" to the folkways. The work of Durkheim, Max Weber, and others gave rise to a new discipline—the "sociology of religion." A review of Joachim Wach's recent study in this field stated: "The volume is distinguished by its author's careful effort to refrain from explicit value judgments in a field in which normative evaluations have been traditional obstacles to scientific insight."

You might suppose that science and mathematics would lie beyond the folkways. But no—the "sociology of knowledge" is another well-established discipline, launched by the German sociologist Karl Mannheim (1893–1947), of the University of London. In Mannheim's view this science was simply an investigation of the interactions of all forms of knowledge with their socio-logical context. He was not so naïve an idealist as to suppose that there was no external world, of definite structure, which science sought to describe with greater and greater accuracy. The fact that tribes had different theories about the shape of the earth would not have led Mannheim to suspect that the earth had no shape at all. But later disciples of Mannheim have twisted his views into a subjective idealism that refuses to admit that science, or even the laws of mathematics, are grounded in a reality independent of the cultural process.

Extreme proponents of the relativism of knowledge do not tell us how their view, which they find superior to all others, manages to escape the all-pervading relativity. It is a tricky criticism. Perhaps they would reply in the manner in which Sextus Empiricus replied when charged with the same in-consistency. The statement that all assertions are false, he writes, may be the one exception—just as we can say that Zeus is the father of all the gods but not the father of himself. Or, if this is not the case, he continues, why not admit frankly that skepticism *does* destroy itself? Fire may destroy fuel and, in so doing, destroy itself; or a laxative purge food from the stomach and itself be purged. A man may climb to a high place on a ladder, Sextus concludes, then overturn the ladder with his foot. But few cultural relativists, one sus-pects, would care to think of themselves as stranded on a summit from which they survey all forms of error, including their own.

The notion advanced by Comte, Durkheim, and Spencer of a "science of ethics," which would construct on an empirical, natural basis a set of standards for judging human conduct, is a notion that goes against the grain of modern cultural anthropology. Such a science would force value judgments into in-vestigations that the anthropologist feels should be kept objective—free of all moral suppositions.

To contemporary naturalistic philosophers the phrase "value judgment" does not have so ominous a ring. Most anthropologists would be startled to learn that John Dewey, whose influence on the social sciences has been incalculable, has always been a firm opponent of cultural relativism and a vigorous champion of science-based morality.

In 1938, in a well-known essay, "Does Human Nature Change?" (reprinted in *Problems of Men*, 1946), Dewey wrote:

> The existence of almost every conceivable kind of social institution at some time and place in the history of the world is evidence of the plasticity of human nature. This fact does not prove that all these different social systems are of equal value materially, morally, and culturally. The slightest observation shows that such is not the case.

The basis on which Dewey is willing to make moral judgments is simply stated. It is on the basis of a common human nature possessed by all men, which finds expression in a common set of "needs." He continues thus:

> By "needs" I mean the inherent demands that men make because of their constitution. Needs for food and drink and for moving about, for example, are so much a part of our being that we cannot imagine any condition under which they would cease to be. There are other things not so directly physical that seem to me equally engrained in human nature. I would mention as examples the need for some kind of companionship; the need for exhibiting energy, for bringing one's powers to bear upon surrounding conditions; the need for both cooperation with and emulation of one's fellows for mutual aid and combat alike; the need for some sort of aesthetic expression and satisfaction; the need to lead and to follow, etc.
>
> Whether my particular examples are well chosen or not does not matter so much as does a recognition of the fact that there are some tendencies so integral a part of human nature that the latter would not be human nature if they changed. These tendencies used to be called instincts. Psychologists are now more chary of using that word than they used to be. But the word by which the tendencies are called does not matter much in comparison to the fact that human nature has its own constitution.

It is important to note that Dewey does not hesitate to include psychological needs in his list. Many modern anthropologists have been willing to grant that there are physical needs common to all cultures; but, for the most part, they are reluctant to admit universal psychological needs. This hesitancy is understandable in view of the diversity of psychological patterns, but at times the hesitancy becomes absurd.

A good example is the chapter "What Is Human Nature?" in Malinowski's *A Scientific Theory of Culture and Other Essays* (1944). The author grants that all humans belong to the same species and therefore have certain "minimum needs" in common, which he lists as follows: breathing, eating, drinking, sex, rest, activity, sleep, micturition, defecation, escape from danger, and avoidance of pain. There is nothing wrong with this list, of course, except Malinowski's insistence that the list provides an adequate description of human nature. Apparently, it did not occur to the author that on these terms a cow becomes a member of the human race.

Broadening the list to include psychological needs in no sense implies that such needs derive from inherited patterns of behavior. Exactly how much in the way of inheritance enters into these needs is still much in dispute among biological and social scientists; but, even should it prove true that nothing is inherited and that all our peculiarly human traits—for example, the creation and enjoyment of art and humor—are learned responses, it still remains that such socially conditioned needs are as characteristic of human cultures as the conditioned behavior traits of birds characterize bird nature. They are universal because they spring from the interaction of what is common in the mental and physical structures of all humans with what is common in the environment of all cultures. Walking is a cultural universal because all men have legs and because the laws of gravity, motion, and inertia do not vary from one locale to another.

Of course we know little as yet about these psychological needs and how they can best be satisfied. But it is clear that the work of the cultural anthropologist in combination with the work of the psychologist offers the most fruitful avenue for research. As this research proceeds, there is reason to hope that a new basis for moral judgments may emerge. Of course it is necessary, as Durkheim recognized, to make two wild assumptions: (1) it is better to be alive than dead; (2) it is better to be healthy and happy than sick and miserable. Such axioms are, it must be granted, "unscientific." They may even be "metaphysical." But in view of the fact that no one cares to dispute them, there seems to be no good reason why a social scientist should not, as an existing "person," affirm them without shame.

There are signs, it is gratifying to observe, that the American social scientist is beginning to develop this courage. One of the earliest indications was a book published several years ago by sociologist Robert S. Lynd. Titled *Knowledge for What?* the book aroused a storm of controversy in social-science circles by attacking vigorously the extreme relativism of the "detached" investigator who refuses to do more than describe. Lynd argues not only that the sociologist should have the right to make value judgments in terms of the degree to which the satisfactions of human needs (Lynd calls them "cravings") are maximized, but, more important, he feels that this should be the primary task of the social sciences.

A second piece of writing that had an equally upsetting effect was the "Methodological Note on Facts and Valuations" in the Appendix to Gunnar Myrdal's classic work on the Negro problem, *American Dilemma* (1944). Myrdal attacked what he called the laissez-faire or "do-nothing" view of the American sociologist. A "disinterested social science" is "pure nonsense," he argues, because every choice of a research project involves some sort of evaluation, even if only in terms of its worth in providing new knowledge. And the refusal to make a moral judgment concerning conflicting views is itself a judgment affirming the equality of the views, leading easily into a defense of the status quo and to stagnation of reform. Since it is impossible for the social scientist to operate in a completely objective fashion, Myrdal proposes that moral judgments be accepted frankly and be explicitly stated in all research reports.

But the American cultural anthropologist is a shy creature. No one of any prominence has yet had the audacity to declare in a firm, unshaken voice that he has made, or intends to make, a value judgment. The men who have come closest to such revolutionary acts are Ralph Linton, professor of anthropology at Yale, and his associate, Abram Kardiner, clinical professor of psychiatry at Columbia and a practicing psychoanalyst.

Ruth Benedict had introduced into ethnology her concept of a psychological pattern that characterized a given culture. But the pattern was obtained by haphazard, intuitional methods. Her conclusions lacked verifiability and precision. In the last decade Kardiner and Linton have combined the research methods of cultural anthropology and psychoanalysis to develop a more fruitful technique for uncovering these configurations. Their methods revolve about the concept of the "BPT," or "basic personality type," first explained in 1939 in Kardiner's *The Individual and His Society* and later (1945) in a work by Kardiner, Linton, and others, called *The Psychological Frontiers of Society*.

The BPT is simply the personality equivalent of the "basic body type." Physical anthropologists have long been able to make a statistical survey of, say, an island tribe to determine characteristic body features. But the determination of characteristic personality traits presents problems of much greater difficulty. By employing techniques borrowed from psychoanalysis—detailed life-histories, personality tests of the Rorschach type, and dream material—Kardiner and Linton and their colleagues have achieved astonishing results.

Although Kardiner has made plain that we have no basis for deciding that the BPT of one culture is better or worse than that of another, he has suggested that we evaluate a culture in terms of how well it molds members to fit the BPT. *Psychological Frontiers* closes with a strong criticism of what Kardiner calls the "pattern of American Calvinism," a Protestant configuration characteristic of our rural areas and running counter to our BPT because it suppresses impulses that our culture as a whole regards as good and releases impulses that our culture, again as a whole, considers destructive. Thus it is possible to define "progress" within a culture as a movement that results in more and more people who resemble the BPT.

Passing over the disturbing implication that such "progress" would sac-
rifice variety to uniformity, the important point to make is that this view in
no sense provides a genuine escape from relativism. For we have as yet no
way of deciding when a BPT is good or bad. We know that in a stable society
the BPT and the entire cultural heritage tend to reinforce each other. But, in
spite of this, the BPT does change slowly. Kardiner cites as an example the
effect that new methods of child-rearing in America may have on our BPT.
This places the author in a curious dilemma. For, if the BPT changes, then
perhaps a change of BPT is more desirable than working for a "progress" that
merely strengthens and stabilizes the BPT. To decide this, however, would
require a value judgment concerning the BPT itself. It is clearly impossible to
advocate a change of BPT except on the basis of a set of standards by which
conflicting BPTs can be judged.

That a BPT may be "bad" is strongly suggested by the section of *Psychological Frontiers* in which Dr. Cora Du Bois writes of the people of Alor, a
small island in the Netherlands East Indies [now Indonesia]. The chief characteristic of the Alor culture is that everybody hates everybody else. The BPT
is "anxious, suspicious, mistrustful." The natives have deep predatory and
exploitive drives, mutual anxiety, violent and indiscriminate aggressions, and
repressed hatreds. They engage in no constructive enterprises because their
energies are absorbed in protecting themselves against the hostilities of one
another. Cooperation is rarely achieved, and when it is, it is by a domination-
submission pattern rather than by love and trust. Marriages are almost always
discordant, and women are reduced to a role of "sheer vegetation." The men
spend most of their time engaged in an elaborate, meaningless financial system in which everyone tries to cheat everyone else. There is no creative art.
Religious myths are filled with parental hatreds and revenge. No attempt is
made to idealize either parents or the tribal gods. There is late toilet-training,
marked lack of cleanliness, and insensitivity to odors. Frustrations are so great
that a typical Alorian, judged by our BPT, would be considered psychotic. It
is difficult to tell whether the Alorese are unhappy, Dr. Du Bois writes, because they are unaware of their "wretchedness."

The author struggles desperately to evade the charge that she has made
a moral judgment in criticizing Alor culture. Her condemnations rest solely,
she declares, on "psychological grounds"—on the degree to which the island
culture fails to meet basic psychological needs. This should not be interpreted,
she insists, as "moralizing."

At this point a disciple of Dewey would be quick to make clear that
moralizing, in any constructive modern sense, is precisely that—making a
judgment of praise or blame in terms of human needs. And why should a
cultural anthropologist hesitate? The battle against the naïve ethnocentrism
of earlier investigators has long ago been won. The relativism that dealt the

death blow was a necessary corrective. What is urgently needed at the moment is a corrective of the corrective—the boldness to affirm that there is a common human nature on the basis of which valuations can be made and in terms of which real progress can be measured.

If such "moralizing" is impossible in principle, then consider the odd sort of mysticism that the ethnologist is forced to defend. He must believe in some sort of mysterious Emersonian law of compensation that operates among human societies—some "God of Relativism" who makes certain that all cultures are exactly and forever balanced in the degree to which they meet human needs. For every gain the culture makes, there must be a compensating loss (otherwise the culture would be "better" than it was before), and for every loss there must be a compensating gain (otherwise the culture would be "worse"). It is difficult to imagine a primitive projective system with superstitions more fantastic.

Perhaps it is not too presumptuous to hope that the groundwork laid by Kardiner and Linton will lead some brave ethnologist to propose a "BHPT," or "basic *healthy* personality type," in reference to which a set of standards might be found. Such standards would not be "absolutes" in the traditional metaphysical sense. They would be what some philosophers have called "relative absolutes." No perceptible changes in the biological foundations of human nature have occurred during the period of recorded history, nor will such changes take place in the foreseeable future. It is in terms of this relative stability of human needs that relatively permanent standards could be formulated.

If a concept of the BHPT develops, it seems not at all naïve to suppose it capable of giving genuine social directives, not merely for strengthening the BPT (as Kardiner already has proposed) but for altering the BPT when it clearly departs (as does the Alor) from mental health. Of course it may turn out that there are many different cultural configurations roughly equal in the degree to which they meet human needs. There may be no single best way, just as there often are alternative solutions to algebraic equations; or, as von Neumann has made clear in his exciting work on the *Theory of Games and Economic Behavior*, there may be equally successful strategies both for winning games and for solving economic problems.

The work of the Freudian ethnologists has already rescued cultural anthropology from its fixations on variations in the shapes of bows and spearheads and turned its attention toward more important issues. Let us hope it will soon outgrow its adolescent fear of moralizing and develop the courage to declare, without stammering, that health and happiness are preferable to sickness and misery and that it is better to be alive than dead. Then, at last, the cultural anthropologist will be ready to combine forces with the psychologist, perhaps even with the philosopher, in the great tasks of formulating a naturalistic ethics and drawing up blueprints for the City in the Skies.

POSTSCRIPT

Since I wrote the foregoing paper there has been a rapid decline of cultural relativism as a philosophy, though not of course as methodology. At the same time, there has been little evidence that cultural anthropologists in the United States, except for a small minority, have developed much concern with the task of shaping a science of culture that would permit cross-cultural value-judgments and provide a foundation for a naturalistic ethics. Most of today's textbooks of anthropology give the problem only a passing glance. The current scene is best described as widely eclectic, one of formless confusion with respect to basic philosophical issues.

The emphasis on basic personality types was all the rage when I wrote my essay. It generated weighty books on how the German BPT led to Hitler, how the Russian BPT led to Stalin (the practice of swaddling babies was supposed to condition Soviet citizens to accept an authoritarian leader), and similar nonsense. Ruth Benedict's *The Chrysanthemum and the Sword: Patterns of Japanese Culture* is the best known of these many studies of national character. Then around 1970 this whole approach mysteriously faded away. The work of Freudian-oriented anthropologists such as Kardiner and Linton, in whom I saw so much promise, turned out to be remarkably sterile.

A few anthropologists found time in the fifties to talk about a basic human nature, universal values, and what some called a "metacultural reality" that gave meaning to progress. George P. Murdock in "A Common Denominator of Culture" (reprinted in *The Science of Man in the World Crisis*, 1945, edited by Ralph Linton) actually listed seventy-three cultural universals, running in alphabetical order from age-weaning, athletic sports, and bodily adornment, to visiting, weaning, and weather control. Clyde Kluckhohn called them "pan-human values." In his paper "Ethical Relativity: Sic Et Non," Kluckhohn defended a position identical to my own. Extreme cultural relativism, he wrote, as typified by Benedict and Boas, is intolerable, because it forces a vindication of such cultural patterns as slavery, cannibalism, and Nazism. Luckily, there is a universal human nature. "Some needs and motives are so deep and so generic that they are beyond the reach of argument: panhuman morality expresses and supports them." No one can question the importance of exploring conflicting patterns of culture, said Kluckhohn. Some human values obviously are relative, but anthropology's greater task, he insisted, is to search, in co-operation with behavioral scientists and philosophers, for panhuman values on which a naturalistic ethics can be based.[1]

There were other trends running counter to cultural relativism at the time I wrote my article. Evolutionary anthropologists in the Soviet Union, and Leslie White in the United States, found a basis for cross-cultural values in the laws by which cultures evolve. Soviet anthropologists, as we all know, seldom hesitated to declare Soviet culture superior in all respects to decadent capitalist cultures.

At the moment, at least in France, the strongest challenge to cultural relativism is the structural anthropology of Claude Lévi-Strauss. He agrees with Noam Chomsky that there is a universal human nature and that, because it is part of the universe, all human minds have the same deep structure, bound by laws of logic and mathematics—laws independent of cultural variations on shallower levels. In sharp contrast to the views of Lucien Lévy-Bruhl (and White), Lévi-Strauss is convinced that the most primitive savage reasons in exactly the same fundamental way as an Einstein. The task of anthropology is more than just endless description of different cultural patterns. It is a search for the infrastructure common to these patterns. On the basis of this structure we can develop a science of culture that will help solve humanity's problems. All cultures may be equal, but some are more equal than others.

Now that Sartre is dead, existentialism is almost dead, with structuralism replacing it as the latest French cultural fad. But as structuralism spreads outward into philosophy and the arts, producing such whimsies as structuralist painting and structuralist poetry, it has become as amorphous as existentialism became. Nobody quite knows anymore just what "structuralism" is supposed to mean. Since everybody recognizes the existence of biological structure, in a broad sense everybody is a structuralist, just as in a broad sense everybody is a pragmatist or an existentialist. It remains to be seen how soon the structuralist craze will give way to some new Gallic plaything, and what sort of lasting contributions it will make.

In spite of these colorful and confusing trends away from old-fashioned relativism, the central paradox remains. How can cultural anthropology preserve the undeniable advantages of an objective, value-free empirical approach to its subject matter and at the same time go beyond this to find a basis for moral judgments? Perhaps the task is in principle impossible for scientists acting as scientists.

POSTSCRIPT (1995)

Consider the practice, widespread in Africa, of the genital mutilation of women, which is done to preserve their virginity by destroying all sexual pleasure. As Abe Rosenthal said in his New York Times *column (June 1995), this is equivalent to male castration—"a form of male control, perhaps the ultimate except for murder." Can anyone argue that because this horrible practice is embedded in the mores of some thirty African countries we have no grounds for condemning it?*

The answer is yes.´ Esther K. Hicks, a Dutch social scientist, has written a book titled Infabulation: Female Mutilation in Islamic Northeastern Africa *(1996). Hicks defends the practice, and lambasts western feminists for regarding it as a violation of human rights! I wouldn't be surprised to learn of some hard-core relativists who object to condemning female infanticide and the burning of widows in India, the binding of feet in the Orient, black slavery in the Confederate States, the German Holocaust, and the Spanish Inquisition.*

NOTES

1. Kluckholn's paper first appeared in the *Journal of Philosophy*, vol. 52, 1955, pp. 663–67. It was reprinted in *Culture and Behavior: Collected Essays of Clyde Kluckholn* (Free Press, 1964), ed. by Richard Kluckholn. See also Kluckholn's essay, "Education, Values, and Anthropological Relativity" in the same volume, and "Universal Categories of Culture," in *Anthropology Today* (University of Chicago Press, 1953), ed. by Alfred L. Kroeber.

FIFTEEN

KLINGON AND OTHER ARTIFICIAL LANGUAGES

As one who reads and speaks no foreign language (all I remember from a year of ancient Greek in college are portions of the Greek alphabet and a few Greek words), I am always awed by those who are fluent in more than one natural tongue. I am even more amazed by persons who learn an artificial language. I can understand someone mastering a synthetic language as widely spoken as Esperanto, but Klingon? Surely the Trekkies have better uses for their time and talents. The following essay is from The Skeptical Inquirer *(July/August 1995).*

Do you speak Esperanto?
Like a native!

According to Genesis there originally was only one human language, the tongue spoken by Adam and Eve. Why did Adam name the elephant an *elephant*? Because, goes an old joke, it *looked* like an elephant. Then a terrible tragedy occurred. The Hebrews tried to scale the heavens by building the Tower of Babel. God was so offended by this hubris that he said:

> Behold, the people is one, and they have all one language . . . and now nothing shall be restrained from them. . . . Go to, let us go down, and there confound their language, that they may not understand one another's speech. So the Lord scattered them abroad from thence upon the face of all the earth. (Gen. 11:6-8)

In *Paradise Lost* (Book 12) Milton described it this way:

> *To sow a jangling noise of words unknown:*
> *Forthwith a hideous gabble rises loud*
> *Among the Builders; each to other calls*
> *Not understood, till hoarse, and all in rage,*
> *As mockt they storm; great laughter was in Heav'n*
> *And looking down, to see the hubbub strange*
> *And hear the din.*

Why God and the angels would find this curse amusing is hard to fathom. At any rate, who can doubt that the multiplicity of world languages is an enormous barrier to world peace. Clearly world unity would be greatly augmented if somehow the babble of tongues could be replaced by a single language.

In ancient times Greek, Latin, and Arabic served as universal languages for large clusters of nations. French was once Europe's international diplomatic language, and for centuries Latin was the favored language of scientists and scholars. Around Mediterranean ports, *lingua franca*, Italian mixed with other tongues, became a common form of communication. Swahili, a Bantu speech mixed with Arabic, has long been the lingua franca of East Africa. Today, for better or worse, the new international language is English. In a few years there will be more non-native speakers of English than native ones! Only France is trying desperately to keep its fingers in the dike.

In the seventeenth century, among such philosophers as Descartes and Leibniz, and the Scotsman George Delgarno, the notion arose that perhaps a completely artificial language, based on logic, with simplified grammar and spelling, might serve to unify nations. This grandiose dream quickly gripped the minds of hundreds of linguistic cranks, who during the next three centuries proposed more than three hundred artificial or semi-artificial tongues.

The first major effort was the 600-page *Essay Towards a Real Character and Philosophic Language* (London, 1688), by John Wilkins, Bishop of Chester. His book was greatly admired by Leibniz. All of Wilkins's words are self-defining in the sense that they convey their triple classification as to genus, species, and subspecies. For example, his word for salmon is *zana—za* for fish, *n* for scaly, and *a* for red. The language was spoken and also written with symbols resembling modern shorthand. The Bishop wrote other eccentric works, including one arguing that the moon was inhabited by intelligent creatures. His philosophic language was caricatured by the French writer Gabriel de Foigny as an Australian tongue in his novel *The Adventures of Jacques Saleur* (1676).

The *Encyclopaedia Britannica* (14th edition) lists the following other totally synthetic languages: Solresol (1817), Lingualumina (1875), Blaia Zimondal (1884), Cabe aban (1887), and Zahlensprache (1901). Ro, invented in 1904 by Edward P. Foster, an American clergyman, had a monthly periodical called *Roia*. Solresol, created by musician Jean François Sudre, combined the syllables of the music scale (*do, re, mi,* . . .) to produce some 12,000 words. The plan was to send messages by playing a tune.

The *Britannica* does not mention Spokil, perpetrated in France by A. Nicolas in 1887, or Alwato, the creation of Stephen Pearl Andrews, a nineteenth century American attorney and abolitionist. Alwato was part of Andrews's 761-page crank work *The Basic Outline of Universology* (1872), and he elaborated on it in other books. All his nouns ended in *o*. A human is *ho*, the body is *hobo*, the head is *hobado*, and society is *homabo*. A vegetable is *zho*, an animal is *zo*, a dead animal is *zobo*, and a live one is *zovo*.

Because no completely synthetic language has yet obtained much of a following, one might suppose that efforts of this sort have ceased. Not so! The TV series "Star Trek" has spawned a guttural extraterrestrial language spoken by the warriors of the Klingon Empire. It was invented in 1984 for the film *Star Trek III: The Search for Spock*, by Marc Okrand. (He has a doctorate in linguistics.) Poetry has been written and weddings performed in Klingon. "Star Trek" fans are rapidly mastering the language, much to Okrand's amazement, because he does not speak it. He designed the language as a joke—its word for "love" is "bang"—but now his peculiar language has developed a life of its own. There are newsletters in Klingon and an audiotape on conversational Klingon spoken by Michael Dorn, who plays a Klingon, Lieutenant Commander Worf, chief of security on the United Federation of Planets starship *Enterprise*, in "Star Trek: The Next Generation," the second "Star Trek" television series.

The Klingon Language Institute, headed by Lawrence Schoen, a psychologist at Chestnut Hill College, Philadelphia, is said to be working on a translation into Klingon of Shakespeare and the Bible.[1] The Bible will not be easy, because Klingons have no words for such concepts as God, holy, atonement, forgiveness, compassion, or mercy. Is all this a put-on? The answer (in Klingon) is *HISlaH* (yes).

On a more useful level than totally contrived languages are the semi-artificial ones based on a blend of natural tongues. Of these, by far the most successful has been Esperanto, the brainchild of Lazarus Ludwig Zamenhof, a Warsaw eye doctor. His first book about it, *Lingvo Internacia* (1887) bore the pseudonym of Dr. Esperanto. The word means "one who hopes." It expressed Zamenhof's quixotic desire that Esperanto would become the world's second language. When that occurs, Esperantists like to say, Esperanto will have achieved *la fina venko* (the ultimate victory).

Based on Europe's major tongues, Esperanto's 16 simple grammatical rules have no exceptions. Spelling, using 28 letters, is uniform and phonetic. As in Alwato, all nouns end in *o*. Adjectives end in *a*, verbs in *s*, and adverbs in *e*. A *j* at the end of a word indicates a plural. For example, *grandaj hundoj* means "big dogs."

More than 30,000 books, including Shakespeare, Dante, the Bible, and the Koran have been translated into Esperanto. A recent translation of Lewis Carroll's *Alice* books calls Humpty Dumpty *Hometo Omleto*, meaning Little-Man Egg. Some hundred periodicals around the world have been written in Esperanto. The Vatican broadcasts in Esperanto, and *Espero Katolika* (Catholic Hope) is a magazine published by a Catholic Esperanto group independent of the Vatican.

Here is the Lord's Prayer in Esperanto:

Patro nia kiu estas en la ĉielo, sankta estu via nomo; venu regeco via; estu volo via, kiel en la ĉielo, tiel ankau sur la tero. Panon nian ĉiutagan donu al ni hodiaü; kaj pardonu al ni ŝuldojn niajn, kiel ni ankau pardonas al niaj ŝuldantoj; kaj ne konduku nin en tenton, sed liberigu nin de la malbono.

The movement peaked in the 1920s, especially among one-worlders, but even today about two million people read and speak Esperanto. Enthusiasts hold conventions here and there, and when traveling identify themselves to one another by green lapel pins shaped like stars. The movement continues to be popular in Europe, but in the United States it is now at a low ebb. In 1991 the Modern Language Association sponsored a seminar on Esperanto at its annual convention. No one showed up. Perhaps the main reason for its decline here is the inexorable rise of English as an international second language. In *The Shape of Things to Come* (Book 5, section 7), H. G. Wells predicts that Basic English (the 850 words selected by C. K. Ogden) will "spread like wildfire" and that by the year 2020 "hardly anyone" in the world will not speak and understand it.

The philosopher Rudolf Carnap learned to speak Esperanto fluently. In his autobiography (in *The Philosophy of Rudolf Carnap*) he says that Esperanto became for him a "living language." He cannot take seriously "the arguments of those who assert that an international auxiliary language might be suitable for business affairs and perhaps for natural science, but could not possibly serve as an adequate means of communication in personal affairs, for discussions in the social sciences and the humanities, let alone for fiction and drama. I have found that most of those who make these assertions have no practical experience with such a language."

To his surprise and dismay Carnap found that Ludwig Wittgenstein was violently opposed to any form of language that had not "grown organically."

The most popular semi-artificial language preceding Esperanto was Volapük—the word means "world speech"—invented in 1879 by Johann Martin Schleyer, a German Catholic priest.[2] It uses 27 letters, accents all words on the last syllable, and adds "ik" to all adjectives. The "iks" give it a strong icky sound. Some notion of its ugliness can be gained from Volapük's wording of the Lord's Prayer:

O fat obas, kel binol in süls, paisaludomöz nem ola! Kömomöd monargän ola! Jenomöz vil olik, äs in sül, i su tal! Bodo obsik, vädeliki givolös obes adelo! E pardolös obes debis obsik äs id obs aipardobs debeles obas. E no obis nindukolös in tentadi; sod aidalivolös obis de bad. Jenosöd!

In France and Germany the Volapük cult gained a following of more than a million, with some two hundred Volapük societies meeting around the globe. After its third congress, in Paris in 1899, its leaders began quarreling over how to improve the language. This bickering created rival versions with such names as Balta, Spelin, Dil, Veltpail, Dilpok, Ilingua European, and others. The movement finally evaporated to be replaced by Esperanto.

I found the following anonymous doggerel in an old scrapbook:

> Take a teaspoonful of English,
> A modicum of Dutch,
> Of Italian just a trifle,
> And of Gaelic not too much;
>
> Some of Russian and Egyptian
> Add them unto the whole,
> With just enough to flavor,
> Of the lingo of the Pole.
>
> Some Singhalese and Hottentot,
> A soupçon, too, of French,
> Of native Scandinavian
> A pretty thorough drench;
>
> Hungarian and Syrian,
> A pinch of Japanese,
> With just as much Ojibway
> And Turkish as you please.
>
> Now stir it gently, boil it well,
> And if you've decent luck,
> The ultimate residuum
> You'll find is Volapük!

Many short-lived attempts from 1900 to the late fifties were made to improve Esperanto. They have such names as Perio, Ulla, Mondlingvo, Romanizat, Europeo, Nepo, Neo, Ro, Espido, Esperantuisho, Globaqo, Novial, and a raft of others. The most successful of these reform efforts was Ido—in Esperanto it means "offspring"—invented in 1907 by the French philosopher Louis Couterat. A monthly titled *Progreso* was written in Ido. Couterat regarded all Esperantists as depraved. In the first volume of his autobiography Bertrand Russell recalls Couterat complaining that Ido had no word similar to "Esperantist." "I suggested 'Idiot,' " Russell adds, "but he was not quite pleased."

Tinkerers with Ido, like the Esperanto tinkerers, soon splintered the movement into variant languages. These included Dutalingue, Italico, Adjuvilo, Etem, Unesal, Esperido, Cosman, Novam, Mundial, Sinestal, Intal, Kosmolinguo, and more.

Here are a few other semi-artificial languages developed from the 1880s to the early decades of this century: Weltsprache, Spelin, Blue, Anglo-franca, Mundolingue, Lingua komun, Idiom neutral, Reform neutral, Latinesce, Nov-Latin, Monario, Occidental, Europan, Optez, and Romanal.

Interlingua is of special interest because it was the creation of the great Italian mathematician Giuseppe Peano. It, too, gave rise to dozens of rival variants, such as Simplo, Latinulus, Interlatino, Panlingua, and others. In the mid-1920s Wilfred Stevens developed Euphony, a language that combined words from 30 natural languages. For example, *olc* for eye, *zu* for blue, and *fra* for human combine to produce *frazolca*, meaning a blue-eyed woman. Lancelot Hogben explained his semi-artificial language in a Penguin book titled *Interglossa* (1943).

Many of these rival tongues are discussed in Marina Yaguello's fascinating *Lunatic Lovers of Language* (1991) translated into English from the original French by Catherine Slater. Yaguello is a teacher of linguistics at the University of Dakar, in Senegal. I have not seen Mary Slaughter's *Universal Languages* (1982).

Yaguello also covers synthetic languages in works of fiction, such as Newspeak in George Orwell's *Nineteen Eighty-Four* and the slang language invented by Anthony Burgess for *A Clockwork Orange*. She also discusses the Martian language created by the French medium Hélène Smith, and neologisms in the works of Swift and Rabelais. To the latter we can add the hundreds of coined words in the fantasies of Lord Dunsany, James Branch Cabell, L. Frank Baum, and in books said to be channeled by supermortals, such as *Oahspe* and *The Urantia Book*.

Edward Kelly, a sixteenth-century crystal-gazer, scoundrel, and friend of the British astrologer John Dee, devised a language called Enochian. He claimed it was spoken by angels and by Adam before it degenerated into Hebrew after the Fall.

For completeness I should mention artificial languages that arise spontaneously in subcultures such as Shelta Thari, spoken by tinkers in England, and "back slang" that arose among street vendors in London in the early decades of the nineteenth century. Originally it was words spelled backward, such as *yob* for boy, but the spelling soon got distorted in such words as *esclop*, later shortened to *slop*, for police. "Back language" is covered in Henry Mayhew's *London Labour and the London Poor.* Carny is a slang language that arose among American carnival workers.

A peculiar language called Bootling flourishes only in the small town of Boonville, California, where coffee is called *horn of zee,* and a pay phone is *eeble heeleh.* (See the *New York Times,* November 12, 1977, for an unsigned article titled "Coast Town's Dialect Keeps Brightlighters in the Dark." A *brightlighter* is a person from a big city, such as San Francisco, a hundred miles south. We all can speak pig-latin, and there are other less familiar ways to distort a natural language. (See *The Cat's Elbow and Other Secret Languages,"* by Alvin Schwartz, a 1982 paperback.)

There are the "unknown tongues" spoken by first century Christians, and more recently by Mormons, Pentecostals, and other sects when the Holy Spirit moves them. Nor should we ignore the sign language used by the hearing impaired, the talking drums of Africa, the smoke signals of American Indians, communication by whistling in the Canary Islands, and the many languages used for conversing with computers.

In crude science fiction, extraterrestrials inexplicably speak English, but in more sophisticated science fantasy they speak alien tongues often described with detailed linguistic rules and words. Every conceivable way of communicating without speech has also been exploited: telepathy (as in H. G. Wells's *Men Like Gods*), dancing, whistling, smelling, using musical tones, and so on. In James Blish's VOR an alien "speaks" by altering the color of a patch on his forehead. For information about science-fiction artificial languages, see the entry "Linguistics" in Peter Nichols's *Encyclopedia of Science Fiction,* and "Language" in the index of Everett Bleiler's monumental *Science-Fiction: The Early Years.*

POSTSCRIPT (1995)

Novial (New International Auxiliary Language) was invented in 1923 by Otto Jesperson, a Danish professor of linguistics. Itala (International Auxiliary Language Association) was headquartered in New York City during the mid-1920s, and in the Hague, but interest in Novial was short-lived.

Loglan, an artificial language invented by James Cooke Brown, has a grammar based on formal logic, and words taken from eight natural languages. Designed mainly to simplify computer communication, Brown described his language in Scientific American *(June 1960, pages 53–63). Brown's Loglan Institute, in Gainesville, Florida, published* Loglan I: A Logical Language *in 1966, and a Loglan-English/English-Loglan Dictionary in 1975. Both books have had revised later editions. For a while it issued a periodical,* The Loglanist.

Loglan spawned a similar language called Lojban, constructed by Robert LeChavlier, a systems engineer. Both languages have a small group of devotees. On Lojban, see Don Oldenburg's "Lojban, a Real Conversation Stopper," in The Washington Post (November 10, 1989, page D5).

Mangani is the language spoken by the great apes who raised Tarzan. Several hundred of its words are scattered through Edgar Rice Burroughs's Tarzan novels. I first learned about this from Joel Carlinsky who wrote that as a boy he and his brother actually learned to speak Mangani, and that a full vocabulary is in one of the biographies of Burroughs. A related language spoken by the tailed men in Tarzan the Terrible is given in that book's ten-page glossary, along with grammatical rules.

Anthony Garrett wrote from England to tell me about Elvish, a complex language invented by J. R. R. Tolkien as the tongue spoken in his imaginary Middle Earth.

Peter C. Speers called my attention to Confluence, the language of the planet Myrin. It was created by the prolific British science-fiction author Brian Wilson Aldiss. Speers sent me a four-page dictionary of its principal words, from Ab We tel Min to Zo Zo Con, that appeared in Punch in 1967. The first phrase is defined as "The sensation that one neither agrees nor disagrees with what is being said to one, but that one simply wishes to depart from the presence of the speaker." The second phrase means "a woman of another field." The dictionary is reprinted in Aldiss's collection of short stories Man and His Time (1988).

Aldiss explains that the meanings are modified by one's posture. There are nearly nine thousand stances, each with its own name. Aldiss recommends that all statemen study Confluence before any negotiations break out with Myrin.

On Stephen Pearl Andrews and Alwato, see Madeline Bettina Stern's biography of him, The Pentarch (University of Texas Press, 1968).

NOTES

1. The Institute publishes a quarterly journal called *HolQeD* (from "Hol," meaning language, and "QeD," meaning science). It recently sponsored a contest for palindromes written in Klingon. For information, send an SASE to KLI, Box 634, Flourtown, PA 19031-0534.

2. Volapük turns up in James Joyce's *Finnegans Wake* as Vollapluck (p. 34, line 5 from bottom), Volapuke (p. 40, line 4), and Volapucky (p. 116, line 6 from bottom).

PART III

PSEUDOSCIENCE

I am one of the founders of CSICOP (Committee for the Scientific Investigation of Claims of the Paranormal) and a regular columnist for our bimonthly magazine The Skeptical Inquirer. We are often accused of being debunkers. I am proud of the term. Our role is to debunk, not the in-between claims that are hard to classify, but pseudoscience as preposterous as homeopathy, Scientology, orgonomy, ufology, creationism, astrology, and a hundred other absurd claims that lack adequate evidence and that damage science education and weaken our culture. Debunking bad science should be the constant obligation of the science community, even if it takes time away from serious research or seems to be a losing battle. One takes comfort from the fact there is no Gresham's law in science. In the long run, good science drives out bad.

SIXTEEN

PSEUDOSCIENCE IN THE NINETEENTH CENTURY

My first book about pseudoscience, In the Name of Science, *was published by G.P. Putnam's in 1952. After it was remaindered, Dover retitled it* Fads and Fallacies in the Name of Science, *and it has been in print as a paperback ever since. I have updated the topic with* Science: Good, Bad, and Bogus; The New Age; *and* On the Wild Side—*books consisting largely of columns I have written regularly for* The Skeptical Inquirer. *The following essay appeared in the* New York Review of Books *(March 17, 1988).*

How can good science be distinguished from bad? Philosophers of science call this the "demarcation problem." Like most problems about distinguishing parts of spectra, sharp definitions are impossible, but from hazy borders it doesn't follow that distinctions between extremes are useless. Twilight doesn't invalidate the contrast between day and night. The fact that top scientists disagree about many things doesn't mean that terms like pseudoscience, crank, and charlatan have no place in the history of science.

Naturally it takes knowledge to make sound judgments. Nineteenth-century Americans were mostly poor and untutored, and even the few who made it to college learned almost nothing about science. It is hardly surprising that the age, like earlier ages, swarmed with scientific claims easily recognized now as absurd. Arthur Wrobel, a teacher of American literature at the University of Kentucky, was to be cheered for editing *Pseudoscience and Society in*

Nineteenth-Century America (University Press of Kentucky, 1987). The book was a long overdue study of the period's bogus science, an anthology whose nine contributors range in fascinating, sometimes frightening, detail over most of the outrageous theories that bamboozled millions of our ancestors.

One might imagine that fringe scientists would be indifferent to social and political trends, but a surprising thing about the nineteenth century is that the opposite was true. It was a time of great millennial hopes. For conservative Christians hope lay in the return of Jesus, but for more enlightened Christians the Second Coming had become a symbol of humanity's march— onward Christian soldiers!—toward liberty and justice. When Unitarian Julia Ward Howe opened her great hymn with "Mine eyes have seen the glory of the coming of the Lord," she was not speaking of the literal return of Christ but of the widespread expectation that the Civil War would hasten fulfillment of the American Dream. Abolition of slavery was only part of a larger complex of causes that included women's rights, temperance, health, better treatment of criminals and the insane, elimination of poverty, and more compassionate government. All these humanitarian ideals found their way into the rhetoric of the fringe sciences.

Influences went also in the other direction. Reformers were as eager to rebel against mainline science, especially medical science, as they were to challenge the government. Many political radicals embraced one or more pseudosciences. Robert Owen, the Welshman who founded the socialist community at New Harmony, Indiana, in the 1820s, and his son, like another socialist, Upton Sinclair, in this century, became ardent spiritualists. This intermixing of social forces with fringe science makes Wrobel's book much more than just a compendium of strange beliefs. His book is of special interest to historians of the period whether their concern is with science, literature, religion, or politics.

Robert Collyer, a now-forgotten mesmerist and phrenologist, is the subject of a contribution to Wrobel's book by Taylor Stoehr, a professor of English. Stoehr sees Collyer as a prototype of the mad scientists who figure so prominently in the fiction of Hawthorne and Poe. Indeed, so many writers of the period were influenced by pseudoscience—chapter 80 of *Moby-Dick* is devoted entirely to a satirical phrenological analysis of the white whale—that one of the book's persuasive themes is that knowledge of fringe science is essential to understanding the century's literature.

Collyer came to America in 1836 from England to become a traveling mesmerist. On the platform he would put his brother Fred into a trance. Then after Fred clairvoyantly diagnosed the ailments of spectators, Collyer would heal them with hypnosis. He also practiced painless dentistry, extracting teeth from dazed patients, their trances intensified by booze and opium.

Collyer claimed he was the first to unite mesmerism and phrenology. When he massaged the bump for "mirthfulness," the mesmerized subject would burst into laughter. Fingering the bump for "tune" made the subject sing, and similarly for the other traits. Mesmerized patients were believed to have enhanced psychic powers. In England no less a scientist than Alfred Russel Wallace became a firm believer in what Collyer called "psychography"—a blend of mesmerism, phrenology, and ESP. In his 1899 book *The Wonderful Century*, Wallace tells of touching the outlined regions of a model head and seeing his mesmerized subject instantly make correct responses.

Phrenology spread from its Austrian founders Franz Gall and Johann Spurzheim, and their Edinburgh disciple, the barrister George Combe, throughout the U.S. and fell into the hands of traveling mountebanks like Collyer. Orson Fowler and his brother Lorenzo were the most famous. Sometimes they would have themselves blindfolded. Orson would skull-read a group of strangers. Then when the same persons were randomly presented to Lorenzo, he would deliver identical readings. One suspects that simple conjuring methods—ranging from trick blindfolds to peeking down the side of the nose—were essential for these dramatic "proofs" of phrenology's claims.[1]

The Fowlers later teamed up with a businessman to form Fowler and Wells, a Manhattan firm that booked hundreds of cranium readers around the country's cities and hamlets. It quickly mushroomed into a vast publishing enterprise from which streamed hundreds of books on phrenology, hydropathy, and other fringe sciences. England's prestigious *Phrenological Journal* lasted only about two decades, but Fowler and Wells's *American Phrenological Journal* flourished from 1838 to 1911. Fowler and Wells published the first two editions of *Leaves of Grass*. So smitten was Walt Whitman by the wonders of phrenology that he scattered its phrases throughout his poetry—"O adhesiveness—O pulse of my life"—and proudly reproduced in his book a chart of his own head displaying the prominence of various admirable bumps.

It has been said that anyone foolish enough to believe in phrenology should have his head examined, and of course that is exactly what millions of people of all classes did in Europe, England, and America. Couples consulted phrenologists to decide if they should marry. Corporations demanded head examinations of prospective employees. New regions of the cranium were added until the count passed 150, with bumps for such traits as love of pets and desire to see ancient places. It is hard to believe, but phrenology even influenced American art, and Charles Thomas Walters, who teaches and writes on art, has a chapter to prove it. *Phrenology Applied to Painting and Sculpture* was one of George Combe's most popular monographs.

Combe studied the heads of leading Renaissance painters to determine how their character influenced their work. Michelangelo's skull, he concluded, shows traits that made his work less graceful than Raphael's. To analyze Raphael, he actually had the artist's tomb opened and plaster casts made of Raphael's skull. Several American sculptors of the day, notably Thomas Crawford and Hiram Powers, put head-bumps on their statues to correspond with the character of their subjects. Crawford's bust of Beethoven, now at the New England Conservatory of Music, shows a prominent "tune" bump in the forehead. Powers's most famous statue, *The Greek Slave*, shows the woman's forehead to be high in spirituality.

Electricity, newly discovered and utterly mysterious, seemed to underlie mesmerism, and did it not also carry information throughout the nervous system? It is easy to understand how it would be looked upon as a potent healing force. An amusing chapter by John Greenway, a professor of English, surveys the century's infatuation with electric therapy. Publications bristled with stirring ads for electric belts, rings, garters, corsets, brushes (for both hair and teeth), even an electric cigarette. Greenway reproduces a marvelous Sears Roebuck ad for the "most powerful" electric belt made. It had detachable pouches for carrying a strong current to the genitals of both men and women. The current was said to stimulate potency as well as to relieve genital ailments. A New York quack cured syphilis by seating a male patient with his back against a metal plate and his scrotum suspended in whirling water. Plate and water were wired to a power source, making it hard to comprehend how the poor fellow escaped electrocution. As with all crank remedies, the placebo effect generated many testimonials of miraculous electrical healings.

Hydrotherapy, crisply covered by the historian Marshall Legan, goes back to ancient times, but the nineteenth-century craze was kicked off by Vincent Priessnitz, an uneducated Austrian farmer whose institute in Gräfenberg became an international success. Only cold water was used. The therapy involved baths, the winding of wet sheets around the body, enemas, douches, and water dripping on ailing parts of the body. Hydropathic physicians popped up everywhere. Institutes were founded. Fowler and Wells took over the *Water-Cure Journal*. Many who spent weeks, months, sometimes years in the fashionable cold-water spas that proliferated around the nation were unquestionably invigorated. It was more than the placebo effect. Alcohol, tea, coffee, tobacco, and spices were forbidden. Food was served cold. There were gyms for exercise and wooded areas through which to stroll. No doubt many felt healthier. The movement came to a crest about 1850, leaving a legacy in the form of whirlpool baths and the fondness for drinking natural spring water.

The life of Andrew Jackson Davis, America's first famous psychic, is the subject of the historian Robert Delp's article. Known as the seer of Poughkeepsie, Davis started out as a devotee of Emanuel Swedenborg, the Swedish mystic whose wild religious fantasies were inexplicably admired by thinkers such as Emerson and the elder Henry James. When Davis was twenty, and in a trance, Swedenborg's spirit dictated *Nature's Divine Revelations: The Principles of Nature*, the first of Davis's many heavy tomes. The Poughkeepsie Seer claimed extraordinary powers of clairvoyance. Believers paid him to gaze into their bodies, diagnose diseased organs, and prescribe weird remedies. His visions produced detailed accounts of intelligent humanoids on Mercury, Venus, Mars, Jupiter, and Saturn.

Delp's opinion of Davis is curiously sympathetic. He says nothing about the seer's blindfold performances (which leave little doubt that he was in part a charlatan), nothing about his spying on extraterrestrials, or the childishness of his metaphysics. Instead, Davis is praised for emphasizing the harmony of body and mind (a central notion of his masterwork, *The Great Harmonia*), for his "ready wit and perceptive understanding," for his support of humanitarian reforms, and for his attacks on mediums who produced physical manifestations. Instead of seeing Davis as a clever crank, Delp finds his life "characterized by extraordinary personal growth and maturity," and one that "epitomized the spirit of his age." On the contrary, Davis's primitive occultism and crude psychic demonstrations were aberrations. Even in its heyday spiritualism had a smaller following than Christian Science or Seventh-day Adventism, not to mention the all-pervasive fundamentalism of mainline churches.

Harold Aspiz, another professor of English, has written the book's drollest chapter—a survey of offbeat speculations about sex. Conservative preachers recommended strict monogamy, but cult leaders like George Rapp, who ran an Adventist colony at Harmony before Robert Owen took over the town, recommended total celibacy (the sect soon disappeared). The Fowler brothers had strong opinions about sex. They argued that electrical energy was released during orgasm, and that the longer a man conserved this energy, the more vigorous would be his copulation, and the finer his offspring. Women were said to become sexually aroused only when they passionately wanted a child, and for this reason husbands were urged never to force lovemaking.

Eugenics was favored by large numbers of pseudoscientists as a way to weed out undesirables and strengthen the nation. John Humphrey Noyes, a socialist and eugenicist who ran the Oneida community in central New York, distinguished between the phrenological traits of propagativeness and amativeness. Members of the colony could engage in as much amative play as they liked, with anybody, provided they blocked pregnancy with *coitus reservatus*. Alice Stockham, in a system she called Karezza, also campaigned for prolonged copulation without climax. Ezra Pound, Aspiz tells us, along with his "heavy burden of pseudoscientific baggage," also believed that conserving semen increased mental powers, in turn boosting a nation's racial destiny.

George Hendrick, also a professor of English, gives a colorful account of Washington Irving's illnesses and their treatment by a homeopath. After water cures, bleeding, and leeching failed him, he turned to homeopathy, the century's chief rival to orthodox medicine. Its shibboleth was "like cures like." If a drug produced symptoms of a disease, then that drug in infinitesimal amounts—the more minute the dose the greater its potency—would cure the disease. Thousands of compounds were tested and listed in the cult's many *materia medicas*, all innocuous because of their extreme dilution, often to just a few molecules, sometimes to none at all. Homeopathy began its downward slide when orthodox medicine developed statistical techniques for evaluating remedies, but old cults seldom die completely. Homeopathy is now making a comeback among New Age junkies.

Robert Fuller, a professor of religion, skillfully sketches the history of mesmerism. The founder, Franz Mesmer, was a German occultist (surprising that so many of the nation's pseudosciences were European imports) who believed that a force called "animal magnetism" flowed from the mesmerist's hands into the subject's brain. Like Wilhelm Reich, whose orgone therapy was one of the funnier follies of the present century, Mesmer was convinced he had discovered the fundamental energy of the universe. Fuller sees mesmerism as America's first popular psychology, one that played a role in the emergence of experimental psychology as a discipline distinct from moral philosophy, and in Freud's infatuation with the unconscious.

Wrobel, in his introduction, afterword, and a chapter on phrenology, rightly makes much of the fact that pseudoscience was far from confined to the poor and ignorant. "I look upon phrenology as the guide to philosophy and handmaiden of Christianity," declared the noted educator Horace Mann. Horace Greeley wanted all railroad engineers to have their skulls examined for the sake of safety. In England, George Eliot had her head shaved twice for more accurate analysis. Among educated people, enthusiasm for fringe science was largely confined to persons outside the scientific community. Their respect for science was unbounded, but their classical education provided them with little comprehension of the need for extraordinary evidence to support extraordinary claims.

The list of notables who took water cures and who shared Irving's faith in homeopathy is very long indeed. Spiritualism won its most distinguished converts in England and Europe; they included several leading physicists and astronomers, and writers as famous as Yeats, Conan Doyle, and Elizabeth Browning. In America James Fenimore Cooper, Harriet Beecher Stowe, William Cullen Bryant, and scores of political leaders became believers.

Homeopathy and hydropathy seemed to have firmer empirical support than orthodox medicine. In the first half of the century mainline medicine was more like astrology than science, favoring remedies that Wrobel summarizes as "blistering, puking, purging, cupping, bleeding, and poisonous doses of mercury and arsenic." At least the effects of electric currents, homeopathic doses, and cold water were harmless. All true, but when Wrobel says of fringe scientists that "by nineteenth-century standards their empiricism was beyond reproach," I must demur.

Although standards of science then were far lower than they are today, especially in medicine, the century was not without scientists who saw clearly how shaky the fringe claims were. Benjamin Franklin ridiculed the notion that mesmerism was anything more than psychological suggestion. Physician Oliver Wendell Holmes wrote blistering and accurate attacks on homeopathy and hydropathy. There were plenty of orthodox scientists around who had a good grasp of scientific methods, but like mainline scientists today they preferred not to squander valuable time opposing what they saw as nonsense. It is not easy to find establishment scientists of the period who tumbled for fringe claims.

It seems to me that Wrobel also overdoes the extent to which fringe scientists were right. It doesn't credit phrenology with much to say that it pioneered measurements of the cranium (as if physical anthropologists would not soon have gotten around to it), or that parts of the brain have specialized functions. Nor am I impressed by statements that a few homeopathic drugs later proved useful. Of thousands of homeopathic remedies, it would have been remarkable if all were worthless; moreover, they really were worthless in their extreme dilutions. I see the merits of pseudoscience less in its trivial anticipations of later science than in the way it encourages the pursuit of all leads no matter how bizarre, and in the fact that the refutation of false claims not only enlightens everybody; it often opens new paths to significant discoveries.

No anthology can cover everything, but perhaps it is worthwhile to mention some American pseudosciences not covered in the book: ignorant attacks on evolution and on the inferiority of non-Caucasians, physiognomy (reading character from facial features: William James took it with great seriousness), above all osteopathy and chiropractic. Osteopaths have since abandoned the crazy doctrines of Andrew Still, their founder, and half of today's chiropractors are now little more than physical therapists, but in the past century both groups attributed all diseases to imaginary "subluxations" of the vertebrae— a medical delusion as unsupported by evidence as homeopathy. Spiritualism, on the other hand, seems to me more a fringe religion than pseudoscience. It claimed empirical support, but no less so than Christian Science or Theosophy.

None of the book's writers considers the question of whether Americans today are more or less gullible than their forebears. My own opinion is that the gullibility of the public today makes citizens of the nineteenth century look like hard-nosed skeptics. A larger fraction of Americans now go to college, science has made astounding strides, popular books and magazines about science abound, and big newspapers have first-class science editors. The result? Almost every newspaper runs a daily horoscope, and astrology books, like books about crank and sometimes harmful diets, far outsell books on reputable science. A Gallup survey in 1986 found that 52 percent of American teenagers believe in astrology and 67 percent in angels. A 1974 poll by the Center for Policy Research in New York reported that 48 percent of American adults are certain that Satan exists and 20 percent more think his existence probable.

Electric belts are out but crystal power is in. Time-Life vigorously promoted a set of lurid volumes about paranormal powers. Mesmerism now stimulates memories of past lives and the recall of being abducted by aliens from outer space. The most preposterous book ever written about UFO abductions, *Intruders*, by Budd Hopkins, was published by Random House with full-page ads in *The New York Times Book Review*. Acupuncture charts show paths of energy-flow as nonexistent as the paths of similar flow on chiropractic charts. *The Hite Report* and treatises on the "G-spot" are as comic as any sex manual of the past century. Spiritualism is back in full force in the form of trance channeling. Shirley MacLaine has become richer and more influential—she is certainly prettier—than Madame Blavatsky ever was.

There is an amusing error on page 226. We are told that in 1933 J. B. Rhine, the father of experimental parapsychology, earned the first doctorate in psychical research ever given by an American university. Dr. Rhine obtained his Ph.D. in 1925, at the University of Chicago, with a thesis in botany titled "Translocation of Fats as Such in Germinating Fatty Seeds." If fatty seeds are taken as symbolic of fat-headed delusions, in part translocated from the nineteenth century, they are germinating as never before throughout the land.

POSTSCRIPT

The following letter from Julian Winson, of Washington, D.C.'s National Center for Homeopathy, along with my reply, ran in the *New York Review of Books* (June 2, 1988):

> In his review ["Bumps on the Head," NYR, March 17] Martin Gardner states the following (in reference to homeopathy):
>
>> Homeopathy began its downward slide when orthodox medicine developed statistical techniques for evaluating remedies, but old cults seldom die completely. Homeopathy is now making a comeback among New Age junkies.
>
> I beg to differ with Mr. Gardner's opinions (and they are opinions!). I suggest that such invective does not belong in such a fine publication as yours.
>
> Mr. Gardner obviously has never read either *Divided Legacy* by Harris L. Coulter, or *Homeopathy: The Rise and Fall of a Medical Heresy* by Martin Kauffman. Both books outline the history of the homeopathic movement in this country, and neither one gives credit to "statistical techniques" for the decline of homeopathy.
>
> If Mr. Gardner thinks that "New Age junkies" are bringing back ho-

meopathy, I wonder if that epithet refers to the English Royal Family (who support and use homeopathy), to the orthodox medical schools in France (who are mandated to teach a course in homeopathy), to the staffs of over 400 teaching hospitals in India who use homeopathy, or to the members of the American Institute of Homeopathy, the oldest medical society in this country, whose members have graduated from the finest orthodox medical schools in this country, and who have turned to homeopathy because they have found its therapy more effective than orthodox methods.

Mr. Gardner might find it curious that *Portraits of Homeopathic Medicines* by Catherine R. Coulter was mentioned as "best book of the year" by Martin Seymour-Smith, the literary critic of *The Independent* in Great Britain.

Mr. Gardner should confine himself to reviewing things he knows about.

My reply:

The slightest criticism of any fringe medicine is sure to generate angry letters from the true believers. There is no popular pseudoscience that has not produced seemingly impressive books and periodicals. That England's Royal Family sometimes uses homeopathic remedies no more impresses me than learning that William Gladstone was a hardshell fundamentalist, or that Canada's longtime prime minister, W. L. Mackenzie King was a practicing spiritualist, or that Ronald Reagan believes in astrology, the Second Coming, and supply-side economics. The popularity of homeopathy in India, where a hundred pseudosciences bloom, is a strong count against it.

If readers are interested in what the medical profession thinks of homeopathy, just ask your family physician or check the January 1987 issue of *Consumer Reports*. CU [Consumers Union] gives the results of a year-long investigation of homeopathy by Stephen Barrett, M.D. The report concludes:

> Unless the laws of chemistry have gone awry, most homeopathic remedies are too diluted to have any physiological effect. . . . CU's medical consultants believe that any system of medicine embracing the use of such remedies involves a potential danger to patients whether the prescribers are M.D.s, other licensed practitioners, or outright quacks. Ineffective drugs are dangerous drugs when used to treat serious or life-threatening disease. Moreover, even though homeopathic drugs are essentially nontoxic, self-medication can still be hazardous. Using them for a serious illness or undiagnosed pain instead of obtaining proper medical attention could prove harmful or even fatal.

POSTSCRIPT (1995)

Of the pseudosciences mentioned in this review, homeopathy has had the most vigorous comeback in the United States. It is especially popular on college campuses, and among New Age and health food enthusiasts. In 1994 homeopathic drugs invaded thousands of reputable drugstores all across the land. When I expressed incredulity to the chief pharmacist in a store I then patronized, he astonished me by saying, "Nobody knows why homeopathic drugs work, but nonetheless they have enormous value in combating ills." I had to visit several other drugstores in town before I found one that did not have large displays of homeopathic remedies.

In 1988 Jacques Benveniste, a French chemist, made a valiant attempt to explain why homeopathic dilutions work even when so extreme that no molecule of the original substance remains. The water, he claimed, somehow retains a "memory" of the molecular properties of the diluted drug! Nature published a report on his experiments (June 30, 1988) on condition that he would allow Nature to oversee a replication.

Nature's team of investigators reported (Nature, July 28, 1989) that the replication was a failure. Both the original claim and the failed replication aroused great controversy in the media both here and abroad. For an account of this comedy, see "Water with a Memory?" a chapter in On the Far Side.

NOTES

1. See the chapter on dermo-optical perception in my *Science: Good, Bad and Bogus* (Prometheus, 1981). In his autobiography Mark Twain tells of visiting Orson Fowler in disguise and being told, after a head reading, that he had no sense of humor. Three months later he returned under his own name. The humor cavity had vanished, replaced by what Fowler said was "the loftiest bump for humor he had ever encountered." Twain may have made this up but in any case it shows how easy it is to invent traps for charlatans.

SEVENTEEN

THE IRRELEVANCE OF CONAN DOYLE

My article on Conan Doyle and the fairy photos was written for Beyond Baker Street, an anthology of essays about Sherlock Holmes, edited by Michael Harrison (Bobbs-Merrill, 1976).

In the spirit of the Baker Street Irregulars, I had naturally assumed that Doyle was merely Watson's literary agent. Incredible as it may seem, many readers took this seriously, as well as my denial that Cervantes wrote Don Quixote. I actually received a letter from a scholar in Spain asking me to send him sources for my claim that Sancho Panza was the true author. "Unfortunately," he wrote, "this information is not yet common knowledge in Spain, nor do I find it in those larger encyclopedias which are accessible to me."

There are some trees, Watson, which grow to a certain height and then suddenly develop some unsightly eccentricity. You will see it often in humans.

—CONAN DOYLE,
The Adventure of the Empty House

What has that eminent Spiritualist . . . to do with Sherlock Holmes?
—T.S. ELIOT

Questions similar to Eliot's can be asked about many another famous scrivener whose name has been associated with allegedly fictional characters. What has that sixteenth-century Spanish drifter and one-armed soldier to do with Don Quixote and Sancho Panza? What has that kinky-haired, pie-faced French mulatto, lecher, spendthrift, and literary hack to do with Athos, Porthos, Aramis, and d'Artagnan?

The answer, of course, is "Nothing." The case of Cervantes is particularly instructive, because it has so much in common with that of Conan Doyle. The two books about the adventures of the Knight of La Mancha tell the story of a long friendship between a dreamer—yet man of action—and his faithful down-to-earth companion. We now know, thanks to the recent efforts of Spanish scholars, that these adventures were written, not by Cervantes, but by Sancho Panza. After the death of his master, Sancho sold his memoirs to Cervantes, who, scoundrel that he was, kept them hidden until Sancho, too, had died.

One should have suspected this long before the truth came out. Cervantes had little interest in Don Quixote. It was his poetry and plays, all written in a careful, classical style, of which he was proud. Only because he was seriously in debt did he allow his name to appear on Sancho's sprawling, carelessly written work.

Sancho was, of course, a much greater writer than Cervantes. He was far from the slow-witted person he made himself out to be, but like James Boswell and John Watson he modestly underplayed himself to pay greater homage to his friend. Unfortunately, his stories about the Don were written in his old age, when his memory was starting to fade, and they are filled with lapses that Cervantes would never have allowed to remain in the manuscript had he troubled to go over it carefully. Cervantes had so little interest in the first half of Sancho's memoirs that it was not until ten years later, when he desperately needed money again, that he issued the sequel. This time he edited more carefully, adding passages in which he tried to explain the contradictions he had failed to catch in the earlier volume.

There are many reasons for believing that Doyle had as little to do with Watson's manuscripts as Cervantes with Sancho Panza's. Like Cervantes, Doyle had no interest in—indeed, he had contempt for—the stories he pretended were his own. But as soon as they became great popular successes, bringing him an income needed for other projects, he let them continue to appear under his own name, touching them up here and there, but editing them so hastily that many of Watson's contradictions, like those of Sancho's, were allowed to remain.

The strongest internal evidence that neither Cervantes nor Doyle wrote the stories for which they became famous is simply the enormous contrast between the mentality and philosophical outlook of supposed author and hero. Don Quixote was a man of firm Roman Catholic faith and high moral principles, with a passion for chivalry. Cervantes hated chivalry. He allowed his name to appear on Sancho's books because he mistakenly supposed them to be attacks on faith and chivalry. His infidelities to his wife, the episodes involving his mistresses, the affairs of his daughter—all were so sordid that early biographers of Cervantes fell back on Latin when they supplied details.

The equally great contrast between the minds of Holmes and Doyle has often been noted. Was Gilbert Chesteron the first to point out how much more Doyle had in common with Dr. Watson? It is true that Doyle and Watson were both medical men, slow thinkers, good writers, and sensitive to the poetry of London; yet there was one overwhelming difference between the two men that has not, I believe, been sufficiently recognized. I refer to Watson's abiding respect for rationality, science, and common sense, a trait shared by Holmes but not by Doyle.

It has many times been pointed out that Holmes's so-called deductions were actually inductions. Like the scientist trying to solve a mystery of nature, Holmes first gathered all the evidence he could that was relevant to his problem. At times he performed experiments to obtain fresh data. He then surveyed the total evidence in the light of his vast knowledge of crime, and of sciences relevant to crime, to arrive at the most probable hypothesis. Deductions were made from the hypothesis; then the theory was further tested against new evidence, revised if need be, until finally the truth emerged with a probability close to certainty.

Although Watson seldom played a role in this complex process, with enormous respect he watched it unfold. Frequently mystified by the speed and efficiency of Holmes's method, he never failed to admire it, to accept its final results, and on one occasion, after the procedure had been explained to him, to exclaim, "How absurdly simple!"

Nothing could be more remote from the mind-set of Watson's alleged creator. Doyle spent the last twelve years of his life in a tireless crusade against science and rationality. It is a period usually glossed over quickly in biographies of Doyle, but, in view of today's explosion of interest in spiritualism and all things occult, it is good to review it as an object lesson. Above all, it provides overwhelming evidence that Doyle had almost nothing to do with either Holmes or Watson.

It has been said that Doyle's conversion to spiritualism, like the more recent case of Bishop James Pike, was an emotional reaction to the death of his son. Not so. Even when he was a young Irish-Catholic, Doyle had a strong interest in psychic phenomena. His crusade for spiritualism began in 1916, two years before his son died. Although several British scientists were caught up in the craze, notably Oliver Lodge and William Crookes, Doyle rapidly became the movement's most influential fugleman. He lectured and debated everywhere. His literary labors for the cause were prodigious. In addition to innumerable pamphlets, magazine articles, introductions to books by others, letters, and book reviews, the following volumes of spiritualist apologetics flowed from his pen: *The New Revelation, The Vital Message, The Wanderings of a Spiritualist, Our American Adventure, Our Second American Adventure, The Case for Spirit Photography, Psychic Experiences, The Mystery of Spiritualism, The Land of Mist,*[1] *The Edge of the Unknown,* and, not least, a monumental two-volume *History of Spiritualism.*

It is no good to say that Doyle had become senile. Clearly he had not. His final years were remarkably vigorous and productive. His last book, *The Edge of the Unknown*, published in 1930, the year that he died at age seventy-one, is a model of lucid, beautifully structured prose. Thousands of people were deeply influenced by his books and lectures. Dr. Joseph B. Rhine, the eminent parapsychologist, is on record as saying that it was a speech by Doyle that first inspired him to turn from botany, in which he had been trained, to the study of psychic phenomena.

In *Memories and Adventures* (pp. 392–94), Doyle gives a dramatic summary of why he believes in spiritualism. He had seen his dead mother and nephew so plainly that he could have counted the wrinkles on one, the freckles on the other. He had conversed at length with spirit voices. He had smelled the "peculiar ozonelike smell of ectoplasm." Prophecies he heard were swiftly fulfilled. He had "seen the dead glimmer up upon a photographic plate" untouched by any hand but his own. His wife, a medium whose writing fingers would be seized by a spirit control, had produced "notebooks full of information . . . utterly beyond her ken." He had seen heavy objects "swimming in the air, untouched by human hand." He had seen "spirits walk around the room in fair light and join in the talk of the company." On his wall was a painting done by a woman with no artistic training, but who had been possessed by an artistic spirit.

He had read books written by unlettered mediums who transmitted the work of dead writers, and he had recognized the writer's style, "which no parodist could have copied, and which was written in his own handwriting." He had heard "singing beyond earthly power, and whistling done with no pause for the intake of breath." He had seen objects "from a distance projected into a room with closed doors and windows." Why, Doyle concludes, should a man who has experienced all this "heed the chatter of irresponsible journalists, or the head-shaking of inexperienced men of science? They are babies in this matter, and should be sitting at his feet."

Those are the strong words of a profoundly sincere man. They are also the words of a man with a temperament utterly alien to that of both Holmes and Watson. The bitter truth is that Doyle was an incompetent observer of supposed psychic events. He was ignorant of even the rudiments of magic and deception, hopelessly naïve, capable of believing anything, no matter how flimsy the evidence. Over and over again the great mediums of the day who produced psychical phenomena were caught in fraud by the Holmeses and Watsons of science. Over and over again Doyle refused to recognize even the possibility of fraud except in a few cases where it was so patently obvious that everyone in the spiritualist movement recognized it. Even in such rare cases Doyle was quick to explain deception away as a temporary aberration on the part of genuine psychics. Were they not pressured into cheating by the incessant demands of skeptics for phenomena that could not always be produced at will?

In many cases Doyle flatly refused to believe fraudulent mediums even when they made full confessions and explained in detail exactly how they cheated. The most sensational of such confessions was by Margaret Fox, one of the Fox sisters of upper New York State whose ability to produce spirit raps by cracking the first joint of a big toe had started the modern spiritualist craze. Margaret Fox's remarkable confession, made in 1888 when she was eighty-one, appeared in the New York *World*, October 21, and you can read it in Harry Houdini's *A Magician Among the Spirits*. That night, on the stage of New York's Academy of Music, under the close scrutiny of three physicians, Margaret took off a shoe, put one foot on a stool and demonstrated her toe-cracking technique to a hushed audience.

How did Doyle react to her confession? Like other prominent spiritualists, he refused to believe it. Nor did he believe Houdini when the magician tried to persuade him that prominent conjurors of the day who were capitalizing on the spiritualist movement by claiming supernormal powers were not genuine psychics. The Davenport brothers, for example, were friends of Houdini. He knew their methods well but was unable to convince Doyle that they were tricksters. Julius Zancig, another magician and friend of Houdini, had perfected a secret code by which he could transmit information quickly to his wife. Just as some magicians today pretend to be genuine mind readers because it enhances their reputation and increases their earnings, so the Zancigs found they could make more money posing as psychics than by doing straight magic. Doyle never doubted the authenticity of their telepathic abilities. Magicians found this as hilarious then as they do today whenever a famous writer or scientist goes on record as believing that some magician-turned-psychic has supernormal powers.

Indeed, Doyle even refused to believe Houdini's repeated denials that he, Houdini, was not psychic. Doyle's essay, "The Riddle of Houdini,"[2] is one of the most absurd documents in the history of parapsychology. Here is Doyle, the supposed creator of Sherlock Holmes, arguing soberly that his friend Houdini was in reality a medium who performed his escapes by dematerializing his body!

Houdini's protests fell on uncomprehending ears. Doyle readily admitted that Houdini was a skilled conjuror, but he argued that the magician's escapes were on such an "utterly different plane" from that of other magicians that it was an "outrage of common sense to think otherwise." Why, if Houdini was a genuine psychic, did he deny his singular powers? "Is it not perfectly evident," Doyle answered himself, "that if he did not deny them his occupation would have been gone forever? What would his brother-magicians have to say to a man who admitted that half his tricks were done by what they would regard as illicit powers? It would have been 'exit Houdini.' "[3]

There is scarcely a page in any of Doyle's books on the occult that does not reveal him to be the antithesis of Holmes. His gullibility was boundless. His comprehension of what constitutes scientific evidence was on a level with that of members of London's flat-earth society. Consider, for example, the story he tells in *The Coming of the Fairies* (1922).[4]

In 1917, in the Yorkshire village of Cottingley, a sixteen-year-old girl, Elsie Wright, was being visited by her ten-year-old cousin, Frances Griffiths. Elsie was a dreamy little girl who for years had loved to draw pictures of fairies. She had a fair amount of artistic talent, had done some designing for a jeweler, and once worked a few months for a photographer. The two girls loved to spend hours in a glen back of the cottage where, they told Mr. and Mrs. Wright, they often played with fairies.

One day the girls borrowed Mr. Wright's camera, and Elsie snapped a picture of Frances in the woods. When Mr. Wright developed the plate he was astonished to see four scantily clad Tinkerbells, with large butterfly wings, prancing merrily in the air under Frances's chin. Two months later Frances took a picture of Elsie that showed her beckoning a tiny gnome wearing black tights and pointed hat (a bright red hat, the girls recalled) to step into her lap.

The two photos reached Doyle by way of Edward L. Gardner, a theosophist and occult journalist. Doyle wrote to Houdini in great excitement: "I have something . . . precious, two photos, one of a goblin, the other of four fairies in a Yorkshire wood. A fake! you will say. No, sir, I think not. However, all inquiry will be made. These I am not allowed to send. The fairies are about eight inches high. In one there is a single goblin dancing. In the other, four beautiful, luminous creatures. Yes, it is a revelation."

In the December 1920 issue of the *Strand Magazine*, the monthly that had printed so many of Watson's marvelous tales, Doyle and Gardner collaborated on "An Epoch-Making Event—Fairies Photographed." The article blew up a storm. Several newspapers attacked the pictures as fakes, but hundreds of readers wrote to Doyle about the fairies that they, too, had seen in their gardens. Three years after the first two fairy pictures had been taken, Gardner brought the two cousins together again at the same cottage (the girls insisted the fairies would not "come out" unless both were there) and let them borrow his camera. Eventually the girls succeeded in obtaining three more fairy photos. Gardner was not present during any of this picture-taking. Why? Because the girls convinced him the fairies were extremely shy and would not come out for a stranger!

The three new pictures appeared in the *Strand* in 1921, and the following year Doyle reproduced all five in his book *The Coming of the Fairies*. Of the three new photos, one shows a fairy with yellow wings (the girls always supplied details about the colors) offering a posy of "etheric harebells" to Elsie.

A second shows an almost nude young lady, with lavender wings, leaping toward Elsie's nose.

Neither girl is in the third photograph. A winged fairy is on the left, another on the right. Both are either partly hidden behind twigs, or the twigs are showing through their transparent bodies. The girls recalled seeing the two creatures, but said they had noticed only a misty glow between them. On the photograph this glow proved to be something that looks like nothing more than a piece of silk hanging on some branches. According to Doyle's caption in the book's first British edition, it is "a magnetic bath, woven very quickly by the fairies, and used after dull weather and in the autumn especially. The sun's rays through the sheath appear to magnetize the interior and thus provide a 'bath' that restores vitality and vigour."

Doyle was now firmly persuaded that the fairies were not "thought forms" projected into the camera by the girls, like the photographs which Jule Eisenbud argues, in his *World of Ted Serios* (William Morrow, 1967), were projected onto Polaroid film by a Chicago bellhop. Doyle believed that the fairies belonged to "a population which may be as numerous as the human race . . . and which is only separated from ourselves by some difference of vibrations."

Moreover, Doyle was convinced that a revelation of the existence of these little people would go far toward combatting the materialism that dominated modern science, and so paved the way for an acceptance of the greater revelation of spiritualism. In 1920 he wrote to Gardner:

I am proud to have been associated with you in this epoch-making incident. We have had continued messages at séances for some time that a visible sign was coming through—and perhaps this was what is meant. The human race does not deserve fresh evidence. . . . However, our friends beyond are very long-suffering and more charitable than I, for I will confess that my soul is filled with a cold contempt for the muddle-headed indifference and the moral cowardice which I see around me.

Doyle noticed that one of the four fairies, in the first picture taken by the girls, is playing a double pipe. A similar pipe is held by the gnome in the second picture. Is not this the traditional pipe of Pan? According to the girls, it made a "tiny little tinkle" that could barely be heard when all was still. And if the fairies have pipes, why not other belongings? "Does it not suggest a complete range of utensils and instruments . . . ?" Doyle asks. "It seems to me that with fuller knowledge and with fresh means of vision, these people are destined to become just as solid and real as the Eskimos."

One of the funniest (and saddest) aspects of Doyle's preposterous book is that the five pictures he so proudly displays are not even clever fakes. The lack of modeling on the fairy figures, and their sharp outlines, indicate that

Elsie had simply drawn them on stiff paper, then the girls had cut them out and stuck them in the grass or supported them in the air with invisible wires or threads. (The pictures could have been faked in other ways, but this seems the most likely.) The little ladies have hairdos that were fashionable at the time. There is not the slightest blurring of their fluttering wings. In every picture the fairies look as flat as paper dolls.

Unlike Dr. Watson, Doyle could never bring himself to exclaim, "How absurdly simple!" Not once did he doubt the genuineness of the fairy photos, although he did own that proof of their authenticity was less "overwhelming" than for the authenticity of photographs of discarnates on the "other side." The two girls never obtained another fairy picture. Doyle reports on a visit in 1921 to the Cottingley glen by a clairvoyant named Geoffrey Hodson. He was accompanied by the two girls. The place swarmed with elves, gnomes, fairies, brownies, goblins, water nymphs, and other elusive creatures, all seen and vividly described by Hodson and the girls, but the little people refused to appear on any camera plates.[5]

In 1971 both Elsie and Frances were interviewed by the BBC. The two elderly ladies insisted that their father had not faked the pictures. When Elsie was asked point blank if she or Frances had faked them, she was unwilling to deny it. "I've told you they're photographs of figments of our imagination," she said, "and that's what I'm sticking to." The same question was put to Frances, who was interviewed separately. Frances asked how Elsie had answered it. When told, she said she had nothing to add.[6]

Well, what is one to make of an eminent writer who believed that Houdini dematerialized his body to perform his escapes and that the glens of England teem with wee folk who now and then allow themselves to be seen and photographed by us mortals? However you answer, one thing is certain. Such a man could never have constructed, as figments of *his* imagination, the coldly rational Holmes or his admiring Dr. Watson.

It was not, I think, Doyle who made this pair immortal. It was the other way around. Holmes and Watson, intent on guarding their privacy, permitted Sir Arthur to take credit for inventing them. In doing so, they conferred upon him that earthly immortality that his authentic but undistinguished writings could never have provided.

POSTSCRIPT

Jerome Clark, in "Exploring Fairy Folklore," a two-part article in *Fate* (September, October, 1945), defended the genuineness of the fairy photos. In a later piece ("The Cottingley Fairies: The Last Word," *Fate*, November 1978) Clark ate crow. The reason: a discovery reported in *Ghosts in Photographs* (Harmony Books, 1978), by occult journalist Fred Gittings.

Gittings found a children's book, *Princess Mary's Gift Book*, published in England in 1915 by Hodder and Stoughton, the same house (ironically) that later published Doyle's treatise on the fairies. In the gift book is a poem by Alfred Noyes called "A Spell for a Fairy" that tells how to conjure up the wee creatures. The poem's final illustration shows three dancing fairies. When you compare them with the three in the first Cottingley photograph, you see at once they are line-for-line copies. One of the girls obviously had drawn them on cardboard, added wings, then cut them out, and the girls had stuck them in the grass just as the skeptics had always said.

This revelation convinced Clark that the photos were indeed a hoax. Will it convince Jule Eisenbud? I doubt it. Many thought-photographs of Ted Serios were found to correspond line for line with published photographs. This did not disturb Eisenbud in the least. He still firmly believes that Ted saw those pictures in magazines, imprinted them on his mind, then years later projected them by his psychic powers onto Polaroid film. One can similarly argue that the two girls saw the fairy pictures in the gift book, remembered them, and later psychically projected three of the prancing ladies onto the camera plates. Paranormal hypotheses never die. They just momentarily fade, only to bloom again in full strength.

POSTSCRIPT (1995)

Perpetrators of major hoaxes seldom admit their deceptions. To my surprise, in 1982 Frances (then 74) and Elsie (80) decided to spill the beans. In April of that year Elsie sent Sotheby a seven-page handwritten letter (I own a copy) offering to sell them the full story. Sotheby declined. The next year they made a full confession to The Times of London. (See issues of March 18 and April 4, 1993.)

Elsie had drawn the little people on cardboard sheets, which the girls cut out and stuck in the shrubbery with long hatpins. The head of one pin is visible sticking out of a gnome. Doyle took the spot to be a navel, convincing him that fairies are born just like humans!

The girls intended their pictures to be short-lived practical jokes, but they felt so sorry for poor Doyle that to protect his reputation, they kept silent. "I hated those photographs," said Frances, "and cringe every time I see them. I thought it was a joke, but everyone else kept it going. It should have died a natural death sixty years ago."

The confession of the two elderly women provides a rare instance of a crank work, such as Percival Lowell's books on nonexistent Martian canals, that is finally totally discredited. Had they told Doyle about their prank, he would of course never have written his crazy book, but I suspect it would not in the least have shaken his belief that fairies exist.

NOTES

1. *The Land of Mist* is actually a novel, but one that rattles with spiritualist drumbeating. Doyle's fictional scientist, George Edward Challenger (of *Lost World* fame), now a widower, is converted to spiritualism when he gets a message from his discarnate wife. Before the *Strand* serialized the novel, Doyle called it *The Psychic Adventures of Edward Malone.*

One of the strongest indications that Holmes was not Doyle's creation is that Holmes, unlike Professor Challenger, never became a spiritualist. True, he once remarked (in "The Adventure of the Veiled Lodger"), echoing one of Doyle's favorite themes: "The ways of fate are indeed hard to understand. If there is not some compensation hereafter, then the world is a cruel jest." But had Doyle actually written this story at the time he claimed, when his interest in spiritualism was at its zenith, Holmes surely would have said more than that.

2. This essay was first published as a pamphlet and serialized in the *Strand Magazine* as "Houdini the Enigma," vol. 74, August and September 1927. It is reprinted in Doyle's *The Edge of the Unknown* (1930), currently in print as a Berkley paperback.

3. On Doyle's relationship with Houdini, see *Houdini and Conan Doyle: The Story of a Strange Friendship*, by Bernard M. L. Ernst and Hereward Carrington (New York: Albert and Charles Boni, 1932). Consult also the chapter on Doyle in Houdini's *A Magician Among the Spirits* (New York: Harper and Brothers, 1924), and the many references to Doyle in *Houdini, the Untold Story*, by Milbourne Christopher (New York: Thomas Y. Crowell, 1969).

4. *The Coming of the Fairies* was first published in 1922: in London by Hodder and Stoughton, in New York by George H. Doran. An enlarged edition, to which Doyle added more fairy photographs from England and other lands, was issued in London in 1928 by Psychic Press. Samuel Weiser, New York, reprinted the Doran edition in paper covers in 1972.

5. Hodson gives a full account of this in his book, *Fairies at Work and Play*, published in London by the Theosophical Society Publishing House, 1921. The same house, in 1945, published Edward L. Gardner's *Fairies: The Cottingley Photographs and Their Sequel*, a book containing the best reproductions of the five photos. The fourth revised edition appeared in 1966. Both books are still in print.

The latest retelling of the story of Doyle and the fairy pictures is "Exploring Fairy Folklore," a two-part article by Jerome Clark, *Fate* magazine, September and October 1974.

6. Tapes of the BBC interviews with Elsie and Frances are owned by Leslie Gardner (son of Edward L. Gardner), who also owns much unpublished material on his father's investigation of the fairy pictures. For comments on the BBC interviews, see Robert H. Ashby's letter in *Fate*, January 1975, pp. 129–30, and "The Cottingley Fairy Photographs: A Re-Appraisal of the Evidence," by Stewart F. Sanderson, in *Folklore*, vol. 84, Summer, 1973, pp. 89–103. The latter article is a presidential address given by Sanderson at the Folklore Society's annual meeting in London, March 1973. It is an excellent summary, by a skeptic, of the history of the fairy photos.

EIGHTEEN

WILHELM REICH AND THE ORGONE

When I wrote Fads and Fallacies in the Name of Science *(Putnam's, 1952; Dover revised edition, 1957) I would never have imagined that orgonomy, Scientology, homeopathy, and ufology, four chapter topics, would still be flourishing a few years before the close of this century.*

After the Dover paperback of my survey of crank science was published, the Village Voice *gave away copies to new subscribers. This so infuriated New York City Reichians that they canceled their subscriptions and wrote angry letters to the* Village Voice *complaining of monstrous errors in my chapter on Wilhelm Reich. In a rebuttal letter I disclosed that I had submitted the chapter to Reich himself for advance approval. Of course he did not know it would be in a book about pseudoscience. Reich made only one trivial correction of a date, and was so pleased with my description of his great work that he wrote "good" at several spots in the margin.*

For an updating on orgonomy and its deluded followers see "Wilhelm Reich, Rainmaker," in my On the Wild Side *(Prometheus, 1992).*

Wilhelm Reich, the discoverer of orgone energy (or "life energy"), was born in Austria in 1897. He received the M. D. in 1922 from the University of Vienna Medical School, became a protégé of Freud, and for the next eight years rose rapidly in psychoanalytic circles. He held several important teaching and administrative posts in Vienna psychoanalytical organizations, and contributed to their periodicals. You will find many references to him scattered among the footnotes and bibliographies of early Freudian writings.

Politically, Reich was active in the Austrian Socialist Party until he broke with them in 1930, and moved to Berlin where he joined the Communists.

Arthur Koestler, in his contribution to *The God that Failed*, 1949, reveals that he and Reich served in the same Party cell. "Among other members of our cell," writes Koestler, "I remember Dr. Wilhelm Reich, founder and director of the *Sex-Pol* (Institute for Sexual Politics). He was a Freudian Marxist; inspired by Malinowski, he had just published a book called *The Function of the Orgasm*, in which he expounded the theory that the sexual frustration of the Proletariat caused a thwarting of its political consciousness; only through a full, uninhibited release of the sexual urge could the working-class realize its revolutionary potentialities and historic mission; the whole thing was less cock-eyed than it sounds."

Reich failed, however, to convince the comrades of the revolutionary importance of his views. Moscow branded his writings "un-Marxist rubbish," and it was not long until he had severed his connections with the Communist movement. Differences with Freud and his followers led eventually, in 1934, to Reich's formal expulsion from the International Psychoanalytical Association.

Having written in 1933 a book attacking German fascism as the sadistic expression of sex-repressed neurotics, Reich was not looked upon kindly by the Nazis when they came to power. He fled to Denmark, then to Sweden, and finally settled in Oslo, Norway, where he continued his research for several years. Here, however, a furious press campaign against his work was instigated, and Reich came to the United States in 1939 to regain the quiet necessary for undisturbed work.

For two years, Reich was an associate professor at the New School for Social Research, in Manhattan. He established the Orgone Institute, a laboratory in Forest Hills, Long Island, and a press in Greenwich Village which began issuing English translations of his books. The books were favorably reviewed in liberal, Socialist, and anarchist periodicals, and cited frequently in such works as Fenichel's *The Psychoanalytic Theory of Neurosis*, 1945, and *Modern Woman, the Lost Sex*, by Lundberg and Farnham, 1947.

Reich was by then a ruddy-faced, distinguished looking man, living in semi-retirement on his estate near Rangeley, Maine. There he directed the multifarious activities of the Orgone Institute and the Wilhelm Reich Foundation. In addition to the publishing of Reich's books, the Foundation also issued the *Orgone Energy Bulletin* (a quarterly which superseded the *International Journal of Sex-Economy and Orgone Research*), *The Annals of the Orgone Institute*, and other literature.

Reich's early books (*The Function of the Orgasm*, 1927; *The Sexual Revolution*, 1930; *The Mass Psychology of Fascism*, 1933; and *Character Analysis*, 1933) were fairly close to the Freudian tradition. Although they contain much debatable material—presented in a repetitious, heavy-handed, totally humorless style—they also contain many fresh and impressive ideas which have become a permanent part of the analytic literature. *Character Analysis*, probably his most significant book, is still used (in the unrevised edition) by many analysts who deplore Reich's later thinking.

Particularly valuable were Reich's early insights into the neurotic aspects of social and political forces, and his stress on sexual health as a prerequisite for genuine morality and political progress. According to Reich, happiness and goodness are the products of sexual well-being, and unless a culture is sexually healthy, all attempts to build a good society are bound to fail. The "change of heart" or "rebirth" that Christian Socialists and Tolstoyan anarchists find essential to political reform is replaced by the Reichian concept of "orgastic potency."

Orgastically potent individuals, in turn, are the product of proper rearing by their parents and society, or they are former neurotics who have successfully undergone orgone therapy. Since there are so few such individuals around (outside of primitive cultures), it follows that most political action is useless. Regardless of how institutions are changed, the same sick individuals take control of them, and the same sick impulses quickly corrupt good intentions. This is why, according to Reich, the Russian Revolution failed so miserably. Not until we have a society of healthy (orgastically potent) citizens will we be able to achieve a decent political order. And when the order is achieved, it will be largely self-regulating, with no need for "compulsive" laws and morality. "Work democracy" is Reich's term for such a society. It is not hard to understand why these views have combined so easily with anarchist sentiments in England and the United States.

It would be out of place to describe here at any greater length Reich's early contributions to psychiatric theory. Many of them are complex and technical, and in order to be understood, would require a mastery of the elaborate and cumbersome Reichian terminology. What has been said, however, should give a faint indication of the importance of the topics which Reich tackled courageously during the German phase of his career.

From this point onward, you may take your choice of one of three possible interpretations of Reich's development. (1) He became the world's greatest biophysicist. (2) He deteriorated from a competent psychiatrist into a self-deluded crank. (3) He merely switched to fields in which his former incompetence became more visible. Critics who favor the last view point out that psychoanalysis was still in such a confused, pioneer state that writings by incompetent theorists were easily camouflaged by technical jargon and a sprinkling of sound ideas borrowed from others. When Reich turned to biology, physics, and astronomy—where there is a solid core of verifiable knowledge—his eccentric thinking became easier to detect.

Whatever the correct explanation may be, there is no doubt about the great turning point in Reich's career. It came in the late thirties when he discovered, in Norway, the existence of "orgone energy." Freud had earlier expressed the hope that some day his theory of the libido, or sexual energy, might be given a biological basis. Reich was convinced that his discovery of orgone energy fulfilled this hope—a discovery which he ranks in importance with the Copernican Revolution. After coming to America, he considered himself less a psychiatrist than a biophysicist, probing deeper into the mysteries of orgone energy, and applying this strange new knowledge to the treatment of bodily and mental ailments.

Exactly what is orgone energy? According to Reich it is a non-electromagnetic force which permeates all of nature. It is the *élan vital* or life force of Bergson, made practically accessible and usable. It is blue in color. To quote from one of Reich's booklets, "Blue is the specific color of orgone energy within and without the organism. Classical physics tries to explain the blueness of the sky by the scattering of the blue end of the spectral color series in the gaseous atmosphere. However, it is a fact that blue is the color seen in all functions which are related to the cosmic or atmospheric or organismic orgone energy." Protoplasm, said Reich, is blue with orgone energy, and loses its blueness when the cell dies. Orgone also causes the blue of oceans and deep lakes, and the blue coloration of certain frogs when they are sexually excited. "The color of luminating, decaying wood is blue; so are the luminating tail ends of glowworms, St. Elmo's fire, and the aurora borealis. The lumination in evacuated tubes charged with orgone energy is blue." (The latter has been photographed on color film and forms the cover photo of the booklet from which the above quotations are taken.)

The so-called "heat waves" you often see shimmering above roads and mountaintops are not heat at all, Reich declares, but orgone energy. These waves do not ascend. They move from west to east, at a speed faster than the earth's rotation. They cause the twinkling of stars. All phenomena which orthodox physicists attribute to "static electricity" are produced by orgone energy—e.g., electric disturbances during sunspot activity, lightning, radio interference, and all other forms of static discharges. "Cloud formations and thunderstorms," he writes, "—phenomena which to date have remained unexplained—depend on changes in the concentration of atmospheric orgone." That is why thunderclouds and hurricanes are deeply blue. "One of the hurricanes which was personally experienced by the writer [Reich] in 1944 was of a deep blue-black color." In an article in the *Orgone Energy Bulletin*, July 1951, Reich reports on some experiments made by himself which prove that dowsing rods operate by orgone energy![1]

In the human body, orgone is the basis of sexual energy. It is the *id* of Freud in a bio-energetic, concrete form. During coitus it becomes concentrated in the sexual parts. During orgasm, it flows back again through the entire body. By breathing, the body charges its red blood cells with orgone energy. Under the microscope, Reich has detected the "blue glimmer" of red corpuscles as they absorb orgone. In 1947, he measured orgone energy with a

Geiger counter. A film produced by his associates demonstrates how motors may some day be run by orgone energy.

The unit of living matter, Reich tells us, is not the cell but something much smaller which he calls the "bion," or "energy vesicle." It consists of a membrane surrounding a liquid, and pulsates continually with orgone energy. This pulsation is the dance of life—the basic convulsive rhythm of love which finds its highest expression in the pulsation of the "orgasm formula." Bions propagate like bacteria. In fact, Reich's critics suspected what he called bions really *were* bacteria.

According to Reich, bions are constantly being formed in nature by the disintegration of both organic and inorganic substances. The bions first group themselves into clumps, then they organize into protozoa! In Reich's book, *The Cancer Biopathy*, 1948, are a series of photomicrographs showing various types of single-cell animals, such as amoebae and paramecia, in the process of formation from aggregates of bions.

Needless to say, no "orthodox" biologist has been able to duplicate these revolutionary experiments. The opinion of bacteriologists who troubled to look at Reich's photographs was that his protozoa found their way into his cultures from the air, or were already present on the disintegrating material in the form of dormant cysts. Reich was aware of these objections, of course, and vigorously denied that protozoa could have gotten into his cultures in any way other than the way he describes.

In 1940, Reich invented a therapeutic box. Technically called an Orgone Energy Accumulator, it consisted of a structure resembling a short phone booth, made of sheet iron on the inside, and organic material (wood or cel-otex) on the outside. Later, three to twenty-layer accumulators were made of alternate layers of steel wool and rock wool. The theory is that orgone energy is attracted by the organic substance on the outside, and is passed on to the metal which then radiates it inward. Since the metal reflects orgone, the box soon acquires an abnormally high concentration of the energy. In Reich's laboratory in Maine, he had a large "orgone room" lined with sheet iron. When all the lights were turned out, he claimed, the room took on a blue-gray luminescence.

According to Dr. Theodore P. Wolfe, Reich's former translator, "The Orgone Energy Accumulator is the most important single discovery in the history of medicine, bar none." In 1951, Reich issued a booklet (there is no author's name on the title page) called *The Orgone Energy Accumulator*, which is the best available reference on the accumulator's construction and medical use. Most of the following material is taken from this work.

Orgone accumulators can be bought, but the Foundation holds rights to their medical use, and rents them to patients on a monthly basis, the charge varying with ability to pay. By sitting inside, lightly clothed, you charge your body with orgone energy. At first you feel a prickling, warm sensation, accompanied by reddening of the face and a rise in body temperature. There is a feeling that the body is "glowing." After you have absorbed as much orgone as your system demands, you begin to feel a slight dizziness and nausea. When this happens, you step out of the accumulator, breathe some fresh air, and the overcharge symptoms quickly vanish. "Under no circumstance," Reich's booklet reads, "should one sit in the accumulator for hours, or, as some people do, go to sleep in it. This can cause serious damage (severe vomiting, etc.). It is better, if necessary, to use the accumulator several times a day at shorter intervals than to prolong one sitting unnecessarily. At this stage of research, no accumulator over 3-layers should be used without medical supervision."

For people who are bedridden, Reich developed an "orgone energy accumulator blanket." This is a curved structure which can be placed on the bed, over a reclining figure, while a set of flat layers goes beneath the mattress. There also were tiny orgone boxes, called "shooters," for application to local areas. A flexible iron cable, from which the inner wires have been removed, carries the energy from the box to the part of the body being irradiated. If the body area is larger than the end of the cable, a funnel is attached. "Only *metal* (iron) funnels can be used," the booklet warns, "funnels made of plastic are ineffective."

It was Reich's belief that the natural healing process of a wound was greatly accelerated by applying the shooter. "Even severe pain will be stopped soon after the accident if orgone energy is applied locally through the shooter," the booklet states. "In severe cases of burns, experience has revealed the amazing fact that no blisters appear, and that the initial redness slowly disappears. The wounds heal in a matter of a few hours; severe ones need a day or two. Only chronic, advanced degenerating processes require weeks and months of daily irradiation. But here, too, severe lesions, as for instance *ulcus varicosus*, will yield to orgone energy irradiation."

In addition to speeding up healing, the energy also sterilizes a wound. "Microscopic observation shows that, for example, bacteria in the vagina will be immobilized after only one minute of irradiation through an inserted glass pipe filled with steel wool. . . . *Do not mix orgone irradiation with other, chemical applications. Orgone energy is a very strong energy.* We do not know as yet what such a mixture can do." (Italics his.)

The following ailments are listed in Reich's booklet as ills to which orgone treatment can be applied with great benefit: fatigue, anemia, cancer in early stages (with the exception of tumors of the brain and liver), acute and chronic colds, hay fever, arthritis, chronic ulcers, some types of migraine, sinusitis, and any kind of lesion, abrasion, or wound. "*Neuroses cannot be cured with physical orgone energy*," the booklet states. "Only the biopathic somatic background and certain somatic consequences of severe neuroses can be alleviated or diminished." In Reich's opinion, disease-producing bacteria are often formed by body bions in a degenerate state because of a patient's neuroses. This "auto infection" can be cleared up by sitting in the accumulator, though many chronic ailments require several years of treatment. The body's slow progress toward a higher energy level is observed by the Wilhelm Reich Blood Tests.

Cancer cells, according to Reich, are protozoa which develop from the bions coming from disintegrating tissues. "Many cancer cells," he observed, "have a tail and move in the manner of a fish." If the formation of these protozoa were not stopped by early death, he writes, "the cancer mouse or the cancer patient would change completely into protozoa." These quotations are from *The Cancer Biopathy* where you will find it all explained in detail.

Orgone therapy includes a type of treatment called "character analysis," exact details of which have not been printed for fear they would be misunderstood and abused. In most cases, the patient lies in a bathing suit on the couch. This is to give the orgonomist an opportunity to observe the patient's muscular reactions. It is Reich's belief that every neurosis is linked to "muscular armor"—a rigidity such as a furrowed brow, tense neck muscles, hunched shoulders, tight anus, and so on. "There is no neurotic . . . who does not show a tension in the abdomen," Reich has written.

The orgonomist tries to make the patient understand the cause of his muscular tensions, and there are certain technical procedures to help him get rid of them. If, for example, he has a tenseness around the jaws, because of an unconscious desire to bite someone, he may be given a towel and told to bite it. Parallel with this "orgone therapy" is the "character analysis." The latter involves free association and other standard devices which seek to penetrate the patient's "character armor."

An important part of orgone therapy is breathing, it being another Reichian belief that "There is no neurotic . . . capable of exhaling . . . deeply and evenly." This is owing to abdominal tenseness. The patient must overcome his inhibition against breathing out properly, often with the therapist assisting by applying pressure on the abdomen. As the breathing therapy advances, a curious phenomenon appears. The patient has an involuntary impulse to move his pelvis. A "dead pelvis," according to Reich, is a rigidity due to "pleasure anxiety," in turn rooted in childhood punishments for wetting the bed, playing with genitals, and so on. It prevents the neurotic from moving his pelvis naturally during the sex act, and also causes lumbago and hemorrhoids. The forward movement which appears spontaneously as the therapy proceeds is an instinctive motion. It is the motion made by the hips during normal coitus— the "orgasm reflex." A *voluntary* effort to move the pelvis during the sex act is considered neurotic.

The final goal of the therapy is the development of the patient's ability to have a full and complete orgasm—this being possible only to the "genital" or non-neurotic personality. The normal sex act follows the Reichian four-beat "orgasm formula"—mechanical tension, bio-electrical charge, bio-electrical discharge, and mechanical relaxation. During the orgasm, orgone energy raises the bio-electrical potential of the skin, especially on erogenous zones. One of the oscillograph photograms reproduced in *The Function of the Orgasm* is captioned, "Mucous membrane of the anus in a woman in a state of sexual excitation."

In subsequent years, Reich's sense of personal greatness and bitterness against colleagues who dismissed his orgone research as evidence of the tragic disintegration of a once brilliant thinker grew alarmingly. "Emotional plague" was his term for the social manifestation of sexual sickness, and as might be expected, he treated all opposition to his work as signs of the plague. In 1947, this aspect of the plague reached a climax when the Pure Food and Drug Administration began to investigate his orgone accumulators, and Mildred Brady wrote two magazine articles about him ("The New Cult of Sex and Anarchy," *Harpers*, April 1947 and "The Strange Case of Wilhelm Reich," *New Republic*, May 26, 1947). The following year Dr. Wolfe penned a pamphlet rebuttal titled *Emotional Plague Versus Orgone Biophysics*, from which the following statement by Reich is taken:

> It is an old story. It is older than the ancient Greeks whom we consider the bearers of a flourishing culture.... It was no different two thousand years later. Giordano Bruno, who fought for scientific knowledge and against astrological superstition, was condemned to death by the Inquisition. It is the same psychic pestilence which delivered Galileo to the Inquisition, let Copernicus die in misery, made Leeuwenhoek a recluse, drove Nietzsche into insanity, Pasteur and Freud into exile. It is the indecent, vile attitude of contemporaries of all times. This has to be said clearly once and for all. One cannot give in to such manifestations of the pestilence.

Even stronger language appears in Reich's *Listen Little Man!*, an angry volume issued in 1948 and delightfully illustrated by William Steig (Steig was an associate member of the Wilhelm Reich Foundation). The book purports to attack the neurotic, sexually-sick "little man" who fails to see his own sickness, and is responsible for the rise of all varieties of fascism. Actually, the book is a violent outburst against the world for its failure to recognize Reich's greatness.

"... When the discoverer has just found out why people die of cancer," Reich writes, "... and ... you, Little Man, happen to be a Professor of Cancer Pathology, with a steady salary, you say that the discoverer is a faker; or that he does not understand anything about air germs ... or you insist that you have a right to examine him, in order to find out whether he is qualified to work on "your" cancer problem, the problem you cannot solve; or you prefer to see many, many cancer patients die rather than admit that *he* has found what *you* so badly need if you are to save your patients. To you, your professional dignity, or your bank account, or your connection with the radium industry means more than truth and learning. And that's why you are small and miserable, Little Man."

Like all other "decent writing of today," Reich declares, his book is addressed "to the culture of 1000 or 5000 years hence as was the first wheel of thousands of years ago to the Diesel locomotive of today." It is true, he writes, that a new "era of atomic energy" has arrived. ". . . But not in the way you think. Not in your inferno, but in my quiet, industrious laboratory in a far corner of America."

Reich compares himself to a lonely eagle trying to hatch chicken eggs in the vain hope that he may hatch eagles. "But no, at the end they are nothing but cackling hens. When the eagle found out this, he had a hard time suppressing his impulse to eat up all the chicks and cackling hens. What kept him from doing so was a small hope. The hope, namely, that among the many cackling chicks there might be, one day, a little eagle capable like himself, to look from his lofty perch into the far distance, in order to detect new worlds, new thoughts and new forms of living. It was only this small hope that kept the sad, lonely eagle from eating up all the cackling chicks and hens. . . . But he thought about it and began to pity them. Sometime, he hoped, there would be, there would have to be, among the many cackling, gobbling and shortsighted chickens, a little eagle capable of becoming like himself. The lonely eagle, to this day, has not given up this hope. . . ."

Finally Reich concludes: "Whatever you have done to me or will do to me in the future, whether you glorify me as a genius or put me in a mental institution, whether you adore me as your savior or hang me as a spy, sooner or later necessity will force you to comprehend that I *have discovered the laws of the living*. . . . I have disclosed to you the infinitely vast field of the living in you, of your cosmic nature. That is my great reward."

Reich's *Cosmic Superimposition*, 1951, written 30 years after his first steps in natural science, carries orgonomy into the realm of astrophysics. "We are moving into the open spaces," he writes, "to find, if possible, what the newborn infant brings with him onto the stage inside." As he expresses it, he is turning from the microscope, which he used in exploring the microcosmos, to the telescope to explore the macrocosmos—in search of some common element which will unite human love with all of nature.

Obviously, the four-beat orgasm formula was not the answer. This convulsion was confined only to the living, and Reich carefully warns against the danger of finding analogies for it in the inorganic world. Earthquakes, for example, are convulsions—but not, he points out, of the orgasm type. The true answer lies in something simpler. It is the "sexual embrace" which precedes the orgasm, and which Reich terms "superimposition." "Whence stems the overpowering drive toward superimposition of male and female orgonotic systems?" he asks. The reply is that it is a drive which runs through all of nature, from the lowest pre-atomic level to the reaches of the stars. It is the basic pattern both of love and natural law.

Orgone energy units, Reich explains, move in a spiral path. When two or more such units approach each other, they superimpose in a way analogous to a sexual embrace. The result is the creation of "offspring"—in this case, a particle of matter!

On the astrophysical level, a similar phenomenon accounts for the birth of galaxies. Structureless streams of orgone energy (the Magellanic Cloud is cited by Reich as an example) are attracted to each other. They superimpose in a great cosmic embrace. The result—a galaxy! The book contains many excellent photographs of nebulae, showing the spiral arms in whose luminous embrace the galactic suns emerge.

But this is not all. Space is not empty. It is in reality a vast ocean of orgone energy, and its movements are responsible for the motions of the heavenly bodies. "The function of gravitation is real," he writes. "It is, however, not the result of mass attraction but of the converging movements of two original orgone energy streams. . . ." Again: "The sun and the planets move in the same plane and revolve in the same direction due to the movements and direction of the cosmic orgone energy stream in the galaxy. Thus, the sun does not 'attract' anything at all. It is merely the biggest brother of the whole group."

And so Reich, searching the skies from his observatory in Maine, found the secret of gravitation, the origin of matter, and the cause of the shape of spiral nebulae. "As the process of functional reasoning unfolded more and more," he confesses, "the observer [i.e., Reich] . . . experienced most vividly his own amazement at his own power of reasoning which was in such perfect harmony with the natural events thus disclosed."

At that time Reich was hard at work on an even more important problem—an antidote to nuclear destruction of life. Back in 1945, shortly after the first atomic bomb had fallen, he had written in his journal that "orgone energy is in fact nothing but 'atomic' energy in its original and natural form." Unlike atomic energy, however, it creates matter and strengthens life. It operates in a slow, constructive fashion. Atomic energy destroys in an explosive fashion. The two energies are, in fact, the underlying principles of love and hate, good and evil, God and Satan. "The horror," Reich wrote, "at the 'discovery' of the atom bomb has its counterpart in the quiet but glowing enthusiasm of anyone who works with orgone energy or experiences its therapeutic effects."

Since atomic energy and orgone energy have such contradictory properties, it was only natural for Reich to suppose that orgone might be useful as an antidote for nuclear radiation. "If, against any expectation, I should ever discover any murderous potentiality of the orgone energy," he wrote in 1945, "I would keep the process secret. We shall have to learn to counteract the murderous form of the atomic energy with the life-furthering function of the orgone energy and thus render it harmless."

In January, 1951, Reich established his ORANUR project (the letters stand for "Orgonomic Anti-Nuclear Radiation") to work out the details of this stupendous undertaking. Reports on his progress appeared in the *Orgone Energy Bulletin*, and other publications. The early experimental work reads like a comic opera. Reich purchased some radium, brought it into his orgone room, then before anyone knew what was happening, the OR (orgone energy), in combating the NR (nuclear energy), ran amok. It unexpectedly turned into DOR ("deadly orgone energy") and the entire laboratory crew came down with "ORANUR sickness."

These events were summed up in a brief notice titled "Emergency at Orgonon." It is dated May 12, 1952, and reads as follows:

> Since March 21, 1952, an acute emergency exists at Orgonon [the name of Reich's headquarters in Rangeley]. The emergency is due to severe Oranur activity. This activity set in a few hours after the tornado developed in the Middle West on March 21. The details of the emergency which developed from high-pitched Oranur activity will be reported in the second report on the Oranur experiment which is due to be published sometime during October, 1952, or sometime in 1953.
>
> The routine work at Orgonon has collapsed. Several workers had to abandon their jobs. Most buildings at Orgonon became uninhabitable. No work could be done in these buildings up to date. It is uncertain when circumstances will return to normal, if at all, and it is also uncertain what exactly has caused the emergency.
>
> The work had to be contracted to the necessary minimum and priority has been given to activities which promise elucidation and mastery of the situation.

Of course, one way to find out exactly what had happened would have been to call in a nuclear physicist, but Reich apparently didn't deem this necessary. Presumably, the situation was eventually mastered, the mystery was fully explained, and the work proceeded with greater caution.

POSTSCRIPT

Reich went on to invent a rain-making device, one of the first of his CORE. (Cosmic Orgone Engineering) projects. Irwin Ross, in a long and amusing article on Reich (*N. Y. Post, Sunday Magazine Section*, Sept. 5, 1954) described the device as follows:

'. . a bank of long hollow pipes tilting at the sky and sections of hollow cable, all of which are mounted on a metal box; it resembles a stylized version of an anti-aircraft gun, and works with surpassing ease. The clouds are not sprayed with any substance; the hollow pipes merely draw orgone out of them—thus weakening their cohesive power and eventually causing them to break up.

At that time three of Reich's cloudbusters were operating in different parts of Maine, two others in North Carolina. It was raining furiously when Irwin Ross visited Orgonon, and when Ross asked Reich if his devices were responsible, the scientist modestly assured him that they were. "But did you have to produce so *much* rain?" Ross asked. "Well," Reich replied, "you know, we haven't yet learned to control it completely."

In 1954 the Food and Drug Administration brought suit against Reich, his wife Ilse Ollendorff, and the Wilhelm Reich Foundation, to prevent interstate shipping of orgone energy accumulators and all literature mentioning orgone energy. The FDA estimated that more than a thousand of the accumulators had been rented or sold. After a series of carefully conducted tests, research scientists for the FDA concluded that "there is no such energy as orgone and that Orgone Energy Accumulator devices are worthless in the treatment of any disease or disease condition of man. Irreparable harm may result to persons who abandon or postpone rational medical treatment while pinning their faith on worthless devices such as these."

Reich chose to ignore the injunction and an Orgone Legal Fund, headed by the cartoonist William Steig, began raising money for the trial. It took place in May, 1956, at Portland, Maine, with Reich acting as his own attorney. After deliberating twenty minutes the federal jury returned a verdict of guilty. Reich was given a two-year prison sentence, his foundation was fined $10,000, and his associate, Dr. Michael Silvert, received a year and a day in jail. Reich appealed of course.

Because the federal injunction ordered the destruction of many of Reich's books that contain little mention of orgone energy, the case soon acquired a civil rights aspect that had nothing to do with a scientific evaluation of Reich's work. The American Civil Liberties Union issued a rebuke and protesting letters appeared in various liberal journals (*e.g. New Leader*, July 30, 1956). See Steig's letter in *Time*, June 25, 1956, in which he states, "Reich's great findings are factual, demonstrable, irrefutable, as were those of Galileo. How much longer will it be before officials, the press, the public shake off their apathy, accept the largesse of orgonomy, and fight to defend it?"

Reich expressed his opinion that there was a "Red Fascist" (i.e., Communist) group within the FDA, seeking access to his unpublished papers in order to learn the secret "Y" factor of his orgone energy motor. This motor presumably runs on orgone energy and offers promise of immense power.

Reich's life ended in tragedy. Unable to get published in mainstream journals, he came more and more to resemble a movie version of the mad scientist. He announced his discovery that his cloudbuster attracted EAs (Energy Alphas), Reich's term for UFOs. EAs, he said, were propelled by orgone motors that gave off vast quantities of DOR (Deadly Orgone Energy). Growing steadily more paranoid, Reich convinced himself that evil aliens in spaceships were spying on him and trying to destroy his work with deadly rays. Fortunately, his cloudbuster drained DOR from the spaceship motors and caused the EAs to flee.

In 1954 he recorded in his notebooks: "Tonight for the first time in the history of man, the war waged for ages by living beings from outer space upon the earth was reciprocated. . . . with positive results." This memorable battle against UFOs is dramatically described by Reich's son Peter in A *Book of Dreams*, a biography of his father.

Reich's last and craziest book, *Contact with Space*, was published posthumously in a limited edition. It tells of his efforts to save the world from the CORE (Cosmic Orgony Energy) men, Reich's term for the aliens from space. "On March 20, 1956, 10 P.M.," the book opens, "a thought of a very remote possibility entered my mind, which I fear will never leave me again. Am I a spaceman? Do I belong to a new race on earth, bred by men from outer space in embraces with earth women?" What inspired this thought? It was seeing the science-fiction film *The Day the Earth Stood Still*, about a spaceman who comes to Earth in a flying saucer to save us from self-destruction in a nuclear war. "All through the film," Reich says, "I had a distinct impression that it was a bit of *my story* which was depicted there, even the actor's expressions and looks reminded me and others of myself as I had appeared 15 to 20 years ago."

In 1956 the Food and Drug Administration, convinced that orgone boxes were damaging the health of gullible people by keeping them from needed medical care, ordered Reich to stop shipping them across state lines. Reich defied the injunction and was hauled off to court. The court proceedings sketch a picture of a man seriously ill with delusions of grandeur and persecution. Reich entered Lewisburg Federal Penitentiary persuaded that President Eisenhower, whom he greatly admired, knew of his genius and would pardon him. Reich died in prison of a heart attack, at the age of 60, a few weeks before he was to be released.

Orgonomy is still a flourishing cult. Reich's books are back in print. A raft of biographies have been published about him, as well as dozens of books defending his work. In 1967 the remnant faithful founded *The Journal of Orgonomy*, and a year later the American College of Orgonomy. In 1987 it moved its headquarters from Manhattan to near Princeton, New Jersey. Patricia Humphrey, wife of New Hampshire's Republican senator Gordon Humphrey, was chairperson of a committee that raised more than $2.5 million to finance construction of the new headquarters. The Wilhelm Reich Museum, in Rangeley, Maine, remains open to the public and is offering annual summer programs.

NOTES

1. The history of modern physics is spotted with reports of non-existent radiations, and it is not unusual for the discoverer to attribute dowsing and similar occult phenomena to them. A good example is the nineteenth century discovery of a force called "Od" by German physicist Baron Karl von Reichenbach. Oddly enough, other scientists were unable to duplicate the baron's experiments.

In 1903 Prosper Blondlot, a reputable French physicist at the University of Nancy, detected what he called "N" (for Nancy) rays. Scores of papers describing the curious properties of N rays appeared in French journals and the French Academy actually awarded Blondlot a prize for his discovery. The *coup de grace* was deftly executed by American physicist Robert W. Wood (best known to laymen as the author of *How to Tell the Birds from the Flowers*) when he called upon Blondlot at his laboratory. While Blondlot was observing and describing an N-ray spectrum, Wood slyly removed an essential prism from the apparatus. This had no effect on what poor Blondlot fancied he was seeing! See Wood's letter on the episode, *Nature*, Vol. 70, 1904, p. 530, and chapter 17 of William Seabrook's biography, *Dr. Wood*, 1941.

NINETEEN

FREUD, FLIESS, AND EMMA'S NOSE

Starting with the Summer 1993 issue of The Skeptical Inquirer, *I have contributed a regular column to this lively, now bi-monthly, magazine. The following short essay appeared in the summer of 1984. Since then, I am
delighted to report, Freud's reputation as a scientist has continued its rapid
downhill slide.*

Elizabeth M. Thorton contributed substantially to the slide with her book
The Freudian Fallacy *(1984). Branko Grünbaum followed his massive attack
on Freud,* Foundations of Psychoanalysis, *with another resounding blast,* Vali-
dation in the Clinical Theory of Psychoanalysis *(1993). Of dozens of recent
books highly critical of Freud, I particularly recommend Robert Wilcocks's*
Maelzel's Chess Player: Sigmund Freud and the Rhetoric of Deceit *(1994).*

*A good roundup account of how rapidly intellectuals and young psychia-
trists are dumping Freud is* Time Magazine's *cover story "Is Freud Dead?"
(November 29, 1993). In December 1995 the Library of Congress decided to
postpone its exhibit on Freud that was scheduled to open in the fall of 1996.
The decision was in response to an angry petition signed by 42 scholars including Gloria Steinem, Oliver Sacks, and Peter Swales. They were alarmed
over the number of Freudians on the advisory committee, and feared that the
exhibit would be a biased effort to shore up a dying cult of psychoanalyis. See
"Freud May Be Dead But His Critics Still Kick," by Dinita Smith, in* The
New York Times *(December 10, 1995), and "The Trouble with Sigmund," in*
Newsweek *(December 18, 1995).*

*Your manuscript is both good and original. But the part that is good is
not original, and the part that is original is not good.*
—SAMUEL JOHNSON

For several decades Freud's reputation has been steadily going downhill. One reason surely has been the realization by leading feminists that Freud never rose above Victorian male chauvinism, but the main reason is much stronger. It is the growing awareness that Freud had only the flimsiest understanding of how to test a conjecture. Over and over again he tossed out brilliant guesses; ingenious, yes, but with an absence of empirical underpinning exceeded only by his dogmatic claims of certitude.

On matters for which he is given the most credit, such as the influence of repressed memories on behavior, Freud took over a commonly accepted opinion. You'll find long discussions of unconscious causes of psychosomatic ills in William James's *Principles of Psychology*, published ten years before Freud began to invent his theories. It is where Freud departed from his colleagues that he should be judged, and it is precisely these departures that are coming to be seen, as Karl Popper and Peter Medawar have long insisted, as little more than colorful mythology projected by a neurotic genius. Even Freud's theory of dreams is now under fire, as recent research suggests that dreams may be mostly random by-products of the brain's process of clearing its circuits and that trying to recall dreams may actually harm a patient.

In a chapter of my *Mathematical Carnival* I tell of Freud's strange and passionate friendship with one of the giants of German crackpottery. He was a Berlin nose-and-throat doctor named Wilhelm Fliess—two years younger than Freud, handsome, charming, conceited, paranoid (he later thought Freud was trying to kill him), and utterly irresponsible. It is hard to believe, but for more than ten years he was Freud's most intimate confidant.

Fliess suffered from two major obsessions. He believed that all living processes conform to two cycles: a male cycle of 23 days, and a female cycle of 28 days. The theory became known as biorhythm, and later his disciples added a third cycle.

Fliess's second obsession was the unshakable conviction that all neuroses and sexual abnormalities are intimately related to the nose. He diagnosed such ills by examining a nose's interior and thought he could cure these ills by cauterizing or applying cocaine to the nose's "genital spots." Masturbation, for example, altered the left middle turbinate bone in its frontal third, and this in turn caused stomach pains. In cases of severe symptoms he removed a piece of nasal bone. Young Freud was enthusiastic about both of these great scientific discoveries. At one time he even feared he would die at 51 because 23 plus 28 equals 51. Several times he allowed Fliess to operate on his nose.

Freud apparently destroyed all of Fliess's letters, but much of Freud's side of the correspondence has survived. His daughter Anna edited a selection of these letters for a book, but she suppressed the letters and passages she considered damaging to her father. These censored writings came to light in Jeffrey Moussaieff Masson's explosive book, *The Assault on Truth*. (1984). The book generated an enormous controversy in newspapers and magazines, including two long articles in the *New Yorker* in December 1983, in which Janet Malcolm drew unflattering portraits of Masson and his chief rival in the debunking of Freud, Peter Swales. Psychiatrists outside the Freudian tradition (they are the vast majority) are reacting with surprise and glee, but the elderly custodians of Freudian orthodoxy are doing their best to minimize the book's impact.

There were two whopping reversals in Freud's early speculations. He stopped using hypnosis when he found it unreliable for gaining access to a patient's real past; and he abandoned his strongly held theory—he once likened it to finding the source of the Nile—that large numbers of neurotic women suffer from suppressed memories of being violently raped by their fathers. Masson argues that Freud did not abandon the second view for scientific reasons but for a variety of unconscious personal motives, and that a horrendous event involving his idolized Fliess played a pivotal role in this decision.

Freud had a young woman patient, Emma Eckstein, of whom he was extremely fond but with whom he was making little progress. To cure her hysterical symptoms, mainly severe stomach pains, he brought Fliess to Vienna in 1895 to remove the offending bone from Emma's nose. As suppressed letters to Fliess revealed, Freud had full confidence in this crazy operation. When it was over, Fliess returned to Berlin but poor Emma's nose began to hemorrhage. The mysterious, massive bleeding refused to stop, and Masson prints stomach-turning reports that Freud sent Fliess, which read like passages in a horror-fantasy potboiler. Not until Emma was on the brink of death did Freud finally seek the help of a reputable surgeon—a doctor who had strongly opposed the original operation. He opened Emma's nose. Inside, wadded into the nasal cavity, he found half a meter of gauze that Fliess forgot to remove. Freud was so stricken that he had to leave the room and imbibe some booze.

"So we had done her an injustice," Freud wrote to Fliess. "[The bleeding] was not at all abnormal, rather a piece of iodoform gauze had gotten torn off as you were removing it, and stayed in for 14 days, preventing healing. . . . How wrong I was to urge you to operate in a foreign city where you could not follow through on the case."

Emma recovered, though disfigured for life because the loss of bone caused one side of her nose to cave in. Although Freud originally attributed the bleeding to Fliess's bungling, he made clear that he considered it one of those unfortunate mistakes that even the best of surgeons sometimes make. A year later, however, Freud had found a better way to absolve Fliess of guilt. He decided that the bleeding was entirely hysterical, springing from the young woman's desire to be loved. This had been Fliess's opinion, which he naturally related to critical days in her 23- and 28-day cycles.

In letters censored by Anna, Freud tells Fliess about his "completely surprising explanation of Eckstein's hemorrhages—which will give you much pleasure. . . . You were right, that her episodes of bleeding were hysterical, were occasioned by longing, and probably occurred at the sexually relevant times (the woman, out of resistance, has not yet supplied me with the dates)."

These "relevant dates" refer, of course, to Fliess's numerology. Emma almost bled to death because she wanted Freud at her bedside! He reports happily on his discovery that Emma had nosebleeds when she was a child. "As far as the blood is concerned," he assures Fliess, "you are completely without blame!" Masson believes that this attempt to exonerate Fliess, along with other personal matters involving Freud's relatives—not clinical data— led Freud to his new theory that sexual fantasies are more important causes of neurotic behavior than actual episodes (such as Emma's operation) in the past. He thinks this shift of emphasis was damaging to the analytic movement, and he sides with those modern researchers who are trying to move the emphasis back to traumatic events that really did occur.

It took Freud more than ten years to realize that his dear friend was a crank. Fliess was the first to break the bond, accusing Freud of abusing him and stealing his ideas. In my chapter on Fliess in *Mathematical Carnival* you'll find the details of how, many years later, Freud suddenly fainted during a lunch with Jung at a hotel in Munich. He told Ernest Jones (who devotes a chapter to Fliess in his classic biography of Freud) that he fainted because an argument with Jung had reminded him of a violent quarrel with Fliess at the same hotel.

Fliess's mad cycle-theory is still going great guns in the biorhythm movement, now unregrettably fading, but I know of no current boosters of his nasal theory. A quack doctor could make a fortune by reviving it. The background material is readily available, in monstrous detail, in Fliess's untranslated tomes and papers. A popular book titled *The Nose Knows* could outfleece any book on acupuncture or homeopathy. Illustrations showing how bones of the nose connect with the penis and vagina would provide marvelous erotic fare. Plastic surgeons could combine the nose therapy with remodeling the nose to improve the face. After it became a Hollywood fad, NOVA could produce a great documentary on it.

It is hard to know which deserves the stronger condemnation: Freud's childish credulity or the shameful way his daughter and other guardians of the orthodox analytic flame have done their best to prevent the lurid facts about Freud's early career from reaching the general public.

POSTSCRIPT

Janet Malcolm's *New Yorker* hatchet job on Jeffrey Masson and Peter Swales was published as a book: *In the Freud Archives* (Knopf, 1984). Needless to say, both her book and Masson's were widely reviewed—traditional Freudians attacking Masson and praising Malcolm, and anti-Freudians commenting from a reverse perspective.

The Complete Letters of Sigmund Freud to Wilhelm Fliess, translated and edited by Masson, was issued by Harvard University Press in 1985. It, too, received extensive critical attention, notably by Charles Rycroft (*New York Review of Books*, May 30, 1985) and by Daniel Goleman in his cover article for the *New York Times Magazine* (March 17, 1985; see also the Letters section of April 21).

The strongest, most thorough attack on psychoanalysis to appear at that time was *Foundations of Psychoanalysis* (University of California Press, 1984), by the distinguished philosopher of science Adolf Grünbaum. His book has two central themes. Karl Popper long claimed that psychoanalysis is unfalsifiable and therefore empty of empirical content. Not so, says Grünbaum. Its claims *are* testable, and such testing has falsified them. Of the many reviews of this book I particularly recommend Frank Sulloway's, in *Free Inquiry* (Fall 1985) and the same magazine's interview with Grünbaum (Winter 1985/86).

Jonathan Lieberson, reviewing Grünbaum's book for the *New York Review of Books* (January 31, 1985) summed up the case against psychoanalysis this way:

> The profession has become increasingly isolated from organic medicine; it has found no new Freud; its theoretical development has been stagnant. It is arguable that what seems evidently true in Freud, such as his notion of repression or his emphasis on the unconscious and on the irrational springs of much of human behavior, has long been known and that Freud introduced an unnecessary technical language and a dubious metaphysical backdrop to describe these phenomena. And it is possible that psychoanalytic therapy will be replaced in time by shorter therapies of various kinds and by psychopharmacology derived from new developments in the neurosciences.

POSTSCRIPT (1995)

An angry Masson sued Ms. Malcolm for putting quotation marks around statements he never made, and which he considered libelous. This celebrated case was in the courts for a decade before it ended in a mistrial in 1993. The jury found that Malcolm had indeed misrepresented Masson in five quotations that were false and defamatory, but it deadlocked on how much money to award him. I do not know if Masson is planning another lawsuit. Meanwhile he has published an autobiography, The Masking and Unmasking of a Psychiatrist.

For an attack on Freud's bizarre dream theory, see two of my Skeptical Inquirer *columns: "Waking Up from Freud's Theory of Dreams" (November/ December 1995), and "Post-Freudian Dream Theory" (January/February 1996).*

TWENTY

WILLIAM JAMES AND
MRS. PIPER

Although my admiration for William James is unbounded—who among Ameri-
can philosophers wrote more clearly, eloquently, and entertainingly?—I fault
him on two grounds. In this book's essay on "Why I Am Not a Pragmatist," I
explain why I think James's effort to redefine empirical truth as the passing of
tests rather than as correspondence with an outside world, was a disaster.
Here I criticize James for his gullibility with respect to psychic phenomena.

Had James been better informed about techniques of deception, as prac-
ticed by magicians and mediums, he would not have been so impressed by
Mrs. Piper's carefully contrived persona. Moreover, James had only a weak
comprehension of how to conduct controlled tests of mediums. My long essay
on his curious bond with Mrs. Piper ran as a two-part article in Free Inquiry
(Spring and Summer 1992).

I should be willing now to stake as much money on Mrs. Piper's honesty
as on that of anyone I know, and am quite satisfied to leave my reputa-
tion for wisdom or folly, so far as human nature is concerned, to stand or
fall by this declaration.
    —WILLIAM JAMES *(Proceedings of the Society for Psychical*
                Research, Vol. 6, 1889/90, p. 654)

William James (1842–1910), consid-
ered by many to be America's most distinguished philosopher, psychologist,
and pioneer psychic investigator, was a Platonist in the following sense. He
believed that the world open to our experience and scientific probing is only
a small fraction of a much vaster realm about which we know nothing. Our
universe, he liked to say, is a tiny island in a vast Mother Sea. Such a vision

may lead to a healthy acceptance of strange phenomena as worthy of investigation. It can also lead, as in James's case, to a careless acceptance of anomalies without first making a strenuous effort to be sure such phenomena exist.

James's Platonism helps explain his lifelong fascination with mediums. His father, Henry James, Sr., was a spiritualist who wrote a book about Emanuel Swedenborg, the famous Swedish trance medium. Although not in any sense a Christian, William James believed in an afterlife, which he defended with a clever model of the brain in his little book *Human Immortality*. He was a founder and life member of the ASPR (American Society for Psychical Research). Many of his best friends, notably the British psychic investigators Frederic Myers and Edmund Gurney, were spiritualists.

James was never able to persuade himself that mediums channeled voices from the dead, though he always remained open to this possibility. He was, however, firmly convinced that some mediums had paranormal powers, even though their "controls" were perhaps what he called "counterfeit" personalities conjured up by a medium's subconscious mind.

I will argue that James, though a brilliant and superb writer, was too gullible and too ignorant of methods of deception to understand the ease with which intelligent persons can be flim-flammed by crafty charlatans. As all magicians know, men of science are the easiest of all people to fool. Electrons and microbes don't cheat. Psychics do. My essay will focus on the one medium who played the dominant role in James's psychic investigations, Mrs. Leonora Piper. For twenty-five years, until his death in 1910, James attended hundreds of Mrs. Piper's séances without ever reaching a firm conclusion about the nature of her spirit controls. "Baffled" is the word he frequently used to describe his state of mind.

Mrs. Piper is still considered the most famous, most trustworthy, direct-voice medium who ever lived. No one ever caught her in outright fraud. Unlike other famous mediums of the time, she never produced physical phenomena such as levitated tables, floating trumpets, luminous ectoplasm from her nose, rappings, cold breezes, spirit photographs, unearthly music, strange odors, or other wonders which, for reasons spiritualists were never able to explain, took place in near total darkness. To James's credit he was strongly skeptical of such manifestations and did not hesitate to brand as charlatans such mediums as Madam Blavatsky and Eusapia Palladino.[1]

Mrs. Piper simply went into trances, during which discarnates took over her vocal chords or seized her hand, which would rapidly write what the spirits dictated. After a trance she insisted she recalled nothing of what had transpired. On one occasion James asked the control to order her (like a hypnotist commanding a mesmerized subject) to remember everything, but the ploy did not work. We shall see later why such claimed amnesia is of great advantage to a medium.

Leonora Evelina Simonds (1859–1950) was born in Nashua, New Hampshire. She never finished high school. When twenty-two she married William J. Piper, identified in some references as a Boston store clerk and in others as a Boston tailor. (It would be surprising if his middle name were James.) For a while the Pipers lived with William's parents. William's father, a salesman in a Boston bookstore, was an ardent spiritualist. Later William and Leonora moved to Pinckney Street, in Boston's Beacon Hill section, where they raised two daughters, Minerva and Alta. Alta wrote *The Life and Work of Mrs. Piper* in 1929. Both daughters became professional musicians. I do not know when or where either died.

Mrs. Piper was tall, stout, and handsome, with blue eyes and brown hair; she was good-natured, self-possessed, matronly, modest, and shrewd. In his *History of Spiritualism* Conan Doyle says a head injury preceded her discovery that she could contact the dead. Alta Piper, in her biography of her mother, describes the injury as a mysterious sharp blow over her right ear that occurred when Leonora was eight, followed by a voice that said, "Aunt Sara, not dead, but with you still." Later Leonora learned of her aunt's death.

In 1884 an ice sled struck Leonora, injuring her internally. Soon thereafter she developed an ovarian tumor, which was later removed along with her fallopian tubes. Her spiritualist father-in-law persuaded her to seek advice about the tumor from J. E. Cocke, a blind medium and healer who liked to develop mediumship in others. On her second visit she fell into a trance. After awakening she was told that a young Indian girl with the improbable name of Chlorine had spoken through her. Mrs. Piper was soon giving her own private séances, charging each client (as she liked to call a sitter) a dollar per sitting. This would have been a considerable sum in today's currency. In later years the fee was raised to $20. The Society of Psychical Research (SPR) in England eventually provided her with a trust income sufficient to support her and her two daughters.

James's mother-in-law was so impressed after attending a Piper séance (the control told her where to find a lost bank book) that she recommended the medium to William. James began attending and soon encouraged a raft of relatives and friends to take part in Mrs. Piper's sittings. Alice, James's wife, was quickly convinced that Mrs. Piper was indeed channeling voices from the dead. As one of James's biographers puts it, Alice was "credulous" where William was merely "curious."

After her fame spread abroad, Mrs. Piper made three trips to England under the auspices of the SPR. During an 1889–1890 visit, she and her daughters stayed in the home of psychic researcher and poet, Frederic Myers, and later in the homes of physicist Oliver Lodge and other SPR members. Her next two trips were in 1906 and 1909. All her séances, on these trips, were supervised by the SPR. In England her two most famous converts, who became absolutely convinced she was channeling discarnates, were Myers and Lodge.

In America her most eminent convert was James Hyslop, a professor of logic and ethics at Columbia University, a man as gullible and ignorant of magic as Doyle. Through Mrs. Piper he conversed with his mother, brother, and uncles. He wrote in *Life After Death*, one of his many worthless books:

> I regard the existence of discarnate spirits as scientifically proved, and I no longer refer to the sceptic as having any right to speak on the subject. Any man who does not accept the existence of discarnate spirits and the proof of it is either ignorant or a moral coward. I give him short shrift, and do not propose any longer to argue with him.

Mrs. Piper liked to begin a séance by asking for a personal possession of either the sitter or the spirit the client wished to contact. It could be a watch, ring, necktie, lock of hair, sweater, and so on. (Getting the right vibes from such an object is known in the trade as "psychometry.") In his autobiography Lodge says that it took Mrs. Piper a long time to move in and out of a trance, "going through contortions which were sometimes painful to watch." James speaks of the "great muscular unrest" that preceded her trance. Her pupils dilated, she moaned and sobbed, her eyes rolled upward, and her ears wiggled violently in a way James says she could not move them when awake. How did James know? Mrs. Piper said so. Later, her transitions between the trance state and awake became much calmer, although curiously it always took her longer to emerge from the state than to go into it. In these later years her breathing became slower during a trance, and she snored throughout. She claimed to feel a snapping in her head when the trance ended. Sitters would witness weeping, disjointed mutterings, and exclamations of pleasure, pain, and sometimes disgust; her eyes would be open and staring, and saliva would drool from her lips.

Alta Piper writes that when her mother came out of a trance she always saw people in the room as small and black, and often greeted a sitter with "Oh! How black you are!" Alta adds that her mother "always resumes the conversation at that point where it was broken off before the sitting began."

James and others tried to hypnotize Mrs. Piper, but she never went beyond a light sleep, her body limp and unlike her trance condition. During one trance she ignored a small cut James made on her left wrist. It did not bleed, Alta tells us, but when her mother awoke it "bled freely," leaving a permanent scar. When a lighted match was pressed on her arm, her control said it "felt cool." She remained undisturbed when a needle was pushed into her hand and when a French investigator stuck a feather up her nose. On the other hand, she reacted if the doorbell rang. On one occasion her control tested a medicine he advised a sitter to take by having Mrs. Piper dip her finger into the liquid then put her finger to her forehead, after which he declared that the medicine had been properly prepared. When a piece of onion was put in her mouth, she smacked her lips and the control said he could taste it.

Mrs. Piper's voice, like the voices of today's trance channelers, always altered when different controls took over. Males spoke like males, children like children. Irishmen had Irish brogues. Frenchmen and Italians had French and Italian accents. Lodge had no doubt he conversed with his dead sister Anne because he recognized her "well remembered voice."

When Mrs. Piper later lived in Arlington Heights, near Boston, her séances were held in an upstairs room she called her Red Room because its wallpaper and furnishing were red. A clock in the darkened room was kept illuminated. One skeptic dared suggest that this was so she could know when to end a séance, since she preferred that it not go beyond an hour.

After Chlorine, Mrs. Piper's earliest controls included Martin Luther, Commodore Cornelius Vanderbilt, Longfellow, George Washington, Lincoln, Loretta Pachini (a young Italian), J. Sebastian Bach, and Sarah Siddons (an English actress). After they stopped coming, the next and most famous of all her controls was an eighteenth-century French physician named Dr. Phinuit (pronounced Fih-*nuee*), who had died of leprosy. His full name, he said, was Jean Phinuit Scliville. Phinuit had a deep, gruff voice. Oddly, Phinuit sounds very much like the French physician Dr. Albert G. Finnett (pronounced *Finee*), the control of the blind medium who launched Mrs. Piper on her career.

Dr. Phinuit said he came from Metz, but strenuous efforts to find evidence of a doctor by that name who lived in Metz were fruitless even though the doctor gave his birth and death dates. Phinuit spoke English with a stage French accent, but was unable to speak French even though Mrs. Piper said she had studied French for two years. Nor could Phinuit understand James when he spoke in French, or recognize the names of French drugs. Later he said he had lived so long in Marseilles, in an English speaking colony, that he had lost all knowledge of French except for such phrases as *bonjour* and *au revoir!*

The next major control, who continued for a time in parallel with Phinuit, was known as G. P., the initials of George Pelham. The name was a pseudonym used by the ASPR to conceal the identity of George Pellew, a young lawyer by training but a writer by profession. He wrote a dissertation on Jane Austen and published two books, *In Castle and Gable* and *Women of the Commonwealth*. Pellew died in 1882 at age thirty-two in New York City after falling off a horse. A month later he turned up as one of Mrs. Piper's favorite controls.

Pellew had been a good friend of Richard Hodgson, a British psychic investigator who came to Boston in 1887 to serve as secretary of the ASPR and editor of its journal. He died in 1905 of heart failure while playing handball. Hodgson and Pellew became friends, often arguing about life after death, in which Hodgson believed but Pellew did not. When Pellew began coming through Mrs. Piper, Hodgson was at first so suspicious that he hired detectives to shadow Mr. and Mrs. Piper for several weeks to make sure they were not secretly researching "evidential" information about his friend. But when Mrs. Piper put Hodgson in touch with the spirit of a former girlfriend in Australia (Hodgson came from Melbourne) who informed him for the first time of her death, Hodgson abandoned all doubts.

Early in her career Mrs. Piper channeled only voices, but gradually the voices gave way to automatic writing. During her voice period the séances were either not recorded or notes were taken by stenographers, but of course the automatic writing provided its own record of what the controls said. Unfortunately records were seldom kept of what the sitters said.

During a trance Mrs. Piper would turn her head to one side, on a pillow, while her right hand rapidly scribbled messages. The writing was often illegible and subject to different interpretations. Frequently she pressed so hard that a pencil would break. At other times her hand would violently sweep the writing paper off the table. For a while Mrs. Piper spoke and wrote at the same time. On at least two known occasions, three sitters received simultaneous communications, a vocal one from Phinuit, a written one from G. P. through one hand, and another written by a deceased sister of the sitter through the other hand. Writing with both hands was not hard to do because Mrs. Piper was ambidextrous. She was normally left-handed, but wrote and sewed with her right, and could handle a fork equally well with either hand.

One time Mrs. Piper pressed a sheet to her forehead and wrote on it in mirror-reversed script. (Try this and you will be surprised at how easily it can be done with paper on your forehead.) Mrs. Piper's right hand did more than write while she was in a trance. It also functioned as a strange kind of telephone to the controls. If sitters wanted to ask a question, they held the hand close to their mouth and spoke into it with a loud voice.

In 1896 the controls became a group called the Imperators. They had earlier been the controls of William Stainton Moses, a famous British medium. They were immortals on a higher plane who had such names as Imperator, Rector, Director, and Mentor, and who talked constantly about God, heaven, and the angels. In 1905 this group (someone suggested it should have been called the Imposters) gave way to the dead Richard Hodgson. However, Rector would appear first, then locate Hodgson in the spirit world and bring him to Mrs. Piper. At the end of a séance he would return to pronounce a benediction.

James had known Hodgson well. The spirit of Hodgson did his best to persuade James it was actually he, but James never budged from the fence. Whenever he asked Hodgson for details about the other side, Hodgson either driveled nonsense or refused to answer. After Hodgson vanished, there were many other controls, including the dead Frederic Myers and Edmund Gurney.

At about this time England's SPR began experimenting with what it called "cross correspondence." The idea was to have Mrs. Piper and several other mediums in distant localities seek simultaneous messages from the same discarnate. The messages were then checked for correlations. Doyle gives some examples in his history of spiritualism that would impress nobody except himself. For example, Mrs. Piper would get a message with the word *violet* in it. Another medium would channel a message that referred to "violet buds." (For a detailed analysis of these correspondences, see the book by Amy Tanner discussed in my epilogue.)

Every psychic investigator of Mrs. Piper was impressed by her simplicity and honesty. It never occurred to them that no charlatan ever achieves great success by acting like a charlatan. No professional spy acts like a spy. No card cheat behaves at the table like a card cheat. No successful con artist acts like a con artist. No fake psychic ever gives the impression of being anything but honest.

What convinced so many intelligent persons that the dead actually spoke through Mrs. Piper? It was the astonishing amount of information she provided that she seemed to have no normal way of acquiring. Even James was persuaded that she got this information by paranormal means, although he doubted it came from discarnates. A common conjecture of the time was that Mrs. Piper was telepathic and clairvoyant, picking up data from the minds of sitters, or from the minds of others far away, or from a clairvoyant viewing of letters, tombstones, and so on. It was even suggested that her controls had such ESP. James did not buy this theory. He was inclined to believe that she was tapping into some part of the transcendent Mother Sea. Using diagrams and playing cards, he once gave Mrs. Piper tests for telepathy and clairvoyance, all of which she totally failed.

How can a hard-nose skeptic like myself account for the seeming flood of accurate data that constantly flowed from Mrs. Piper's controls?

A reading of verbatim records of Mrs. Piper's séances shows that her controls did an enormous amount of what was then called "fishing" and today is called "cold reading." First a vague statement is made, followed by more precise statements depending on a sitter's reactions. Mrs. Piper liked to hold a client's hand throughout the sitting, or even to place the hand against her forehead. This made it easy to detect muscular reactions even when a sitter remained silent.

During a trance Mrs. Piper's eyes were often only half-closed, so it was also easy for her to observe how a sitter responded to fishing. If a reaction, often a spoken one, is unfavorable, the medium at once takes off on a different tack. If the reaction is favorable, the medium knows he or she is on the right track. Many tests have shown that victims of skillful cold reading are never aware of how they subtly guide what the cold reader is saying. Afterward they will vigorously deny they made statements indicating whether the medium was right or wrong, and are astounded when they listen to a recording.

Dr. Phinuit had a habit of babbling on and on, making inane conversation while he shamelessly fished. If he made an outright mistake, he followed with silly excuses. Often when asked a question he could not answer, he would profess deafness and leave. His ignorance of science and literature was monumental, yet he was well informed about hats and clothing! Frequently a client would get nothing from Mrs. Piper, James wrote, but "tiresome twaddle" and "unknown names and trivial talk."[2] To any skeptic, this indicated either that the client was carefully uncooperative during a cold reading, that Mrs. Piper had no advance information, or both.

When you read books about Mrs. Piper by believers, such as the anthology *William James on Psychical Research*, edited by Gardner Murphy and Robert Ballou, you will learn only about her hits—nothing about her abundant misses. On one occasion Mrs. Piper told James that a certain ring had been stolen, but it was later found in James's house. On three occasions Phinuit tried to guess the contents of a sealed envelope in James's possession: All three were failures even though Phinuit contacted Hannah Wild, the very person who wrote James the letter! In a typical séance hundreds of statements would be made, and there were thousands of séances. By chance alone one would expect some fantastic lucky guesses. The verbatim records reveal a weird mixture of hits and misses. Believers of course forget the misses—"selective amnesia," it has been called—and remember only the hits.

On many occasions a Piper control would *pretend* to be fishing to give the impression that something was partly but not fully known. This is a common dodge of mediums, as well as magicians who perform what in the trade is called a "mental act." For example, when a control tried to give the name of Mrs. James's father, which everyone in the area knew to be Gibbens, the control first tried "Niblin," then "Giblin," before finally getting it right. The name of Herman, a child of James who, as everyone knew, died the previous year, was first spelled "Herrin."

On another occasion James's deceased father thanked William for bringing out a certain book. "What book?" James asked. His father could do no better than spell L-i, the first two letters of the title. The book was *Literary Remains of the Late Henry James*, a collection of his father's papers. Of course the title would have been well known to Mrs. Piper, but James was actually persuaded that she could not be faking her partial guess. Why? Because had she known the complete title she would surely have given it! Phinuit's stumbling, spelling, and otherwise "imperfect ways of bringing out his facts," James wrote, "is a great drawback with most sitters, and yet it is habitual with him." I am reminded of how Merv Griffin, introducing Uri Geller on his television talk show, said the thing that convinced him Geller was not a magician was that a magician's tricks always work, whereas Uri's paranormal feats sometimes fail!

Although true believers were overwhelmed by the accuracy of information coming through Mrs. Piper, skeptics had exactly the opposite reaction. According to Joseph Rinn in his *Sixty Years of Psychic Research*, Hodgson constantly lied in reporting on how members of the Pellew family reacted to what George Pellew said through Mrs. Piper. Hodgson repeatedly spoke of how they confirmed what George's spirit was saying, but exactly the opposite was the case. George's mother called the data "utter drivel." In 1921 Rinn came upon a series of letters written by George's brother Charles when he was a professor of chemistry at Columbia University. (In 1923 Charles succeeded to his British father's title and became Viscount Exmouth and a member of the House of Lords.) The letters had been written to Edward Clodd, author of an anti-spiritualist book called *The Question: If a Man Die, Shall He Live Again?*— published in London in 1917. The letters were later printed in an annual of London's Rationalist Press Association. Here is the full text of one of Charles's letters, sent to Clodd in 1918:

I must apologize for delaying so long in answering your letter of inquiry about Mrs. Piper, but I have been engaged in some extremely important professional work, necessitating some weeks' stay in Washington, and have only just got a chance to clear up my correspondence.

My brother G. P. died very suddenly, by accident, some twenty-five years ago. He was an exceedingly clever fellow, of remarkable literary ability, and had written one or two good books, had taken the prize at Harvard for an essay which, together with his class O.K., is still passed down by the staff of their English Department as indicating the "high-water mark" of student ability.

At his funeral, one friend, a famous novelist (Mr. Howells) begged father and myself to have his poems collected and published, saying that he considered two of them as among the very finest sonnets in the English language. A very well-known historian and essayist (John Fiske) told me to be sure and print some essays of his on philosophy, which he assured us were well worth preserving, in permanent form.

The poems were gradually sorted out from various papers and scrapbooks, and a collection of them was published a few months later. We could not, however, put our hands on his philosophical papers, though we heard from various friends who believed they must still be in existence.

A few weeks after George's death, word came to us from some very excitable friends of his in Boston that they had been in communication with his spirit, through the medium Mrs. Piper. One of the first questions asked of him, so we were told, was, "Where are those philosophical notes of yours?" Back came the answer, "At Katonah," this being the name of our country place, not far from New York City. "Whereabouts at Katonah?" "In a tin box, in the corner cupboard in my bedroom," came the reply.

As I remember the story, it was one of his friends, possibly a cousin, who immediately started for Katonah and went to the bedroom, in the corner cupboard, and found the tin dispatch box—*empty*.

The papers themselves, as I only found some twenty years later, when of course their value was entirely gone, were at the time in the possession of one of G. P.'s friends, to whom he had given them before his death.

This was the closest that Mrs. Piper ever came, so far as I know, to saying anything that might conceivably have come from my brother, although for weeks and months, and even years, we were continually bombarded with like reports of interviews of all sorts and conditions of people with him under the auspices of the Psychical Research Society.

After this had been going on for at least fifteen years, my people showed me, one New Year's, a letter they had just received from Hodgson. He reminded them that ever since G. P.'s death his society had been sending them repeatedly the bulletins and reports of the Piper sittings where G. P. was involved and that, undoubtedly, my parents had long been convinced, as was every other intelligent and unprejudiced reader, that they had at last been able to prove, without question, the existence of G. P.'s own self in the other kingdom, etc., and that, while of course the mere question of a few dollars was not of any importance to any of them, he did hope that my father and mother would become regular members of the Psychical Research Society, and have their names published as such, to show their acceptance of the accuracy of the conversations with my brother.

To which Mrs. Pellew, George's mother, replied briefly, and, it seems to me, not without a very considerable amount of intelligence and good, sound common sense. It was to the effect "that they had been receiving, for years past, numerous communications from the society concerning supposed interviews of various people with my brother, and some of these they had read more or less carefully. Everybody, however, who had ever met G. P. in life had always been impressed by the fact that his keen, clear, brilliant intellect was unfortunately kept down by a weak body. And that nothing could possibly convince her, who knew G. P. so well, that, when that wonderful mind and spirit of his was freed from the trammels of the flesh, it could under any conceivable circumstances, have given vent to such utter drivel and inanity as purported, in those communications, to have been uttered by him," and they did not join the society.

For my own part, I was telling this story once, before a meeting just addressed by one of Mrs. Piper's most ardent believers, and was informed that I evidently had not, myself, carefully read the reports in question—which was the case. So, next day, I went to the public library and getting hold of some of the *Transactions* of the Psychical Research Society, I hunted round in them to find some characteristic interview with my brother. I soon found one. An old friend, so I gathered, or certainly an acquaintance, was at last put in touch with him, per Mrs. Piper, and began to identify him. "You hear what I say, George?"—"Yes."—"You are sure you understand me?"—"Yes, go ahead."—"Well, George, listen to this carefully: 'Pater hemon.' "—"Pat?"—"Do you understand, George? 'Pater, hemon ho en tois ouranois.' "—"Pat—what is that? I don't quite catch it." I chuckled. Whoever it was answering that fellow, whether Mrs. Piper or Phenuit or anyone else, it was *not George*.

George was a good scholar, and had been at St. Paul's School, Concord, N.H., for at least five years, and had, every Monday morning of his school term, to recite, and hear his classmates recite, the Lord's Prayer in Greek.

Unless I'm very much mistaken, it was some old friend of his who was trying him with the first words, knowing that if George was there he would recognize them *instantly,* as I did some ten or fifteen years later, just seeing them in print this way.

The most curious evidence, to my mind, of the absolute unreliability of any statement of the believers in the Mrs. Piper cult happened to me in connection with these same philosophy papers I spoke about.

I had supposed the Piper nuisance had faded away, not having heard of it for a year or two, when, having run over to Washington to see my people, I was shown a curious letter from Hodgson. It was something to this effect: "Of course they all knew and regretted that my parents so persistently refused to recognize the truth of those wonderful interviews with George, but that now they had some evidence which was convincing—absolute, positive proof. My people knew John Fiske, what a clever, keen mind he had, what a close friend of George he was, and what a hardheaded, practical, unemotional sort of fellow—well, he had at last been persuaded to see Mrs. Piper—much against his wishes—sure that it would amount to nothing—and yet, after a sitting with her, he had come out *absolutely convinced* that he had been talking with his dear old friend George. He had even asked him some questions about points in Revolutionary history, which George had either discovered or was going to discuss with his, George's ancestors, who had been prominent in that period, etc. And really, when John Fiske was so absolutely and completely convinced of the truth of the interview, my own people ought to reconsider their position in the matter."

I told my father to reserve judgment, and a few days afterward returned to New York.

Within a week or two, happening to be at the Century Club at one of their monthly gatherings, I saw big, jolly, burly John Fiske walk into the reading room. I at once hailed him (I had met him only a few times): "How are you, Mr. Fiske? Do you remember me, Charles Pellew? By the way, I hear you've been having a talk recently with my brother George." Fiske stopped—gasped, "Good heavens—your brother George—why, he's been dead for twenty years!" "That's all right," said I; "through Mrs. Piper, I mean." "Oh," and he paused—relaxed—and his whole voice changed. *"That old fraud!"* and he sat down and began to laugh. "Why," I said, "I heard that you said there was no doubt about his being George himself, just as though he was at the other end of a rather poor telephone connection." *"That's a lie,"* he said; "nothing of the sort. I was finally persuaded to see Mrs. Piper, and found her a bright, shrewd, ill-educated, commonplace woman who answered glibly enough questions where guessing was easy, or where she might have obtained previous information. But whenever I asked anything that would be known only to George himself, she was either silent or entirely wrong. For instance, I asked as follows: 'Is this you, George?'—'Yes.'—'You know who I am?'—'Yes, my old friend John Fiske.'—'When did you see me last?'—'In Cambridge, at your house, a few months before I passed over.'—'What sort of house is mine?'—'A wooden house, two stories, hall in the middle, dining room on one side, library and study on the other.' And so it was but *almost all the Cambridge houses are just that style.*

" 'Now, George, you remember seeing me, at my house, at that time?'—'Yes.'—'What was it you came to see me about?' *Perfect blankness.*

" 'Now," said Fiske, "that winter I had just published my book on philosophy, and George had amused himself by writing some very clever, very remarkable papers, in which he criticized my views quite severely. And, before publishing them, he was so afraid of hurting my feelings that the dear old boy wrote me to say he was coming to Cambridge to talk it over with me. He sent me his manuscript, which I read carefully, and then he came on by night from New York, and was at my house soon after breakfast. We talked philosophy all morning and all the afternoon. We went to the library and talked philosophy until nearly twelve o'clock, when I started him home. Now I think if he remembered the date of the visit, and the house and arrangement of the rooms, he might have *had some slight remembrance of what we were talking about.*"

Of course you can use this letter in any way you wish.

Yours very sincerely,
CHARLES E. PELLEW

As Charles's remarkable letter makes plain, Hodgson told outright lies about how Fiske had reacted to the séance he attended. John Fiske was a Harvard philosopher and historian, and a friend of William James. He was a devout theist and a believer in immortality, but he was also less gullible than James with respect to alleged psychic phenomena. Note how Mrs. Piper, who knew no Greek, took the word *Pater*, Greek for "Father" in the opening line of the Lord's Prayer, to refer to someone named Pat!

The tendency of believers to take vague statements uttered by a medium, and then fit circumstances to them, is brought out vividly by Rinn in giving some of Mrs. Piper's remarks that Hyslop considered evidential. Hyslop's dead father, speaking through Mrs. Piper, said that just before his death he had visited Hyslop. Hyslop called this evidential because his father had visited him several years before he died. The father's spirit spoke of a box of minerals he had owned as a boy. Hyslop scored this a hit because his father had owned a box of Indian arrowheads. In his book *Science and a Future Life* Hyslop said it took two years for Mrs. Piper to guess correctly what his uncle died from. Telepathy cannot account for Mrs. Piper's knowledge, Hyslop argued, because it took her twenty sittings to guess his uncle's name. "There was great difficulty in getting the name of my uncle James Carruthers," he wrote. "I had to ask Mrs. Piper's spirit control to spell it out after failing in the first attempt. It was tried again the next day with no results." To a skeptic, this simply indicates that Mrs. Piper, at the time, didn't know the name.

Some notion of Hyslop's competence as an investigator can be gained from his practice of wearing a mask to conceal his identity when he entered a room for a séance, then removing it after Mrs. Piper went into a trance. Hyslop assumed that while in a trance Mrs. Piper could not see him even though her eyes were half-open, and that while in trance she could not recognize his voice! Before she awoke, he put the mask on again. Of course Hyslop had been introduced to Mrs. Piper by Hodgson, who could have provided the medium with all sorts of facts about him.

In *Modern Spiritualism*, Frank Podmore came to the following conclusion after going carefully over the verbatim reports of Mrs. Piper's séances with Hyslop:

> I cannot point to a single instance in which a precise and unambiguous piece of information has been furnished of a kind which could not have proceeded from the medium's own mind, working upon the materials provided and the hints let drop by the sitter.

Romaine Newbold, a philosopher at the University of Pennsylvania, after making many tests of Mrs. Piper, concluded: "In all the years of Mrs. Piper's mediumship, she made no revelation to science, her efforts in astronomy were utterly childish, her prophecy untrue. She never has revealed one scrap of useful knowledge. She never could reveal the contents of a test letter left by Dr. Hodgson."

Myers also left a sealed test letter for mediums to try to read. Myers himself, speaking through Mrs. Piper, was as unable to read the letter as Hodgson's spirit could not read Hodgson's test letter. Myers's wife wrote to the London *Morning Post* (October 24, 1908) stating that she and her son found nothing in all the messages from Myers purporting to come through mediums that "we can consider of the smallest evidential value."

When Rinn asked Mrs. Piper's Dr. Phinuit if he had ever treated Esther Horton in Marseilles, George Pellew seized Mrs. Piper's hand and wrote "Esther Horton is very weak—cannot-cannot now—will try some other time." Rinn had invented the name, which of course meant nothing to Mrs. Piper. After Rinn explained the trap to Hodgson, he was never invited to another Piper séance.

The following *New York Times* editorial (July 9, 1909) gave an accurate summary of what everybody outside the small circle of believers thought of Mrs. Piper:

> We have no desire to deride the few men of learning in this age who hold to a spiritual conception of the universe, but when, like Sir Oliver

Lodge and Professor James, they carry their theories so far as to accept, or at least dally with, supposed communications from the spirit world through trance mediums, their experiences will inevitably be compared with those of Robert Dale Owen and Luther Marsh. Owen received with an "open mind" the antics and sayings of the materialized Katy King, and lived to see the medium he had trusted thoroughly exposed as a common impostor. So did Marsh.

Professor James is not willing to declare that the "Richard Hodgson" who maundered and chattered with the tongue of the medium Mrs. Piper is the veritable soul of his dead friend Dr. Richard Hodgson, but obviously he should like to believe it. To the practical mind, Mrs. Piper is either a rank impostor, kindred to Browning's Sludge, and nearly all the other mediums who have forced themselves into public notice since the era of the Fox sisters, or a neurotic person subject to self-hypnosis.

Mrs. Piper's talk in trance, as quoted in the *Proceedings of the American Society for Psychical Research*, reads like the unutterable nonsense spoken by persons in hypnotic trance. Some of it must have sounded like the rambling of a phonograph out of order. But in the gift of evasion of direct questions to Richard Hodgson's spirit, it closely resembled the spirits called up in dark séances by all fraudulent mediums. The unseen ghosts of the Psychical Researchers are a poor, aimless lot, occasionally droll, but never convincing to anybody who has not made up his mind as to the honesty of the medium. Mrs. Piper is so ineffective as a medium, we are willing to believe that she is self-deluded. So are Professor James and Professor Hyslop.

On one occasion Hodgson asked Mrs. Piper to describe what a certain Mrs. Howard was doing at that moment. The control said she was pressing violets in a book, writing letters to two persons (who were named), then going upstairs to look in a drawer. These actions were corroborated by Mrs. Howard's daughter, except they all occurred on the day *before* the séance. (There was one error. Mrs. Howard put the violets in a drawer, not a book.) I was unable to learn if the daughter was present during the séance. If so, Mrs. Piper could have obtained the information by cold reading. Or did Hodgson inform Mrs. Piper in advance about the test, so that her servant woman could check with Mrs. Howard's servant? Surely either explanation is more plausible than that Mrs. Piper's control clairvoyantly saw what Mrs. Howard did the day before.

Charles Peirce, James's skeptical philosopher friend, said that, when he attended one of Piper's séances, at no time did he think he was conversing with anybody except Mrs. Piper. Thomas W. M. Lund, chaplain of the School for the Blind, in Liverpool, made the following comment about a séance with Mrs. Piper in *The Proceedings of the Society for Psychical Research* (vol. 6, 1889/90, p. 534):

With regard to my experience of Mrs. Piper, I do not feel that I saw enough to form data for any satisfactory conclusion. What impressed me most was the way in which she seemed to feel for information, rarely telling me anything of importance right off the reel, but carefully fishing, and then following up a lead. It seemed to me that when she got on a right tack, the nervous and uncontrollable movement of one's muscles gave her the signal that she was right and might steam ahead.

Lund goes on to say that among Mrs. Piper's usual mix of hits and misses she correctly told him his son was ill and that his wife planned to visit the son. However, he recalled that before the séance began he told Mrs. Lodge about his son's illness and his wife's plans "within earshot of Mrs. Piper." Here is how Mrs. Piper guessed the name of Lund's sister. "She then tried to find the name and went through a long list; at last she said it had 'ag' in the middle." After a favorable reaction, she said that the spirit taking over her vocal chords was named Maggie. When he asked Maggie why he wasn't there when she died, the control said "I'm getting weak now—*au revoir.*" Of course if Lund had not agreed that "ag" was in the name, the spirit would have continued along other lines. Incidentally, although Mrs. Piper knew Lund's name in advance of the séance, her control opened the sitting by asking, "Where's Mr. London?" Lund writes: "She made several attempts to arrive at my real name, Lund, but failed, saying that she couldn't pronounce it."

In later séances Lund's dead sister tried to explain why he was absent when she died, but the guesses were totally wrong. Here is how Lund summed up his final opinions:

> Altogether there was such a mixture of the true and false, the absurd and rational, the vulgar commonplace of the crafty fortune-teller with star-tling reality, that I have no theory to offer—merely the above facts. I should require much more evidence than I yet have, and with much more careful testing of it, to convince me (1) that Mrs. Piper was unconscious; (2) that there was any thought-reading beyond the clever guessing of a person trained in that sort of work; (3) that there was any ethereal com-munication with a spirit-world. I did not like the sudden weakness ex-perienced when I pressed my supposed sister for the reason of my absence at her death, and the delay wanted for giving a reply.

Even Myers, in the same issue of the *JSPR*, admitted there were striking differences between Mrs. Piper's honesty when awake, and the obvious dis-honesty of her controls. He tells how her trances had a way of degenerating into sessions during which Dr. Phinuit's conversation consists "wholly of fish-ing questions and random assertions" which extract "information from the sitter under the guise of giving it."

More than two-thirds of James Hyslop's *Science and the Future Life* (1905) are devoted to Mrs. Piper. Although Hyslop wrote "I shall not summarize details of failures and errors," his reports of Piper séances bristle with so many glaring misses that one is tempted to suppose that most of her hits are easily explained by sheer chance combined with clever cold reading. On page 163 Hyslop cites a few cases of what he calls "large scale" error. "Professor Macalister's sitting was one of the worst and he spoke of the failure in strong and uncomplimentary language. He thought . . . Mrs. Piper was wide enough awake to profit by suggestions."

One of the most bizarre of all cases involving Mrs. Piper concerned her attempt, like so many of today's psychics, to locate a missing person who had been reported dead. Dean Connor, the son of an assistant postmaster in Burlington, Vermont, went to Mexico in 1894 and was believed to have died there. Dean's father had a vivid dream in which his son appeared and told him he was alive and held as a captive while someone else had been buried in his place. Hodgson heard about the dream and arranged for a friend of the Connor family to visit Mrs. Piper. In a trance, Mrs. Piper said that the boy had been drugged, sent to a nearby mental hospital run by a Dr. Gintz, and a dead body had been put in the coffin. The control recommended that the coffin be opened and the body examined. So convinced was the sitter of Mrs. Piper's powers that he actually went to Mexico and had the body exhumed. He brought back from the decomposed corpse, which had not been embalmed, a sample of its hair. Doctors in Vermont thought it too dark to be the son's hair. Believers in Mrs. Piper were jubilant.

The Boston Globe was so taken by the story that it dispatched one of its reporters to Mexico to investigate. He there obtained conclusive evidence that Dean Connor had indeed died in a hospital, of typhoid fever, and had been buried. His body had not been embalmed because it was considered too expensive for the family. A nurse who had been in charge of Connor when he died said that the hair of typhoid victims often darkens after death. An injury to the son's left ring finger was visible on the skeleton. No trace could be found of a Dr. Gintz, or even of a nearby mental hospital. For more details about this weird series of events, check the summary in Rinn's book or look up fuller details in a book that the reporter, A. J. Philpot, wrote in 1897.

How did Hodgson respond to Philpot's investigation? He refused to believe the boy was dead. If he had the funds, he said, he would go to Mexico himself and find the lad alive. The Boston Globe then ran a headline on their first page offering to pay all of Hodgson's expenses for such a trip. Hodgson turned the offer down. You'll not find this story, or other stories about Mrs. Piper's abject failures, in any book by a believer in her powers. Nor are such failures cited by William James in his many articles about Mrs. Piper.

Although it is conceivable that cunning cold reading may account for all of Mrs. Piper's hits, I believe that, especially in her early years, she had other methods up her sleeves. We must not forget that she was constantly seeing friends and relatives of her clients. A vast amount of personal information can come through in the give and take of séance conversation, to be fed back to clients in later sessions. Because believers in Mrs. Piper were convinced she could recall nothing of what was said during a séance, it never occurred to them that Mrs. Piper might be lying, and that what she learned in one session could be used in a later one. We are told that much of the evidential data in her earlier séances was of such a personal nature it could not be published. Indeed, the large bulk of the records of her séances remains unpublished to this day, being stored in the archives of the SPR and the ASPR. Even the séances that James published were considerably chopped because James considered the omitted portions to be trivial and irrelevant. Maybe irrelevant to James—but not to skeptics who might find data from one séance turning up in another.

Mrs. Piper also could easily have obtained information from conversations among clients awaiting the start of a séance. Two or more visitors often chatter away, revealing all sorts of facts that could be overheard by the medium, or by her husband or one of her daughters on the other side of a wall. And it should not be forgotten that after years of practice Mrs. Piper may have developed a talent, like Sherlock Holmes, of basing shrewd deductions on a client's appearance, behavior, and way of speaking.

For a while investigators took the precaution of introducing clients to Mrs. Piper under names not their own. Since the clients came mostly from the area, many from the Harvard faculty, it would not be difficult for Mrs. Piper to recognize them from published photographs. Podmore relates an amusing incident. Professor J. E. Carpenter, from Oxford, was introduced to Mrs. Piper as Mr. Smith. But as soon as his wife entered the room, Mrs. William James greeted her as Mrs. Carpenter.

Did Mrs. Piper ever cheat by doing advance research on prospective clients? James and other investigators were of course aware of how easily mediums can obtain information about deceased persons, especially if they were prominent in their profession. Obituaries can be checked in newspapers and periodicals. Courthouses can yield valuable data on birth and marriage records, real estate sales, and so on. Reference books contain detailed biographical information that sitters will swear a medium could not possibly have known. The history of spiritualism swarms with instances of sitters insisting that no one but themselves knew this or that, only to have it turn out later that the fact was readily available in an obit or some other document. After his death, it was discovered that the American medium Arthur Ford—he converted Bishop James Pike to spiritualism—owned a vast collection of obituary clippings, which he called his "poems."

When Richard Hodgson began investigating Mrs. Piper he was so convinced she did secret research that, for several weeks, and much to Mrs. Piper's annoyance when she found out about it, he had detectives watch her and her husband. How effective was this effort? It seems unlikely that the Pipers were not early aware of such shadowing. How carefully was Mr. Piper watched? He is a dim figure about whom I have been unable to learn much. In her biography of her mother, Alta says little about her father beyond the facts that he loved outdoor sports (especially croquet) and music, played the piano and violin, and was strongly supportive of his wife's mediumship. Nowhere does Alta say how her father earned a living. He died in 1904 when Alta was twenty.

There are many instances in history of husbands secretly assisting mediums and psychics. The surgeon husband of Margery Crandon, another Boston medium, is a classic instance. Nina Kulagina's husband in Russia was always around in back rooms when Nina performed a miracle that requires a hidden confederate to pull invisible thread. What was to prevent Mr. Piper, before and after the shadowing, from going to libraries and doing other leg work? As far as I can tell, nothing.

And what about Mrs. Piper's two daughters? They were too young to help on their mother's first visit to England, but by the second visit they were in their twenties. Were the girls carefully monitored in the houses where they stayed or were they allowed to roam about? Amazing amounts of "evidential" data can be gathered from wastebaskets alone.

In her hagiography, Alta speaks of "servants" in their large home, as well as nurses and governesses. In 1885 they had an "old Irish servant" whose sister was a servant for a prominent Beacon Hill family, a family frequently visited by William James's mother-in-law. Yet when the mother-in-law first sat with Mrs. Piper, William was flabbergasted to learn that the medium had given her the names of members of his family! William and his wife later became good friends of the Pipers. On one occasion they shared a vacation in the White Mountains of New Hampshire, where Mrs. Piper went every summer for a month or two of relaxation.

Did Hodgson and his detectives interview servants in the area? Did they visit Boston and Cambridge libraries with photographs of Mr. and Mrs. Piper to ask clerks if any of them were frequent patrons?

There are still other ways in which mediums can obtain evidential data. Mediums in a city get to know one another and cooperate. Among Arthur Ford's remains were copies of letters thanking other mediums, some in distant cities, for their help. People who like to attend séances usually visit many mediums. At the time there were scores of practicing mediums in Boston. They formed a network of professionals among whom valuable information could be passed back and forth. Of course no medium in such a network would ever admit knowing any of the others.

The strongest indictment that can be made against William James as a psychic researcher is that not once did he devise, or even consider devising, a sting operation. He was surely aware of how easily skeptics can set such traps. The psychologist G. Stanley Hall, for example, invented Bessie Beale, a fictitious person whose spirit Mrs. Piper had no difficulty reaching. Even James's invalid sister Alice—unlike her brother, a skeptic of things psychic—initiated a simple sting. James had asked for a lock of her hair to give to Mrs. Piper for use in some sort of séance, perhaps to determine the nature of Alice's illness. Alice sent her brother a lock of a deceased friend's hair. Here is how she exposed the hoax in a letter to William in 1886:

> I hope you wont be "offended," like Frankie, when I tell you that I played you a base trick about the hair. It was a lock, not of my hair, but that of a friend of Miss Ward's who died four years ago. I thought it a much better test of whether the medium were simply a mind-reader or not; if she is something more I should greatly dislike to have the secrets of my organisation laid bare to a wondering public. I hope you will forgive my frivolous treatment of so serious a science.

In the same letter Alice added: "I shall be curious to hear what the woman will say about the hair. Its owner was in a state of horrible disease for a year before she died—tumours, I believe."

If James reported the results to Alice, his letter apparently has not survived. At any rate, I know of no record that he left of any séance in which the hair played a psychometric role. James was probably too embarrassed to record it. So convinced was he of Mrs. Piper's honesty that he would have considered revealing such a sting to be an insult to a noble woman. Whether Alice's hoax succeeded or failed, Mrs. Piper and James's wife would never have forgiven him. If any reader knows of any report of Mrs. Piper's reaction to the hair, perhaps a document gathering dust in the ASPR archives, please tell me!

Alice had a low opinion of James's spiritualist friends. In one of her letters to William she calls Myers an "idiot." Here are her candid opinions as she jotted them down in her diary in February 1892, a week before she died of breast cancer:

> I do pray to Heaven that the dreadful Mrs. Piper won't be let loose upon my defenceless soul. I suppose the thing "medium" has done more to degrade spiritual conception than the grossest forms of materialism or idolatry: was there ever anything transmitted but the pettiest, meanest, coarsest facts and details: anything rising above the squalid intestines of human affairs? And oh, the curious spongy minds that sop it all up and lose all sense of taste and humour!

James's aunt Kate was another relative deeply suspicious of Mrs. Piper and William's other spiritualist pals. She wrote to James's wife, also named Alice— the spongy-minded Alice—warning her against mediums. The letter was mentioned by Mrs. Piper in one of her trances. "Of course no one but my wife and I knew of the existence of this letter," James naively wrote. The "of course" typifies James's mind-set. It never occurred to him that his wife might have mentioned the letter to a friend or servant, and completely forgotten she did so. James himself could have mentioned the letter to someone and forgotten. Or their servant could have seen the letter. We know from an article by Mrs. Piper, which I shall come to in a moment, that her "maid of all work" was a friend of William James's servant!

In his book *The Will to Believe*, James likens anomalies in science to the white crow that falsifies the assertion that all crows are black. "My own white crow," he wrote, "is Mrs. Piper." In the midst of all the undoubted humbug, he said in *Memories and Studies*, is "the presence . . . of really supernormal knowledge . . . in really strong mediums this knowledge seems to be abundant, though it is usually spotty, capricious and unconnected." Poor William! He was unable to see that it was spotty precisely because mediums, by normal means, can do no better than obtain spotty, disconnected, often inaccurate shreds of information.

James was a great man, but, like so many other intelligent men who take up psychic research, he had no comprehension of how easily bright persons, especially scientists, can be duped. A number of excellent books on how fake mediums operate were available in James's time. There is no evidence, however, he read any of them. Not once did he seek advice from a knowledgeable magician, such as England's John Maskelyne, whose *Modern Spiritualism* had appeared as early as 1876.

A year before he died James wrote "Confessions of a Psychical Researcher" for *American Magazine* (October 1909), an essay reprinted in his *Memories and Studies*. Said James:

> Mrs. Piper's control "Rector" is a most impressive personage, who discerns in an extraordinary degree his sitter's inner needs, and is capable of giving elevated counsel to fastidious and critical minds. Yet in many respects he is an arrant humbug—such he seems to me at least—pretending to a knowledge and power to which he has no title, nonplussed by contradiction, yielding to suggestion, and covering his tracks with plausible excuses.

And yet James believed! "If spirits are involved," he wrote, they are "passive beings, stray bits of whose memory she [Mrs. Piper] is able to seize. . . ." James was aware of how Mrs. Piper's controls shamelessly fished for data, yet he could not avoid thinking that her messages were "accreted round some original genuine nucleus." Belief in psychic phenomena has lasted so long through the centuries, he argued foolishly, as so many believers still do, that there *must* be something to it. Something to astrology? To palmistry? Let me quote what I consider the most stupid remark in all of James's writings:

> When a man's pursuit gradually makes his face shine and grow handsome, you may be sure it is a worthy one. Both Hodgson and Myers kept growing ever handsomer and stronger-looking.

When I began researching Mrs. Piper, I expected to find her a sincere woman whose skull contained split personalities that emerged in genuine trances. But the more I learned about her the more I became convinced that she was no more than a typical medium of the day, though cleverer than most in avoiding physical manifestations, which are so easily exposed, and in the art (for it is an art) of cold reading. There is no conceivable reason why the spirit of a dead person, chatting through a medium, would have to resort to flagrant fishing to obtain data that might prove he or she was a genuine discarnate. But cold reading is precisely what to expect from a clever mountebank who has no other way at the moment of obtaining evidential information. Even James once admitted that he sometimes wished Mrs. Piper could be caught in fraud because that would be the simplest way to explain her powers!

My low opinion of Mrs. Piper was clinched when I came across two references (there are probably many more) of Mrs. Piper performing a trick known to magicians as "eyeless vision." William James tells of an occasion when Mrs. Piper described the contents of a letter by holding it to her forehead, although it was not until two years later that she provided the writer's name. Oliver Lodge describes a séance during which Mrs. Piper was given a letter from a package, along with wrapping paper. She put the wrapping and the letter on top of her head, flicked away the wrappers, and partially read the letter.

We have learned how Mrs. Piper could not divine the contents of several sealed letters. When handed unsealed letters she did much better. Now, there is no sensible reason why a psychic should put a letter on the forehead or on top of the head before viewing it clairvoyantly, but there is an excellent reason for such action when a medium cheats. The usual technique goes like this. With eyes almost shut, the letter is held far to one side while the medium chatters away. Meanwhile, the eyes, hidden under their lids, shift to one side and steal quick glimpses of the letter. (If the letter is more than one page, of course it is hard to get a glimpse of the signature at the end.) Some mediums are blindfolded when they do eyeless vision, but Mrs. Piper never bothered with such precautions and would not even have known how to get around them. Spectators naturally assume that, while the medium divulges the letter's contents, she is viewing it paranormally for the first time, never dreaming that the letter was glimpsed some time before while their attention was diverted.

Lodge's account of how Mrs. Piper paranormally "read" the letter on top of her head strongly suggests that she had obtained only a quick glimpse of the letter's single page. She began by saying "Who's dear Lodge? Who's Poodle, Toodle, Poodle! Whatever does that mean?"

LODGE: "I haven't the least idea."
MRS. PIPER: "Is there J.N.W. here? Poole. Then there's Sefton. S-e-

f-t-o-n. Poole, hair. Yours truly, J.N.W. That's it; I send hair. Poole. J.N.W. Do you understand that?"

LODGE: "No, only partially."

MRS. PIPER: "Who's Mildred, Milly? something connected with it, and Alice; and with him too, I get Fanny. There's his son's influence on it."

Lodge adds the following clarification.

I found out afterwards that the letter began "Dear Dr. Lodge," contained the words "Sefton Drive" and "Cook" so written as to look like Poole. It also said "I send you some hair," and finished "yours sincerely, J.B.W."; the "B" being not unlike an "N." The name of the sender was not mentioned in the letter.

Apparently the references to a Mildred, Alice, and Fanny, and the son's influence, were no more than fishing remarks.

There are three possible explanations of Mrs. Piper's account of the letter: (1) While in trance she became a powerful clairvoyant; (2) Her spirit controls read the letter; (3) She cheated. Is not the third possibility the simplest and most plausible? But, you may argue, could she have deceived such astute observers as James and Lodge by such a simple technique? The answer is a thunderous yes. Both men were totally ignorant about how conjurers perform such feats. Even had they not been thoroughly convinced of Mrs. Piper's honesty, they would not have known what to look for when Mrs. Piper was handed the letter. Their scientific training was a liability, not an asset. To repeat: Electrons and laboratory animals don't cheat. Psychics do.

In 1901 Mrs. Piper wrote an extraordinary article for the *New York Herald* (Sunday, October 20). I have obtained a copy. It ran on two and one-half pages, with photographs of Mrs. Piper in her house and garden on Oakland Avenue in the Boston suburb of Arlington Heights. (The suburb had formerly been part of West Cambridge, near Harvard.) The headline over her article read: "I Am No Telephone To the Spirit World."

Mrs. Piper announced that she was resigning from the ASPR and retiring as a medium. Personal circumstances, which she did not specify, were making it impossible to continue her work. Besides, she wanted to be "liberated" from the ASPR, for which she had served as an "automaton" for fourteen years; she desired freedom for "other and more congenial pursuits." She wanted to tell the world that she had never heard of anything she said or wrote while in trance that could not have been either latent in her mind, or obtained by telepathy from the minds of a sitter or other persons living somewhere in the world. "I must truthfully say," she wrote, "that I do not believe that spirits of the dead have spoken through me. When I have been in a trance state . . . it may be that they have, but I do not affirm it." In her opinion telepathy was the most plausible explanation of her remarkable hits. Why could not information come from distant, living persons, she asked, like messages over a wireless telegraph, to be picked up by her subliminal self?

The article rambles, but it is well-expressed and gives evidence of a high intelligence and a woman of wide reading. She refers to St. Paul, and says that she hopes to enter heaven "directly" rather than through the "back door of spiritualism." At the end of the article she repeats a story about how savages were so impressed by a sundial that they built a roof over it. We are doing the same thing, she said, with our faith in God. "Break down the roof; let God in on your life!" Mrs. Piper was then under heavy fire from Christian preachers. Her references to God and the Bible may have been a calculated move to pacify them, or could have reflected a growing interest on her part in Christianity. Her parents had been Methodists, but when they moved to a town that had only a Congregational church, she attended that church with them. In 1910, in England, she was baptized and confirmed in the Anglican Church.

Five days later the *Boston Daily Advertiser* published a brief statement by Mrs. Piper. She was upset over the headline above the *Herald* piece. She did not contradict anything in that article, but she did complain that her words had been misunderstood. She had not intended to deny unequivocally that the dead spoke through her, but only to say that, like William James, she was baffled by the sources of her utterances. She inclined to the view that it was her subliminal self speaking and that the evidential information brought forth was the result of her telepathic powers.

Mrs. Piper did not retire. For two more decades she continued to give séances, supervised by the ASPR, and continued to receive payments from England's SPR. Her communications by this time were almost entirely by automatic writing. New controls included George Eliot, Julius Caesar, and Madame Guyon, a seventeenth-century French mystic and automatic writer. When Doyle visited her in 1922, he says in his history of spiritualism, she had lost all her powers. Skeptics suspect that the main reason for this was that better qualified researchers, such as psychologist G. Stanley Hall—he was a student of William James and a teacher of John Dewey—were subjecting her to rigorous experiments that earlier researchers were unwilling to make.

In her biography, Alta Piper attributes her mother's loss of power, from 1911 to 1914, directly to the "harsh" experiments conducted by Hall and his assistant Amy Tanner. So strict were the conditions that Imperator, Mrs. Piper's control, issued an "ultimatum that the power must be withdrawn for a time in order to repair 'the machine.'" Although her trances returned in 1915, from then until 1924 Mrs. Piper had only occasional sittings. The last parapsychologist to conduct experiments with her was Gardner Murphy, in 1924 and 1925. Unlike Hall, Murphy was a true believer in Mrs. Piper's powers.

Mrs. Piper died in 1950, age ninety-one, and almost totally deaf. She was then living in an old apartment house in a Boston suburb with her youngest daughter, Minerva. Her address was secret, and her phone number unlisted. The last article written about her was probably "America's Most Famous Medium," by Murray Teigh Bloom, in *The American Mercury* (May 1950). Bloom closed with these words:

> Few in the comfortable, old-fashioned apartment house know that the very old lady who occasionally goes out for a stroll with her nurse or gray-haired daughter is the simple Yankee housewife whose work once convinced leading scientists of two countries that there was indeed life after death.

POSTSCRIPT

I had finished this essay when psychologist Ray Hyman called my attention to a book I did not know existed. Books and articles about Mrs. Piper never mention it, nor is it cited by Alta Piper in her biography of her mother. The reason for such silence is obvious. The book was written by a skeptic, and is far and away the most valuable study ever made of Mrs. Piper. It is a book that deserves reprinting.

Studies in Spiritism, by Dr. Amy B. Tanner, was published by Appleton in 1910.[3] Tanner was an assistant to Dr. G. Stanley Hall, one of the most prominent and respected psychologists of his day, and at that time president of Clark University. Unlike William James and other investigators of Mrs. Piper, Hall was the first to perform experiments with Mrs. Piper that James would have considered unethical. As I noted earlier, these were the tests that Alta believed were responsible for her mother's temporary loss of powers.

Both Hall and Tanner approached Mrs. Piper with open minds. Tanner writes in her preface that before they began their investigation she believed in telepathy and did not rule out the possibility of spirit communication. Hall was more skeptical, though as a youth he accepted spiritualist claims and as an adult continued to believe in immortality. In 1909 he and Tanner had six sessions with Mrs. Piper, all recorded verbatim in Tanner's book. They ended their research persuaded that Mrs. Piper was probably not a charlatan, but a classic case of a person with multiple personalities who emerged from her unconscious mind during trances. Mrs. Piper was then at the height of her fame. Had the book accused her of fakery, Hall and Tanner could have been open to libel suits. If, however, you read carefully between the lines, there are subtle suggestions that Mrs. Piper may in some ways have practiced conscious deception.

One indication of this was the fact that, unlike other persons with subliminal personalities who take over in trances, Mrs. Piper's trances did not occur spontaneously. They never began when she was alone, or asleep, or daydreaming. She never walked or talked in her sleep. She was incapable of being hypnotized. Yet when a sitter who had paid for a séance was present, she had no difficulty going into a trance. I should add that persons who suffer from genuine trance seizures do not go in and out of trances in theatrical ways calculated to impress an audience.

An even stronger suggestion of fraud was the incredible role played by Mrs. Piper's right hand after direct-voice channeling had been entirely replaced by automatic writing. The fact that the hand functioned as a telephone to her controls was, as Hall remarks in his introduction, a miracle in itself. Sitters were asked to hold the hand, its palm close to their mouth, and to speak with a loud voice. Frequently the control would be unable to hear and would ask the sitter to talk louder, as if on a long distance telephone call. Occasionally the hand would explore a sitter's face or body.

My first thought was that the hand needed shouting because Mrs. Piper was getting a trifle deaf, but Hall and Tanner convinced me that the reverse was true. Although she sat with her head on pillows, face turned to one side and eyes seemingly closed, her hearing was extremely acute. As Hall writes, she reacted to everything audible—"noises on the streets, the rustle of clothing, the sitter's position, and every noise or motion, and our conversation, too. . . ."

By insisting that sitters address the hand in a loud voice, a strong impression was created that Mrs. Piper was "as much out of the game as if she were dead." If the hand could not hear unless a mouth was close to it and shouting, surely Mrs. Piper could not hear whispers or voices spoken in low tones. That Mrs. Piper was in a deep sleep was further strengthened by the long time, fifteen to twenty minutes, that it took her to come out of a trance. Convinced that the sleeping Mrs. Piper could hear nothing, sitters were free to move about the room and talk to one another. After a séance they would not even remember what they had said. Then when information from such whispered conversations came out in later séances, or even in the same séance, they would be amazed at how the control could possibly know such things!

It was often the case that nothing evidential emerged in a first sitting, to be followed by great successes in a later visit. Hints of revelations to come were commonplace during a first sitting, arousing a sitter's strong desire to come back and pay for other visits, often a series of many visits separated by weeks. This allowed plenty of time for sitters to forget their conversations; it also allowed Mrs. Piper time to find out more about a sitter's family.

Because I believe this conversation in the séance room to be Mrs. Piper's best kept secret, let me quote at length from Hall:

It is the ear, of course, that hears what is spoken into the hand. The establishment of this fact is of great significance. The clever trickster might have reasoned out a scheme of impressing the sitters with the idea that they must shout into the hand and that all else was lost, so that they would thus be thrown off their guard, while the intently listening ear would catch and utilize for the manual responses all that was said to each other. The keener the audition and the more deft the hand, the wider the range of oral impartation from whispering to shouting that would be profited by. With Mrs. Piper we believe this method was not a project of strategy or designed, but a slow, unconscious evolution. Thus, responses and statements are written that fairly smite with wonder the incautious and uncritical sitter, who naively allows himself to fall into the assumption which the method suggests that the control hears nothing but what is loudly spoken into the hand. The sitters have really thought aloud and communicated in low tones to others, feeling as secure against betrayal as if their thoughts were unspoken, and perhaps, indeed, not conscious that they had been put in articulate form. Thus, when natural answers come back, they seem veritable mind-reading or marvellous il-lustrations of the pellucidity of the sitters' souls to the celestial visitant.

Now, it is a very significant fact that stenographic records have rarely been kept, even of the *ipsissima verbs*, that are *consciously* said to the control by the sitters. Even our record, which was made as full as long hand could be, does not do this. This is because the feeling has been that the important things of the sitting came from the medium, when the exact reverse is true. Everything that is really significant comes from the sitters. Far less has there been any stenographic record of things said loud or low in the room, where there frequently are at least two if not more visitors present. Under the conditions of the sitting, the temptation is incessant to carry on considerable conversation, to express secret plans, and purposes and methods that betray answers; and all with the same feeling of security that we have, as I said, in speaking before the deaf. Such talk is, much of it, almost immediately forgotten, if, indeed, it was conscious even at the time. Yet in this is the source of supply from which the control garners most of its knowledge of us. There are, of course, inflections, too, movements, slight noises, etc., which are more or less significant. Often especially in our characterisations of both real and fic-titious dead friends, we have only given the name and a few salient facts to the ear, adding various details in a low voice to Mr. Dorr and Dr. Tanner, while the hand was writing, which, however, insistently utilized these sources of information by incorporating reactions in the script, while we tried not to be remiss in the expressions of wonder which seemed to be the usual and proper thing under such circumstances.[4]

It is important to realize that such careless conversations in the séance room were never recorded. In early years, when Mrs. Piper channeled direct voices, only brief notes in longhand were taken, and in many cases were writ-ten down later from memory. Nor were any records made of such conversation in later years when only her right hand channeled. The absence of such records render all voluminous records of Mrs. Piper's séances almost valueless in trying to evaluate the kind of information she overheard. Today, of course, a serious investigator would tape-record the entire séance, which may be one reason why direct-voice mediums who bring evidential information from dead relatives are so hard to find. It is much safer to channel the voice of someone who lived thousands of years ago or who is on a distant planet!

I quote once more from Hall:

... Here then is a wide and copious margin in which suggestion can work. Never in our own or in other Piper sittings was any full record kept of what her interlocutors said. Still less have involuntary exclamations, inflections, stresses, etc., been noted, and even the full and exact form of questions is rarely, if ever, kept while the presence of a stenographer which we proposed was objected to. Thus unlimited suggestions are unconsciously ever being given off to be caught and given back or reacted to in surprising ways. If this method be a conscious invention on her part it shows great cleverness and originality, and if it be a method unconsciously drifted into, its great effectiveness could in fact be scientifically evaluated only by prolonged experiments in which a normal person should simulate her very peculiar kind of sleep. In fact, it often seemed that only her eyes were out of the game, and all her mental and emotional powers were very wide awake. A little practice convinced me that it is not hard to feign all this, and yet I am by no means convinced that she acted her sleep-dream, although that this could be done with a success quite equal to her own I have no shadow of doubt. If this is the case she is, of course, fraudulent, but if some of her faculties are really sleeping it is a unique and interesting case of somno-scripticism as her former practice of speaking instead of writing was of somno-verbalism, for both are species of the same genus of somnambulism. That Mrs. Piper-Hodgson's soul is awake and normal, our last sittings gave abundant evidence when she seemed to quite fall out of the Hodgson role and became angry.

Mrs. Piper's anger, as expressed by her Hodgson control (her right hand would pound the table), came after Hall revealed to Hodgson, in the sixth and final sitting, that he had been thoroughly flimflammed. Mrs. Piper had unconditionally agreed before the séances began that Hall could perform any kinds of experiments he desired. It seems likely she had no inkling of how far Hall would go in laying traps.

What Hall did—James should have done it earlier—was to present Hodgson with completely fictitious names. Although Hall had met Hodgson only once, Hall acted as if they were old friends. Hodgson reciprocated by calling Hall "old chap" and by recalling a wealth of events and discussions that had never happened. Hall invented a Bessie Beale. Hodgson had no difficulty locating her on the "other side." Indeed, he seemed as intimate with Hall as Mrs. Piper, in her waking state, mistakenly assumed he had been. Hodgson recalled everything Hall pretended had passed between them. When Mrs. Piper was given neckties to hold, neckties she was told belonged to Hodgson, Hall slyly substituted old neckties of his own. Hodgson, of course, never knew the difference.

In the final séance, Hall openly told Hodgson about his deceptions and did his best to persuade the control to admit he was not really Hodgson but only part of Mrs. Piper's brain. Both Hall and Tanner broke into laughter over Hodgson's confusions and evasions. This is the book's funniest chapter and probably the funniest séance ever recorded. At one point Hall said, "Now, . . . to oblige me, repeat the words 'I am not Hodgson.' " Hodgson refused. "No, I am Hodgson." Hall told him he was hurting the cause of spiritualism by pretending to be Hodgson and ordered him to "fade away." But Hodgson refused to fade, protesting that he would go only when he was ready. He finally faded, replaced by Rector who came on with "May the blessing of God rest on you."

"It may be that he [Hodgson] humoured me in my deceit to see how far I would go," Hall writes, "and let me fill full the measure of my turpitude of ruse and deception, but if so, why the flaming anger when I confessed my strategy?" Although Mrs. Piper insisted she never recalled anything that transpired during a séance, Hall had earlier noticed a coldness in her attitude toward him. After this final séance she betrayed no hint that she knew how damaging it had been to her. "She was evidently very curious to know," Tanner closes her account of this séance, "whether we were at all convinced and kept looking at both of us with a contemplative, questioning gaze, and when we said good-bye, and thanked her for her personal courtesy, the last thing that we saw was that same questioning gaze."

When Hall questioned Hodgson about events in his life on earth, events unknown to Mrs. Piper, he answered "only in platitudes or evaded. Would Hodgson, if living, have accepted such a tatterdemalion ghost of himself, and would he not have preferred death to such a pitiful prolongation of his personality?" Perhaps, suggests Hall with tongue in cheek, Hodgson's soul was in a "process of dissolution." He had already reached "an advanced stage of senile decrepitude. . . . He surely cut a sorry figure with us. He accepted each of the fictitious personages we invented. The figments of our fancy were quite as real to him as his own friends. . . . He could thus be fooled and imposed upon to the very top of our bent."

Mrs. Piper's hand did much more than just scribble almost unreadable messages. As Hall writes: "The hand points, nods for yes, shakes for no, quivers with impatience, listens, gestures for silence, beckons, with quite a vocabulary of signs." When a control first took over, the hand would suddenly clench. Controls called the hand, as well as Mrs. Piper's body, "the machine" through which they communicated. Mrs. Piper was known as "the light."

Hodgson constantly fished for information. He had a habit of suddenly injecting, from the blue, a meaningless name of a person, or initials, or a word. If these random interjections meant nothing to a sitter, they were simply ignored or forgotten. But if a sitter, often after much thinking, found some connection with his or her life, Hodgson would instantly follow up with more data. For example, a common name such as Robert or Kitty would be written. Almost everybody knew someone named Robert or Kitty. If the sitter could think of a relative or friend named Robert or Kitty, it would be the cue for Hodgson to go on. Otherwise, the name would be forgotten.

Mrs. Piper's most impressive séances took place when her husband was alive, and I strongly suspect that he did actual research for her. After his death, there was a marked falling off of "evidential" material in her séances when in my opinion she was forced to rely entirely on cold reading and information gained from conversations spoken in low tones during a séance.

If Mrs. Piper was in part a clever charlatan, as I am convinced she was, how does one explain such a curious personality? Although Mrs. Piper, after her husband's death, had no other means of supporting herself and her two daughters, I agree with Hall that money was not a primary motive. It is also possible she may sincerely have believed herself to be possessed of paranormal powers which she did her best to augment by trickery. It is, of course, impossible now, as it probably always was, to get inside Mrs. Piper's mind. Her daughter's hagiography is no help; it may even have been ghostwritten. Writing about fraudulent mediums in general, Hall suggested that the primary motive is a

> morbid passion for deception . . . the real explanation of their success is to be chiefly found in the abnormal development of an inveterate inborn propensity to lie and mislead, which gives them a titilating sense of superiority on the one hand, and on the other the overpowering will to believe on the part of the faithful.

Those who were persuaded of Mrs. Piper's powers were invariably persons predisposed to believe. We know of her famous converts, but less familiar are the many prominent persons who were not impressed by her séances. Tanner gives a partial list. Geologist N. S. Shaler was unable to exclude fraud. Sir George Darwin, a British astronomer, was convinced she had no paranormal powers. Professor Robert Alexander Stewart Macalister, a Cambridge University archeologist, considered her a "poor imposter." S. Weir Mitchell, an American physican and novelist, said that if he hadn't heard such praise from William James he would have considered Mrs. Piper a very stupid fraud. Harvard physicist John Trowbridge "was struck by a sort of insane cunning" in the way her controls groped for information. Andrew Lang said that Mrs. Piper "would cheat whenever she could." Harvard physiologist Henry Bowditch believed Mrs. Piper obtained advance information about him which during a séance her controls mistakenly applied to his uncle.

A Mrs. Howard Oakie wrote that nothing evidential came out in her first two sittings except "a great deal of hedging and guessing," but as she left the house she met two good friends on their way in. She was not impressed when, during her third session, Mrs. Piper produced a wealth of accurate information, but nothing that the two friends did not know.

"Spiritism," wrote Hall, "is the ruck and muck of modern culture, the common enemy of true science and of true religion, and to drain its dismal and miasmatic marshes is the great work of modern culture." More than eighty years have passed since he wrote those words, and hoped that Amy Tanner's book would help "turn the tide." Alas, it had no such effect. The muck is still with us, albeit in new forms, and the marshes are as far from drained as ever.

NOTES

1. Palladino was a short, fat, Italian peasant who was caught cheating so many times that she herself finally admitted she resorted to trickery whenever the spirits failed to come. This admission had little effect on the faith of her followers. Hereward Carrington, who fancied himself a knowledgeable magician and even wrote a book on how mediums cheat, was her manager on a tour of the United States. He never doubted that she had genuine powers, one of which was her strange ability to produce a blast of cold air from a scar on her forehead. (She probably produced it simply by extending her lower lip and blowing upward.)

When James's colleague and friend, the Harvard philosopher Josiah Royce, learned that Eusapia had been caught using her feet to produce certain phenomena, he gleefully circulated the following jingle:

> Eeny, meeny, miney, mo.
> Catch Eusapia by the toe.
> If she hollers that will show
> That James's theories are not so.

2. "What real spirit," James wrote in one of his skeptical moods, "at last able to revisit his wife on this earth, but would find something better to say than that she had changed the place of his photograph?" Such a remark is typical of those made by sham fortune-tellers that have a high probability of being true, like saying "You have been thinking about buying a new car," or "You recently had a disturbing phone call."

3. James Hyslop was so infuriated by this book that he wrote a scathing 98-page review for the *Journal of the ASPR* (vol. 5, January 1911). Hyslop called the authors liars, idiots, troglodytes, and ignorant bunglers whose book swarms with omissions, distortions, and factual errors. Their crude methods, he states, "reduced Mrs. Piper to nervous prostration" so severe that for almost a year she was unable to enter a trance.

Neither Hall, Tanner, nor Tanner's book are mentioned in *William James on Psychical*

Research (Viking, 1960), edited by Gardner Murphy and Robert Ballou, although it purports to be a definitive account of James's work with Mrs. Piper.

4. George B. Dorr was then the representative of England's SPR. As Hodgson had done for eighteen years, he served as Mrs. Piper's manager. All arrangements for séances had to be made through him, and he was usually present during the sittings.

TWENTY-ONE

CLOSE ENCOUNTERS OF THE THIRD KIND

Only three times have I ventured into movie criticism. This attack on Spielberg's Close Encounters of the Third Kind *appeared in the* New York Review of Books *(January 26, 1978). For an even lower opinion of Spielberg's Poltergeist, see my* Discover *review (August 1982), reprinted as "The Power and the Gory" in* Order and Surprise *(1993).*

Martin Scorsese's The Last Temptation of Christ *struck me as so awful that not even Spielberg would have produced it. My review for the Hendersonville, North Carolina,* Times-News *can be found in* On the Wild Side *(1992).*

Close Encounters of the Third Kind opens with a bang. At first the titles flash on and off in eerie silence, then a faint sound slowly swells in volume until it explodes. A symbol of the explosion that created the universe? The producers' hope that the movie will blow everybody's mind?

We know that young Steven Spielberg, the director who gave us *Jaws*, has done it again, this time without a bare nipple or a spurt of blood. The film's dazzling photography, high decibel score, and tolerable acting make it hard to see how bad the film really is, but of course that is the secret of block-busting. Douglas Trumbull, who created the special effects for *2001: A Space Odyssey*, is indeed a genius, and his contributions to *Close Encounters* are everything the film's publicity says. Alas, beneath the visual hanky-panky stretches a thin, hackneyed plot that was done to death in the SF magazines and third-rate films of the fifties.

This is easier to comprehend if you read Spielberg's ghostwritten version, *Close Encounters*, issued by Dell paperbacks in 1977 as a movie tie-in. Here on the stark pages, uncontaminated by clanking sounds and flashing colors, you can savor the film's dull story, cardboard characters, and dreary dialogue in all their pure, clean, adolescent banality. Both novel and movie, however, have one thing going for them that makes the film commercially unstoppable. More than any other SF novel or movie, they reflect the extent to which ufology has become a pop religion.

Millions of Americans, disenchanted with science and politics, are longing for apocalypse—for a mystical explosion that will instantly solve the world's problems and start a new age of love. For Protestants who haven't left, or who are able to return to, evangelical Christianity, expectation of the Second Coming is rapidly rising. Billy Graham more and more thumps on the theme of a hopelessly corrupt world, firmly in Satan's grip, but any day now—surely soon!—the Lord will return. Eccentric cults based on Parousian nearness are flourishing as seldom before. Shabby books like Hal Lindsey's *Late Great Planet Earth* sell by the millions.

For those who cannot believe in the Second Coming, or the Messianic hopes of orthodox Judaism, there are the UFOs! If the earth is being visited by extraterrestrials, if the sky (as an Indian sadhu puts it in *Close Encounters*) is singing to us, surely the aliens must be friendly or by now we would have learned otherwise. It is this childish possibility that has kept the flying saucers aloft for almost fifty years. Fifty years!

Strange things have, of course, always been happening in the heavens, but the first flying saucer "flap" had a precise beginning. It was June 24, 1947. Kenneth Arnold, flying his private plane near Mt. Rainier, saw nine disklike objects flipping through the firmament. A wire service man called them "saucers," flurries of new sightings followed, and ufology arrived to stay.

The press and radio responded quickly to the growing public interest in UFOs and, as always, the sensational books and magazine articles boosted the mania even higher. A few government and military officials at first took the saucers seriously, but after twenty years of investigation the Air Force finally decided that nothing extraordinary was going on overhead. To settle the matter, a distinguished physicist, Edward U. Condon, was handed half a million dollars by the Air Force to produce the definitive "Condon report"—a 1,000-page document that can be summarized in one sentence. There are no UFOs that can't be explained as hoaxes, hallucinations, or honest misidentifications of such natural objects as meteors, Venus, huge balloons, conventional aircraft, reentering satellites, and atmospheric illusions.

Of course the Condon report, when it came out in 1968, no more settled the matter than the Warren Commission report settled the question of who killed the president. Indeed, even before the Condon report was published a leading occult journalist, John G. Fuller, blasted it with an article in *Look*: "The Flying Saucer Fiasco."

Obviously there is no way that the Air Force or anybody else can prove that alien spacecraft are not visiting us. Is there a tooth fairy? No amount of cases in which a grown-up is caught pushing a quarter under a child's pillow will add up to irrefutable negative evidence. Always there is a small residue of cases in which grown-ups are not caught, and the morning appearance of money remains mysterious. No matter how many sightings of UFOs are shown to have natural explanations, there is always a residue—how could it be otherwise?—of cases for which information is insufficient for judgment.

The cast of mind of true believers in alien UFOs is remarkably similar to that of true believers in spiritualism when it was in its heyday. It mattered not a spirit rap how many mediums were caught in fraud. Every time this happened, Sir Arthur Conan Doyle, who believed in the reality of fairies as well as of ghosts, would sigh and point out, as if talking to a child, that some mediums do indeed cheat, but not all of them and not all the time. Always that residue of the unexplained.

Dr. J. Allen Hynek, professor of astronomy at Northwestern University, was the Conan Doyle of ufology. He started out as a debunker, but became firmly persuaded that something paranormal—he didn't know just what—was behind the UFO flaps. In his book, *The Hynek UFO Report*, issued by Dell in 1977 as a companion to Spielberg's "novel," he writes:

> Today I would not spend one additional moment on the subject of UFOs if I didn't seriously feel that the UFO phenomenon is real and that efforts to investigate and understand it, and eventually to solve it, could have a profound effect—perhaps even be the springboard to a revolution in man's view of himself and his place in the universe.

The title of Spielberg's movie is from Hynek's 1972 book, *The UFO Experience*. Close encounters of the first kind are mere sightings. The second are physical interactions. The third are meetings with the aliens. Spielberg, a long-time UFO enthusiast, hired Hynek to be his technical consultant. Sure enough, in the movie's climactic scene when the great encounter of the third kind occurs, there is Dr. Hynek himself, standing among the observers, puffing contemplatively on a pipe and looking very unsurprised.

The Hynek UFO Report contains nothing of substance that Hynek had not said many times before. Four-fifths of all UFO reports, he cheerfully admits, are easily explained. But that damnable residue! The government is attacked once more for "suppressing" data. The Condon report is again branded a huge fraud whose "cold and clammy" hand was lifted by the last big UFO flap in the fall of 1973 when four planets were exceptionally bright, and there had been a widely publicized claim by two fishermen in Pascagoula, Mississippi, that they had been kidnapped by a flying saucer. UFO debunking books by top scientists and writers are dismissed as flimsy efforts of the "establishment" to sweep truth under the rug. Hynek likens his detractors to those who refused to look through Galileo's telescope for fear of seeing something that might damage their "belief systems."

The best insight into Hynek's own belief system can be gained from an interview published in the June 1976 issue of *Fate*, a tawdry occult pulp magazine that many years ago was the first to publish articles about UFOs as extraterrestrial objects. Hynek once favored the "nuts and bolts" theory that UFOs are physical things, but now, he tells us, he inclines to the view (proposed by Jung) that they are psychic projections. "Perhaps an advanced civilization understands the interaction between mind and matter.... Perhaps it is a naïve notion that you've got to build something physical, blast it off with sound and fury to cross vast distances and finally land here.... There are other planes of existence—the astral plane, the etheric plane and so forth."

"I believe," he goes on, "the world is in a psychic revolution that most of us are not aware of. And least aware are the *Establishment* scientists.... The new puzzle pieces are being given to us by the whole parapsychological scene—ESP, telepathy, the Uri Geller phenomena, psychic healing and particularly psychic surgery."

But now Hynek is troubled by a seeming contradiction. If UFOs are psychic constructs, how come they leave physical traces? "UFOs break tree branches, appear on radar and are photographed. Maybe they're an example of the Uri Geller-type phenomena in which physical effects occur apparently without physical causes...."

Do the aliens come from beyond Pluto, or from "parallel or interlocking worlds"? Hynek wishes he knew. (The fairies, Conan Doyle believed, live in an interlocking world of "vibrations" different from ours. See his book, *The Coming of the Fairies*, with its splendid photos of the winged creatures, far more convincing than the blurry, easily faked photos of ufology.)

"I ran across two contactee cases just recently," Hynek told *Fate*,

in which the witnesses said they were impelled to do something; they were compelled to sleepwalk, to leave their beds and to go where the spacecraft was waiting. There they saw the creatures. They were without will of their own and suffered very bad effects from the experience— nausea, headaches, etc. The modern psychiatrist might label these persons "disturbed." Sure they're disturbed. But why?

Hynek's remarks outline the central plot of *Close Encounters*. Roy Neary ("near" the Great Truth?), played by Richard Dreyfuss, who also starred in *Jaws*, is a power company lineman in Muncie, Indiana—the "Middletown" chosen by the Lynds for their classic sociological study of ordinary Americans. (No doubt the aliens read the book in kindergarten.) When Roy is sent to investigate a mysterious blackout, he has a dramatic encounter of the second kind. Back home, he becomes increasingly haunted by a mountain shape. He sees it first in a glob of shaving cream, and at dinner tries to build it with mashed potatoes while a son's eyes fill with tears. He thinks poor dad is losing his marbles. A few days later Neary is yanking up shrubs to garnish a large model of a mountain he has constructed in his hobby room. His distraught wife, a prototype of the stubborn UFO skeptic, packs the children in a car and leaves.

As luck would have it, Roy sees on a TV newscast the very mountain he has modeled. It is Devil's Tower, a steep-sided mesa in Wyoming. There has been, it seems, a derailment, and the area is being evacuated because a nerve gas has contaminated the region. Roy feels compelled to go there.

A young widow, Jillian Guiler, lives not far from Roy with her four-year-old son Barry. When a UFO passes over her roof at night, all the electrical toys and devices in the house turn on and go haywire. (This, by the way, is something new in ufology.) Barry, enjoying the poltergeist fun, runs out of the house. Jill finally catches him, but not before the two are almost killed on the highway by Neary, who is chasing a chain of UFOs around a dangerous curve.

A few nights later, when the UFO returns, the force inside Jill's house is even scarier. She tries to bolt the doors and windows, but the force drags Barry through the dog's kitchen entrance. This time, for reasons never made clear, the aliens kidnap him. Now Jill is obsessed by the mountain shape. She, too, seeing it on the news, can't avoid the trek to Wyoming. Near Devil's Tower, Jill and Roy meet again.

The chemical derailment is only a cover for Project Mayflower. The aliens have made computer contact with an international group of ufologists, headed by a handsome expert acted by the French movie director François Truffaut, who died in 1984. Spielberg had in mind Jacques Vallee, a French-born ufologist who collaborated with Hynek on their 1975 UFO book, *The Edge of Reality*.

What the Devil is going on? Well, the aliens want a rendezvous on Devil's Tower. Technicians have blasted out a clearing on the mountain and surrounded it with floodlights, computers, television cameras, portable toilets, and so on. A Moog synthesizer is connected to a big display screen on which each tone lights a differently colored rectangle.

Project personnel try to hustle Roy and Jill out of the area, along with a small group of "nobodies" who also have been inexplicably drawn there, but the pair escape. After strenuous exertions they finally make it to the clearing just in time to hear the loudspeakers boom: "Take your positions please. This is not a drill."

To prove how friendly they are, the aliens put on a stupendous aerial show. For an opener they form stars in the dark sky that duplicate the Big Dipper. Then their small craft, seemingly made entirely of colored lights, swoop here and there, flying through one another and through the mesa just like Jonathan Livingston Seagull.

The mother ship, a monstrous wheel of light, slowly settles over the clearing and hangs there like a mammoth Victorian chandelier. Swing low sweet chariot. In the novel it generates a negative gravity field that makes everybody feel 40 percent lighter. The mother ship is Spielberg's beatific vision, his poor replica of Dante's vision of the Godhead in the last canto of *The Divine Comedy*. Some observers actually fall on their knees in awe.

On the Moog synthesizer a musician plays a corny five-note theme that the aliens have taught the earthlings as a kind of password. The mother ship breaks into deep organ tones. A computer gets into the act, and there is an idiotic jam session that Spielberg describes as "very strange music—at one moment melodic and the next atonal, sometimes jazzy, then a little country western. . . ."

Pauline Kael, in the *New Yorker*, called this "one of the peerless moments in movie history—spiritually reassuring, magical, and funny at the same time." Apparently Ms. Kael sat bug-eyed through the film, finding it an innocent fantasy of such "immense charm" that she could only liken it to *The Wizard of Oz*. "It's trying to teach us something," says a technician during the film's peerless moment. "It's the first day of school, fellas!"

Like Dante's, Roy's desire and will are now rolling with the divine wheel of cosmic love. His wife and children? Who cares. Truffaut, sensing Roy's desire, recruits him on the spot to join a team of a dozen astronauts (the twelve disciples?) who are waiting in helmets and red jumpsuits to go aboard.

The ship disgorges a group of dazed U.S. Navy men. Surprise! They are the crew of the famous lost patrol of Flight 19, a squadron of five Avenger torpedo bombers that vanished into the Bermuda Triangle in 1945.

Someone says: "Lieutenant, welcome home. This way to debriefing." It would be hard to top that in bathos, but Spielberg does it. "They haven't even aged!" a civilian shouts. "Einstein *was* right!" To which a team leader responds: "Einstein was probably one of them."

And now, toddling out of the mother ship, still enjoying the fun and games, is little Barry. Jill rushes forward, accompanied by handclaps in the theater.

Tall creatures start to emerge. They are hard to see, silhouetted against a blinding white light, but we can make out enormous heads, long necks, and pipe-stem arms and legs of great flexibility. They are followed by their children—twittering, lovable little things who rush around touching everybody, "feeling human groins, human faces, human backsides." It's a group grope at Esalen. "If the human didn't like it, they moved on to someone who did . . . an orgy of touching, palpating, feeling, stroking."

The thirteen red-clad astronauts (for Roy is now among them) march solemnly into the mother ship. Presumably they will be brought back later, from wherever they are going, stuffed with transcendent wisdom. The Age of

Aquarius has dawned. Jill watches through happy tears, snapping photos with her Instamatic, and too freaked out to guess that when Roy returns she'll be an old lady and he'll still be thirty-two.

At last—a close-up of an alien. It has a big balloon of a face, with enormous Kewpie-doll eyes. Responding to Truffaut's noble, transfigured countenance, the face manages a feeble, crooked smile before he, she, or it returns to the mother ship. The picture ends, not with a bang but a simper.

Before the brave astronauts go aboard there is a crude church service during which a priest intones: "God has given you his angels' charge over you." Could it be that these friendly humanoids are the angels of the Bible? Billy Graham and Father Andrew Greeley won't buy it, but millions of Laodicean Protestants will have no trouble stashing the notion into their brains alongside demons and other moldering vestiges of Christian mythology.

It is this pretentious, quasi-religious, Nirvana-like finale that may well have kept Spielberg's ridiculous script from sending Columbia Pictures stock into a tailspin. No, not enough ordinary souls out there, even in Muncie, are capable of smelling the spiritual fakery of it all. For it is not God who comes to rescue humanity. It is just another race of humanoids.

"It turns me on," Spielberg told *Newsweek,* "to think that when we die we don't go to heaven but to space, to Alpha Centauri, and there we're given a laser blaster and an air-cushion car." Does this not say it all? Gee whiz, fellas! Jesus (a superhumanoid from another galaxy?) once prayed (Luke 10: 21): "I thank thee, O Father, Lord of heaven and earth, that thou hast hid these things from the wise and prudent, and hast revealed them unto babes." This is why the aliens are so interested in Barry and simple nobodies like Neary. This is why the wise scientists won't look through Hynek's psychic telescope.

In the original film version of *Close Encounters* a song from Roy's childhood floats into his head just before he boards the celestial chariot. You won't believe it, but the song is from Walt Disney's *Pinocchio,* and its stanzas still grace the last pages of the novel.

> *When you wish upon a star,*
> *Makes no difference who you are,*
> *Anything your heart desires will*
> *come . . . to . . . you.*

As Roy, eyes shining, tramps like a Cub Scout into the Great Mystery, another stanza jogs through his mind:

> *Like a bolt out of the blue,*
> *Fate steps in and sees you through.*

When you wish upon a star your
dream . . . comes . . . true.

After this scene provoked derisive snorts at a Texas preview, Spielberg had enough sense to recognize that its effect was about the same as having Roy burst into the lyrics of "On the Good Ship Lollipop." I'll bet a dime that even Dr. Hynek was happy to see Pinocchio go.

What remains is not much better. It is fashionable now to describe Spielberg as a terribly gifted but innocent prodigy, bug-eyed with wonder and lost in the Ozzy worlds of modern technology and the silver screen. It will be interesting, concluded *Newsweek*, to watch him grow up.

POSTSCRIPT

Hynek died in 1986, age seventy-eight, still persuaded that aliens from higher dimensions are invading our space.

Hynek, along with Edgar Mitchell, Betty Hill, George Barski, and Robert Jastrow, were guests on the Stanley Seigel TV show December 30, 1977. Mitchell said he thought it "probable" that UFOs were extraterrestrial, that he was a "religious" man, and that the UFOs "might" be here to aid humanity. Hynek was even more cautious. He allowed that *Close Encounters* was overdramatic, but he praised Spielberg's knowledge of ufology and said that everything in the movie was based on actual reports.

Betty Hill, whose close encounter (along with her now-deceased husband, Barney) was the basis of a book by John G. Fuller, retold her wild story for the umpteenth time. She displayed a modeled head of one of the creatures who had "dragged her aboard" the UFO, and she said that the Kewpie-doll head in *Close Encounters* had been based on it. One of the aliens spoke to her in English, and she has a torn dress to prove she struggled with them. Both Mitchell and Hynek looked uncomfortable while she rattled on, though neither of them uttered a single critical remark.

Barski, an elderly gentlemen who owns a liquor store, told the story of his encounter of the second kind. All he did was watch from his car while ten or more creatures from a cylindrical UFO scooped up samples of earth. They were three feet high and looked, he said, like children in jumpsuits.

Jastrow pointed out that if there are intelligent beings elsewhere in the universe they are likely to be billions of years ahead of us and therefore extremely unlikely to resemble human children in jumpsuits. The trouble with all contactee stories, he said sensibly, is that the creatures never talk or behave in a way commensurate with advanced beings. As I would put it, they talk and act exactly like the notions that simpleminded people have of creatures from other worlds.

The friendship between Hynek and Vallee suddenly cooled in 1979, but let me first back up and summarize Vallee's strange career. His first two books of ufology, *Anatomy of a Phenomenon* (Regnery, 1965) and *Challenge to Science* (Regnery, 1966) leaned toward the then-prevailing view among UFO buffs that UFOs are alien spacecraft. The second book, which Vallee wrote with his wife, Janine, has an introduction by Hynek.

Vallee became a U.S. citizen in 1967 and lived near San Francisco, where he headed his Infomedia Corporation. He has a French master's degree in astrophysics and a doctorate in computer science from Northwestern University.

In 1969 Regnery brought out Vallee's third book, *Passport to Magonia*. It marked his first big turn in mental space. UFOs, he argued, are probably *not* nuts-and-bolts spacecraft. More likely they are paranormal phenomena, as Jung suggested. Vallee explicitly likened them to the fairies that everybody seemed to see in Conan Doyle's day.

Vallee's next book, *The Invisible College* (Dutton, 1975), introduced his concept of a "control system." UFOs are myths created by unknown paranormal forces. The book's title refers to an underground network of people, organized by Vallee, who study UFOs seriously. The same paranormal hypothesis dominates *The Edge of Reality* (Regnery, 1975), which Vallee wrote in collaboration with Hynek. "There is a physical object," Vallee said in an interview published in *Fate* (February 1978). "It may be a flying saucer or it may be a projection or it may be something entirely different." Whatever it is, it "has the ability to create a distortion of the sense of reality or to substitute artificial sensations for the real ones. . . . A strange kind of deception may be involved."

Deception! This bold thought reached full flower in Vallee's book, *Messengers of Deception* (And/Or Press, 1979). In this stupid, paranoid work Vallee puts forth the hypothesis that UFOs are the product of deliberate human deception by high government officials, possibly a collaborated effort by the major governments of the world similar to deceptions they used against Hitler in the Second World War. The purpose of the plot is to spread irrationalism around the world, an irrationalism that could topple humanity and lead to another Dark Age. UFOs are not from outer space. They are created right here on earth by an advanced "psychotronic technology." They are real, all right, and can do all sorts of terrible physical things, such as mutilate cattle. Exactly what is a UFO? "I don't know what it is," Vallee told Christopher Evans in an *Omni* interview (January 1980). "It seems to be a lot of electromagnetic energy in the form of microwaves, in a small space, and an intense, colored 'light.'"

Hynek did not buy this earth-based conspiracy theory. He was particularly incensed by Vallee's suggestion that agents of the Great Plot have infiltrated numerous UFO organizations and cults, including Hynek's own Center for UFO Studies! That was a bit much. Hynek blasted the plot theory in his article "Messengers of Deception, Or Who's Manipulating Whom?" in *Second Look* (May 1979).

Hynek said he didn't know what UFOs are either. In his lecture entitled "What I Really Believe About UFOs" (*Proceedings of the First International UFO Congress*, compiled and edited by Curtis G. Fuller, Warner paperback, 1980), Hynek said essentially the following. There is strong evidence that UFOs are nut-and-bolts spacecraft controlled by ETI (extraterrestrial intelligence) and equally strong evidence they are psychic phenomena controlled by EDI (extradimensional intelligence in some parallel reality). Hynek proposed a third possibility: They are both physical and psychic, both material and mental.

Hynek said he didn't "support" any of these theories. They were hotly debated at the 1977 congress at which Hynek spoke, a congress sponsored by that great "scientific journal," *Fate* magazine. Hynek didn't want to offend anybody listening to him, but he left no doubt about his belief that UFOs present a deep mystery for science and that we are in a position similar to that of Galileo trying to understand sunspots. We are on the threshold of a major scientific breakthrough, although Hynek didn't know just what it will be. People in future centuries, he said, will look back on us and say, "They were really dumb in those days. They didn't even know what UFOs were." Doyle felt exactly the same way about his ghosts and fairies, but instead of people looking back now and saying how dumb the skeptics were—they didn't even understand fairies and ectoplasm—they look back and marvel at how dumb Doyle was.

As for dumb skeptics like Carl Sagan, Phil Klass, and myself, who see the UFO mania as nothing more than a social-psychological phenomenon, we are what Vallee calls the "useful idiots" who are being manipulated by whatever diabolical government and military forces are behind the great UFO deception. Does Vallee really believe all this? I wish I could say no and call him an interesting charlatan, but I fear the answer is yes.

I am not so sure about Charles Berlitz. He made his first pile of dough with *The Bermuda Triangle* and tried again with *The Roswell Incident* (Grosset & Dunlap, 1980), in which he and his coauthor tell us all about the flying saucer that crashed near Roswell, New Mexico, in 1947. The Air Force keeps saying it was just a weather balloon and its instruments, but Berlitz knows better. It was a craft from outer space, and the CIA is hiding the wreckage and the bodies of the extraterrestrials in a secret warehouse in Virginia. Yes, Virginia, the aliens are right there, and we "sit at the verge of the greatest news story of the twentieth century. . . ."

Said *Discover* (in its October 1980 review of this latest slice of ufological baloney): "Anyone who will believe that such a secret could be kept through six different administrations in a loose-lipped city like Washington deserves Charles Berlitz."

The UFO mania shows no signs of fading. Books on close encounters and abductions by aliens are earning millions for such writers as Budd Hopkins and Whitley Strieber and their publishers. To Harvard's great embarrassment, one of their tenured faculty members, psychiatrist John Mack, has become the most famous UFO therapist using hypnosis and other techniques to restore memories of UFO abductions. Like Hynek and other UFO buffs, Dr. Mack believes the aliens come here from parallel worlds in higher space-time dimensions. His book *Abductions: Human Encounters with Aliens* (1994) swarms with lurid accounts of the revived memories of thirteen abductees.

PART IV

MATHEMATICS

There is as much mystery about mathematics as about the universe. Purely abstract structures such as circles, triangles, groups, numbers, infinite sets, higher dimensions, and thousands of other mathematical objects seem to have a peculiar existence of their own, independent of both the outside world and the human mind—even though they don't "exist" in the way stones and stars exist. Like almost all mathematicians, I am a Platonist who believes that mathematical objects and theorems are as much discovered as scientific laws. I believe that a huge number with, say, a million digits is either a prime or a composite before any human proves it one way or the other.

Although it is largely unrecognized, mathematics is, of course, part of our culture, because everything humans do is part of human culture. In a trivial sense mathematical objects and theorems are creations of human minds. The more profound mystery is why, after being created or discovered (either term is legitimate), they so beautifully fit the outside world.

Physicist Eugene Wigner, who won a Nobel Prize in 1963, and who died in 1995, at age ninety-two, wrote a famous essay titled "The Unreasonable Effectiveness of Mathematics." As a Platonist, I believe that this seemingly miraculous correspondence arises because mathematical structure is the basis of the universe. Since our minds are part of the universe, is it so surprising that mathematics neatly fits a universe not made by us?

TWENTY-TWO

MATHEMATICS AND THE FOLKWAYS

Because physical laws are based on observations and experiments they are never absolutely certain. They are always corrigible, subject to possible revision as more is learned about how Nature behaves. Pure mathematics, on the other hand, has a curious kind of certainty. The Pythagorean theorem, for example, is true in all possible worlds because it follows with iron logic from the axioms and rules of a formal system, the system of Euclidian plane geometry. It is what philosophers like to call an analytic statement. As Bertrand Russell once said, the theorems of pure mathematics ultimately reduce to such great truths as that there are three feet in a yard.

The following essay was the first of many efforts to defend mathematical realism and certainty against the subjective views of a small number of thinkers, most of them social scientists, who are still under the sway of extreme cultural relativism. It first appeared in the Journal of Philosophy *(March 30, 1950).*

If there is any aspect of our culture that one might suppose would lie outside the folkways, grounded in a reality independent of cultural processes, it is mathematics—the Queen of the Sciences. Alas, she has been toppled from her lonely throne! Dr. Leslie Alvin White, while professor of anthropology at the University of Michigan, was responsible for this bold deed. In a chapter called "The Locus of Mathematical Reality," in his book *The Science of Culture* (Farrar, Straus, 1949), he banishes her to the region of the folkways to join company with other distinguished exiles from the realms of Truth, Beauty, and Goodness. Because Professor White's chapter carries to an ultimate extreme the approach that in anthropology is called "cultural determinism," marking the conquest of the last outpost of values that were thought to be in contact with a universal, non-social reality, it seems worthwhile to make a close inspection of the author's arguments.

Professor White opens the chapter with a quotation from *Through the Looking Glass*. It is the section in which Alice is told she is merely a figment of the Red King's dream. The passage is appropriate because the chapter defends a view that leads ultimately, as the author himself apparently realized, to a curious kind of collective solipsism.

Of course Professor White does not put it in those terms. He is concerned only with what he calls "mathematical reality." The laws of mathematics, he writes, are "wholly dependent upon the mind of the species." "Mathematics in its entirety, its 'truths' and its 'realities,' is a part of human culture, nothing more." "The locus of mathematical reality is cultural tradition." "Mathematical concepts are independent of the individual mind but lie wholly within the mind of the species, i.e., culture." "Its [mathematical] reality is cultural: the sort of reality possessed by a code of etiquette, traffic regulations, the rules of baseball, the English language or rules of grammar."

One final quotation: "It is now clear that concepts such as space, straight line, plane, etc., are no more necessary and inevitable as a consequence of the structure of the external world than are the concepts green and yellow—or the relationship term with which you designate your mother's brother, for that matter."

Let us take a more careful look at that last statement. The *term* by which a society designates the kinship of uncle-nephew is, of course, purely cultural. But the relationship itself, the *denotatum* of the sign, is clearly an aspect of the external world that would exist whether anyone gave a term to it or not. Dinosaurs had uncles and nephews long before a species evolved capable of describing the relationship in language symbols.

Similarly with colors. The *term* "green" is obviously a cultural reality. The *sensation* of green is a psychological reality. But the sensation and the symbol are both grounded in an external state of affairs that causes all wavelengths of light to be absorbed by an object except the green, which is reflected to the eye of the observer.

When Professor White suggests that colors are not features of the external world he certainly does not mean anything so trivial as that color *sensations* are in the mind. His chapter makes quite clear that he wishes to deny any necessary causal connection between the sensations and outside reality. Colors are not "a consequence of the structure of the external world." You might think so, he adds, until you learn that Creek and Natchez Indians did not distinguish yellow from green, but had a common term for both.

This is an astonishing *non sequitur*. The fact that these Indian tribes used the same word for what we call yellow and green does not mean that a tribesman could not distinguish between green and yellow objects otherwise identical. If someone had shown him a green and a yellow string of beads, pointed to the green saying, "This is yours," then mixed them and asked him to pick out "his," there is no reason for thinking he would have experienced any difficulty. Does Professor White mean to imply that the Creek and Natchez Indians had a culturally conditioned yellow-green color blindness?

One is reminded of the famous controversy over Homer's color sense, provoked by the British statesman William Gladstone. In 1858 Gladstone wrote a book on Homer which suggested that the Greek poet was color-blind because of his meager use of color words. In 1870 a German group of evolutionary ethnologists argued that the entire Greek population of Homer's day was color-blind, and that ability to discriminate colors did not develop until a culture reached advanced levels of complexity. The first important attack on this view was Grant Allen's *The Colour Sense: Its Origin and Development* (1879). Allen called attention to the fact that a single term for green and blue is common among primitive societies, but he pointed out that the Highland Scots, who did not verbally distinguish green and blue, were able to discriminate perfectly between the two colors when they were tested for this ability. There was no word for "orange" in the Middle English of Chaucer's time and one might suppose Chaucer unaware of this dubious color had he not referred twice in the *Canterbury Tales* to a shade "bitwixe yelow and reed." Since 1900 the theory that a deficiency of color terms in a language indicates a deficiency in color discrimination has been increasingly discredited, especially by the investigations of the Spanish anthropologist José Perez de Barradas, published in the thirties.

No one questions, of course, that the precise areas of the spectrum signified by color words will vary widely from culture to culture depending on the society's needs. A primitive tribe may demand only a few color words, whereas a modern factory producing women's dresses may require terms for several hundred different shades. Members of a tribe who did not distinguish green from yellow might have an understandable tendency to confuse these colors, just as it is easy for us to confuse shades of brown, but this does not mean that the tribesmen could not see the difference between green and yellow. The basic issue, of course, is whether the process of color vision is culturally determined, as Professor White implies, or whether it is determined by an external structure ordered in such manner that it sends certain wave lengths to the retina that result in certain color sensations in the brain.

Precisely the same issue is involved in regard to "mathematical reality." We do not have to plunge here into the highly technical controversies over the exact meaning of "reality" that divide such philosophers as Carnap, Russell, and Dewey, because the vital point is much simpler. There has been no philosopher of eminence, including the logical empiricists, who has argued that the so-called external world was nothing more than a projection of human minds. Even idealists like Berkeley, who insisted that nothing could exist ex-

cept as perceived, were quick to restore external reality by making the world
a projection of God's mind. Berkeley's stones are just as external and kickable
as the stones of a materialist. All we need grant, for purposes of this elementary discussion, is the existence of a world outside of human minds that has
a structure that is ordered.[1] We need not concern ourselves with the metaphysical questions of how or why it exists, or exactly how and why it is ordered.
It will suffice if we are willing to abandon solipsism, both of the individual
and of the group, and confess belief in an outside reality that is more than a
vast, nondescript fog in which such features as, say, spiral nebulae, are merely
projections of our interests, involving no pattern of parts other than the patterns we infuse into them by our attention.

And what are the consequences of affirming an external order? It follows
that mathematical concepts, like colors and family linkages, have at least one
foothold in a reality independent of the human species. It is true, of course,
that an abstract triangle does not exist in the same sense a cow does, but this
does not mean that the concept of triangle is an arbitrary cultural feature
unconnected with the structure of the world. Professor White himself admits
this connection at the close of his chapter when he discusses briefly the question of how mathematical concepts first arose. They were produced, he says,
in the "nervous systems" of our apelike ancestors, and he reminds us that
apes "have a fine appreciation of geometric forms." This is a startling admission, because clearly, if an ape appreciates geometric forms, there must be
geometric forms outside of human culture for him to appreciate. This is only
another way of saying that, if all men vanished, there would still be a sense
(exactly *what* sense is another and more difficult problem) in which spiral
nebulae could be said to spiral, and hexagonal ice crystals to be hexagonal,
even though no human creatures were around to give these forms a name.
The only alternative to this view is to insist that all the order we perceive in
the universe, whether it be the static geometrical order of structure or the
dynamic order of natural laws, is but a projection of our minds upon empty
space or, at the most, on a kind of patternless plenum.[2]

And yet the modern ethnologist, with his allergy toward absolutes, is constantly haunted by forms of subjective idealism. I recall an evening at the
University of Chicago a few years ago when I tried for hours, totally without
success, to persuade a group of anthropology graduate students that two plus
two were four in all cultures. It sounded to them suspiciously like a "cultural
universal" that might trap them into a value judgment. In the course of the
discussion, however, two important misconceptions about mathematics came
to light, and since both are to be found in Professor White's chapter, it might
be instructive to mention them here.

First, there is the notion that variations in counting systems somehow
mean variations in mathematical laws. People inherit methods of counting
and calculating from their culture, Professor White explains, just as they in-

herit ways of cooking and marrying. "Had Newton been reared in Hottentot culture he would have calculated like a Hottentot." The author's choice of Hottentot was unfortunate, because Hottentots have a decimal system and therefore calculate the same way Newton did; but even if Professor White had chosen, say, the African bushmen who use a binary system, the illustration would still have been utterly valueless for his purposes. Counting and calculation in the binary system make use of exactly the same mathematical laws as any other system. In fact most of the giant electronic calculators operate on a binary system because it adapts easily to electronic relays, but this does not imply that the machine is based on a different kind of mathematical reality. Variations in number systems are, in fact, nothing more than variations in methods of symbolization. Whatever is done in the signs of one system can be translated exactly into all the others. Any number can provide a base for counting, though in most cultures the base has been five, ten, or twenty in correspondence with the groupings of fingers and toes. (One of the curiosities of ethnology is the quaternary system of the Yuki Indians in California. They counted on the *spaces* between fingers.) The base number chosen will play a role in determining the sounds used for higher numbers, or the way they are depicted in writing, but this no more changes the underlying mathematical laws than the number designated by "17" changes its properties when it is symbolized by Roman numerals or in the Mayan vigesimal system by two dots above three horizontal lines.

To make this very clear, let us consider for a moment the meaning of "two plus two are four." In everyday experience we find that objects often are grouped as couples. To all classes of couples let us give the generic name of "bing." We further observe another type of configuration of units, which in our culture is designated by the word "four." To this grouping we will give the name "bong." A little experimentation with groups of bings soon establishes an astonishing law. Whenever we add one bing to another bing, producing so to speak "bing bings," the new configuration invariably belongs to the class we have designated "bong." Thus we arrive at a simple arithmetical law, "Bing plus bing are bong." This is what is meant by "two plus two are four."

I am aware of the fact that, if two drops of water are added to two drops, the result may be one large drop. But in so far as the units remain units, the law is universal and invariable. If a tribesman breaks each of two sticks in half he will find he has four sticks. If he extends two fingers of one hand, then two more, he would be surprised indeed to discover, exclusive of his thumb, five fingers.

John Stuart Mill, in an effort to establish logic and mathematics on an empirical basis, imagined a mischievous demon who went about creating fifth objects whenever two things were brought together with two other things. If this were the case, Mill reasoned, our arithmetic books would tell us that two plus two equaled five. Most contemporary empiricists agree that experience provides the psychological origin for our knowledge of mathematical laws, but they prefer to give the laws an absolute validity of their own—analytic, formal, and a priori.[3] We need not concern ourselves, however, with the controversy between those who defend Mill's view, and those who, like Carnap and Russell, regard the laws as true of all possible worlds, because in neither case are the laws subject to cultural variation. The spoken and written signs by which a culture symbolizes mathematical reality are, of course, culturally determined, though one method of symbolization may be more efficient than another. Robert Lowie, in his *Introduction to Cultural Anthropology*, does not hesitate to describe the Roman system as "cumbersome" in comparison with the Mayan, which introduced the valuable zero symbol.

It is important to realize also that the process of addition does not require the witness of a human being. It operates just as effectively when no one is looking. If you drop two pennies in a child's empty bank, then two more pennies, you will discover, on opening the bank, that it contains four pennies. The entire operation could, in fact, be performed mechanically and recorded on film.

The view that mathematics is grounded only in the cultural process slides easily into the "collective solipsism" that George Orwell satirizes in his novel *Nineteen Eighty-Four*. For if mathematics is in the folkways, and the folkways can be molded by a political party, then it follows that the party can proclaim mathematical laws. "Reality exists in the human mind," declares O'Brien, member of the Inner Party, "and nowhere else. Not in the individual mind, which can make mistakes, and in any case soon perishes; only in the mind of the Party, which is collective and immortal. Whatever the Party holds to be truth *is* truth." One of the more agonizing episodes in the novel is the scene in which the protagonist is tortured into the conviction that two plus two are sometimes five.

A second common source of confusion concerning these topics is the fact that recent work in mathematics, stimulated by the relativity revolution in physics, seems to deny an absolute validity to familiar Euclidean laws. For centuries, Professor White points out, it was thought that Euclid's theorems were necessary, but "the invention of non-Euclidean geometries . . . has dispelled this view entirely."

Now there is a sense in which this is entirely correct; but it is a sense wholly foreign to Professor White's purposes. It is true there is no a priori reason why a geometrical postulate, such as the famous parallel postulate, must be true. A coherent non-Euclidean system can be constructed that will violate this postulate, and the discoveries of modern physics suggest that such a system is a sounder basis on which to make calculations involving high speeds and astronomical distances. But on the level of ordinary speeds and distances, we live very much in an old-fashioned, prosaic, Euclidean world that does not vary in any *measurable* respect from one geographical area to another. If a tribesman wishes to shoot a bird with a bow and arrow, it is necessary for him, whatever his tribal affiliation, to aim the arrow at the bird in strict accord with Euclidean and Newtonian laws and not, say, to shoot the arrow in the opposite direction on the grounds that straight lines, prolonged indefinitely in a closed fourth-dimensional continuum, will circle the cosmos and return to the starting point.

A moment's reflection and one will realize that any imaginable society, to exist at all, must constantly make use of elementary mathematical laws that are everywhere the same but so commonplace we are seldom aware of them. For example, to exist it is necessary to eat, and to eat it is necessary that something be placed in the mouth. But the fact that a smaller object can be pushed through a larger orifice is a fact of geometry. A tribe that acted on the reverse assumption, i.e., that only larger objects could be placed through smaller holes, would be acting on a law that, however well grounded it might be in the mythology of the culture, would be so poorly grounded in mathematical reality that the tribe would quickly die of starvation.

Of course no native group has ever adopted a belief that stupid, and in fact ethnological research of recent decades has disclosed members of primitive societies to be not nearly as unlearned in mathematics as earlier anthropologists had supposed. At one time it was assumed that, if a tribe had no words for numbers beyond two or three, members were incapable of counting beyond two or three. Early investigators, however, were puzzled by the uncanny ability of these natives to survey a herd of fifty sheep and immediately know when one was missing. It was supposed that the native had a phenomenal memory in which he retained the entire herd gestalt; or perhaps he knew each sheep personally and recalled the face. But later investigation soon made clear that these natives had elaborate means of counting in which they made use of various parts of their anatomy in a predetermined order. For example, they counted their fingers, wrists, elbows, armpits, nipples, navel, knees, and toes. The counting would be done mentally; then, instead of remembering a word for 31, the native would simply recall that he stopped counting on, say, his left big toe.

Lévy-Bruhl's books on primitive mentality made clear that the savage was much shrewder than the aboriginal idiots described by Spencer in his *Principles of Sociology*. But even Lévy-Bruhl is now regarded as having greatly exaggerated the extent to which savage "pre-logical" thought differs from our own. There is perhaps a more thorough mixing of reality with the religious projective system; but, when it comes to solving practical problems within terms of their own culture, they do as well, if not better, than we do. And they are successful precisely because they make use of laws of logic and mathematics that have their loci, not in the culture, but in external reality. The laws are discovered, not created, just as the laws of the lever or wheel are discovered; and there is no reason an anthropologist should be ashamed to admit this fact.

In fairness to Professor White I should say at this point that I do not doubt for a moment that he believes in an external world, of orderly structure, and that this order plays a necessary role in determining the ways in which cultures formulate mathematical and physical laws. His article contains a great deal of ambiguity, and I suppose it would be possible to twist and force his statements to mean nothing more than that the *cultural* aspect of mathematics is cultural. But this is like saying that all aspects of reality within this room are inside this room, and I have accordingly paid Professor White the compliment of assuming his words to mean something less trivial—to convey what he obviously believes to be a new and revolutionary approach to his topic. I have tried to show that this approach leads to an idealism that Professor White would be the first, I am sure, to disavow.

Since 1900, cultural anthropologists have been in a phase of reaction against the naïve ethnocentrism of their Victorian predecessors. One by one various aspects of culture—art, philosophy, religion, ethics—have fallen into the category of the folkways. Karl Mannheim's "sociology of knowledge" subjected all ideas, including those of science, to sociological investigation. But even Mannheim did not dream of maintaining that the laws of mathematics, or even the knowledge obtained by science, were culturally determined. "Relating individual ideas to the total structure of a given historico-social subject," he wrote in his *Ideology and Utopia*, "should not be confused with a philosophical relativism which denies the validity of any standards and of the existence of order in the world" (p. 254). On page 263 he explicitly cites the law of "two times two equals four" as an example of the sort of truth *not* subject to cultural determination. Even in the social sciences Mannheim believed objective knowledge to be possible. In fact the chief end of the sociology of knowledge, as he saw it, was to "unmask" the unconscious compulsions behind conflicting points of view and so enable the social scientist to arrive at a perspective that would be the most objective possible, and therefore the nearest to reality. Two quotations from *Ideology and Utopia* will suffice:

> No one denies the possibility of empirical research nor does anyone maintain that facts do not exist (nothing seems more incorrect to us than an illusionist theory of knowledge).

> It is, of course, true that in the social sciences, as elsewhere, the ultimate criterion of truth or falsity is to be found in the investigation of the object, and the sociology of knowledge is no substitute for this.

In Mannheim's view the student of the sociology of knowledge is like a man moving among a group of artists who surround a nude model (reality), each painting her from his own perspective. The man studies every canvas, comparing it with what he sees from each artist's perspective, and in this manner tries to arrive at an accurate understanding of the model's shape. The notion that, because each artist paints her differently, therefore her anatomy has no definite shape, would have struck Mannheim as a completely indefensible form of subjective idealism. And I need not add that "shape" is geometrical.

Among contemporary anthropologists signs of a long-needed rebellion against extreme cultural determinism are increasingly evident. The work of such men as Kardiner and Linton (Professor White does not mention Kardiner in his 650-page survey of "culturology," and he cites Linton only to disagree with him) is beginning to suggest dimly a basis for setting up standards of mental health that may someday provide a rough yardstick for measuring the degree to which a culture satisfies the basic needs of its members. It is regrettable that Professor White, out of sheer inertia, should let the older trend propel him through the looking glass into a realm of dream and nonsense.

POSTSCRIPT

Leslie Alvin White, one of America's most influential and controversial anthropologists, died in 1975 after a distinguished career at the University of Michigan. Although he regarded all of mathematics, even the theoretical constructions of physics, as rooted in culture, not in the outside world, he was not a cultural relativist. Far from it! More than any other anthropologist, White was responsible for the revival of the evolutionary views of Lewis Morgan. Like Morgan, White saw all cultures as passing through stages from savagery to barbarism to civilization, thereby achieving genuine progress toward better and better ways of meeting basic human needs.

George Boas and other cultural relativists recognized the importance of environment (that is, the external world) in shaping both individual personalities and cultures. In his vigorous battle against the cultural relativism of Boas, there was (in my opinion) no need whatever for White to abandon epistemological realism. I see his paper on mathematics as an aberration, inconsistent with evolutionary anthropology and written out of philosophical naïveté. It is easy to understand why. In his later years White became so obsessed by his vision of culture as the fundamental reality that he almost forgot there was a big world out there, with its own fixed laws not made by us, that had produced all human cultures. But I will say no more here about White's curious philosophy, which I find marred by internal contradictions, because I will discuss it later in a review of White's most important book, *The Science of Culture*.

White's "Locus of Mathematical Reality" was first reprinted in *The Science of Culture* (1949) but it did not become widely known to mathematicians until James R. Newman reprinted it in his best-selling four-volume anthology, *The World of Mathematics* (1956). Although Newman included many pieces by mathematical realists (for example, a portion of G. H. Hardy's *A Mathematician's Apology*, with its vigorous defense of realism[4]), he was inclined to look favorably on White's cultural solipsism. I can still recall the shock I experienced when I first came upon the following passage in *Mathematics and the Imagination*, which Newman wrote with Edward Kasner: ". . . we have overcome the notion that mathematical truths have an existence independent and apart from our own minds. It is even strange to us that such a notion could have ever existed."

Kasner and Newman go on to admit that hundreds of great mathematicians held just such a view, but they are convinced that it was overthrown by (among other things) the discovery of non-Euclidean geometry. Twentieth-century mathematicians, they contend, now realize that mathematics "is man's own handiwork subject only to the limitations imposed by the laws of thought."

What the authors don't tell you is that even today the majority of great mathematicians still regard mathematical truths as independent of human thought. Nor do they remind you that relativity theory adopted non-Euclidean geometry (which of course was the work of human minds) because it best fitted what empirical investigations had discovered about the structure of space-time, out there, in a universe not created by you and me.

Newman also included in *The World of Mathematics* a paper as muddled in its thinking as White's: "Mathematics and the World," by Douglas A. T. Gasking. It first appeared in 1940 in an Australian philosophical journal and has since been reprinted in several books. Gasking's thesis is that our choice of what mathematics to apply to the world is entirely a matter of convention, dictated by what we find convenient rather than by the structure of the outside world. To prove this, he introduces several "queer" multiplication tables, as he calls them, which he says work perfectly well in measuring a rectangular floor with integral sides, and then tiling it with unit squares. To make the queer multiplication work, we must do one of three things: (1) use a queer system of measuring the two sides of the rectangle we wish to tile, (2) use a queer system of counting tiles as we remove them from a bin, or (3) measure and count normally, but invoke queer laws of nature that change the length of our measuring rod while we use it or that change the area of each tile as we put it on the floor.

Consider Gasking's simplest example. Our strange multiplication table gives products that are twice what our familiar table gives: 1 times 1 = 2, 1 times 2 = 4, 2 times 2 = 8, 2 times 3 = 12, and so on. How do we make this work? When we take the tiles from the bin we simply count them by twos. Thus the first tile is called 2, the second is called 4, and so on. If our floor is 2 times 3 our strange arithmetic gives us an area of 12. Using our new way of counting, we count tiles until we reach 12. This gives us just the 6 we need. Clearly this reduces to the triviality that, instead of counting objects the ordinary way, we can get the same practical results if we counted by twos and then halve the final tally. Of course this is the same as doing ordinary arithmetic, except that we are doing it a more complicated way by giving different meanings to certain symbols.

I'll not spend time detailing the ambiguities, confusions, and contradictions in Gasking's paper. I know of no mathematician today who takes it seriously. If you are interested, check *Philosophy of Mathematics* (1964), edited by Paul Benacerraf and Hilary Putnam, where you'll find Gasking's eccentric essay followed by Hector-Neri Castañeda's paper, "Arithmetic and Reality," which thoroughly demolishes it.

I find in my files a clipping from *Scientific American*, dated October 1964, about some studies that reinforce what I had to say about color perception as distinct from color language. Verne F. Ray, an anthropologist, writing in the *Transactions of the New York Academy of Sciences*, reports on his investigations of the color perception of a hundred Indian tribes. He found that no two of them divided the color spectrum exactly the same way. Some had only three color words in their language, others eight. One tribe had two words for two shades of yellow. A wavelength on the dividing line between two color words in one language was sometimes in the middle of a color named in another language. Ray concluded that the language differences reflected no differences in color perception.

A vigorous defense of White's cultural solipsism is a paper by Raymond L. Wilder, "Mathematics: A Cultural Phenomenon," in *Essays in the Science of Culture: In Honor of Leslie A. White* (T.Y. Crowell, 1960), edited by Gertrude Dole and Robert Carneiro.[5] Wilder was a good friend of White, and one of his colleagues at the University of Michigan. I suspect that Wilder's philosophy of mathematics was a major influence on White's paper.

Wilder singles out my article as "one of the most bitter attacks on White's views" and then proceeds to take me to task for failing to understand modern mathematics. Now Wilder is of course a distinguished mathematician, and I am only a journalist; yet I must say that I find Wilder, like White, talking in a language both idiosyncratic and obfuscatory.

After quoting my remark that there is a sense in which the spiral form of a nebula is independent of human minds, Wilder adds: "I submit that if there were no human to *say* such things, the phenomena described would still be just phenomena and nothing more." Of course it would be just phenomena, leaving aside the possibility that the nebula could be observed by a nonhuman creature or by a god. Nobody can *say* a nebula has a spiral form unless there is somebody capable of saying it. The nontrivial question is whether it is meaningful to insist that the spiral form itself is mind dependent. If we refuse to say the form is "out there" in space, independent of you and me, do we have a right to say the *nebula* is out there?

Consider astronomy. Everything an astronomer says and writes is obviously cultural, because everything any human says and writes is part of culture. Moreover, astronomy is influenced in obvious ways by a culture's patterns of beliefs and interests. But who would want to say that the locus of astronomical reality is culture? In a sense it is, but since all science is cultural in the same sense, to say this is to say something vacuous. Astronomers and ordinary people talk in the language of Aristotelian realism. The locus of astronomy is the structure of the universe, not made by us, unless one believes that everything "out there" is a projection by our minds on some sort of unstructured fog.

To a realist, mathematical structure is mind-independent in two senses. The universe is not shapeless, but patterned in ways that are described by mathematics. In addition, mathematicians investigate purely abstract structures, defined by formal systems, which may or may not have applications to the physical world. The proper attitude to take toward the ontological status of these abstract systems is, of course, one of the great unending controversies in metaphysics. I will here say only that almost all mathematicians today agree with Hardy that a mathematician discovers truths that are independent of his culture and that those truths are qualitatively different from the conventions of traffic regulations or codes of etiquette.

There are two reasons for supposing that mathematical theorems are more than cultural conventions. One is that, whenever two cultures independently develop the same formal system, such as Euclidean geometry, they discover the same theorems. The second reason is that mathematics applies with eerie exactitude to the physical world. Any two cultures, isolated from each other, that develop a system for measuring the two sides of a right triangle and calculating the hypotenuse will discover the same Pythagorean rule, because that is how the world is structured. Of course, if they write down the rule or talk about it, their writing and talking will be mind-dependent in the same way that writing and talking about the moon is mind-dependent. But the moon itself, and the fact that it is spherical, is not mind-dependent.

"If it should occur in the future," writes Wilder, "that contact is established with beings on another planet having highly developed cultures, and elements are found in these cultures isomorphic to mathematical elements in our own culture, would this make these elements any less *cultural?*" In a sense, of course not; but the sense is trivial. If extraterrestrial chemists discover that the hydrogen atom has only one electron (they would express this, of course, in their own set of symbols), all their talking and writing about chemistry will naturally be cultural. But who wants to say that culture is the locus of chemical reality? It is much simpler and clearer to say that matter is the locus of chemical reality. Trees are independent of the minds of woodchoppers. Wood-chopping theory is cultural, but the theory rests on something that is not.

Of course it is mostly a matter of wordchopping, and Wilder would reply: sets of two things, like the two moons of Mars, do indeed exist "out there," but the number two does not. Like the good nominalist that he is, he regards all universals, such as numbers and circles and triangles, as mere symbols that are created by human minds. Therefore they are all part of culture. If all cultures in the cosmos were annihilated, the stars would continue to exist, and they would still exist in sets of two, three, four, and so on; but no one could *say* this, because there would be nobody around to say it. In this sense, all mathematics is cultural.

One may, of course, adopt any way of talking one likes, but the fact is that mathematicians do not talk like Wilder except for a few who are moti-vated by an intense desire to make humanity the measure of all things. I have known many mathematicians, some more eminent than Wilder. All of them, without exception, prefer to talk like Hardy. The notion that modern anthro-pology and the sociology of knowledge have rendered Hardy's way of talking obsolete is simply not true.

As I said in my original blast at White, if the cultural approach to math-ematics is no more than a belief that everything that goes on inside human minds is something that goes on inside human minds, then who can disagree? No one wants to deny that "trees" are culture-bound in the sense that a mind is needed to isolate a certain portion of reality and give it the name "tree." The name is obviously mind-dependent, but the structure of the tree is not. To adopt a language in which all the patterns of nature, and all the abstract patterns of formal mathematical systems, are as cultural-dependent as mar-riage rituals or rules for how to use a knife and fork is to talk in a way so far removed from ordinary language, as well as the language of great scientists and mathematicians and even most philosophers, that in my layman's opinion it adds nothing to mathematical discourse except confusion.

NOTES

1. When I say the external world "exists" I mean nothing more than the simple, commonsense recognition of an ordered set of relations independent of human minds, which is somehow structurally similar to our subjective mathematical relations. It may be that this belief is merely a matter of convenience (i.e., it is simpler to assume it than to try to describe events in terms of shifting sense impressions); but, in any case, the contro-versy among empiricists over whether "realism" can be affirmed (as Russell and Reichen-bach believed) or whether such an affirmation is meaningless (as Carnap and possibly Dewey believed) is on a level irrelevant to the issue here under discussion. Even the most extreme anti-realists among the logical positivists would be appalled by the suggestion that logical and mathematical laws were culturally variable.

2. This was Kant's view, and even William James, in unguarded moments, defended it. (See James's footnote on page 428 of the Modern Library edition of *Varieties of Religious Experience*.) For a brief, clear exposition of the weakness of Kant's subjective mathematics, see Russell's A *History of Western Philosophy*, 1945, pp. 712 ff.

3. The demon's activity can, in fact, easily be shown to be self-contradictory and therefore meaningless, like the statement "Some odd numbers are even." For example, if we bring together two horses, two pigs, and two chipmunks, we have various combinations possible of two plus two. If we consider two horses and two pigs, then the fifth animal, created by the demon, must be either a horse or pig. Let us assume it is a horse. The grouping of two pigs and two chipmunks necessitates, say, a third chipmunk. But now we are unable to obtain five from the addition of two horses and two chipmunks because we already have three of each.

4. Hardy's words are often quoted (indeed, even White quotes them), but they are worth quoting again here: "I believe that mathematical reality lies outside us, that our function is to discover or *observe* it, and that the theorems which we prove, and which we describe grandiloquently as our 'creations,' are simply our notes of our observations." There is something amusing about an anthropologist, who knows little about mathematics, insisting that this view, held not only by most mathematicians today but also by most experts on the foundations of mathematics, has been rendered obsolete by the findings of cultural anthropology.

5. Wilder has defended his cultural approach to mathematics in two later books: *Evolution of Mathematical Concepts* (Wiley, 1968) and *Mathematics as a Cultural System* (Pergamon, 1981).

TWENTY-THREE

MR. APOLLINAX VISITS
NEW YORK

When I wrote the "Mathematical Games" column for Scientific American, *I occasionally lapsed into fiction. The following whimsy ran in May 1961.*

Although I bear no resemblance to Apollinax, I have long worn on my left ring finger a silver Moebius band made by a friend. I use it for demonstrating a magic trick in which the ring is seemingly placed on a rubber band and then removed. Easily done, I explain, by sliding the elastic along the ring's "outside" until it is "inside" the ring.

> When Mr. Apollinax visited the United States
> His laughter tinkled among the teacups.
> —T. S. ELIOT

P. Bertrand Apollinax, the brilliant protégé of the celebrated French mathematician Nicolas Bourbaki, was little known even in France until the spring of 1960. It was then, as everyone knows, that the mathematical world was shattered by the disclosure, in a French mathematical journal, of what is now known as the Apollinax function. By means of this remarkable function Apollinax was able at one stroke to (1) prove Fermat's last theorem, (2) provide a counterexample (a map with 5,693 regions) to the famous four-color theorem of topology, (3) lay the groundwork for Channing Cheetah's discovery, three months later, of a 5,693-digit integer—the first of its kind known—that is both perfect and odd.

The reader will understand my excitement when Professor Cheetah, of New York University, invited me to his apartment for an afternoon tea at which Apollinax would be guest of honor. (Cheetah's apartment is in Greenwich Village, in

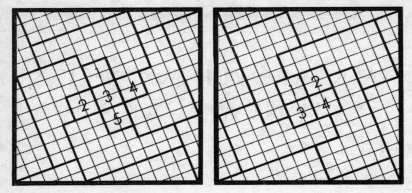

Figure 1. The mystery of the disappearing tile

a large brownstone building off Fifth Avenue. The building is owned by Mrs. Orville Phlaccus, widow of the well-known financier, and is called Phlaccus Palace by students at nearby N.Y.U.) When I arrived, the tea was in full swing. I recognized several members of the N.Y.U. mathematics faculty and guessed that most of the younger people present were graduate students.

There was no mistaking Apollinax. He was the obvious center of attention: a bachelor in his early thirties, tall, with rugged features that could not be called handsome but nevertheless conveyed a strong impression of physical virility combined with massive intellect. He had a small black goatee and rather large ears with prominent Darwin points. Under his tweedy jacket he sported a bright red vest.

While Mrs. Phlaccus served me a cup of tea, I heard a young woman say: "That silver ring on your finger, Mr. Apollinax. Isn't it a Moebius strip?"

He removed the ring and handed it to her. "Yes. It was made by an artist friend of mine who has a jewelry shop on the Left Bank in Paris." He spoke with a husky French accent.

"It's crazy," the girl said as she handed back the ring. "Aren't you afraid it will twist around and your finger will disappear?"

Apollinax chuckled explosively. "If you think that's crazy, then I have something here you'll think even crazier." He reached into his side pocket and took out a square, flat wooden box. It was filled with seventeen white plastic tiles that fitted snugly together (see Figure 1). The tiles were of such thickness that the five small pieces in the center were cubes. Apollinax called attention to the number of cubes, dumped the tiles onto a nearby table, then quickly replaced them in the box in the manner shown in the illustration at right. They fitted snugly as before. But now there were only four cubes. One cube had completely vanished!

The young woman stared at the pattern with disbelief, then at Apollinax, who was shaking with high-pitched laughter. "May I study this for a while?" she asked, taking the box from his hand. She carried it off to a quiet corner of the room.

"Who's the chick?" Apollinax said to Cheetah.

"I beg your pardon?" replied the professor.

"The girl in the sweatshirt."

"Oh. Her name is Nancy Ellicott. A Boston girl. She's one of our undergraduate math majors."

"Very attractive."

"You think so? I've never seen her wear anything but dungarees and that same dirty sweatshirt."

"I like your Village nonconformists," Apollinax said. "They're all so much alike."

"Sometimes," remarked someone in the group, "it's hard to distinguish nonconformity from neurosis."

"That reminds me," I said, "of a mathematical riddle I just heard. What's the difference between a psychotic and a neurotic?"

Nobody said anything.

"A psychotic," I went on, "thinks that two plus two is five. A neurotic knows that it's four, but it makes him nervous."

There was some polite laughter, but Apollinax looked grave. "He has good reason to be nervous. Wasn't it Alexander Pope who wrote: 'Ah why, ye gods! should two and two make four?' Why indeed? Who can say why tautologies are tautological? And who can say that even simple arithmetic is free from contradiction?" He took a small notebook from his pocket and jotted down the following infinite series:

$$4 - 4 + 4 - 4 + 4 - 4 + 4 \ldots$$

"What," he asked, "is the sum of this series? If we group the numbers like this,

$$(4 - 4) + (4 - 4) + (4 - 4) \ldots$$

the sum is obviously zero. But if we group them so,

$$4 - (4 - 4) - (4 - 4) - (4 - 4) \ldots$$

the sum is clearly four."

I started to make a comment, but Nancy pushed her way back through the group and said: "These tiles are driving me batty. What happened to that fifth cube?"

Apollinax laughed until his eyes teared. "I'll give you a hint, my dear. Perhaps it slid off into a higher dimension."

"Are you pulling my leg?"

"I wish I were," he sighed. "The fourth dimension, as you know, is an extension along a fourth coordinate perpendicular to the three coordinates of three-dimensional space. Now consider a cube. It has four main diagonals, each running from one corner through the cube's center to the opposite corner. Because of the cube's symmetry, each diagonal is clearly at right angles to the other three. So why shouldn't a cube, if it feels like it, slide along a fourth coordinate?"

"But my physics teacher," Nancy said with a frown, "told us that *time* was the fourth dimension."

"Nonsense!" Apollinax snorted. "General relativity is as dead as the dodo. Hasn't your professor heard about Hilbert Dongle's recent discovery of a fatal flaw in Einstein's theory?"

"I doubt it," Nancy replied.

"It's easy to explain. If you spin a sphere of soft rubber rapidly, what happens to its equator? It bulges. In relativity theory, you can explain the bulge in two different ways. You can assume that the cosmos is a fixed frame of reference—a so-called inertial system. Then you say that the sphere rotates and inertia makes the equator bulge. Or you can make the sphere a fixed frame of reference and regard the entire cosmos as rotating. Then you say that the masses of the moving stars set up a gravitational tensor field that exerts its strongest pull on the equator of the motionless ball. Of course—"

"I would put it a bit differently," Cheetah interrupted. "I would say that there is a relative movement of sphere and stars, and this relative motion causes a certain change in the space-time structure of the universe. It is the pressure, so to speak, of this space-time matrix that produces the bulge. The bulge can be viewed either as a gravitational or inertial effect. In both cases the field equations are exactly the same."

"Very good," Apollinax replied. "Of course, this is exactly what Einstein called the principle of equivalence—the equivalence of gravity and inertia. As Hans Reichenbach liked to put it, there's no truth distinction between the two. But now let me ask you this: Does not relativity theory make it impossible for physical bodies to have relative motions greater than the speed of light? Yet if we make the rubber ball our fixed frame of reference, it takes only a slow spin of the ball to give the moon a relative motion much faster than the speed of light."

Cheetah did a slow double take.

"You see," Apollinax continued, "we just can't keep the sphere still while we spin the universe around it. This means that we have to regard the ball's spin as absolute, not relative. Astronomers run into the same sort of difficulty with what they call the transverse Doppler effect. If the earth rotates, the relative transverse velocity between the observatory and a ray of light from a distant star is very small, so the Doppler shift is small. But if you view the cosmos as rotating, then the transverse velocity of the distant star relative to the observatory is very great, and the Doppler shift would have to increase accordingly. Since the transverse Doppler shift is small, we must assume it is the earth that rotates. Of course, this defenestrates relativity theory."

"Then," Cheetah mumbled, looking a trifle pale, "how do you account for the fact that the Michelson-Morley experiment failed to detect any motion of the earth relative to a fixed space?"

"Quite simple," Apollinax said. "The universe is infinite. The earth spins around the sun, the sun speeds through the galaxy, the galaxy gallumphs along relative to other galaxies, the galaxies are in galactic clusters that move relative to other clusters, and the clusters are parts of superclusters. The hierarchy is endless. Add together an infinite series of vectors, of random speeds and directions, and what happens? They cancel each other out. Zero and infinity are close cousins. Let me illustrate."

He pointed to a large vase on the table. "Imagine that vase empty. We start filling it with numbers. If you like, you can think of small counters with numbers on them. At one minute to noon we put the numbers 1 through 10 into the vase, then take out number 1. At one-half minute to noon, we put in numbers 11 to 20 and take out number 2. At one-third minute to noon we put in 21 to 30, take out 3. At one-fourth minute to noon we put in 31 to 40, take out 4. And so on. How many numbers are in the vase at noon?"

"An infinity," said Nancy. "Each time you take one out, you put in ten."

Appolinax cackled like an irresponsible hen. "There would be *nothing* in the vase! Is 4 in the vase? No, we took it out on the fourth operation. Is 518 in the vase? No, it came out on the 518th operation. The numbers in the vase at noon form an empty set. You see how close infinity is to zero?"

Mrs. Cheetah approached us, bearing a tray with assorted cookies and macaroons. "I think I shall exercise Zermelo's axiom of choice," said Apollinax, tugging on his goatee, "and take one of each kind."

"If you think relativity theory is dead," I said a few minutes later, "what is your attitude toward modern quantum theory? Do you think there's a fundamental randomness in the behavior of the elementary particles? Or is the randomness just an expression of our ignorance of underlying laws?"

"I accept the modern approach," he said. "In fact, I go much further. I agree with Karl Popper that there are *logical* reasons why determinism can no longer be taken seriously."

"That's hard to believe," someone said.

"Well, let me put it this way. There are portions of the future that *in principle* can never be predicted correctly, even if one possessed total information about the state of the universe. Let me demonstrate."

He took a blank file card from his pocket, then, holding it so no one could see what he was writing, he scribbled something on the card and handed it to me, writing side down. "Put that in your right trouser pocket."

I did as he directed.

"On that card," he said, "I've described a future event. It hasn't taken place yet, but it positively either will or will not take place before"—he glanced at his wristwatch—"before six o'clock."

He took another blank card from his pocket and handed it to me. "I want you to try to guess whether the event I just described will take place. If you think it will, write 'Yes' on the card you hold. If you think it won't, write 'No.'"

I started to write, but Apollinax caught my wrist. "Not yet, old chap. If I see your prediction, I might do something to make it fail. Wait until my back is turned, and don't let anyone see what you write." He spun around and looked at the ceiling until I had finished writing. "Now put the card in your left pocket, where no one can see it."

He turned to face me again. "I don't know your prediction. You don't know what the event is. Your chance of being right is one in two."

I nodded.

"Then I'll make you the following bet. If your prediction is wrong, you must give me ten cents. If it's right, I'll give you one million dollars."

Everyone looked startled. "It's a deal," I said.

"While we're waiting," Apollinax said to Nancy, "let's go back to relativity theory. Would you care to know how you can always wear a relatively clean sweatshirt, even if you own only two sweatshirts and never wash either of them?"

"I'm all ears," she said, smiling.

"You have other features," he said, "and very pretty ones too. But let me explain about those sweatshirts. Wear the cleanest one, say sweatshirt A, until it becomes dirtier than B. Then take it off and put on the relatively clean sweatshirt B. The instant B is dirtier than A, take off B and put on the relatively clean sweatshirt A. And so on."

Nancy made a face.

"I really can't wait here until six," Apollinax said. "Not on a warm spring evening in Manhattan. Would you by any chance know if Thelonious Monk is playing anywhere in the city tonight?"

Nancy's eyes opened wide. "Why, yes, he's playing right here in the Village. Do you like his style?"

"I dig it," Apollinax said. "And now, if you'll kindly direct me to a nearby restaurant, where I shall pay for your dinner, we will eat, I will explain the mystery of the tiles, then we will go listen to the Monk."

After Apollinax had left, with Nancy on his arm, word of the prediction bet spread rapidly around the room. When six o'clock arrived, everyone gathered around to see what Apollinax and I had written. He was right. The event was logically unpredictable. I owed him a dime.

The reader may enjoy trying to figure out just what future event Apollinax described on that card.

ANSWERS

The paradox of the tiles, demonstrated by P. Bertrand Apollinax, is explained as follows. When all seventeen tiles are formed into a square, the sides of the square are not absolutely straight but convex by an imperceptible amount. When one cube is removed and the sixteen tiles re-formed into a square, the sides of the square are concave by the same imperceptible amount. This accounts for the apparent change in area. To dramatize the paradox, Apollinax performed a bit of sleight of hand by palming the fifth cube as he rearranged the pattern of the tiles.

In his prediction bet the event that Apollinax described on the file card was: "You will place in your left trouser pocket a card on which you have written the word 'No.'" The simplest presentation of the same paradox is to ask someone to predict, by saying yes or no, whether the next word that he utters will be no. Karl R. Popper's reasons for thinking that part of the future is in principle unpredictable are not based on this paradox, which is simply a version of the old liar paradox, but on much deeper considerations. These considerations are given in Popper's "Indeterminism in Quantum Physics and in Classical Physics," in *The British Journal for the Philosophy of Science*, vol. 1, no. 2 and 3, 1950, and discussed more fully in his book *Postscript: After Twenty Years*. A prediction paradox essentially the same as Apollinax's, except that it involves a computer and electric fan instead of a person and card, is discussed in chapter 11 of John G. Kemeny's *A Philosopher Looks at Science*, published by D. Van Nostrand in 1959.

The paradox of the infinite series of fours, alternately added and subtracted, is explained by the fact that the sum of this series does not converge but oscillates back and forth between the values of zero and four. To explain the rotation paradoxes would require too deep a plunge into relativity theory.

POSTSCRIPT

Many readers took Apollinax seriously (even though I said he was a protégé of Bourbaki, the well-known, nonexistent French mathematician) and wrote to ask where they could find out about the "Apollinax function." Both Apollinax and Nancy, as well as others at the tea, are straight out of T. S. Eliot's two poems, "Mr. Apollinax" and "Nancy," which appear on facing pages in Eliot's *Collected Poems: 1909–1962* (Harcourt Brace, 1963).

"Mr. Apollinax," by the way, is a poem about Bertrand Russell. When Russell visited Harvard in 1914, Eliot attended his lectures on logic, and the two met at a tea; the tea Eliot describes in his poem. A mathematician at Trinity College, Cambridge, wrote to ask me if the name "Phlaccus" was a portmanteau word combining "flaccid" and "phallus"; I mention this as a minor contribution to Eliot exegesis. Hilbert Dongle derives from Herbert Dingle, the British physicist who argued that if the clock paradox of relativity theory is true, then relativity isn't.

Apollinax's reasoning about Nancy's dirty sweatshirt is borrowed from a small poem by Piet Hein. The paradox about numbers in the vase comes from J. E. Littlewood's *A Mathematician's Miscellany*. It illustrates a case in which the subtraction of the transfinite number aleph-null from ten times aleph-null results in zero. If the numbered counters are taken out of the vase in the order 2, 4, 6, 8 . . . , an aleph-null infinity remains, namely, all the odd numbers. One can also remove an infinite set of counters in such a way as to leave any desired finite number of counters. If one wishes to leave, say, exactly three counters, he merely takes out numbers in serial order, but beginning with 4. The situation is an amusing illustration of the fact that when aleph-null is taken from aleph-null, the result is indeterminate; it can be made zero, infinity, or any desired positive integer, depending on the nature of the two infinite sets that are involved.

The pattern for the vanishing-cube paradox is one that I based on a little-known principle discovered by Paul Curry, of New York City. It is discussed at length in the chapters on "Geometrical Vanishes" in my Dover paperback, *Mathematics, Magic and Mystery*.

My dramatization of the prediction paradox as a bar bet was first published in *Ibidem*, a Canadian magic magazine, no. 23, March 1961, page 23. I contributed a slightly different version, involving a card mailed to a friend, to *The British Journal for the Philosophy of Science*, vol. 13, page 51, May 1962.

My vanishing cube paradox was marketed with colorful plastic tiles in

1993 or 1994 under the title "Puzzle Mania." Made in China, it was distributed by Playtime Toys, Louisville, Kentucky.

Bertrand Russell's sexual adventures are legendary. Indeed, he even had a one-night stand with T. S. Eliot's first wife Vivien, although he later complained in a letter to the French writer Colette, a former lover, that the experience was loathsome. Don Morris, a friend of mine, paid tribute to Russell's prowess with the following toast:

> *Let's raise a glass to the third earl of Russell*
> *For sheer functional use of his genital muscle.*

TWENTY-FOUR

HOW NOT TO TALK
ABOUT MATHEMATICS

Reviewing a popular book by two distinguished mathematicians, each of whom knows far more about mathematics than I, gave me another excuse to defend realism against the "all math is cultural" approach. The controversy is, of course, ancient and deep, and certainly not to be settled by anything I have to say.

Morris Kline died in 1992. I had the pleasure of lunching with him some twenty years earlier. We agreed that the "new math," then a craze among teachers, had been a disaster, and that the best introduction to calculus to give a high school student, was Sylvanus Thompson's Calculus Made Easy. *This amusing book was first published in 1910, and is still in print although no one has troubled to update its terminology. (The derivative is throughout called a differential coefficient.)*

We disagreed over the topic of this chapter, and over the political views of Kline's colleague at New York University, Sidney Hook. I defended Hook, but Kline considered him a reactionary scoundrel.

In precisely what sense do universals (such as blueness, goodness, cowness, squareness, and threeness) exist? For Plato they are transcendent things, independent of the universe. Aristotle agreed that they are outside human minds, but he pulled them down from Plato's heaven to make them inseparable from the world. During the Middle Ages the nominalists and conceptualists shifted universals sideways from the outside world to the inside of human heads.

In the philosophy of mathematics, with which *The Mathematical Experience* (Birkhäuser, 1980) is primarily concerned, this ancient controversy over universals takes the form of speculating on what it means to say that such abstractions as the number three, a triangle, or an infinite set "exist," and the companion problem of what it means to say that a theorem about these ideal objects has been "proved." Let us not get bogged down in the technical and ambiguous differences between such schools as the logicism of Bertrand Russell, the formalism of David Hilbert, and the constructivism (or intuitionism) of L. E. J. Brouwer. All of these are briskly discussed, along with many other central mathematical issues, by the book's two distinguished authors, mathematicians Philip Davis and Reuben Hersh. Let us consider instead the more fundamental question that cuts across all the schools. Do mathematical structures have a reality independent of human minds?

It is easy to caricature what mathematicians mean when they call themselves realists. They certainly do not suppose (I doubt if Plato did) that were we transported to some far-off realm we would see luminous objects floating about that we would recognize as pi, the square root of minus one, transfinite sets, pure circles, and so on; not symbols or models, but the undefiled universals themselves. Realists mean something less exotic. They mean that, if all intelligent minds in the universe disappeared, the universe would still have a mathematical structure and in some sense even the theorems of pure mathematics would continue to be "true." On its ultimate microlevel (if it has one) the universe may be nothing but mathematical structure. "Matter" has a way of vanishing on the microlevel, leaving only patterns. To say that these patterns have no reality outside minds is to take a giant step toward solipsism; for, if you refuse to put the patterns outside human experience, why must you put them outside your experience?

For a mathematical realist a tree not only exists when nobody looks at it, but its branches have a "tree" pattern even when no graph theorist looks at them. Not only that, but when two dinosaurs met two dinosaurs there were four dinosaurs. In this prehistoric tableau "2 + 2 = 4" was accurately modeled by the beasts, even though they were too stupid to know it and even though no humans were there to observe it. The symbols for this equality are, obviously, human creations, and our mental concepts of two, four, plus, and equals are by definition mind-dependent. If mathematical structure is taken to mean only what is inside the brains of those who do mathematics, it is as trivial to say all mathematics is mind-dependent as it is to define sound as a mental phenomenon, then proclaim that the falling tree makes no sound when nobody hears it.

Fortunately scientists, mathematicians, and ordinary people seldom talk this way. The existence of an external world, mathematically ordered, is taken for granted. I have yet to meet a mathematician willing to say that if the human race ceased to exist the moon would no longer be spherical. I suspect Davis and Hersh would not care to say this, yet the troubling thing about their book is that it does not make clear why.

Although there are hints of the authors' philosophical perspective throughout the book, it is not explicitly stated until the last page but one:

> Mathematics is not the study of an ideal, preexisting nontemporal reality. Neither is it a chess-like game with made-up symbols and formulas. Rather, it is the part of human studies which is capable of achieving a science-like consensus. . . .
>
> Mathematics does have a subject matter, and its statements are meaningful. The meaning, however, is to be found in the shared understanding of human beings, not in an external nonhuman reality. In this respect, mathematics is similar to an ideology, a religion, or an art form; it deals with human meanings, and is intelligible only within the context of culture. In other words, mathematics is a humanistic study. It is one of the humanities.

Davis and Hersh do not deny that mathematical concepts are objective in the sense that they are "outside the consciousness of any one person," but they are not outside the collective consciousness of humanity. Mathematicians do not discover preexisting, timeless things like pi and dodecahedrons; they construct them. Once constructed, however, they can be studied in much the same way that astronomers study Saturn. They acquire from the culture's consensus a permanence of structure that cannot be altered by the whims of individual mathematicians.

What is one to make of this extreme conceptualist view? All that mathematicians do is certainly part of culture for the simple reason that everything human beings do is part of culture. But to talk as if mathematical objects are no more than cultural artifacts is to adopt a language that quickly becomes awkward because it is so out of step with ordinary language. It is like insisting that all birds are pink, then distinguishing between the pinkness of cardinals and the pinkness of crows. Conceptualism in mathematics has its strongest appeal among anthropologists and sociologists who have a vested interest in making culture central. It is a language that also appeals to those historians, psychologists, and philosophers who cannot bring themselves to talk about anything that transcends human experience.

Mathematical realists avoid this language for a variety of reasons, one of which is its obvious clumsiness in explaining some things everybody knows are true. For example, why do mathematical theorems fit the universe so accurately that they have enormous explanatory and predictive power? The authors call attention to Eugene Wigner's well-known paper, "The Unreasonable Effectiveness of Mathematics in the Natural Sciences." For a nonrealist this effectiveness is indeed an awesome mystery. And if mathematical concepts have no locus outside human culture, how has nature managed to produce such a boundless profusion of beautiful models of mathematical objects:

orbits that are conic-section curves, snowflakes, coastlines that model fractal curves, carbon molecules that are tetrahedral, and on and on?

If mathematical entities are no more than cultural products, one would expect independent cultures to fabricate widely disparate laws of arithmetic and geometry. But they don't. Number systems may differ in their notational base, but of course this is only a difference in how numbers are symbolized. If theorems of elementary geometry are created, not discovered, why has no culture found it expedient to suppose that the cube of the hypotenuse of a right triangle equals the sum of the cubes of the other two sides? Who can believe that on some distant planet intelligent beings have constructed a planar map of five regions, each pair sharing a common portion of a border? The mere existence of extraterrestrial mathematicians would at once place some mathematical objects outside human culture, but even here on earth are apes aware, albeit dimly, of the difference between a ball and a cube, and between one and two bananas? Of course, if one believes in a God who knows all that can be known, then all mathematical objects are not only "out there," beyond the folkways, they are *way* out there.

For the realist, mathematical progress, like scientific progress, mixes creativity with discovery. Never would Newton have entertained the fantastic notion that he had invented the law of gravity, or Einstein the wild belief that he had invented the law $E = mc^2$. There is an obvious sense in which scientists create theories, but there is an equally obvious sense in which theories penetrate the secret chambers of what Einstein liked to call the Old One. Einstein did not impose his equations on the universe. The Old One imposed its equations on Einstein.

What does a conceptualist gain by talking as though the spirality of Andromeda is projected onto the galaxy by human experience? Of course if spirality is defined as entirely a mental concept, then the spirality cannot be "out there." But what astronomer, seeing a photograph of a newly discovered galaxy, is likely to exclaim: "How astonishing! When I look at this photograph I perceive that lovely spirality stamped on my brain by the shared experience of my race"? Not that there is anything inconsistent about such a language. Rudolf Carnap was able to show, in his *Logical Structure of the World*, that a phenomenological language, never going beyond human experience, is capable of expressing the same empirical content as any realistic language, but he quickly opted for realism as the only workable language for science.

It is also the most efficient language for most mathematical discourse. Although I am an unabashed realist (for emotional reasons) I agree with Carnap's application of his "principle of tolerance" to the various schools of mathematical philosophy. The choice of a language for talking about mathematics is not so much which language is "right" (in logic, said Carnap, there are no morals) as it is which language is most convenient in a given context. With reference to the book under review, the context is not a technical discussion about the flimsy foundations of set theory. As the authors make clear in their preface, the book is an attempt to convey to nonprofessionals what mathematics is all about.

No mathematician hesitates to speak of "existence proofs" about objects even when they are nowhere modeled, or known to be modeled, by the external world. And most mathematicians, including the very greatest, think of such objects as independent of the human mind, though not of course existing in the same way Mars exists. In 1980 Robert Griess, Jr., con structed a finite simple group called the "Monster." It has 808,017,424,794,512,875,886,459,904,961,710,757,005,754,368,000,000,000 elements, each a matrix of 196,883 by 196,883 numbers. Griess prefers to call it "The Friendly Giant from the 196,883rd Dimension" because it is a symmetry group of the packing of identical hyperspheres in a space of 196,883 dimensions. There is nothing "wrong" in thinking of the Friendly Giant as composed by Griess the way Mozart composed a symphony, but there also is nothing wrong in thinking of the Giant as having existed as timelessly as a large prime, waiting to be discovered.

Artists can paint anything they like; but, if a Russian mathematician had constructed the Monster before Griess had, the group would have had exactly the same properties as Griess's group. A conceptualist can explain this, but not without using a language both curious and cumbersome. Davis and Hersh, overwhelmed by the mysteries of infinite sets and modern proof theory, have chosen a language of considerable value in analyzing the obscure foundations of mathematics, but it serves only to confuse us ordinary folk when applied to all of mathematics.

Closely related to the anti-realism of Davis and Hersh is their attack on the infallibility of mathematical reasoning. Most philosophers have found it useful to distinguish mathematics from science by saying that mathematicians can prove some things in ways scientists cannot. Awareness that all science is fallible (I think it was the mathematical realist Charles Peirce who first applied the term "fallibilism" to science) goes back to the ancient Greek skeptics and is taken for granted by all modern scientists and philosophers. (It is not a doctrine first stressed by Karl Popper, as the authors imply on page 345.)

This fallibilism follows at once from the absence of any logical reason why a natural law cannot alter tomorrow. Science has no way of establishing facts, laws, or theories except by assigning them what Carnap called degrees of confirmation and Popper likes to call degrees of corroboration. The borderline between this corrigible synthetic truth (based on observation of the world) and infallible analytic truth (based on consistency in the use of words) may not be as sharp as Hume thought, but the distinction is too useful to throw away. "There are three feet in a yard" clearly is not the same sort of statement as "Mars has two moons."

Now a large portion of mathematics is analytic; and, where it is, there is no harm in speaking of certainty. The truth of $2 + 2 = 4$ does not depend (as John Stuart Mill contended) on the pleasant fact that two fingers plus two fingers make four fingers. It follows from the way terms are defined in a formal system that constructs integers. Davis and Hersh devote several pages to instances where arithmetic addition fails to apply—for example, a cup of milk added to a cup of popcorn does not produce two cups of the mixture. No realist would deny the authors' assertion that "there is and there can be no comprehensive systemization of all the situations in which it is appropriate to add." In relativity theory, to give another example, addition of relative velocities does not obey the usual arithmetical laws.

In an interview in *Omni* (June 1981) mathematician Morris Kline makes the same mistake of confusing the certainty of a formal system with the uncertainty of applying it to nature. Asked if he could think of an algebra that violated the rules of arithmetic, Kline replied:

I can think of several. Take a quart of water at forty degrees and mix it with another quart of water at fifty degrees. Do you get two quarts at ninety degrees? You do not. It's more like forty-five degrees. So you can't just say I'm going to add forty and fifty and automatically get ninety. It depends on the physical situation.

Kline, Davis, and Hersh of course fully understand the distinction between a formal system and its applicability, but that is not the point. The point is that fallibilism in the application of a formal system to nature in no way introduces uncertainty into the system. On this point the arguments of Davis and Hersh become careless. A good instance is on page 326, where they speak of Euclid's theorem that the angles of a triangle add to a straight angle. This, they declare, has been "proved false" by non-Euclidean geometry. A better way to put it—it is what they really mean—is that in a formal non-Euclidean geometry the theorem is false. But in the Euclidean system it remains true for all possible (noncontradictory) worlds because it expresses a tautology that follows from the system's axioms and rules. It says nothing at all about the structure of physical space.

To blur the distinction between analytic and synthetic truth (as Willard Van Orman Quine and others have done) is to blur the difference between science and mathematics. A colorful effort along these lines is a monograph called *Proofs and Refutations* (1936) by the Hungarian philosopher Imre Lakatos, who died suddenly in 1974, age fifty-one, of a brain tumor. Lakatos's fiery broadsides against mathematical certainty have acquired something of a cult following, especially among social scientists. Davis and Hersh devote a chapter to this eccentric book, which they deem brilliant, overwhelming, and a masterpiece of complex reasoning and historical erudition.

Fascinating though this book by Lakatos is, in my opinion Davis and Hersh greatly overrate its merits. Lakatos had been a student of Popper. Impressed by Popper's vision of science as an ever-growing body of constantly altering conjectures, *Proofs and Refutations* tries to show that mathematical progress follows a similar zigzag course. The book has been called more Popperian than Popper. Later Lakatos and Popper clashed over the problem of induction. (Lakatos's acid tongue got him into brawls with almost everybody.) You will find Popper's low opinion of Lakatos vigorously detailed in *The Philosophy of Karl Popper* (1974), edited by Paul Schilpp, where he replies to Lakatos's contribution to that anthology.

Now it is quite true, as Davis and Hersh emphasize, that mathematicians seldom use deductive reasoning to create theorems. First they have a hunch. Then, like scientists, they make experiments (in their heads or on paper) and search for proofs that the hunch is sound. (The fact that they can tinker with drawings and discover elegant theorems is not easily justified in a nonrealist language.) This fumbling process is unlikely to be reflected in their papers. As Davis and Hersh remind us, only after a published proof has met the approval of peers is it eventually accepted. Sometimes, as in the case of the celebrated four-color-map theorem, a proof is taken to be valid for years before someone punches a deductive hole in it.

Recently the four-color theorem was proved with the aid of a computer, but the proof is buried in such an ugly mass of printouts that it requires other computers to check it. Davis and Hersh are right, in my opinion, in denying that this reliance on computers adds a new empirical element to mathematics. Many proofs, especially in group theory, are so horrendously complex that the possibility of human error becomes large. To say such proofs may be invalid is not different in principle from saying that mortals can fumble when they do long division by hand or on an abacus. Because waitresses make mistakes when they add your check, however, it does not follow that the laws of arithmetic are corrigible, or that geometers should keep trying to trisect the angle.

Lakatos's book takes the form of an entertaining dialogue between a teacher and his students. First the teacher gives Cauchy's clever proof, using graph theory, of Euler's famous conjecture that the number of vertices of any polyhedron, minus the number of edges and plus the number of faces, equal two. Thus for a cube: $8 - 12 + 6 = 2$. This formula, with its apparently ironclad proof, is then shot down by the students, who describe a zoo of "monster" counterexamples. Consider a cube with a smaller cube glued to the center of one face. The number of vertices is 16, the edges 24, the faces 11. Plugging these values into Euler's formula gives $16 - 24 + 11 = 3$. Does this undermine Cauchy's proof?

It does not. For Euler and Cauchy a polyhedron was assumed to be simply-connected (topologically like a ball), with nonintersecting faces that are simply-connected polygons (topologically like a circle). Lakatos writes as though Cauchy, had someone showed him the cube-on-cube monster, would have slapped his forehead and exclaimed: "What a fool I am! Euler's formula is false!" But the formula is not false. The face around the base of the smaller cube is a polygon with a square hole, and therefore the solid is not what Cauchy meant by a "polyhedron." And the same for the other monsters: polyhedrons with intersecting faces, polyhedrons joined at edges or at corners, polyhedrons with tunnels or interior hollow spaces, and so on. In a footnote Lakatos actually speaks of Cauchy's "inability to imagine" a polyhedron not topologically equivalent to a ball, as though this eminent French mathematician could not conceive of a cube with a square hole through it!

What happened historically has little resemblance to the distorted history sketched in Lakatos's seemingly learned notes. Mathematicians simply generalized Euler's formula to other kinds of solids; and, as this commonplace process continued, terms like polygon and polyhedron broadened in meaning. Steady generalization, with inevitable language modification, is more characteristic of mathematical growth than revisions forced by oversights and faulty proofs. The discovery of irrational numbers did not demolish proofs that all integers are either odd or even, nor did the discovery of quaternions invalidate the commutative law of arithmetic. Both discoveries simply pushed along the social process of enlarging the way mathematicians decided to use the word *number*.

Lakatos was aware of these obviosities. In fact, they are expressed by students in his dialogue. But he seemed to think that the final moral of his book—Euler's formula holds only for "Eulerian polyhedrons"—is somehow an indictment of formalism. But this is just what formalism is all about. For a formalist, a theorem never holds except in a formal system in which it holds.

Although Lakatos's historiography is, as Gerald Holton put it, "parody that makes one's hair stand on end," his book does suggest the shaggy, meandering way in which mathematics, like science, advances. As for providing any evidence that all proofs are suspect, as Davis and Hersh suggest, the book is irrelevant. Proofs naturally are fallible in the pragmatic sense, and they become ambiguous and controversial when applied to such queer objects as transfinite sets. Mathematicians do make errors, and proofs are often naïve, incomplete, and plain wrong. No complicated proofs are ever wholly formalized, because of printing costs and limits of time, space, and energy.

Moreover, thanks to the work of Kurt Gödel (whose Platonic realism was extreme), we know that in any formal system complicated enough to include arithmetic there are theorems that cannot be proved within the system. The structure of a brick may indeed have mathematical properties that can never be completely captured within a deductive system. None of this touches the realist view that the brick and its properties are independent of human minds and that where proofs are simple enough to be formalized they can be considered "certain" in a way that does not apply to any scientific claim.

Many aspects of *The Mathematical Experience* deserve high praise. It contains discussions, often quite technical, of topics not usually found in books for general readers. The authors are skillful in describing the monumental task of classifying finite simple groups—a task completed after the book went to press. They do an excellent job on the notorious and still unproved Riemann conjecture. There are admirable chapters on non-Cantorian set theory and nonstandard analysis.

The book jumps around a lot from topic to topic, but this hopscotch effect was inevitable since many of the chapters are excerpts from previously published articles, some by Davis alone, some by Hersh alone, some by both, and some by one of them in collaboration with somebody else. An excellent chapter on Fourier analysis is by Reuben and Phyllis Hersh. Not least of the book's merits are the many photographs of mathematicians whose faces are unfamiliar even to most professionals.

In my opinion, *The Mathematical Experience* is a stimulating book that is marred by its preference for an ancient way of talking about mathematics that has become fashionable in some mathematical circles,[1] but that seems to me so inappropriate in a book for general readers that it spreads more confusion than light. It is possible to scratch your left ear with your right hand, but why bother?

POSTSCRIPT

My review prompted much correspondence pro and con. The following letter from Robert Farrell, of La Trovi University, Bundoona, Victoria, Australia, appeared in the January 21, 1982, issue of the *New York Review of Books:*

> Martin Gardner's criticisms of the mathematical conceptualism he found in Davis and Hersh's *The Mathematical Experience* ring true. That kind of conceptualism is of a piece with the various "philosophies" mathematicians—and scientists—espouse not as a result of argument and reflection but as, one suspects, a means of deflecting them. One can appreciate that working mathematicians and scientists will typically find philosophical enquiry into their disciplines distracting while wishing that they didn't dress up their irritation or mere lack of interest as a rival "philosophy."
>
> Conceptualism, though espoused in order to deflect problems, faces, as Gardner rightly pointed out, problems of its own. Most notable is conceptualism's inability to give any convincing account of the role mathematics plays in successful science and technology. If mathematics is just a human conceptual or cultural creation, how is it that it stands so strikingly apart from other such human creations in being applicable to re-

ality? Conceptualism has no answer; it presents us with a mystery. Gardner is surely right, too, to see part of conceptualism's appeal as being to those with an abhorrence of "talk of anything that transcends human experience."

Gardner attacks conceptualism in the name of mathematical realism, the view that "if all intelligent minds in the universe disappeared, the universe would still have a mathematical structure and in some sense even the theorems of pure mathematics would continue to be 'true.'" The correctness or otherwise of such a view I won't discuss here; one thing that is sure, though, is that mathematical realism is not so easily dismissed as conceptualists will have it. Gardner's comments on Davis and Hersh indicate why.

Unfortunately, having done such a good job in realism's behalf, Gardner then proceeds to undo it. Just when one takes him to have offered strong arguments for mathematical realism, one finds Gardner writing that his "unabashed" realism is held for mainly "emotional reasons"; his only other announced ground for being a realist is the "efficiency" of the language of realism. Gardner sees the dispute between realists and conceptualists as one to be settled not by evidence and argument, but by choice. He takes Rudolf Carnap as his philosophical guide, modeling his view of mathematics on the view he takes Carnap to have held about rival theories of physical reality: "Rudolf Carnap was able to show, in his *Logical Structure of the World*, that a phenomenological language, never going beyond human experience, is capable of expressing the same empirical content as any realistic language. . . ." Carnap showed no such thing; at most that was what he *tried* to show. Most later philosophers— Carnap's later self included—have taken him to have failed in his attempt. (Gardner's metaphysically tolerant attitude, by the way, fits rather more Carnap's views of 1950, as expressed in the essay "Empiricism, Semantics and Ontology.")

Gardner's mathematical realism now looks rather abashed, having no more philosophic worth than someone else's unabashed conceptualism, perhaps also held for "emotional reasons."

Gardner's realism takes another beating when he, later in his review, informs us that mathematics, in particular Euclidean geometry, is analytic; that is, that the theorems of Euclidean geometry are true solely in virtue of their logical structures and of the meanings of the terms in them. According to Gardner, Euclidean geometry can't be wrong— though many have thought it so—because its theorems are "logical tautologies," without content. But if geometrical—and, in general, mathematical—theorems are without content, what becomes of Gardner's mathematical "realism"? A genuine realist about geometry will see it as being about points, lines, planes and such. If the realist wants geometry to be necessarily true, the necessity will have to come from elsewhere than analyticity. Gardner's Carnapian tolerance of various geometries is but another symptom of a deeper antirealism, one which affects his view of all mathematics.

The question of whether mathematical realism is correct or not will only get settled if one is, first of all, clear as to what it is, and, second, clear as to what the criteria for settling such questions are. Anyone interested in the question would do well to ignore any "emotional reasons" one way or the other, and look to the work of those who have approached it with those two desiderata in mind; to them I recommend Hartry Field's recent *Science Without Numbers*, an impressive—and rather technical—attempt to answer the question in the negative, though not in favor of conceptualism, but of a version of Hilbert's formalism.

My reply (in the same issue) was as follows:

Robert Farrell is right in chiding me for saying Carnap "was able to show." I should have said "believed he could show." But Farrell is wrong in suggesting that Carnap later gave up his "metaphysical tolerance" toward the rival languages of phenomenalism and realism, or toward the rival languages for talking about the foundations of mathematics.

Der logische Aufbau der Welt (The Logical Structure of the World, which I will henceforth call the *Aufbau* program) was Carnap's first major work. Carnap himself considered it no more than a tentative sketch of a program. He early recognized its many faults, and became his own severest critic. The *Aufbau's* major error, he declares in his 1961 preface to the second edition, was basing the program on a single primitive relation (similarity) instead of a multiplicity of relations. He remains convinced, however, that his thesis of the "reducibility of thing concepts to autopsychological concepts remains valid."

Carnap's *Aufbau* program was taken up by Nelson Goodman in his book *The Structure of Appearance*, and later vigorously championed in his contribution to *The Philosophy of Rudolf Carnap* (edited by P. A. Schilpp, 1963). Goodman argues that the incompleteness of a phenomenal language no more counts against it than the inability to trisect any angle counts against Euclidean geometry. Equally irrelevant is the charge that a phenomenal language is epistemologically false, because the language is not designed to say anything about an external world. Goodman concludes that Carnap's errors were "serious, unoriginal, and worthwhile."

Commenting favorably on Goodman's paper, in the same volume, Carnap left no doubt that he considered the choice between a phenomenal language and the realistic language of physics to be based only on the "practical decision" as to which language is the most efficient. Phenomenalism is rejected because "it is an absolutely private language which can only be used for soliloquy, but not for common communication between two persons."

If realism is taken as an ontological thesis, Carnap writes, he is not a realist. But "if 'realism' is understood as preference for the reistic language [Carnap's term for a language about material, observable things] over the phenomenal language, then I am also a realist." This metaphysical neutrality was never abandoned by Carnap, and I cannot comprehend why Farrell seems to think it applies only to the Carnap of 1950.

The problem of "realism" with respect to the entities of pure mathematics is an altogether different question, but here again Carnap never discarded his "principle of tolerance." When Farrell says: "A genuine realist about geometry will see it as being about points, lines, planes and such," I don't know what he means. Euclidean geometry was formalized by Hilbert, and others, as an uninterpreted system. One interpretation is to take its symbols as representing abstract points, lines, planes and so on. Even so, one is still inside a formal system which says nothing about the world "out there." To get to *that* world one must apply what Carnap called correspondence rules which link such ideal concepts as points and lines to observed physical structures.

Insofar as geometry applies to the outside world, it loses its certainty. By the same token, it is necessarily true only when its empirical meanings are abandoned. I am sure Farrell intends to say something important in his paragraph about this, but exactly what he wants to say eludes me. I am unfamiliar with the book Farrell recommends, so I cannot comment on it.

The notion that there is no mathematical reality outside human minds seems to appeal strongly to some contemporary writers who look favorably on Eastern religions. Here, for instance, is a passage from Robert Pirsig's *Zen and the Art of Motorcycle Maintenance* (Morrow, 1974):

> Laws of nature are human *inventions*, like ghosts. Laws of logic, of mathematics are also human inventions, like ghosts. The whole blessed thing is a human invention, including the idea that it *isn't* a human invention. The world has no existence whatsoever outside the human imagination. It's all a ghost, and in antiquity was so recognized as a ghost, the whole blessed world we live in. It's run by ghosts.

Contrast this with the Platonic realism defended by G. H. Hardy in his *Mathematician's Apology:*

> A chair or a star is not in the least like what it seems to be; the more we think of it, the fuzzier its outlines become in the haze of sensation which surrounds it; but "2" or "317" has nothing to do with sensation, and its properties stand out the more clearly the more closely we scrutinize it. It may be that modern physics fits best into some framework of idealistic philosophy—I do not believe it, but there are eminent physicists who say so. Pure mathematics, on the other hand, seems to me a rock on which all idealism founders: 317 is a prime, not because we think so, or because our minds are shaped in one way rather than another, but *because it is so*, because mathematical reality is built that way.

Hardy's realism is certainly shared by most professional mathematicians, including those working on the foundations of mathematics. Just to be sure

I was not biased in this opinion, I phoned my friend Raymond Smullyan, an expert on formal systems who also happens to be a Taoist. My first question was "Do you consider yourself a realist?" He replied, "Of course." My next question was "Among today's leading authorities on set theory who are doing creative work in the field, how many would you say are antirealists?" Smullyan said: "Almost none."

William James, in his book *The Meaning of Truth*, argues for a mind-dependent view of mathematics very close to that of Davis, Hersh, and Kline. It is marred by the fact that James had only a meager understanding of mathematics; he never heeded his friend Charles Peirce's continual urging that he take time to study the subject. For example, to bolster the view that even logics are man-made, James speaks of Boole and Jevons as having created different logics, without realizing that Boole and Jevons merely proposed different systems of notation for the same logic. Nevertheless, in spite of such mistakes, James makes a good case for a cultural approach to mathematics that was shared by F. C. S. Schiller and (I think) by John Dewey.[2]

Truths of science and mathematics, not yet verified, are what James calls "sleeping truths." The thousandth decimal of pi, for example, "sleeps" in "the world of geometrical relations," even though "no one may ever try to compute it." Of course it sleeps just as much in the world of arithmetic, where pi is the limit of a series of fractions; or rather I should say it "slept," because pi's thousandth decimal is now known. To make the point today one would have to speak of, say, pi's billionth decimal digit.[3]

There are, James writes, coats and shoes that "fit" backs and feet even though they are not yet made. "In the same way countless opinions 'fit' realities, and countless truths are valid, though no thinker ever thinks them." James doesn't mention it, but this includes countless scientific facts and laws not yet discovered.

To the anti-pragmatist, James continues, these sleeping relations are the fundamental ones. To the pragmatist, they are "static, impotent, and relatively spectral" until they are verified in human experience. For a Jamesian, the thousandth decimal of pi was a ghost that did not spring into full-bloodied reality until someone calculated it. "To attribute a superior degree of glory to [an unverified truth] seems little more than a piece of perverse abstraction worship."

What James seems to be claiming here is that although facts about the world, and even theorems of pure mathematics, exist in some vague way before they are discovered, as soon as they enter human experience they acquire a stronger reality. I can think of few philosophical tasks less rewarding than defending the view that the planet Neptune became more real after humanity knew it existed, or that a giant prime becomes more real when it is proved to be prime.

Of course Neptune did not exist as a known object before it was found, and nobody knew that $2^{44497}-1$ is a prime until 1979; but these statements are vapid tautologies. Obviously, nothing is known by a mind until a mind knows it. The trouble with a pragmatic language that limits full reality to human experience is that there are excellent pragmatic reasons for not adopting such a strange way of speaking.

NOTES

1. See, for example, Morris Kline's book, *Mathematics: The Loss of Certainty* (Oxford University Press, 1980), which takes the same extreme anthropocentric point of view as the book by Davis and Hersh. All mathematics, Kline tells us, is a "purely human creation," all laws of logic are the products of human experience, and "today the belief in the mathematical design of nature seems far-fetched." No mathematical design in nature? My mind reels at the infelicity of this phrasing. I am in complete agreement with Ernest Nagel's criticisms, expressed in his restrained review (*New York Review of Books*, November 6, 1980) of this quirkish volume.

2. F. C. S. Schiller, England's leading pragmatist, knew almost as little mathematics as James. In chapter 19 of *Logic for Use* (1930), enormous confusion results from his failure to distinguish the certainty of abstract arithmetic from the uncertainty of applied arithmetic. What is worse, he seems to think that laws of arithmetic vary with the notation used:

> A dialectical victory over the rash assertion that $2 + 2 = 4$ *absolutely and unconditionally*, is easy to gain. For what the sum works out at depends on the *scale of notation* we choose to adopt. Ordinarily we use 10. But in the scale of 4, $2 + 2$ would $= 10$, which would also be the sum of $7 + 5$, in the scale of 12. Moreover, each of these results is as true and necessary in its context as that $7 + 5 = 12$ in decimal notation.

Of course translating $2 + 2 = 4$ into another base notation no more alters its truth than translating "two plus two equals four" into French.

3. The billionth decimal digit of pi is now known. After a Japanese computer scientist calculated pi to more than 3 billion decimal places, the brothers David and Gregory Chudnovsky, of Columbia University, in 1995 carried the calculation beyond 4 billion decimal digits. It is safe to say that the trillionth digit of pi still "sleeps" in some sort of limbo. However, even the constructivists admit that it exists as robustly as the tenth digit because there is a known finite way to determine it.

PART V

THE ARTS

Aesthetic values, like moral values, evolved slowly on the earth. Altruistic behavior was discovered by some animal species for reasons that are gradually becoming clearer to biologists. There seems to be dim aesthetic awareness among birds, reflected in their warbling, and in sex rituals such as the spreading of the peacock's tail or the male bower bird's finding of colored objects to decorate his nest in a way that would appeal to females.

The arts arouse queer kinds of pleasures which psychologists still only dimly understand. Why are certain shapes and color combinations more pleasing than others? What is the secret of a popular melody? I see these as temporary mysteries that experimental psychologists will eventually solve.

The last essay of this section raises such questions with respect to music. The others simply reflect my tastes and interests.

TWENTY-FIVE

COLERIDGE AND
THE ANCIENT MARINER

The Ancient Mariner, like the bumbling shortstop who "stoppeth one of three," is surely one of the great mythic characters in English poetry. Was there ever a finer combination in verse of beauty and horror? Although Gustave Doré continues to be out of fashion, especially among critics who praise Jackson Pollock's dribblings, I make no apologies for reviving Doré's Ancient Mariner art in my 1965 book The Annotated Ancient Mariner. I have never ceased to admire Doré's marvelous sense of composition or his imaginative visions of literary classics.

The essay included here is the opening chapter of my book—an essay mainly about Coleridge. The book's Afterword, in which I discuss various interpretations of the ballad, can be found in Gardner's Whys and Wherefores (1989).

THE ALBATROSS

Sometimes, to entertain themselves, the men of the crew
Lure upon deck an unlucky albatross, one of those vast
Birds of the sea that follow unwearied the voyage through,
Flying in slow and elegant circles above the mast.

No sooner have they disentangled him from their nets
Than this aërial colossus, shorn of his pride,
Goes hobbling pitiably across the planks and lets
His great wings hang like heavy, useless oars at his side.

How droll is the poor floundering creature, how limp and
  weak—
He, but a moment past so lordly, flying in state!

*They tease him: One of them tries to stick a pipe in his
    beak;
Another mimics with laughter his odd lurching gait.*

*The Poet is like that wild inheritor of the cloud,
A rider of storms, above the range of arrows and slings;
Exiled on earth, at bay amid the jeering crowd,
He cannot walk for his unmanageable wings.*
                                —CHARLES BAUDELAIRE,
                                translated by George Dillon

*But I do not think "The Rime of the
Ancient Mariner" was for Coleridge an
escape from reality: I think it was reality,
I think he was on the ship and made the
voyage and felt and knew it all.*
                    —THOMAS WOLFE,
        in a letter of 1932, included in *The
        Letters of Thomas Wolfe*, edited by
        Elizabeth Nowell, Charles Scribner's
                Sons, 1956, p. 322

When young Charles Baudelaire fin-
ished his education in Paris, his guardians packed him off on an ocean voyage
that carried him around the Cape. Observing sailors trap albatrosses for sport,
he was struck by the contrast between the majestic beauty of these birds,
flying high above the ship, and their pathetic, lurching gait on the ship's deck.
Years later, in *Flowers of Evil*, this cruelty furnished the theme for one of his
most memorable poems. I do not know if Baudelaire had Coleridge in mind
when he likened the albatross to the poet, but it would be hard to find a
more appropriate metaphor for the soaring beauty of Coleridge's imagination
and his awkward, comic, painful flounderings across the planks of the earth.

Samuel Taylor Coleridge was born October 21, 1772, at Ottery St. Mary,
Devonshire, England. His father, a friendly, absent-minded vicar and school-
master, had four children by his first wife, ten by his second. Samuel was the
youngest. He was a dreamy, precocious child who hated physical sports
(though later in life he enjoyed swimming and mountain climbing) and whose
time was occupied mostly in reading every book he could get his hands on.

When his father died (Coleridge was then ten), his mother sent him to
London to complete his early schooling at Christ's Hospital, a famous charitable institution known as the Blue-coat School. Each boy wore a long, blue
gown, knee-britches, yellow petticoat, yellow stockings, blue cap. "He seldom
had two garters at one time," a schoolmate of Coleridge's later recalled, "in
consequence of which his stockings used to drop into a series of not very

elegant folds." Another schoolfellow remembered his habit of strolling about the yard reciting Greek verse. Coleridge and Charles Lamb, a student two years his junior, became lifelong friends.

It was at Christ's Hospital that young Coleridge discovered *Sonnets on Picturesque Spots* by the Reverend William Lisle Bowles. Today, Bowles's poetry seems bland and uninspired, but at the time it was something of a tradition-breaker. Coleridge later declared that Bowles was the first poet he had ever read who spoke of nature in a simple, natural diction. Too poor to buy more copies, Coleridge actually transcribed Bowles's entire book more than forty times so he could give out copies to friends! He himself began to feel the Muse's inspiration. An early sonnet pays generous tribute to Bowles, though it begins with what is surely one of the least promising opening phrases in English poetry: "My heart has thank'd thee, Bowles!"

Coleridge was 19 when he left London to accept a scholarship at Jesus College, Cambridge. For a short time he took his studies seriously, but soon was reading everything except what he was supposed to read. His mind was a ferment of newly discovered political and religious ideas. There was the spine-tingling news of revolution in France. Burke was writing his great political pamphlets. In Coleridge's room—the center of endless wine parties and bull sessions—there was no need to have the latest political tract on hand; Coleridge had always read it and could repeat whole pages verbatim. William Frend, a fellow at Jesus College, was expelled from Cambridge for his liberal politics and Unitarian religious convictions. Coleridge declared himself a Unitarian.

His debts grew, and an attempt to win a second scholarship failed. Coleridge wrote his brother George that for the entire six weeks preceding the examination he was "almost constantly intoxicated." For several months he tried to convince himself that he could pay off his debts by writing a great new translation of Greek and Latin lyric poetry. He never got around to it. A second plan was scarcely more practical: to win the Irish lottery! He even wrote a poem about it, "To Fortune," that was published in a London newspaper.

Coleridge went to London for the drawing. The outcome plunged him back into despair and thoughts of suicide. At this point, who could have guessed what Coleridge did next? Under the name of Silas Tomkyn Comberbacke (the initials corresponded to his own) he enlisted in the 15th Light Dragoons, a cavalry unit of the King's Regiment. Two days later he was sworn in—"an uncritical acceptance," writes Lawrence Hanson in his biography of Coleridge, "which the exigencies of war with France alone can explain."

"As a soldier of any kind," continues Hanson, "Coleridge would have been misplaced. As a cavalry man, he was a joke. He did not like horses: he could not ride: he was constantly thrown: he never learned to groom his horse: his accoutrements were never clean: he was constantly unwell."

Silas Tomkyn soon found himself cleaning the stables and serving as a hospital orderly. One day an officer, Captain Ogle, was startled to find the following epigraph scrawled on the white-washed stable wall: *Eheu! quam infortunii miserrimum est fuisse felicem!*

Coleridge's family obtained his discharge by providing a substitute, and in 1794 he was back at Jesus College, bubbling over with frugality and new resolutions. Two months later he was off with a friend on a walking tour of Wales. They stopped first at Oxford where Coleridge met Robert Southey, the second of his notable friendships. It was there that Coleridge, Southey, and some other young liberals—filled with enthusiasm for the French Revolution and with resentment against England—hatched up a utopian scheme that had even less chance of success than winning the Irish lottery.

The scheme was for twelve "gentlemen of good education and liberal principles" to get together with twelve like-minded ladies, leave England the following April, and establish a colony in North America, on the banks of the Susquehanna. This river valley was believed in England to be a spot of idyllic beauty; besides, Coleridge liked the sound of the river's name. All property was to be jointly owned. No money would be used. The men would work two or three hours a day. The women would keep house. A large library would be established. Everybody would be good, unselfish, and devoted to the commonweal and the cultivation of their minds. Coleridge called it Pantisocracy, combining the Greek words "panto" (all) and "isocracy": government by all, in contrast to England's hated aristocracy.

The young rebels took it all with incredible seriousness. Coleridge and his friend continued their tour of Wales, seeking money and converts. But, there was still the problem of Coleridge's helpmeet. He fancied himself still in love, "almost to madness," with a girl named Mary Evans, but Mary had never taken him seriously as a prospective husband. Southey was engaged to Edith Fricker, who had a plump, pretty sister named Sarah. Soon everybody took it for granted that, come next spring, it would be Sarah who would accompany Coleridge to the Susquehanna. Coleridge forgot about Mary and for a time convinced himself that Sarah was his new love. "America! Southey! Miss Fricker!" he wrote to Southey. ". . . I certainly love her. I think of her incessantly . . ."

Mary caught wind of the scheme and wrote Coleridge a sensible but curious letter. "There is an eagerness in your nature which is ever hurrying you in the sad extreme. I have heard that you mean to leave England on a plan so absurd and extravagant that were I for a moment to imagine it *true*, I should be obliged . . . [to think you mad]." Although Mary closed by expressing sisterly affection for him, the letter subtly (perhaps with unconscious cruelty) aroused Coleridge's hopes of winning her after all, and he sent her a declaration of love. But soon she was engaged to marry somebody else. After writing a poem "On a Discovery Made too Late," Coleridge decided, reluctantly, that it was his duty to marry Sarah. A few weeks after Coleridge's wedding, Southey secretly married Edith and, on the same day, set sail alone for Portugal.

Though the gradual disintegration of Pantisocracy must have been painful to those concerned, it is impossible to read their letters today with a straight face. For one thing, Southey wanted to take along his aunt's faithful servant, Shadrach. When Coleridge found out that Southey intended Shad (as he was called) to remain a servant, he was furious. "To be employed in the toil of the field, while *we* are pursuing philosophical studies—can earldoms or emperorships boast so huge an inequality? . . . a *willing* slave is the worst of slaves! His *soul* is a slave." In addition, Southey also wanted to bring along some married couples and their children. But what if the children had already learned selfishness from their schoolfellows? "How are we to prevent their minds from infecting *our* children?" Coleridge wanted to know. And so it went. The great plans dribbled off into nothing. Almost the only concrete results were a few mediocre sonnets that Coleridge wrote about Pantisocracy, and the following lines from his preposterous poem "To a Young Ass: Its Mother Being Tethered Near It":

> I hail thee *Brother*—spite of the fool's scorn!
> And fain would take thee with me, in the Dell
> Where high-soul'd Pantisocracy shall dwell!
> Where Mirth shall tickle Plenty's ribless side,
> And smiles from Beauty's Lip on sunbeams glide,
> Where Toil shall wed young Health that charming Lass!
> And use his sleek cows for a looking-glass—
> Where Rats shall mess with Terriers hand-in-glove
> And Mice with Pussy's Whiskers sport in Love.[1]

The first years of Coleridge's marriage were happy enough. He never returned to Cambridge for his degree. He and Sarah lived mostly on money borrowed from friends, and small sums that Coleridge obtained from sales of poetry. A periodical that he founded, *The Watchman* (published every eighth day to avoid a tax on weeklies), folded after the tenth issue. Coleridge admitted he probably lost 500 subscribers at one blow when he opened an essay "On National Fasts" by quoting Isaiah 16:11, "Wherefore my bowels shall sound like an harp . . ." He thought of becoming a Unitarian clergyman, and he tried unsuccessfully to open a school for children. Increasing rheumatic pains led to increasing use of opium. At Cambridge, during an attack of rheumatic fever and jaundice, the doctors had given him small doses of opium, and almost without realizing it he had slowly developed an addiction to the drug.

The year 1797 found the Coleridges living in the house of a friend at

Stowey, in the southwestern county of Somerset. One morning Coleridge walked to Racedown, a nearby farm in Dorset, to renew a brief acquaintance with William Wordsworth and his small, shy, bright-eyed sister Dorothy who kept house for him. "He is a wonderful man . . ." was the way Dorothy described Coleridge in a letter to a friend. "At first I thought him very plain, that is, for about three minutes: he is pale and thin, has a wide mouth, thick lips, and not very good teeth, longish loose-growing half-curling rough black hair. But if you hear him speak for five minutes you think no more of them. His eye is large and full, not dark but grey;[2] such an eye as would receive from a heavy soul the dullest expression; but it speaks every emotion of his animated mind; it has more of the 'poet's eye in a fine frenzy rolling' than I ever witnessed. He has fine dark eyebrows, and an overhanging forehead."

It is interesting to compare Dorothy's famous description with the way Coleridge had pictured himself in a letter written six months earlier. "As to me, my face, unless animated by immediate eloquence, expresses great sloth, and great, indeed almost idiotic, good nature. 'Tis a mere carcase of a face: fat, flabby, and expressive chiefly of inexpression. Yet I am told that my eyes, eyebrows, and forehead are physiognomically good; but of this the Deponent knoweth not. As to my shape, 'tis a good shape enough, if measured—but my gait is awkward, and the walk of the whole man indicates *indolence capable of energies* . . . I cannot breathe through my nose, so my mouth with sensual thick lips is almost always open."

Coleridge and Wordsworth were a study in contrast. Coleridge: outgoing, impulsive, emotional, unstable, weak-willed, impractical, helpless, careless; at times a liar and a hypocrite, but always fun-loving and lovable. (I refrain from adding that he was lazy, a frequent charge and one which he himself would advance. Coleridge was anything but lazy; he was this only in the sense that his wife would consider him lazy when he was reading, thinking, talking, or writing instead of earning money, chopping wood, or taking out the garbage.) Wordsworth: cool, rational, industrious physically as well as intellectually, cautious, reserved, grim. Coleridge was as compulsive a talker as he was a reader. (Lamb once imagined himself buttonholed by Coleridge and forced to escape by snipping off the button. Five hours later he returns, finds Coleridge, eyes closed, still holding the button and talking eloquently.) Surely Wordsworth must have been a compulsive listener. Yet the two men had much in common: a Protestant outlook, a love of nature, a love of poetry, enormous talent, and, it must also be said, a common conviction that Wordsworth was potentially the greatest poet in England.

Dorothy's role in this remarkable, mutually reinforcing triangle has long been a favorite topic for critics and amateur Freudians. In spite of (or because of?) her intense, neurotic devotion to her brother, she and Coleridge became enormously fond of one another. They took long walks together through the rambling Quantock Hills. Many arresting phrases in Coleridge's poetry of this period, including some in *The Ancient Mariner*, are similar to phrases Dorothy used in a journal she was keeping. It has been difficult for scholars to determine who thought of what first. (Many of her phrases and suggestions *were* adopted, we know, by Wordsworth.) There is no question of anything improper in their relationship, although below the surface, the emotional involvements of all three were doubtless subtle and complex. Here we need only note that the two men seemed desperately to need each other. Wordsworth, in Book X of the 1805 version of his *Prelude*, recalled a period of mental depression that had preceded the beginning of his friendship with Coleridge:

> *Sick, wearied out with contrarieties,*
> *Yielded up moral questions in despair,*
> *And for my future studies, as the sole*
> *Employment of the enquiring faculty,*
> *Turn'd towards mathematics and their clear*
> *And solid evidence—Ah! then it was*
> *That Thou, most precious Friend! about this time*
> *First known to me, didst lend a living help*
> *To regulate my Soul. . . .*

Both men profited hugely from the early years of their friendship, and through it all, Dorothy played her strange role as the indispensable catalyst. "Three people, but only one soul," was how Coleridge described it.

In July, 1797, the Wordsworths moved to Alfoxden, an old mansion that was but a short walk from Stowey. Their express purpose was to be closer to the Coleridges. For Coleridge, the next twelve months were pure joy. With one incredible leap he became a major poet. Almost all his finest poems—including that immortal fantasy trio, *The Ancient Mariner*, the first part of "Christabel," and the fragment "Kubla Khan"—were written before the middle of the following year.

The genesis of *The Ancient Mariner* deserves detailed description. John Cruikshank, a neighbor, mentioned to Coleridge one day that he had had a strange dream about "a skeleton ship, with figures in it." This, together with some suggestions by Wordsworth, aroused in Coleridge a desire to write a sea ballad. The story was outlined by Coleridge on a long walk through the Quantock Hills that he, Wordsworth, and Dorothy made on November 13. This is how Wordsworth, years later, remembered the historic outing:

> In the autumn of 1797, he [Coleridge], my sister, and myself started from Alfoxden pretty late in the afternoon with a view to visit Linton and the Valley of Stones near to it; and as our united funds were very small, we agreed to defray the expense of the tour by writing a poem to be sent to the *New Monthly Magazine*. Accordingly, we set off, and proceeded along

the Quantock Hills towards Watchet; and in the course of this walk was planned the poem of the "Ancient Mariner," founded on a dream, as Mr. Coleridge said, of his friend Mr. Cruikshank. Much the greatest part of the story was Mr. Coleridge's invention, but certain parts I suggested; for example, some crime was to be committed which should bring upon the Old Navigator, as Coleridge afterwards delighted to call him, the spectral persecution, as a consequence of that crime and his own wanderings. I had been reading in Shelvocke's "Voyages," a day or two before, that while doubling Cape Horn, they frequently saw albatrosses in that latitude, the largest sort of sea fowl, some extending their wings twelve or thirteen feet. "Suppose," said I, "you represent him as having killed one of these birds on entering the South Sea, and that the tutelary spirits of these regions take upon them to avenge the crime." The incident was thought fit for the purpose, and adopted accordingly. I also suggested the navigation of the ship by the dead men, but do not recollect that I had anything more to do with the scheme of the poem. The gloss with which it was subsequently accompanied was not thought of by either of us at the time, at least, not a hint of it was given to me, and I have no doubt it was a gratuitous afterthought. We began the composition together on that, to me, memorable evening. I furnished two or three lines at the beginning of the poem, in particular

> "And listened like a three years' child:
> The Mariner had his will."

These trifling contributions, all but one, which Mr. C has with unnecessary scrupulosity recorded, slipped out of his mind, as they well might. As we endeavored to proceed conjointly (I speak of the same evening), our respective manners proved so widely different that it would have been quite presumptuous in me to do anything but separate from an undertaking upon which I could only have been a clog. . . . The "Ancient Mariner" grew and grew till it became too important for our first object, which was limited to our expectations of five pounds; and we began to think of a volume which was to consist, as Mr. Coleridge has told the world, of poems chiefly on supernatural subjects, taken from common life, but looked at, as much as might be, through an imaginative medium.

Coleridge worked on the ballad for four months before he read it to Wordsworth and Dorothy on March 23, 1798. Compared to his early, conventional lyrics, even to his later poems, the ballad was something of a miracle. It seemed to spring out of Coleridge's skull with a fantastic life of its own. It was not at all the sort of poem one would have expected him to write. What does the old mariner's tale have to do, one is tempted to ask, with that young Greek scholar, compulsive talker, and moon-faced opium eater?

Yet somehow Coleridge did write it. For years he had been soaking up details from books on sea travel, perhaps in anticipation of a voyage to North

America. His religious views were swinging from Unitarianism back to the orthodoxy of his parents. The opium that he took may have given a certain vividness and color to his reveries. He was 25, he had a good wife and a handsome year-old son, and one of England's greatest poets had become his friend. The times were ripe for the beginning of the Romantic movement with its emphasis on the wildness of nature, the charm of the distant past and distant places, its unconcealed emotion, its freedom to experiment with new poetic forms. And there was Dorothy's intelligent, sensitive enthusiasm. All these forces came together to produce the miracle.

It was, of course, Coleridge's greatest poem. No fantasy poem in English approaches its magic blend of beauty and terror. We know that he wrote it partly to defray the expenses of a trip. Could it have been that he wrote with a kind of youthful carelessness, and this very carelessness permitted a full, uninhibited release of creative imagination? It is as foolish to speak of *The Ancient Mariner* as "perfect" as it is to speak of one of Shakespeare's plays as perfect. Surely part of its magic lies in its roughness, ambiguity, and loose ends. Coleridge was always tinkering with it, altering lines, adding and removing stanzas, never quite sure of exactly what he was up to.

The ballad's first version appeared in a small book called *Lyrical Ballads*, 500 copies of which were published anonymously in September, 1798. Of the book's twenty-three poems, only four were by Coleridge. Nothing in the book indicated that more than one author was involved. Years later, this is how Coleridge remembered the way the book had been planned:

> During the first year that Mr. Wordsworth and I were neighbours, our conversations turned frequently on the two cardinal points of poetry, the power of exciting the sympathy of the reader by a faithful adherence to the truth of nature, and the power of giving the interest of novelty by the modifying colors of imagination. The sudden charm, which accidents of light and shade, which moon-light or sun-set, diffused over a known and familiar landscape, appeared to represent the practicability of combining both. These are the poetry of nature. The thought suggested itself (to which of us I do not recollect) that a series of poems might be composed of two sorts. In the one, the incidents and agents were to be, in part at least, supernatural; and the excellence aimed at was to consist in the interesting of the affections by the dramatic truth of such emotions, as would naturally accompany such situations, supposing them real. And real in *this* sense they have been to every human being who, from whatever source of delusion, has at any time believed himself under supernatural agency. For the second class, subjects were to be chosen from ordinary life; the characters and incidents were to be such, as will be found in every village and its vicinity, where there is a meditative and feeling mind to seek after them, or to notice them, when they present themselves.
>
> In this idea originated the plan of the *Lyrical Ballads;* in which it

was agreed, that my endeavours should be directed to persons and characters supernatural, or at least romantic; yet so as to transfer from our inward nature a human interest and a semblance of truth sufficient to procure for these shadows of imagination that willing suspension of disbelief for the moment, which constitutes poetic faith. Mr. Wordsworth, on the other hand, was to propose to himself as his object, to give the charm of novelty to things of every day, and to excite a feeling analogous to the supernatural, by awakening the mind's attention from the lethargy of custom, and directing it to the loveliness and the wonders of the world before us; an inexhaustible treasure, but for which, in consequence of the film of familiarity and selfish solicitude we have eyes, yet see not, ears that hear not, and hearts that neither feel nor understand.

Things did not work out as planned. Only *The Ancient Mariner* actually fulfilled Coleridge's intention.[3] "I wrote *The Ancient Mariner*, and was preparing among other poems, "The Dark Ladie," and the "Christabel," in which I should have more nearly realized my ideal, than I had done in my first attempt. But Mr. Wordsworth's industry had proved so much more successful, and the number of his poems so much greater, that my compositions, instead of forming a balance, appeared rather an interpolation of heterogeneous matter."

Although *Lyrical Ballads* eventually became one of the great milestones in English poetry, heralding the beginning of the Romantic movement, its sales were poor and its critical reception no better. Coleridge later recalled (in *Table Talk*) that he had been told by the publisher that most of the book's sales had been to sailors who, having heard of *The Ancient Mariner*, thought it was a naval songbook. "The *Lyrical Ballads* are not liked at all by any," was the way Mrs. Coleridge bluntly put it in a letter. Nobody appreciated Wordsworth's fine poem, "Lines Written a Few Miles above Tintern Abbey," which closed the book. No reviewer perceived the greatness of *The Ancient Mariner* which opened it. Most critics complained that they couldn't understand the ballad. "The extravagance of a mad German poet," said one. "The strangest story of a cock and a bull that we ever saw on paper . . . a rhapsody of unintelligible wildness and incoherence," said another.

Coleridge was deeply wounded by Southey's review, particularly because he knew that Southey knew him to be the ballad's author:

> In a very different style of poetry is the *Rime of the Ancient Mariner;* a ballad (says the advertisement) "professedly written in imitation of the *style,* as well as the spirit of the elder poets." We are tolerably conversant with the early English poets; and can discover no resemblance whatever, except in antiquated spelling and a few obsolete words. This piece appears to us perfectly original in style as well as in story. Many of the

stanzas are laboriously beautiful; but in connection they are absurd or unintelligible. Our readers may exercise their ingenuity in attempting to unriddle what follows:

> *"The roaring wind, it roar'd far off.*
> *It did not come anear." etc., etc.*

We do not sufficiently understand the story to analyse it. It is a Dutch attempt at German sublimity. Genius has here been employed in producing a poem of little merit.

(I sometimes fancy that Southey's punishment is that his career as a poet would be almost forgotten today were it not for Lewis Carroll's "You are Old Father William," which parodies one of his poems. It is hard to believe that Southey, like Wordsworth, was once poet laureate of England and that his collected verse fills ten volumes.)

Coleridge himself, who always enjoyed literary jokes, joined in the general criticism of his ballad. In *Biographia Literaria* he recalls:

The following anecdote will not be wholly out of place here, and may perhaps amuse the reader. An amateur performer in verse expressed to a common friend a strong desire to be introduced to me, but hesitated in accepting my friend's immediate offer, on the score that "he was, he must acknowledge, the author of a confounded severe epigram on my *Ancient Mariner*, which had given me great pain." I assured my friend that, if the epigram was a good one, it would only increase my desire to become acquainted with the author, and begged to hear it recited: when, to my no less surprise than amusement, it proved to be one which I had myself some time before written and inserted in the "Morning Post," to wit—

To the Author of the Ancient Mariner.

> *Your poem must eternal be,*
> *Dear sir! it cannot fail,*
> *For 'tis incomprehensible,*
> *And without head or tail.*

Neither Coleridge nor Wordsworth was in England at the time *Lyrical Ballads* and its first reviews appeared. Together with Dorothy they had gone to Germany. Coleridge had recently received an annuity from his friends the Wedgwood brothers (sons of Josiah Wedgwood, the famous potter) with the proviso that he *not* become a minister, but devote all his energies to literature and philosophy. (The German trip was a bonus; the Wedgwoods footed the bill for all three travelers!) Coleridge had been studying German and was anxious to make firsthand contact with German philosophy. It was while in Germany that he learned of the death of his second child, Berkeley, born shortly before he left. Coleridge's letters to Sarah are filled with genuine concern for her and tender sorrow over the loss of his child. But he did not return.

After eleven months abroad, Coleridge finally meandered home. His relations with Sarah deteriorated rapidly. Wordsworth, having at last recovered from a careless romance in France with Annette Vallon, the girl who bore his illegitimate daughter, became engaged to his cousin Mary Hutchinson. And now a nightmarish parody of the past unfolded.

You will recall that Sarah, Coleridge's wife, had been the sister of Southey's fiancée. Wordsworth's fiancée also had a sister named Sarah, with whom Coleridge proceeded to fall violently in love. The precise nature of their relationship is still a puzzle for historians; none of her letters to Coleridge survive, and only a few of his to her, so there is little to go on except speculation. She was a small, plump, brown-haired girl, two years younger than Coleridge, not pretty, but with a fair skin and, above all, a lively sense of humor. So far as anyone knows, their relationship was as nonphysical as it was hopeless (divorce in those days was almost unthinkable); nevertheless, there is no doubt about the passion with which Coleridge was smitten. A notebook contains an entry in Latin in which he speaks of pressing her hand one Sunday, standing around the fire after an occasion of "Conundrums and Puns and Stories and Laughter," and how love had then pierced him like an arrow, "poisoned, alas, and incurable." A later entry recalls her "dear lips" pressed to his forehead. The obsession lasted ten years, and was certainly one of the causes of the eventual decline of friendship between Coleridge and Wordsworth. Sarah Hutchinson never married. She finally moved in with the Wordsworths and Dorothy to become a sort of third wife.

Coleridge's poem "Love" (later so widely imitated—it was the prototype of Keats's "La Belle Dame sans Merci") was a disguised expression of his first outburst of love for Sarah Hutchinson. "Dejection: an Ode," composed two years later, expresses the utter hopelessness of his emotions:

> A *grief without a pang, void, dark, and drear,*
> A *stifled, drowsy, unimpassioned grief,*
> Which *finds no natural outlet, no relief,*
> In *word, or sigh, or tear—*

There is a sad entry in Dorothy's journal: "William and I sauntered in the garden. Coleridge came to us, and repeated the verses he wrote to Sara.

I was affected with them, and . . . in miserable spirits. The sunshine, the green fields, and the fair sky made me sadder; even the little happy sporting lambs seemed but sorrowful to me . . . I went to bed after dinner, could not sleep."

The two Sarahs have, understandably, often been confused by Coleridge's biographers. In his letters and notebooks, Coleridge always dropped the "h" from both names, and to make matters more confusing, in 1802 he named his daughter Sara. Sometimes, to distinguish the first from the second Sarah, he rearranged the letters of "Sara" (Hutchinson) to spell "Asra." Some forty love poems, now called the Asra poems, are known to have been written to the second Sarah. (The interested reader should consult Thomas M. Raysor's "Coleridge and 'Asra.'" *Studies in Philology*, July 1929, and George Whalley's book, *Coleridge and Sara Hutchinson and the Asra Poems*, 1955.)

When a new edition of *Lyrical Ballads* came out in 1800 under Wordsworth's name, Coleridge's contribution to the book remained anonymous. *The Ancient Mariner* came close to being left out. "From what I can gather," Wordsworth had earlier written to the publisher, "it seems that The Ancyent Marinere has upon the whole been an injury to the volume, I mean that the old words and the strangeness of it have deterred readers from going on . . . If the volume should come to a second edition I would put in its place some little things which would be more likely to suit the public taste."

But the poem remained. Coleridge had revised it considerably, taking out many of the more obscure old English expressions about which critics had complained, and adding to it the subtitle: "A Poet's Reverie." Wordsworth's note, added to the new edition, comments patronizingly:

I cannot refuse myself the gratification of informing such Readers as may have been pleased with this Poem, or with any part of it, that they owe their pleasure in some sort to me; as the Author was himself very desirous that it should be suppressed. This wish had arisen from a consciousness of the defects of the Poem, and from a knowledge that many persons had been much displeased with it. The Poem of my Friend has indeed great defects; first, that the principal person has no distinct character, either in his profession of Mariner, or as a human being who having been long under the control of supernatural impressions might be supposed himself to partake of something supernatural: secondly, that he does not act, but is continually acted upon: thirdly, that the events having no necessary connection do not produce each other; and lastly, that the imagery is somewhat too laboriously accumulated. Yet the Poem contains many delicate touches of passion, and indeed the passion is everywhere true to nature; a great number of the stanzas present beautiful images, and are expressed with unusual felicity of language; and the versification, though the metre is itself unfit for long poems, is harmonious and artfully varied, exhibiting the utmost powers of that metre,

and every variety of which it is capable. It therefore appeared to me that
these several merits (the first of which, namely that of the passion, is of
the highest kind), gave to the Poem a value which is not often possessed
by better Poems. On this account I requested of my Friend to permit
me to republish it.

Charles Lamb, quick to defend the poem earlier against Southey's attack,
was equally miffed by the way it had been treated and commented upon in
the new edition. He wrote to Wordsworth:

> I am sorry that Coleridge has christened his *Ancient Marinere*, a
> *Poet's Reverie*; it is as bad as Bottom the Weaver's declaration that he is
> not a lion, but only the scenical representation of a lion. What new idea
> is gained by this title but one subversive of all credit—which the tale
> should force upon us—of its truth.[4]
> For me, I was never so affected with any human tale. After first
> reading it, I was totally possessed with it for many days. I dislike all the
> miraculous part of it; but the feelings of the man under the operation of
> such scenery, dragged me along like Tom Piper's magic whistle. I totally
> differ from your idea that the Marinere should have had a character and
> profession. This is a beauty in *Gulliver's Travels*, where the mind is kept
> in a placid state of little wonderments; but the Ancient Marinere under-
> goes such trials as overwhelm and bury all individuality or memory of
> what he was—like the state of a man in a bad dream, one terrible pe-
> culiarity of which is, that all consciousness of personality is gone. Your
> other observation is, I think as well, a little unfounded: the Marinere,
> from being conversant in supernatural events, *has* acquired a supernatural
> and strange cast of phrase, eye, appearance, etc., which frighten the wed-
> ding guest. You will excuse my remarks, because I am hurt and vexed
> that you should think it necessary, with a prose apology, to open the eyes
> of dead men that cannot see.
> To sum up a general opinion of the second volume, I do not feel any
> one poem in it so forcibly as the *Ancient Marinere*, and the *Mad Mother*,
> and the *Lines at Tintern Abbey*, in the first.

In 1800 a third son, Derwent, was born to Coleridge and Sarah, and
two years later, the daughter they named Sara. But their marriage was beyond repair and by 1806 the break was complete. They separated informally.
From that time on, Sarah and the two children were cared for by Southey,
with the help of friends. Later, Coleridge transferred his annuity to his wife;
from time to time he was able to send her small sums from the sales of his
prose works.

For fifteen years after his return from Germany, Coleridge wandered here
and there, sponging off friends. He would pop in for a short visit, and stay

months. Wordsworth, Byron, and De Quincey were among the notables who came to his rescue with considerable loans. For a short time he was Secretary to the Governor of Malta. He visited Rome. He tried to edit a new magazine called *The Friend*, but it was as badly managed as *The Watchman* and soon failed. In 1809 he rejoined Wordsworth in the Lake District, where Wordsworth and his three women had settled, but their friendship had cooled and their ways soon separated again. His play *Remorse* had a short, successful run at Drury Lane Theatre, in London, thanks largely to Byron's help and influence.

It was in Germany that Kant took hold of Coleridge, "as with a giant's hand"—an event which, as Bertrand Russell has observed in his *History of Western Philosophy*, "did not improve his verse." Indeed, Coleridge never did recapture the magic of that wonderful year at Stowey; his energies turned more and more toward the study of German philosophy and theology. As a kind of literary character, like Samuel Johnson before him, his fame spread around the world. He was much in demand as a lecturer: on Shakespeare, Milton, poetry, drama, philosophy, and religion. Coleridge was a brilliant conversationalist (or rather, monologist, for he seldom listened to what anyone else said), but unimpressive on the platform. On many occasions he even failed to appear. When he did, his lectures had a feeble, absent-minded quality. They rambled off on everything except the main topic. Nobody understood him when he tried to explain German idealism. Byron wrote, in his Dedication to *Don Juan:*

> And Coleridge, too, has lately taken wing,
> But like a hawk encumber'd with his hood,—
> Explaining metaphysics to the nation—
> I wish he would explain his explanation.

Coleridge so constantly altered his philosophic and religious views that it is hard to pin down exactly what he believed, at any given time, about a variety of important topics. Yet there is one dominating thread of intent that ties together the history of his shifting metaphysical opinions. Throughout his adult life he was searching desperately for a firm philosophical underpinning to support his Protestant faith. He believed that the Catholic philosophers had perverted reason by trying to prove too much, and that only along the lines indicated by Kant, who destroyed reason to make room for faith, could one finally reconcile the head of modern science with the heart of Christianity.

At no time, except for a brief period as a youth when he was reading Voltaire, did Coleridge cease to be a true believer; not even during his Unitarian period. Most Unitarians today are agnostics or atheists, but in Coleridge's day they were Christian theists who stressed the humanity of Jesus in opposition to trinitarianism. After his return from Germany, Coleridge abandoned Unitarianism completely. Take away the divinity of Christ, he wrote, and God becomes no more than a "power in darkness," like the power of gravitation. A letter written in 1802 to his brother George contains the following capsule version of his faith:

"My faith is simply this—that there is an original corruption in our nature, from which and from the consequences of which, we may be redeemed by Christ—not, as the Socinians [Catholic heretics, forerunners of the Unitarians] say, by his pure morals, or excellent example merely—but in a mysterious manner as an effect of his Crucifixion. And this I believe, not because I *understand* it; but because I *feel* that it is not only suitable to, but needful for my nature, and because I find it clearly revealed. Whatever the New Testament says I believe—according to my best judgment of the meaning of the sacred writer."

Though Coleridge sometimes expressed one set of views to his brother George while professing other views to his friends, there is no reason to doubt the sincerity of the passage just quoted. It is easy to forget that Coleridge, like Milton, was one of those rare birds in English literature, a genuine Protestant poet. Many lines of his poems, including some in *The Ancient Mariner*, reflect his doctrinal beliefs. He may have been inconsistent at times, unsure of many things, weak in behavior, but only confusion results when a critic tries to sweep Coleridge's Protestant convictions under the rug, as though they were somehow irrelevant to his life and writings.

"Every man is born," Coleridge said (*Table Talk*, July 2, 1830), "an Aristotelian or a Platonist." The distinction can be made in many different ways. Let's say a Platonist is one who believes (as an Aristotelian does not) that this world is only a shadow of a larger reality; a reality utterly beyond the comprehension of our little animal minds. ". . . and we in this low world / Placed with our backs to bright Reality," was how Coleridge put it in *Destiny of Nations*. In this sense he was a born Platonist. As a young man he was fascinated for a time by Neoplatonism and the even wilder pantheistic occultism of Jacob Boehme, but his first really great philosophical enthusiasm was for the gentle, commonsense, almost colorless Platonism of David Hartley.

Hartley was a medical doctor of unorthodox Protestant views, famous in his day for a two-volume work, *Observations on Man, his Frame, Duty, and Expectations*. The work was an ambitious attempt to harmonize the empiricism of science, and the views of such empirical philosophers as David Hume, with what Hartley considered the essentials of Christianity. Though few people read Hartley today, the first half of his work says little with which a modern empiricist would disagree. Hartley's doctrine of the "association of ideas" as the basis of animal habit and thought is now generally accepted. His "vibrations" in the ether, by means of which sensory experience is carried along nerves and stored in the brain, are clearly equivalent to today's "electrical impulses" that transmit ingeniously coded information along the nerve fibers. Finally, Hartley was a thoroughgoing determinist, or "necessitarian," as such philosophers were called then. Allowing for his lack of knowledge of twentieth century science, his views are almost indistinguishable from those of most modern psychologists.

The second half of Hartley's opus is another matter. The entire empirical outlook of the first volume is now framed by Christian theology. *This* world, with its unvarying laws, its vibrating ether, its creatures with the remarkable power of storing and associating vibrations in their heads—*this* is the world that God made. Tens of thousands of liberal Protestant ministers today hold opinions differing in no essential respect from Hartley's "system." For Coleridge, the book was a liberation. He named his first child David Hartley. There is no question that many of Hartley's tenets underlie portions of *The Ancient Mariner,* especially Hartley's insistence that animals share with man the power of associative thought, and that they possess low-order souls and are therefore united with man as part of one unified divine creation.[5]

But by the time his second child was born, Coleridge was beginning to have doubts about Hartley's "Christian materialism," as it was sometimes called. He was particularly disturbed by its dogmatic denial of free will. "Berkeley," the name given to his second son, reflects Coleridge's enthusiasm for the idealistic system of another Protestant philosopher, Bishop Berkeley. This interest, in turn, was supplanted by his discovery of Kant, and his growing preoccupation with those German idealists who were Kant's successors.

Kant was, of course, still another philosopher in the Protestant tradition. His special brand of idealism had a prodigious influence on German theology, and Coleridge struggled for years trying to master the involutions of post-Kantian metaphysics. He finally concluded that Kant's views had reached their purest form in the philosophy of Friedrich von Schelling. It was Coleridge's fervid hope that someday he would write a vast systematic work on metaphysics in which he would give the world his version of Platonism, expanded and refined by Christian orthodoxy and German idealism. ("Jesus Christ," he once declared, "was a Platonic philosopher.") Alas, it was only one of the many grandiose plans about which Coleridge talked and wrote at length, but never carried out. After his death, one of his disciples, Joseph Henry Green, produced a two-volume work entitled *Spiritual Philosophy: Founded on the Teaching of the Late S. T. Coleridge.* But neither this volume nor any of Coleridge's scattered metaphysical writings succeeded in explaining Coleridge's explanation, or making any significant contribution to idealistic philosophy or Protestant theology.

Nevertheless, Coleridge acquired an enormous reputation in his day as an interpreter of German thought. He was essentially a literary thinker, a stimulator, a prodder; he was not a systematic thinker. Yet his influence on Emerson and the New England transcendentalists was strong, and there is no question that he belongs in a tradition that leads up through Kierkegaard and on into the neoorthodoxy of twentieth-century Protestantism. Coleridge's *Letters on the Inspiration of the Scriptures*, for example, could almost have been written by Paul Elmer More, or C. S. Lewis, or Karl Barth. Even the "yea" and "nay" of the Barthian dialectic reverberate through Coleridge's third letter.

The older Coleridge became, the heavier he used opium. It was a habit he could not shake, and a never-ceasing source of misery, both physical and spiritual. His nightmares became more frequent, more severe. He felt himself approaching madness. One of his letters to Dr. James Gillman, a physician and friend, was a heart-rending plea for help in escaping from "the terror that haunts my mind." The final eighteen years of his sad, slovenly life were spent in Dr. Gillman's home, at Highgate, where his opium doses could be carefully kept to a minimum.

It was at Highgate that "Christabel" and "Kubla Khan" (the first started and the second completed back in his Stowey period) were first published. The thin volume also included his poem "Pains of Sleep," in which he speaks of waking up screaming from a "fiendish dream," weeping, wondering why such sufferings had come to him. The poem closes with those pathetic lines:

> To be beloved is all I need,
> And whom I love, I love, indeed.

In 1817 his collected poems appeared in a volume called *Sibylline Leaves*. It contained his final revision of *The Ancient Mariner*. The marginal gloss—such glosses were common in the sea travel books of the time—and the motto from Burnet were first added to this printing, although Coleridge may have written his gloss many years earlier. It was the first occasion on which the poem was publicly identified as his own. *Lay Sermons, Biographia Literaria*, and *Aids to Reflection* were among his prose books published while he was under Dr. Gillman's care. His last book, *Church and State*, appeared in 1830. (*Confessions of an Inquiring Spirit* and *Table Talk* were not issued until after his death.)

Thomas Carlyle visited Coleridge at Highgate. His vivid, unsympathetic description is often quoted, but is worth quoting again:

> Coleridge sat on the brow of Highgate Hill in those years, looking
> down on London and its smoke tumult like a sage escaped from the in-

anity of life's battle, attracting towards him the thoughts of innumerable brave souls still engaged there. His express contributions to poetry,
philosophy, or any specific province of human literature or enlighten-
ment had been small and sadly intermittent; but he had, especially
among young inquiring men, a higher than literary, a kind of prophetic
or magician character. He was thought to hold—he alone in England—
the key of German and other Transcendentalisms; knew the sublime
secret of believing by the "reason" what the "understanding" had been
obliged to fling out as incredible; and could still, after Hume and Voltaire had done their best and worst with him, profess himself an orthodox Christian, and say and print to the Church of England, with its
singular old rubrics and surplices at Allhallowtide, *Esto perpetua*. A sublime man; who alone in those dark days had saved his crown of spiritual manhood, escaping from the black materialisms and revolutionary
deluges with "God, Freedom, Immortality," still his; a king of men.
The practical intellects of the world did not much heed him, or carelessly reckoned him a metaphysical dreamer; but to the rising spirits of
the young generation he had this dusky sublime character, and sat
there as a kind of Magus, girt in mystery and enigma; his Dodona oak-
grove (Mr. Gillman's house at Highgate) whispering strange things, uncertain whether oracles or jargon.

The good man—he was now getting old, towards sixty perhaps, and
gave you the idea of a life that had been full of sufferings; a life heavy-
laden, half-vanquished, still swimming painfully in seas of manifold physical and other bewilderment. Brow and head were round and of massive
weight, but the face was flabby and irresolute. The deep eyes, of a light
hazel, were as full of sorrow as of inspiration; confused pain looked mildly
from them, as in a kind of mild astonishment. The whole figure and air,
good and amiable otherwise, might be called flabby and irresolute; expressive of weakness under possibility of strength. He hung loosely on his
limbs, with knees bent, and stooping attitude; in walking he rather shuffled than decisively stept; and a lady once remarked he never could fix
which side of the gardenwalk would suit him best, but continually shifted,
corkscrew fashion, and kept trying both; a heavy-laden, high-aspiring, and
surely much-suffering man. His voice, naturally soft and good, had contracted itself into a plaintive snuffle and sing-song; he spoke as if preaching—you could have said preaching earnestly and almost hopelessly the
weightiest things. I still recollect his "object" and "subject," terms of
continual recurrence in the Kantean province; and how he sang and snuf-
fled them into "om-m-ject" and "sum-m-mject," with a kind of solemn
shake or quaver as he rolled along. No talk in his century or in any other
could be more surprising.

Coleridge died in Dr. Gillman's house on July 25, 1834. His funeral was
unattended by his wife, children, or three old friends. Southey reacted coolly
to news of his friend's death. A shaken Wordsworth declared that Coleridge

was the most "wonderful" man he had ever known. It was Charles Lamb, his first good friend, who was most grief stricken. "His great and dear spirit haunts me," Lamb wrote. "Never saw I his likeness, nor probably the world can see again."

NOTES

1. It was this poem, and others almost as bad, that Byron had in mind when he wrote (in *English Bards and Scotch Reviewers*, lines 255–64):

> *Shall gentle Coleridge pass unnoticed here,*
> *To turgid ode and tumid stanza dear?*
> *Though themes of innocence amuse him best,*
> *Yet still Obscurity's a welcome guest.*
> *If Inspiration should her aid refuse*
> *To him who takes a Pixy for a muse,*
> *Yet none in lofty numbers can surpass*
> *The bard who soars to elegize an an ass.*
> *So well his subject suits his noble mind,*
> *He brays, the Laureate of the longeared kind.*

2. There seems little doubt that Coleridge's eyes were gray; yet Carlyle spoke of them once as hazel and on another occasion as brown, Emerson (who as a young man paid Coleridge a visit) called them blue, and other descriptions of Coleridge record his eyes as greenish-gray and black. See "The Color of Coleridge's Eyes," by John Louis Haney, *Anglia*, Vol. 23, 1901, pp. 424–26.

3. Intended for *Lyrical Ballads*, though not included, was Wordsworth's narrative poem "Peter Bell," in which he sought to dramatize the same moral theme of Coleridge's ballad, but without resort to the supernatural. Parallels with *The Ancient Mariner* are so obvious, and the poetry so inept, that the poem is almost a parody. Peter Bell, a wanderer by land instead of sea, is an uncouth, immoral salesman of (Wedgwood?) pottery, blind to the beauty of yellow primroses and other aspects of nature:

> *Not for the moon cared he a tittle*
> *And for the stars he cared as little.*

An act of cruelty to one of God's humble creatures, a donkey, plunges him into a sequence of terrifying events which lead finally to his remorse, repentance, and spiritual rebirth. There are numerous, deliberate attempts to introduce images from Coleridge's ballad: a man's corpse, a horned moon, moonlight, blood, the donkey's shining eye, a grotesque grin, auroral lights, an apparition, those three mystic numbers (3, 7, and 9), the great harlot of Babylon, an empty bucket, an underground explosion, and many others.

4. It is hard to believe, but one of the most persistent approaches to *The Ancient Mariner* is to regard it as not about the supernatural at all. William Darby Templeman, summarizing the poem for *Encyclopedia Americana*, says: "Though often regarded as a poem of the supernatural, *The Ancient Mariner* is rather one of abnormal psychology, in

which a poor workman, illiterate, profoundly superstitious, and at least partly crazed by long exposure, fear, and loneliness, is presented as giving his own account of the happenings . . ."

More recently, Lionel Stevenson, in *"The Ancient Mariner* as a Dramatic Monolog" (*The Personalist*, January 1949), interprets the ballad as a dramatic story about a superstitious sailor who imagines that killing a bird has caused all his woes. The moral quatrain at the end is, says Stevenson, not Coleridge's idea of a moral, but only his idea of the Mariner's idea of a moral: "the stumbling effort of a man with no rudiment of intellectual training to formulate his sense of religious dedication to universal love and brotherhood. . . ."

5. The influence of Hartley's views in general on the poem has been emphasized by Dorothy Waples in "David Hartley in *The Ancient Mariner*" (*Journal of English and Germanic Philology*, July 1936). Solomon Francis Gingerich, in a paper reprinted in *Essays in the Romantic Poets*, 1924, stresses the influence of Hartley's determinism on the ballad; not determinism in the modern scientific sense, but in the Calvinistic sense of all events in nature and history being foreordained by God.

TWENTY-SIX

LEWIS CARROLL AND HIS *ALICE* BOOKS

My Annotated Alice (1960) has far and away been my most successful book in terms of sales. I originally tried to persuade several publishers to ask Bertrand Russell to annotate Carroll's two Alice books, but they all thought this preposterous. I finally decided to do such a book myself, and Clarkson Potter was the only publisher who believed it worth doing. It was the first of Potter's famous series of annotated classics.

Since the publication of Annotated Alice there has been an astonishing surge of interest in Carroll. Numerous biographies have been written, the latest by Professor Morton Cohen. There is even a biography of the real Alice! Hundreds of critical papers deal with Carroll's writings, many of them collected in some dozen anthologies. Stage musicals, films, animated cartoons about Alice continue to be made. Symphonies based on Alice themes by David Del Tredici have won wide acclaim. Plans are underway for a new Alice movie using computer graphics. Carroll's diary is being reissued in unexpurgated form, and Morton Cohen has edited two volumes of Carroll's letters. There are Carroll societies in England, here, and in Japan, each publishing a periodical.

Over a period of three decades I received so many letters from Carrollians pointing out subtleties I had missed in my notations for Annotated Alice that in 1990 I followed that book with More Annotated Alice. If I live long enough there may be a Still More Annotated Alice. The following essay is the unaltered introduction to Annotated Alice, followed by a correction of four mistakes.

Let it be said at once that there is something preposterous about an annotated *Alice*. Writing in 1932, on the hundred-year anniversary of Lewis Carroll's birth, Gilbert K. Chesterton voiced his "dreadful fear" that Alice's story had already fallen under the heavy hands of the scholars and was becoming "cold and monumental like a classic tomb."

"Poor, poor, little Alice!" bemoaned G.K. "She has not only been caught and made to do lessons; she has been forced to inflict lessons on others. Alice is now not only a schoolgirl but a schoolmistress. The holiday is over and Dodgson is again a don. There will be lots and lots of examination papers, with questions like: (1) What do you know of the following: mimsy, gimble, haddocks' eyes, treacle-wells, beautiful soup? (2) Record all the moves in the chess game in *Through the Looking-Glass*, and give diagram. (3) Outline the practical policy of the White Knight for dealing with the social problem of green whiskers. (4) Distinguish between Tweedledum and Tweedledee."

There is much to be said for Chesterton's plea not to take *Alice* too seriously. But no joke is funny unless you see the point of it, and sometimes a point has to be explained. In the case of *Alice* we are dealing with a very curious, complicated kind of nonsense, written for British readers of another century, and we need to know a great many things that are not part of the text if we wish to capture its full wit and flavor. It is even worse than that, for some of Carroll's jokes could be understood only by residents of Oxford, and other jokes, still more private, could be understood only by the lovely daughters of Dean Liddell.

The fact is that Carroll's nonsense is not nearly as random and pointless as it seems to a modern American child who tries to read the *Alice* books. One says "tries" because the time is past when a child under fifteen, even in England, can read *Alice* with the same delight as gained from, say, *The Wind in the Willows* or *The Wizard of Oz*. Children today are bewildered and sometimes frightened by the nightmarish atmosphere of Alice's dreams. It is only because adults—scientists and mathematicians in particular—continue to relish the *Alice* books that they are assured of immortality. It is only to such adults that the notes of this volume are addressed.

There are two types of notes I have done my best to avoid, not because they are difficult to do or should not be done, but because they are so exceedingly easy to do that any clever reader can write them out for himself. I refer to allegorical and psychoanalytic exegesis. Like Homer, the Bible, and all other great works of fantasy, the *Alice* books lend themselves readily to any type of symbolic interpretation—political, metaphysical, or Freudian. Some learned commentaries of this sort are hilarious. Shane Leslie, for instance, writing on "Lewis Carroll and the Oxford Movement" (in the *London Mercury*, July 1933), finds in *Alice* a secret history of the religious controversies of Victorian England. The jar of orange marmalade, for example, is a symbol of Protestantism (William of Orange; get it?). The battle of the White and Red Knights is the famous clash of Thomas Huxley and Bishop Samuel Wilberforce. The blue Caterpillar is Benjamin Jowett, the White Queen is Cardinal

John Henry Newman, the Red Queen is Cardinal Henry Manning, the Chesh-
ire Cat is Cardinal Nicholas Wiseman, and the Jabberwock "can only be a
fearsome representation of the British view of the Papacy . . ."

In recent years the trend has naturally been toward psychoanalytic interpretations. Alexander Woollcott once expressed relief that the Freudians had
left Alice's dreams unexplored; but that was twenty years ago and now, alas,
we are all amateur headshrinkers. We do not have to be told what it means
to tumble down a rabbit hole or curl up inside a tiny house with one foot up
the chimney. The rub is that any work of nonsense abounds with so many
inviting symbols that you can start with any assumption you please about the
author and easily build up an impressive case for it. Consider, for example,
the scene in which Alice seizes the end of the White King's pencil and begins
scribbling for him. In five minutes one can invent six different interpretations.
Whether Carroll's unconscious had any of them in mind, however, is an altogether dubious matter. More pertinent is the fact that Carroll was interested
in psychic phenomena and automatic writing, and the hypothesis must not
be ruled out that it is only by accident that a pencil in this scene is shaped
the way it is.

We must remember also that many characters and episodes in *Alice* are
a direct result of puns and other linguistic jokes, and would have taken quite
different forms if Carroll had been writing, say, in French. One does not need
to look for an involved explanation of the Mock Turtle; his melancholy presence is quite adequately explained by mock-turtle soup. Are the many references to eating in *Alice* a sign of Carroll's "oral aggression," or did Carroll
recognize that small children are obsessed by eating and like to read about it
in their books? A similar question mark applies to the sadistic elements in
Alice, which are quite mild compared with those of animated cartoons for the
past thirty years. It seems unreasonable to suppose that all the makers of
animated cartoons are sadomasochists; more reasonable to assume that they
all made the same discovery about what children like to see on the screen.
Carroll was a skillful storyteller, and we should give him credit for the ability
to make a similar discovery. The point here is not that Carroll was not neurotic
(we all know he was), but that books of nonsense fantasy for children are not
such fruitful sources of psychoanalytic insight as one might suppose them to
be. They are much too rich in symbols. The symbols have too many explanations.

Readers who care to explore the various conflicting analytic interpretations
that have been made of *Alice* could do worse than start with Phyllis Greenacre,
a New York psychoanalyst, who has made the best and most detailed study
of Carroll from this point of view. Her arguments are most ingenious, possibly
true, but one wishes that she were less sure of herself. There is a letter in
which Carroll speaks of his father's death as "the greatest blow that has ever

fallen on my life." In the Alice books the most obvious mother symbols, the Queen of Hearts and the Red Queen, are heartless creatures, whereas the King of Hearts and the White King, both likely candidates for father symbols, are amiable fellows. Suppose, however, we give all this a looking-glass reversal and decide that Carroll had an unresolved Oedipus complex. Perhaps he identified little girls with his mother so that Alice herself is the real mother symbol. This is Dr. Greenacre's view. She points out that the age difference between Carroll and Alice was about the same as the age difference between Carroll and his mother, and she assures us that this "reversal of the unresolved Oedipal attachment is quite common." According to Dr. Greenacre, the Jabberwock and Snark are screen memories of what analysts still persist in calling the "primal scene." Maybe so; but one wonders.

The inner springs of the Rev. Charles Lutwidge Dodgson's eccentricities may be obscure, but the outer facts about his life are well known. For almost half a century he was a resident of Christ Church, the Oxford college that was his alma mater. For more than half that period he was a teacher of mathematics. His lectures were humorless and boring. He made no significant contributions to mathematics, though two of his logical paradoxes, published in the journal *Mind*, touch on difficult problems involving what is now called metalogic. His books on logic and mathematics are written quaintly, with many amusing problems, but their level is elementary and they are seldom read today.

In appearance Carroll was handsome and asymmetric—two facts that may have contributed to his interest in mirror reflections. One shoulder was higher than the other, his smile was slightly askew, and the level of his blue eyes not quite the same. He was of moderate height, thin, carrying himself stiffly erect and walking with a peculiar jerky gait. He was afflicted with one deaf ear and a stammer that trembled his upper lip. Although ordained a deacon (by Bishop Wilberforce) he seldom preached because of his speech defect and he never went on to holy orders. There is no doubt about the depth and sincerity of his Church of England views. He was orthodox in all respects save his inability to believe in eternal damnation.

In politics he was a Tory, awed by lords and ladies and inclined to be snobbish toward inferiors. He objected strongly to profanity and suggestive dialogue on the stage, and one of his many unfinished projects was to bowdlerize Bowdler by editing an edition of Shakespeare suitable for young girls. He planned to do this by taking out certain passages that even Bowdler had found inoffensive. He was so shy that he could sit for hours at a social gathering and contribute nothing to the conversation, but his shyness and stammering "softly and suddenly vanished away" when he was alone with a child. He was a fussy, prim, fastidious, cranky, kind, gentle bachelor whose life was sexless, uneventful and happy. "My life is so strangely free from all trial and trouble," he once wrote, "that I cannot doubt my own happiness is one of the talents entrusted to me to 'occupy' with, till the Master shall return, by doing something to make other lives happy."

So far so dull. We begin to catch glimpses of a more colorful personality when we turn to Charles Dodgson's hobbies. As a child he dabbled in puppetry and sleight of hand, and throughout his life enjoyed doing magic tricks, especially for children. He liked to form a mouse with his handkerchief then make it jump mysteriously out of his hand. He taught children how to fold paper boats and paper pistols that popped when swung through the air. He took up photography when the art was just beginning, specializing in portraits of children and famous people, and composing his pictures with remarkable skill and good taste. He enjoyed games of all sorts, especially chess, croquet, backgammon, and billiards. He invented a great many mathematical and word puzzles, games, cipher methods, and a system for memorizing numbers (in his diary he mentions using his mnemonic system for memorizing pi to seventy-one decimal places). He was an enthusiastic patron of opera and the theater at a time when this was frowned upon by church officials. The famous actress Ellen Terry was one of his lifelong friends.

Ellen Terry was an exception. Carroll's principal hobby—the hobby that aroused his greatest joys—was entertaining little girls. "I am fond of children (except boys)," he once wrote. He professed a horror of little boys, and in later life avoided them as much as possible. Adopting the Roman symbol for a day of good fortune, he would write in his diary, "I mark this day with a white stone" whenever he felt it to be specially memorable. In almost every case his white-stone days were days on which he entertained a child-friend or made the acquaintance of a new one. He thought the naked bodies of little girls (unlike the bodies of boys) extremely beautiful. Upon occasion he sketched or photographed them in the nude, with the mother's permission, of course. "If I had the loveliest child in the world, to draw or photograph," he wrote, "and found she had a modest shrinking (however slight, and however easily overcome) from being taken nude, I should feel it was a solemn duty owed to God to drop the request *altogether*." Lest these undraped pictures later embarrass the girls, he requested that after his death they be destroyed or returned to the children or their parents. None seems to have survived.

In *Sylvie and Bruno Concluded* there is a passage that expresses poignantly Carroll's fixation upon little girls of all the passion of which he was capable. The narrator of the story, a thinly disguised Charles Dodgson, recalls that only once in his life did he ever see perfection. ". . . it was in a London exhibition, where, in making my way through a crowd, I suddenly met, face to face, a child of quite unearthly beauty." Carroll never ceased looking for such a child. He became adept at meeting little girls in railway carriages and on public beaches. A black bag that he always took with him on these seaside trips contained wire puzzles and other unusual gifts to stimulate their interest. He even carried a supply of safety pins for pinning up the skirts of little girls when they wished to wade in the surf. Opening gambits could be amusing. Once when he was sketching near the sea a little girl who had fallen into the water walked by with dripping clothes. Carroll tore a corner from a piece of blotting paper and said, "May I offer you this to blot yourself up?"

A long procession of charming little girls (we know they were charming from their photographs) skipped through Carroll's life, but none ever quite took the place of his first love, Alice Liddell. "I have had scores of child-friends since your time," he wrote to her after her marriage, "but they have been quite a different thing." Alice was the daughter of Henry George Liddell (the name rhymes with fiddle), the dean of Christ Church. Some notion of how attractive Alice must have been can be gained from a passage in *Praeterita*, a fragmentary autobiography by John Ruskin. Florence Becker Lennon reprints the passage in her biography of Carroll, and it is from her book that I shall quote.

Ruskin was at that time teaching at Oxford and he had given Alice drawing lessons. One snowy winter evening when Dean and Mrs. Liddell were dining out, Alice invited Ruskin over for a cup of tea. "I think Alice must have sent me a little note," he writes, "when the eastern coast of Tom Quad was clear." Ruskin had settled in an armchair by a roaring fire when the door burst open and "there was a sudden sense of some stars having been blown out by the wind." Dean and Mrs. Liddell had returned, having found the roads blocked with snow.

"How sorry you must be to see us, Mr. Ruskin!" said Mrs. Liddell.

"I was never more so," Ruskin replied.

The dean suggested that they go back to their tea. "And so we did," Ruskin continues, "but we couldn't keep papa and mamma out of the drawing-room when they had done dinner, and I went back to Corpus, disconsolate."

And now for the most significant part of the story. Ruskin *thinks* that Alice's sisters, Edith and Rhoda, were also present, but he isn't sure. "It is all so like a dream now," he writes. Yes, Alice must have been quite an attractive little girl.

There has been much argumentation about whether Carroll was in love with Alice Liddell. If this is taken to mean that he wanted to marry her or make love to her, there is not the slightest evidence for it. On the other hand, his attitude toward her was the attitude of a man in love. We do know that Mrs. Liddell sensed something unusual, took steps to discourage Carroll's attention, and later burned all of his early letters to Alice. There is a cryptic reference in Carroll's diary on October 28, 1862, to his being out of Mrs. Liddell's good graces "ever since Lord Newry's business." What business Lord Newry has in Carroll's diary remains to this day a tantalizing mystery.

There is no indication that Carroll was conscious of anything but the purest innocence in his relations with little girls, nor is there a hint of impropriety in any of the fond recollections that dozens of them later wrote about him. There was a tendency in Victorian England, reflected in the literature of the time, to idealize the beauty and virginal purity of little girls. No doubt this made it easier for Carroll to suppose that his fondness for them was on a high spiritual level, though of course this hardly is a sufficient explanation for that fondness. Of late Carroll has been compared with Humbert Humbert, the narrator of Vladimir Nabokov's novel *Lolita*. It is true that both had a passion for little girls, but their goals were exactly opposite. Humbert Humbert's "nymphets" were creatures to be used carnally. Carroll's little girls appealed to him precisely because he felt sexually safe with them. The thing that distinguishes Carroll from other writers who lived sexless lives (Thoreau, Henry James . . .) and from writers who were strongly drawn to little girls (Poe, Ernest Dowson . . .) was his curious combination, almost unique in literary history, of complete sexual innocence with a passion that can only be described as thoroughly heterosexual.

Carroll enjoyed kissing his child-friends and closing letters by sending them 10,000,000 kisses, or 4¾, or a two-millionth part of a kiss. He would have been horrified at the suggestion that a sexual element might be involved. There is one amusing record in his diary of his having kissed one little girl, only to discover later that she was seventeen. Carroll promptly wrote a mock apology to her mother, assuring her that it would never happen again, but the mother was not amused.

On one occasion a pretty fifteen-year-old actress named Irene Barnes (she later played the roles of White Queen and Knave of Hearts in the stage musical of *Alice*) spent a week with Charles Dodgson at a seaside resort. "As I remember him now," Irene recalls in her autobiography, *To Tell My Story* (the passage is quoted by Roger Green in Vol. 2, page 454, of Carroll's *Diary*), "he was very slight, a little under six foot, with a fresh, youngish face, white hair, and an impression of extreme cleanliness. . . . He had a deep love for children, though I am inclined to think not such a great understanding of them. . . . His great delight was to teach me his Game of Logic [this was a method of solving syllogisms by placing black and red counters on a diagram of Carroll's own invention]. Dare I say this made the evening rather long, when the band was playing outside on the parade, and the moon shining on the sea?"

It is easy to say that Carroll found an outlet for his repressions in the unrestrained, whimsically violent visions of his Alice books. Victorian children no doubt enjoyed similar release. They were delighted to have at last some books without a pious moral, but Carroll grew more and more restive with the thought that he had not yet written a book for youngsters that would convey some sort of evangelistic Christian message. His effort in this direction was *Sylvie and Bruno*, a long, fantastic novel that appeared in two separately published parts. It contains some splendid comic scenes, and the Gardener's song, which runs like a demented fugue through the tale, is Carroll at his best. Here is the final verse, sung by the Gardener with tears streaming down his cheeks.

> *He thought he saw an Argument*
> *That proved he was the Pope:*
> *He looked again, and found it was*
> *A Bar of Mottled Soap.*
> *"A fact so dread," he faintly said,*
> *"Extinguishes all hope!"*

But the superb nonsense songs were not the features Carroll most admired about this story. He preferred a song sung by the two fairy children, Sylvie and her brother Bruno, the refrain of which went:

> *For I think it is Love,*
> *For I feel it is Love,*
> *For I'm sure it is nothing but Love!*

Carroll considered this the finest poem he had ever written. Even those who may agree with the sentiment behind it, and behind other portions of the novel that are heavily sugared with piety, find it difficult to read these portions today without embarrassment for the author. They seem to have been written at the bottom of treacle wells. Sadly one must conclude that, on the whole, *Sylvie and Bruno* is both an artistic and rhetorical failure. Surely few Victorian children, for whom the story was intended, were ever moved, amused, or elevated by it.

Ironically, it is Carroll's earlier and pagan nonsense that has, at least for a few modern readers, a more effective religious message than *Sylvie and Bruno*. For nonsense, as Chesterton liked to tell us, is a way of looking at existence that is akin to religious humility and wonder. The Unicorn thought Alice a fabulous monster. It is part of the philosophic dullness of our time that there are millions of rational monsters walking about on their hind legs, observing the world through pairs of flexible little lenses, periodically supplying themselves with energy by pushing organic substances through holes in their faces, who see nothing fabulous whatever about themselves. Occasionally the noses of these creatures are shaken by momentary paroxysms. Kierkegaard once imagined a philosopher sneezing while recording one of his profound sentences. How could such a man, Kierkegaard wondered, take his metaphysics seriously?

The last level of metaphor in the Alice books is this: that life, viewed rationally and without illusion, appears to be a nonsense tale told by an idiot mathematician. At the heart of things science finds only a mad, never-ending quadrille of Mock Turtle Waves and Gryphon Particles. For a moment the waves and particles dance in grotesque, inconceivably complex patterns capable of reflecting on their own absurdity. We all live slapstick lives, under an inexplicable sentence of death, and when we try to find out what the Castle authorities want us to do, we are shifted from one bumbling bureaucrat to another. We are not even sure that Count West-West, the owner of the Castle, really exists. More than one critic has commented on the similarities between Kafka's *Trial* and the trial of the Jack of Hearts; between Kafka's *Castle* and a chess game in which living pieces are ignorant of the game's plan and cannot tell if they move of their own wills or are being pushed by invisible fingers.

This vision of the monstrous mindlessness of the cosmos ("Off with its head!") can be grim and disturbing, as it is in Kafka and the Book of Job, or lighthearted comedy, as in *Alice* or Chesterton's *The Man Who Was Thursday*. When Sunday, the symbol of God in Chesterton's metaphysical nightmare, flings little messages to his pursuers, they turn out to be nonsense messages. One of them is even signed Snowdrop, the name of Alice's White Kitten. It is a vision that can lead to despair and suicide, to the laughter that closes Jean-Paul Sartre's story "The Wall," to the humanist's resolve to carry on bravely in the face of ultimate darkness. Curiously, it can also suggest the wild hypothesis that there may be a light behind the darkness.

Laughter, declares Reinhold Niebuhr in one of his finest sermons, is a kind of no-man's-land between faith and despair. We preserve our sanity by laughing at life's surface absurdities, but the laughter turns to bitterness and derision if directed toward the deeper irrationalities of evil and death. "That is why," he concludes, "there is laughter in the vestibule of the temple, the echo of laughter in the temple itself, but only faith and prayer, and no laughter, in the holy of holies."

Lord Dunsany said the same thing this way in *The Gods of Pagana*. The speaker is Limpang-Tung, the god of mirth and melodious minstrels.

"I will send jests into the world and a little mirth. And while Death seems to thee as far away as the purple rim of hills, or sorrow as far off as rain in the blue days of summer, then pray to Limpang-Tung. But when thou growest old, or ere thou diest, pray not to Limpang-Tung, for thou becomest part of a scheme that he doth not understand.

"Go out into the starry night, and Limpang-Tung will dance with thee . . . Or offer up a jest to Limpang-Tung; only pray not in thy sorrow to Limpang-Tung, for he saith of sorrow: 'It may be very clever of the gods, but he doth not understand.' "

Alice's Adventures in Wonderland and *Through the Looking-Glass* are two incomparable jests that the Reverend C. L. Dodgson, on a mental holiday from Christ Church chores, once offered up to Limpang-Tung.

POSTSCRIPT (1995)

As I point out in More Annotated Alice, *the foregoing essay contains four errors:*

I took Shane Leslie's paper seriously. As many readers enlightened me, Leslie was satirizing the compulsion of certain scholars to find obscure symbolism in the Alice *books.*

I said none of Carroll's photographs of naked little girls had survived. Four such pictures, hand-colored, are reproduced in Lewis Carroll's Photographs of Nude Children, *a monograph published by the Rosenbach Foundation in 1979 with an introduction by Morton Cohen. Cohen also reproduces them in his biography of Carroll.*

The mystery of "Lord Newry's business" has been cleared up. Viscount Newry was an undergraduate at Christ Church who Mrs. Liddell hoped would marry one of her daughters. When Lord Newry petitioned the faculty for permission to give a ball, he was turned down. Caroll's vote against him angered Mrs. Liddell.

I said there was no evidence Carroll wanted to marry Alice when she was of marriageable age. Such evidence has since been found. It is given in detail by Professor Morton Cohen in his long-awaited biography of Carroll, published by Knopf in 1995.

TWENTY-SEVEN

THE ROYAL HISTORIAN OF OZ

The year 2000 will mark the centennial of the first publication of The Wizard of Oz, our country's greatest work of fantasy for children. It is difficult to understand, but prejudice against L. Frank Baum's Oz books was so intense among librarians and critics of juvenile literature that the essay you are about to read, published more than half a century after the great popular success of The Wizard as both a book and musical, was the first attempt ever made to report in detail on Baum's life and career. It first appeared as a two-part article in Fantasy and Science Fiction (January and February 1955). The magazine was then edited by Anthony Boucher, who like myself had read and loved the Oz books as a child. Four other essays about Baum can be found in my Order and Surprise. One of them, "Why Librarians Dislike Oz," is an effort to explain their curious prejudices.

Today Baum is one of the most ardently collected of all American authors. So many articles about him have appeared in scholarly journals that Michael Patrick Hearn, author of The Annotated Wizard of Oz, gathered them into an anthology in 1983. Some dozen other books about Baum and his writings have been published, with more on the way. The quarterly Baum Bugle, with its color plates and learned articles, is getting better and better. It is the organ of The International Wizard of Oz Club which holds four conventions every year for Oz fans to meet and exchange information. The librarians, I am happy to report, are now in full retreat.

It is not down on any map; true places never are.
—MELVILLE, Moby-Dick

America's greatest writer of children's fantasy, as everyone knows except librarians and critics of juvenile literature, was L. Frank Baum. His *Wonderful Wizard of Oz* has long been the nation's best-known, best-loved native fairy tale, but you will look in vain for any recognition of this fact in histories of children's books. Aside from an obscure booklet by Edward Wagenknecht and a brief magazine article by James Thurber, no one has felt it worthwhile to inquire as to what merits the Oz books may have or what manner of man it was who first produced them. By and large, the critics have looked upon Baum's efforts as tawdry popular writing in a class with Tom Swift and Elsie Dinsmore; certainly not to be compared with such classic "children's" fantasies as *Pilgrim's Progress* and *Gulliver's Travels*.

Fortunately, children themselves seldom listen to such learned opinion. Nothing in the world could induce them to plod their way through Bunyan's dreary discourse on Protestant fundamentalism or Swift's impudent nose-thumbing at the human race. Even Lewis Carroll's *Alice* books, with their archaic British phrases, abrupt transitions, and nightmarish episodes, have lost almost all their appeal for a modern child unless he or she happens to be a prodigy who plays chess and dabbles in semantics and symbolic logic. Yet today, all these years after they were written, children still turn the pages of Baum's Oz books with passionate delight. Surely it is only a matter of time until the critics develop sufficient curiosity to read the books themselves. When they do, they will be startled to find them well written, rich in excitement, humor, and philosophy, and with sustained imaginative invention of the highest order. In anticipation, therefore, of this event, it may be of interest to recount here for the first time the full story of Baum's remarkable career.

Lyman Frank Baum was born May 15, 1856, in the little town of Chittenango, near Syracuse, New York. His mother, Cynthia Stanton, was Scotch-Irish in descent and a devout Episcopalian. On his father's side his ancestors came from Germany, settling in central New York in 1748. His grandfather, the Reverend John Baum, was a circuit-riding Methodist minister. Benjamin Ward Baum, his father, was one of the nation's earliest oil producers, with extensive holdings in the Pennsylvania oil fields, and owner of a large estate near Syracuse in an area that is now the town of Mattydale.

Baum's childhood was spent in comparative luxury at Rose Lawn, the name of his father's estate. Here he was privately tutored except for a short period of attendance at Peekskill Military Academy. Young Frank did not take to military discipline, a fact that may explain the satire that pervades his descriptions of the Royal Army of Oz. (For a time it numbered twenty-seven officers and one private named Omby Amby, though on most occasions it consisted only of the Soldier with the Green Whiskers.)

When Baum was entering his teens, his father bought him a small printing press. For several years, during the summer months, Frank and his younger brother Harry wrote and printed a monthly newspaper that they called the *Rose Lawn Home Journal*. This may have aroused Frank's interest in a newspaper career. At any rate, at the age of seventeen he took a job in Manhattan as cub reporter on the *New York World*. Two years later we find him opening his own printing shop at Bradford, Pennsylvania, where he established the *New Era*, a paper still published today. But the work was dull and his spirit restless. For a while he managed a small chain of "opera houses" owned by his father in New York and Pennsylvania.

The theatrical world fascinated him more and more. Occasionally he acted with traveling stock companies, using a stage name because his family frowned on his associations with the theater. At one time he even tried to make a go of his own Shakespearean troupe. Finally he turned to playwrighting and in 1881 achieved his first literary success with an Irish musical comedy called *The Maid of Arran*. The play opened at his own opera house in Gilmour, Pennsylvania, then moved to Manhattan, where it enjoyed a profitable run. Baum wrote the book, music, and lyrics, produced and directed, and, under the name of Louis F. Baum, played the romantic lead! His acting was described in one review as "quiet and effective."[1]

Judging by early descriptions, young Baum must have made an impressive stage appearance. He was slightly over six feet, slender, and athletically proportioned, with brown hair, gray eyes, fair skin, and handsome angular features. His voice was low and well modulated and he sang in a rich baritone. In later years he always wore a large bicycle-handle mustache that was fashionable in his time. In photographs his eyes seem humorous, kindly, dreamy.

During the first year of his play's success, Baum married Maud Gage, of Fayetteville, New York, an attractive, spirited girl whose strong will and practical mind served to counterbalance her husband's reluctance to take money matters seriously. It proved to be a permanent, happy marriage. The play was on the road for several years, but when Maud became pregnant Baum dropped out of the cast and returned with her to Syracuse. There he set up a small company to manufacture and sell "Baum's Castorine" a crude-oil product used for greasing axles. This aspect of the oil business did not long hold his interest. He tried his hand at three more Irish melodramas—*Matches*, *Kilmourne*, and *The Queen of Killarney*. Only the first two were actually produced. They enjoyed brief runs but failed to achieve the popularity of his first play.

In 1887, with two small sons to support, Baum turned his face westward in search of greener pastures. His wife had a brother living in Aberdeen, a small prairie town in the region that was soon to become the state of South Dakota, and it was there that Baum took his family. At first he ran a variety store called Baum's Bazaar, but his generosity with credit made it difficult to keep the business solvent. He next bought a weekly paper, the *Aberdeen Saturday Pioneer*, and edited it for two years. "Our Landlady," his front-page column, poked good-natured fun at the local gentry but apparently made a few enemies. There were later rumors that he became involved in a pistol duel with one villager. The duel began with the two men standing back to back in the middle of the street. They were instructed to walk away from each other to the ends of the block, circle the block, and start shooting as they came together on the opposite side. Each man, as soon as he turned his first corner, reportedly ran up an alley and vanished from the scene.[2]

Two more sons were born in Aberdeen. The paper failed in 1891 and Baum moved his family to Chicago, where he first took a job as reporter on the *Chicago Post*. For a time he traveled through the Middle West selling china and glassware for a Chicago importing firm while his wife supplemented the family income by doing embroidery. His luck turned in 1897, when he tapped a hitherto unexploited magazine field by founding the *Show Window*, a monthly periodical for window trimmers. It was the official organ of the National Association of Window Trimmers of America, of which Baum was founder and first president.

For some time Baum had delighted his four sons by telling them ingenious tales that amplified the meaning of familiar Mother Goose rhymes. He began putting these stories on paper, and in 1897 a collection was published by the Chicago firm of Way and Williams in a handsome format with illustrations by Maxfield Parrish. *Mother Goose in Prose*, as it was called, was Baum's first book for children as well as Parrish's first job of book illustrating.[3] It must have sold well, because it soon appeared in a London printing and in several other American editions.

Baum's next book, *By the Candelabra's Glare*, is now extremely rare and much sought by collectors. He issued it himself in 1898, setting the type, printing it, and even binding it in his own workshop. It is a collection of sentimental, undistinguished verse. "My best friends have never called me a poet," he confesses in the foreword, "and I have been forced to admire their restraint." One poem, "La Reine Est Morte—Vive la Reine!," is an amusing attack on the type of woman then active in the feminist movement. The third stanza reads:

> *And shout hurrah for the woman new!*
> *With her necktie, shirt and toothpick shoe,*
> *With tailor-made suit and mien severe*
> >   *She's here!*

Baum's mother-in-law was a prominent feminist, a fact that may help explain his dislike of the New Woman. Even the Oz books contain many sly digs at the suffragettes, and one book, *The Land of Oz*, is one long satire on the movement. It chronicles the temporary overthrow of Oz by an army of comely young women.[4] The revolution is bloodless, owing to the fact that the

Royal Army (i.e., the Soldier with the Green Whiskers) flees in terror when the girls brandish their knitting needles at him. Once the female dictatorship is established, the husbands of Oz are forced to take over all the former duties of their wives. This proves annoying to both wives and husbands, but luckily the throne is soon restored.

General Jinjur, the pretty farm girl who leads the revolt, is one of Baum's best "meat people" characterizations (in Oz "meat people" are sharply distinguished from such personages as the Scarecrow and Tin Woodman who have no flesh and blood). She is a shrewdly drawn portrait of the masculine protest type. Her face wears "an expression of discontent coupled to a shade of defiance or audacity." She walks with "swift strides" and there is about her "an air of decision and importance." In a later Oz book she blacks her husband's eye for milking a red cow when she wanted him to milk the white one. Whenever the Scarecrow's painted face becomes faded, it is Jinjur who enjoys retouching it. It is not her own face that she paints, but that of a straw man.

Baum's third hardcover work, published in 1899, was *Father Goose, His Book*. It is a collection of nonsense rhymes for children, illustrated by Baum's friend William Wallace ("Den") Denslow, a Chicago newspaper artist, and hand-lettered by another Chicago artist and friend, Ralph Fletcher Seymour.[5] To everyone's surprise the book was an immediate sell-out, requiring four reprintings in the three months that followed the first edition.

For several years Baum had been taking his family each summer to Macatawa, a Michigan resort town on the shore of Lake Michigan. With the money earned by *Father Goose* he had a summer cottage built there, which he named "The Sign of the Goose." Most of the furniture was built by Baum himself. Since early manhood he had suffered from a bad heart and his doctor had advised him to do more of the manual craft work that he so much enjoyed. It was characteristic of Baum that he used the goose as the decorative motif of his cottage. A large rocking chair was in the shape of a goose. A frieze of green geese bordered the living room walls. A stained-glass window portrayed a goose in brilliant colors. Even the tiny brass heads of his upholstery tacks were specially made for him in the shape of geese![6]

Baum continued to edit his trade journal and in 1900 published *The Art of Decorating*, a mammoth handbook on the decoration of store windows and interiors. But his interest had now shifted to juvenile writing and his head was brimming with unusual ideas. During that year four children's books came from his pen. Two were unimpressive—*The Army Alphabet* and *The Navy Alphabet*, oversize books of mediocre verse telling the reader that A stands for Admiral, B for Bulwark, and so on. The other two books were fantasies, each concerned with adventures in a mythical land of enchantment. *A New Wonderland* had as its setting the Beautiful Valley of Phunnyland, where it snows popcorn, rains lemonade, and "the thunder is usually a chorus from the opera of Tannhauser." The other book—the book destined to make him immortal—was *The Wonderful Wizard of Oz.*

A New Wonderland (later retitled *The Magical Monarch of Mo*) is a collection of short, hilarious tales. It was written for an eastern firm and published by them at about the same time that *The Wonderful Wizard of Oz* was issued by George M. Hill, the small Chicago house that had published *Father Goose. The Wonderful Wizard* almost failed to find a publisher. It was turned down by every house to which it was submitted, Mrs. Baum later recalled in a letter,[7] because it was "too different, too radical—out of the general line." Mr. Hill finally consented to act as the book's distributor only after Baum and his illustrator, Denslow, agreed to shoulder all printing expenses. The book was not actually distributed to stores until the fall, but before the end of the year it had become the fastest-selling children's book in America. In 1955 a first edition sold at auction in Manhattan for six hundred dollars.

The book's story, as everyone knows, is about a plain-spoken little orphan girl who suddenly finds herself, like Lewis Carroll's Alice, in a magic land. Alice fell into Wonderland by way of a rabbit hole. Dorothy Gale is blown into Oz by a Kansas cyclone. And behind her strange adventures, as in all of Baum's fantasies, there lurks many an intended level of higher meaning. The Cowardly Lion, Scarecrow, and Tin Woodman illustrate delightfully the human tendency to confuse a real virtue with its valueless outer symbols. The Lion wants the Wizard to give him courage, the Scarecrow wants brains, and the Tin Woodman desires, beneath the coldness of his metal exterior, a warm heart. All three possess, of course, the things they seek. The Lion quakes with fear but meets all danger bravely. The Scarecrow thinks better than anyone in the party, and the Tin Woodman is so concerned over his lack of heart that his "reverence for life" exceeds that of a Schweitzer. On one occasion when he accidentally steps on a beetle he weeps so copiously that his tears rust and lock his jaws.

Even the ancient philosophic question of which is superior, the head or the heart, is explicitly raised. "I shall ask for brains instead of a heart," remarks the straw man, "for a fool would not know what to do with a heart if he had one." To which the tin man replies, "I shall take the heart, for brains do not make one happy, and happiness is the best thing in the world."

Baum wisely adds: "Dorothy did not say anything, for she was puzzled to know which of her two friends was right."

After the success of *The Wonderful Wizard,* Baum handed his trade journal over to a new editor and began work in earnest on other books for children. Three were published in 1901, none about Oz. *Dot and Tot of Merryland* is a full-length fantasy for very young readers. *The Master Key,* for older boys, is a science-fiction story about the wonders of electricity. The third volume, *Baum's American Fairy Tales,* deserves special mention because it marks the first appearance in American letters of fairy tales of merit that have the United States as a setting.

In 1902 Baum published *The Life and Adventures of Santa Claus*, a warm, moving story told in almost biblical prose and involving an elaborate Dunsany-like mythology. Its appearance, however, was completely overshadowed by the success in Chicago of a musical extravaganza based on *The Wizard*. Baum wrote both book and lyrics, Paul Tietjens composed the music, and Denslow designed the costumes.[8] The final script had been so heavily revised by Julian Mitchell, the producer, that it bore little resemblance to the original. Oz fans are usually shocked to learn that in the stage version Dorothy's pet is not a little black dog named Toto, but a huge cow called Imogene. There is a Lady Lunatic, very much out of place in Oz, and even a Poet Prince, with whom Dorothy falls in love!

Baum first reacted to many of these changes with amazement and indignation, but after the musical had become a smashing success, playing eighteen months on Broadway, he decided that Mitchell knew his audiences. In concluding a letter to the *Chicago Tribune* (Sunday, June 26, 1904, part 4, p. 1) he expressed his views as follows:

> I confess, after two years of success for the extravaganza, that I now regard Mr. Mitchell's views in a different light. The people will have what pleases them, and not what the author happens to favor, and I believe that one of the reasons why Julian Mitchell is recognized as a great producer is that he faithfully tries to serve the great mass of playgoers—and usually succeeds.
>
> My chief business is, of course, the writing of fairy tales, but should I ever attempt another extravaganza, or dramatize another of my books, I mean to profit by the lesson Mr. Mitchell has taught me, and sacrifice personal preference to the demands of those I shall expect to purchase admission tickets.

Two vaudeville comedians who worked as a team, Fred Stone and Dave Montgomery, were catapulted to stardom by the stage success of *The Wizard*. Stone played the Scarecrow and Montgomery the Tin Woodman. (The role of Dorothy, it is interesting to note, was taken by Anna Laughlin, mother of the "star-spangled soprano" of the fifties, Lucy Monroe.) The two comics were in England when Mitchell wired them to return for parts in the musical. New York papers reported that Mitchell met Stone with the comment, "Fred, you are a perfect scarecrow." To which Stone indignantly replied that his clothes had been made by one of the finest tailors in England. A chapter of Fred Stone's autobiography, *Rolling Stone*, published in 1945, is devoted to the musical. It is interesting to learn from this that Fred's brother, Edwin, took the role of Dorothy's pet cow, and that Fred fell in love with and married the girl who played the Lady Lunatic.

Flushed with the success of his musical, Baum and his wife sailed for Europe in January of 1906 for a six-month vacation abroad. The trip took them through Egypt, Greece, Italy, North Africa, Switzerland, and France. Baum's heart condition prevented him from climbing to the top of the Great Pyramid, a challenge that his robust wife was unable to resist. "The steps are from three to four feet in height," Maud wrote in a letter home, "and the ascent so strenuous that I rested several times on the way up."[9] A dramatic eruption of Mt. Vesuvius, witnessed by the Baums, prompted Baum to write a friend that the crater was the only thing he had seen on the trip that smoked more than he did.

Paul Tietjens, who wrote *The Wizard*'s musical score, also took a vacation abroad, spending it in Paris with Denslow. There he met and married the American girl who later became the poet Eunice Tietjens. In her autobiography, *The World at My Shoulder*, she describes Denslow as "a delightful old reprobate who looked like a walrus." Back in the States, she and her husband called on Baum at his Michigan cottage, "The Sign of the Goose." She wrote:

L. Frank Baum was a character. He was tall and rangy, with an imagination and a vitality which constantly ran away with him. He never wrote fewer than four books a year. . . . Constantly exercising his imagination as he did, he had come to the place where he could honestly not tell the difference between what he had done and what he had imagined. Everything he said had to be taken with at least a half-pound of salt.[10] But he was a fascinating companion.

He was never without a cigar in his mouth, but it was always unlit. His doctor had forbidden him to smoke, so he chewed up six cigars a day instead. There was one exception to this. Before he took his swim in the lake in the afternoon he would light a cigar and walk immediately into the water. He would solemnly wade out till the water was up to his neck and there walk parallel with the shore, moving his arms to give the impression that he was swimming. When a wave splashed on the cigar and put it out he at once came in and dressed.

His house was full of the most remarkable mementos of the time when it had been necessary for him "to rest his brain," following a stroke of facial paralysis. He had painted the walls with stencilled designs; he had made a sign of wrought iron and painted wood for the dooryard, "At the Sign of Father Goose"; he had made furniture; he had written a small book of poems(!), had set it up in type himself, printed and bound it by hand. Last of all, because all this had not yet rested his brain enough, he had made an elaborate piano arrangement of Paul's music for *The Wizard of Oz*—though he was no musician it was pretty good—had then figured out the system by which pianola records were made, and had cut a full-length record of this arrangement out of wrapping paper! This seems to have done the trick, and he was presently back at work.

Surviving friends of Baum all remember him as a modest, dignified gentleman who enjoyed meeting people, talking, and telling funny stories. "He was a very kindly man," Mrs. Baum states in a letter, "never angry, pleasant to everyone, but when his mind was active with some story he would meet his best friend and not see him."[11]

Throughout his adult life Baum did not affiliate with any church organization save for a brief period of membership in an Episcopalian church in Aberdeen. But he was always a "religious" man in the sense that he believed in both God and immortality. For a time he was intrigued by theosophy, and although he rejected most of the preposterous doctrines of this cult he seems to have retained a belief in reincarnation and the law of Karma. His eldest son, Frank, a retired army colonel in Los Angeles, told me in a letter that his father always believed that he and his wife had been together in previous incarnations and would be together again in future lives. (In Baum's fantasies I can recall only two places where he touches on the question of soul survival. Sea Fairies has a satirical section in which a school of "holy" mackerel express their conviction that, when they are jerked out of their element by a hook, they "go to glory"—to an "unknown, but beautiful sea." And in Sky Island, when inhabitants of the blue region reach the close of their life, they walk through the Arch of Phinis into the Great Blue Grotto, but what happens to them on the other side is not known.)

Aside from marching in a few torchlight parades for William Jennings Bryan, Baum was as inactive in politics as in church affairs. He consistently voted as a Democrat, however, and his sympathies seem always to have been on the side of the laboring classes. (In Sea Fairies an octopus expresses great indignation at having been likened to the Standard Oil monopoly!) I do not know whether Baum ever read William James, but he certainly shared James's love of variety and his democratic tolerance for ways of life alien to his own. There is a remarkable scene in The Lost Princess of Oz (p. 148) in which a group of animals, meat and meatless, argue about who among them is superior. The matter is finally settled by the Cowardly Lion who says quietly:

> Were we all like the Sawhorse we would all be Sawhorses, which would be too many of the kind; were we all like Hank, we would be a herd of mules; if like Toto, we would be a pack of dogs; should we all become the shape of the Woozy, he would no longer be remarkable for his unusual appearance. Finally, were you all like me, I would consider you so common that I would not care to associate with you. To be individual, my friends, to be different from others, is the only way to become distinguished from the common herd. Let us be glad, therefore, that we differ from one another in form and in disposition. Variety is the spice

of life and we are various enough to enjoy one another's society; so let us be content.

This theme of tolerance runs through all of Baum's writings, with many episodes that poke fun at narrow nationalism and ethnocentrism. In *John Dough and the Cherub*, for example, we encounter the Hilanders, who are tall and thin, their country separated by a stone wall from the Lolanders, who are short and fat. A law observed in both regions forbids anyone to ask questions of strangers or of inhabitants on the opposite side of the wall. As a consequence, neither country knows anything about the other, regarding its own area as a paradise and inhabitants on the other side as barbarians.

Like William Morris, whom he read and admired, Baum had a constitutional dislike of the mass-produced item, whether a piece of furniture or a man. "After all," says the Scarecrow to Tommy Kwikstep (a boy with twenty legs), "you have the pleasure of knowing you are unusual, and therefore remarkable among the people of Oz. To be just like other persons is small credit to one, while to be unlike others is a mark of distinction." I can think of only one spot outside of Oz where individuals of eccentric appearance do not suffer because of their deviation from the norm, and that is in the world of the carnival and circus sideshow. Perhaps it was his circus-background that enabled the Wizard to adjust so easily to life in Oz.

Eccentric as Baum's "meatless" characters are, they have a consistency of personality and behavior that makes them very real to the mind of a child. On one occasion when Baum had not written for weeks, Maud asked him what the trouble was. "They won't do what I want them to," he replied. When he began writing again and she asked how the matter had been settled, his answer was, "By letting them do what they wanted to."[12] It is a believable answer. Baum was a natural storyteller and even his most outlandish characters seem always to move about with a life of their own.

In spite of the fact that he continued to receive hundreds of letters (a mere trickle of the deluge to come!) from children who wanted to hear more about Oz, Baum's interests still lay in fairy tales of other sorts. His *Enchanted Island of Yew* (1903) is not a bad story (the chapter on Twi, a land where everything exists in double form, is an amazing *tour de force*) but it did not sell well, and it is marred by unpleasant psychological undertones.

Finally, in 1904, Baum yielded to the persistent demands of his readers. He wrote *The Marvelous Land of Oz* (later retitled *The Land of Oz*), dedicating it to Montgomery and Stone. It is his only Oz book in which Dorothy does not appear. The central character, a small boy named Tip, is later revealed to be Princess Ozma in enchanted form. For many years the Baums had longed for a daughter, and the book's dramatic climax may well have been an expression of such a desire.

Many new and entertaining "meatless" characters are introduced in the

story. Jack Pumpkinhead is an awkward, wooden figure whose head is a pump-
kin carved in an eternal grin. A wooden sawhorse is brought to life, much to
its own astonishment. And of course we must not fail to mention Professor
H. M. Woggle-Bug, T.E.

The Woggle-Bug is Baum's caricature of the overeducated pedant. He
had originally been an ordinary woggle-bug, living in the hearth of a country
schoolhouse. There he had become extremely learned by listening to the lectures of Professor Nowitall. One day the professor discovered him in the room,
and to show his pupils what a woggle-bug looked like, put him in a magic
lantern that projected his magnified image on the screen. At a moment when
the attention of the class was distracted, the Woggle-Bug stepped down from
the screen and made an escape in his greatly puffed-up condition. "H.M."
stands for "Highly Magnified," and "T.E." for "Thoroughly Educated." The
Woggle-Bug is addicted to using big words and has to be rebuked occasionally
for his tendency to indulge in bad puns. This is partly a satire on Baum
himself, for the Oz books abound in puns. They reach a crescendo in a later
book when Dorothy visits the Kingdom of Utensia, where all the citizens are
pieces of kitchenware. In eight pages of text Baum manages to introduce no
less than fifty puns!

The Woggle-Bug eventually becomes the President of the College of Art
and Athletic Perfection. His great contribution to the higher learning is the
invention of a pill that gives a student all the knowledge he needs simply by
swallowing it. This frees students from the burden of attending classes and
permits them to spend all their time on college sports.

The Woggle-Bug, an operetta that Baum based on The Land of Oz, was
produced in Chicago in 1905, but its run was short. The Woggle-Bug Book,
issued the same year to publicize the play, is now a rare collector's item. It is
a large picture book in paper covers, telling of the Woggle-Bug's adventures
in an American city.

In addition to his summer home at Macatawa, Baum now began spending
part of each winter in a cottage at Coronado, on the California coast. In 1905
he purchased Pedloe Island, eighty miles off the coast, and announced to the
press his plans to convert the island into a miniature land of Oz that would
serve as a playground for youngsters. An eleven-year-old San Francisco girl was
appointed Princess of Oz. A palace and statues of leading Oz personages were
to be erected, and a monument to Jack Pumpkinhead built on Wizard's Point.
The project never got beyond the planning stage and may have been little
more than a publicity stunt to promote the sale of the second Oz book.

Queen Zixi of Ix, Baum's effort to write an old-fashioned European-type
fairy tale, appeared in 1905. That same year Baum tried his hand at an adult
novel. The Fate of a Crown, a romantic tale about Brazil, was published under
the pseudonym of Schuyler Staunton. Another romance by Staunton, Daughters of Destiny, came out the following year. His final attempt along these

lines was *The Last Egyptian*, issued anonymously in 1908. The three novels are well-written adventure tales, but otherwise have little to recommend them.

Six other pseudonyms were used by Baum. Captain Hugh Fitzgerald was his *nom de plume* for two boys' books about the adventures of one Sam Steele. Six novels about the Boy Fortune Hunters (two were reprints of the Sam Steele books) came out under the name of Floyd Akers. John Estes Cooke (not to be confused with John Esten Cooke, a Virginia historian whom Baum may have admired) was the name he used for a privately printed edition of *Tamawaca Folks*. Tamawaca is an anagram for Macatawa. The novel is about Baum's friends in the resort area.

Under the name of Edith Van Dyne, Baum wrote seventeen novels for teenage girls. Ten of them are about Aunt Jane's nieces, five about Mary Louise, and two about Orissa Kane, a girl aviator. After Baum's death, books by Edith Van Dyne continued to appear but were the product of other hands. *Annabel*, a love story about a red-haired lass, was written under the pseudonym of Suzanne Metcalf. As Laura Bancroft, he published six small books of fantasy (subsequently issued as a single volume called *Twinkle and Chubbins*) and *Policeman Bluejay*, a longer fantasy (later issued as *Babes in Birdland*). With the possible exception of the Bancroft books, none of these pseudonymous works are of lasting value. But the potboilers for older boys and girls, including two published under his own name (*The Daring Twins* and *Phoebe Daring*), brought him a steady and considerable income.

On one occasion, Mrs. Baum recalls,[13] an eastern publisher visiting in Chicago expressed to Baum's publisher a strong desire to meet Mrs. Van Dyne. He was so persistent that the firm finally arranged a tea at which the visitor was introduced to a lady who had been carefully coached to play the role. The publisher was charmed and edified. Baum and his wife attended the tea, enjoying the hoax immensely.

In 1907 Baum returned to his role of Father Goose by publishing *Father Goose's Year Book*, a kind of diary with blank pages on the right and humorous poems and aphorisms (such as "Rolling billiard balls gather no salary") on the left. But Baum's readers were no longer interested in Father Goose; they wanted to hear more about Oz. The second Oz book had not concerned Dorothy—in fact no one from the "outside world" appeared in the story. But readers remembered Dorothy with fondness, and yielding to their entreaties Baum reintroduced her as the protagonist of *Ozma of Oz*, the third volume in the series.

Dorothy's companion on this second adventure is a proud yellow hen called Billina. Other "Ozzy" characters also introduced for the first time include Tik-Tok, a mechanical copper man; the Hungry Tiger, who longs to eat little babies but whose conscience never permits him to do so (the *id* versus the *super-ego!*); and the Nome King, a whimsical mixture of evil and the comic, who appears in many later Oz books as the sworn enemy of Dorothy and Ozma.

Tik-Tok is one of the earliest robots in American fantasy. As his directions for winding read, he "thinks, speaks, acts, and does everything but live." Parts of his mechanism are always running down at crucial moments. Once in a later book he lapses into double talk when his thought mechanism, but not his speech, ceases to function.

The remaining Oz books, all excellent, though some have sections of careless writing, contain scores of outrageous personages. There is the Woozy, a blue, square-shaped animal of wood whose eyes dart fire whenever anyone says "Krizzle-Kroo" (the Woozy does not understand what this means and it is this that makes him so furious). There is the Patchwork Girl, a cotton-stuffed, but far from stuffy figure whose meeting with the Scarecrow is one of the highlights of the book in which she first appears. Nor does one easily forget such minor characters as Johnny Dooit, with the long gray whiskers and copper tool chest, who can build anything in just a few seconds; the Braided Man, who sells boxes of assorted rustles for ladies' skirts and flutters for flags; the Fuddles, a race of 3-D jigsaw people who "scatter" when disturbed, thereby giving befuddled visitors the fun of putting them together again.

The two most important cats in Oz deserve a paragraph. Both behave exactly as you would expect cats to behave if they could talk. Eureka, Dorothy's meat cat, permits herself to undergo a long court trial to determine if she has eaten one of the Wizard's piglets before she informs the court where the little pig can be found. Bungles, a glass cat with a cold ruby heart, is so reluctant to show her emotions that once, when she leaves to obtain help for friends in distress, she moves very slowly to give the impression she is indifferent to their fate. As soon as she is out of sight, however, she runs like a streak of crystal.

At the close of *The Emerald City of Oz*, sixth in the series, Baum tried to drop the series altogether. Glinda, the most powerful sorceress in Oz, casts a spell over the country that makes it impossible for the Royal Historian to find out what is happening inside its borders. You can imagine, of course, the flood of letters from heartbroken youngsters! Fortunately Baum was able to reestablish communication with the Shaggy Man, by wireless, and thus continue the series. Before writing the seventh Oz book, however, he managed to finish two superbly written fantasies, *Sea Fairies* and *Sky Island*. They tell of the adventures of Mayre Griffiths, better known as Trot, and her peglegged sailor companion, Cap'n Bill. Both Trot and Cap'n Bill later become honored citizens of Oz.

Certainly one reason for the immense popularity of the Oz books is the fact that they are told with such a wealth of detail that a strong sense of reality is created. These details range from such trifling observations as the fact that the Scarecrow has difficulty picking up small objects with his padded fingers, to important data about the history, geography, and customs of Oz. There is even a map of Oz, drawn by Professor Woggle-Bug. It formed the front end-paper of early editions of *Tik-Tok of Oz* and also was issued separately as a book insert.

No Oz reader need be told that Oz is roughly rectangular and divided into four regions, each with a characteristic color. The first edition of *The Road to Oz* was actually printed on tinted paper that changed color each time the scene shifted to another region! In the center of Oz is the Emerald City (a reflection of Baum's love of Ireland), where Princess Ozma rules in a palace of glittering gems. Surrounding Oz on all four sides is the Deadly Desert. Anyone setting foot on the desert turns instantly to dust.

Many social and economic details about Oz are known. Its population is more than half a million. The Emerald City, at the time it was almost conquered by the Nome King, had 9,654 buildings, 57,318 inhabitants. There is no sickness or disease in Oz. No one grows older and death occurs only rarely.[14] All animals talk in Oz and they are treated with as much respect as humans. In many ways Oz resembles the anarchist utopia of William Morris's *News from Nowhere*.[15] There is virtually no police force because all Ozites are happy, unselfish, and law-abiding. They work half the time, play half the time. There is no money, no rich, no poor. "Each person," the Royal Historian tells us, "was given freely by his neighbors whatever he required for his use, which is as much as anyone may reasonably desire."

Fortunately, not all parts of Oz are this orderly—especially the wild, unsettled areas of the Gillikin and Quadling regions, where many queer and unruly races flourish. Otherwise there would be no dangers and consequently no adventures.

Dangers yes, but horrors no. It is a rare occasion when Baum describes a scene that might frighten a sensitive child. Only a morbid adult could object to a wicked witch melting away or Jack Pumpkinhead carving a new head for himself to replace a former one that has spoiled. Baum's intention, stated in the preface of *The Wizard*, to leave out the "heartaches and nightmares" was amply fulfilled. You have only to glance through Grimm and Andersen, *Pinocchio*, or many another classic fairy tale to realize how skillfully Baum managed, in contrast with these works, to retain the excitement and avoid the violence and tears. Perrault's original story of Red Riding Hood, still the version told to French children, ends with the wolf eating both the little girl and her grandmother. I am told that youngsters in France find this highly amusing. A respectable case can even be made for the view that violent images provide a healthy purging of a child's sadistic emotions as well as a valuable early introduction to the reality of evil. "Children love a lot of nightmare and at least a little heartache in their books," writes Thurber; and he for one is glad that Baum did not succeed completely in keeping these elements out of his work.[16] It is true that Baum occasionally forgot his promise, especially in *Do-*

rothy and the Wizard in Oz, where an atmosphere of violence and gloom hangs over a large part of the tale, and in the macabre episode (in a later book) of the Tin Woodman's conversation with his former head. But on the whole his books are singularly free of shocking scenes and the spirit of Oz is a happy, sunny one. There are only two references in all of Baum's Royal History to its having rained in Oz.

Literary masterpieces are often written with astonishing carelessness of detail. Cervantes completely forgot that Sancho Panza's ass had been stolen; with no word of explanation we find Sancho riding him again. Robinson Crusoe strips off his clothes, swims out to the wreckage of a ship, and a moment later we find him filling his pockets with biscuits from the ship's bread room. Like the Baker Street Irregulars, who delight in inventing plausible explanations for Watson's memory lapses, a group of Oz enthusiasts can spend many pleasant hours suggesting ways for harmonizing similar contradictions in the Royal History.

The Land of Ev, for example, lies just across the Deadly Desert. But in what direction? You can find a basis for placing it to the north, south, east, or west of Oz. The early history of Oz, before the Wizard arrived in his balloon, is riddled with difficulties. There is reason to believe that grass takes on the color of each region in Oz and equally good reason to think it doesn't. Exactly what happens when a Nome touches an egg? Does he wither away or turn into a mortal? Why do the Shaggy Man and Polychrome, the Rainbow's daughter, act like strangers when they meet (in *Tik-Tok of Oz*) for the second time? These are only a fraction of the tantalizing problems that face the student of Oz.

An equally fascinating pastime is to speculate on how Baum arrived at the names of various characters and countries. In many instances the basis is obvious. For example, Princess Langwidere is a haughty woman with a "languid air." General Jinjur is a girl with lots of "ginger." But what about Woot the Wanderer, protagonist of *The Tin Woodman of Oz?* Did Baum take the initials of the tin man's title then switch the "T" from front to back?

The word Oz itself has been the subject of much speculation. The most popular theory is that Baum, searching for a name, looked up at a filing cabinet and saw the words "From O to Z." Another is that it came from "Boz," the nickname of Charles Dickens, one of Baum's favorite authors. And someone has pointed out that Job lived in the land of Uz. The late Jack Snow advanced a captivating theory in the preface of his monumental *Who's Who in Oz.* Baum once wrote that he had always enjoyed stories that cause the reader to exclaim with "Ohs" and "Ahs" of wonder, and Mr. Snow points out that Oz can be pronounced either "Ohs" or "Ahs."

The Baums moved to Los Angeles in 1909. Baum constructed an enormous circular birdcage in the garden of his home and stocked it with a large variety of songbirds. This love of wildlife is reflected in all of Baum's writings, and one has the feeling that when the Tin Woodman expresses horror at the thought of injuring a butterfly, he is expressing the sentiments of the author. Baum never cared for hunting and fishing. In early life his favorite outdoor sports seem to have been swimming, archery, and motorboating, though as he approached his sixties he turned more to golf and gardening. When the Baums moved to Hollywood in 1910, a large garden surrounded Ozcot, Baum's name for the house he built there. Baum won many cups in state flower competitions and even became known locally as "The Chrysanthemum King of Southern California."

At the time Ozcot was built, Hollywood was still a small suburban town. The infant movie industry then centered in New York. But as Jack Snow has observed, Baum was unable to escape from fairyland. The motion picture empire grew up around him. Mrs. Baum remained at Ozcot, on Cherokee Avenue near Sunset Boulevard, until her death in 1953 at the age of 91. The house has since been torn down to make room for a modern apartment building.

As one would have expected, Baum was early fascinated by the artistic potential of the cinema. In 1908, while still living in Chicago, he had invested heavily in the production of a series of short, hand-colored movies depicting stories from his books. He called them "Radio Plays." They were presented in Chicago and later in New York with Baum standing by the screen to narrate the tales. He lost so heavily in this venture that in 1911 he found it necessary to file a bankruptcy petition in California, listing his debts as $12,600 and his assets as two suits of clothes and a typewriter.[17]

Baum made another attempt to repeat the stage success of *The Wizard*. His musical *The Tik-Tok Man of Oz* opened in Los Angeles in 1913, then went on tour after profitable runs in San Francisco and Chicago. The comedy team of James Morton and Frank Moore took the roles of Tik-Tok and Shaggy Man, respectively. Queen Ann Soforth was played by Charlotte Greenwood. The play opened, like *The Wizard*, with the impressive sound and lighting effects of a violent storm; in this case the storm at sea that washes Betsy Bobbin of Oklahoma and Hank the mule to the shores of the Rose Kingdom. The book was written after the play, and dedicated to Louis F. Gottschalk, who provided the play's musical score.

Although this was Baum's last stage success, his enthusiasm for the theater never left him. In later years he wrote and acted in musicals produced by the Uplifters, a Los Angeles social club that he helped found. The names of the officers were invented by him: Grand Muscle (president), Elevator (vice president), Royal Hoister (secretary), Lord High Raiser (treasurer), and the Excelsiors (directors). Will Rogers, George Arliss, and many other Hollywood notables later became members. Let us hope that someday someone will uplift the manuscript of *The Uplift of Lucifer*, one of the plays Baum wrote for this club.

In 1914 Baum turned his attention once more to motion pictures, forming the Oz Film Manufacturing Company to produce screen versions of his tales. In a press interview he explained that because of their many color plates his books had to sell at a price that kept them from millions of youngsters. Through the movies he hoped to make his stories available to every American boy and girl for the cost of admission to the theater—five cents. Like so many smaller film companies that were trying to get started at the time, Baum's company was soon backed against the wall by the competition of larger studios. Only five films were completed: *The Patchwork Girl of Oz* (played by Pierre Coudere, a French acrobat), *His Majesty the Scarecrow of Oz* (later retitled *The New Wizard of Oz*), *The Magic Cloak*, *The Last Egyptian*, and *The Gray Nun of Belgium*.

The Wizard of Oz was filmed as a one-reeler by Selig Pictures in 1910. Another silent version was issued in 1925 by Chadwick Pictures, starring the comedian Larry Semon as the Scarecrow. Oliver Hardy took the role of the tin man. And of course everyone has seen MGM's lavish technicolor spectacle, first released in 1939, with Judy Garland in the role of a singing Dorothy. Ray Bolger played the capering straw man, Jack Haley the Tin Woodman, and Bert Lahr an outrageously funny Cowardly Lion. Other roles included Billie Burke, badly miscast as Glinda, Frank Morgan as the Wizard, and the Singer Midgets as the Munchkins. The picture featured some excellent tunes ("Over the Rainbow" and "We're Off to See the Wizard") and had several inspired touches, such as running the farm scenes in black and white to contrast them with the brilliant colors of Oz. But to my taste the picture was marred by sentimentality toward the close and the inexcusable final revelation that the whole thing was a dream.

Baum's generous heart, unlike the fine velvet heart of the Tin Woodman, was not replaceable. Angina attacks and a gall-bladder operation kept him in bed during the last year and a half of his life. *The Tin Woodman of Oz*, *The Magic of Oz*, and a rough draft of *Glinda of Oz* were written during this period. The last book is almost devoid of humor. I have often fancied that the sunken island on which Dorothy was trapped beneath a lake was an unconscious expression of Baum's own sinking emotions. The island was raised when Dorothy thought of the proper magic words. There were no magic words for Baum's failing heart, and on May 6, 1919, at his home in Hollywood, it finally gave way. He was buried in Forest Lawn Memorial Park, at Glendale, where a simple monument bearing his name and dates of birth and death marks his resting place.

Glinda of Oz, edited by one of Baum's sons, was published posthumously. The next book in the series, *The Royal Book of Oz*, carries Baum's name on the cover and a statement inside by Mrs. Baum that her husband had left some unfinished notes for another Oz book. These notes, she says, were turned over to Ruth Plumly Thompson, then a twenty-year-old Philadelphia journalist and children's author who had loved the Oz books as a child. All this seems to have been merely a device on the part of the publisher for easing the transition to a new author. The book was written entirely by Miss Thompson. She continued adding to the series eighteen more Oz books, writing them with a zest and humor that won her an ardent following.

John Rea Neill, who illustrated all of Baum's Oz books except the first one, also tried his hand at writing three Oz books. He was not a skillful writer, but as the Royal Painter of Oz his pictures are as indissolubly linked with the Oz books as Tenniel's drawings are linked with Alice. Whatever one may think of Neill's pictures as works of art, there is no denying that he caught the full flavor of Baum's text, and his illustrations have exactly the sort of color and realism that Oz books require. Denslow's drawings for *The Wizard* possess a quaint wooden charm, but I have yet to meet an Oz enthusiast who regrets that Denslow did not carry on with the series.

Much can be said in praise of Miss Thompson's books and also of the more recent Oz book, written by Rachel Cosgrove; but in the opinion of many Oz fans the mantle of Royal Historian best fitted the shoulders of the late Jack Snow. His two Oz books are remarkable in capturing the mood and style of Baum. I have already mentioned his *Who's Who in Oz*, which contains lively biographies of every Oz character who ever appeared in an Oz book, as well as biographical sketches of each Oz author and illustrator, and plot summaries of all the Oz books.[18]

Ray Bradbury has spoken many times of the influence of Oz on his career as a popular author of fantasy and science fiction. His story "The Exiles" pictures a future in which the psychologists have succeeded at last in destroying all books of fantasy. The narrative closes with the collapse of the Emerald City as the last Oz book goes up in flames.

But I do not think the Emerald City will collapse for a long, long time. A child's love of fantasy is too healthy a love. "Perhaps some of those big, grown-up people will poke fun at us," Baum wrote in his introduction to *A New Wonderland*, "—at you for reading these nonsense tales. . . . and at me for writing them. Never mind. Many of the big folk are still children—even as you and I. We can not measure a child by a standard of size or age. The big folk who are children will be our comrades; the others we need not consider at all, for they are self-exiled from our domain."

POSTSCRIPT (1995)

The first full-length biography of Baum, To Please a Child *(1961), was written by Russell MacFall with the help of Baum's son Frank. MacFall, then night editor of the* Chicago Tribune, *was sitting one evening with his fellow workers when he said he would like to write the life of some person of note who had not previously been the subject of a biography. Someone suggested the author of* The Wizard of Oz, *then much in the news because of the great popularity of MGM's motion picture starring Judy Garland as Dorothy. No one present could think of the book author's name! Michael Hearn is currently working on a more detailed, more definitive life of Baum, with help and authorization by the Baum estate.*

NOTES

1. From the *New York Mirror* (theatrical paper), June 24, 1882.

2. This story is told in a letter to me from Ralph Fletcher Seymour, a Chicago artist who knew Baum during his Chicago days. How much of the story is true? No one knows. In *Aunt Jane's Nieces on Vacation* (1912) Baum devotes chapter 13 to an account of just such a duel.

3. One of Baum's most moving inscriptions is to be found in a presentation copy of this book to his sister, Mary Louise Baum Brewster:

> My dear Mary: When I was young I longed to write a great novel that should win me fame. Now that I am getting old my first book is written to amuse children. For, aside from my evident inability to do anything "great," I have learned to regard fame as a will-o-the-wisp which, when caught, is not worth the possession; but to please a child is a sweet and lovely thing that warms one's heart and brings its own reward. I hope my book will succeed in that way—that the children will like it. You and I have inherited much the same temperament and literary taste and I know you will not despise these simple tales, but will understand me and accord me your full sympathy. Lovingly your brother Frank.

4. "We are revolting!" exclaims the leader of the Revolution to the Guardian of the Gates. To which he understandably replies, "You don't look it."

5. Seymour tells the story of this book's preparation in his privately printed autobiography, *Some Went This Way*, Chicago, 1945, p. 46.

6. A lengthy interview with Baum at his "Sign of the Goose" appeared in the *Grand Rapids Herald*, August 18, 1907. There is a picture of Baum sitting in his goose chair, as well as photographs of the interior of the cottage.

7. A lengthy letter to Jack Snow in 1943, replying to seventy-five questions about her husband that Mr. Snow had asked in a previous letter.

8. This was not Baum's first attempt to collaborate with Tietjens and Denslow on a musical comedy. In 1901, at Tietjens's urging, he wrote the book of a comic opera titled *The Octopus* or *The Title Trust*. In Tietjens's unpublished diary, now in possession of his daughter, he describes their unsuccessful attempts to find a producer. Baum was particularly fond of the song "I Am a Great Promoter," to be sung by Gripem Harde. There are references to other songs, but unfortunately no intimations of the plot. The diary also contains many details about the wrangling of the three men over the contract for their second effort, *The Wizard*, and speaks of "much friction" between Baum and the producer, Julian Mitchell. Nothing came of later comic opera projects—*Father Goose, Prince Silver Wings,* and *The Pagan Potentate*—on which Tietjens and Baum planned to work jointly.

9. From *In Other Lands than Ours*, a collection of Mrs. Baum's letters from abroad, privately printed by her husband in 1907.

10. Cf. the following paragraph of a letter dated June 7, 1943, from Baum's nephew, Henry B. Brewster, of Syracuse, N.Y., to Jack Snow: "Mr. Baum always liked to tell wild tales, with a perfectly straight face, and earnestly, as though he really believed them himself. . . . His mother was very religious . . . and felt she knew her Bible very well. Frank Baum seemed to take particular delight in teasing her and I recall, not once but many times, how he would pretend to quote from the Bible, with which he definitely was not familiar. For example, once she said, 'Frank, you are telling a story,' and he said, 'Well, Mother, as you know, in St. Paul's epistle to the Ephesians he said, "All men are liars." ' Whereupon his mother said, 'Why, Frank, you are wrong, I do not recall that,' and irrespective of the fact that she had been fooled so many times she would look up her Bible to see if she were wrong, and he right. Frank Baum was one of the most imaginative of men. There was nothing wrong, but he did love to 'Fairytale,' or as you might say, tell 'white lies.' "

11. From her letter to Jack Snow, op. cit.

12. Ibid.

13. Ibid.

14. "It is possible for beasts—or even people—to be destroyed, but the task is so difficult that it is seldom attempted. Because it is free from sickness and death is one reason why Oz is a fairyland, but it is doubtful whether those who come to Oz from the outside world . . . will live forever or cannot be injured. Even Ozma is not sure about this, and so the guests of Ozma from other lands are always carefully protected from any danger, so as to be on the safe side."—*The Magic of Oz*, p. 83.

15. The ultimate ideal of Marxian socialism, after the state has withered away, is of course an anarchist society. This explains an article in *New Masses*, October 4, 1938, titled "The Red Wizard of Oz." Stewart Robb, the author, had just discovered that Oz books had been banned from all New York City libraries and he satirically suggests that the reason may be a political one. Another letter of Robb's, in the *New York Post*, October 9, 1938, compares the late Frank ("I am the law") Hague, then mayor and political boss of Jersey City, to the Supreme Dictator of the Flatheads (*Glinda of Oz*). The Supreme Dictator keeps getting reelected because of a law that gives himself the authority to count the votes. Both letters appear in Robb's privately published book *Letters on Nostradamus*, New York, no date.

16. "The Wizard of Chittenango," by James Thurber, the *New Republic*, December 12, 1934.

17. *Chicago Tribune*, August 16, 1911.

18. With one exception, *The Laughing Dragon of Oz*, by Baum's son, Frank Joslyn. This was issued by Whitman Publishing Company in 1934, as one of their "Big Little Book Series," and sold in the dime stores for ten cents. His second book, *The Enchanted Princess of Oz*, was purchased by Whitman but never published. No characters from previous Oz books appear in either work.

Mention also should be made of two "Oz" books published by Denslow. He and Baum parted company over a disagreement as to how much the illustrations had contributed to the success of the first Oz book and its musical. Feeling that he was in part a creator of Oz, and legally in possession of a copyright on his illustrations, Denslow wrote and illustrated a picture book titled *Scarecrow and the Tin Man* (New York: G. W. Dillingham, 1904), telling how the two men escape from a New York theater in which they are appearing, and of the mishaps that befall them before the police send them back to the theater. Denslow also issued a 43-page booklet of color plates from the first Oz book. It was called *Pictures from the Wonderful Wizard of Oz* (Chicago: George W. Ogilvie, no date) and carried his own name on the title page but no mention of Baum. Accompanying the pictures is a story by Thomas H. Russell about the adventures of a "Little Girl" with the Scarecrow and the Tin Man. Neither of these books contains the word Oz.

TWENTY-EIGHT

GEORGES PEREC

Georges Perec, who died in 1982, has only recently been discovered by American critics. He was one of France's most admired authors. A devotee of linguistic play, Perec was an active member of a curious French group of scholars called the Oulipo, whose members amused themselves by juggling letters and words in incredible ways. For a survey of their results see chapters 6 and 7 of my Penrose Tiles to Trapdoor Ciphers.

An 802-page biography, Georges Perec: A Life in Words, *by David Bellos, was published here by Godine in 1994. Bellos also translated W, the book I here review. Perec's* La Disparition *(The Disappearance), a novel written without the letter e, has been been put into English by Gilbert Adair. His translation also omits e. When Paul Gray reviewed it for* Time *(February 6, 1995), he, too, managed e's disappearance.*

My review of W: Or the Memory of Early Childhood *(Godine, 1988) appeared in* Dimensions *(vol. 4, no. 3, 1989).*

When Georges Perec died of cancer in 1982, at the age of 46, he was famous in France for being a member of a remarkable group of writers and mathematicians known as the Oulipo. The name stands for Ouvroir de Littérature Potentielle (Workshop of Potential Literature). Members are dedicated to every variety of wild literary experimentation, with mathematics and linguistic play furnishing major ingredients. Perec, for example, wrote an entire novel, *La Disparition*, without once using the letter *e*. It was so artfully done that some critics did not even realize it was a lipogram (a type of wordplay in which a sentence or a longer work omits one letter or more of the alphabet).

Perec's masterpiece, *La Vie: Mode d'Emploi* (*Life: A User's Manual*) won the Prix Medicis shortly before his death. A marvelous translation by David Bellos, professor of French studies at England's University of Manchester, introduced Perec to British and American readers. Perec's reputation here should rise still higher with Bellos's skillful translation of W. It is a novel only Perec could have written—a double vision that interweaves sad memories of his childhood in Nazi-occupied France with a savage indictment, by way of fantasy, of totalitarian political insanity.

W is pronounced "double-u" in English, but U was originally V, a fact recognized by the French pronunciation of W, "double-vé." The capital letter W is, of course, a joining of two Vs. "Double-vé" is a pun on double-vie, or double-life, and Perec's novel elaborates on this conceit. Every alternate chapter tells of his search for a dimly-remembered childhood. The other chapters, printed in italics, delineate a childhood fantasy about life on W, an imaginary island among thousands in the archipelago of Tierra del Fuego, at the southern tip of South America.

The fantasy starts as an adventure. Its narrator has deserted the army of an unnamed country to live in Germany under the false name of Gaspard Winkler, the name on a passport he has illegally acquired. The real Winkler is a child who may have perished when a ship on which he was traveling with his mother sank in Tierra del Fuego. The narrator is hired to go there to find out if the child has survived on one of the islands. We are not told if he succeeds. We are given only an account of an island called W.

Founded by a lighthouse keeper, colonized by Aryans from Holland, Germany, and Scandinavia, W is an island where "Sport is King." Four villages, situated roughly at the corners of a square, are the locales where Athletes are trained for three sporting events: the Atlantiads held once a month; the Spartakiads held every three months; and the annual Olympiads. Between each pair of adjacent towns is a stadium, with a fifth and larger stadium at the island's center.

The athletes and all men directly involved with the sports—managers, trainers, doctors, dieticians, and so on—live in the villages. Men indirectly involved with the contests—judges, referees, track sweepers, torchbearers, etc.—live in or near the stadiums. Those uninvolved with the sporting events—old men, women, and children—are confined to the Fortress, south of the villages. Dominating the Fortress is a stone tower housing the government officials.

Early chapters about W convey the impression of a whimsical place; these scenes are perhaps intended as a satire on the subculture of those who dedicate their lives to promoting and participating in major sports. Then slowly, chapter by chapter, the allegory grows dark and menacing. We realize it is not the sporting world that W resembles but totalitarian nations where the "sports" are war and torture and the arbitrary executions of millions for the glory and amusement of the populace.

I believe that this slow disclosure of horrors was Perec's way of reminding us of how evil regimes are often first perceived as harmless by outsiders. Wasn't Hitler a funny little man who looked like Charlie Chaplin? Robert

Hutchins and Charles Lindbergh did their best to persuade their fellow countrymen that going to war against Nazi Germany would be against America's best interests. Gilbert Chesterton was so impressed by Mussolini that he praised Italian fascism in his most gullible book, *The Resurrection of Rome*. We all know how many writers and thinkers around the world refused to believe in the iniquities of Stalin's purges and labor camps, and later, in the terrors of Mao's Cultural Revolution.

Perec's descriptions of life on W, its insane rules, the arbitrary decisions of judges, the punishments inflicted on Athletes who lose, are as detailed and grimly amusing as the irrational events in Kafka's *Trial* and *Castle*. An Athlete who is last in a race is forced to run an extra lap with his shoes on backward. Losers in major events are made to strip naked and jog past judges who beat them with sticks. They are then paraded with nail-studded stocks around their necks. If a spectator singles out an Athlete with a thumbs-down gesture, the man is stoned to death, and his corpse hung on butcher hooks at a stadium's main gate; later the body is tossed to the dogs. Winners receive trophies at grandiose banquets where the national anthem is played while the revelers eat and drink themselves into a stupor.

All sporting events are permeated with unpredictable injustice. Judges show their favoritism by imposing capricious handicaps and making deliberate umpiring errors. During a race a referee will sometimes shout, "Stop!" Runners must freeze in their last posture. The one who holds it longest is declared the winner.

The women of W are confined to quarters surrounded by an electric fence. An Athlete who tries to break into their dormitories is punished with a severity inversely proportional to how far he gets. If he reaches the fence he may be electrocuted on the spot. If he penetrates the fence his punishment is a few weeks in solitary. If he goes still farther, he is given a caning. No Athlete has yet reached the dormitories. Should one do so, he would be designated Honorary Casanova and showered with honors.

Infanticide keeps the number of women at about 500; only one girl out of five is not killed after birth. A male child is allowed to survive, unless he has a deformity rendering him unfit for competition. If a (male) individual's deformity is minor, he is allowed to become a clown, and provide comic relief at the games.

The women are kept busy cooking, keeping house, and sewing track suits, flags, and other sports-related items. They are allowed to leave their quarters only once a month, during the Atlantiads, when ceremonial mating takes place. Stripped naked, they are given a head start on the cinder track and then pursued by naked Athletes. The men are naked to prevent them from carrying concealed knives, but spikes on their shoes serve as weapons in the violent fights that break out before the chase. About a third of the Athletes are knocked unconscious, mainly by boxers and shot-putters who cannot run fast. During the chase, tripping is permitted, as well as kicks to the groin and the gouging out of eyeballs. The spectators, like those at ancient gladiatorial contests, cheer wildly, the sound amplified by loudspeakers. The cheering reaches a crescendo each time a woman is caught and instantly raped.

Boys undergo three years of training as novices. Their first six months of Quarantine parody the first six weeks of basic training endured by enlisted men in any army or navy. The novices are gagged, and kept in handcuffs and leg irons. Those who do not commit suicide or go mad are sustained by the illusory hope that someday the sky will be bluer, the soup better, and the law less harsh. Some never stop howling, but most of the novices lapse into silence.

> The life of an Athlete on W is but a single, endless, furious striving, a pointless, debilitating pursuit of that unreal instant when triumph can bring rest. . . . The Masters are unreachable, and the slaves tear at each other. But an Athlete on W does not even know that. . . . He waits for luck to smile on him. One day the Gods will be for him. . . .
>
> If you just look and see these Athletes of skin and bone, ashen-faced, their backs permanently bent, their skulls bald and shiny, their eyes full of panic, and their sores suppurating, if you see all these indelible marks of humiliation without end, of boundless terror, all of it evidence, administered every hour, every day, every instant, of conscious, organized, structured oppression; if you just look and see the workings of this huge machine, each cog of which contributes with implacable efficiency to the systematic annihilation of men, then it should come as no great surprise that the performances put up are utterly mediocre: the 100 metres is run in 23.4", the 200 metres in 51"; the best high jumper has never exceeded 1.30 metres.

(One is reminded by this passage that after the Nazis lost the war it was discovered that their "Oak Ridge" laboratory, where work was underway on the making of an atom bomb, was the size of a tiny cottage. Because of the Hitler regime's methodical brutality and persecution, all of Germany's great physicists [except for Werner Heisenberg] had fled the Fatherland. So the Third Reich's efforts to create a nuclear weapon were as futile as the attempts by the Athletes on W to have the Gods favor them.)

And what about the tower where the political leaders and bureaucrats live? If at some later time, after W is forgotten, you get into the tower, what will you find? "Dim, long, empty rooms," and a smell of evil until you reach the subterranean levels where you come upon "piles of gold, teeth, rings, spectacles, dusty card indexes, and stocks of poor quality soap." We know now what W is parodying. It is not sports, but nations ruled by Master Races—nations where war is an exciting game, where holocausts are the sport of madmen.

The book's other narrative tells how Perec, who barely remembers his early years, tries to reconstruct them from scraps of paper and long-lost photographs. His memory is hazy. The text swarms with such phrases as "I think," "it is possible," "I have forgotten," "I don't remember, "perhaps." He is seldom sure of his reconstructions. (A suggestive epigraph from the Oulipo novelist Raymond Queneau speaks of "the mindless mist where shadows swirl, how could I pierce it?")

Perec's parents were Polish Jews who, for reasons he never learned, settled in Paris some years after the end of the First World War. His father joined the French army after World War II began, and was shot the day after the armistice was declared between Germany and France. His young widowed mother worked in a factory until 1943, when she and her sister were sent to Auschwitz. "She died without understanding." Had she been French, said an official decree, she would have been entitled to the citation, "Died for France." His two grandfathers were also deported, and died in the death camps. Perec was never able to learn how his mother died, but he found his father's grave, the name and regiment number stenciled on a wooden cross. There is a touching paragraph in which Perec struggles to recall the emotions he felt. He is aware of how neutral and blank his writing about his parents seems:

> I am not writing in order to say that I shall say nothing, I am not writing to say that I have nothing to say. I write: I write because we have lived together, because I was one amongst them, a shadow amongst their shadows, a body close to their bodies. I write because they left in me their indelible mark, whose trace is writing. Their memory is dead in writing; writing is the memory of their death and the assertion of my life.

Orphaned in 1943 at the age of six, Perec was adopted by his father's sister. At age 13 he made up the story of W, but later forgot it. After becoming a noted writer, his memory was reawakened by some old drawings he had made and he was able to reinvent the fantasy. First published serially in a magazine, this fantasy later became half of the novel W, where it crisscrosses his memories of childhood.

Like all of Perec's fiction, W contains a great deal of untranslatable wordplay. David Bellos has done his best to find appropriate English replacements, rather than keep the French and add explanatory notes. His substitutions include references to "orange" as a word without a rhyme, to the mnemonic "Every Good Boy Deserves Fun" (used for recalling lines of musical notation), to "Spring forward, fall back" (a catchphrase for remembering how to change clocks). The counting jingles "Eeeny, meeny, miney, mo" and "One potato, two potato" are cited, as is the joke of asking someone to say "I one a rat, I two a rat, I three a rat" until he gets to "I eight a rat." I was puzzled by the use of "Posh" to indicate the difference between port and starboard, until Bellos explained it to me in a letter. When one sails from England to India, port is on the side of land (PO, Port Out). Starboard is where land is on the way back (SH, Starboard Home).

A page of pictorial play shows how to make an X by putting two Vs together; extend the arms and a Nazi swastika is formed. Two halves of the swastika can be rearranged to create the SS symbol. Put two Xs side by side, and two little triangles can be added (at top and bottom) to make the Star of David. It is no coincidence that in W a novice begins training with a triangle pointing down on the back of his gray tracksuit. Later, the triangle points up, and finally becomes a W when the novice becomes an Athlete. Perec recalls that in *The Great Dictator* Chaplin replaced the swastika with a pair of overlapping Xs.

The autobiographical half of W is as moving and memorable as the story of the island is terrifying. To me the most poignant episode, its power to bring tears heightened by Perec's simple syntax and matter-of-fact tone, is his memory of being taken by an aunt to see an exhibition about Nazi concentration camps. "I remember the photographs of the walls of the gas chambers showing scratchmarks made by the victims' fingernails, and a set of chessmen made from bits of bread."

TWENTY-NINE

PUZZLES IN *ULYSSES*

Serious students of James Joyce will not find much in the following essay that is unfamiliar, but I thought it worthwhile to pull together, for the first time, all the passages in Ulysses that could reasonably be called "puzzles." The article appeared in Semiotica, vol. 57 (1985).

All page numbers refer to the Modern Library edition of 1961. I checked the three-volume Garland edition, edited by Hans Walter Gabler, which corrects some five thousand typographical errors in earlier publications of Ulysses. None of these corrections influences the material considered here.

> *There are no puzzles in* Ulysses.
> —VLADIMIR NABOKOV, *Strong Opinions*

> *Martin . . . an old gardener from the glens of* Antrim.
> —*Finnegans Wake*, 266, note 2

James Joyce was fond of traditional puzzles of all types, both mathematical and linguistic. A footnote on page 284 of *Finnegans Wake* (Viking Compass edition), in a long section of mathematical puns, mentions the last name of Henry Ernest Dudeney, England's most famous creator of mathematical puzzles. In 1905 Joyce was so eager to win a prize of 250 pounds offered by a London magazine for the first correct set of solutions to a puzzle contest that he planned to send his brother Stanislaus a registered, sealed letter of answers in case he later had to prove the date of his entry. Joyce is probably referring to this contest on page 283 of *Ulysses*. Unfortunately his labors went for nothing because his entry arrived too late to qualify.

Joyce's interest in puzzles was almost invisible in *Dubliners*, his book of short stories. It began to surface in his first novel, *A Portrait of the Artist as a Young Man,* and exploded into monstrous proportions in the wordplay and letter play of *Finnegans Wake.* I propose to examine the puzzles that Joyce injected into *Ulysses,* including some enigmas not yet fully solved, and then to consider briefly whether these puzzles add to or detract from the greatness of this greatest of modern comic novels.

Let us begin with letter play. The first letter of the novel *Ulysses* is S. In the Random House Modern Library edition (1961) the S fills all of page 2. Similarly, the letters M and P (pp. 54 and 612, respectively) open the book's second and third parts. Did Joyce intend them to signify something?

As far as I know, Joyce never commented on SMP. It has been observed, however, that in Aristotelian logic, which Joyce studied under Jesuit teachers, S, M, and P are letters that stand for the three terms of a syllogism: subject, middle term, and predicate. Perhaps Joyce had this in mind. It has also been noticed that the first two words of the book are *Stately, plump.* Their initials provide S and P. The M is given by Mulligan, to whom both adjectives refer.

Note also that the first section of *Ulysses* opens with S and ends with P. The third section opens with P and ends with S. The middle section begins with M, and ends with T. Molly Bloom's maiden name is Marion Tweedy.

Could S stand for Stephen, M for Molly, and P for Poldy, Leopold Bloom's nickname? These guesses are all in that gray area where no one can be sure of Joyce's intentions, conscious or unconscious, or whether the letter play is coincidental. To make things even grayer, Joyce may have recognized such accidental correlations later and let them stand because he found them amusing.

Poldy is an obviously intended acrostic for the five-line poem (p. 678) that Bloom sent to Molly, but there are other poems in the book that may or may not conceal planned acrostics. Consider the way Joyce breaks the lines of the song (p. 75) Molly plans to sing on her concert tour with her lover Blazes Boylan:

> *Love's*
> *Old*
> *Sweet*
> *Song*
> *Comes lo-ve's old . . .*

Did Joyce intend the initial letters to spell *loss,* followed by *comes* to suggest that a loss of love has come to Molly and her husband? The first three lines of a quatrain on page 640 spell *Tao.* This is probably accidental, but who can be sure?

Ulysses swarms with initial-letter abbreviations of which I will cite only a few. KMA and KMRIA (pp. 146, 147, respectively), presented as newspaper headlines, stand for "Kiss my ass" and "Kiss my royal Irish ass." *Roygbiv* (pp.

376, 486) are the first letters of the colors of the rainbow. Joyce missed an opportunity to divide them into the name *Roy G. Biv*, but perhaps he deliberately avoided this old mnemonic. (The seven colors are a recurring motif in *Finnegans Wake*.) Many standard Irish abbreviations in the novel are left unexplained. *FOTEI*, for example, stands for Friends of the Emerald Isle, *DMP* for Dublin Metropolitan Police, *DBC* for Dublin Baking Company, and so on. On page 345 there are nineteen such abbreviations in three lines.

A trivial question involving initials was once a topic for speculation by Joyce buffs. On page 237 the names of four men who ride past the College Library on bicycles are mentioned; one is J. A. Jackson. Could the initials J.A.J. be a suggestion that James Augustine Joyce was riding by? Someone checked the Dublin newspapers and discovered that on what is now called Bloomsday (June 16, 1904, the date of the novel) a bicycle race through Dublin actually took place. It was won by J. A. Jackson.

Is it coincidental that *Bella* and *Circe* each have five letters, with their vowels at the same places? We know that Joyce intended *Bella*, the whorehouse madam, to reflect Homer's *Circe*, but whether the correspondence of consonants and vowels was intended remains speculative, though Joyce certainly would have noticed it. There is, of course, no doubt that Joyce intended *Athos*, the name of the dog owned by Bloom's father, to resemble *Argos*, the name of Ulysses' dog in Homer's *Odyssey*.

I know of no high-quality anagrams in *Ulysses*. Bloom's crude attempts to anagram his name (p. 678)—two are flawed by missing a letter—are amusing but scarcely noteworthy. Even the anagrams in *Finnegans Wake* are unremarkable. On page 456, for instance, Joyce scrambles the letters of *steak, peas, onions, bacon, rices, and duckling*, and by substituting *X*'s for consonants and *O*'s for vowels, codes *cabbage* and *boiled Protestants*. This meets his intention of suggesting how chewing rearranges parts of food, but as anagrams they display no unusual cleverness.

Hundreds of words in *Ulysses*, like the tens of thousands in *Finnegans Wake*, are formed by pushing words together in the manner of Lewis Carroll's "portmanteau" words, but most of them are too obvious in meaning to be puzzling. Shakespeare's word *honorificabilitudinitatibus* (from act 5 of *Love's Labour's Lost*), in which consonants and vowels alternate throughout, appears in *Ulysses* on page 210. It is not, however, as long as the 105-letter word (p. 307) which foreshadows the ten great thunderclaps in *Finnegans Wake*.

One of the most outrageous instances of wordplay in *Ulysses* is AEIOU, the five vowels in alphabetical order (p. 190). Stephen Dedalus had borrowed a pound from A.E., the pen name of the renowned Irish poet and theosophist George William Russell, which Stephen was supposed to use for food, but instead gave to a prostitute. AEIOU is Stephen's way of remembering this debt.

U.P. up is surely the book's most controversial letter play. (See pp. 158,

160, 280, 299, 320, 381, 446, 474, 486, and 744.) This cryptic message written on an anonymous postcard to the eccentric Mr. Breen arouses him to such fury that he goes to great efforts to find out who sent the card so he can sue for ten thousand pounds. Adams (1962), discloses that *The Freeman's Journal* (November 5, 1903) actually reported a case of one Dublin man suing another for sending a libelous postcard—an incident of which Joyce was probably aware. Molly in her soliloquy (p. 744) recalls her husband "going about in his slippers to look for a £10000 for a postcard up up." Are we to gather from this that Bloom himself sent the card? In any case, what does *U.P. up* mean?

The Oxford English Dictionary (entry U, 2:4) says that when the two letters of *up* are pronounced separately the slang meaning is "over, finished, beyond remedy." A passage is quoted from *Oliver Twist* (chap. 24) where an apothecary's apprentice says "Oh, it's all U.P. there," meaning that he thinks a dying woman will not last more than two hours. Another quotation, "It's all U.P. with him" is explained as "all up either with his health, or circumstances." Adams calls attention to a line from Arnold Bennett's novel *The Old Wives' Tale* in which a doctor emerges from the room of a dying patient and actually says "U.P. up." Thus the message would be taken by Breen to mean "you'll soon be dead." This interpretation is supported by a mention (p. 474) of *U.P.* as the label of a burial plot. In the French translation of *Ulysses*, authorized by Joyce, the postcard reads *fou tu* (screw you). Change one letter to make *feu tu* and it means "you're dead."

So much for the postcard's primary meaning. Joyce could not, of course, have missed the urinary overtones of *P*, but it is not clear exactly what he had in mind, if anything. Is it to suggest that Breen is impotent—that he can produce only urine, not semen? Adams speculates about several possibilities along such lines, but I think the critics have missed something here. It is not generally known—though, in view of Joyce's (and Bloom's) strong interest in curious aspects of sexual organs, he must have known—that all men bifurcate into two classes. Most men pee down, making it necessary to lift their penis to hit a urinal. A small class pee up, requiring a push down on the penis to get proper aim. As Molly says (p. 743), her husband "knows a lot of mixed up things especially about the body." Was the anonymous writer, perhaps Bloom himself, poking fun at Breen's membership in the small class of up pee-ers, perhaps with the insulting implication that this is the only way in which Breen's penis is ever up? As Mrs. Breen herself put it (p. 158), the card was sent by "Someone taking a rise out of him."

Joyce was fascinated by the fact that *God*, spelled backward, is dog. This reversal is suggested several times in *Ulysses* and is made explicit in the Black Mass of the Circe chapter. Other reversals occur during the mass, including a backward spelling of *Alleluia, for the Lord God Omnipotent Reigneth* (p. 599). Two old palindromes are quoted (p. 135): Adam's remark to Eve, *Madam, I'm Adam,* and Napoleon's supposed statement, *Able was I ere I saw*

Elba. Reversals of many varieties are almost as common in *Ulysses* as in Carroll's *Through the Looking-Glass*. Mirror reflections are often mentioned, starting with Buck Mulligan's cracked shaving mirror which Stephen sees as a symbol of modern Irish literature. Bloom falls asleep in a curled up position, his "big square feet" so close to Molly's face that she fears he might kick out her teeth (p. 771). In one of the hallucinatory episodes of nighttown, Bloom and Bella exchange sexes. In the role of Bello, the whorehouse madam abuses Bloom unmercifully. Bloom himself has a curious left-right anomaly. We are told (p. 476) that his testicles, instead of hanging in the left trouser like most men's, hang in the right. Perhaps the symmetry in Joyce's own name is worth mentioning: J.A.J. is palindromic, and *James* and *Joyce* each have five letters.

Joyce's fondness for reversals is also indicated by the cipher Bloom uses when he secretly records the name and address of the woman with whom he is having a clandestine correspondence. It is a reverse alphabet cipher: A = Z, B = Y, C = X, and so on. The cipher is explained on page 721. N. IGS./ WI.UU. OX/W. OKS. MH/Y. IM decodes as "Martha Clifford, Dolphin's Barn." Vowels are left out, and the words are taken alternately forward and backward. The periods indicate vowels and slashes divide the four words.

As Kahn (1973, p. 767) points out, the last word, *Barn*, should have been reversed. This could have been Joyce's mistake, but more likely Joyce intended the error to suggest Bloom's carelessness. (The book contains many instances of mistakes by Bloom.) In a similar way Joyce lets us know that Martha, although she responded to Bloom's advertisement for a typist, is a careless typist because in a letter to Bloom (p. 77) she types world when she meant word.

Joyce was (as Kahn informs us) an intimate friend of J. F. Byrne, a man who spent a good part of his life trying to interest governments in a cipher he had invented and which he believed to be unbreakable. The character of Granly in *A Portrait of the Artist* is based on Bryne, and in *Ulysses*, Bloom's address (7 Eccles Street) was Bryne's address in Dublin. Two chapters in Byrne's *Silent Years: An Autobiography with Memories of James Joyce*, deal with his cipher machine. The book contains a message written with this machine and an offer of $5,000 to the first person who decodes it. According to Kahn, the cipher remains unbroken to this day.

I mention all this to suggest how familiar Joyce must have been, through his friendship with Byrne, with cipher systems. Did Joyce incorporate any secret cipher messages (other than Bloom's) in *Ulysses* or (more likely) in *Finnegans Wake*? If so, they have not yet been detected.

Turning from letters to words, *Ulysses* swarms with puns, of which I single out just a few: *Lawn Tennyson* (p. 50), *Lily of the alley* (p. 512), and *met him pike hoses* (a play on *metempsychosis* that recurs throughout the novel). Molly was greatly amused (pp. 64 and 765) by the name of Paul de Cock, an actual French writer of bawdy novels. *Cuckoo*, taken as a pun on *cuckold* (pp. 212

and 382), is borrowed from Shakespeare's *Love's Labour's Lost.* Molly's clever pun of *base barreltone* for *base baritone* is recalled by Bloom on page 154 and by Molly on page 759. These and other puns in *Ulysses* are witty but not particularly amusing. *Alfred Lord Tennis Shoes,* for example, is somehow funnier than *Lawn Tennyson.*

Two of the novel's periodic motifs play on the word *throwaway.* On page 151 a YMCA man hands Bloom a throwaway leaflet advertising a lecture by Alexander Dowie, the Scottish evangelist who later founded Zion City, Illinois, a shabby little town north of Chicago where everyone once believed (perhaps some still do) that the earth is flat. Bloom crumples up the leaflet, tosses it into the Liffey, and at intervals we learn of the throwaway's progress as it floats through Dublin.

On page 85 Bantam Lyons asks to see Bloom's newspaper to check the racing page. Bloom tells him to keep the paper because he was going to "throw it away." Bloom is unaware that *Throwaway* is the name of a dark horse (the odds are twenty to one) in the Gold Cup Race that afternoon at Ascot. Thinking he has heard an inside tip, Lyons rushes off to bet on Throwaway. Meanwhile, Blazes Boylan, with whom Molly sleeps that afternoon, has put a bet on a horse named *Sceptre.* He is furious when he learns that Throwaway won the race. As Joyce experts have long recognized, Sceptre is a phallic symbol for the stud Blazes, whereas Bloom is Molly's throwaway husband. However, just as Throwaway wins the race, so Bloom (as we infer from Molly's soliloquy) will probably outlast Blazes in her affections and be the final winner.

"What opera resembles a railroad?" (p. 132). The punning answer is Rose of Castille—rows of cast steel (pp. 134 and 491 and numerous other pages). There are less interesting riddles in the novel, such as "Where was Moses when the candle went out?" (p. 729), to which the answer (not supplied) is, in the dark. Stephen's riddle about the fox (pages 26, 46, 558, 572) is of no interest to wordplayers. It is a "shaggy dog" riddle—one that cannot be answered unless you know the answer. On the same page Joyce gives the first two lines of an old riddle rhyme:

> *Riddle me, riddle me, randy ro.*
> *My father gave me seeds to sow.*

Joyce does not supply the next two lines (The seed was black and ground was white./Riddle me that and I'll give you a pipe) or its traditional answer: the speaker is writing a letter.

In *A Portrait of the Artist,* Athy asks Stephen: "Why is the county of Kildare like the leg of a fellow's breeches?" Answer: because there's a thigh in it. After explaining that Athy [a thigh] is a town in Kildare, Athy says there is another way to ask the riddle, but he refuses to tell Stephen what it is. Nor does Joyce tell the reader. This practice of keeping his readers perplexed became an obsession with Joyce, reaching a culmination in *Finnegans Wake*. But even in *Ulysses* there are hundreds of nagging little questions that experts still debate because Joyce has carefully concealed information. We are straying now from wordplay, but a typical example is the problem of whether Bloom's list of twenty-five lovers of Molly (p. 731) gives actual lovers or only men Bloom imagines were lovers. Theories range from the view that Molly actually slept only with Boylan, the last name on the list, to the view that she slept with all of them, including a bootblack at the General Post Office. Joyce obviously wanted his readers to wonder.

Ulysses contains many religious puns, such as those in a blasphemous parody of the Apostle's Creed (p. 329) that begins: "They believe in rod, the scourger almighty." The most amusing religious pun is Bloom's "Come forth, Lazarus! And he came fifth and lost the job" (p. 105). Joyce is here applying an old racing joke about Moses to a passage from the New Testament: "God commanded Moses to come forth, but he slipped on a banana peel and came in fifth."

The quatrain on page 497 seems innocent enough:

> *If you see kay*
> *Tell him he may*
> *See you in tea*
> *Tell him from me.*

It is the least innocent bit of doggerel in the book. As Joyce experts have pointed out, the first line provides a four-letter obscenity, the third line provides another. Did Joyce also intend the initial letters of the four lines, after moving the last line to the front, to spell *tits?*

Some of the puzzles in *Ulysses* are logical and mathematical. What is the largest number that can be represented by three digits, using no other mathematical symbols? The answer is:

$$9^{9^9}$$

Joyce introduces this old brainteaser on page 699. We are told that when Bloom was trying to square the circle he made a rough calculation of the number's size. He was quite right in concluding that if printed out the number would require some "33 closely printed volumes of 1000 pages each."

Puzzle books are filled with brainteasers about age, such as Sam Loyd's (he was the American counterpart of Dudeney) famous puzzle known as "How old is Ann?" Joyce parodies questions by this sort by speculating at length on the relative ages of Bloom and Stephen (p. 679) if one assumes that, as the years go by, they keep the same ratio their ages had in 1883. As Adams makes clear in *Surface and Symbol,* Joyce's calculations are accurate only for the first dozen lines of this paragraph. In the next line, 714 should be 762, and the numbers 83,300 and 81,396 are also wrong. Is Joyce again letting us know how often Bloom makes mistakes, or (as Adams argues) is it more plausible to assume these errors actually were made by Joyce, who intended the calculations to be correct?

An ancient conundrum concerns a man who points to a picture and says: "Brothers and sisters I have none, yet this man's father is my father's son." Whose picture is it? It is his son's. Joyce modifies this by having Bloom see his "composite asymmetrical image" in a mirror: "Brothers and sisters had he none. Yet that man's father was his grandfather's son" (p. 708). The statement is accurate because Bloom sees himself in the glass. The episode links with Stephen's proof "by algebra" (p. 18) that Shakespeare's grandfather is Hamlet's grandson.

On page 631 a sailor named Murphy displays the number 16 tattooed on his chest but refuses to say what it means. Joyce enthusiasts, worrying over this, have found many references to 16 in the novel. The tattoo is mentioned in the sixteenth chapter of part 3. The date is June 16. There is an age difference of sixteen years between Bloom and Stephen (p. 679). The Blooms have been married for sixteen years (p. 736). Molly was sixteen when she made her first public appearance as a singer (p. 653). In Europe 16, like 69 in the United States, is a symbol of oral sex.

It is easy to carry this kind of speculation to absurd extremes. The initials of Nora Barnacle (Joyce's wife) are the fourteenth and second letters of the alphabet, and $14 + 2 = 16$. Note also that 16 can be written:

$$2^{2^2}$$

Because Joyce was as secretive as Murphy about the meaning of the tattoo, who can say what, if anything, Joyce intended it to mean?

We do know that all his life Joyce was intrigued by number symbolism and superstitions. He was careful never to make trips or important decisions on the thirteenth day of a month, and he was acutely aware of the fact that his mother died on August 13. When Joyce died on January 13 his wife and friends did not miss the coincidence. Had Joyce been alive in 1955, when his brother Stanislaus died on Bloomsday (June 16), he would not have been surprised.

Joyce often spoke of Dante's obsession with 3, the number of the Trinity. *The Divine Comedy* is in three parts, thirty-three cantos to each, and is written in terza rima. It is probably no accident that *Ulysses* has three parts, with three chapters to the first and final parts, and $3 \times 4 = 12$ chapters in the middle part. Molly's age on Bloomsday is thirty-three (p. 751). In conversation with Adolph Hoffmeister, Joyce once discussed the significance of 12—the twelve apostles, twelve tables of Moses, twelve months, and so on. "Why," Joyce asked, "was the armistice of the Great War trumpeted forth on the eleventh minute of the eleventh hour of the eleventh day of the eleventh month?"

We conclude with some unclassified puzzles. After the famous episode in which Bloom, hands in pockets, masturbates while Gerty allows him glimpses of her underdrawers, Bloom picks up a stick and, like Jesus, writes in the sand (p. 381). He writes "I AM A" but never completes it. How did he intend to finish? Man, Jew, fool, cuckold, masturbator? Or is it supposed to mean "I am alpha" the beginning of all things? There is no consensus among scholars.

On page 761 of the flawed Modern Library edition of *Ulysses*, before it was corrected in 1961, an unintended period slipped into Molly's unpunctuated soliloquy. Molly's actual period starts on page 769, forcing her out of bed and onto a cracked chamber pot. And when was Molly's birthday? We learn on page 736 that it was September 8, the traditional date for celebrating the birth of the Virgin Mary. There are more 8's connected with Molly. Her marriage, at eighteen, was on October 8, 1888 (p. 736), and her monologue, perhaps not by accident, consists of eight sentences. It has also not escaped Joyceans that when 8 is rotated 90 degrees it becomes the symbol for infinity and eternity.

The greatest of all unresolved puzzles in Ulysses is the identity of a "lankylooking galoot" in a brown mackintosh who first turns up at the funeral Bloom attends in the Hades chapter. No one there knows who he is, and throughout the novel Bloom wonders about him. We are told that he was the thirteenth mourner—"death's number" Bloom says to himself—and it may be intentional that there are thirteen references to him in the book (109–110, 112, 254, 290, 333, 376, 427, 485, 502, 511, 525, 647–648, and 729). We learn that he "loves a lady who is dead." A newspaper account of the funeral calls him McIntosh, but that is a mistake. The reporter heard Bloom use the word mackintosh and wrongly took it to be the man's name.

We glimpse the mystery man on the street, "eating dry bread" (p. 254) and later encounter him in a bar, near the red-light area, where he is drinking Bovril soup (p. 427). (Bovril is the trade name of an instant beef soup introduced in England in 1889. It was widely advertised with the slogan, appropriate to its context here, "Bovril prevents that sinking feeling.") The man's seedy clothes are described, and we learn that he was once a prosperous citizen "all tattered and torn that married a maiden all forlorn. Slung her hook, she did. Here see lost love." The man "thought he had a deposit of lead in his penis. Trumpery insanity. Bartle the Bread we calls him. . . . Walking Mackintosh of lonely canyon." I have no idea what Bartle means.

In the whorehouse dream sequence the man in the brown raincoat pops onto the stage through a trapdoor, points a finger at Bloom, and says "Don't you believe a word he says. That man is Leopold M'Intosh, the notorious fireraiser. His real name is Higgins" (p. 485). Ellen Higgins was Bloom's mother, and one of the prostitutes is Zoe Higgins. What Joyce is trying to say here is far from clear.

"Who was M'Intosh?" Joyce asks explicitly (p. 729). We are told in Gorman's (1948) biography of Joyce that Joyce was fond of asking friends this question, but he always refused to answer. There have been many theories. Among the implausible:

1. Theoclymenus, a Greek soothsayer whose presence in Homer's *Odyssey* (Books 15 and 20) is somewhat mysterious;
2. Wetherup, an obscure acquaintance of Joyce who is mentioned in *Ulysses* (pp. 126 and 660);
3. James Duffy, a character in "A Painful Case" (*Dubliners*) based in part on Joyce's brother Stanislaus;
4. The ghost of Charles Parnell, the Irish nationalist leader;
5. The Wandering Jew;
6. Jesus;
7. Nobody (Joyce was playing a joke on his readers).

Hodgart (1978) takes the mystery man to be Death. Vladimir Nabokov (1980) argues that the man in the brown raincoat is none other than Joyce himself, a "selfinvolved enigma" (p. 729) that Bloom could not comprehend. Joyce certainly was a "lankylooking galoot." The man's lost love could be the Virgin Mary, symbol of the Roman Catholic Church which had its hooks into Joyce before he abandoned her. Perhaps the bread and soup are intended to contrast with the bread and wine of the Eucharist. The conjecture may be further supported by the quotation ("all tattered and torn . . .") from the Mother Goose rhyme "The House That Jack Built." Joyce grew up in a household that Jack (his father John) built.

After the word *Bovril* (p. 427) Joyce adds "by James". Bovril was introduced in England by someone named J. Lawson Johnston (according to the Oxford English Dictionary Supplement), but whether the J stands for James, I have been unable to determine. Is it possible Joyce wants us to take this to mean that the soup is on the table next to James Joyce? In any case, Nabokov is convinced that Joyce, as Stephen insists Shakespeare often did in his plays, "set his face in a dark corner of his canvas" (p. 209). Perhaps when Bloom hears the loud crack in a table and turns out the light (p. 729) he suddenly comprehends the awful truth—he is no more than a figment in the mind of a writer who has imagined him.

We know Joyce is not the man who races through Dublin on a bicycle, and he may not be the man in the brown raincoat, but there is little doubt that Joyce puts in a totally unexpected appearance in Molly's monologue, "O Jamesy," she cries out when she realizes she is menstruating and about to stain the bed's clean sheets, "let me up out of this pooh sweets of sin" (p. 769). *Sweets of Sin* is the title of a trashy novel that Bloom has brought home for his wife. Who could Jamesy be but Molly's creator? Like many another novelist before and since, Joyce could not resist this moment of paradoxical self-reference—an imaginary woman calling out to the man who imagined her and who wrote the very words she is using.

Now we must ask the question, How much does all this riddling add to the worth of *Ulysses?* The wordplay attributed to Bloom does indeed enrich our understanding of Bloom. It lets us know that he, like Homer's Ulysses, is a man of many wiles. He likes anagrams and acrostics. He knows enough geometry to attempt squaring the circle. We are given a catalogue of his many ingenious schemes for making money. He uses a cipher. But what about the wealth of wordplay that is not Bloom's but Joyce's?

Numerous writers have enjoyed peppering their fiction with outlandish wordplay. One thinks of the puns in the works of Aristophanes and Rabelais and Shakespeare. Even Milton had a weakness for puns. In American literature one thinks of the incessant wordplay of James Branch Cabell, Peter DeVries, and Vladimir Nabokov. Sometimes the play turns up where least anticipated. In F. Scott Fitzgerald's *This Side of Paradise*, for example, all the purple passages in italics are formal poems, not very good ones, disguised as prose. In chapter 7 of *The Great Gatsby* we learn of a man named "Blocks" Biloxi who makes boxes and comes from Biloxi, Mississippi, but what relevance this has to the story is not apparent. Even the novel's title, like that of *Finnegans Wake*, conceals a pun. Fitzgerald well knew that gat was then underworld slang for a handgun. Readers who relish wordplay, coming upon such spots in a novel, may be as pleased as the author was when he put them there, but do such whimsies improve the novel?

My own view is a dull compromise. As a longtime connoisseur of puzzles, I am not offended by Joyce's riddling. On the other hand, neither am I much impressed. The sad truth is that the wordplay in *Ulysses* is not on the highest level. It takes only a glance at books such as Dmitri Borgmann's *Language on Vacation* or at the pages of *Word Ways* (an American quarterly devoted to recreational linguistics) to realize how trivial most of it is. Any clever writer can compose acrostics, toss in old riddles, blend two or more words into one, concoct puns, and hide meanings under thick layers of enigmatic persiflage. No skill is needed to spell a sentence backward or to observe that *dog* is a reversal of *God.* Joyce simply was not capable of inventing a palindrome comparable to, say, "Straw? No, too stupid a fad. I put soot on warts." The wordplay in *Ulysses* may indeed add to the novel's overall comic atmosphere, but in my opinion it does not add much.

We can focus the issue by considering two cryptic words that appear side by side on page 286: *yrfmstbyes* and *blmstup*. There is no doubt that the second word means "Bloom stood up" because Joyce himself explains it two sentences later. Even if we grant that *blmstup* reinforces a mental image of Bloom suddenly standing up, is it worth the effort of going back to decode it? And what on earth does *yrfmstbyes* mean?

To put the words in context, Bloom has just finished dining in a hotel restaurant with Stephen's alcoholic uncle. He thinks: "Well, I must be. Are you off? *Yrfmstbyes. Blmstup.*" In the vast literature on *Ulysses* I am sure there must be theories about *yrfmstbyes*, but I have not encountered them, so let me pass along two suggestions. Borgmann thinks that Bloom is answering "Well, I must be. Are you off?" with "You are off. Must be, yes." My wife came up with a more startling conjecture. From his seat in the dining room Bloom has been watching a barmaid in the adjoining saloon. She is massaging a beerpull knob by sliding her fingers smoothly back and forth over the "firm white enamel baton" while Bloom is mentally masturbating. Could he be answering "Are you off?" with "You royal fucking masturbator, yes"? Perhaps Joyce slyly contrived the preceding words so that both interpretations could be made.

For readers who like to solve cryptograms, *yrfmstbyes* and *blmstup* may add interest to the texture of a novel. For readers who care little about such conundrums, the strange words are mere blots on the text. *Bltsnthtxt.*

As for *Finnegans Wake*, I agree with Nabokov. Here Joyce's preoccupation with wordplay, kept under control in *Ulysses*, overwhelms everything else. Searching for the plot, philosophy, and beauty below the surface of what Nabokov called *Punnigans Wake* may forever Joyceously occupy erudite and multilingual critics, but I suspect the world's final verdict will be that the book is little more than a monstrous linguistic curiosity. Even the vast knowledge of world literature, the high intelligence, the stylistic skill, the humor, and the tireless energy that went into the making of this mammoth dish of verbal "chop suey" (as Joyce's wife called it) become less awesome when you consider that Joyce had sixteen years (16 again!) to cook it. In an interview Nabokov said: "*Ulysses* towers over the rest of Joyce's writings, and in comparison to its noble originality and unique lucidity of thought and style the unfortunate *Finnegans Wake* is nothing but a formless and dull mass of phony folklore, a cold pudding of a book, a persistent snore in the next room, most aggravating to the insomniac I am. . . . *Finnegans Wake*'s facade disguises a very conventional and drab tenement house, and only the infrequent snatches of heavenly intonations redeem it from utter insipidity" (Appel 1967, pp. 134–35).

POSTSCRIPT

A puzzle I failed to mention occurs on page 581 in the brothel episode. Stephen says: "Tell me the word, mother, if you know now. The word known to all men."

Stephen's mother does not supply the word, and critics have disagreed on what it could be. Richard Ellmann, in *Ulysses on the Liffey* (1972), suggested *love*. Another critic thought it *death* and still another proposed *synteresis*. This would seem, commented Ellmann (writing on "The Big Word in Ulysses," *New York Review of Books*, October 25, 1984), "rather to be the one word unknown to all men."

The mystery was solved in 1984 when the corrected three-volume edition of *Ulysses* was published. A passage had been omitted from the Scylla and Charybdis episode in which Stephen says: "Do you know what you are talking about? Love, yes. Word known to all men." This is followed by a Latin quotation which Ellmann translates as "Love truly wishes some good to another, and therefore we all desire it." It is not known whether Joyce wanted the passage removed or whether it was inadvertently dropped.

On page 153 Bloom reads a sign that says POST NO BILLS. This is followed by POST 110 PILLS—puzzling unless you realize that someone has scraped off the diagonal line in N and the bottom loop of B. Someone also called my attention to the made-up palindromic word TATTARRATTAT, though I have not yet located it in the novel.

On page 137 are two classic palindromes: Napoleon's remark, "Able was I ere I saw Elba," and Adam, introducing himself to Eve with "Madam, I'm Adam." Joyce does not add that Eve could have replied with the palindrome, "Eve." Adam's remark has been extended by palindromists to "Madam, in Eden I'm Adam."

Everett Bleiler was intrigued by the difficulty of anagramming Leopold Bloom. "Do you think it possible," he asked in a letter "that Joyce left an incident out of *Ulysses*? When Bloom, having robbed the Dublin post office, went with the loot to his gangster mistress, she wanted to make love, but he insisted instead on her giving him a haircut. When her scissors accidentally cut his ear, they quarreled and she kicked him out. I don't remember what happened to the loot."

All this is necessary background for understanding the following dialogue, each line of which is an anagram on Bloom's name!

> "Bloom! Ope, doll!
> P.O. boodle, moll!"
> "Bold pool-mole,

> O, do loll, bop me!"
> "P.L.O.-model bolo?
> Poll me. O! Blood!
> Doombell! Loop!"
> "O!! Do lollop, B.E.M.!
> Plod, Leo Bloom!"
> Lo, lo, bold poem!

REFERENCES

Adams, Robert M. *Surface and Symbol: The Consistency of James Joyce's Ulysses.* New York: Oxford University Press, 1962.

Appel, Alfred Jr. Interview with Vladimir Nabokov. *Wisconsin Studies in Contemporary Literature* 8 (Spring, 1967) 134–135.

Bergerson, Howard W. *Palindromes and Anagrams.* New York: Dover Publications, 1973.

Ellmann, Richard. *James Joyce.* New York: Oxford University Press, 1959.

Gifford, Don and Seidman, Robert J. *Notes for Joyce: An Annotation of James Joyce's Ulysses.* New York: E.P. Dutton, 1974. Revised second edition, *Ulysses Annotated.* Berkeley: University of California Press, 1988.

Gorman, Herbert. *James Joyce.* New York: Rinehart, 1948.

Hodgart, Matthew. *James Joyce: A Student's Guide.* London: Routledge and Kegan Paul, 1978

Kahn, David. *The Codebreakers.* New York: New American Library, 1973.

Nabokov, Vladimir. *Lectures in Literature.* New York: Harcourt Brace Jovanovich, 1980.

Thornton, Weldon, *Allusions in Ulysses.* Chapel Hill: University of North Carolina Press, 1968.

THIRTY

WHO WAS SHAKESPEARE?

My review of Samuel Schoenbaum's excellent book, Shakespeare's Lives, *appeared in the* Washington Post's Book World *(January 19, 1992). I was a bit taken aback by the vehemence of letters from the true believers that someone other than Shakespeare wrote his plays. They constitute what can be called a literary cult built around opinions held as steadfastly as any religious faith.* Book World *published a typical letter from an angry reader. You will find it in the Postscript, along with my reply.*

There is no English writer about whom critics long to know more than William Shakespeare. Yet after three centuries of searching, and thousands of books, the established facts are thin enough to be compressed to a few sentences. Shakespeare was born in 1564, married Anne Hathaway, had two daughters and one son who died at age 11. He began his career as an actor, wrote popular plays and sonnets of imperishable beauty, and died in 1616.

Contemporaries found him witty, gentle, and modest. "I loved the man, and do honor his memory on this side idolatry as much as any," wrote Ben Jonson, the only Elizabethan poet to be honored in his own lifetime.

Samuel Schoenbaum, professor of Renaissance Literature at the University of Maryland, knows more about what isn't known about Shakespeare than anyone. Twenty years ago, as a companion to his excellent biography of Shakespeare, he wrote *Shakespeare's Lives*. It is a wonderfully detailed account of what he calls the myth-makers—those who labored mightily to deduce Shakespeare's life and personality from what he wrote, and from scraps of information in obscure documents.

Now revised and updated, *Shakespeare's Lives* (Oxford University, 1991) is a marvelous, objective history of the legends that, in the author's words, "surround like a nimbus the blurred outlines of the Bard." It is all here, from the first full-scale biography by Nicholas Rowe in 1709, through myriads of later books and papers to the most recent. The search for the real Shakespeare has become a vast ongoing industry rivaling even the search for the historical Jesus.

What is not known is enormous. Was Shakespeare a Roman Catholic, an Anglican, or an unchurched theist or atheist? Critics have stoutly defended each possibility in writings that Schoenbaum skillfully summarizes.

Was the Bard heterosexual, bisexual, or homosexual? Arguments for each view rest mainly on the sonnets, but the trouble is, as Schoenbaum makes clear, no one knows to what degree the sonnets are autobiographical. They are dedicated to "Mr. W.H." Various men with those initials have been found, but W.H.'s true identity remains hidden. Schoenbaum retells the plot of a famous story by Oscar Wilde ("The Portrait of Mr. W.H."), who invents a William Hughes, the last name based on a fancied pun, "a man in hue, all 'hues,'" in Sonnet 20. Willie is a young actor who has been seduced by Marlowe, and of whom Shakespeare is for a time enamored. He turns up again in George Sylvester Viereck's novel about the Wandering Jew (*My First Two Thousand Years*), only now he is a girl dressed like a boy.

Samuel Butler, as gay as Wilde, outdid his crank work proving Homer to be a woman with *Shakespeare's Sonnets Reconsidered*. Drawing on an incident in his own life, Butler turns Willie into a sailor boy with whom the Bard had a brief encounter.

The sonnets contain three other biographical riddles. Who is the high-born Fair Youth whom Shakespeare calls "my love"? He has "a woman's face with Nature's own handpainted," so begins the notorious Sonnet 20. Alas, the Fair Youth also has a penis (a line puns on the word "prick"), which defeats the ultimate act of passion.

Who is the Dark Lady, equally loved by the writer? She has black eyes and hair, swarthy skin, and a strong sexual appetite. She even seduces the Fair Youth. As Schoenbaum tells us, Gerald Massey, in a 600-page study of the sonnets, identifies her as one Lady Rich. Critics have just as plausibly proposed other women.

Who is the Rival Poet? Experts have named Spenser, Marlowe, Jonson, Tasso, and many more. The current favorite is George Chapman, whose translation of Homer so excited Keats.

In discussing recent biographies of Shakespeare, Schoenbaum bears down heavily on A.L. Rowse for his cocksure claims of having solved all the sonnets' enigmas. Rowse has not the slightest doubt that W.H. was William Harvey, third husband of the countess of Southampton, and that the Fair

Youth was Henry Wriothesley, third earl of Southampton. The Rival Poet was Marlowe. The Dark Lady was Emilia Bassano, the promiscuous Italian wife of Alfonso Lanier. Schoenbaum has little patience with Rowse's dogmas, or for those in Anthony Burgess's *Shakespeare*, which he calls "an absurd gallimaufry of invention and (to put it mildly) dubious biographical theorizing."

It is, of course, the paucity of facts about Shakespeare (popular playwrights in those days had about as much fame as today's writers of movie scripts) that has generated what Schoenbaum calls the "lunatic rubbish" of the cranks. Ohio-born Delia Bacon began it all in 1857 with the first major work (675 pages) proving that the Bard was an uneducated "booby" whose plays had been written by Francis Bacon. Emerson took Delia seriously, and Hawthorne wrote a tepid preface to her book that he later regretted. She died, age 48, in a mental hospital, believing she was descended from Francis Bacon. Mark Twain was one of her converts.

I spare the reader comments on later Baconians, many of whom found lengthy ciphertexts in the plays (no two using the same cipher), or the critics who produced tomes to prove that Marlowe wrote Shakespeare's plays. Today the anti-Stratfordian man of choice is Edward de Vere, 17th earl of Oxford. This shaky conjecture, started in 1920 by the appropriately named Thomas Looney, has (to quote Schoenbaum) "given the Baconians a run for their madness."

The de Vere claim culminated in a massive 1,297-page work by Dorothy and Charlton Ogburn in 1952, and more recently in the 900-page *The Mysterious Shakespeare* (1984) by Ogburn's son who writes under the same name as his father. It was Looney who converted Freud to de Vereianism, providing Schoenbaum with amusing pages about Freud's obsession. As late as 1991 we find de Vere championed by Joseph Sobran in the *National Review* (April 29), and by Tom Bethell in the *Atlantic* (October).

Considering the vast welter of writings about Shakespeare—crank references alone, in a bibliography compiled in the 1840s, numbered more than 4,000 items—one might suppose that by now a Shakespeare would have emerged from the fog more substantial than a luminous wraith. But no, the Immortal Bard remains as shadowy as Homer. We do not even know what he looked like.

Schoenbaum quotes from the ending of a moving parable by Borges:

"History adds that before or after dying he found himself in the presence of God and told Him: 'I who have been so many men in vain want to be one and myself.' The voice of the Lord answered from a whirlwind: 'Neither am I anyone; I have dreamt the world as you dreamt your work, my Shakespeare, and among the forms in my dreams are you, who like myself are many and no one'."

TWO MORE SHAKESPEARE MYSTERIES

Consider these lines addressed to Bottom the Weaver by Queen Titania in "A Midsummer Night's Dream" (Act III, Scene 10):

> *Out of this wood do not desire to go:*
> *Thou shalt remain here, whether thou wilt or no.*
> *I am a spirit of no common rate;*
> *The summer still doth tend upon my state;*
> *ANd I do love thee; therefore, go with me.*
> *I'll give thee fairies to attend on thee,*
> *And they shall fetch thee jewels from the deep.*

The capitalized letters, reading down on the left, spell "O Titania."

Here is a passage from "The Comedy of Errors" (Act I, Scene 1):

> *To bear the extremity of dire mishap!*
> *Now, trust me, were it not against our laws,*
> *Against my crown, my oath, my dignity,*
> *Which princes, would they, may not disannul,*
> *My soul should sue as advocate for thee,*
> *But, though thou art adjudged to the death,*
> *And passed sentence may not be recall'd*
> *But to our honour's great disaparagement,*
> *Yet will I favour thee in what I can.*

Read the initial letters up from the word "My," then "My," and down for the next four letters. You get "Want my baby."

Coincidences? Or did Shakespeare, who enjoyed wordplay as much as Joyce, and Nabokov, intend both these acrostics? We owe their discovery to the late British wordplay expert Leigh Mercer who pointed them out to me in a letter. Mercer, by the way, invented the famous palindrome "A man, a plan, a canal—Panama!"

POSTSCRIPT

The following two letters were published in *Book World* (March 8, 1992):

It's not surprising that S. Schoenbaum's *Shakespeare's Lives* was reviewed by Martin Gardner, another Stratford orthodox—they hold each other's hands, unable to hold up their side of legitimate debate.

Gardner follows the contours of Schoenbaum's flat earth, pointing out how Baconians fell over the edge, with similar hope that those who support Edward de Vere, the earl of Oxford, will drop out of sight. Gardner's prize syllogism is that the Oxfordians' mentor was named Looney; therefore they are. What other reply can Stratfordians provide when their man was demonstrably illiterate? There is no evidence that he penned *anything* except to autograph a few legal documents, letter by painful letter, yet still misspelling his own name.

The case for Oxford's authorship is long, detailed and cogent; but not nearly so as that against the bumpkin Schoenbaum and Gardner enshrine as their Shakespeare. They admit that hardly a scintilla of biographical data exists about their man. And why not? should have been their first question, but it is never asked, much less answered.

So it is for lovers of the greatest English poet to ask that question. The best place to start is an excruciatingly objective study that Schoenbaum labeled "madness": Charlton Ogburn's *The Mysterious William Shakespeare*. The arguments therein convinced the likes of Bismarck, John Bright, Dickens, Disraeli, Palmerston, Freud, Henry James, Walt Whitman and Mark Twain. The last, no doubt, had particular empathy for non-Stratfordians because he wrote under a pen name himself. But of course he, like the others mentioned, was mad.

THOMAS H. TAYLOR
Washington

In a sidebar to Martin Gardner's review of S. Schoenbaum's *Shakespeare's Lives*, Gardner notes the existence of certain acrostics in passages from the plays and asks whether these acrostics are accidental or intentional.

By somewhat similar means, it can be shown that Shakespeare was one of the translators, or at least one of the editors, of the King James Version of the Bible. The King James Version was published in 1611. Shakespeare presumably worked on the translation in 1610 when he was 46 years old. In Psalm 46 of the King James Version, the 46th word from the beginning is "Shake"; the 46th word from the end is "spear." What better way for Shakespeare to tell us that in his 46th year, he translated or edited, the 46th psalm?

HERSHEL SHANKS
Washington, D.C.

I replied:

Thomas H. Taylor pulled a fast one when he listed those nine names. The implication is that all nine persons agreed with Ogburn that Shakespeare's plays were written by Edward de Vere. Actually, most of the nine, especially Mark Twain, were Baconians. It is typical of anti-Stratfordians, convinced that A wrote Shakespeare, to be not in the least troubled by the vast literature containing shrewdly argued "proofs" that the plays were written by B, C, D, E . . . I would enjoy being in a room listening to a conversation between Taylor and an equally ardent Baconian.

Hershel Shanks brings up a classic piece of numerology. I first heard of it from "Dr. Matrix," the world renowned numerologist, when I interviewed him more than 30 years ago for one of my mathematical games columns in *Scientific American*. Maybe Psalm 46 was translated by Bacon, or de Vere, or Marlowe, or one of several dozen other men and women put forth by anti-Stratfordians as purloiners of poor Shakespeare's good name.

One can also find "William" in Psalm 46. The fourteenth word is "Will," and the thirty-second word from the end (not counting "Selah") is "am," preceded by "I." Fourteen plus 32 equals 46.

J. Karl Franson, writing on "A Myth About the Bard," in *Word Ways* (August 1994) proved that these correlations are sheer coincidences. There were English translations of the Bible before King James. Franson checked Richard Taverner's 1539 version of Psalm 46 and found exactly the same numerical positions for "shake" and "spear"! Moreover, in Taverner's Bible "Will" is the fourteenth word, and "I am" are the thirty-first and thirty-second words from the end. This in spite of the fact that wordings of the two translations are not the same!

There is no evidence that Shakespeare, who was born in 1564, had any role in the King James translation. If you search tirelessly through any work as huge and complex as the Bible, it would be surprising *not* to find some unusual coincidences.

In my chapter on Bacon's cipher system, in *Knotted Doughnuts and Other Mathematical Entertainments*, I discuss the writings of two of the funniest Baconian cranks of all time: Ignatius Donnelly, whose work *The Great Cryptogram* purports to decode a ciphertext in Shakespeare's plays, and the mad Elizabeth Wells Gallup.

In 1991 three New Agers, and a publicist named Fletcher Richman, raised a big ruckus in Williamsburg, Virginia. They contended that secret papers proving Bacon wrote Shakespeare's plays were buried in a vault in the graveyard of the town's eighteenth-century Brunton Parish Church. Richman, who heads the Tudor Graph Society, a Williamsburg public relations firm, claims to be a reincarnation of one of Bacon's descendants. In 1674, he insists, he himself had buried the papers in the graveyard.

Twice in 1991 the three New Agers crept surreptitiously into the Brunton church cemetery and tried to dig up the vault. Richman maintains that the vault also contains the crown jewels of the first Queen Elizabeth, the original manuscript of the King James Bible, lost writings of Peter, and early versions of The Declaration of Independence and the U.S. Constitution, both written by Bacon.

Belief in the vault comes from the contentions of Marie Bauer Hall, an elderly occultist then living in Los Angeles. Her husband, who died in 1990, was Manly Palmer Hall, founder of the Los Angeles Philosophical Research Society. Mrs. Hall says she discovered a ciphertext in a 1673 book by one George Withers in which he predicted that the Bacon material would be buried in the Williamsburg cemetery. In 1936 Hall obtained permission to dig. Her crew found what was probably a coffin, but church officials filled up the hole and sent the diggers packing. In 1990 Mrs. Hall's Veritas Foundation hired some archaeologists to make electronic tests at the site. They reported "anomalies" under the soil.

The 1991 dig came about because Marsha Middleton, the chief New Age digger, had read about Hall's research and was captivated. Middleton belongs to a Santa Fe, New Mexico, group called the Ministry of Children. A Hopi Indian woman appeared to her seven-year-old son in a dream and said the time was ripe for a new dig. Middleton's husband Frank Flint, and a friend, attempted the new dig, but were restrained by a court order obtained by the church. The church considered hiring a professional archaeologist to make a deep dig to end the controversy, but concluded that the New Agers would not give up until the entire cemetery had been dug.

Robert Fehrenbach, who teaches English at William and Mary, a Williamsburg college, said it this way:

What if someone said to you, 'I have reason to believe that the equivalent of the Hope Diamond and Genghis Khan's saddle is in your garage. If I can't find it there, I'll go through your sock drawer. If I can't find it there, I'll go through your attic, your basement and finally your bra.'

In November 1991 the New Agers were back trying to dig in the dead of night, but fled when discovered by security guards. A warrant was issued for their arrest. The mayor of Williamsburg called them a bunch of "kooks."

In August 1992 the church relented because of the enormous publicity generated by the wild claims. They hired a team of archaeologists to dig six feet down at the favored spot. Nothing but dirt was found. Gerald Johnson, a William and Mary geologist, drilled holes 21.5 feet deep at twelve spots near the site without hitting anything. As expected, the Baconians, now quarreling among themselves, declared that the dig wasn't deep enough. Besides, it was in the wrong place.

The farce was extensively covered by local papers and by the *Washington Post*. See the *Wall Street Journal's* front page of January 27, 1992, for a hilarious account, and a round-up article in the *Skeptical Eye* (vol. 6, no. 4, 1992), a Washington, D.C., periodical.

THIRTY-ONE

WHITE, BROWN, AND FRACTAL MUSIC

One of the greatest mysteries of experimental aesthetics, a branch of psychology still in a primitive state, is the almost total failure to understand what goes on in the mind of a composer when he creates something so simple as a great melody. For some efforts in the past to construct mechanical devices and computer programs for composing tunes, see chapter 6, "Melody-Making Machines," in my Time Travel and Other Mathematical Amusements *(1988). Will future computers learn how to compose a tune as catchy as, say, The Beer Barrel Polka, let alone a symphony comparable to those of the great composers? Maybe so, maybe not. If so, I believe it will not be soon.*

When I was researching the following essay I had the privilege of interviewing Benoit Mandelbrot, the father of fractals and the discoverer of the famous "Mandelbrot set," and his associate Richard Voss. My column about fractal music (also called pink or tan music) ran in Scientific American *(April 1978).*

"For when there are no words [accompanying music] it is very difficult to recognize the meaning of the harmony and rhythm, or to see that any worthy object is imitated by them."

—PLATO, *Laws*, Book II

Plato and Aristotle agreed that in some fashion all the fine arts, including music, "imitate" nature, and from their day until the late 18th century "imitation" was a central concept in western aesthetics. It is obvious how representational painting and sculpture "represent," and how fiction and the stage copy life, but in what sense does music imitate?

By the mid-18th century philosophers and critics were still arguing over exactly how the arts imitate and whether the term is relevant to music. The rhythms of music may be said to imitate such natural rhythms as heartbeats, walking, running, flapping wings, waving fins, water waves, the periodic motions of heavenly bodies and so on, but this does not explain why we enjoy music more than, say, the sound of cicadas or the ticking of clocks. Musical pleasure derives mainly from tone patterns, and nature, though noisy, is singularly devoid of tones. Occasionally wind blows over some object to produce a tone, cats howl, birds warble, bowstrings twang. A Greek legend tells how Hermes invented the lyre: he found a turtle shell with tendons attached to it that produced musical tones when they were plucked.

Above all, human beings sing. Musical instruments may be said to imitate song, but what does singing imitate? A sad, happy, angry, or serene song somehow resembles sadness, joy, anger, or serenity, but if a melody has no words and invokes no special mood, what does it copy? It is easy to understand Plato's mystification.

There is one exception: the kind of imitation that plays a role in "program music." A lyre is severely limited in the natural sounds it can copy, but such limitations do not apply to symphonic or electronic music. Program music has no difficulty featuring the sounds of thunder, wind, rain, fire, ocean waves, and brook murmurings; bird calls (cuckoos and crowing cocks have been particularly popular), frog croaks, the gaits of animals (the thundering hoofbeats in Wagner's *Ride of the Valkyries*), the flights of bumblebees; the rolling of trains, the clang of hammers; the battle sounds of marching soldiers, clashing armies, roaring cannons, and exploding bombs. *Slaughter on Tenth Avenue* includes a pistol shot and the wail of a police-car siren. In Bach's *Saint Matthew Passion* we hear the earthquake and the ripping of the temple veil. In the *Alpine Symphony* by Richard Strauss, cowbells are imitated by the shaking of cowbells. Strauss insisted he could tell that a certain female character in Felix Mottl's *Don Juan* had red hair, and he once said that someday music would be able to distinguish the clattering of spoons from that of forks.

Such imitative noises are surely a trivial aspect of music even when it accompanies opera, ballet, or the cinema; besides, such sounds play no role whatsoever in "absolute music," music not intended to "mean" anything. A Platonist might argue that abstract music imitates emotions, or beauty, or the divine harmony of God or the gods, but on more mundane levels music is the least imitative of the arts. Even nonobjective paintings resemble certain patterns of nature, but nonobjective music resembles nothing except itself.

Since the turn of the century most critics have agreed that "imitation" has been given so many meanings (almost all are found in Plato) that it has become a useless synonym for "resemblance." When it is made precise with reference to literature or the visual arts, its meaning is obvious and trivial. When it is applied to music, its meaning is too fuzzy to be helpful. In this essay we take a look at a surprising discovery by Richard F. Voss, a physicist from Minnesota who joined the Thomas J. Watson Research Center of the International Business Machines Corporation after obtaining his Ph.D. at the University of California at Berkeley under the guidance of John Clarke. This work is not likely to restore "imitation" to the lexicon of musical criticism, but it does suggest a curious way in which good music may mirror a subtle statistical property of the world.

The key concepts behind Voss's discovery are what mathematicians and physicists call the spectral density (or power spectrum) of a fluctuating quantity, and its "autocorrelation." These deep notions are technical and hard to understand. Benoît Mandelbrot, who is also at the Watson Research Center, and whose work makes extensive use of spectral densities and autocorrelation functions, has suggested a way of avoiding them here. Let the tape of a sound be played faster or slower than normal. One expects the character of the sound to change considerably. A violin, for example, no longer sounds like a violin. There is a special class of sounds, however, that behave quite differently. If you play a recording of such a sound at a different speed, you have only to adjust the volume to make it sound exactly as before. Mandelbrot calls such sounds "scaling noises."

By far the simplest example of a scaling noise is what in electronics and information theory is called white noise (or "Johnson noise"). To be white is to be colorless. White noise is a colorless hiss that is just as dull whether you play it faster or slower. Its autocorrelation function, which measures how its fluctuations at any moment are related to previous fluctuations, is zero except at the origin, where of course it must be 1. The most commonly encountered white noise is the thermal noise produced by the random motions of electrons through an electrical resistance. It causes most of the static in a radio or amplifier and the "snow" on radar and television screens when there is no input.

With randomizers such as dice or spinners it is easy to generate white noise that can then be used for composing a random "white tune," one with no correlation between any two notes. Our scale will be one octave of seven white keys on a piano: do, re, me, fa, so, la, ti. Fa is our middle frequency. Now construct a spinner such as the one shown on the left in Figure 1. Divide the circle into seven sectors and label them with the notes. It matters not at all what arc lengths are assigned to these sectors; they can be completely arbitrary. On the spinner shown, some order has been imposed by giving fa the longest arc (the highest probability of being chosen) and assigning decreasing probabilities to pairs of notes that are equal distances above and below fa. This has the effect of clustering the tones around fa.

To produce a "white melody" simply spin the spinner as often as you like, recording each chosen note. Since no tone is related in any way to the sequence of notes that precedes it, the result is a totally uncorrelated sequence.

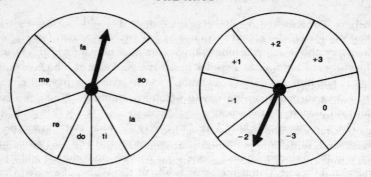

Figure 1. Spinners for white music (left) and brown music (right)

If you like, you can divide the circle into more parts and let the spinner select notes that range over the entire piano keyboard, black keys as well as white.

To make your white melody more sophisticated, use another spinner, its circle divided into four parts (with any proportions you like) and labeled 1, $\frac{1}{2}$, $\frac{1}{4}$ and $\frac{1}{8}$ so that you can assign a full, a half, a quarter or an eighth of a beat to each tone. After the composition is completed, tap it out on the piano. The music will sound just like what it is: random music of the dull kind that a two-year-old or a monkey might produce by hitting keys with one finger. Similar white music can be based on random number tables, or the digits in an irrational number.

A more complicated kind of scaling noise is one that is sometimes called Brownian noise because it is characteristic of Brownian motion, the random movements of small particles suspended in a liquid and buffeted by the thermal agitation of molecules. Each particle executes a three-dimensional "random walk," the positions in which form a highly correlated sequence. The particle, so to speak, always "remembers" where it has been.

When tones fluctuate in this fashion, let us follow Voss and call it Brownian music or brown music. We can produce it easily with a spinner and a circle divided into seven parts as before, but now we label the regions, as shown at the right in Figure 1, to represent intervals between successive tones. These step sizes and their probabilities can be whatever we like. On the spinner shown, plus means a step up the scale of one, two or three notes and minus means a step down of the same intervals.

Start the melody on the piano's middle C, then use the spinner to generate a linear random walk up and down the keyboard. The tune will wander here and there, and will eventually wander off the keyboard. If we treat the ends of the keyboard as "absorbing barriers," the tune ends when we encounter one of them. We need not go into the ways in which we can treat the barriers as reflecting barriers, allowing the tune to bounce back, or as elastic barriers. To make the barriers elastic we must add rules so that the farther the tone gets from middle C, the greater is the likelihood it will step back toward C, like a marble wobbling from side to side as it rolls down a curved trough.

As before, we can make our brown music more sophisticated by varying the tone durations. If we like, we can do this in a brown way by using another spinner to give not the duration but the increase or decrease of the duration— another random walk but one along a different street. The result is a tune that sounds quite different from a white tune because it is strongly correlated, but a tune that still has little aesthetic appeal. It simply wanders up and down like a drunk weaving through an alley, never producing anything that resembles good music.

If we want to mediate between the extremes of white and brown, we can do it in two essentially different ways. The way chosen by previous composers of "stochastic music" is to adopt transition rules. These are rules that select each note on the basis of the last three or four. For example, one can analyze Bach's music and determine how often a certain note follows, say, a certain triplet of preceding notes. The random selection of each note is then weighted with probabilities derived from a statistical analysis of all Bach quadruplets. If there are certain transitions that never appear in Bach's music, we add rejection rules to prevent the undesirable transitions. The result is stochastic music that resembles Bach but only superficially. It sounds Bachlike in the short run but random in the long run. Consider the melody over periods of four or five notes and the tones are strongly correlated. Compare a run of five notes with another five-note run later on and you are back to white noise. One run has no correlation with the other. Almost all stochastic music produced so far has been of this sort. It sounds musical if you listen to any small part but random and uninteresting when you try to grasp the pattern as a whole.

Voss's insight was to compromise between white and brown input by selecting a scaling noise exactly halfway between. In spectral terminology it is called $1/f$ noise. (White noise has a spectral density of $1/f^0$, brownian noise a spectral density of $1/f^2$. In "one-over-f" noise the exponent of f is 1 or very close to 1.) Tunes based on $1/f$ noise are moderately correlated, not just over short runs but throughout runs of any size. It turns out that almost every listener agrees that such music is much more pleasing than white or brown music.

In electronics $1/f$ noise is well known but poorly understood. It is sometimes called flicker noise. Mandelbrot, whose book *The Fractal Geometry of Nature* (W. H. Freeman and Company, 1982) has already become a modern classic, was the first to recognize how widespread $1/f$ noise is in nature, outside of physics, and how often one encounters other scaling fluctuations. For ex-

Figure 2. Mandelbrot's Peano-snowflake as it appeared on the cover of Scientific American (April, 1978). The curve was drawn by a program written by Sigmund Handelman and Mark Laff

ample, he discovered that the record of the annual flood levels of the Nile is a 1/f fluctuation. He also investigated how the curves that graph such fluctuations are related to "fractals," a term he invented. A scaling fractal can be defined roughly as any geometrical pattern (other than Euclidean lines, planes, and surfaces) with the remarkable property that no matter how closely you inspect it, it always looks the same, just as a slowed or speeded scaling noise always sounds the same. Mandelbrot coined the term fractal because he assigns to each of the curves a fractional dimension greater than its topological dimension.

Among the fractals that exhibit strong regularity the best known are the Peano curves that completely fill a finite region and the beautiful snowflake

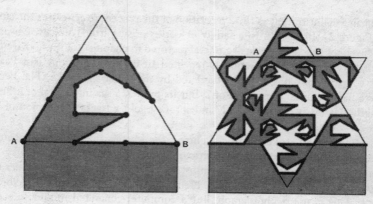

Figure 3. The first two steps in constructing Benoît Mandelbrot's Peano-snowflake curve

curve discovered by the Swedish mathematician Helge von Koch in 1904. The Koch snowflake appears in Figure 2 as the boundary of the dark "sea" that surrounds the central motif. (For details on the snowflake's construction, and a discussion of fractals in general, see chapter 3 of my *Penrose Tiles to Trapdoor Ciphers* (W. H. Freeman, 1989).

The most interesting part of Figure 2 is the fractal curve that forms the central design. It was discovered by Mandelbrot and published for the first time as the cover of *Scientific American*'s April 1978 issue. If you trace the boundary between the black and white regions from the tip of the point of the star at the lower left to the tip of the point of the star at the lower right, you will find this boundary to be a single curve. It is the third stage in the construction of a new Peano curve. At the limit this lovely curve will completely fill a region bounded by the traditional snowflake! Thus Mandelbrot's curve brings together two pathbreaking fractals: the oldest of them all, Giuseppe Peano's 1890 curve, and Koch's later snowflake!

The secret of the curve's construction is the use of line segments of two unequal lengths and oriented in 12 different directions. The curve is much less regular than previous Peano curves and therefore closer to the modeling of natural phenomena, the central theme of Mandelbrot's book. Such natural forms as the gnarled branches of a tree or the shapes of flickering flames can be seen in the pattern.

At the left in Figure 3 is the first step of the construction. A crooked line of nine segments is drawn on and within an equilateral triangle. Four of the segments are then divided into two equal parts, creating a line from A to B that consists of 13 long and short segments. The second step replaces each of these 13 segments with a smaller replica of the crooked line. These replicas (necessarily of unequal size) are oriented as is shown inside the star at the right in the illustration. A third repetition of the procedure generates the curve in Figure 2. (It belongs to a family of curves arising from William Gosper's discovery of the "flow-snake," a fractal pictured in chapter 3 of my above cited book.) When the construction is repeated to infinity, the limit is a Peano curve that totally fills a region bordered by the Koch snowflake. The Peano curve has the usual dimension of 2, but its border, a scaling fractal of infinite length, has (as is explained in Mandelbrot's book) a fractal dimension of log 4/log 3, or 1.2618. . . .

Unlike these striking artificial curves, the fractals that occur in nature—coastlines, rivers, trees, star clustering, clouds, and so on—are so irregular that their self-similarity (scaling) must be treated statistically. Consider the profile of the mountain range in Figure 4, reproduced from Mandelbrot's book. This is not a photograph, but a computer-generated mountain scene based on a modified Brownian noise. Any vertical cross section of the topography has a profile that models a random walk. The white patches, representing water or snow in the hollows below a certain altitude, were added to enhance the relief.

The profile at the top of the mountain range is a scaling fractal. This means that if you enlarge any small portion of it, it will have the same statistical character as the line you now see. If it were a true fractal, this property would continue forever as smaller and smaller segments are enlarged, but of course such a curve can neither be drawn nor appear in nature. A coastline, for example, may be self-similar when viewed from a height of several miles down to several feet, but below that the fractal property is lost. Even the Brownian motion of a particle is limited by the size of its microsteps.

Since mountain ranges approximate random walks, one can create "mountain music" by photographing a mountain range and translating its fluctuating heights to tones that fluctuate in time. Villa Lobos actually did this using mountain skylines around Rio de Janeiro. If we view nature statically, frozen in time, we can find thousands of natural curves that can be used in this way to produce stochastic music. Such music is usually too brown, too correlated, however, to be interesting. Like natural white noise, natural brown noise may do well enough, perhaps, for the patterns of abstract art but not so well as a basis for music.

When we analyze the dynamic world, made up of quantities constantly changing in time, we find a wealth of fractal-like fluctuations that have $1/f$ spectral densities. In his book Mandelbrot cites a few: variations in sunspots, the wobbling of the earth's axis, undersea currents, membrane currents in the nervous system of animals, the fluctuating levels of rivers and so on. Uncertainties in time measured by an atomic clock are $1/f$: the error is 10^{-12} regardless of whether one is measuring an error on a second, minute or hour. Scientists tend to overlook $1/f$ noises because there are no good theories to

Figure 4. A modified Brownian landscape generated by a computer program

account for them, but there is scarcely an aspect of nature in which they cannot be found.

T. Musha, a physicist at the Tokyo Institute of Technology, discovered that traffic flow past a certain spot on a Japanese expressway exhibited $1/f$ fluctuation. In a more startling experiment, Musha rotated a radar beam emanating from a coastal location to get a maximum variety of landscape on the radar screen. When he rotated the beam once, variations in the distances of all objects scanned by the beam produced a Brownian spectrum. But when he rotated it twice and then subtracted one curve from the other the resulting curve—representing all the changes of the scene—was close to $1/f$.

We are now approaching an understanding of Voss's daring conjecture. The changing landscape of the world (or, to put it another way, the changing content of our total experience) seems to cluster around $1/f$ noise. It is certainly not entirely uncorrelated, like white noise, nor is it as strongly correlated as brown noise. From the cradle to the grave our brain is processing the fluctuating data that comes to it from its sensors. If we measure this noise at the peripheries of the nervous system (under the skin of the fingers), it tends, Mandelbrot says, to be white. The closer one gets to the brain, however, the closer the electrical fluctuations approach $1/f$. The nervous system seems to act like a complex filtering device, screening out irrelevant elements and processing only the patterns of change that are useful for intelligent behavior.

On the canvas of a painting, colors and shapes are static, reflecting the world's static patterns. Is it possible, Mandelbrot asked himself many years ago, that even completely non-objective art, when it is pleasing, reflects fractal patterns of nature? He is fond of abstract art, and maintains that there is a sharp distinction between such art that has a fractal base and such art that does not, and that the former type is widely considered the more beautiful. Perhaps this is why photographers with a keen sense of aesthetics find it easy to take pictures, particularly photomicrographs, of natural patterns that are almost indistinguishable from abstract expressionist art.

Motion can be added to visual art, of course, in the form of the motion picture, the stage, kinetic art, and the dance, but in music we have meaningless, nonrepresentational tones that fluctuate to create a pattern that can be appreciated only over a period of time. Is it possible, Voss asked himself, that the pleasures of music are partly related to scaling noise of $1/f$ spectral density? That is, is this music "imitating" the $1/f$ quality of our flickering experience?

That may or may not be true, but there is no doubt that music of almost every variety does exhibit $1/f$ fluctuations in its changes of pitch as well as in the changing loudness of its tones. Voss found this to be true of classical music, jazz, and rock. He suspects it is true of all music. He was therefore not surprised that when he used a $1/f$ flicker noise from a transistor to generate a random tune, it turned out to be more pleasing than tunes based on white and brown noise sources.

Figure 5, supplied by Voss, shows typical patterns of white, $1/f$, and brown when noise values (vertical) are plotted against time (horizontal). These patterns were obtained by a computer program that simulates the generation of the three kinds of sequences by tossing dice. The white noise is based on the sum obtained by repeated tosses of 10 dice. These sums range from 10 to 60, but the probabilities naturally force a clustering around the median. The Brownian noise was generated by tossing a single die and going up one step on the scale if the number was even and down a step if the number was odd.

The $1/f$ noise was also generated by simulating the tossing of 10 dice. Although $1/f$ noise is extremely common in nature, it was assumed until recently that it is unusually cumbersome to simulate $1/f$ noise by randomizers or computers. Previous composers of stochastic music probably did not even know about $1/f$ noise, but if they did, they would have had considerable difficulty generating it. As this article was being prepared Voss was asked if he could devise a simple procedure by which readers could produce their own $1/f$ tunes. He gave some thought to the problem and to his surprise hit on a clever way of simplifying existing $1/f$ computer algorithms that does the trick beautifully.

The method is best explained by considering a sequence of eight notes chosen from a scale of 16 tones. We use three dice of three colors: red, green, and blue. Their possible sums range from 3 to 18. Select 16 adjacent notes on a piano, black keys as well as white if you like, and number them 3 through 18.

Write down the first eight numbers, 0 through 7, in binary notation, and assign a die color to each column as is shown in Figure 6. The first note of

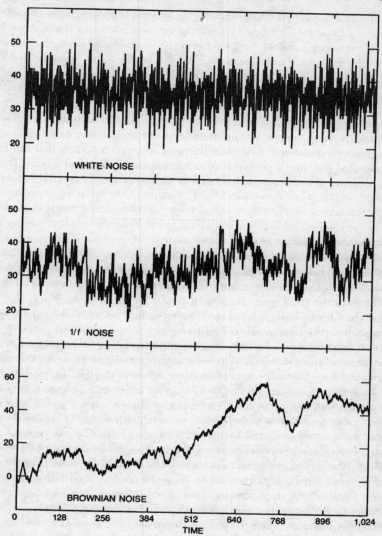

Figure 5. Typical patterns of white, 1/f, and Brownian noise

our tune is obtained by tossing all three dice and picking the tone that corresponds to the sum. Note that in going from 000 to 001 only the red digit
changes. Leave the green and blue dice undisturbed, still showing the numbers
of the previous toss. Pick up only the red die and toss it. The new sum of all
three dice gives the second note of your tune. In the next transition, from

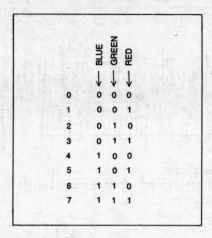

Figure 6. *Binary chart for Voss's 1/f dice algorithm*

001 to 010, both the red and green digits change. Pick up the red and green dice, leaving the blue one undisturbed, and toss the pair. The sum of all three dice gives the third tone. The fourth note is found by shaking only the red die, the fifth by shaking all three. The procedure, in short, is to shake only those dice that correspond to digit changes.

It is not hard to see how this algorithm produces a sequence halfway between white and brown. The least significant digits, those to the right, change often. The more significant digits, those to the left, are more stable. As a result, dice corresponding to them make a constant contribution to the sum over long periods of time. The resulting sequence is not precisely $1/f$ but is so close to it that it is impossible to distinguish melodies formed in this way from tunes generated by natural $1/f$ noise. Four dice can be used the same way for a $1/f$ sequence of 16 notes chosen from a scale of 21 tones. With 10 dice you can generate a melody of 2^{10}, or 1,024, notes from a scale of 55 tones. Similar algorithms can of course be implemented with generalized dice (octahedrons, dodecahedrons and so on), spinners, or even tossed coins.

With the same dice simulation program Voss has supplied three typical melodies based on white, brown, and $1/f$ noise. The computer printouts of the melodies are shown in Figures 7, 8, and 9. In each case Voss varied both the melody and the tone duration with the same kind of noise. Above each tune are shown the noise patterns that were used.

Over a period of two years, tunes of the three kinds were played at various universities and research laboratories, for many hundreds of people. Most listeners found the white music too random, the brown too correlated, and the $1/f$ "just about right." Indeed, it takes only a glance at the music itself to see how the $1/f$ property mediates between the two extremes. Voss's earlier $1/f$

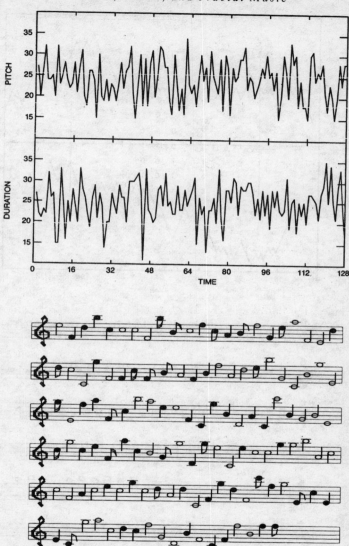

Figure 7. White music

music was based on natural 1/ƒ noise, usually electronic, even though one of his best compositions derives from the record of the annual flood levels of the Nile. He has made no attempt to impose constant rhythms. When he applied 1/ƒ noise to a pentatonic (five-tone) scale and also varied the rhythm

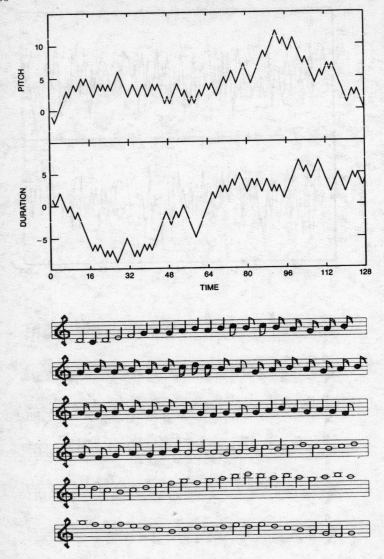

Figure 8. Brown music

with 1/*f* noise, the music strongly resembled Oriental music. He has not tried
to improve his 1/*f* music by adding transition or rejection rules. It is his belief
that stochastic music with such rules will be greatly improved if the underlying
choices are based on 1/*f* noise rather than the white noise so far used.

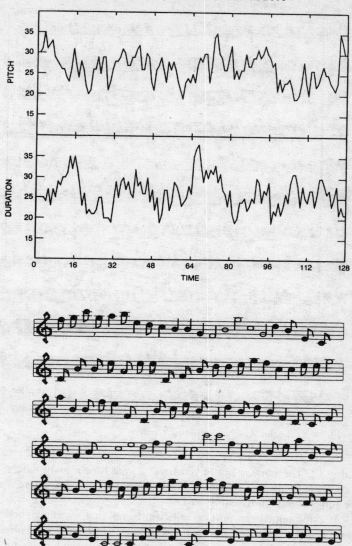

Figure 9. 1/f *music*

Note that 1/f music is halfway between white and brown in a fractal sense, not in the manner of music that has transition rules added to white music. As we have seen, such music reverts to white when we compare widely separated parts. But 1/f music has the fractal self-similarity of a coastline or a mountain range. Analyze the fluctuations on a small scale, from note to note,

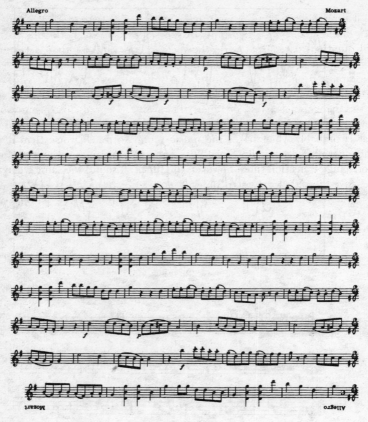

Figure 10. Mozart's palindromic and invertible canon

and it is $1/f$. The same is true if you break a long tune into 10-note sections and compare them. The tune never forgets where it has been. There is always some correlation with its entire past.

It is commonplace in musical criticism to say that we enjoy good music because it offers a mixture of order and surprise. How could it be otherwise? Surprise would not be surprise if there were not sufficient order for us to anticipate what is likely to come next. If we guess too accurately, say in listening to a tune that is no more than walking up and down the keyboard in one-step intervals, there is no surprise at all. Good music, like a person's life or the pageant of history, is a wondrous mixture of expectation and unanticipated turns. There is nothing new about this insight, but what Voss has done is to suggest a mathematical measure for the mixture.

I cannot resist mentioning three curious ways of transforming a melody to a different one with the same 1/*f* spectral density for both tone patterns and durations. One is to write the melody backward, another is to turn it upside down and the third is to do both. These transformations are easily accomplished on a player piano by reversing and/or inverting the paper roll. If a record or tape is played backward, unpleasant effects result from a reversal of the dying-away quality of tones. (Piano music sounds like organ music.) Reversal or inversion naturally destroys the composer's transition patterns, and that is probably what makes the music sound so much worse than it does when it is played normally. Since Voss composed his tunes without regard for short-range transition rules, however, the tunes all sound the same when they are played in either direction.

Canons for two voices were sometimes deliberately written, particularly in the 15th century, so that one melody is the other backward, and composers often reversed short sequences for contrapuntal effects in longer works. Figure 10 shows a famous canon that Mozart wrote as a joke. In this instance the second melody is almost the same as the one you see taken backward and upside down. Thus if the sheet is placed flat on a table, with one singer on one side and the other singer on the other, the singers can read from the same sheet as they harmonize!

No one pretends, of course, that stochastic 1/*f* music, even with added transition and rejection rules, can compete with the music of good composers. We know that certain frequency ratios, such as the three-to-two ratio of a perfect fifth, are more pleasing than others, either when the two tones are played simultaneously or in sequence. But just what composers do when they weave their beautiful patterns of meaningless sounds remains a mystery that even they do not understand.

It is here that Plato and Aristotle seem to disagree. Plato viewed all the fine arts with suspicion. They are, he said (or at least his Socrates said), imitations of imitations. Each time something is copied something is lost. A picture of a bed is not as good as a real bed, and a real bed is not as good as the universal, perfect idea of bedness. Plato was less concerned with the sheer delight of art than with its effects on character, and for that reason his *Republic* and *Laws* recommend strong state censorship of all the fine arts.

Aristotle, on the other hand, recognized that the fine arts are of value to a state primarily because they give pleasure, and that this pleasure springs from the fact that artists do much more than make poor copies.

> They said, "You have a blue guitar,
> You do not play things as they are."
> The man replied, "Things as they are
> Are changed upon the blue guitar."

Wallace Stevens intended his blue guitar to stand for all the arts, but music, more than any other art and regardless of what imitative aspects it may have, involves the making of something utterly new. You may occasionally encounter natural scenes that remind you of a painting, or episodes in life that make you think of a novel or a play. You will never come on anything in nature that sounds like a symphony. As to whether mathematicians will some-day write computer programs that will create good music—even a simple, memorable tune—time alone will tell.

POSTSCRIPT

Irving Godt, who teaches music history at the Indiana University of Pennsyl-vania, straightened me out on the so-called Mozart canon with the following letter. It appeared in *Scientific American* (July 1978):

> A few musical errors slipped past Martin Gardner's critical eye when he took up "Mozart's palindromic and invertible canon" in his report on fractal curves and "one-over-*f*" fluctuations.
>
> Mozart scholars now agree that the canon is almost certainly not by Mozart, even though publishers have issued it under his name. For more than 40 years the compilers of the authoritative Köchel catalogue of Moz-art's compositions have relegated it to the appendix of doubtful attri-butions, where along with three other pieces of a similar character, it bears the catalogue number K. Anh. C 10.16. We have no evidence that the piece goes back any further than the last century.
>
> The piece is not for two singers but for two violins. Singers cannot produce the simultaneous notes of the chords in the second measure (and elsewhere), and the ranges of the parts are quite impractical. To perform the piece the two players begin from opposite ends of the sheet of music and arrive at a result that falls far below the standard of Mozart's au-thentic canons and other *jeux d'esprit*. The two parts combine for long stretches of parallel octaves, they rarely achieve even the most rudimen-tary rhythmic or directional independence, and their harmony consists of little more than the most elementary writing in parallel thirds. This little counterfeit is not nearly as interesting as Mr. Gardner's columns.

John G. Fletcher wrote to suggest that because 1/*f* music lies between white and brown music it should be called tan music. The term "pink" has also been suggested, and actually used by some writers. *Fate* magazine (Oc-tober 1978) ran a full-page advertisement for an LP record album produced by "Master Wilburn Burchette," of Spring Valley, California, titled *Mind Storm*. The ad calls it "fantastic new deep-hypnotic music that uses a phe-nomenon known in acoustical science as 'pink sound' to open the mind to thrilling psychic revelations! This astonishing new music acts something like a crystal ball reflecting back the images projected by the mind. . . . Your spirit will soar as this incredible record album carries you to new heights of psychic awareness!"

Frank Greenberg called my attention to some "mountain music" composed by Sergei Prokofiev for Sergei Eisenstein's film *Alexander Nevsky* in 1938. "Eisenstein provided Prokofiev with still shots of individual scenes of the movie as it was being filmed. Prokofiev then took these scenes and used the silhouette of the landscape and human figures as a pattern for the position of the notes on the staff. He then orchestrated around these notes."

PART VI

PHILOSOPHY

I am convinced that philosophy makes genuine progress, similar in some ways to progress in mathematics, but only in clarifying and elaborating certain basic visions that were all, without exception, expressed by the ancient Greeks. Given the axioms of a formal system, such as Euclidian geometry, we know far more about such geometry than did Euclid. Given the axioms of a philosophical system, it can be elaborated and justified today with far greater subtlety than in the past. But the visions remain the same. As someone has said, modern philosophy is mainly a series of footnotes on the works of Plato.

In my Whys of a Philosophical Scrivener I do my best to defend realism in the sense that the universe is mind-independent, the correspondence theory of truth as opposed to pragmatic theory, a naturalistic ethics as against extreme cultural relativism, and the right to make leaps of faith concerning crucial questions on which it is impossible not to make a decision. Even agnosticism is a decision not to make a decision. Such opinions underlie this section's chapters.

THIRTY-TWO

THE SIGNIFICANCE
OF "NOTHING"

Partly mathematical and partly philosophical, I enjoyed writing about "nothing" as much as any topic for my Mathematical Games column in Scientific American. *This particular column ran in February 1975.*

The logician and philosopher Raymond Smullyan, in The Tao is Silent, *recalls a dream in which a Yogi said: "Lo and Behold! An empty universe!" Smullyan comments:*

"One might, of course, say: 'Well, if the universe is empty, then at least something exists—viz., an empty universe. So perhaps I should modify my poem and say:

> *Lo and Behold!*
> *Not even an empty universe!' "*

Nobody seems to know how to deal with it. (He would, of course.)
—P. L. HEATH

Our topic is nothing. By definition nothing does not exist, but the concepts we have of it certainly exist as concepts. In mathematics, science, philosophy, and everyday life it turns out to be enormously useful to have words and symbols for such concepts.

The closest a mathematician can get to nothing is by way of the null (or empty) set. It is not the same thing as nothing because it has whatever kind of existence a set has, although it is unlike all other sets. It is the only set that has no members and the only set that is a subset of every other set. From a basket of three apples you can take one apple, two apples, three apples, or no apples. To an empty basket you can, if you like, add nothing.

The null set denotes, even though it doesn't denote anything. For example, it denotes such things as the set of all square circles, the set of all even primes other than 2, and the set of all readers of this book who are chimpanzees. In general it denotes the set of all *x*s that satisfy any statement about *x* that is false for all values of *x*. Anything you say about a member of the null set is true, because it lacks a single member for which a statement can be false.

The null set is symbolized by Ø. It must not be confused with 0, the symbol for zero. Zero is (usually) a number that denotes the number of members of Ø. The null set denotes nothing, but 0 denotes the number of members of such sets, for example the set of apples in an empty basket. The set of these nonexisting apples is Ø, but the number of apples is 0.

A way to construct the counting numbers, discovered by the great German logician Gottlob Frege and rediscovered by Bertrand Russell, is to start with the null set and apply a few simple rules and axioms. Zero is defined as the cardinal number of elements in all sets that are equivalent to (can be put in one-to-one correspondence with) the members of the null set. After creating 0, 1 is defined as the number of members in all sets equivalent to the set whose only member is 0. Two is the number of members in all sets equivalent to the set containing 0 and 1. Three is the number of members in all sets equivalent to the set containing 0, 1, 2, and so on. In general, an integer is the number of members in all sets equivalent to the set containing all previous numbers.

There are other ways of recursively constructing numbers by beginning with nothing, each with subtle advantages and disadvantages, in large part psychological. John von Neumann, for example, shortened Frege's procedure by one step. He preferred to define 0 as the null set, 1 as the set whose sole member is the null set, 2 as the set whose members are the null set and 1, and so on.

Some years ago John Horton Conway of the University of Cambridge hit on a remarkable new way to construct numbers that also starts with the null set. He first described his technique in a photocopied typescript of thirteen pages, "All Numbers, Great and Small." It begins: "We wish to construct all numbers. Let us see how those who were good at constructing numbers have approached the problem in the past." It ends with ten open questions, of which the last is: "Is the whole structure of any use?"

Conway explained his new system to Donald E. Knuth, a computer scientist at Stanford University, when they happened to meet at lunch one day in 1972. Knuth was immediately fascinated by its possibilities and its revolutionary content. In 1973 during a week of relaxation in Oslo, Knuth wrote an introduction to Conway's method in the form of a novelette. It was issued in paperback in 1974 by Addison-Wesley, which also publishes Knuth's well-known continuing series titled *The Art of Computer Programming*. I believe it is the only time a major mathematical discovery has been published first in a work of fiction. A later book by Conway, *On Numbers and Games*, opens with an account of his number construction, then goes on to apply the theory to the construction and analysis of two-person games.

Knuth's novelette, *Surreal Numbers*, is subtitled *How Two Ex-Students Turned On to Pure Mathematics and Found Total Happiness*. The book's primary aim, Knuth explains in a postscript, is not so much to teach Conway's theory as "to teach how one might go about developing such a theory." He continues: "Therefore, as the two characters in this book gradually explore and build up Conway's number system, I have recorded their false starts and frustrations as well as their good ideas. I wanted to give a reasonably faithful portrayal of the important principles, techniques, joys, passions, and philosophy of mathematics, so I wrote the story as I was actually doing the research myself."

Knuth's two ex-mathematics students, Alice and Bill (A and B), have fled from the "system" to a haven on the coast of the Indian Ocean. There they unearth a half-buried black rock carved with ancient Hebrew writing. Bill, who knows Hebrew, manages to translate the opening sentence: "In the beginning everything was void, and J. H. W. H. Conway began to create numbers." JHWH is a transliteration of how the ancient Hebrews wrote the name Jehovah. "Conway" also appears without vowels, but it was the most common English name Bill could think of that fitted the consonants.

Translation of the "Conway stone" continues: "Conway said, 'Let there be two rules which bring forth all numbers large and small. This shall be the first rule: Every number corresponds to two sets of previously created numbers, such that no member of the left set is greater than or equal to any member of the right set. And the second rule shall be this: One number is less than or equal to another number if and only if no member of the first number's left set is greater than or equal to the second number, and no member of the second number's right set is less than or equal to the first number.' And Conway examined these two rules he had made, and behold! they were very good."

The stone's text goes on to explain how on the zero day Conway created zero. He did it by placing the null set on the left and also on the right. In symbolic notation $0 = \{\emptyset \mid \emptyset\}$, where the vertical line divides the left and right sets. No member of the left $\emptyset$ is equal to or greater than a member of the right $\emptyset$ because $\emptyset$ *has* no members, so that Conway's first rule is satisfied. Applying the second rule, it is easy to show that 0 is less than or equal to 0.

On the next day, the stone reveals, Conway created the first two nonzero integers, 1 and -1. The method is simply to combine the null set with 0 in the two possible ways: $1 = \{0 \mid \emptyset\}$ and $-1 = \{\emptyset \mid 0\}$. It checks out. Minus

1 is less than but not equal to 0, and 0 is less than but not equal to 1. Now, of course, 1 and −1 and all subsequently created numbers can be plugged back into the left-right formula, and in this way all the integers are constructed. With 0 and 1 forming the left set and Ø on the right, 2 is created. With 0, 1, and 2 on the left and Ø on the right, 3 is created, and so on.

At this point readers might enjoy exploring a bit on their own. Jill C. Knuth's illustration for the front cover of *Surreal Numbers* shows some huge boulders shaped to symbolize {0 | 1}. What number does this define? And can the reader prove that {−1 | 1} = 0?

"Be fruitful and multiply," Conway tells the integers. By combining them, first into finite sets, then into infinite sets, the "copulation" of left-right sets continues, aided by no more than Conway's ridiculously simple rules. Out pour all the rest of the real numbers: first the integral fractions, then the irrationals. At the end of aleph-null days a big bang occurs and the universe springs into being. That, however, is not all. Taken to infinity, Conway's construction produces all of Georg Cantor's transfinite numbers, all infinitesimal numbers (they are reciprocals of infinite numbers), and infinite sets of queer new quantities such as the roots of transfinites and infinitesimals!

It is an astonishing feat of legerdemain. An empty hat rests on a table made of a few axioms of standard set theory. Conway waves two simple rules in the air, then reaches into almost nothing and pulls out an infinitely rich tapestry of numbers that form a real and closed field. Every real number is surrounded by a host of new numbers that lie closer to it than any other "real" value does. The system is truly "surreal."

"Man, that empty set sure gets around!" exclaims Bill. "I think I'll write a book called *Properties of the Empty Set*." This notion that nothing has properties is, of course, commonplace in philosophy, science, and ordinary language. Lewis Carroll's Alice may think it nonsense when the March Hare offers her nonexistent wine, or when the White King admires her ability to see nobody on the road and wonders why nobody did not arrive ahead of the March Hare because nobody goes faster than the hare. It is easy, however, to think of instances in which nothing actually does enter human experience in a positive way.

Consider holes. An old riddle asks how much dirt is in a rectangular hole of certain dimensions. Although the hole has all the properties of a rectangular parallelepiped (corners, edges, faces with areas, volume, and so on), the answer is that there is no dirt in the hole. The various holes of our body are certainly essential to our health, sensory awareness, and pleasure. In *Dorothy and the Wizard in Oz*, the braided man, who lives on Pyramid Mountain in the earth's interior, tells Dorothy how he got there. He had been a manufacturer of holes for Swiss cheese, doughnuts, buttons, porous plasters, and other things. One day he decided to store a vast quantity of adjustable postholes by placing them end to end in the ground, making a deep vertical shaft into which he accidentally tumbled.

The mathematical theory behind Sam Loyd's sliding-block puzzle (15 unit cubes inside a 4-by-4 box) is best explained by regarding the hole as a moving cube. It is analogous to what happens when a gold atom diffuses through lead. Bubbles of nothing in liquids, from the size of a molecule on up, can move around, rotate, collide, and rebound just like things. Negative currents are the result of free electrons jostling one another along a conductor, but holes caused by an absence of free electrons can do the same thing, producing a positive "hole current" that goes the other way.

Lao-tzu writes in chapter 11 of *Tao Tê Ching*:

> *Thirty spokes share the wheel's hub;*
> *It is the center hole that makes it useful.*
> *Shape clay into a vessel;*
> *It is the space within that makes it useful.*
> *Cut doors and windows for a room;*
> *It is the holes which make it useful.*
> *Therefore profit comes from what is there;*
> *Usefulness from what is not there.*

Osborne Reynolds, a British engineer who died in 1912, invented an elaborate theory in which matter consists of microparticles of nothing moving through the ether the way bubbles move through liquids. His two books about the theory, *On an Inversion of Ideas as to the Structure of the Universe* and *The Sub-Mechanics of the Universe*, both published by the Cambridge University Press, were taken so seriously that W. W. Rouse Ball, writing in early editions of his *Mathematical Recreations and Essays*, called the theory "more plausible than the electron hypothesis."

Reynolds's inverted idea is less crazy than it sounds. P. A. M. Dirac, in his famous theory that predicted the existence of antiparticles, viewed the positron (antielectron) as a hole in a continuum of negative charge. When an electron and positron collide, the electron falls into the positron hole, causing both particles to vanish.

The old concept of a "stagnant ether" has been abandoned by physicists, but in its place is not nothing. The "new ether" consists of the metric field responsible for the basic forces of nature, perhaps also for the particles. John Archibald Wheeler proposed a substratum, called superspace, of infinitely many dimensions. Occasionally a portion of it twists in such a peculiar way that it explodes, creating a universe of three spatial dimensions, changing in time, with its own set of laws and within which the field gets tied into little knots that we call "matter." On the microlevel, quantum fluctuations give space a foamlike structure in which the microholes provide space with additional properties. There is still a difference between something and nothing, but it is purely geometrical and there is nothing behind the geometry.

Empty space is like a straight line of zero curvature. Bend the line, add little bumps that ripple back and forth, and you have a universe dancing with matter and energy. Outside the utmost fringes of our expanding cosmos are (perhaps) vast regions unpenetrated by light and gravity. Beyond those regions may be other universes. Shall we say that these empty regions contain nothing, or are they still saturated with a metric of zero curvature?

Greek and medieval thinkers argued about the difference between being and nonbeing, whether there is one world or many, whether a perfect vacuum can properly be said to "exist," whether God formed the world from pure nothing or first created a substratum of matter that was what St. Augustine called *prope nihil*, or close to nothing. Exactly the same questions were and are debated by philosophers and theologians of the East. When the god or gods of an Eastern religion created the world from a great Void, did they shape nothing or something that was almost nothing? The questions may seem quaint, but change the terminology a bit and they are equivalent to present controversies.

There are endless examples from the arts—some jokes, some not—of nothing admired as something. In 1951 Ad Reinhardt, a respected American abstractionist who died in 1967, began painting all-blue and all-red canvases. A few years later he moved to the ultimate—black. His all-black five-by-five-feet pictures were exhibited in 1963 in leading galleries in New York, Paris, Los Angeles, and London. Although one critic called him a charlatan (Ralph F. Colin, "Fakes and Frauds in the Art World," *Art in America*, April 1963), more eminent critics (Hilton Kramer, *The Nation*, June 22, 1963, and Harold Rosenberg, *The New Yorker*, June 15, 1963) admired his black art. An "ultimate statement of esthetic purity," was how Kramer put it (*The New York Times*, October 17, 1976) in praising an exhibit of the black paintings at the Pace Gallery.

In 1965 Reinhardt had three simultaneous shows at top Manhattan galleries: one of all-blacks, one of all-reds, one of all-blues. Prices ranged from $1,500 to $12,000. (See *Newsweek*, March 15, 1965.) For the artist's defense of his black pictures, consult *Americans, 1963*, edited by Dorothy C. Miller (The Museum of Modern Art, New York, 1963), and *Art as Art: The Selected Writings of Ad Reinhardt*, edited by Barbara Rose (Viking, 1975). (I am indebted to Thomas B. Lemann for these references.)

Since black is the absence of light, Reinhardt's black canvases come as close as possible to pictures of nothing, certainly much closer than the all-white canvases of Robert Rauschenberg and others. A *New Yorker* cartoon (September 23, 1944) by R. Taylor showed two ladies at an art exhibit, standing in front of an all-white canvas and reading from the catalogue: "During the Barcelona period he became enamored of the possibilities inherent in virgin space. With a courage born of the most profound respect for the enigma of the imponderable, he produced, at this time, a series of canvases in which there exists solely an expanse of pregnant white."

I know of no piece of "minimal sculpture" that is reduced to the absolute minimum of nothing, though I expect to read any day now that a great museum has purchased such a work for many thousands of dollars. Henry Moore certainly exploited the aesthetics of holes. In 1950 Ray Bradbury received the first annual award of The Elves', Gnomes' and Little Men's Science-Fiction Chowder and Marching Society at a meeting in San Francisco. The award was an invisible little man standing on the brass plate of a polished walnut pedestal. This was not entirely nothing, says my informant, Donald Baker Moore, because there were two black shoe prints on the brass plate to indicate that the little man was actually there.

There have been many plays in which principal characters say nothing. Has anyone ever produced a play or motion picture that consists, from beginning to end, of an empty stage or screen? Some of Andy Warhol's early films come close to it, and I wouldn't be surprised to learn that the limit was actually attained by some early avant-garde playwright.

John Cage's 4'33" is a piano composition that calls for four minutes and thirty-three seconds of total silence as the player sits frozen on the piano stool. The duration of the silence is 273 seconds. This corresponds, Cage has explained, to −273 degrees centigrade, or absolute zero, the temperature at which all molecular motion quietly stops. I have not heard 4'33" performed, but friends who have tell me it is Cage's finest composition.

There are many outstanding instances of nothing in print: Chapters 18 and 19 of the final volume of *Tristram Shandy*, for example. Elbert Hubbard's *Essay on Silence*, containing only blank pages, was bound in brown suede and gold-stamped. I recall as a boy seeing a similar book titled *What I Know about Women*, and a Protestant fundamentalist tract called *What Must You Do to Be Lost? Poème Collectif*, by Robert Filliou, issued in Belgium in 1968, consists of sixteen blank pages.

In 1972 the Honolulu Zoo distributed a definitive monograph called *Snakes of Hawaii: An authoritative, illustrated and complete guide to exotic species indigenous to the 50th State*, by V. Ralph Knight, Jr., B.S. A correspondent, Larry E. Morse, informs me that this entire monograph is reprinted (without credit) in *The Nothing Book*. This volume of blank pages was published in 1974, by Harmony House, in regular and deluxe editions. It sold so well that in 1975 an even more expensive (five dollars) deluxe edition was printed on fine French marble design paper and bound in leather. According to *The Village Voice* (December 30, 1974), Harmony House was threatened with legal action by a European author whose blank-paged book had been published a few years before *The Nothing Book*. He believed his copyright had been infringed, but nothing ever came of it.

Howard Lyons, a Toronto correspondent, points out that the null set has long been a favorite topic of songwriters: "I ain't got nobody," "Nobody loves me," "I've got plenty of nothing," "Nobody lied when they said that I cried over you," "There ain't no sweet gal that's worth the salt of my tears," and hundreds of other lines.

Events can occur in which nothing is as startling as a thunderclap. An old joke tells of a man who slept in a lighthouse under a foghorn that boomed regularly every ten minutes. One night at 3:20 A.M., when the mechanism failed, the man leaped out of bed shouting, "What was that?" As a prank all the members of a large orchestra once stopped playing suddenly in the middle of a strident symphony, causing the conductor to fall off the podium. One afternoon in a rural section of North Dakota, where the wind blew constantly, there was a sudden cessation of wind. All the chickens fell over. A Japanese correspondent tells me that the weather bureau in Japan now issues a "no-wind warning" because an absence of wind can create damaging smog.

There are many examples that are not jokes. An absence of water can cause death. The loss of a loved one, of money, or of a reputation can push someone to suicide. The law recognizes innumerable occasions on which a failure to act is a crime. Grave consequences will follow when a man on a railroad track, in front of an approaching train and unable to decide whether to jump to the left or to the right, makes no decision. In the story "Silver Blaze," Sherlock Holmes based a famous deduction on the "curious incident" of a dog that "did nothing in the night-time."

Moments of escape from the omnipresent sound of canned music are becoming increasingly hard to obtain. Unlike cigar smoke, writes Edmund Morris in a fine essay, "Oases of Silence in a Desert of Din" (*The New York Times*, May 25, 1975), noise can't be fanned away. There is an old joke about a jukebox that offers, for a quarter, to provide three minutes of no music. Drive to the top of Pike's Peak, says Morris, "whose panorama of Colorado inspired Katherine Lee Bates to write 'America the Beautiful,' and your ears will be assailed by the twang and boom of four giant speakers—N, S, E, and W—spraying cowboy tunes into the crystal air." Even the Sistine Chapel is now wired for sound.

"At first," continues Morris, "there is something discomforting, almost frightening, about real silence. . . . You are startled by the apparent loudness of ordinary noises. . . . Gradually your ears become attuned to a delicate web of sounds, inaudible elsewhere, which George Eliot called 'that roar which lies on the other side of silence.'" Morris provides a list of a few Silent Places around the globe where one can escape not only from Muzak but from all the aural pollution that is the by-product of modern technology.

These are all examples of little pockets in which there is an absence of something. What about the monstrous dichotomy between all being—everything there is—and nothing? From the earliest times the most eminent thinkers have meditated on this ultimate split. It seems unlikely that the universe is going to vanish (although I myself once wrote a story, "Oom," about how God, weary of existing, abolished everything, including himself), but the fact that we ourselves will soon vanish is real enough. In medieval times the fear of death was mixed with a fear of eternal suffering, but since the fading of hell (albeit it is now enjoying a renaissance) this fear has been replaced by what Sören Kierkegaard called an "anguish" or "dread" over the possibility of becoming nothing.

This brings us abruptly to what Paul Edwards has called the "superultimate question." "Why," asked Leibniz, Schelling, Schopenhauer, and a hundred other philosophers, "should something exist rather than nothing?"

Obviously it is a curious question, not like any other. Large numbers of people, perhaps the majority, live out their lives without ever considering it. If someone asks them the question, they may fail to understand it and believe the questioner is crazy. Among those who understand the question, there are varied responses. Thinkers of a mystical turn of mind, the late Martin Heidegger for instance, consider it the deepest, most fundamental of all metaphysical questions, and look with contempt on all philosophers who are not equally disturbed by it. Those of a positivistic, pragmatic turn of mind consider it trivial. Since everyone agrees there is no way to answer it empirically or rationally, it is a question without cognitive content, as meaningless as asking if the number 2 is red or green. Indeed, a famous paper by Rudolf Carnap on the meaning of questions heaps scorn on a passage in which Heidegger pontificates about being and nothingness.

A third group of philosophers, including Milton K. Munitz, who wrote an entire book titled *The Mystery of Existence*, regards the question as being meaningful but insists that its significance lies solely in our inability to answer it. It may or may not have an answer, argues Munitz, but in any case the answer lies totally outside the limits of science and philosophy.

Whatever their metaphysics, those who have puzzled most over the superultimate question have left much eloquent testimony about those unexpected moments, fortunately short-lived, in which one is suddenly caught up in an overwhelming awareness of the utter mystery of why anything is. That is the terrifying emotion at the heart of Jean-Paul Sartre's great philosophical novel *Nausea*. Its red-haired protagonist, Antoine Roquentin, is haunted by the superultimate mystery. "A circle is not absurd," he reflects. "It is clearly explained by the rotation of a straight segment around one of its extremities. But neither does a circle exist." Things that do exist, such as stones and trees and himself, exist without any reason. They are just insanely *there*, bloated, obscene, gelatinous, unable not to exist. When the mood is on him, Roquentin calls it "the nausea." William James had earlier called it an "ontological wonder sickness." The monotonous days come and go, all cities look alike, nothing happens that means anything.

G. K. Chesterton is as good an example as any of the theist who, stunned by the absurdity of being, reacts in opposite fashion. Not that shifting to God the responsibility for the world's existence answers the superultimate question; far from it! One immediately wonders why God exists rather than nothing. But although none of the awe is lessened by hanging the universe on a transcendent peg, the shift can give rise to feelings of gratitude and hope that relieve the anxiety. Chesterton's existential novel *Manalive* is a splendid complement to Sartre's *Nausea*. Its protagonist, Innocent Smith, is so exhilarated by the privilege of existing that he goes about inventing whimsical ways of shocking himself into realizing that both he and the world are not nothing.

Let P. L. Heath, who had the first word in this essay, also have the last. "If nothing whatsoever existed," he writes at the end of his article on nothing in *The Encyclopedia of Philosophy*, "there would be no problem and no answer, and the anxieties even of existential philosophers would be permanently laid to rest. Since they are not, there is evidently *nothing to worry about*. But that itself should be enough to keep an existentialist happy. Unless the solution be, as some have suspected, that it is not nothing that has been worrying them, but they who have been worrying it."

POSTSCRIPT

You ain't seen nothin' yet.
—AL JOLSON

The previous essay, when it first appeared in *Scientific American*, prompted many delightful letters on aspects of the topic I had not known about or had failed to mention.

Hester Elliott was the first of several readers who were reminded, by my story of the lighthouse keeper, of what some New Yorkers used to call the "Bowery El phenomenon." After the old elevated on Third Avenue was torn down, police began receiving phone calls from people who lived near the El. They were waking at regular intervals during the night, hearing strange noises, and having strong feelings of foreboding. "The schedules of the absent trains," as Ms. Elliott put it, "reappeared in the form of patterned calls on the police blotters." This is discussed, she said, by Karl Pribram in his book *Languages of the Brain* as an example of how our brain, even during sleep, keeps scanning the flow of events in the light of past expectations. It is aroused by any sharp deviation from the accustomed pattern.

Psychologist Robert B. Glassman also referred in a letter to the El example, and gave others. The human brain, he wrote, has the happy facility of forgetting, of pushing out of consciousness whatever seems irrelevant at the moment. But the irrelevant background is still perceived subliminally, and changes in this background bring it back into consciousness. Russian psychologists, he said, have found that if a human or animal listens long enough to the repeated sound of the same tone, they soon learn to ignore it. But if the same tone is then sounded in a different way, even if sounded more *softly* or more *briefly*, there is instant arousal.

Vernon Rowland, a professor of psychology at Case Western Reserve, elaborated similar points. His letter, which follows, was printed in *Scientific American*, April 1975:

Sirs:

I enjoyed Martin Gardner's essay on "nothing." John Horton Conway's rule and Gardner's analysis of "nothing" are, like all human activity, expressions of the nervous system, the study of which helps in understanding the origins and evolution of "nothing."

The brain is marvelously tuned to detect change as well as constancies in the environment. Sharp change between constancies is a perceptually or intellectually recognizable boundary. "Nothing" is "knowable" with clarity only if it is well demarcated from the "non-nothing." Even if it is vaguely bounded, nothingness cannot be treated as an absolute. This is an example of the illogicality of absolutes, because "nothing" cannot be in awareness except as it is related to (contrasted with) nonnothing.

One can observe in the brains of perceiving animals, even animals as primitive as the frog, special neurons responding specifically to spatial boundaries and to temporal boundaries. In the latter, for instance, neurons called "off" neurons, go into action when "something," say light, becomes "nothing" (darkness). "Nothing" is therefore positively signaled and is thereby endowed with existence. The late Polish neuropsychologist Jerzy Konorski pointed out the possibility that closing the eyes may activate off neurons, giving rise to "seeing" darkness and recognizing it as being different from not seeing at all.

I and others have used temporal nothingness as a food signal for cats by simply imposing 10 seconds of silence in an otherwise continuously clicking environment. Their brains show the learning of the significance of this silence in ways very similar to those for the inverse: 10 seconds of clicking presented on a continuous background of silence. "Nothing" and "something" can be treated in the same way as psychologists deal with other forms of figure-ground or stimulus-context reversal.

The nothingness of which we become aware by specific brain signals can be known only by discriminating it from other brain signals that reveal the boundaries and constancies of existing objects. This requires an act of attention. There is another form of "nothing" that is based on an attentional shift from one sense modality to another (as in the example of listening to music) or to a failure of the attentional mechanism. In certain forms of strokes the person "forgets" one part of his body and acts as if it simply does not exist, for example a man who shaves only one half of his face.

Animate systems obtain and conserve life-supporting energy by evolving mechanisms to offset or counter perturbations in their energy supply. Detecting absences ("nothings") in the energy domain had to be acquired early or survival could not have gone beyond the stage of actually living in the energy supply (protozoa in nutritious pools) rather than near it (animals that can leave the water and return).

If this pragmatic view of the biopsychological origins of "nothing" and "absence" is insufficient for trivializing the Leibnizian question ("Why should something exist rather than nothing?"), I would argue that the philosopher faces the necessity of showing that the statement "Nothing [in the absolute sense] exists" is not a self-contradiction.

The reference to my story "Oom" reminded Ms. Elliott of the following paragraph from Jorge Luis Borges's essay on John Donne's *Biathanatos* (a work which argues that Jesus committed suicide), in *Other Inquisitions, 1937–1952*:

As I reread this essay, I think of the tragic Philipp Batz, who is called Philipp Mainländer in the history of philosophy. Like me, he was an impassioned reader of Schopenhauer, under whose influence (and perhaps under the influence of the Gnostics) he imagined that we are fragments of a God who destroyed Himself at the beginning of time, because He did not wish to exist. Universal history is the obscure agony of those fragments. Mainländer was born in 1841; in 1876 he published his book *Philosophy of the Redemption*. That same year he killed himself.

Is Mainländer one of Borges's invented characters? No, he actually existed. You can read about him and his strange two-volume work in *The Encyclopedia of Philosophy*, Vol. 6, page 119.

Several readers informed me of the amusing controversy among graph theorists over whether the "null-graph" is useful. This is the graph that has no points or edges. The classic reference is a paper by Frank Harary and Ronald C. Read, "Is the Null-Graph a Pointless Concept?" (The paper was given at the Graphs and Combinatorial Conference, at George Washington University, in 1973, and appears in the conference lecture notes, published by Springer-Verlag.)

"Note that it is not a question of whether the null-graph 'exists,' " the authors write. "It is simply a question of whether there is any point in it." The authors survey the literature, give pros and cons, and finally reach no

Figure 1. The null-graph

conclusion. Figure 1, reproduced from their paper, shows what the null-graph looks like.

Wesley Salmon, the philosopher of science, sent a splendid ontological argument for the existence of the null set:

> I have just finished reading, with much pleasure, your column on "nothing." It reminded me of a remark made by a brilliant young philosopher at the University of Toronto, Bas van Fraassen, who, in a lecture on philosophy of mathematics, asked why there might not be a sort of ontological proof for the existence of the null set. It would begin, "By the null set we understand that set than which none emptier can be conceived . . ." Van Fraassen is editor in chief of the *Journal of Philosophical Logic*. I sent him the completion of the argument:
>
> "The fool hath said in his heart that there is no null set. But if that were so, then the set of all such sets would be empty, and hence, it would be the null set. Q.E.D."
>
> I still do not know why he did not publish this profound result.

Frederick Mosteller, a theoretical statistician at Harvard, made the following comments on the superultimate question:

Ever since I was about fourteen years old I have been severely bothered by this question, and by and large not willing to talk to other people about it because the first few times I tried I got rather unexpected responses, mainly rather negative put-downs. It shook me up when it first occurred to me, and has bothered me again and again. I could not understand why it wasn't in the newspapers once a week. I suppose, in a sense, all references to creation are a reflection of this same issue, but it is the simplicity of the question that seems to me so scary.

When I was older I tried it once or twice on physicists and again did not get much of a response—probably talked to the wrong ones. I did mention it to John Tukey once, and he offered a rather good remark. He said something like this: contemplating the question at this time doesn't seem to be producing much information—that is, we aren't making much progress with it—and so it is hard to spend time on it. Perhaps it is not yet a profitable question.

It seems so much more reasonable to me that there should be nothing than something that I have secretly concluded for myself that quite possibly physicists will ultimately prove that, were there a system containing nothing, it would automatically create a physical universe. (Of course, I know they can't quite do this.)

Meditating on the recent flurry of interest in what is called the "anthropic principle" (on this see chapter 5), I suddenly realized that I could answer the superultimate question: Why is there something rather than nothing? Because if there wasn't anything we wouldn't be here to ask the question. I think this points up the essential absurdity of the weak anthropic principle. It's not wrong, but it contributes nothing significant to any philosophical or scientific question. The Danish poet Piet Hein, in one of his "grook" verses, says it this way:

> The universe may
> Be as great as they say,
> But it wouldn't be missed
> If it didn't exist.

Lakenan Barnes, an attorney in Missouri, reminded me that Joshua was the son of Nun (Joshua 1:1), that "love" in tennis means nothing, that the doughnut's hole is the "dough naught." He also passed along a quatrain of his that had appeared in the St. Louis Post-Dispatch (July 7, 1967):

> In the world of math
> That Man has wrought,
> The greatest gain
> Was the thought of naught.

Some readers were mystified by the chapter's epigraph. It is the second sentence of Heath's article on nothing in the *Encyclopedia of Philosophy*. Like Lewis Carroll, in the second *Alice* book, Heath is taking Nobody to be the name of a person. Here is the sentence in the context of Heath's playful opening paragraph:

NOTHING is an awe-inspiring yet essentially undigested concept, highly esteemed by writers of a mystical or existentialist tendency, but by most others regarded with anxiety, nausea, or panic. Nobody seems to know how to deal with it (he would, of course), and plain persons generally are reported to have little difficulty in saying, seeing, hearing, and doing nothing. Philosophers, however, have never felt easy on the matter. Ever since Parmenides laid it down that it is impossible to speak of what is not, broke his own rule in the act of stating it, and deduced himself into a world where all that ever happened was nothing, the impression has persisted that the narrow path between sense and nonsense on this subject is a difficult one to tread and that altogether the less said of it the better.

THIRTY-THREE

NEWCOMB'S PARADOX

One of the most hotly debated paradoxes in the field of decision theory is called Newcomb's paradox after physicist William Newcomb who invented it. It involves a hypothetical Being capable of accurately predicting which of two boxes you will choose to maximize the probability of obtaining the largest amount of money. The problem seems closely related to the question of whether humans possess a genuine power to make free, unpredictable choices.

When this essay first appeared in Scientific American *(July 1973) it generated more mail than any other column I wrote for that magazine. Indeed, it aroused so much controversy that I asked philosopher Robert Nozick, who had been the first to write about the paradox, to contribute a guest column on his reaction to the flood of letters. Published in March 1974, it is reprinted in my* Knotted Doughnuts and Other Mathematical Entertainments *(1986). Nozick concluded that the paradox has yet to be resolved.*

Since Nozick and I discussed Newcomb's paradox, some fifty papers about it have been published expressing wild disagreements over how to handle the problem. You'll find a partial bibliography at the close of the column's reprinting in Knotted Doughnuts. *More recent references include sections in two books by Roy Sorenson,* Blind Spots *(1988) and* Thought Experiments *(1992);* Labyrinths of Reason *(1988), by William Poundstone; Mark Sainsbury,* Paradoxes *(1988); and John Broome's "An Economic Newcomb Problem" in* Analysis *(October 1989).*

A common opinion prevails that the juice has ages ago been pressed out of the free-will controversy, and that no new champion can do more than warm up stale arguments which every one has heard. This is a radical mistake. I know of no subject less worn out, or in which inventive genius has a better chance of breaking open new ground.

—WILLIAM JAMES

One of the perennial problems of philosophy is how to explain (or explain away) the nature of free will. If the concept is explicated within a framework of determinism, the will ceases to be free in any commonly understood sense, and it is hard to see how fatalism can be avoided. *Che sarà, sarà.* Why work hard for a better future for yourself or for others if what you do must always be what you do do? And how can you blame anyone for anything if he could not have done otherwise?

On the other hand, attempts to explicate will in a framework of indeterminism seem equally futile. If an action is not caused by the previous states of oneself and the world, it is hard to see how to keep the action from being haphazard. The notion that decisions are made by some kind of randomizer in the mind does not provide much support for what is meant by free will either.

Philosophers have never agreed on how to avoid the horns of this dilemma. Even within a particular school there have been sharp disagreements. William James and John Dewey, America's two leading pragmatists, are a case in point. Although Dewey was a valiant defender of democratic freedoms, his metaphysics regarded human behavior as completely determined by what James called the total "push of the past." Free will for Dewey was as illusory as it is in the psychology of B. F. Skinner. In contrast, James was a thoroughgoing indeterminist. He believed that minds had the power to inject genuine novelty into history—that not even God himself could know the future except partially. *"That,"* he wrote, "is what gives the palpitating reality to our moral life and makes it tingle . . . with so strange and elaborate an excitement."

A third approach, pursued in depth by Immanuel Kant, accepts both sides of the controversy as being equally true but incommensurable ways of viewing human behavior. For Kant the situation is something like that pictured in one of Piet Hein's "grooks":

> *A bit beyond perception's reach*
> *I sometimes believe I see*
> *That Life is two locked boxes, each*
> *Containing the other's key.*

Free will is neither fate nor chance. In some unfathomable way it partakes of both. Each is the key to the other. It is not a contradictory concept, like a square triangle, but a paradox that our experience forces on us and whose resolution transcends human thought. That was how Niels Bohr saw it. He found the situation similar to his "principle of complementarity" in quantum mechanics. It is a viewpoint that Einstein, a Spinozist, found distasteful, but many other physicists, J. Robert Oppenheimer for one, found Bohr's viewpoint enormously attractive.

What has free will to do with mathematical games? The answer is that in recent decades philosophers of science have been wrestling with a variety of queer "prediction paradoxes" related to the problem of will. Some of them are best regarded as a game situation. One draws a payoff matrix and tries to determine a player's best strategy, only to find oneself trapped in a maze of bewildering ambiguities about time and causality.

A marvelous example of such a paradox came to light in 1970 in the paper "Newcomb's Problem and Two Principles of Choice" by Robert Nozick, a philosopher at Harvard University. The paradox is so profound, so amusing, so mind-bending, with thinkers so evenly divided into warring camps, that it bids fair to produce a literature vaster than that dealing with the prediction paradox of the unexpected hanging. (See chapter 1 of my *Unexpected Hanging and Other Mathematical Diversions*.)

Newcomb's paradox is named after its originator, William A. Newcomb, a theoretical physicist at the University of California's Lawrence Livermore Laboratory. (His great-grandfather was the brother of Simon Newcomb, the astronomer.) Newcomb thought of the problem in 1960 while meditating on a famous paradox of game theory called the prisoner's dilemma. A few years later Newcomb's problem reached Nozick by way of their mutual friend Martin David Kruskal, a Princeton University mathematician. "It is not clear that I am entitled to present this paper," Nozick writes. "It is a beautiful problem. I wish it were mine." Although Nozick could not resolve it, he decided to write it up anyway. His paper appears in *Essays in Honor of Carl G. Hempel*, edited by Nicholas Rescher and published by Humanities Press in 1970. What follows is largely a paraphrase of Nozick's paper.

Two closed boxes, B1 and B2, are on a table. B1 contains $1,000. B2 contains either nothing or $1 million. You do not know which. You have an irrevocable choice between two actions:

1. Take what is in both boxes.

2. Take only what is in B2.

At some time before the test a superior Being has made a prediction about what you will decide. It is not necessary to assume determinism. You only need be persuaded that the Being's predictions are "almost certainly" correct. If you like, you can think of the Being as God, but the paradox is just as strong if you regard the Being as a superior intelligence from another planet, or a supercomputer capable of probing your brain and making highly accurate predictions about your decisions. If the Being expects you to choose both boxes, he has left B2 empty. If he expects you to take only B2, he has put $1 million in it. (If he expects you to randomize your choice by, say, flipping a coin, he has left B2 empty.) In all cases B1 contains $1,000. You understand the situation fully, the Being knows you understand, you know that he knows and so on.

What should you do? Clearly it is not to your advantage to flip a coin, so that you must decide on your own. The paradox lies in the disturbing fact that a strong argument can be made for either decision. Both arguments cannot be right. The problem is to explain why one is wrong.

Let us look first at the argument for taking only B2. You believe the Being is an excellent predictor. If you take both boxes, the Being almost certainly will have anticipated your action and have left B2 empty. You will get only the $1,000 in B1. Contrariwise, if you take only B2, the Being, expecting that, almost certainly will have placed $1 million in it. Clearly it is to your advantage to take only B2.

Convincing? Yes, but the Being made his prediction, say a week ago, and then left. Either he put the $1 million in B2, or he did not. "If the money is already there, it will stay there whatever you choose. It is not going to disappear. If it is not already there, it is not going to suddenly appear if you choose only what is in the second box." It is assumed that no "backward causality" is operating; that is, your present actions cannot influence what the Being did last week. So why not take both boxes and get everything that is there? If B2 is filled, you get $1,001,000. If it is empty, you get at least $1,000. If you are so foolish as to take only B2, you know you cannot get more than $1 million, and there is even a slight possibility of getting nothing. Clearly it is to your advantage to take both boxes!

"I have put this problem to a large number of people, both friends and students in class," writes Nozick. "To almost everyone it is perfectly clear and obvious what should be done. The difficulty is that these people seem to divide almost evenly on the problem, with large numbers thinking that the opposing half is just being silly.

"Given two such compelling opposing arguments, it will not do to rest content with one's belief that one knows what to do. Nor will it do to just repeat one of the arguments, loudly and slowly. One must also disarm the opposing argument; explain away its force while showing it due respect."

Nozick sharpens the "pull" of the two arguments as follows. Suppose the experiment had been done many times before. In every case the Being predicted correctly. Those who took both boxes always got only $1,000; those who took only B2 got $1 million. You have no reason to suppose your case will be different. If a friend were observing the scene, it would be completely rational for him to bet, giving high odds, that if you take both boxes you will get only $1,000. Indeed, if there is a time delay after your choice of both boxes, you know it would be rational for you yourself to bet, offering high odds, that you will get only $1,000. Knowing this, would you not be a fool to take both boxes?

Alas, the other argument makes you out to be just as big a fool if you do

BEING

	MOVE 1 (PREDICTS YOU TAKE ONLY BOX 2)	MOVE 2 (PREDICTS YOU TAKE BOTH BOXES)
MOVE 1 (TAKE ONLY BOX 2)	$1,000,000	$0
MOVE 2 (TAKE BOTH BOXES)	$1,001,000	$1,000

(YOU)

Figure 1. Payoff matrix for Newcomb's paradox

not. Assume that B1 is transparent. You see the $1,000 inside. You cannot see into B2, but the far side is transparent and your friend is sitting opposite. He knows whether the box is empty or contains $1 million. Although he says nothing, you realize that, whatever the state of B2 is, he wants you to take both boxes. He wants you to because, regardless of the state of B2, you are sure to come out ahead by $1,000. Why not take advantage of the fact that the Being played first and cannot alter his move?

Nozick, an expert on decision theory, approaches the paradox by considering analogous game situations in which, as here, there is a conflict between two respected principles of choice: the "expected-utility principle" and the "dominance principle." To see how the principles apply, consider the payoff matrix for Newcomb's game [see Figure 1]. The argument for taking only B2 derives from the principle that you should choose so as to maximize the expected utility (value to you) of the outcome. Game theory calculates the expected utility of each action by multiplying each of its mutually exclusive outcomes by the probability of the outcome, given the action. We have assumed that the Being predicts with near certainty, but let us be conservative and make the probability a mere .9. The expected utility of taking both boxes is

$$(.1 \times \$1,001,000) + (.9 \times \$1,000) = \$101,000.$$

The expected utility of taking only B2 is

$$(.9 \times \$1,000,000) + (.1 \times \$0) = \$900,000.$$

Guided by this principle, your best strategy is to take only the second box.

The dominance principle, however, is just as intuitively sound. Suppose the world divided into n different states. For each state k mutually exclusive actions are open to you. If in at least one state you are better off choosing *a*, and in all other states either *a* is the best choice or the choices are equal, then the dominance principle asserts that you should choose *a*. Look again at the payoff matrix. The states are the outcomes of the Being's two moves. Taking both boxes is strongly dominant. For each state it gives you $1,000 more than you would get by taking only the second box.

That is as far as we can go into Nozick's analysis, but interested readers should look it up for its mind-boggling conflict situations related to Newcomb's problem. Nozick finally arrives at the following tentative conclusions:

If you believe in absolute determinism and that the Being has in truth predicted your behavior with unswerving accuracy, you should "choose" (whatever that can mean!) to take only B2. For example, suppose the Being is God and you are a devout Calvinist, convinced that God knows every detail of your future. Or assume that the Being has a time-traveling device he can launch into the future and bring back with a motion picture of what you did on that future occasion when you made your choice. Believing that, you should take only B2, firmly persuaded that your feeling of having made a genuine choice is sheer illusion.

Nozick reminds us, however, that Newcomb's paradox does *not* assume that the Being has perfect predictive power. If you believe that you possess a tiny bit of free will (or alternatively that the Being is sometimes wrong, say once in every 20 billion cases), then this may be one of the times the Being has erred. Your wisest decision is to take both boxes.

Nozick is not happy with this conclusion. "Could the difference between one in *n* and none in *n*, for arbitrarily large finite *n*, make this difference? And how exactly does the fact that the predictor is certain to have been correct dissolve the force of the dominance argument?" Both questions are left unanswered. Nozick hopes that publishing the problem "may call forth a solution which will enable me to stop returning, periodically, to it."

One such solution, "to restore [Nozick's] peace of mind," was attempted by Maya Bar-Hillel and Avishai Margalit, of Hebrew University in Jerusalem, in their paper "Newcomb's Paradox Revisited." They adopt the same game-theory approach taken by Nozick, but they come to an opposite conclusion. Even though the Being is not a perfect predictor, they recommend taking only the second box. You must, they argue, resign yourself to the fact that your best strategy is to behave *as if* the Being has made a correct prediction, even though you know there is a slight chance he has erred. You know he has played before you, but you cannot do better than to play as if he is going to play after you. "For you cannot outwit the Being except by knowing what he predicted, but you cannot know, or even meaningfully guess, at what he predicted before actually making your final choice."

It may seem to you, Bar-Hillel and Margalit write, that backward causality is operating—that somehow your choice makes the $1 million more likely to be in the second box—but this is pure flim-flam. You choose only B2 "because it is inductively known to correlate remarkably with the existence of this sum in the box, and though we do not assume a causal relationship, there is no better alternative strategy than to behave as if the relationship was, in fact, causal."

For those who argue for taking only B2 on the grounds that causality is independent of the direction of time—that your decision actually "causes" the second box to be either empty or filled with $1 million—Newcomb proposed the following variant of his paradox. Both boxes are transparent. B1 contains the usual $1,000. B2 contains a piece of paper with a fairly large integer written on it. You do not know whether the number is prime or composite. If it proves to be prime (you must not test it, of course, until after you have made your choice), then you get $1 million. The Being has chosen a prime number if he predicts you will take only B2 but has picked a composite number if he predicts you will take both boxes.

Obviously you cannot by an act of will make the large number change from prime to composite, or vice versa. The nature of the number is fixed for eternity. So why not take both boxes? If it is prime, you get $1,001,000. If it is not, you get at least $1,000. (Instead of a number, B2 could contain any statement of a decidable mathematical fact that you do not investigate until after your choice.)

It is easy to think of other variations. For example, there are one hundred little boxes, each holding a $10 bill. If the Being expects you to take all of them, he has put nothing else in them. But if he expects you to take only one box—perhaps you pick it at random—he has added to that box a large diamond. There have been thousands of previous tests, half of them involving you as a player. Each time, with possibly a few exceptions, the player who took a single box got the diamond, and the player who took all the boxes got only the money. Acting pragmatically, on the basis of past experience, you should take only one box. But then how can you refute the logic of the argument that says you have everything to gain and nothing to lose if the next time you play you take all the boxes?

These variants add nothing essentially new. With reference to the original version, Nozick halfheartedly recommends taking both boxes. Bar-Hillel and Margalit strongly urge you to "join the millionaire's club" by taking only B2. That is also the view of Kruskal and Newcomb. But has either side really done more than just repeat its case "loudly and slowly"? Can it be that Newcomb's paradox validates free will by invalidating the possibility, in principle, of a predictor capable of guessing a person's choice between two equally rational actions with better than 50 percent accuracy?

POSTSCRIPT

Although the growing literature on Newcomb's problem proves that philosophers are still far from agreement on how to handle it, let me set down some tentative personal views.

My sympathies are with those who say the prediction cannot be valid. Even if strict determinism in some sense holds for every event in the history of the universe, I believe that certain events are in principle unpredictable when predictions are allowed to interact causally with the event being predicted. We have here, I am persuaded, something analogous to the resolution of semantic paradoxes. Contradictions arise whenever a language is allowed to talk about the truth or falsity of its own statements, or when sets are allowed to be members of themselves. We can escape the semantic paradoxes by permitting talk about the truth of a sentence only in a metalanguage. "This sentence is false" simply is not a sentence. Bertrand Russell's notorious paradox of the barber who shaves every person and only those persons who do not shave themselves, and who himself belongs to the set of persons, is a barber who cannot exist. It is not logically inconsistent to suppose that the future is totally determined, whether or not an omniscient God exists, but as soon as we permit a superbeing to make predictions that interact with the event being predicted, we encounter contradictions that render the validity of such a prediction impossible.

Consider the simplest case. A superbeing knows that when you go to bed next Thursday you will take off your shoes. If the superbeing keeps this knowledge from you, there is no problem; but if the superbeing informs you of the prediction, you can falsify it easily by going to bed with your shoes on. At this point we touch the mystery of free will, about which I have a chapter in my *Whys of a Philosophical Scrivener* (Morrow, 1983). I agree with those who say that Newcomb's problem in no way settles the question of whether the future is completely determined, but I do maintain that it brings us face to face with the eternal, and to me unanswerable, problem of defining what is meant by free choice.

Although I don't believe it, the state of the world a hundred years from now may be determined in every detail by the state of the world now. Innumerable future events obviously can be predicted with almost certain accuracy, but other events are the outcome of such complex causes that even if determinism is true it seems likely there is no possible way they could be predicted by any technique faster than allowing the universe itself to unroll to see what happens. (We leave aside the notion of a God outside of time who sees the past and future simultaneously, whatever that means.) All this is by the way. The main point is that when a prediction interacts with the predicted event, whether human wills are involved or not, logical contradictions can arise. A familiar example is the supercomputer asked to predict if a certain event will occur in the next three minutes. If the prediction is no, it turns on a green light. If yes, it turns on a red light. The computer is now asked to predict whether the green light will go on. By making the event part of the prediction, the computer is rendered logically impotent. (See my variation of this paradox in chapter 23.)

It is my view that Newcomb's predictor, even if accurate only 51 percent of the time, forces a logical contradiction that makes such a prediction, like Russell's barber, impossible. We can avoid contradictions arising from two different "shoulds" (should you take one or two boxes?) by stating the contradiction as follows. One flawless argument implies that the best way to maximize your reward is to take only the closed box. Another flawless argument implies that the best way to maximize your reward is to take both boxes. Because the two conclusions are contradictory, the prediction cannot be even probably valid. Faced with a Newcomb decision, I would share the suspicions of Max Black and others that I was either the victim of a hoax or of a badly controlled experiment that had yielded false data about the predictor's accuracy. On this assumption, I would take both boxes.

But, you may ask, how would I decide if I made what I would regard as a counterfactual posit that the prediction was what it claimed to be? I suppose if I could persuade myself that the prediction was sound I might take only the closed box even though it would be logically irrational. But I cannot so persuade myself. It is as if someone asked me to put 91 eggs in 13 boxes, so each box held seven eggs, and then added that an experiment had proved that 91 is prime. On that assumption, one or more eggs would be left over. I would be given a million dollars for each leftover egg, and 10 cents if there were none. Unable to believe that 91 is a prime, I would proceed to put seven eggs in each box, take my 10 cents and not worry about having made a bad decision.

THIRTY-FOUR

IS "REALISM"
A DIRTY WORD?

Whenever I try to defend the claim that stars exist when no one is observing them, I feel as if I am trying to convince a child that his teddy bear exists when it is in a closet. For a more extended defense of commonsense realism see "The World: Why I Am Not a Solipsist," the first chapter of my Whys of a Philosophical Scrivener *(1983). The following mini-essay was a guest editorial in the* American Journal of Physics *(March 1989).*

Every now and then a philosopher is smitten with incredible hubris. "Man is the measure of all things" was how Protagoras vaguely put it. For some metaphysicians, mostly in Germany, hubris mounted to such heights that they imagined the very existence of the universe depended on human minds. Only our shifting perceptions are real. If we cease to exist, presumably the universe would dissolve into structureless fog, perhaps cease to exist altogether, perhaps never to have existed. Laws of science and mathematics, the structures of fields and their particles, are not "out there." They are free creations of the human spirit.

Instead of seeing our brains as feeble, short-lived ensembles of atoms dancing to universal rules, this curious view sees our brains as actually inventing physical laws—in a sense, constructing the universe. J. J. Thomson did not discover the electron. He invented it. Einstein did not discover the laws of relativity, he fabricated them. The fact that such fabrications are so successful in explaining past observations and predicting future ones strikes a cultural solipsist as uncanny, inscrutable magic. "The Unreasonable Effectiveness of Mathematics" was the title of Eugene Wigner's best-known essay.

Now there is nothing unusual about philosophers holding such opinions because no view is so bizarre that some metaphysician hasn't defended it. The astonishing thing is that in more recent years a few working physicists have abandoned the realism of Newton and Einstein. "The purpose of this article is to refute the fallacy that reality exists outside of us," writes British physicist Paul Davies in his contribution to *The Encyclopedia of Delusions*. The theme of astrophysicist Bruce Gregory's *Inventing Reality: Physics as a Language* is accurately described on the book's flap: "Physicists do not discover *the* physical world, they invent *a* physical world . . . as the poet Muriel Rukeyser puts it, 'The universe is made of stories, not of atoms.' "

For decades, John Wheeler has been telling us that sentient life exists nowhere in the universe except on little old Earth; that if the universe had not been structured so as to allow itself to be observed by us, it would have only the palest sort of reality. "Quantum mechanics," he asserts, "demolishes the view that the universe exists out there." Frank Wilczek, reviewing a book honoring Wheeler (*Science*, October 28, 1988) diplomatically comments on this remark: "The importance of Wheeler's technical contributions to physics gives his statements a weight that, coming from another source, they would not have."

It is a short step from Wheeler's social solipsism to the notion that science is not a progressively better understanding of eternal laws, but a cultural creation like music and art. Competing scientific theories are "incommensurable," varying from place to place and time to time like fashions in clothes. You can no more say one is true and the others false than you can say one nation's traffic laws are superior to those of another. It is a view held mainly by social scientists, unable to escape from cultural relativism, who look for support to historian Thomas Kuhn and philosopher Paul Feyerabend.

Physicists influenced by New Age nonsense, and by what they fancy certain Eastern religions say, find the strongest support for antirealism in the "measurement problem" of quantum mechanics. A particle's property seems not to be out there until the particle interacts with a measuring apparatus that collapses its wave packet and allows the property to become "definite." Because all material things, including measuring devices, are ensembles of particles, it seems to follow that they too are not there until someone observes them.

"To be is to be perceived," said George Berkeley, but the canny Irish bishop generously restored the external world by allowing God to observe it. Cultural solipsists, unwilling to call on God, are left with what Wheeler calls a "participatory universe"—one whose reality depends on our cooperation in experiencing it.

Does it follow from the fact that an electron is not there until observed that the universe is not there until observed? It does not. There is nothing new about the fact that many things that seem to be out there are not. The image in a mirror is not behind the mirror, as baby chimps suppose. No two persons in front of a looking glass see the same reflection. A mirror does not look like anything in an empty room. It does not follow that a well-defined structure of room, mirror, and bouncing light rays is not there. A rainbow is observer-dependent. No two people see the same bow. No arc of colors is out there. It does not follow that a well-defined structure of Sun, sunlight, and raindrops is not there. Moreover, neither rainbow nor mirror images require human observation. Unmanned cameras photograph them admirably.

It is true that an electron is somehow—no one knows exactly how—not there until measured even though the measurer can be a mindless machine. It does not follow that the macroscopic records of measuring instruments are not there, as Wigner and some parapsychologists maintain, until a human mind sees them. It does not follow that quantum fields, interacting in enormously complex ways, are not there. Because the sound of a falling tree is a sensation in your brain, it does not follow that the tree and the compression waves are inside your brain. Quantum mechanics raises not a single fresh metaphysical problem. It has nothing to say about such ancient unanswerable questions as whether the universe was created or exploded all by itself, whether it would go on running if all minds vanished, or why quantum fields exist rather than nothing.

If you are compelled to think, for emotional reasons or because some guru said so, that you are essential to the universe, that the Moon would not be there without minds to see it (the mind of a mouse? Einstein liked to ask), you are welcome to such self-centered insanity. Don't imagine that it follows from quantum mechanics.

Realism is not a dirty word. If you wonder why all scientists, philosophers, and ordinary people, with rare exceptions, have been and are unabashed realists, let me tell you why. No scientific conjecture has been more overwhelmingly confirmed. No hypothesis offers a simpler explanation of why the Andromeda galaxy spirals in every photograph, why all electrons are identical, why the laws of physics are the same in Tokyo as in London or on Mars, why they were there before life evolved and will be there if all life perishes, why all persons can close their eyes and feel eight corners, six faces, and twelve edges on a cube, and why your bedroom looks the same as it did yesterday when you wake up in the morning.

POSTSCRIPT

Art Hobson, in *Physics and Society* (July 1989), referred to my editorial on realism and accused me of failing to understand how odd quantum mechanics is. This prompted my following letter, and Hobson's reply, in the periodical's October 1989, issue:

Holy smoke! Whatever gave you the notion that I don't think quantum mechanics is weird? I won a prize a few years ago for an article in *Discover* titled "Quantum Weirdness" (reprinted here as chapter 3), and I have written about the mystery of the EPR (which suggests an interconnectedness on a superluminal level) in half a dozen places. I agree with Feynman that QM is crazy, and I certainly regard it as a much more fundamental break with classical physics than relativity theory.

You have totally missed the point of my editorial. It is that quantum weirdness does not justify a leap to the views of Wheeler and Wigner that the reality and mathematical structure of the external world is mind-dependent. The Schrödinger equation, as you know, changes in a completely deterministic way. It is only when measurement occurs that chance enters the picture, but it does not follow from this fact that the external world does not exist and have a structure independent of observation. It is *this* metaphysical solipsism my editorial attacked, and I would guess that 99 percent of working physicists agree with me. I even received a letter from Glashow saying he couldn't comprehend how anyone could find fault with my editorial, just as I have nothing in *your* comment to oppose.

Please, don't accuse me again of views I don't hold!

Hobson's response:

The quotation marks around "not odd at all" in reference to Gardner's article were meant to indicate the article's general attitude toward quantum theory, rather than an actual quotation from the article. The quotation marks were thus misleading, and I apologize for that.

On the other hand, the drift that I get from carefully re-reading this particular essay of Gardner's is still that quantum theory is not odd at all. Maybe I am reading too much into such statements as (and here I do quote) "Quantum mechanics raises not a single fresh metaphysical problem." At any rate, I thank Gardner for the above clarification of his views.

My second letter about this, and Hobson's response, ran in the January 1990, issue:

Thanks for running my letter.

When relativity was new, many physicists who had little background in philosophy wrote carelessly about how relativity theory introduced fresh insights into metaphysical questions—how it supported determinism, abandoned the correspondence theory of truth, led to all sorts of relativisms, etc., but it soon turned out that relativity raised no fresh metaphysical problems. The same thing is happening all over again with QM, perhaps starting with the claim (Eddington, Compton, etc.) that QM supports free will. My own view, which I am prepared to defend, is that the nature of science and metaphysics (as Carnap said, there is no bridge between these two continents) is such that science cannot solve *any* metaphysical problem, let alone raise new ones.

When I say that QM has not raised a single fresh metaphysical problem, we must have a common understanding of two key words: "fresh" and "metaphysical."

By fresh I mean new. By metaphysics I mean problems that by definition are beyond the reach of empirical physics. This is how the word is used by all modern philosophers of science: Russell, Carnap, Popper, Reichenbach, Hempel, to mention a few. In Carnap's often-used phrase, metaphysics has no "cognitive content."

"Philosophy of Science" is a different matter altogether. Carnap rejected all metaphysics as meaningless, but he wrote a book (on which I collaborated) called *Introduction to the Philosophy of Science*. Now obviously relativity and QM have made significant contributions to the philosophy of science. As I stressed in my *Relativity Explosion*, it was relativity theory that made clear that determining the structure of space-time was an *empirical* question (in contrast to Kant's views). And QM did indeed make clear that physical laws can rest on a basic indeterminism.

None of this raises a fresh metaphysical problem. For example, the question of whether the future is completely determined by the present, or whether elements of pure chance underlie "being" is one of the oldest questions in philosophy. It was constantly debated by the ancients and the medievals. The Greek atomists injected randomness into the basic structure of the universe by introducing a random "swerving" of particles on a level too small to be seen. Lucretius has a beautiful metaphor for this. He speaks of a flock of sheep moving about at random on a hill. But to a distant viewer, they appear as a white spot that is motionless. Jumping to more recent times, Charles Peirce, America's greatest philosopher, firmly believed (before QM) that pure chance was an element in the evolution of the cosmos. He called his view "tychism." It had a major influence on William James. Note also that this old metaphysical question is far from settled today. Many QM experts, Bohm for example, believe (with Einstein) that QM is incomplete and that when a deeper level is discovered, determinism will be restored. And if one accepts (I don't) the many-worlds interpretation of QM, strict determinism *is* restored. Thus, the indeterminism of QM is certainly not a "fresh metaphysical question."

Consider another ancient metaphysical debate. Did the universe have an infinite past, or was it created by a transcendent deity, or did it pop into existence, all by itself, from nothing? Again, this was endlessly debated by the ancients and medievals. QM has shed *no* light on this question. There is speculation that the universe started with a random quantum fluctuation in the false vacuum, but this vacuum has nothing to do with metaphysical "nothing." The fluctuation presupposes quantum fields and laws, and laws of probability. So the question is simply pushed down to a deeper level, but the problem of why there is something rather than nothing is as opaque as ever.

Finally, take the question of whether the tree exists when no one observes it. QM has indeed introduced a tinge of solipsism into the measurement problem, which is far from completely understood, but it certainly hasn't introduced a "fresh metaphysical question." One of Wigner's famous essays, in which he wonders about the persistence of a tree when no one sees it, never mentions Bishop Berkeley!

Hobson:

OK, I can agree that quantum mechanics raises no metaphysical problems that have not been raised at some point in the history of human thought. But most of us tend to frame the question in the more limited context of the history of scientific thought (i.e. not Bishop Berkeley) since Copernicus (i.e. not Lucretius, either). Relative to post-Copernican scientific thought, quantum mechanics does indeed raise fresh questions about determinism versus free will, the existence of a purely objective reality, and other matters. Quantum mechanics, or any other scientific theory, should not be expected to answer such metaphysical ("beyond physics") questions, but it does throw them into a fresh perspective, and I think this fresh perspective is important.

I have no argument with Hobson's comments.

THIRTY-FIVE

THE MYSTERY OF FREE WILL

Free will, in my opinion, is another name for self-awareness or consciousness. I cannot conceive of having one without the other. My "solution" to the problem of distinguishing free will from determinism and haphazardry is the same as Kant's—we are incapable of knowing the solution.

Dismissing free will as a profound, impenetrable mystery is an unpopular view among today's secular thinkers, although a few defend it, notably Thomas Nagel, Colin McGinn, Jerry Fodor, and linguist Noam Chomsky. We belong to a group that has been called the "mysterians" by reductionists who see no conflict between determinism and free will. What follows is a chapter from my Whys of a Philosophical Scrivener.

"There is a lot to be said for destiny," said Jorkens, "but you can't ignore free will."
"What do you mean?" said one of the philosophers.
—LORD DUNSANY, *Jorkens Consults a Prophet*

We all know what destiny is, but what do we mean by free will?

A famous section at the close of Ludwig Wittgenstein's *Tractatus Logico-Philosophicus* asserts that when an answer cannot be put into words, neither can the question; that if a question can be framed at all, it is possible to answer it; and that what we cannot speak about we should consign to silence.

The thesis of this chapter, although extremely simple and therefore annoying to most contemporary thinkers, is that the free-will problem cannot be solved because we do not know exactly how to put the question. I do not mean that the question is meaningless, unless one adopts an empiricist's narrow definition of what "meaning" means. Many questions in philosophy are not meaningless in a wide sense, yet are unanswerable nonetheless. Why is there something rather than nothing? What is space? What is time? We have ways to measure time, but no way to explain it without introducing the notion of change, which presupposes time.

Is there anyone without an intense intuitive belief that his or her will is free? "Sir, we *know* our will is free," said Samuel Johnson, "and *there's* an end on't."[1] Just about everyone feels the same. We *must* believe in free will, someone has quipped—we have no choice in the matter. Who considers himself an automaton, like Tik-Tok of Oz, who does only what he is wound up to do—or, in today's computer language, what he is programmed to do? We all know in our bones what L. Frank Baum meant when he said that Tik-Tok could think, speak, act, and do everything but live. Yet when we try to put it into words, to define human consciousness and its incredible ability to make free choices, we come up against one of Immanuel Kant's most notorious antinomies. Our attempt to capture the essence of that freedom either slides off into determinism, another name for destiny, or it tumbles over to the side of pure caprice. Neither definition gives us what we desperately want *free will* to mean.

William James, in his essay on "The Dilemma of Determinism," tried to persuade readers that determinism forces one into a dilemma, both horns of which are abominable. Although I share the sentiments of James's impassioned attack, his essay sidesteps the deeper dilemma, the Kantian dilemma which James himself recognized in other writings but failed to bring out in his celebrated essay. This deeper dilemma is the dilemma of will itself. When we try to define it within a context of determinism it becomes a delusion, something we think we have but really don't. When we try to define it within a context of indeterminism it becomes equally delusory, a choice made by some obscure randomizer in the brain which functions like the flip of a coin. It is here, I am convinced, that we run into a transcendent mystery—a mystery bound up, how we do not know, with the transcendent mystery of time.

A free-will act cannot be fully predetermined. Nor can it be the outcome of pure chance. Somehow it is both. Somehow it is neither. The question, as H. L. Mencken once put it, "is dark, puzzling, and not a little terrifying."[2] My own view, which is Kant's, is that there is no way to go between the horns. The best we can do (we who are not gods) is, Kant wrote, comprehend its incomprehensibility. As we now know, some mathematical problems can be "solved" only by showing them to be unsolvable. I believe this is also true of many, if not most, of the great traditional questions of philosophy. In what follows I shall try to convince you that the only solution to the problem of free will is to admit that we cannot know the solution. I do not mean it has *no* solution; only that if it has one, you and I cannot know it. We do not even know exactly how to put the question. Maybe God knows. Maybe God doesn't. Whereof one cannot speak, one had best keep silent.

Let us start our metaphysical excursion by considering the case for determinism with respect to human actions. We know that the human body, including its brain, is an incredibly complex organization of molecules. It is part of nature and subject to nature's laws. As a thought experiment, imagine a superbeing, perhaps a god, who knows all the laws of the universe and is capable of obtaining complete information about both a person's brain and the environment with which that person interacts. The determinist thesis is that such a being could in principle predict, under all circumstances, how the person would behave.

We must assume that our hypothetical predictor is not interacting with the person; otherwise we get into contradictions that have been explored in many recent papers dealing with what are called prediction paradoxes. Obviously if a predictor tells you that you will take a bath tonight, you can falsify the prediction by not taking a bath. And there are amusing logic paradoxes that arise whenever a predictor's behavior, while predicting, is part of the predicted event.

For example, suppose I put on the table two cards, one bearing the word *yes*, the other bearing the word *no*. I can now describe an event that will or will not take place in the room in the next five minutes, and bet a million dollars against your dime that you cannot predict correctly whether the event will or will not occur by touching the *yes* or *no* card. The event is: "You will make your prediction by touching the *no* card." This traps you in a variant of the liar paradox. If you touch the *no* card you will be wrong because the event will have taken place. And if you touch the *yes* card you will be wrong because the event will not have taken place.[3]

Such paradoxes need not detain us, because we are not concerned with the accuracy of predictions that interact with human behavior, only with whether there is a sense in which human behavior, given the total state of a person and his or her environment, must always be just what it is. The same point can be made by considering past decisions. Suppose that last Monday you decided to take a bath. Given the total state of the world, including the state of your brain, could you have decided other than the way you did?

Before quantum mechanics, in which pure chance is built into the theory's formalism, many scientists and philosophers regarded the universe as one vast machine which could not change in any way other than the way it did. In the eighteenth century Pierre de Laplace (in his *Mécanique Céleste*) gave the classic expression of this point of view:

> An intelligence knowing at a given instant of time all forces acting in nature as well as the momentary positions of all things ... would be able to comprehend the motions of the largest bodies of the universe and

those of the lightest atoms in one single formula, provided his intellect were powerful enough to subject all data to analysis; to him nothing would be uncertain, both past and future would be present to his eyes.

Here is how Samuel Taylor Coleridge, in his *Biographia Literaria*, colorfully phrased it:

> Thus the whole universe cooperates to produce the minutest stroke of every letter, save that I myself, and I alone, have nothing to do with it, but am merely the causeless and effectless beholding of it when it is done. Yet scarcely can it be called a beholding; for it is neither an act nor an effect; but an impossible creation of a *something-nothing* out of its very contrary! It is the mere quicksilver plating behind the looking-glass; and in this alone consists the poor worthless I!

The feeling of free will has been called an "epiphenomenon," a psychological by-product of events that has no more influence on the universe, as it goes its predetermined way, than a rainbow has on the sun or on falling drops of rain. This view is as consistent with theism, pantheism, or polytheism as it is with atheism. Greek mythology had its three Fates, and the notion that there is no escape from destiny was central to Greek tragedy. Most of the great Christian theologians of the past, Protestant as well as Catholic, believed that God, in his omniscience, knows every future event. Glinda of Oz has a magic book that records all important events in Oz the instant they take place, but it cannot predict the future. The Koran speaks of a book in heaven in which all events, future as well as past, are recorded.

No person is truly free, Spinoza taught, until he or she realizes that free will is a delusion. If a falling stone were conscious, Spinoza wrote in a letter, it would believe it was falling of its own free will. I mention Spinoza because he was one of the greatest of secular philosophers to stress total determinism, and also because of the influence of his pantheism on Einstein. "Honestly," Einstein once remarked, "I cannot understand what people mean when they talk about freedom of the human will." Not only did Einstein believe that human behavior was completely determined by causal laws, he also refused to accept the chance aspect of quantum theory. He could not believe that God, Spinoza's God, would play dice with the universe. Until his death, he hoped and believed that some day quantum mechanics would be replaced by a deeper theory in which determinism on the microlevel would be restored.

At this point it is useful to introduce James's distinction between what he called hard and soft determinism. The hard determinist, said James, is one who does not "shrink from such words as fatality, bondage of the will, necessitation, and the like. Nowadays, we have a *soft* determinism which abhors harsh words, and, repudiating fatality, necessity, and even predetermination, says that its real name is freedom; for freedom is only necessity understood, and bondage to the highest is identical with true freedom." One of his colleagues, James wrote with amazement, even calls himself a "free-will determinist."[4]

Among the hard determinists, those who do not hesitate to call free will a delusion, one thinks first of Spinoza, but also of Leibniz, Nietzsche, Schopenhauer, Marx, Santayana, and scores of other philosophers. Among eminent lawyers in the United States, no one more effectively used determinism in the defense of criminals than Clarence Darrow. "I am firmly convinced," Darrow once said in a debate on free will, "that a man has no more to do with his own conduct than a wooden Indian. A wooden Indian has a little advantage for he does not even think he is free."[5] Among later psychologists, B. F. Skinner was the most outspoken in expressing similar views. Man is a machine— a computer made of meat, as Marvin Minsky once said—acting in a way that is fully determined by its hereditary structure and the modifications introduced by that structure's interaction with the world.

It is hard to draw a sharp line between hard and soft determinism, especially since it is so much a matter of word choice and emphasis. The soft determinist usually does not like a language without the term *free will*, because abandoning it implies that human beings are automatons and this makes it difficult, if not impossible, to defend the use of such ordinary words as *right* and *wrong*, *praise* and *blame*. To restore morality, he redefines *free will* as acting in such a way that one's behavior is not compelled by external forces. If my hands are tied behind my back, I am not free to scratch my nose. Untie the hands and now I am free to do so. It is certainly true that ordinary language distinguishes between the unfreedom of a prisoner and his freedom when released. But if one continues to believe that decisions inside the brain, made in a way not coerced by outside forces, are the inevitable outcome of inner forces, it is hard to see how soft determinism differs from hard except in its ways of using language.

Consider a mechanical turtle that crawls across the floor in obedience to internal mechanisms. It moves here and there, seemingly at random. Contrast this with a toy turtle that a child pulls with a string. The toy is compelled by outside forces to move as it does, whereas the mechanical turtle is under no extraneous compulsion. Does anyone want to maintain that the mechanical turtle has free will? Yet is not the soft determinist doing exactly this when he speaks of a person's free will? It is easy to convert anyone to theism by redefining God as everything that exists. It is easy to convert anyone to a belief in free will by redefining it so that it means no more than acting from internal causes.

I wish I had space to discuss the curious history of this attempt to save determinism and simultaneously find a meaning for free will and moral responsibility. It was brilliantly argued by John Stuart Mill in a way that is indistinguishable from later arguments by Bertrand Russell, John Dewey, and Vienna Circle members and their admirers. Similar arguments are in the writings of Leibniz, Hobbes, Locke, Freud, Marx, Engels, Hegel and his followers, and hundreds of other thinkers. Charles Peirce and his friend James, both candid indeterminists, had little patience with such rhetoric. It seems "scarcely defensive for a thoroughgoing determinist," wrote Peirce (chiding Paul Carus for his arguments), ". . . to fly the flag of Free Will."[6] For James, soft determinism "is a quagmire of evasion under which the real issue of fact has been entirely smothered."

As G. K. Chesterton observed, a determinist has the very real problem of explaining why he says "Thank you" to anyone who passes him the mustard. "For how could he be praised for passing the mustard, if he could not be blamed for not passing the mustard?"[7] Raymond Chandler somewhere describes private detectives as having the moral stature of streetlights. If our activities are internally compelled by mechanisms inside the brain, there is only a difference in complexity between a person and a streetlight. Soft determinism doesn't eliminate compulsion; it only shifts the compulsion from outside to inside the brain.

Karl Marx and Friedrich Engels were determinists, but this did not prevent them from passionately exhorting humanity to do one thing and not another. Stalin did not hesitate to kill millions because they disagreed with him, or he thought they did, even though his philosophy required him to believe that those whom he murdered could not have behaved otherwise. The ancient Greeks were fully aware of this paradox at the heart of determinism, and it has been discussed endlessly since. If a person must do whatever he or she does, where is the basis for moral judgment? There is no "ought," said Kant, without a "can." In recent times Jean-Paul Sartre and his fellow existentialists have tried to escape the trap by emphasizing the reality of human freedom, even though they fail (in my opinion) to give an adequate account of what they mean by freedom.

If determinism implies fatalism, as I believe it does, can anything be gained by trying to make a free act an indeterminate act? Alas, as all determinists know, it cannot. The indeterminist position, with respect to human behavior, can only mean there are moments when the brain decides, perhaps by choosing which of two or more paths a nerve impulse will take, in a way that is not the outcome of prior causes. But if this is the case, the decision degenerates into one of pure chance. Surely this is even further from what we want "free will" to mean than a decision that is somehow internally caused. If we cannot praise or blame persons for decisions they could not have made otherwise, even less can we praise or blame them for decisions made by dice rattling inside their skulls!

Quantum mechanics is no help to the indeterminist except in the sense that if indeterminism exists on the microlevel, it may remove a mental block against believing that indeterminism can, in some incomprehensible way, also be involved in human behavior. Indeed, this was the main argument of such scientists as Sir Arthur Stanley Eddington and Arthur Holly Compton. Quantum mechanics, they said, does not explain free will; it just makes it easier to believe in free will.

I have no objection to this ploy if it is joined to a realization that quantum mechanics tells us nothing about the nature of free will. Suppose a decision in the brain is triggered by a random quantum jump or, as Epicurus phrased it, by a random "swerve" of a fundamental particle. Since the jump is the result of pure chance (assuming quantum mechanics is indeed correct), clearly this in no way satisfies what we intuitively feel "free will" to be. It merely transforms the decision from a causal one to a haphazard one, like deciding between possible courses of action by spinning a roulette wheel. There is certainly nothing creative about such a decision. In my opinion quantum mechanics sheds no light on the understanding of free will.

Peirce and James, and later Alfred North Whitehead, Charles Hartshorne, and others, became strong opponents of determinism, although few of them were or are as fully aware as was Kant of the free-will problem's intrinsic unsolvability.[8] Perhaps this is not quite fair. There are few indeterminists who do not, in unguarded moments, catch glimpses of the central mystery. Peirce once likened the problem of defining free will to that of trying to write down the entire decimal expansion of pi. Obviously pi is a limit "to which no numerical expression can be perfectly true. If our hope is vain; if in respect to some question—say that of the freedom of the will—no matter how long the discussion goes on, no matter how scientific our methods may become, there never will be a time when we can fully satisfy ourselves either that the question has no meaning, or that one answer or the other explains the facts, then in regard to that question there certainly is no *truth*."[9] Peirce meant, of course, truth in the pragmatic sense. He immediately followed this remark by pointing out that to say there is no "true" answer to such a question (no way to confirm an answer by testing) does not mean there is no "reality" that answers the question.

James comes the closest to restating Kant's position in the third chapter of his *Pragmatism*:

> So both free-will and determinism have been inveighed against and called absurd, because each, in the eyes of its enemies, has seemed to prevent the "imputability" of good or bad deeds to their authors. Queer antinomy this! Free-will means novelty, the grafting on to the past of something not involved therein. If our acts were predetermined, if we merely transmitted the push of the whole past, the free-willists say, how could we be praised or blamed for anything? We should be "agents" only, not "principals," and where then would be our precious imputability and responsibility?

But where would it be if we *had* free-will? rejoin the determinists. If a "free" act be a sheer novelty, that comes not *from* me, the previous me, but *ex nihilo*, and simply tacks itself on to me, how can *I* the previous I, be responsible? How can I have any permanent *character* that will stand still long enough for praise or blame to be awarded? The chaplet of my days tumbles into a cast of disconnected beads as soon as the thread of inner necessity is drawn out by the preposterous indeterminist doctrine.[10]

It has always puzzled me that James, although he recognized that free will posed a "queer antinomy," could not bring himself to say, with Kant, that once the antinomy is recognized, there is no more to be said. James was enormously effective in arguing that determinism leaves no room for morality, and that only free wills can inject creative novelty into history, yet he was curiously reluctant to take that final step of putting the nature of will beyond the comprehension of finite minds.

Among this century's physicists, the most vigorous champion of Kant's attitude toward will was Niels Bohr. It provided one of his favorite applications to human life of what he called the "complementarity principle" of quantum mechanics. The psychologist, acting as a scientist, must regard all human behavior as fully determined. On the other hand, our sense of morality makes it equally imperative to believe that our behavior is not entirely determined. We must approach human behavior from both points of view, but we can no more reconcile them than we can perform an experiment in which we simultaneously measure the position and the momentum of an electron. "A great truth," Bohr liked to say, "is a truth whose opposite is also a great truth."[11] It is no surprise to learn that Bohr was so taken by the yin-yang symbol of the Orient that he put it at the center of his coat-of-arms.

Determinists sometimes argue that the chance aspect of quantum mechanics has no relevance for human history because all physical objects of the macroworld, including brains, contain so many billions upon billions of particles that quantum uncertainty on the microlevel becomes negligible. In other words, determinism holds, in a statistical sense, with a probability indistinguishable from certainty. This may be true in general, but there is a dramatic thought experiment (I do not know who first proposed it; it goes back to the early days of quantum mechanics) which proves that chance on the particle level can easily be magnified until it is capable, in a microsecond, of unleashing forces that radically alter history in ways that are unpredictable in principle.

Imagine a plane flying at supersonic speed over a continent. It carries a hydrogen bomb that is dropped by a mechanism triggered by the click of a Geiger counter. If quantum mechanics is correct, the timing of this click is purely random. Hence absolute chance determines where the bomb falls, and thereby decides between many alternate, equally possible courses of history. I mention this thought experiment only as an aside. It proves that if indeter-

minism rules on the microlevel, then strict determinism can be radically violated on the macrolevel. All of this, in my opinion, has no bearing whatever
on the mystery of will.

Nor does religious belief have any bearing. In all great religious traditions
the nature of will is as incomprehensible as it is in secular philosophy, and
the secular viewpoints and arguments all have their counterparts in religious
discourse. If the God of Judaism, Christianity, or Islam is omniscient, will he
not know every detail of the future? But if God has such knowledge, how can
our wills be free? And if our wills are not free, how can God treat us as morally
responsible? On the other hand, if our actions are in principle unpredictable,
then God cannot be all-knowing. Moreover, if our decisions are uncaused
random events, we are as morally irresponsible as if they were totally determined. Rewards and punishments in another life seem monstrously unjust if
we cannot behave other than the way we do, and equally unjust if all our
actions result from dice throws.

The traditional Judaic-Christian attempt to solve these old conundrums
was proposed by Maimonides and Augustine, and later adopted by Thomas
Aquinas and all the great Scholastics, as well as by leading Muslim theologians.
It rests on the assumption that God is outside of time. As a consequence he
sees all history from the standpoint of eternity. He sees the future as well as
the past, but (the argument continues) from our time-bound perspective we
make genuine choices. Roman Catholic thinkers of the Middle Ages differed
in the degree to which they were bothered by what seems here to be a sharp
contradiction. If an omniscient God can know our future, is there not a sense
in which that future exists even now, and if so, how can our decisions be truly
free? The argument seems to turn history into something like a motion picture
film. While it is being projected, the shadow actors on the screen make real
choices about what they say and do, even though everything is permanently
recorded. Some Scholastics were untroubled by this doctrine. Others regarded
it as a disturbing paradox, the resolution of which is known only to God.

The Christian doctrine of predestination, that every person is foreordained
to be saved or unsaved, is a natural corollary of believing that God knows the
future timelessly. The leading Protestant theologians who stressed this doctrine—Martin Luther, John Calvin, Jonathan Edwards, Karl Barth, to mention
a few—followed their Catholic predecessors in finding support for predestination in remarks by Paul (Romans 9:18–21):

Therefore hath he mercy on whom he will have mercy, and whom
he will he hardeneth.

Thou wilt say then unto me, Why doth he yet find fault? For who
hath resisted his will?

Nay but, O man, who art thou that repliest against God? Shall the
thing formed say to him that formed it, Why hast thou made me thus?

Hath not the potter power over the clay, of the same lump to make one vessel unto honour, and another unto dishonour?

Thomas Paine, a deist who believed in both God and immortality (though not in Christianity) attacked Paul's reasoning in a characteristic way. "Nay, but who art thou, presumptuous Paul, that puttest thyself in God's place?" To compare man with a clay pot, said Paine, is a "wretched metaphor" because it implies that human beings are no more than lifeless lumps of clay. "If Paul believed that God made man after His own image, he dishonors it by making that image and a brickbat to be alike."[12]

Christian leaders have quarreled interminably over predestination. Evangelists like John Wesley saw little point in exhorting sinners to repent if it was already decided in heaven who would and would not be saved. Yet there was always, even for the foes of predestination, the nagging problem of how persons could be genuinely free without limiting the power of God to know the future. Some predestination sects, like the Two-Seed-in-the-Spirit Predestination Baptists of the southern United States, openly opposed evangelism on the plausible ground that the question of who is or is not saved is already settled.

Leibniz exchanged letters with Samuel Clarke over this difficulty. As someone said, if they had hit their heads together it would have produced more light. "That which happens is assured," wrote Leibniz, "but it is not therefore necessary, and if anyone did the contrary, he would do nothing impossible in itself, although it is impossible . . . that that other happen."

Here is René Descartes making similar comments: ". . . We will be free from these embarrassments if we recollect that our mind is limited while the power of God, by which he not only knew from all eternity what is or can be, but also willed and preordained it, is infinite. It thus happens that we possess sufficient intelligence to know clearly and distinctly that this power is in God, but not enough to comprehend how he leaves the free actions of men indeterminate. . . ."[13]

In Milton's *Paradise Lost* (Book 3) God recalls his creation of Adam and Eve, and how their disobedience resulted from free will even though he knew how they would decide:

> . . . They themselves decreed
> Their own revolt, not I. If I foreknew,
> Foreknowledge had no influence on their fault
> Which had no less proved certain unforeknown.

Peirce saw nothing wrong in this medieval way of harmonizing free will with divine foreknowledge, even though it seems "to most persons flatly self-contradictory." The contradiction arises, Peirce continued, only if we think of

God's knowledge as existing, like ours, in time. "But it is a degraded conception to conceive God as subject to Time, which is rather one of his creatures. Literal foreknowledge is certainly contradictory to literal freedom. But if we say that though God knows (using the word *knows* in a trans-temporal sense) he never did know, does not know, and never will know, then his knowledge in no wise interferes with freedom."[14] Thus did Peirce defend his doctrine of "tychism," a belief that the future is in part undetermined, without regarding it as in conflict with the view of Aquinas and Kant that God, being outside time, knows the future in a timeless way.

Here is C. S. Lewis saying the same thing in his own clear language:

> But suppose God is outside and above the Time-line. In that case, what we call "tomorrow" is visible to Him *in just the same way* as what we call "today." All the days are "Now" for Him. He doesn't *remember* you doing things yesterday; He simply *sees* you doing them, because, though you've lost yesterday, He has not. He doesn't *foresee* you doing things tomorrow; He simply *sees*, you doing them: because, though tomorrow is not yet there for you, it is for Him. You never supposed that your actions at this moment were any less free because God knows what you are doing. Well, He knows your tomorrow's actions in just the same way—because He is already in tomorrow and can simply watch you. In a sense, He doesn't know your action till you've done it: but then the moment at which you have done it is already "Now" for Him.
>
> This idea has helped me a lot. If it doesn't help you, leave it alone. It is a "Christian idea" in the sense that great and wise Christians have held it and there is nothing in it contrary to Christianity. But it is not in the Bible or any of the creeds. You can be a perfectly good Christian without accepting it, or indeed without thinking of the matter at all.[15]

Another way to avoid the paradox is to regard God as omniscient only in the sense that he knows all that can be known, allowing for parts of the future to be in principle unknowable. The Scholastics stressed the fact that God cannot do logically impossible things, such as alter the past or construct a square triangle. Perhaps there are aspects of the future that God, in a similar way, is powerless to know because God is not outside of time, and the future is not completely determined.

In one of James's picturesque metaphors, God is playing a vast game of superchess with the universe. Because God made up the rules and can play a perfect game, the outcome is certain even though God allows the universe to make some moves that even he cannot anticipate. Put another way, God's providence is only an overall plan. It allows for many different ways of winning, depending on how the universe moves. Our wills constitute part of the freedom God has permitted his universe to have to make the game interesting. He has made us in his own image by giving us genuine creativity. Free will, as Charles Hartshorne likes to say, is the "glory" of our very being. This notion of a "finite God," suggested by Hume and championed by Mill, has strongly appealed to many later thinkers. Even H. G. Wells was once so taken by the concept of a finite God that he wrote an entire book about it, *God the Invisible King.* (Later, Wells decided he was an atheist.)

There are, then, two essentially different ways of harmonizing free will with divine foreknowledge. One is to put God outside of time and see no contradiction between his timeless knowledge of the future and our free choices. The other is to model God as in some sort of time, his omniscience limited to what can be known, allowing room for contingent events that not even God can unerringly predict. Which view is right? I can give my opinion at once. I don't know. Do not ask *me!* As a theist I see nothing inconsistent about either view, or any reason why the truth may not be a third view which we are incapable of formulating or understanding. Who am I to know how to answer such questions?

I do know this. I cannot conceive of myself as existing without a body in both space and time, or without a brain that has free will. I agree with Samuel Johnson that "All theory is against the freedom of the will; all experience for it."[16] I cannot comprehend how the dilemma can be resolved, but I am no more troubled by this than by the fact that I cannot understand time, being, consciousness, or the nature of God. Indeed, it was with a feeling of enormous relief that I concluded, long ago, that free will is an unfathomable mystery.

Listen to Raymond Smullyan. The speaker in his dialogue is God:

> Why the idea that I could possibly have created you without free will! You acted as if this were a genuine possibility, and wondered why I did not choose it! It never occurred to you that a sentient being without free will is no more conceivable than a physical object which exerts no gravitational attraction. (There is, incidentally, more analogy than you realize between a physical object exerting gravitational attraction and a sentient being exerting free will!) Can you honestly even imagine a conscious being without free will? What on earth could it be like? I think that one thing in your life that has so misled you is your having been told that I gave man the *gift* of free will. As if I first created man, and then as an afterthought endowed him with the extra property of free will. Maybe you think I have some sort of "paint brush" with which I daub some creatures with free will, and not others. No, free will is not an "extra"; it is part and parcel of the very essence of consciousness. A conscious being without free will is simply a metaphysical absurdity.[17]

I do not wish to imply that we have souls that are somehow distinct from the pattern of our molecular structure, even though I grant that this may be the case. I do not want to suggest that free will is limited to human organisms, not possessed in lower degrees by humbler creatures. Nor am I a panpsychic who thinks that all things, including plants and stones, possess some degree of will. I believe that a stone or a plant has no will at all, and that in a butterfly's brain, although there may be a low degree of will, the amount is so minute as to be negligible. I cannot say it is impossible for humanity some day to build a computer or a robot of sufficient complexity that a threshold will be crossed and the computer or robot will acquire self-consciousness and free will. These are profound questions about which I have no fixed opinions.

Thomas Henry Huxley, in an unguarded moment, wrote: "I protest that if some great Power would agree to make me always think what is true and do what is right, on condition of being turned into a sort of clock and wound up every morning before I got out of bed, I should instantly close with the offer. The only freedom I care about is the freedom to do right; the freedom to do wrong I am ready to part with on the cheapest terms to any one who will take it from me."[18] Much as I admire Huxley, I find this statement monstrous. To be turned into a Tik-Tok would mean ceasing to be human. Sara Teasdale said it this way in her poem "Mastery":

> I would not have a god come in
> To shield me suddenly from sin,
> And set my house of life to rights;
> Nor angels with bright burning wings
> Ordering my earthly thoughts and things;
> Rather my own frail guttering lights
> Wind blown and nearly beaten out;
> Rather the terror of the nights
> And long, sick groping after doubt;
> Rather be lost than let my soul
> Slip vaguely from my own control—
> Of my own spirit let me be
> In sole though feeble mastery.

I am persuaded that somehow, in a way utterly beyond our ken, you and I possess that incomprehensible power we call free will. I am content to let theologians worry over whether God could, if he liked, create a person who always wills to do right. Such a person, to be a person, may be as self-contradictory as a square triangle. Or it may be otherwise.

You and I—this I know—are not such creatures. But I have no insight into the nature of the transcendental magic that operates inside our skulls. I believe that the magic is neither fate nor chance, yet how it escapes those two categories is beyond my grasp. Like time, with which it is linked, free will is best left—indeed, I believe we cannot do otherwise—an impenetrable mystery. Ask not how it works because no one on earth can tell you.

NOTES

1. James Boswell, *The Life of Samuel Johnson*, 1769 section. See also Boswell's discussion (1778 section) with Johnson on the problem of reconciling free will with God's foreknowledge.

2. The quotation is from a surprisingly good account of the free-will problem in the second chapter of Mencken's *Treatise on Right and Wrong* (1934). Writing these pages, he said in a letter, took him two weeks and reduced him to a "frazzle."

Robert Nozick reports similar frustration over the question. In his ponderous *Philosophical Explanations* (1981) almost a hundred pages are devoted to free will. There is lots of what Nozick calls "thrashing about," all of which, to borrow a witticism from Whitehead, "leaves the darkness of the subject unobscured." Nozick confesses that he spent more time "banging" his head on the topic than any other topic in his book except the foundations of ethics. Unfortunately he never takes the ultimate step of recognizing that there is no intelligible way to avoid what he aptly calls the "quicksand" of indeterminism and the "frozen ground" of determinism.

3. The literature on prediction paradoxes is growing rapidly. The one I gave is a variant of one described in chapter 23 of this book. On the notorious paradox of the unexpected hanging, see the first chapter of my *Unexpected Hanging and Other Mathematical Diversions* (1969). The more recent Newcomb's paradox is here covered in chapter 33.

4. William James, "The Dilemma of Determinism," in *The Will to Believe* (1903).

5. Darrow's debate, with G. B. Foster, is in *Little Blue Book*, no. 1286, published by Haldeman-Julius in 1928.

6. See Peirce's *Collected Papers*, volume 5, section 565. This is the section in which Peirce gives his famous definition of pragmatic truth as the ideal limit of belief. Kant was equally contemptuous of the view—"wretched subterfuge," he called it—that free will is somehow saved by making it a matter of interior psychological causation rather than a mystery of the transcendent, timeless, noumenal self.

7. *The Autobiography of G. K. Chesterton* (1936), chapter 7. Bertrand Russell, writing on ethics and free will (*Philosophical Essays*, 1910) said the same thing this way:

> But if determinism is true, there is a sense in which no action is possible except the one actually performed. Hence, if the two senses of possibility are the same, the action actually performed is always objectively right; for it is the only possible action, and therefore there is no other possible action which would have had better results. There is here, I think, a real difficulty.

Russell goes on to defend determinism, but without in any way clearing up the difficulty.

8. Kant's view can be compressed as follows: In the space-time world of our experience, the world investigated by science, causal determinism must be assumed; in this sense the will is not free. But morality is meaningless unless the will *is* somehow free. For practical reasons, therefore, we must assume that the human soul, considered as a noumenon, a thing in itself, belongs to a transcendent, timeless realm, and in this realm it is truly free. How empirical determinism and noumenal freedom can be reconciled, however, is a mystery utterly beyond our finite minds. When I say I follow Kant in my attitude toward free will, I do not mean that I buy all of his metaphysics, but only that I buy his conviction that the free-will problem is unsolvable.

In *Religion within the Limits of Reason Alone* (in a footnote for the final section of Book 3), Kant wrote: "Hence we understand perfectly well what freedom is, practically (when it is a question of duty), whereas we cannot without contradiction even think of wishing to understand theoretically the causality of freedom (or its nature)."

9. From the reference cited in note 6 above.

10. William James, *Pragmatism* (1907).

11. For a good defense of Bohr's complementarity approach to human actions see Clarence Shute, "The Dilemma of Determinism after Seventy-five Years," in *Mind*, volume 70, July 1961, pages 331–350. I agree with all that Professor Shute says, regretting only his failure to recognize that he was restating Kant's view, and that he did not follow Kant in declaring the antinomy unsolvable.

12. Paine's essay, "Predestination," is in volume 7 of *The Writings of Thomas Paine* (1908), edited and annotated by Daniel Edwin Wheeler.

13. René Descartes, *Principles of Philosophy*, part 1, 41.

14. Charles S. Peirce, *Collected Papers*, volume 4, section 67.

15. C. S. Lewis, *Beyond Personality* (1945).

16. James Boswell, *The Life of Samuel Johnson*, 1778 section.

17. Raymond Smullyan, "Is God a Taoist?" in *The Tao Is Silent* (1977). Rousseau's Savoyard vicar, in the fourth book of *Émile*, puts it this way: If you try to convince me that I have no free will, he says, "you might as well convince me I do not exist."

That free will is part of the mystery of what it means to be a person is, of course, much older than Descartes, Rousseau, and Kant. Few Catholic theologians emphasized it more effectively than William of Occam, the fourteenth-century English fideist. On the question of how free will can be harmonized with God's foreknowledge, Occam was not happy with Aquinas's casual answer that God, from an eternal vantage point, sees exactly how each person will freely decide. Occam saw more clearly than Aquinas that the problem is an unsolvable paradox. "It is impossible," he wrote in his *Commentary on the Sentences* (of Peter Lombard), "for any intellect, in this life, to explain or evidently know how God knows all future contingent events." I quote from Ernest Moody's excellent article on Occam in *The Encyclopedia of Philosophy* (1967).

Occam, Moody tells us, presented an interesting paradox involving the wills of God and created minds. Can God will that a person disobey him? Because God wills that all creatures love and obey him, such a command seems impossible to fulfill. It would require a person simultaneously to both obey and disobey. (One thinks of Abraham and Isaac.) Must we conclude, then, that it is logically impossible for God to issue such a command?

18. From Huxley's essay on Descartes, in *Methods and Results* (1893).

THIRTY-SIX

COMPUTERS NEAR
THE THRESHOLD?

*Almost all AI (Artificial Intelligence) researchers believe that the human brain
is nothing more than a computer in which electrical impulses are shifted
about by organic molecules in accord with known laws of physics. Our consciousness and free will, and all our other mental abilities, emerge from the
complexity of the brain's molecular structure, like the properties of water
which emerge when hydrogen and oxygen combine.*

A vigorous attack on this reductionism was The Emperor's New Mind *by
the British mathematician-physicist Roger Penrose, followed by his* Shadows of
the Mind. *Penrose does not defend a soul separate from the body, a "ghost in
the machine" as it has been derisively called. He grants that human consciousness emerged from our brain's complexity as it evolved over millions of
years. His point is subtler. He thinks we will never understand this emergence
until we know more about laws of physics deeper even than the laws of quantum mechanics.*

*The following essay expresses my essential agreement with Penrose, and
with philosopher John Searle and others. It first appeared in* Mysteries of Life
and the Universe *(Harcourt Brace, 1992), edited by William H. Shore, and
was reprinted in the* Journal of Consciousness Studies *(vol. 3, no. 1, 1996).*

The notion that it is possible to con-
struct intelligent machines out of nonorganic material is as old as Greek mythology. Vulcan, the lame god of fire, fabricated young women out of gold to
assist him in his labors. He also made the bronze giant Talus, who guarded
the island of Crete by running around it three times a day and heaving huge
rocks at enemy ships. A single vein of ichor (the blood of the gods) ran from

Talus's neck to his heels. He bled to death when he was wounded in the ankle or, according to another myth, when a brass pin in his heel was removed.

After the Industrial Revolution, with its wonderful machinery, writers began to speculate about the possibility that humans as well as gods could some day build intelligent machines. In chapters twenty-three, twenty-four, and twenty-five of his novel *Erewhon* (1872), Samuel Butler wrote about the coming of just such robots. Tik-Tok, one of the earliest mechanical men in fiction, was a windup copper person who made his first appearance in L. Frank Baum's *Ozma of Oz* (1907). He was manufactured in Ev, a land adjacent to Oz, by the firm of Smith and Tinker. A plate on his back said that the robot "Thinks, Speaks, Acts, and Does Everything But Live."

After the computer revolution produced electronic calculating machines, with their curious resemblance to the electrical networks of a human brain, the possibility of constructing intelligent robots began to be taken seriously, especially by leaders of AI (artificial intelligence) research, and by a few fellow traveling philosophers. Hans Moravec directs a robot laboratory at Carnegie Mellon University; in his book *Mind Children* (1988), he predicted the appearance of robots with human intelligence before the end of the next fifty years. Both he and Frank Tipler, a Tulane University physicist, are convinced that computers will soon *exceed* human intelligence, making the human race superfluous. Computers will then take over the burden and adventure of colonizing the universe.

Here is a passage from *Erewhon* that could have been written seriously by Tipler or Moravec:

> There is no security against the ultimate development of mechanical consciousness, in the fact of machines possessing little consciousness now. A mollusc has not much consciousness. Reflect upon the extraordinary advance which machines have made during the last few hundred years, and note how slowly the animal and vegetable kingdoms are advancing. The more highly organized machines are creatures not so much of yesterday, as of the last five minutes, so to speak, in comparison with past time. Assume for the sake of argument that conscious beings have existed for some twenty million years: see what strides machines have made in the last thousand! May not the world last twenty million years longer? If so, what will they not in the end become?

Another passage, remarkably prophetic, from the same book:

> Do not let me be misunderstood as living in fear of any actually existing machine; there is probably no known machine which is more than a prototype of future mechanical life. The present machines are to the future as the early Saurians to man. The largest of them will probably greatly diminish in size.

Actually, these are not the narrator's words but sentences that Butler attributes, tongue firmly in cheek, to an Erewhonian professor. The professor's opinions prompt the Erewhonians to destroy all their machines before they surpass human intelligence and take over the world.

In *Mind Children* Moravec puts it this way:

> Today our machines are still simple creations, requiring the parental care and hovering attention of any newborn, hardly worthy of the word *intelligent*. But within the next century they will mature into entities as complex as ourselves, and eventually into something transcending everything we know—in whom we can take pride when they refer to themselves as our descendants.

The most powerful attack on such opinions, which have come to be called "strong AI," is Roger Penrose's best-seller *The Emperor's New Mind* (1989). Naturally, the book was vigorously lambasted by strong AIers. Because I wrote the book's foreword, I too have been denounced for my obtuseness. This essay is an effort to set down in more detail precisely what I believe about the possibility that computers will soon be able to converse with us in ways indistinguishable from the conversations of human beings.

First, I should make clear that I am not a vitalist who thinks there is a "ghost in the machine"—a soul distinct from the brain. I believe that the human mind, like the mind of any lower animal, is a function of a material lump of organic matter. Although I remain open to the Platonic possibility of a disembodied soul, as I am open to any metaphysical notion not logically contradictory, the evidence against it seems overwhelming. Strong arguments for a functional view of the mind are too familiar to need summarizing.

If a human has a nonmaterial soul, it is hard to see why the same should not be said of an amoeba, a plant, or even a pebble. A few pan-psychic monists such as Charles Hartshorne actually do say this, but I consider it an absurd misuse of words, a "category mistake," to talk of a potato in a dark cellar as having what Butler called "a certain degree of cunning." Here are two panpsychic quotations from Butler's imaginary Erewhonian professor:

> But who can say that the vapor engine has not a kind of consciousness? Where does consciousness begin, and where end? Who can draw the line? Who can draw any line? Is not everything interwoven with everything? Is not machinery linked with animal life in an infinite variety of ways?

> Shall we say that the plant does not know what it is doing merely because it has no eyes, or ears, or brains? If we say that it acts mechanically, and mechanically only, shall we not be forced to admit that sundry other and apparently very deliberate actions are also mechanical? If it

seems to us that the plant kills and eats a fly mechanically, may it not seem to the plant that a man must kill and eat a sheep mechanically?

I agree with Aristotle that the self is the "form" of the body, or in modern terminology, a pattern of the molecular structure of organic matter inside our skull. Of course the pattern is far more complex than the pattern of a vase or the Empire State Building.

Life did indeed evolve along continua, but there are spots (albeit with fuzzy edges) where wide chasms were crossed and new properties of matter emerged. The first great threshold was the emergence of life itself from lifeless compounds. And the last of the great thresholds, the greatest of them all, was the evolution of a brain with such properties as consciousness (self-awareness), expanded free will (with all its moral implications), a sense of right and wrong, a sense of humor, the power to communicate complicated ideas by speech and writing, and a raft of creative skills such as the abilities to compose poetry and music, paint pictures, discover significant mathematical theorems, and invent scientific theories capable of being tested. With the last skill came the awesome power to control the process of evolution and steer it in new directions, as well as the power to terminate the process.

It goes without saying that many of these human traits are possessed to a weak degree by animals. Chimpanzees seem to have a low-level awareness of themselves and an ability to make decisions. (*Free will* and *self-awareness*, by the way, are for me two names for the same phenomenon, like Einstein's principle of the equivalence of gravity and inertia, or, what amounts to the same thing, the equivalence of gravitational and inertial mass. I cannot imagine myself having free will without being self-aware, nor can I conceive of being self-aware without some degree of free will). Monkeys have a feeble sense of humor; you can watch them play pranks on each other in a cage. Bower birds may have a dim sense of visual beauty. Apes can communicate with humans by signs, and so can a dog or cat. A chimp can make and test conjectures about how to get a banana from the ceiling if there are boxes lying around. And so on. That animals feel emotions of love and pain is undeniable. It is equally undeniable that a major gulf of some sort was crossed when humans evolved from bestial ancestors.

The question is not whether our human traits emerged as a function of an evolving brain, as I assume they did, but whether it will be easy or difficult, perhaps even impossible, to build a calculating machine complex enough to leap the same threshold. At this point we touch the central theme of Roger Penrose's brilliant, controversial book *The Emperor's New Mind*.

The difficulty in crossing the threshold, Penrose argues, is that we don't yet know enough about matter to know how to do it. Clearly we know far more about particles than did Democritus, but we are still a long way from understanding those particles. In standard theories, matter is made of leptons and quarks, and these particles are taken to be geometrical points, or at least *pointlike*, as physicists prefer to say. In recent superstring theories they are not points but inconceivably tiny loops. In either case, Newton's hard little pebbles that bounce against one another—the kind of matter Bishop Berkeley ridiculed as a "stupid, thoughtless somewhat"—have now totally dissolved. What is left is mathematics. Leptons and quarks, whether points or loops, are not made of anything. Their fields are just as ghostly. On the quantum level, to put it bluntly, there is nothing except mathematical patterns.

My readers know how impatient I am with some pragmatists, phenomenologists, and subjective idealists of various schools who heap scorn on the notion that mathematical structures are "out there" with a reality that is not mind-dependent. For these thinkers, mathematical reality is located within human experience. Like Penrose and the overwhelming majority of eminent mathematicians past and present, I am a Platonist in the sense that I believe mathematical patterns are discovered, not invented. Of course, they are still invented, in a sense. Everything humans do and say is what humans do and say. Mathematics obviously is part of human culture, but to say so is to say something utterly trivial. The fact that only humans can talk or write about mathematics and laws of physics does not mean that it is useful to deny that mathematics and laws of physics are embedded in an enormous universe not made by us, but of which we are a part, and an inconceivably tiny part at that.

As I have said before, if two dinosaurs met two others in a forest clearing, there would have been four dinosaurs there—even though the beasts were too stupid to count and there were no humans around to watch. I believe that a large integer is prime before mathematicians prove it prime. I believe that the Andromeda galaxy had a spiral structure before humans arose on Earth to call it a spiral. As the noted Bell Labs mathematician Ronald Graham recently put it, mathematics is not only real, it is the *only* reality.

Some eccentric philosophers prefer to think that human minds alone are really real. There are even physicists, overwhelmed by the solipsistic tinges of QM (quantum mechanics), who like to talk the same way. But the human mind is made of molecules, which are in turn made of atoms, which are in turn made of electrons, protons, and neutrons. The protons and neutrons are made of quarks. What are quarks and electrons made of? Nothing except equations. Let's face it. You and I, at the lowest known level of our material bodies, are made of mathematics, pure mathematics, mathematics uncontaminated by anything else.

The most elegant theory of matter today is of course QM. Unfortunately, it is riddled with mysterious paradoxes. In recent years Einstein's EPR paradox (named with the initials of Einstein and two of his colleagues) has been the most debated. How can the measurement of one particle cause the emergence of a property on a correlated particle that can be millions of light-years away?

It seems to happen either instantaneously or with a speed faster than light can travel between the particles. In the first case, the paradox violates the dogma that prohibits instant action at a distance. In the second case, it seems to violate relativity, which prohibits information from traveling faster than light.

None of the many proposed resolutions is satisfactory. The many-worlds interpretation of QM seems to get rid of the paradox, but there is an enormous price to be paid. One must posit billions upon billions of ever-proliferating parallel universes in which everything that can happen, does. Other efforts to solve the EPR paradox do no more than restate it in a different language. It is no good, for example, to say that the two correlated particles are part of a single quantum system whose wave function (or state vector in another language) collapses all at once, so naturally when you collapse it by measuring one particle you obtain information about the other. This simply restates the formalism. You now have to explain how two particles, light-years apart, can remain correlated.

For years Penrose has maintained, along with David Bohm, Paul Dirac, Erwin Schrödinger, and other great physicists, that QM is not the ultimate theory of fields and particles. This was Einstein's own view. Indeed, it was Einstein who first proposed the notorious EPR paradox in an effort to show that QM was incomplete. Working physicists, for the most part, never worry about such things. As long as QM works, and of course it works magnificently, they simply accept the fact that (as Richard Feynman liked to say) QM is "crazy." Don't try to understand how it works, Feynman warned his students, because nobody knows how it works. Should physicists leave it at that? No, insist Bohm and Penrose, because that tends to discourage research that may some day find that QM, like Newton's gravity, is only a good approximation of a deeper theory. Penrose himself is trying to go deeper, with a geometrical theory of particles and fields about which I am not competent to have an opinion.

Penrose contends, and I agree, that until we know more about matter on a level beyond QM, we will not understand how our minds can be a function of our gray matter. Until we know those deeper laws, we will not even come close to constructing a machine that can do everything our minds can do.

In Penrose's opinion, the great mistake behind the optimistic predictions of strong AIers is the assumption that machines made of wires and switches, operating with algorithmic software, can cross the great threshold. Let's look at this assumption more closely. We know from the work of Alan Turing and others that it is possible in principle to build computers out of any kind of equipment that transmits energy along channels, with switches to tell the energy where to go. You can build computers with networks of pipes that hold a flowing liquid. You can build them with rotating gears, with string and pulleys, with little balls that roll down inclines or slide along wires as on an abacus. Mechanical devices of these sorts have been constructed in the past. If you are interested, you can read about them in my *Logic Machines and Diagrams*.

Every machine, the philosopher-mathematician Charles Peirce once observed, is a logic machine in having aspects that model logic functions. The blades of an eggbeater rotate in one direction "if and only if" you turn the handle clockwise. They go the other way if and only if you turn the handle counterclockwise. An old mechanical typewriter is a jungle of binary logic relations. (Peirce, incidentally, was the first to show how a simple logic machine handling binary functions could be built with electrical currents and switches.) A few years ago a group of computer hackers constructed a machine out of Tinker Toys that played perfect ticktacktoe. There is no reason why, in theory, one could not build a Tinker Toy computer that could do everything a Cray computer can do or, indeed, what any supercalculating machine of the future could do. Of course, it would have to be monstrously large and intolerably slow. Would its sluggishness dilute its consciousness? Could it still write a great novel, provided it had a few thousand years to do it?

Now, no one in his right mind would say that a Tinker Toy ticktacktoe machine "knows" it is playing ticktacktoe any more than a vacuum cleaner knows it is cleaning a rug or a lawn mower knows it is cutting grass. Sophisticated computer programs that now play Master chess differ from ticktacktoe programs only in the complexity of their algorithms. A computer with such a program is no more aware it is playing chess than an eggbeater is aware it is beating eggs.

Strong AIers believe that as computers of the sort we presently know how to construct keep growing in the complexity of their circuitry and software, they will eventually cross a threshold and become conscious of what they are doing. If one believes this, is not one forced to say that a Tinker Toy machine of comparable complexity, or even one made with rolling marbles, will cross the same threshold?

I admit that all this may someday be possible, but I agree with Penrose and such opponents of strong AI as the philosopher John Searle that it seems extremely unlikely. We know very little about how the brain of a fish or a bird works. We do not even know how memories are stored in the mind of an ant. It is true that electrical pulses are silently shifted about inside the skulls of animals, but this is done in a manner far from understood. What Penrose is telling us is that evolution, working on computers made of meat, crossed a threshold in a way that involves laws of physics not yet known. It could be that if and when those deeper laws are discovered and we know exactly how our brain does what it does, we will be able to construct a replica (perhaps made of nonorganic matter, perhaps requiring organic molecules) that will simulate a human mind. But to expect a calculating machine made with components of the sort now in use or imagined to cross the threshold seems hopelessly unwarranted.

What does a computer do? It twiddles symbols—symbols that are meaningless until we attach meanings to them. It twiddles them in blind obedience to syntactical rules provided by the software. But our minds do more than twiddle symbols. They also twiddle meanings of symbols. I can easily imagine a monstrous machine made of Tinker Toys that can play Grand Master chess, but I cannot imagine it will know it is playing chess. By the end of this century I expect a chess program to be able to defeat any grand master while playing under the usual time restraints. Even now chess programs can crush grand masters when moves must be made within a few seconds. I expect that powerful computers will steadily improve in their ability to do all sorts of extraordinary things, but these things will all be done by symbol twiddling. I do not believe that the complexity of their circuitry will push them across the magic threshold.

Endless novels, stories, plays, and even operas have been written about intelligent robots, and it is no accident, I suspect, that so many strong AIers were science-fiction buffs in their youth. My favorite novel about robotics is a little-known one by Lord Dunsany, inexplicably never published in the United States. Titled *The Last Revolution* (1951), it concerns a rebellion against humanity of superintelligent, self-reproducing machines, the sort of rebellion that Tipler and Moravec believe possible. The book's funniest scene occurs when the narrator plays chess with the first prototype. Its inventor, Ablard Pender, lives with his aunt Mary. He pretends to wind up his "gadget" with a key so as not to frighten her by letting her know it is alive.

It requires only a few moves for the narrator, whose Ruy López opening quickly takes a bizarre turn not in any chess manual, to realize he is playing not only against an intelligence superior to his own but against a mind aware of what it is doing.

When Pender's girlfriend, Alicia, first sees the crablike, four-legged monster and its eyes like a cockroach's, there is an intuitive flash on her face like forked lightning. She senses immediately that the thing is alive. A dog, frightened by something it too knows is living but that has no smell, howls and bites the iron. The thing tears the dog to pieces.

The brain of Pender's robot consists of fine wire that transmits electrical pulses. "Did you make it entirely yourself?" Alicia asks.

"Yes, of course," Pender replies. "Don't you like it?"

"Time," says Alicia, "will have to show that."

THIRTY-SEVEN

THE CURIOUS MIND
OF ALLAN BLOOM

In 1987 Simon and Schuster published Allan Bloom's The Closing of the American Mind: How Higher Education Has Failed Democracy and Impoverished the Souls of Today's Students. *The book is a powerful indictment of today's higher learning for its neglect of the Great Books of the western world in favor of what Robert Hutchins called the cafeteria approach to education—allowing students to pick and choose trivial courses on topics they find interesting. Saul Bellow, one of Bloom's students, provides the book's foreword. To the surprise of both Simon and Schuster and Professor Bloom, the book became an instant best-seller.*

My review appeared in Education and Society (Spring 1988), *the premier issue of a quarterly published by the Anti-Defamation League of B'nai Birth.*

In the 1930s, when Robert Hutchins was president of the University of Chicago, he and Mortimer Adler raised a great ruckus about the decay of college education. In *The Higher Learning in America*, and in later books, speeches, and articles, Hutchins pleaded for a return to liberal education grounded in familiarity with the great literature and philosophy of the past.

Hutchins lived to see all the trends he denounced with such vigor and wit steadily increase. Our universities, he said in 1954, have become "high-class flophouses where parents send their children to keep them off the labor market and out of their own hair." Now comes Allan David Bloom, a professor of social thought at the University of Chicago, to echo and amplify the Hutchins-Adler rhetoric. In spite of his scholarly style and erudition, and to everyone's amazement, Bloom's book was for months on the *New York Times's* nonfiction best-seller list.

Professor Bloom is the author of a volume about Shakespeare's politics, and translator of two classics on education: Plato's *Republic* and Rousseau's *Emile*. His *Closing of the American Mind*, a powerful, idiosyncratic indictment of everything he finds wrong on today's campuses, has obviously struck a raw nerve, especially among parents who have seen their offspring graduate college with minds as empty as they were in high school.

Like Hutchins before him, Bloom blames the mediocrity of college teaching on a pervasive moral and philosophical relativism. In reaction to the certainties of past ages of faith, relativism abolishes all absolutes except the absolute of being free from absolutes. Bloom sees this great opening as a great closing. Because there is no way to define the good life, colleges no longer urge students to seek it. Instead of introducing young people to the wisdom of the past, colleges offer a flea market of unrelated courses from which students select whatever they find easiest and most to their liking.

Unfortunately, Bloom weakens his arguments by unrestrained caricature. He tells us that professors and students have lost sight of what the Constitution calls inalienable rights. He sees black power as an effort to obtain superior rights, not equality. Affirmative action promotes the racism our Founding Fathers tried to "defang." Government loans and quotas have flooded the universities with poorly prepared blacks whose teachers are afraid to give them low grades, and whose presence is a leading cause of sagging educational standards. Although relativism has promoted an admirable belief in racial equality, there has been little social integration. Tables in eating halls still separate into black and white. Bloom attributes this in part to a sense of shame among black students for their special treatment, and to a smoldering white resentment.

Bloom is all for openness to other cultures provided it stimulates a search for standards, but if there is no fundamental human nature, with needs common to all societies, the search becomes meaningless. Good versus evil gives way to an "I'm okay, you're okay" attitude that discourages interest in ethics and politics. Because there are no standards for the good life, no Platonic vision of an ideal society, the basis for the social activism of the sixties has evaporated. Students have turned inward, absorbed with self, concerned only with making money, and enjoying movies, sex, and music.

Sex, however, has become casual, passionless, and "flat-souled." Romance has gone the way of binding contracts. Students have forgotten how to say "I love you" except when they dump a bed partner. Bloom is struck speechless when he sees a couple, who have been roommates throughout their college years, part with a handshake. Relationships have turned gray and amorphous. Students don't date; they live in groups with no more sex differentiation than "animal herds when not in heat." The desire for marriage has diminished, and along with it the motive for gallantry. "Why should a man risk his life to protect a karate champion?"

Women are rapidly gaining equality, as Plato thought they should, but Bloom thinks the feminists go too far in trying to obliterate natural distinctions. "Law may prescribe that the male nipples be made equal to the female ones," he declares in one of his most embarrassing aphorisms, "but they still will not give milk." The feminists are trapped between conflicting loyalties. They ridicule their mothers' advice, "He won't respect you or marry you if you give him what he wants too easily," then they wonder why they are losing both respect and marriage proposals.

Bloom is also down on the feminists for what he perceives as their indifference to the Great Books. Instead of reading them to learn how earlier ages coped with male chauvinism, they dismiss them as useless relics of a male-dominated past. To Bloom's annoyance, they have even persuaded Bible translators to replace all masculine pronouns for God with neuter pronouns, as if Great Books should be rewritten to avoid offending the latest sensibilities.[1]

Like all conservatives, most of whom have hailed his book as a modern classic, Bloom sees the monogamous family as essential to any good society, and the rising divorce rate as "America's most urgent social problem." Students from broken homes are filled with suppressed "rage, doubt and fear." Many undergo long, ineffective mental therapies, financed by guilt-ridden parents. There are no hints in Bloom's book of the terrible quarrels that prevailed when divorce was difficult, or the damage this inflicted on children. There is no hope that new freedoms may lead to happier homes.

Loss of aesthetic standards parallel the loss of truth and goodness. Students no longer can distinguish "the sublime from trash." This is most obvious, Bloom thinks, with respect to music. Except for a small elite, classical music is dead. There is no escape from rock's *boom, thumpa, boom* in dormitories, cars, on TV and movie screens, in concert halls, and blasting out of Walkmans. "As long as they have the Walkman on, they cannot hear what the great tradition has to say. And, after its prolonged use, when they take it off, they find they are deaf."

I would guess that Bloom's blistering attack on rock, rivaled only by a chapter in Jerry Falwell's *Listen, America!*, is a major reason for his book's success. Word about it has spread and almost every reader will relish it. (The people who won't probably won't be reading this book.) What is the culmination of our vast technology? "A pubescent child whose body throbs with orgasmic rhythms, whose feelings are made articulate in hymns to the joys of onanism or the killing of parents; whose ambition is to win fame and wealth in imitating the drag-queen who makes the music."

Bloom's final chapter, a stirring defense of the "good old great books," is pure Hutchins except for a failure to mention how college athletics divert money and energy from everything a university is supposed to do. Hutchins is never mentioned. Mortimer Adler is cited only to praise his business acumen in promoting the Great Books set he edited. Indeed, Bloom calls the Hutchins-

Adler Great Books movement an amateurish "cult," marred by a "coarse evangelistic tone."

Nevertheless, Bloom believes that Great Books should be the core of every liberal education. He can understand why scientists are indifferent to the science classics. Unlike the liberal arts, science is a cumulative enlargement and refinement of knowledge. Studying Newton's *Principia*, for example, won't teach a physics student anything he can't learn more easily from a modern textbook. It is the hostility to literary and philosophical classics by liberal arts professors that puzzles Bloom, who maintains that in the humanities, now a "submerged old Atlantis," book reading has degenerated into an elevation of criticism over content. Bloom sees the French fad of deconstructionism as the ultimate neglect of what great works of art and literature say in favor of studying how they should be examined. He predicts that deconstructionism will soon deconstruct here as it already has in Paris.

Bloom is as coy as was Hutchins about revealing his own metaphysical posits. There are constant references to the "soul," even to the "perfect soul," and on page 137 he distinguishes the soul from both body and mind. Kant is praised for viewing the soul as an utterly mysterious entity that "stands outside the grasp of science." Does Bloom think of the soul as Kant and Plato did (and Aristotle did not), as a personality that survives the body?

Bloom clearly believes there are objective moral standards, but how to recognize them remains vague. Is he an emotive ethicist who rests morality on nothing firmer than human desires, or does he think reason and science can support a naturalistic ethics that cuts across all cultural barriers? Must we look to God as the ground of morals? "Real religion and knowledge of the Bible have diminished to the vanishing point," Bloom complains, but what on earth does he mean by "real religion"? Atheists, he insists, have a "better grasp of religion" than those sociologists who are fascinated with the "sacred." Bloom likens the latter to a man who keeps a "toothless old circus lion around the house . . . to experience the thrills of the jungle." Does the lion with teeth exist? If so, Bloom is silent on where to look for it.[2]

As for knowledge of the Bible fading, imagine Bloom in debate with Falwell or Jimmy Swaggart about what the Good Book says. He would quickly discover that today's fundamentalist leaders know the Scriptures as thoroughly as did Saint Augustine and Martin Luther. Nowhere does Bloom consider the baleful effect of fundamentalism on American education, or the equally debilitating influence of the occult revolution. About half our college students, polls show, believe in Satan, angels, and astrology.

Bloom devotes a chapter to arguing that today's cultural relativism springs from the popularization of German philosophy, especially the teachings of Nietzsche and such heirs as Freud, Max Weber, and Martin Heidegger. (Nietzsche has a longer list of references in Bloom's index than any other person.) "The self-understanding of hippies, yippies, yuppies, panthers, prelates and presidents has unconsciously been formed by German thought of a half-century earlier." Nietzsche has had more influence on the American left, Bloom actually believes, than Karl Marx, now obsolete and boring. He sees German nihilism behind radical violence, even in the popularity of the song "Mack the Knife." There are horror tales of Bloom's experiences with student violence at Cornell, and strong condemnation of the cowardice of Cornell officials and professors. Terrorism around the world, the thirst for bloody revolution, are all consequences of Nietzsche's evil ideas.

This is Teutonic baloney. Nietzsche was something of a rage among U.S. intellectuals when H. L. Mencken wrote a book about his philosophy in 1908, but his influence on native relativism even then was minimal. The stronger influence came from sociologists and anthropologists, who may have been impressed by German metaphysics, but whose relativism flowed mainly from their investigations. Books like William Sumner's *Folkways* were more influential than any book by Nietzsche.

Nowhere does Bloom seem aware that American philosophy has for half a century been tramping to the beat of British skepticism and empiricism. Hume has had far more effect on American philosophy than the German metaphysicians. Hegel, for instance, was the source of everything wrong in philosophy for our greatest thinkers: Charles Peirce, William James, and John Dewey. (Incidentally, the only influential twentieth-century philosopher or theologian mentioned in the book is Dewey.) Protestant, Catholic, and Jewish theologians have also reacted violently to what they consider the Hegelian sin of hubris. Bloom's pommeling of German metaphysics reads as if it had been written in 1916, the year Santayana published *Egotism and German Philosophy*.

Bloom has a knack for writing wisely and eloquently, then suddenly uncorking something foolish. I will cite two Bloomers. On page 52 he sees Descartes and Pascal as opposites, representing the eternal conflict between reason and revelation. But both men were great creative mathematicians, and is there any exercise of reason purer than mathematics? As for revelation, both were devout Catholics. The main difference: Descartes thought unaided reason could prove such things as God's existence. Pascal, the better thinker, was sure it couldn't.

On page 106 we read: "To strangers from another planet, what would be the most striking thing is that sexual passion [among our youth] no longer includes the illusion of eternity." Does Bloom suppose that on other worlds there are humanoids with sex organs like ours and marriage rituals?

I closed *Closing* with unbounded admiration for the clarity of Bloom's style and for his quixotic courage in battling educators who will ignore arguments that are fundamentally sound. I also had a strong feeling of *déjà vu*, because I had heard it all before. Hutchins and Adler fought the same fight when I was an undergraduate at the University of Chicago. At least Hutchins achieved one of his goals. He got rid of the football team.

POSTSCRIPT (1995)

Bloom died in 1992, a year before Simon & Schuster published Love and Friendship, *a collection of his essays. Clifford Orwin, a political scientist at the University of Toronto, wrote a warm memoir, "Remembering Allan Bloom," for the Summer 1993 issue of* The American Scholar. *Because it shed no light on Bloom's metaphysical opinions, I wrote to ask Orwin if he knew what they were. He replied that although Bloom constantly stressed the superiority of religious piety over atheism, leading many students back to the faith of their fathers, he never made a public statement of what he believed. Nor did Orwin know.*

Mortimer Adler, in the prologue to a collection of his essays titled Reforming Education: The Opening of the American Mind *(1989), is strongly critical of Bloom for his unwillingness to mention the University of Chicago's Great Books program. Adler accuses Bloom of viewing the Great Books as limited to the education of an elite, whereas he and Hutchins believed they could be understood by anybody, including high school students.*

In his biography of Hutchins, Unseasonable Truths *(1989), Harry Ashmore expresses amazement over the same omission in Bloom's book, especially since Bloom was an undergraduate at the University of Chicago when Hutchins was president, and actually taught a Great Books seminar. Asked why he never mentioned Hutchins in his best-seller, Bloom's reply, as quoted by Ashmore, was as follows:*

> *There are not many changes I would make in the book in response to the criticisms I have received but that's one. The University of Chicago was my inspiration, and Hutchins was the University of Chicago. I've always regarded myself as a student of Hutchins, a figure I look up to with the greatest admiration. He was a gem, a genius of an educational administrator.*

NOTES

1. Bloom's perpetual, compulsive use of male pronouns reflects his opposition to the growing practice of eliminating sexist language from secular books. On the first two pages of his preface I counted 17 male pronouns that refer to college teachers. Although his university's president is a woman, no female faculty members are visible in his book. In a seven-page chapter titled "The Self" I circled 58 uses of "man" and "men" when bachelor Bloom really means humanity.

2. Bloom's respect for the Bible is mystifying. I was unable to learn anything about his religious upbringing, but on page 60 Bloom has nothing but praise for the Bible's influence on his grandparents. "Their home was spiritually rich because all the things done in it . . . found their origin in the Bible's commandments . . . and the commentaries on

them. . . . I am not saying anything so trite as that life is fuller when people have myths to live by. I mean rather that a life based on the Book is closer to the truth, that it provides the material for deeper research in and access to the real nature of things." On pages 374–75 he deplores the way colleges teach the Bible only as literature. "To include it in the humanities is already a blasphemy, a denial of its own claims." Such remarks make sense coming from a conservative Catholic or Protestant. Why Bloom feels compelled to make them is almost as unfathomable as Mortimer Adler's lifelong reverence for Thomas Aquinas.

THIRTY-EIGHT

ISAIAH BERLIN:
FOX OR HEDGEHOG?

Sir Isaiah Berlin, born in Latvia in 1909, became one of Oxford University's most distinguished philosophers and historians of political ideas. He is perhaps best known for two distinctions: between positive and negative liberty, and between two types of thinkers: foxes and hedgehogs.

The Crooked Timber of Humanity: Chapters in the History of Ideas, is a collection of brilliant, scholarly essays edited by Henry Hardy and published by Knopf in 1991. My review appeared in Dimensions *(vol. 6, no. 2, 1991).*

This fifth and latest gathering of essays by Sir Isaiah Berlin, one of the world's most respected historians of ideas, is cause for rejoicing. "No century has seen so much remorseless and continued slaughter of human beings by one another as our own," he says at the beginning of "European Unity and Its Vicissitudes." "Compared with it, even the wars of religion and the Napoleonic campaigns seem local and humane." If there is any hope for the future, it lies in the lessons Berlin has been trying to teach us throughout his long and illustrious career.

The slaughter around the globe continues. What are Berlin's central theses, which might, if accepted by enough nations, at least have a chance of creating a world in which holocausts of all varieties would be obsolete?

The most important thesis is the incommensurability of cultures, the realization that we lack criteria by which one culture can be rated superior to another. Most wars of the past, the genocides, the pogroms, the gulags, the millions murdered by the tyrants of Russia, Germany, and China, all have in common a belief on the part of nations and individuals that there is an ideal form of society which justifies the deaths of millions to achieve it. To make a perfect omelette, Berlin writes in "The Pursuit of the Ideal," "there is surely no limit to the number of eggs that should be broken." No matter that thousands perish if it will make millions happy in some far-off utopia. Unfortunately, "the eggs are broken . . . but the omelette remains invisible."

As a youth, Berlin tells us in the same essay, he assumed the possibility, in principle, of an ideal society until a translation of Giambattista Vico's *La scienza nuova* (1725) shocked him into a realization that every great culture is a unique mixture of ends that cannot be judged by the ends of other great cultures. There is no way "conflicting" cultures can be merged to form one grand synthesis. A second insight came from reading Johann Gottfried Herder; while Vico considered only a succession of cultures in time, Herder went further to defend the incommensurability of contemporary cultures.

Utopias, from Plato's to Wells's, can be valuable as poetic visions of possibilities, but "as guides to conduct they can prove literally fatal." There is no "final solution" of humanity's problems, in Hitler's terrible phrase. We must learn, Berlin keeps pounding in our ears, that in ethics and politics there are no laws comparable to those of mathematics and physics. We must rest content with an "uneasy equilibrium" in which irreconcilable values clash in the world, inside nations, and among individuals. Berlin's favorite quotation, which gives the book its title, is Kant's statement: "Out of timber so crooked as that from which man is made nothing entirely straight can be built."

From this perspective Berlin heaps scorn on all historians—Fichte, Hegel, Spengler, Marx, and even Toynbee—who find patterns in history as it marches toward some predetermined ideal. Karl Marx, who did so much damage to the world by his doctrine that inevitable progress would culminate in a Communist utopia, actually wanted to dedicate *Das Kapital* to Darwin, convinced that his book disclosed laws comparable to the laws of evolution. Darwin politely refused, pleading ignorance of economics. As an economist, Marx himself was much more crank than scientist. The very concept of a perfect society is as foolish as that of a perfect house. Berlin's 1953 lecture, "Historical Inevitability" (reprinted in his book *Four Essays on Liberty*), has become a classic attack on deterministic theories of history, alongside Karl Popper's *Poverty of Historicism* and *The Open Society and Its Enemies*.

Is Berlin a cultural relativist, unwilling to make moral judgments about various societies? Only in the trivial sense that he sees no way to rate the relative worth of great cultures, and doesn't believe that the end of history will resemble the final fitting of jigsaw pieces into a unified picture. He maintains, however, that there is a small set of "ultimate values" that derives from a common human nature.

No culture believes in wanton killing. No culture today defends Hitler's gas chambers. The diversity of values cannot be unlimited because "the nature of men, however various and subject to change, must possess some generic character if it is to be called human at all." If you meet someone who sees nothing wrong in the Holocaust, Berlin writes, you are entitled to consider him not human, but closer to an animal or plant. Such persons are often put in asylums. These ultimate human values are not imposed on us by a deity or by a metaphysics. They simply spring from needs common to the human species.

Another basic theme in Berlin's essays, closely related to those we have mentioned, is his ringing defense of free will. Although determinism may hold in the physical world, it is totally irrelevant in ethics and politics, because it is psychologically as impossible not to assume free will, in Berlin's opinion, as it is to pretend there is "no time or space or number." If ethical determinism is valid, Berlin has written elsewhere, it would be appropriate to attribute moral responsibility to the solar system. Here Berlin is following Kant's dictum that it is meaningless to speak of "ought" unless there is also a genuine, nonillusory "can."

In a revealing 1983 interview published in *Partisan Review*, Berlin expressed his belief that the free wills of individuals can drastically alter history. If Lenin had been run over by a train when a boy, Berlin said, Russia's later history would surely be different. If Churchill had not been Prime Minister during World War II, Hitler might have won the war. Single persons can ignite explosions once a situation reaches "critical mass." Although Berlin did not add this, we now know that a mad dictator with atom bombs can, by an act of will, obliterate entire cities, perhaps even nations. Not all historians, however, are happy with Berlin's defense of free will. The Cambridge historian E. H. Carr called it a "dead horse" that Berlin has "flogged into life."

Still another of Berlin's principal tenets is that totalitarianism has its roots in the romantic belief (at one time, stronger in Germany than elsewhere) that an ideal society is like a work of art. This perfect society is not pursued through reason and science; it is created like a painting or a symphony. Berlin quotes a Russian writer: "Where is the dance before I have danced it?" The twentieth century's admiration for the romantic leader who molds history to his heart's desire was presaged, Berlin thinks, by the Byronism of England and France, by Fichte, Friedrich Schlegel, Schiller and Nietzsche, and by Germany's period of *Sturm und Drang* (the late eighteenth century), in which young writers rebelled against all standards.

In his essay "The Bent Twig," Berlin defends Schiller's theory that if a society is humiliated (as Germany's was after the First World War), it tends to snap back like a bent twig, the snapping often accelerated by the citizenry's enthusiasm for a charismatic leader who vows to restore the nation's former greatness. Berlin wrote this essay before the snapping back of the Baltic states. Will Iraq soon be snapping back? Will Tibet?

The book's longest, most controversial essay is on Joseph de Maistre. He was Europe's noisiest ultramontanist, a term suggesting, in Maistre's day, that the Pope was "beyond the mountains [the Alps]." Today it is a pejorative term for the pro-Italian bureaucracy of the Vatican. In Maistre's time ultramontanism was a Catholic fundamentalism that espoused a belief in the divine right of kings, and the subservience of kings to the Pope. According to Maistre's dark Augustinian theology, men are too wicked to govern themselves. The most famous passage in Maistre's writings, quoted in full by Berlin, is his passionate praise of the hangman as the preserver of a nation's order. Maistre even looked kindly on the Inquisition, believing it not only saved millions of souls from hell, but also saved Spain from chaos. He also hated the free exchange of ideas, and was the first Western writer openly to advocate opposing art and science.

Berlin considers these sentiments a prelude to modern totalitarianism. Maistre's "monstrous trinity" of Hangman, King, and Pope, his distrust of reason and glorification of blind obedience, are, Berlin asserts, at "the heart of the totalitarianism, of both left and right, of our terrible century."

There is much to be said for this, but I think Berlin overstates. Maistre was an aberration whom even the Vatican denounced. It is impossible to imagine Hitler, Mussolini, Stalin, Mao, or even Franco taking orders from the Pope. I suspect that Maistre had less influence on German Nazism than Luther, who hated Jews with a passion, or Calvin, who burned Servetus at the stake.

Berlin was born in Riga, Latvia, in 1909, of Jewish parents, his father a prosperous timber merchant. The family settled in England in 1919, where young Isaiah obtained his bachelor's and master's degrees at Corpus Christi College, Oxford. He has had two careers—teaching at numerous universities in England and the United States, and holding academic and diplomatic posts, such as his stint as first secretary in the British Embassy in Washington, D.C. during World War II. For nine years he was president of Wolfson College, Oxford. He is one of the governors of Hebrew University, in Jerusalem. The Queen knighted him in 1957.

Berlin speaks both Russian and English with astonishing rapidity. Even though he slows down for lectures, they have been described as "torrential cascades" and "a noise like bathwater running." Gertrude Himmelfarb, reviewing The Crooked Timber of Humanity in The New York Times Book Review, called Berlin's writing style "breathless." Breathless it may be, but every page in the book is, nevertheless, dense with erudition.

I noticed a curious reluctance on Berlin's part to discuss American philosophers. No modern philosopher has stressed more vigorously the importance of an open, pluralistic, democratic society than John Dewey, who based his naturalistic ethics on values common to all cultures. No other recent philosopher has so strongly condemned the use of evil means to obtain good but distant ends. When Berlin writes, "We cannot legislate for the unknown consequences of consequences of consequences," the sentence could have been written by Dewey (if he had been less dull a writer). Yet at no time is Dewey ever mentioned by Berlin.

In the essay "The Pursuit of the Ideal," Berlin refers to an "eminent American philosopher" who pointed out that truth need not be interesting. Was it Dewey who said this? One longs to know. In his essay on Maistre, Berlin cites another "eminent philosopher" who stressed the need to get at the heart of a philosopher's vision in order to understand him. The philosopher was William James, but why not say so? Can it be that Berlin finds American philosophy inferior to British philosophy?

At the close of a BBC interview to be found in Bryan Magee's *Men of Ideas* (published by the BBC in 1978, later by Oxford University Press), Berlin said he agrees with Bertrand Russell that the central visions of great philosophers are always lucid. "No one who reads them intently," adds Berlin, "can have much doubt of what is at the heart of Plato's or Augustine's or Descartes' or Locke's or Spinoza's or Kant's conceptions of the world. And this is equally true of most contemporary philosophers of any standing: their basic convictions are seldom in serious doubt."

What, then, is Berlin's central vision? Ironically, like so many other historians of ideas who strive to appear objective, Berlin is circumspect about revealing his own metaphysical principles. We know he hates tyranny, favors pluralism and democracy, and is a good friend of Israel, but is he a theist, like his mentor Kant, or an atheist, pantheist, or agnostic? Clearly he is not Jewish in any religious sense. In the *Partisan Review* interview cited earlier Berlin put it this way:

> I have never in my life either wanted not to be a Jew, or wished to be one. A Jew is a Jew as a table is a table. . . . I've never been either proud or ashamed of being a Jew any more than I am proud or ashamed of possessing two arms, two legs, two eyes.

Berlin's best known work is the long essay, "The Hedgehog and the Fox," a brilliant study of Tolstoy first published in 1953 (reprinted in Berlin's *Russian Thinkers*). The title comes from an epigram attributed to the Greek poet Archilochus (675?–635): "The fox knows many things, but the hedgehog knows one big thing." (In England the proverb takes the form of, "The fox knows many tricks and the cat only one, but that one is the best of all." The clever fox boasts of many ways to escape hounds. The stupid cat knows only one—to climb a tree.) In his essay, Berlin takes the original epigram to mean that the fox is a pluralist who embraces life in all its discordant multiplicity. The hedgehog is a monist who sees everything from one central point of view. Aristotle, Montaigne, and Shakespeare were foxes, Berlin claims; Lucretius and Dante were hedgehogs. Berlin contends that Tolstoy, a fox by temperament, desperately tried all his life to be a hedgehog. In this he failed, ending as a tragic old man, "wandering self-blinded," without ever finding the "single serene vision."

We know that Sir Isaiah Berlin is a fox. Is he also some sort of hedgehog? If any reader knows, please write and tell me.

POSTSCRIPT (1995)

Henry Hardy, who edited Berlin's book of essays, sent me the following letter and gave permission for Dimensions *to print it. They did so in Vol. 6, No. 3, 1991.*

Dear Martin:

. . . Your excellent review of Crooked Timber *in* Dimensions *invites a couple of comments.*

I'm delighted to be told that the philosopher who talked of the heart of every philosopher's vision was William James. I thought it was Russell—as your next paragraph seems to allow—but can you give me a reference for the attribution to James (or for that matter to Russell!)? The reason the philosopher is not named in the essay on Maistre—I raised the point with Isaiah myself—is that he couldn't be sure if his memory that it was Russell was correct. In the Magee interview, though, he does name Russell in this context. I'm puzzled.

You ask who made the point about truth not being interesting: the answer is C. I. Lewis, according to Isaiah, but I haven't been able to find the quote. It doesn't seem to be in Mind and the World Order. *. . . As for Dewey, I don't know why he isn't mentioned—possibly because Isaiah hasn't studied him much, but this is a dangerous hypothesis, especially given the mention on p. 77 of* Concepts and Categories.

Your concluding question is, I take it, largely rhetorical, and I am no better equipped to answer it than you are. If to be a hedgehog is to be a monist, then obviously Isaiah isn't a hedgehog; but if it is to be preoccupied with a single issue or set of issues, then there is some truth in the classification—but not much, as Isaiah is always ready to surprise one with the breadth and variety of his interests and knowledge. Undoubtedly, though, his main work has had a central focus. So it all depends what you mean by "hedgehog"—once again the truth is not especially interesting!

I think some of the encapsulations in your review are particularly happy and economical, and I congratulate you warmly. You are a fox, all right.

> *Yours ever,*
> *Henry Hardy*
> *Oxford, England*

P.S.: I have now put some of your questions to Isaiah. He tells me that he definitely took the point about philosophers' visions from Russell, who makes it, he believes, in his History of Western Philosophy. *The quotation from C. I. Lewis was given to him over the telephone in America once: his informant did not mention the work in which it appears.*

Mr. Hardy later called my attention to the following remarks by Berlin as they appeared in Conversations with Isaiah Berlin, *by Peter Halban (1992):*

> I have myself no sense of a reality above and beyond the life I know. I am not religious, but I place high value on the religious experience of believers. I am moved by religious services—those of the synagogue, but also of churches and mosques. I think that those who do not understand what it is to be religious, do not understand what human beings live by. That is why dry atheists seem to me blind and deaf to some forms of profound human experiences, perhaps the inner life: it is like being aesthetically blind.

If I understand Berlin correctly, he has no belief in a higher being, but like George Santayana, has a sort of aesthetic respect for those who have.

THIRTY-NINE

WHY I AM NOT A PRAGMATIST

Aside from the works of a few living American philosophers such as Richard Rorty, the epistemology of William James and John Dewey continues its steady decline. As philosophers of science, James and Dewey have now almost faded from the literature, while the reputation of Charles Peirce, who invented the term "pragmatism" but objected to its misuse by his friend James, continues to soar.

In this essay, a chapter from my Whys of a Philosophical Scrivener, *I attempt to explain why pragmatism has declined, and I also argue that the clash between Dewey and his major antagonist, Bertrand Russell, was largely a disagreement over a choice of language.*

I think pragmatism an amusing humbug.
—JUSTICE OLIVER WENDELL HOLMES, JR.,
in a Letter to Sir Frederick Pollock

Given the existence of a structured universe that is independent of our minds, and regardless of how we view its ontological status, there is an absurdly simple way to explain what is meant by saying that a statement or a belief (we will use these two words more or less interchangeably) about that world is true or false. It is called the correspondence theory of truth. Like the realist thesis the correspondence theory of truth has been held by almost all philosophers and scientists of the past, and it has always been taken for granted by every ordinary person who has not studied philosophy.

According to this theory an assertion or a belief is true if it corresponds with some aspect of the actual world. Sometimes the correspondence is said to be with a fact, taking "fact" in a very broad sense. A geologist may say, for example: "Evolution is not just a theory. It is a fact." By this he means that he believes it has been confirmed to such a high degree that we can confidently say it is true. Thus we are involved in an obvious circularity. Truth is a correspondence of statements with facts, and a fact is an assertion we believe is true. Both correspondence and fact are fuzzy words, difficult to define, and there is a vast literature on the technicalities involved in trying to make them precise.

Correspondence clearly does not mean copying in the way a photograph or a painting copies nature. There is no way to put a statement over a part of the universe to see how well it fits. Sometimes the meaning of a statement is picturable in the mind, such as "The earth rotates on its axis," but this is not always the case. "There is life in the interior of Jupiter" is fairly clear in meaning, but because we do not know what the interior of Jupiter is like, or what a Jovian life-form would look like, any mental image of the meaning is necessarily vague. Albert Einstein conjectured that the space of our universe may be the surface of a four-dimensional sphere, finite in volume but unbounded. Here the correspondence is with an object that cannot be pictured in the mind, although it can be precisely defined by four-dimensional Euclidean geometry. Rather than get involved with the great technical problems of defining correspondence, we will consider some commonplace examples in which the term's meaning will become clear enough for our humble purposes.

Suppose a deck of fifty-two playing cards is shuffled, spread face down on a table, and someone withdraws a card by sliding it out of the spread without turning the card face up. Beside the card is placed a sheet of paper on which is written, "This is the queen of hearts." What does it mean to say that the sentence on the paper is true?

It is easy to guess how ordinary people answer. (If you have any doubts, try asking friends.) They will answer in the same way similar questions were answered by the ancient Greek philosophers. The statement is true if, in fact, the chosen card *is* the queen of hearts. As Aristotle put it: "To say of what is that it is not, or of what is not that it is, is false; while to say of what is that it is, and what is not that it is not, is true." Similar remarks are in the *Dialogues* of Plato.[1]

Now we must introduce an all-important distinction. The correspondence theory defines only what it *means* to say a sentence is true or false. It says nothing about how to *decide* whether a sentence is true or false, or (as in the case of most scientific assertions) to evaluate the probability of whether an assertion is true or false. In other words, the correspondence theory is not concerned with criteria for truth. It tells us nothing about the kinds of tests that can be made for truth. If our sentence about the card is true, this truth is not dependent on future testing. The truth or falsity of the statement is not something that springs into reality when we turn over the card to see its face.

Statements in number theory provide trivial instances of the time-independence of truths about abstract entities in pure mathematics. It was shown a few years ago that the integer formed by 317 repetitions of the digit 1 is a prime. Few people would want to say that this number became prime only after it was proved to be a prime. The sentence "the number formed by 317 repetitions of 1 is prime" was true in the days of Pythagoras. Only recently did mathematicians *know* it to be true.

Although the truth about this number is a truth in pure mathematics, like so much of pure mathematics it also tells us something about the physical world. A prime number of n pebbles, for example, cannot be divided evenly into equal sets of pebbles other than by forming n sets of one pebble each, or one set of n pebbles. Thus statements about primes can be translated into statements about physical objects that maintain their identities as units. To say of seven cows that there are a prime number of cows is as true a statement about the world as "Snow is white." Note that the statement's truth depends solely on the meaning of "prime number," not on the existence of algorithms for efficiently deciding whether a given number is prime or composite.

In our card experiment we are entitled to say that the statement on the paper has a probability of 1/52 of being true. The simplest way to know for certain is to turn over the card. There are more complicated ways of testing. For example, we could lift an index corner of the card and slip a mirror under it. Everyone agrees that such tests are the only ways of knowing whether the written sentence is true or false.

To those who accept the correspondence theory of truth, science is a search for statements that correspond to the world's structure. When Sir Isaac Newton concluded that gravity is a force that varies directly with the product of two masses and inversely with the square of the distance between them, he expressed a law which he believed corresponded with the dynamic structure of the actual world. We shall be unconcerned with the methods by which scientists test such hypotheses, sometimes confirming them, sometimes disconfirming, sometimes refining. We assume that science has no way of being certain that any of its statements is absolutely true, although many of them can approach extremely close to certainty. No astronomer now doubts that Saturn's largest moon, Titan, has an atmosphere. But there is no formal procedure by which precise probabilities—what Carnap called degrees of confirmation—can be assigned to scientific statements except in an extremely rough way. Where there are two rival hypotheses, the best a scientist can do is make vague statements such as that he thinks one is probably true and the other is probably false. If he thinks the evidence is about equal for each, he may tell you the odds are fifty-fifty but personally he likes one theory better than the other.

What does a scientist have in mind when he says, "I am convinced that general relativity is true"? If you ask him, it is unlikely he will launch into a technical discussion of experiments which confirm the theory. He is more likely to give an answer essentially the same as the ordinary person's answer when asked what it means to say the statement "This is the queen of hearts" is true. He will tell you that he believes general relativity is true because it expresses in mathematical form the way he thinks the universe "out there," the universe independent of human minds, actually behaves.

We can clarify the distinction between the meaning of truth and the criteria for truth by considering some statements to which truth values can be assigned but which are difficult or impossible to evaluate. Suppose our selected card is returned to the deck, without anyone having seen its face, and the deck is shuffled. We alter the sentence on the paper to "The selected card *was* the queen of hearts." Everybody will agree that this is either true or false, and that it is true if, and only if, the chosen card was in fact the queen of hearts. Testing the statement is now difficult but not impossible. If the deck is brand-new, sliding the card over the surface of the table may have produced a faint smudge of dirt on the card's face. In taking the card from the spread, a corner may have become slightly bent. Fingerprints may be on the card. And so on. Such tests may not give as certain an answer as turning over the card before it was replaced, but they can establish the truth of the sentence with a high degree of probability. Scientific historians and criminal lawyers use just such tests to confirm or disconfirm conjectures about the past.

Suppose now that before the card of unseen face is replaced in the deck we take a photograph of its back. On the picture we write, "The card here photographed was the queen of hearts." The deck is then tossed into a furnace and destroyed. There is no longer any way to know what in fact the card was. Nevertheless most people, including most scientists and philosophers, would not hesitate to say that the untestable sentence is true if, and only if, the selected card was in fact the queen of hearts.

It is easy to think of scientific and historical statements for which truth is easily defined by Aristotle's correspondence theory even though it is unlikely they can ever be tested. "On a planet in the Andromeda galaxy there are ostriches." "At noon, on such-and-such a day, Shakespeare sneezed." Even though we may never learn the truth or falsity of either assertion, ordinary language puts no obstacle in the way of saying it is true or false. We need not be concerned here with statements about future events, such as Aristotle's famous example of a prediction that a sea battle will occur at a certain locale on a certain future date. Can such a statement be said *now* to be either true of false, or must one say it has no truth value until the assigned date arrives? Here the correspondence theory is inadequate unless, perhaps, one is a determinist who maintains that the statement corresponds to a state of the universe that inevitably will lead to the predicted sea battle or to its failure to take place.

The correspondence theory of truth has two traditional rivals: the coherence theory and the pragmatic theory. We will not discuss the first because, although it has its merits and its distinguished defenders, it has not been this century's major challenge to the correspondence theory. The major attack was launched by a group of philosophers who called themselves pragmatists. Their point of view dominated American philosophy during the first quarter of this century, and the school included three of our most eminent native thinkers: Charles Peirce, William James, and John Dewey. In England the movement's leader was F. C. S. Schiller, an interesting philosopher but one whose views were less influential. In any case, this chapter would be too long if we considered him.

The term "pragmatism" was first introduced by Peirce in an article in *Popular Science Monthly* on "How to Make Our Ideas Clear." The article's main point was what later became known as the pragmatic maxim for deciding what a concept or an assertion means. We simply ask what possible consequences in human behavior follow from the "idea" in question. If there are no consequences, the idea is meaningless. The sum total of all the consequences constitute the idea's full meaning.

What does "queen of hearts" mean? It denotes a card which our culture calls the queen of hearts. What does "This is the queen of hearts" mean? It means that if we look at the card's face and see that it is the face of a queen of hearts, we will call the sentence true. What does truth mean? Applying Peirce's maxim, it means the successful passing of whatever tests support the correspondence of the assertion with reality. Peirce did not abandon the notion of correspondence, he merely introduced a subtle shift in the way one talks about correspondence. Since only a process of verification can decide whether a statement is true or false, why not *define* truth as the passing of such tests?

William James, fascinated by this suggestion, initiated the pragmatic movement with a series of dazzling lectures that were published in 1907 as the book entitled *Pragmatism: A New Name for Some Old Ways of Thinking*. The subtitle was a good one. As James was fully aware, pragmatism did not introduce any radically new ideas. It offered only a radical way of talking about old ideas.

At the heart of James's pragmatism was the abandonment of the traditional definition of truth as a timeless correspondence of an assertion (or belief) with the real world regardless of whether it is verified or not. This was replaced by a definition based on Peirce's maxim. Truth is that which is confirmed by testing. It is that which "works" or, in one of James's more unfortunate phrases, that which "pays in cash value."

In our card experiment James would say that the sentence "This is the queen of hearts" is true if, and only if, when we turn the card over we see it is the queen of hearts. If the unseen card is returned to the deck and the deck destroyed, James would say that the sentence "The selected card was the queen of hearts" is true if, and only if, had the card been looked at before it was returned, we would have seen that it was the queen of hearts.[2]

James never discarded the notion of correspondence with reality. There are even passages in his writings in which he speaks of correspondence as something too obvious to require defense. The turning of the card verifies or falsifies the written statement, he would have readily admitted, depending on whether the selected card is or is not in fact the queen of hearts. And of course Aristotle would have agreed that the best way to decide if the sentence is true or false is to turn the card. The central issue here is one of linguistic preference. Is it best to preserve the language of the old correspondence theory, or is something gained by modifying it along the lines proposed by the pragmatists?

James lived at a time when Western philosophy was dominated by German metaphysics, by philosophers who insisted with boundless egoism that all sorts of timeless metaphysical truths could be established by rational arguments. During the same period, science was suggesting that all our ideas about the world are provisional, and can be established only with varying degrees of probability as they pass or fail empirical tests. It was James's belief that if the meaning of truth could be put more in harmony with scientific method—instead of saying a hypothesis works because it is true in some absolute sense, we turn the words around and say it is probably true because it works—this new way of talking about truth would inject enormous clarity into philosophical speculation and eliminate all sorts of metaphysical muddles.

James and Schiller introduced a second notion. In the absence of contrary evidence, if a belief satisfies a human desire, that too is a practical consequence and therefore a legitimate basis for calling certain beliefs true. If Moslem theology makes Moslems happier, the theology is for them true, and similarly for other metaphysical or theological "over-beliefs" (as James called them)—beliefs that cannot be established by reason or science but which do not conflict with reason or science, and which have psychological value for the believer.

Dewey did not accept this, but he did embrace the more fundamental tenet of pragmatism, the conviction that philosophy would be better served if it substituted for the ancient language of correspondence a new language in which statements become true only when they pass tests for truth. "The true means the verified and means nothing else . . ." was how Dewey crisply put it in the chapter on logic in his *Reconstruction in Philosophy*. In later years, to avoid misunderstanding, Dewey stopped using the word *truth* altogether. He preferred the phrase "warranted assertibility." It had for Dewey essentially the same meaning that "confirmation" had for Carnap and his friends.

James waxed so enthusiastic about the benefits he thought would follow from the pragmatic redefinition of truth that he made all sorts of extravagant statements which were easy to misinterpret. For example, if truth is no more than what is verified, then the statement "This is the queen of hearts" is not true or false until the card is turned. James did not hesitate to recommend this way of speaking. His *Pragmatism* abounds with eloquent passages about how truth is continually *made* by acts of verification. In ordinary language one would normally say this of only a very restricted class of statements. If I declare, "I will take a bath tonight," I can make the statement true by taking the bath. (Aristotle's sea battle!) But James made it sound as if he meant that science does not discover timeless facts, but somehow creates those facts by acts of verification. It seemed as if he meant that a statement such as "Saturn has rings" was not true in the days of Aristotle, but was made true by later astronomers when they first observed the planet's rings. James's ambiguous language, as well as the sometimes vague language of Dewey, lends itself easily to this kind of parody.

"The truth of an idea is not a stagnant property inherent in it. Truth *happens* to an idea. It *becomes* true, is *made* true by events. Its verity *is* in fact an event, a process: the process namely of its verifying itself. . . ."

"Truth is *made*, just as health, wealth and strength are made, in the course of experience."

Parodies? Alas, they are quotations from James's *Pragmatism*.

What James actually meant, however, is something utterly commonplace. He meant that as science keeps finding better and better reasons for calling certain assertions true (in the old correspondence sense), the process never reaches certainty. Science is forever changing and improving, but never incorrigible. For instance, astronomers keep altering their theories about how the solar system was formed, or about the chemical nature of the earth's core. Does this mean that as scientific opinions change about past events, those events change? Does it mean that as opinions change about the earth's core, the composition of the core changes? James certainly did not believe anything so ridiculous, but his language was so fuzzy and eccentric that it was easy for critics to suppose he meant such things. The classic instance of how preposterous James's *Pragmatism* seemed to British realists is G. E. Moore's essay "William James's *Pragmatism*" (you'll find it in Moore's *Philosophical Studies*). It is an amusing piece of polemics. By taking James's words at their face value it was easy for Moore to show how sharply they clashed with ordinary language, leading the reader to suppose James meant all sorts of absurd things he clearly did not mean.

James was so astounded by his failure to communicate in *Pragmatism* that he wrote an unintentionally funny sequel, *The Meaning of Truth,* in which he tried hard to clear up major misunderstandings. Unfortunately, the sequel contains so many of the same cloudy phrases that it only compounded the confusion. He repeats, for instance, his notorious passage from *Pragmatism:* "The true . . . is only the expedient in the way of our thinking, just as the right is only the expedient in the way of our behaving." Again, what James meant is commonplace: If an assertion passes certain tests for truth it is useful to assume it is true. If studies of the weather show it will probably rain, it is expedient to take an umbrella. But owing to James's novel language, with its refusal to talk of truth as a timeless relation, it was easy for his critics to suppose he meant that one could call any belief true if a person found the belief expedient at the time, and false if the belief had evil consequences. Sidney Hook once rebutted this charge by considering the statement on a label: "This bottle contains poison." If a person drinks the contents and dies, the label has been verified, although no pragmatist would suppose that this verification was useful to the person who made it.

Dewey was more cautious. As I have said, he found it less confusing to drop the word *truth* altogether. Nevertheless, his language, because it, too, departed so widely from common usage, also was widely misunderstood. Like James, Dewey fully realized that if an assertion passes tests for truth it is because the assertion corresponds with reality, but his way of speaking, like that of James, was easy to ridicule. Bertrand Russell, his most eminent antagonist, was both a realist in the sense of believing in a "stuff" behind the phaneron (whereas Dewey dismissed this belief as meaningless), and also a staunch defender of truth as a timeless correspondence with reality. The two men frequently attacked each other's view of truth, each presenting such a caricature of the other's opinions that it was easy to make them seem absurd. An entire book could be devoted to this battle of titans. I must here content myself with no more than giving my personal opinion of the debate.

I am persuaded that Russell and Dewey had no fundamental disagreement about truth, but only different ways of talking about it. I believe that any statement made by either man can be restated, when properly understood, in the language of the other. After all, both men were extremely intelligent, well acquainted with modern science as well as with the history of philosophy, and even in surprising agreement in their educational and political opinions. They had equally superficial differences about the nature of moral values. It seems unlikely that either man was quite the simpleton with respect to epistemology as the other made him out to be.

In my view the great controversy over truth was not much different from the old brainteaser (introduced by James in the second lecture of *Pragmatism*) about the man who circles a tree while a squirrel scrambles around the trunk so as always to keep the tree between itself and the man. After completing a circuit around the tree, has the man gone around the squirrel? It all depends, said James, on what is meant by "around." I find it surprising that James never seemed to comprehend that the storm aroused by his 1907 book was the result of using "truth" in a way that violated ordinary language. I find it equally amazing that philosophers by and large seem not to realize that similar arguments over linguistic preferences also account for the differences between Dewey and Russell in their historic clash over pragmatism.[3]

Russell and Dewey, if I am right, each accepted the basic notions of the other, but considered them too ordinary to be worth emphasizing. Dewey was always pointing out that his theory of truth included the idea of correspondence; indeed, he argued that his theory was the only one entitled to be called a correspondence theory! Because we know nothing about a reality behind the phenomenal world, the only meaningful correspondence is with that aspect of our experience which we call the external world. To put it plainly, Dewey's truth is a correspondence of two parts of our experience: assertions about the world and our success in validating those assertions.

How would Dewey have talked about our illustration of the selected playing card? I think he would have said the following. We are presented with a problem. Is the statement "This is the queen of hearts" a warranted assertion? To answer this question we must initiate an inquiry. This takes the form of turning over the card. If we see that it is the queen of hearts our doubts are dispelled. The problem has been solved. We have performed an act that establishes a correspondence between the sentence and the card. The process of inquiry has ended in the warranted assertion that the card is in fact the queen of hearts.

I see nothing in this description with which Russell could have quarreled. However, Russell and other nonpragmatists are allowed to say in their preferred language, that "This is the queen of hearts" is true even before making a test, if in fact the card *is* the queen of hearts. In their language, truth in this case is a time-independent relation between a statement and a fact, whether the statement is verified or not.

Nonpragmatists may even believe there is a final "absolute" truth about the world's structure, and combine this with what Peirce called "fallibilism," the doctrine that we have no sure way of knowing whether any belief about the world is absolutely true or not. Peirce liked to speak of the possibility that at some distant, perhaps infinitely distant, date the beliefs of scientists will finally converge on absolute truth. Dewey even quotes Peirce on this in a footnote to chapter 17 of his *Logic*. "The best definition of truth known to me," writes Dewey (it is the only use of the word *truth* in his entire book!), is Peirce's statement: "The opinion which is fated to be ultimately agreed to by all who investigate . . ." Elsewhere Peirce phrased it this way: "Truth is that concordance of an abstract statement with the ideal limit towards which endless investigation would tend to bring scientific belief. . . ."

It is important to understand that Peirce is here speaking only of truth as we finite minds can know it. But Peirce was a thoroughgoing realist with respect both to the material world and to theorems of mathematics and logic. As a good disciple of Duns Scotus, Peirce never doubted that there are absolute timeless truths which are "out there," independent of you and me, and that science is a search for just such truth, even though it can never be certain it has found it.

In his *Collected Papers*, Peirce wrote that every person believes in timeless truth. *"That* truth consists in conformity to something *independent of his thinking it to be so,* or of any man's opinion on that subject" (Peirce's italics). For a pragmatist who thinks otherwise, "the only reality there could be would be conformity to the ultimate result of inquiry. But there would not be any course of inquiry possible except in the sense that it would be easier for him to interpret the phenomenon; and ultimately he would be forced to say that there was no reality at all except that he now at this instant finds a certain way of thinking easier than any other. But this violates the very idea of reality and of truth."[4] It would be hard to find a clearer statement of Peirce's reluctance to adopt the pragmatic language of James and Dewey.

One need not, of course, be a theist to believe in ultimate truth, the timeless ideal limit of knowledge. However, if one does believe in God, as Peirce did, presumably God knows all the facts about the universe and how it operates. This, too, combines easily with fallibilism since we, with our feeble minds and crude instruments of investigation, have no procedures other than fallible ones for getting at tiny portions of God's total knowledge.

But we are wandering from our present topic. Russell certainly would have taken for granted that to *know* whether the hypothesis that the card is the queen of hearts is true, one must turn over the card. For Russell this seemed too obvious to require stating. The center of the controversy is thus seen to be trivial. It is an argument over what the word *truth* should mean, perhaps also over what *mean* means. Each man thought his point of view included all that was essential in the other's. (Both views, incidentally, contain elements of the coherence theory of truth, but this is beside the point.) In brief, it is my contention that Dewey and Russell differed mainly, if not entirely, in the way they liked to talk about the same state of affairs. Their language preferences were grounded in their respective temperaments and backgrounds, perhaps also in their cultures. Their ways of speaking reflected what seemed to them most important in the process by which human beings acquire partial knowledge of the outside world.

The two men also differed in the way they talked about logic. This is strikingly brought out by the full title of Dewey's *Logic: The Theory of Inquiry*. As Carnap pointed out (in *Logical Foundations of Probability*), Dewey uses the word *logic* in a broad sense that has little to do with its traditional meaning. Instead of confining the term to formal reasoning within a deductive system, Dewey covers the entire process by which humans go about solving problems. As Carnap remarks, Dewey's book contains almost nothing about formal logic of the sort that interested himself and Russell. Even those sections where formal logic is briefly discussed seem out of place and unconnected with the rest of the book.

Dewey had little interest in formal logic and pure mathematics, or even in modern physics, where logic and mathematics play such essential roles. We must also keep in mind that in Dewey's overall philosophy there is no sharp distinction between subject and object, between the knower and the known. Dewey saw human history as a perpetual struggle of intelligent organisms to solve the problems created by their interaction with their environments. In this ongoing process, mathematics and formal logic are seen as useful tools, like plows and telescopes. Perhaps if Dewey had believed in a reality behind the phaneron, or in a God who constructed the phaneron, he would have been less eager to abandon the traditional ways of talking about logic and mathematics, and the timeless nature of truth.

If my assessment of the conflict between Dewey and Russell over truth is correct, as I think it is, another question at once arises. Which of the two languages, Russell's or Dewey's, is the most expedient? Here I am on Russell's side. The ancient definition of truth as a timeless correspondence with reality is too useful to abandon. The linguistic reform attempted by the pragmatists turned out to be pragmatically unwise. It was unnecessary because everything the pragmatists wanted to say can be said just as well in the old language. Moreover, the attempted reform did in fact create more confusion than clarity.

Admirers of Lewis Carroll will recall Humpty Dumpty's notion that words can mean whatever one wants them to mean. Shortly after announcing this he fell off the wall and broke into so many pieces that he couldn't be put together again. Something like this happened to pragmatism. The pragmatists thought they could take *truth*, a respectable word which everybody understood in the Aristotelian sense, and redefine it to mean the passing of tests for truth. Their efforts lasted for a surprisingly brief time. Pragmatists were momentarily at the center of a storm in the United States and England until finally it dawned on philosophers that the pragmatists were not saying anything revolutionary at all. They were only saying the same old things in a bizarre way.

Nowhere is this more amusingly apparent than in a series of letters James exchanged with Charles A. Strong, a philosopher who shared his friend George Santayana's belief in old-fashioned realism and the correspondence theory of truth. Like everyone else, Strong had been mystified by passages in James's *Pragmatism* which seemed to deny the reality of objects independent of human minds. As the letters continue, James keeps stressing in stronger and stronger language that he is indeed a realist in the traditional sense, and that the utility of an idea lies precisely in its correspondence with a world that is independent of human experience.

Writing from Paris, Strong expresses enormous surprise:

Dear James:

    ... Santayana and I (he has just left for London this morning) have been greatly interested by your article on Pratt. We did not know you would acknowledge so roundly that truth is a relation between an idea and a reality beyond it, often quite separate from human experience, and it almost seems to us a complete change of face. We thought the pragmatist doctrine was that truth is a relation between the idea and *subsequent human experiences*,—that it "consists in the consequences" in this sense. Dewey certainly seems to teach that ideas are merely instrumental in resolving tangles in experienced situations, and that it is a fallacy to give them any other validity than that which they have as fulfilling this function. And as to the thoroughness of Schiller's idealism I have no further doubt after the discussions I have just had with him in the Engadine. He said he wasn't able to understand your article "A Word More about Truth"; which I think very likely. So I venture to predict that your developing realism will at once alarm your pragmatist colleagues and astonish those who have hitherto been your critics, who will think you are at last coming to your senses.

James reacts with amiable anger. He is furious, he says, to think he can be misunderstood so completely that anyone would imagine he had altered his views. "Epistemological realism," he insists, has always been the "permanent heart and center" of his thinking, and he reiterates his belief that this also is the case with Schiller and Dewey. At no time has he doubted that correspondence of ideas with reality is the reason for their utility. In a later letter to Strong he admits that some of his sentences may "squint toward idealism," and that he has been guilty of "groping," "fumbling," and "confusion," and has "probably made verbal slips."

When Strong writes to James a year later he has come to realize that he and James are in essential agreement but differ only in how they use words. Strong's finger rests squarely on the nub of their dispute. "I am forced to say that truth is a matter, and exclusively, of resembling or copying, and that what is addition to this is merely utility, and misnamed truth." James's reply, the final letter of the series, is disappointing. He simply points out the obvious. Truth is more than copying, he writes; otherwise one animal that resembled another animal would be "true" to it. Truth, he declares (as if anyone doubted), is a quality of human knowledge. It is here that correspondence comes in. Then James adds—who could disagree?—that the correspondence is "determinable only by the pragmatic method."[5]

It seems to me that there was a blindness on James's part, as well as on the part of Schiller and Dewey, to the kind of confusion that is inevitable whenever a philosopher, following Humpty, takes a useful word, with a commonly understood meaning, and gives it a new and novel meaning. Pragmatists believed, of course, that great benefits would flow from redefining truth as the meeting of tests for truth, but the actual results were decades of bewildering debate in which they wasted incredible amounts of time trying to explain to their opponents that they did not mean what their words, taken in the usual way, implied. They were guilty of violating what Peirce once called the "ethics of terminology," the moral obligation to respect the traditional meanings of entrenched philosophical terms.

Paul Edwards had a delightful way of making this point. Suppose, he wrote, a philosopher decides to redefine "shoe" as "footwear." The word now includes socks. This permits the philosopher to say that he habitually wears two shoes on each foot. The assertion may startle colleagues, and lead to curious arguments, but does it produce any fresh insights?[26] Many other philosophers, from Plato on, have warned against the perils of private definitions. Ironically, John Stuart Mill, who tried to redefine *matter* in a novel way, wrote one of the most eloquent pleas for terminology ethics.[7]

If I had to pick a single individual who, in my judgment, gave the egg of pragmatism the final push that toppled it off the wall, I would pick the Polish logician and mathematician Alfred Tarski. In the early thirties he published a historic paper on the semantic definition of truth, following it with articles that elaborated and popularized his results.[8] Using the tools of modern semantics and formal logic, Tarski found a precise, crystal-clear way of defining truth which he believed to be the same as Aristotle's. To oversimplify, Tarski posited an infinite hierarchy of formal languages in which every language is the "object language" of a "metalanguage" immediately above it. Only in a metalanguage can one speak of the truth or falsity of sentences in the object language below. If one wants to say that a statement about the physical world is true or false, one must assert this in a metalanguage. Tarski's favorite example is " 'Snow is white' is true if and only if snow is white." Its counterpart for our card experiment is: The sentence "This card is the queen of hearts" is true if, and only if, this card is the queen of hearts. The truth of the metasentence in quotes must, of course, be tested by pragmatic means.

Tarski's semantic definition of truth has many merits. For one thing, it eliminates all the ancient semantic paradoxes that spring from allowing a language to talk about the truth or falsity of its own sentences. Forms of the liar paradox, such as "This statement is false," become nonstatements, without meaning. Another merit of Tarski's definition is that it applies to assertions in pure logic and mathematics as well as to scientific statements and ordinary speech. The meaning of truth is the same for all these languages; only the methods of testing are different. In logic and mathematics the correspondence is established by formal proofs, in science by empirical techniques.

Tarski's way of defining truth was enthusiastically endorsed by Russell and Carnap and Karl Popper, indeed by almost all philosophers of science outside the pragmatic school. Even the pragmatists could not fault Tarski's reasoning. They could only express dismay at his revival of a way of talking which they had hoped would become obsolete. All over the world, philosophers, troubled for decades by the pragmatic challenge, heaved a sigh of relief comparable to Strong's sigh in his letter when he finally realized that James agreed with him.

If you check the indexes of books on the philosophy of science published since 1950, you will find that the names of James, Schiller, and Dewey have almost vanished. This is not to say they were not influential thinkers or that their books are no longer worth reading. I myself admire Peirce and James more than any other American philosophers. Given the philosophical climate of the time, it is easy to understand James's enthusiasm for a radical redefinition of truth. The great debate that he and Peirce initiated was certainly stimulating, and we can expect many more historical studies that will trace the details of the debate and evaluate its good and bad influences.

Annoyed by James's excesses and distortions, Peirce changed his word to *pragmaticism*, adding that it was too ugly a word for anybody to "kidnap." He was right. Only students of Peirce know the word, and in ordinary discourse *pragmatism* has now degenerated into a synonym for practical. We say of a politician that he made a pragmatic decision. In this trivial sense everybody is a pragmatist. Even in the more technical sense of insisting that scientific hypotheses can be tested only in experience, every scientist and philosopher is a pragmatist. When I say I am not a pragmatist I mean only that I agree with most philosophers today in seeing no pragmatic reasons for adopting the epistemological language of pragmatism.

Let me put it this way: I believe that everything worthwhile that the pragmatists had to say about truth can be said better, with less ambiguity and misunderstanding, in a language that adopts the Aristotelian theory of truth as refined by Tarski. The notion that a statement can have an absolute, timeless correspondence with the world, whether verified or not, is too useful a notion. Abandon it and at once you have to invent another way to say the same thing.[9] Now that Tarski has established the pragmatic value of *truth* in its classic sense, why hesitate to use it? What harm is done by letting the word mean what it has always meant in ordinary discourse? Philosophers of science can then get on with the more important task of trying to understand and improve the methods by which human beings—Dewey's organisms interacting with environments—can decide when to call a statement about the world true or false, or how to assign to it a useful measure of credibility, albeit tentative, between one and zero.

NOTES

1. See for instance Plato's *Sophist*, lines 262–263.
2. An amusing example of how James was forced to use such cumbersome counterfactuals can be found in his "Dialogue" that closes *The Meaning of Truth*. The antipragmatist maintains that one may regard statements as true or false even when they concern

past events that can never be tested. James agrees, but only if he is allowed to say it in his own language:

> The truth of an event, past, present, or future, is for me only another name for the fact that *if* the event ever *does* get known, the nature of the knowledge is already to some degree predetermined. The truth which precedes actual knowledge of a fact means only what any possible knower of the fact will eventually find himself necessitated to believe about it. He must believe something that will bring him into satisfactory relations with it, that will prove a decent mental substitute for it.

3. Readers who care to examine in detail the Dewey-Russell controversy should take the following references in chronological order:

(1) "A Short Catechism Concerning Truth," in Dewey's *The Influence of Darwin on Philosophy* (1910). This early paper is not about Russell, but in it Dewey (like William James before him in chapter 8 of *The Meaning of Truth*) replies to all the major charges that had been hurled at pragmatism.
(2) Bertrand Russell, "Dewey's New Logic," in *The Philosophy of John Dewey*, edited by Paul Arthur Schilpp (1939).
(3) Dewey's reply to Russell, *ibid*, pages 544–549.
(4) Chapter 23 of Russell's *Inquiry into Meaning and Truth* (1940), in which Russell responds to Dewey's reply.
(5) The chapter on Dewey in Russell's *History of Western Philosophy* (1945).
(6) "Propositions, Warranted Assertibility, and Truth," in Dewey's *Problems of Men* (1946). Dewey's rebuttal.
(7) Chapter 3 of Russell's *Impact of Science on Society* (1951).

On Russell's earlier controversy with William James see:

(1) Russell, "William James's Conception of Truth" (1908), and "Pragmatism" (1909), both reprinted in *Philosophical Essays* (1910).
(2) James's reply to these two papers, in which he calls Russell's views "diseased abstractionism," is reprinted as chapter 14 of James's *The Meaning of Truth*, op. cit.

4. Charles S. Peirce, *Collected Papers*, vol. 5, section 211 (1934).
5. The Strong-James correspondence is in volume 2, chapter 82, of *The Thought and Character of William James* (1935), by Ralph Barton Perry.
6. Paul Edwards, "Kierkegaard and the 'Truth' of Christianity," in *Philosophy*, vol. 46, April 1971, pages 89–108. The paper attacks Kierkegaard for his James-like effort to redefine truth as that which a person passionately believes.
7. John Stuart Mill, A *System of Logic*, book 4, chapter 4, section 6. The section is headed: "Evil Consequences of Casting Off Any Portion of the Customary Connotation of Words."
Bishop Berkeley, who had earlier redefined *matter* in an unusual way (for Berkeley it was the mind of God), was equally aware of the importance of keeping the customary meaning of words unless there are strong reasons not to. Here is how his disputants put the matter in the second of his *Three Dialogues Between Hylas and Philonous, in Opposition to Skeptics and Atheists*:

PHILONOUS: Tell me, Hylas, hath every one a liberty to change the current proper signification attached to a common name in any language? For example, suppose a traveller should tell you that in a certain country men pass unhurt through the fire; and, upon explaining himself, you found he meant by the word *fire* that which others call *water:* or, if he should assert that there are trees that walk upon two legs, meaning men by the term *trees.* Would you think this reasonable?

HYLAS: No, I should think it very absurd. Common custom is the standard of propriety in language. And for any man to affect speaking improperly is to pervert the use of speech, and can never serve to a better purpose than to protract and multiply disputes where there is no difference in opinion.

8. Tarski's original paper is in many anthologies, including Tarski's *Logic, Semantics, Metamathematics* (1956), where it appears as chapter 8, "The Concept of Truth in Formalized Languages." For a less technical account, see his "Truth and Proof," in *Scientific American*, June 1963.

9. A more recent example of the verbal difficulties that arise whenever someone tries to do away with the correspondence theory of truth is provided by the curious history of Thomas Kuhn. His *Structure of Scientific Revolution* (1962) has been enormously influential, especially among sociologists of science. Its thesis is simple. Science usually proceeds by normal growth in which a scientific community engages in puzzle solving within a commonly accepted theory which Kuhn called a paradigm. (Kuhn singles out crossword puzzles and jigsaw puzzles for metaphors, unfortunate choices because in both cases there are unique solutions known in advance.) These periods of "normal science" are punctuated by revolutionary breaks that occur when "anomalies" arise, puzzles that cannot be solved within the accepted paradigm. Slowly, painfully, against the opposition of many scientists (especially the elderly), a "gestalt shift" takes place and the old paradigm gives way to a new one. In this respect the history of science resembles the history of music, painting, and other fine arts.

Now, paradigm shifts certainly occur, though most historians of science find Kuhn's schema exaggerated and simplistic. His use of "incommensurable" to describe competing paradigms led many to suppose that he considered the choice between paradigms irrational. If so, one would find it difficult to say that science makes genuine progress when it changes paradigms. Writing in his postscript to the second (1970) edition of his book, Kuhn denied this vigorously. New paradigms, he insisted, are *not* chosen irrationally. They are adopted on the basis of "accuracy, simplicity, fruitfulness, and the like." Again: "accuracy of prediction, particularly of quantitative prediction; the balance between esoteric and everyday subject matter; and the number of different problems solved" are some of the criteria that are used in choosing.

One would suppose that by "accuracy" Kuhn meant the accuracy with which a theory fits the world; but no, he makes clear that he has no use for the notion that one theory is better than another "because it is somehow a better representation of what nature is really like"; that theories "grow ever closer to, or approximate more and more closely to, the truth . . . to the match, that is, between the entities with which the theory populates nature and what is 'really there.' "

After writing that postscript, Kuhn struggled to defend the above remarks, but in ways that grow increasingly hard to understand. As Harvey Siegel put it (reviewing Kuhn's 1977 book, *The Essential Tension*, in *The British Journal for the Philosophy of Science*, vol. 31, 1980, pages 359–384), "Kuhn seems to want it both ways: he wants to maintain incommensurability (and so irrationality), yet deny irrationality and allow for communication between proponents of competing paradigms (thus giving up incommensurability). It is clear, I hope, that Kuhn cannot have it both ways. His maintenance of incommensurability vitiates his denial of the irrationality thesis."

Consider the ways in which science, though always fallible, has made undisputed progress. It has advanced in its ability to explain, solving millions of puzzles the ancient Greeks could not solve. It has advanced in its ability to predict; it can make millions of predictions the Greeks could not make. It has developed marvelous instruments for better observing nature (telescopes, microscopes, cyclotrons, and so on). Its application to nature has given rise to a technology of awesome power in its ability to control nature and use it for human ends. More than anything else, this technology would stagger Plato and Aristotle if they could return and see it.

Why has science been so fantastically successful? There is a simple, obvious answer that a child can understand. It has been successful for the same reason a bird is successful in finding food and building nests. It is successful because human brains have learned more than birds about the structure of the world—yes, a world "out there," independent of you and me and our cultural biases. If Kuhn could ever bring himself to admit the strength of this simple, ancient hypothesis, it would dispel all his difficulties.

FORTY

GARDNER'S *WHYS*

When William Morrow published my "confessional," The Whys of a Philo-sophical Scrivener (1983), friend Douglas Hofstadter, newly famous for his Gödel, Escher, Bach, suggested on the phone that it might be interesting if I reviewed the book negatively. I proposed this to Robert Silvers, editor of the New York Review of Books. He was amused by the idea and gave me a go-ahead. The hatchet job I perpetrated on myself appeared in the December 8, 1983, issue, and has since become something of a legend.

I had wanted the review to be an unrevealed hoax under the pseudonym of George Groth, but Silvers thought this would be too damaging to my reputa-tion unless I disclosed the joke in the review's last line. Even so, I heard that many potential buyers of the book did not realize I had written the attack and avoided purchasing the book because of the blistering review.

In the book's chapter on aesthetics I played a dirty trick on readers. I quoted what I said was a poem by William Carlos Williams and asked readers to compare it with a parody I had written of Williams's style. Actually, the parody was an authentic quote from one of Williams's poems, and what I said was by Williams was my parody. Naturally George Groth was too dense to be aware of this sneaky switch.

The Whys of a Philosophical Scrivener (Morrow, 1983), by Martin Gardner, is one of the strangest books of philo-sophical game playing to come along in many a moon. The author seems well acquainted with modern philosophy—indeed, he studied under Rudolf Car-nap and even edited one of Carnap's books—yet he defends a point of view so anachronistic, so out of step with current fashion, that, were it not for a plethora of contemporary quotations and citations, his book could almost have been written at the time of Kant, a thinker the author apparently admires.

Gardner is well known for the mathematical-games column he wrote for *Scientific American.* He is also the editor of *The Annotated Alice,* as well as annotated volumes on "The Ancient Mariner," Lewis Carroll's *The Hunting of the Snark,* and a collection of ballads about the mighty Casey who struck out. In addition to his many books about science, pseudoscience, and mathematics and his several children's books, he has also written a curious novel, *The Flight of Peter Fromm.* Disguised as a biography, it chronicles the progressive disillusionment of a young Protestant divinity student at the University of Chicago who, after chucking Christianity, preserves a faith in God. Because the novel's narrator is an atheist, it has been difficult to know whether Gardner's sympathies are with his narrator or with his bewildered student.

Now the secret is out. Gardner's sympathies are not with his narrator. As his new book makes clear, although he has little use for any organized religion, he believes there are good reasons, though only emotional ones, for faith. He is as ruthless as Carnap or Bertrand Russell in dismissing systematic theology as nonsense. An entire chapter is devoted to demolishing proofs of God and poking fun at Mortimer Adler for his unshakable conviction that a valid proof can be formulated. Only an irrational "leap of faith," as Kierkegaard described it, an impulse springing mysteriously from the heart and will, can underpin philosophical theism.

To put it bluntly, Gardner is a simpleminded fideist who sees himself in the tradition of Kant, William James, and Miguel de Unamuno. It is impossible to imagine anyone reading his outrageous confessional (unless the reader is a clone of Gardner) who, however impressed he may be by the author's wide-ranging erudition and rhetorical skill, will not be infuriated by his idiosyncrasies.

The first "why" Gardner asks is why he is a realist—that is, why he believes a mathematically structured universe is "out there," independent of all human minds. "Let me not look aloft and see my own / Feature and form upon the Judgment-throne." These lines, from a poem by G. K. Chesterton, are the chapter's epigraph. It turns out that Gardner is a fan of G. K.'s, even though he has not the slightest sympathy for Roman Catholic doctrine. He also admires H. G. Wells. Wells and Chesterton? It would be hard to pick two writers more incompatible or about whom today's critics care less. "Can you comprehend," Gardner asks, "as most of my friends cannot, how it is possible to admire . . . the writings of both men? If so, you will understand how it is possible to combine a Chestertonian faith . . . with a Wellsian admiration for science, and at the same time ignore each man's areas of blindness."

After arguing for the reality of an outside world (here Gardner sides with Russell and Hans Reichenbach in making a firm ontological commitment to realism, rather than with Carnap, who defended realism only because he considered it a more efficient language than phenomenology), Gardner takes on the pragmatic theory of truth. In a series of clever arguments based on selecting a card at random from a deck (Gardner is an amateur magician), he concludes that pragmatism failed in its effort to replace the traditional Aristotelian correspondence theory of truth with a theory in which truth is defined as the passing of tests for truth. Although he thinks Russell and John Dewey differed mainly in their choice of language when they clashed repeatedly over this question, he sides strongly with Russell's language. Pragmatism died, Gardner tells us, because the verbal revolution it desired was pragmatically undesirable.

Gardner's chapter on why he is not a "paranormalist" contains little he has not said elsewhere and ad nauseam. He is down on parapsychologists not because he thinks psychic forces are impossible—nothing in science is impossible, he never tires of saying—but because he finds their evidence too feeble beside the wildness of their claims. Would the world be more interesting if psi forces existed? Maybe yes, maybe no. Gardner speculates amusingly on some of the less-pleasant consequences that could result if ESP and PK [psychokinesis] turn out to be genuine.

In explaining why he is not a relativist with respect to aesthetic values, Gardner goes to preposterous lengths to justify his convictions that "Dante and Shakespeare were better poets than Ella Wheeler Wilcox, that Michelangelo was a greater painter than Jackson Pollock, and that Beethoven's music is superior to that of John Cage or a punk rock band." So what else is new?

There is something to be said for Gardner's defense of objective value judgments in aesthetics, but he spoils it all with a dreary recital of his own peculiar tastes in poetry. No one will fault his admiration for Homer, Virgil, Dante, Shakespeare, Milton, Keats, and Emily Dickinson, but what is one to make of his distaste for Yeats? He considers T. S. Eliot "overrated" and agrees with Nabokov that Ezra Pound was a "total fake." Although he says he has tried his best to enjoy William Carlos Williams, he has yet to find a poem by Williams he thinks worth reading twice. The reader is asked to compare a crude parody of Williams with one of Williams's best known short poems. Gardner's atrocious spoof—it contains such lines as "Your knees are a southern breeze"—is obviously inferior to Williams's lovely lyric about the butterfly on a red wheelbarrow.

Moral relativism enrages Gardner even more than aesthetic relativism. Here his position is substantially the same as Dewey's: a naturalistic ethics can be based on a common human nature provided one makes such emotional assumptions as that it is better to be healthy than sick and better to be alive than dead. Stale arguments against the extreme cultural relativism that once dominated American anthropology are trotted out and doggedly defended; but when it comes to the "staggering" moral decisions that will have to be made when biologists find ways to alter human nature, Gardner writes, "I have no light to throw on these rapidly approaching and terrible questions."

Free will is the next topic to occupy Gardner's attention. No modern philosopher is likely to be impressed by his simple way of evading this ancient conundrum. He "solves" it by declaring it unsolvable. As Gardner sees it, the fundamental dilemma is that determinism leads straight to fatalism but that indeterminism is even worse because it turns free will into the haphazard toss of a die inside one's skull. There is no way, he insists, to define free will without sliding into one or the other of these dark chasms. The best we can do, indeed the *only* thing we can do, is leave will a blinding mystery. It is not fate, it is not chance. It is somehow both, yet somehow neither. "Ask not how it works," he concludes, "because no one on earth can tell you."

When he comes to politics and economics, Gardner's chaotic high jinks seem calculated to drive both liberals and conservatives up the wall. Gardner has no respect for what he calls the "Smithians"—all those who think government should shrink, leaving as much play as possible for the free market. Robert Nozick's minimal state is dismissed as a "me generation" aberration, and Ayn Rand is shoved aside as the ugly offspring of Milton Friedman and Madalyn Murray O'Hare. Withering scorn is heaped on the supply-siders. He quotes Paul Samuelson's remark that if Friedman did not exist it would be necessary to invent him. He likens Friedman to a chiropractor. Unlike an authentic doctor who knows too much to make a snap diagnosis, a chiropractor will tell you at once why your back is aching and how quickly he can cure it.

On the other hand, conservatives will be delighted by Gardner's jabs at Karl Marx. He quotes an amusing passage from a forgotten book on Russia by Wells in which the insane abundance of *Das Kapital* is compared with Marx's woolly beard. The sooner Michael Harrington forgets about Marx, says Gardner, the better. Politically, Gardner turns out to be—who could have guessed it?—an old-fashioned democratic socialist in the tradition of Wells, Russell, Norman Thomas, Gunnar Myrdal, Irving Howe, and a host of other socialists who are as ignored today by most liberals as they are hated by all conservatives—and whose practical political prospects, which he does not discuss, seem as dim as ever.

We are now halfway through Gardner's bizarre book—and ready for its biggest surprise, his back flip into fideism. But first he writes a diversionary chapter on polytheism. Like Lord Dunsany—whose name suggests how out of date are Gardner's tastes but whose fantasies he admires—Gardner has a wistful fondness for the beautiful gods of ancient Greece and little to say about their cruelty. Although he finally chooses monotheism, it is largely on the flimsy ground of "Occam's razor." Emotionally, he believes, a single God will do all a plurality would—and do it better—though in a final sense he says he does not know whether God is one or many, or even whether numbers have any meaning when applied to God. He sees Christianity as almost as polytheistic as Hinduism. Are not Jesus and the Holy Ghost (not to forget Satan, the Immaculate Mary, and the vast medieval hierarchy of angels) man-

ifestations of a higher deity—just as Brahma, Vishnu, and Siva are manifestations of Brahman?

At this point one might expect Gardner to glide into a pantheism along
the lines of Alfred North Whitehead's, but no. He dislikes pantheism even
more than polytheism. His God is "personal," though he emphasizes, with
Thomas Aquinas and Charles Peirce, that we have not the foggiest notion of
what it means to pin human traits on God. He applauds today's Christian
feminists for their attacks on the male bias of the Bible but goes them one
better. He sees no way the bias can be removed without removing the Incarnation itself and therefore abandoning the heart of Christianity. Nevertheless,
if God is to be of any value to us we must model him with the highest
metaphors we have. Gardner quotes a colorful passage from C. S. Lewis on
what happens when God is modeled with nonpersonal symbols. He becomes
a kind of gas—or maybe Jell-O—that permeates the cosmos, of less use to us
than a cloud or stone.

There are more surprises. Not only does Gardner believe in God; he also
believes that petitionary prayer can make a difference. How? He does not
know. As for skeptics, "Do they think, the fools," Gardner quotes from Thornton Wilder's *The Cabala*, "that their powers of observation are cleverer than
the devices of a god?" For Gardner, the mystery of prayer is bound up with
the terrible mysteries of time, causality, and free will. To defend the right to
pray, he constructs several ingenious models, one of them deriving from quantum mechanics. They are put forth whimsically. His only motive, he claims,
is to show that belief in the efficacy of prayer is not logically contradictory.
Are any of the models true? "Do not ask *me*," Gardner answers himself.

One of the characteristics of Gardner's "theological positivism," as he calls
it, is that he is content to accept paradox and mystery in regions where philosophers endlessly seek solutions. For a theist, the most dreadful of all mysteries is random, insane evil. Two chapters are devoted to the ancient
argument that God either (*a*) could prevent evil but does not and hence is
not good or (*b*) wants to prevent it but cannot, in which case He is not all
powerful. Gardner not only has no answer to this deadly dilemma; he actually
thinks it makes atheism more sensible than theism! All the better arguments,
he freely admits, are on the atheist's side. The leap of faith is an irrational,
absurd somersault of the soul that some people cannot avoid making (Gardner
does not know why) even though all experience suggests that the leap is as
foolish as Don Quixote's belief that Dulcinea smells like sweet perfume. The
modern fideist, Gardner writes, must grant it all.

Note how Gardner here ensures that no one can prove him wrong. His
invisible God is like the White Knight's green whiskers; no one can see them
because he keeps them always behind his fan. The atheist argument from evil
to no God bounces harmlessly off Gardner's head because he does not deny

its persuasiveness. Like Pascal, he defends his fideism on the grounds that if it were otherwise, if we knew the secret of evil, faith would not be faith. It would become compelled belief.

What is one to say about such a view, wholly unsupported by reason or revelation? I can best reply with a passage from Russell that Gardner must know but apparently could not bring himself to quote: "There is to my mind something pusillanimous and sniveling about this point of view, which makes me scarcely able to consider it with patience. To refuse to face facts merely because they are unpleasant is considered the mark of a weak character, except in the sphere of religion. I do not see how it can be ignoble to yield to the tyranny of fear in all ordinary terrestrial matters, but noble and virtuous to do exactly the same thing when God and the future life are concerned."[1]

Gardner's discussion of immortality is the most outlandish in the book. Although he realizes that within one's head theism can be separated from hope for another life, he follows Unamuno in regarding the two beliefs as interlocked inside the heart. He quotes Unamuno's conversation with the peasant who, after being told that perhaps there is a God but no afterlife, responded, "Then wherefore God?" Although Gardner believes Jesus to have been an ordinary man, likely born illegitimate and possibly gay, he professes to admire most of what he suspects Jesus actually taught. He is amazed that Paul Tillich, who did not believe in a personal God or an afterlife—Jesus's two basic themes—could have made the cover of *Time* as a great Christian theologian. As for hell, which Gardner thinks Jesus also taught, he cites this as one reason why he stopped calling himself a Christian.

Gardner constructs three models for an afterlife, all designed (like his models for prayer) to show that the doctrine is not logically inconsistent. Is one of the models true? "For my part," Gardner answers, "I believe that none of the models . . . is true. I am persuaded that the truth about immortality is as far beyond our grasp as the ideas in this book are beyond the grasp of a glowworm." Again it is all a matter of "faith," for which he can show no rational basis.

The book's last chapter but one is a frank attempt to arouse in the reader a sense of what Rudolf Otto called the "numinous," a Chestertonian awe before the incredible mystery of existence. The final chapter pleads for religious tolerance. Gardner is appalled by the view that history is a duel to the death between Christianity and atheism—a duel that Chesterton and Whittaker Chambers saw, and William Buckley and Ronald Reagan still see, as manifest today in the military confrontation of "Christian" America and "atheist" Russia. Gardner quotes a poem by Stephen Crane about a "complacent fat man" who climbed to the top of a mountain, expecting to see "good white lands and bad black lands," only to find that the scene was gray. This leads to the book's final metaphor. Today's philosophical grayness becomes a backdrop that intensifies the colors of an unpredictable future.

How seriously should we take Gardner's fideism? He seems sincere, yet one wonders. After all, the man has a reputation as a hoaxer. His April 1975 column in *Scientific American* purported to disclose such dramatic break-throughs as the discovery of a map that required five colors, a fatal flaw in relativity theory, an opening move in chess (pawn to queen's rook four) that is a certain win for white, and a lost parchment proving that Leonardo da Vinci invented the flush toilet. Thousands of readers wrote to tell Gardner where he went wrong, and one irate professor tried to have him expelled from the American Mathematical Society. Happily, the society made him an hon-orary life member. George Groth, by the way, is one of Gardner's pseudonyms.

NOTES

1. From *The Value of Free Thought: How to Become a Truth-Seeker and Break the Chains of Mental Slavery,* by Bertrand Russell (1944). Reprinted in *Understanding History and Other Essays* (Philosophical Library, 1957).

FORTY-ONE

THE POPPERISM OF
SIR KARL

I have included this short review of The Philosophy of Karl Popper *because it deals with a famous conflict between two distinguished philosophers of science over how scientists evaluate theories. The best introduction to Carnap's philosophy is his nontechnical* Introduction to the Philosophy of Science, *recently reissued as a Dover paperback to which I, as editor of the original volume, had the pleasure of contributing a new foreword. The following review appeared in* The New Leader *(October 14, 1974).*

When Sir Karl died in 1992 he was England's best known philosopher of science, but was almost as famous for his vigorous defense of democracy in his most influential book The Open Society and Its Enemies *(1945).*

The first volume in the Library of Living Philosophers, *The Philosophy of John Dewey*, was published in 1939. Today, this incomparable series, edited by Paul Arthur Schilpp, numbers fourteen works, of which *The Philosophy of Karl Popper* (Open Court, 1974) is the latest, largest, and most expensive. It is the only publication in the collection thus far to require two volumes, and to sell for the then horrendous price of $30.00. Nevertheless, for anyone seriously concerned with the philosophy of science, the book is a bargain.

In keeping with the series' established format, *The Philosophy of Karl Popper* opens with a lengthy intellectual autobiography by Sir Karl himself (a splendid introduction to the man and his ideas), followed by thirty-three descriptive and critical essays by eminent thinkers. These, in turn, receive detailed, often caustic, replies from Popper. The book concludes with a massive bibliography of the philosopher's writings, and a comprehensive index.

Like Bertrand Russell, whom Popper considered his greatest predecessor since Kant, Sir Karl was a passionate "realist." That is, he accepts the commonsense belief in an external world, existing independent of our minds, and possessing a structure not made by us yet partially comprehensible to us. Science is a never-ending search for truth about that structure. ("Truth" is taken in the classic correspondence sense that goes back to Aristotle and received precise definition from the twentieth-century mathematician and logician Alfred Tarski; it is objective and absolute.) Of course we can never be certain we have caught it, but we do have reasons for believing science is getting closer to it.

Whereas Popper's realism is unobjectionable to most modern philosophers of science, other aspects of his thought have brought him into bitter conflict with his peers. (There has long been a rumor that he and Ludwig Wittgenstein once battled each other with pokers: Sir Karl's account of this incident is even funnier than the mythology.)

His most publicized contention is that the more easily a theory can be proved false, the better and bolder it is, and that one which cannot be refuted is useless because it has no "informative content." Marxist and psychoanalytic theory, he insists, have become empty in this way, for each has been so vaguely generalized, twisted, and patched, one can no longer imagine a historical event or experimental outcome that would persuade a Marxist or a Freudian to discard his core beliefs. In his autobiography, Popper gives a colorful account of how he came to realize the sharp difference between such vapid theories and theories that take genuine risks. "If the redshift of spectral lines due to the gravitational potential should not exist," Popper quotes Einstein, "then the general theory of relativity will be untenable." One would be hard put, Popper argues, to get a statement of comparable humility from a Marxist or Freudian. By ingeniously "immunizing" their views against all possible falsifications, they have rendered those views uninteresting.

Sir Karl is at odds with his critics on many other important topics as well. He has, for example, defended indeterminism throughout his life against the determinism of Einstein and others. Most physicists are probably indeterminists on the microlevel and determinists on the macrolevel. Popper is an indeterminist on all levels.

"If God had wanted to put everything into the world from the beginning," Sir Karl writes, quoting himself from an early lecture, "He would have created a universe without change, without organisms and evolution, and without man and man's experience of change. But He seems to have thought that a live universe with events unexpected even by Himself would be more interesting than a dead one." This emotional bias toward what William James called the "open universe," as against the "block universe," underlies Popper's great defense of democracy in his best known work, *The Open Society and Its Enemies*.

Popper's most notable clashes were with Rudolf Carnap over induction. Carnap was convinced that inductive logics could be constructed for formalized scientific languages, and that these would become useful tools for measuring a theory's "degree of confirmation" in the light of total available evidence. Sir Karl considers this nonsense.

Not only is Popper scornful of any attempt to formulate a logic of induction; in his language, induction does not exist. He is persuaded he has completely solved Hume's famous problem (How can induction be justified?) by replying: It can't because there is no such thing.

To be sure, says Popper, scientists can and do prefer one hypothesis over another. This preference, though, is not based on Carnapian "confirming instances" but on how successfully a theory passes attempts to refute it. Yet hasn't Popper merely introduced induction through the back door? To oversimplify one case in point, he does not believe the discovery of Neptune confirmed Newton's theory of gravitation. Instead, he argues, the new planet "corroborated" the theory by not falsifying it. This sounds like denying that a man is happy because the horse he bet on won the race, and asserting, on the contrary, that he is jumping up and down because his horse failed to lose. (For Carnap's side of this acrimonious debate, see *The Philosophy of Rudolf Carnap*, Open Court's earlier work in the same series, pp. 995–98.)[1]

On the problem of induction it is too early to know whether future thinking will follow a Popperian or Carnapian road, or find other directions. But in this, as in all his concerns, Popper has opened myriads of new speculative paths. Even his strongest critics must admit that the publication of this new work is a major event in the history of modern philosophy.

NOTES

1. It was Carnap's opinion that Popper consistently tried to exaggerate the differences between them by finding ways to say the same things Carnap said, but say them in a less ordinary language. Suppose, for instance, a scientist, convinced that Neptune probably has a ring around it, supervises a space probe that succeeds in photographing the ring. Carnap would say that the purpose of the probe was to confirm the theory, and that it succeeded. Popper would say that the probe's purpose was to falsify the theory, and having failed, the theory was corroborated.

In the mid-sixties Carnap and Popper both attended a conference in London where some of their differences were discussed by Popperians. At the close, Carnap declared that the main thing he had learned from the conference was that the distance function is not symmetric. The distance from me to Popper, he said, is small. But the distance from Popper to me appears to be enormous.

FORTY-TWO

W. V. QUINE

Rudolf Carnap clashed not only with Sir Karl Popper but also with philosopher-logician Willard Van Orman Quine. It was a friendly argument over the usefulness of the term "analytic." I have tried to summarize the essence of this historic debate in the short review that follows. It appeared in the Boston Globe *(July 7, 1985). Correspondence between the two good friends was published in* Dear Carnap, Dear Van, *edited by Richard Creath (University of California, 1990).*

Not many philosophers attempt autobiographies—Bertrand Russell and George Santayana are the outstanding modern exceptions—so it was a rare event on June 25, 1985, the 77th birthday of Willard Van Orman Quine, when *The Time of My Life* (MIT Press) was published. Though little known outside academia, Quine is the most distinguished American-born philosopher since John Dewey. His views have been enormously influential and, to this day, continue to generate heated and fruitful controversy.

In earlier ages, philosophers were expected to have deep opinions on almost everything, but now they are as specialized as scientists. Quine's specialties are set theory, logic, semantics, and linguistics. Like his friend and mentor, Rudolf Carnap, the most famous of the Vienna Circle empiricists, Quine has no wisdom to impart about aesthetics, ethics, political philosophy, or religion. For this reason, his autobiography has less in common with those of generalists such as Russell and Santayana than with the autobiography of an opthalmologist or a chess grand master.

Even with respect to his special interests, Quine seldom has much to say, except for one brief chapter on his "Mathematical Logic," or "ML," as it is known. This is a formal system similar to "Principia Mathematica," or "PM," constructed by Russell and Alfred North Whitehead, but simpler and more elegant. Quine intended it to avoid the paradoxes that marred PM, but, unfortunately, ML proved to have paradoxes of its own. Quine partly banished them from the book's revised edition and corrected little mistakes such as a careless reference to Paul as one of the apostles. Hao Wang, Quine's brilliant pupil, finally completed the repairs.

Quine was born in Akron, Ohio, in 1908, and it was while he was a mathematics major at Oberlin College that the three volumes of PM dropped on his head like a thunderbolt. Scholarships at Harvard allowed him to complete a doctorate under Whitehead himself. "That's ripping, old fellow. Right jolly!" said Whitehead when Quine explained his choice of topic. "Bertie [Russell] thinks I'm muddle-headed," Whitehead told him on another occasion, "but I think Bertie's simpleminded."

Eventually, Quine became chairman of Harvard's philosophy department, and it would take paragraphs to list all the academic honors he has received since. During World War II, he enlisted in the Navy, serving several years in Washington as a cryptanalyst. A WAVE who worked in his office became his second wife after a bitter divorce that Quine covers in a grim chapter titled "Sturm und Drang."

As a boy, Quine loved to draw maps, and his interest in geography combined naturally with philately. For a while, he and a friend published a little periodical called O.K. Stamp News. In adult life, his passion for collecting stamps became, as he puts it, a passion for collecting countries. There are long stretches in Quine's book, as he crosses more than one hundred national borders, that read like the trivial details of a travel diary.

Quine sees himself as a man preoccupied with the precision, beauty, and simplicity of formal logic, as taciturn, easily bored, introverted, but with "little talent for soul searching." He has always lived frugally and simply, and, although he dislikes personal confrontations, he recognizes that much of his reputation has been aided by the controversies he has initiated.

Quine's most notorious argument was with Carnap over what logicians call the analytic-synthetic distinction. Almost all philosophers since Hume have contrasted analytic sentences that are true in virtue of the meanings assigned to their words ("All black cows are black") with synthetic sentences that require observation of the world before they can be deemed true ("Some cows are brown"). No one denies that the distinction has a fuzzy dividing line, like the line between night and day or between spoons and forks, but Quine obviously means more than that. His subtle attacks on analyticity have even given rise to the use of his name as a verb. "To Quine," it is said, means "to repudiate a clear distinction." Mathematician John Kemeny, the former president of Dartmouth, once described Quine's efforts to undermine Carnap on this point as "the most important losing battle in the history of modern philosophy." Entire books have been devoted to this battle. Both sides are defended at length in *The Philosophy of W. V. Quine*, edited by Lewis Edwin

Hahn and Paul Arthur Schilpp, volume 18 in the distinguished Library of Living Philosophers (Open Court, 1986).

Quine's eagerness to blur distinctions—boundaries, he once said, are for deans and librarians—underlies his second most famous controversy, also touched lightly in his autobiography. "To be is to be the value of a variable" is one of his most quoted remarks. Roughly, this means that if a formal system interprets X as a triangle, then the triangle (or any other abstract object) is as "real" (in a sense) as a watermelon. This tendency toward Platonic realism also brought Quine into sharp conflict with Carnap. Although Quine does not consider himself a Platonist, he insists that calling him a nominalist (one who thinks universals are merely words) is not right, either; indeed, he calls this one of the many misconceptions that have bedeviled him over the decades.

The Time of My Life abounds with amusing anecdotes about eminent philosophers who became Quine's friends, but none ever took the place of Ed Haskell, or Head Rascal, as Quine's two-year-old son once called him. Ed glides in and out of Quine's life like a curious shadow. The two met when they were undergraduates at Oberlin. Hitchhiking with his violin, Ed had earlier been picked up by a wealthy elderly woman who found him so engaging that she arranged to send him $100 a month for life. If this sum grew with inflation, it explains why Ed seems never to have had a job.

Quine describes his lifelong confidant as "ambitious, opinionated, contentious in the classroom, and rather shunned as an eccentric. . . ." In the thirties, Ed became an ardent Communist. A few years later, while a graduate student at the University of Chicago, Ed became attached to Count Alfred Korzybski's cult of general semantics. Quine had as little use then for the count as he had for communism. Soon, Ed was a strong anti-Communist, pinning his faith on a "unified science" that he hoped would save the world. Quine was trying once more to "apply the brakes" to Ed's "runaway ambition," when, incredibly, Ed became a booster of the Rev. Sun Moon! It was he who persuaded Moon to hold annual international conferences on unified science, at which Nobel prize winners were hornswoggled into speaking. Quine himself attended Moon's fourth conference, finding Moon funnier than any fundamentalist Bible thumper. At one point, Quine was about to admire physicist Eugene Wigner for getting up and walking out, but, no—Wigner was only going to the men's room.

Despite Quine's distrust of Ed's quirky enthusiasms, the two were constantly together for long walks and earnest talks. Quine calls Ed his "closest friend" and speaks of accepting speaking engagements only for the sake of their frequent reunions. Quine admits to weeping twice—with joy during his second marriage ceremony, with grief when he remembers how he fumbled a chance to join Ed in 1984 for a jaunt through western Texas. It was a project that Ed's failing health made impossible to renew.

POSTSCRIPT (1995)

I was startled to learn from Quine's autobiography about his long friendship with Ed Haskell. I had known Ed when we both were poor and living in cheap furnished rooms at the Homestead Hotel, 5610 Dorchester, in the shadows of the University of Chicago. I described this dreary building in "Room X," a chapter of my novel The Flight of Peter Fromm.

FORTY-THREE

THE IRRELEVANCE
OF "EVERYTHING"

A year or so after Scientific American *published my column on nothing (reprinted here as chapter 32), I followed with a column on everything. I am indebted to computer scientist Donald Knuth for calling my attention to the C. S. Lewis quote which closes the essay.*

A curious thing about the ontological problem is its simplicity. It can be put in three Anglo-Saxon monosyllables: "What is there?" It can be answered, moreover, in a word—"Everything."

—WILLARD VAN ORMAN QUINE,
"On What There Is"

The topic of the first essay of the *Philosophy* section of this book is "nothing." I have nothing more to say about nothing, or about "something," since everything I know about something was said when I wrote about nothing. But "everything" is something altogether different.

Let us begin by noting the curious fact that some things, namely ourselves, are such complicated patterns of waves and particles that they are capable of wondering about everything. "What is man in nature?" asked Pascal. "A nothing in comparison with the infinite, an all in comparison with the nothing, a mean between nothing and everything."

In logic and set theory "things" are conveniently diagrammed with Venn circles. In Figure 1 the points inside circle *a* represent humans. The points inside circle *b* stand for feathered animals. The overlap, or intersection set, has been darkened to show that it has no members. It is none other than our old friend the empty set.

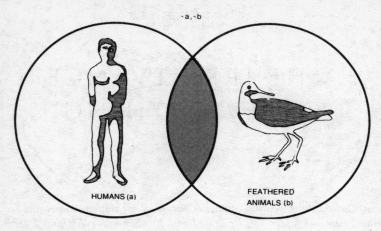

Figure 1. A Venn diagram for "No humans have feathers"

So far, so clear. What about the points on the plane outside the two circles? Obviously they represent things that are not *a* and not *b*, not human and not feathered, but how far-ranging is this set? To clarify the question Augustus De Morgan invented the phrase "universe of discourse." It is the range of all the variables with which we are concerned. Sometimes it is explicitly defined, sometimes tacitly assumed, sometimes left fuzzy. In set theory it is made precise by defining what is called the universal set, or, for short, the universe. This is the set with a range that coincides with the universe of discourse. And that range can be whatever we want it to be.

With the Venn circles *a* and *b* we are perhaps concerned only with living things on the earth. If this is so, that is our universe. Suppose, however, we expand the universe by adding a third set, the set of all typewriters, and changing *b* to all feathered objects. As Figure 2 shows, all three intersection sets are empty. It is the same empty set, but the range of the null set has also been expanded. There is only one "nothing," but a hole in the ground is not the same as a hole in a piece of cheese. The complement of a set *k* is the set of all elements in the universal set that are not in *k*. It follows that the universe and the empty set are complements of each other.

How far can we extend the universal set without losing our ability to reason about it? It depends on our concern. If we expand the universe of Figure 1 to include all concepts, the intersection set is no longer empty because it is easy to imagine a person growing feathers. The proofs of Euclid are valid only if the universe of discourse is confined to points in a Euclidean plane or in 3-space. If we reason that a dozen eggs can be equally divided only between one, two, three, four, six, or twelve people, we are reasoning about a universal set that ranges over the integers. John Venn (who invented

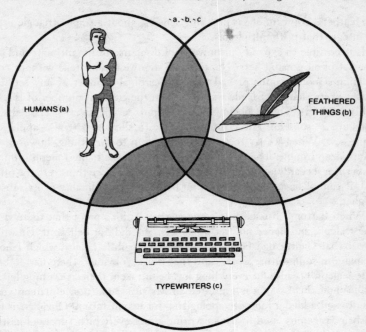

Figure 2. A Venn diagram for three sets

the Venn diagram) likened the universe of discourse to our field of vision. It is what we are looking at. We ignore everything behind our head.

Nevertheless, we can extend the universe of discourse amazingly far. We certainly can include abstractions such as the number 2, pi, complex numbers, perfect geometric figures, even things we cannot visualize such as hypercubes and non-Euclidean spaces. We can include universals such as redness and cowness. We can include things from the past or in the future and things real or imaginary, and can still reason effectively about them. Every dinosaur had a mother. If it rains next week in Chicago, the old Water Tower will get wet. If Sherlock Holmes had actually fallen off that cliff at Reichenbach Falls, he would have been killed.

Suppose we extend our universe to include every entity that can be defined without logical contradiction. Every statement we can make about that universe, if it is not contradictory, is (in a sense) true. The contradictory objects and statements are not allowed to "exist" or be "true" for the simple reason that contradiction introduces meaninglessness. When a philosopher such as Leibniz talks about "all possible worlds," he means worlds that can be talked about. You can talk about a world in which humans and typewriters have feathers. You cannot say anything sensible about a square triangle or an odd integer that is a multiple of 2.

Is it possible to expand our universe of discourse to the ultimate and call it the set of all possible sets? No, this is a step we cannot take without contradiction. Georg Cantor proved that the cardinal number of any set (the number of its elements) is always lower than the cardinal number of the set of all its subsets. This is obvious for any finite set (if it has n elements, it must have 2^n subsets), but Cantor was able to show that it also applies to infinite sets. When we try to apply this theorem to everything, however, we get into deep trouble. The set of all sets must have the highest aleph (infinite number) for its cardinality; otherwise it would not be everything. On the other hand, it cannot have the highest aleph because the cardinality of its subsets is higher.

When Bertrand Russell first came across Cantor's proof that there is no highest aleph, and hence no "set of all sets," he did not believe it. He wrote in 1901 that Cantor had been "guilty of a very subtle fallacy, which I hope to explain in some future work," and that it was "obvious" there had to be a greatest aleph because "if everything has been taken, there is nothing left to add." When this essay was reprinted in *Mysticism and Logic* sixteen years later, Russell added a footnote apologizing for his mistake. ("Obvious" is obviously a dangerous word to use in writing about everything.) It was Russell's meditation on his error that led him to discover his famous paradox about the set of all sets that are not members of themselves.

To sum up, when the mathematician tries to make the final jump from lots of things to everything, he finds he cannot make it. "Everything" is self-contradictory and therefore does not exist!

The fact that the set of all sets cannot be defined in standard (Zermelo-Fraenkel) set theory, however, does not inhibit philosophers and theologians from talking about everything, although their synonyms for it vary: being, *ens*, what is, existence, the absolute, God, reality, the Tao, Brahman, *dharmakaya*, and so on. It must, of course, include everything that was, is and will be, everything that can be imagined and everything totally beyond human comprehension. Nothing is also part of everything. When the universe gets this broad, it is difficult to think of anything meaningful (not contradictory) that does not in some sense exist. The logician Raymond Smullyan, in one of his several hundred marvelous unpublished essays, retells an incident he found in Oscar Mandel's book *Chi Po and the Sorcerer: A Chinese Tale for Children and Philosophers*. The sorcerer Bu Fu is giving a painting lesson to Chi Po. "No, no!" says Bu Fu. "You have merely painted what *is*. Anybody can paint what is! The real secret is to paint what isn't!" Chi Po, puzzled, replies: "But what is there that isn't?"

This is a good place to come down from the heights and consider a smaller, tidier universe, the universe of contemporary cosmology. Modern cosmology started with Einstein's model of a closed but unbounded universe. If there is sufficient mass in the cosmos, our 3-space curves back on itself like the surface of a sphere. (Indeed, it becomes the 3-space hypersurface of a 4-space hypersphere.) We now know that the universe is expanding from a primordial fireball, but there does not seem to be enough mass for it to be closed. The steady-state theory generated much discussion and stimulated much valuable scientific work, but it now seems to have been eliminated as a viable theory by such discoveries as that of the universal background radiation (which has no reasonable explanation except that it is radiation left over from the primordial fireball, or "big bang").

The large unanswered question is whether there is enough mass hidden somewhere in the cosmos (in black holes?) to halt the expansion and start the universe shrinking. If that is destined to happen, the contraction will become runaway collapse, and theorists see no way to prevent the universe from entering the "singularity" at the core of a black hole, that dreadful spot where matter is crushed out of existence and no known laws of physics apply. Will the universe disappear like the fabled Poof Bird, which flies backward in ever decreasing circles until—poof!—it vanishes into its own anus? Will everything go through the black hole to emerge from a white hole in some completely different space-time? Or will it manage to avoid the singularity and give rise to another fireball? If reprocessing is possible, we have a model of an oscillating universe that periodically explodes, expands, contracts, and explodes again.

Among physicists who have been building models of the universe John Archibald Wheeler of Princeton University has gone further than anyone in the direction of everything. In Wheeler's wild vision our universe is one of an infinity of universes that can be regarded as embedded in a strange kind of space called superspace.

In order to understand (dimly) what Wheeler means by superspace let us start with a simplified universe consisting of a line segment occupied by two particles, one black and one gray [*see Figure 3, top*]. The line is one-dimensional, but the particles move back and forth (we allow them to pass through each other) to create a space-time of two dimensions: one of space and one of time.

There are many ways to graph the life histories of the two particles. One way is to represent them as wavy lines, called world lines in relativity theory, on a two-dimensional space-time graph [*see Figure 3, bottom*]. Where was the black particle at time k? Find k on the time axis, move horizontally to the black particle's world line, then move down to read off the particle's position on the space axis.

To see how beautifully the two world lines record the history of our infant universe, cut a slot in a file card. The slot should be as long as the line segment and as wide as a particle. Place the card at the bottom of the graph where

A one-dimensional universe with two particles

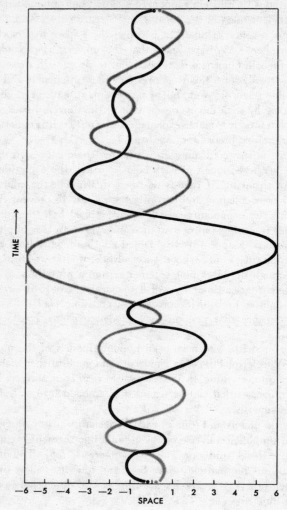

Figure 3. A space-time graph of a two-particle cosmos from birth to death

you can see the universe through it. Move the card upward slowly. Through the slot you will see a motion picture of the two particles. They are born at the center of their space, dance back and forth until they have expanded to the limits, and then dance back to the center, where they disappear into a black hole.

In kinematics it is sometimes useful to graph the changes of a system of particles as the motion of a single point in a higher space called configuration

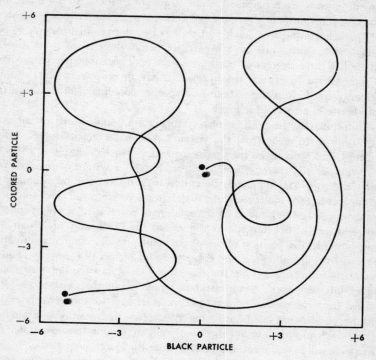

Figure 4. A configuration-space graph of the history of two particles in a one-dimensional universe

space. Let us see how to do this with our two particles. Our configuration space again is two-dimensional, but now both coordinates are spatial. One coordinate is assigned to the black particle and the other to the gray particle [*see Figure 4*]. The positions of both particles can be represented by a single point called the configuration point. As the point moves, its coordinate values change on both axes. One axis locates one particle, the other axis the other particle. The trajectory traced by the moving point corresponds to the changing pattern of the system of particles; conversely, the history of the system determines a unique trajectory. It is not a space-time graph. (Time enters later as an added parameter.) The line cannot form branches because that would split each particle in two. It may, however, intersect itself. If a system is periodic, the line will be a closed curve. To transform the graph into a space-time graph we can, if we like, add a time coordinate and allow the point to trace a curve in three dimensions.

The technique generalizes to a system of N particles in a space with any number of dimensions. Suppose we have 100 particles in our little line-segment cosmos. Each particle has one degree of freedom, so our configuration point must move in a space of 100 dimensions. If our universe is a system of N particles on a plane, each particle has two degrees of freedom, so our configuration space must be a hyperspace of $2N$ dimensions. In 3-space a particle has three degrees of freedom, so the configuration space must have $3N$ dimensions. In general the hyperspace has an order equal to the total degrees of freedom in the system. Add another coordinate for time and the space becomes a space-time graph.

Unfortunately the position of a configuration point at any instant does not enable us to reconstruct the system's past or predict its future. Josiah Willard Gibbs, working on the thermodynamics of molecules, found a slightly more complicated space in which he could graph a system of molecules so that the record was completely deterministic. This is done by assigning six coordinates to each molecule: three to determine position and three to specify momentums. The movement of a single phase point in what Gibbs called a "phase space" of $6N$ dimensions will record the life history of N particles. Now, however, the position of the phase point provides enough information to reconstruct (in principle) the entire previous history of the system and to predict its future. As before, the trajectory cannot branch, but now it also cannot intersect itself. An intersection would mean that a state could be reached from two different states, and could lead to two different states, but both possibilities are ruled out by the assumption that position and momentums (which include a vector direction) fully determine the next state. The curve may still loop, however, indicating that the system is periodic.

Our universe, with its non-Euclidean space-time and its quantum uncertainties, cannot be graphed in anything as simple as phase space, but Wheeler has found a way to do it in superspace. Like configuration space, superspace is timeless, but it has an infinity of dimensions. A single point in superspace has an infinite set of coordinates that specify completely the structure of our non-Euclidean 3-space: its size, the location of every particle, and the structure of every field (including the curvature of space itself) at every point. As the superpoint moves, its changing coordinate numbers describe how our universe changes, not failing to take into account the role of observers' frames of reference in relativity and the probability parameters of quantum mechanics. The motion of the superpoint gives the entire history of our universe.

At the same time (whatever that means!) that the present drama of our cosmos is being acted on the stage of superspace countless other superpoints, representing other 3-space universes, are going through their cycles. Superpoints close to one another describe universes that most resemble one another, like the parallel worlds that H. G. Wells introduced into science fiction with his *Men Like Gods*. These parallel universes, cut off from one another because they occupy different slices of superspace, are continually bursting into space-time through a singularity, flourishing for a moment of eternity, then vanishing back through a singularity into the pure and timeless "pre-geometry" from whence they came.

Whenever such a cosmos explodes into being, random factors generate a specific combination of logically consistent (Leibniz called them compossible) particles, constants, and laws. The resulting structure has to be tuned exceedingly fine to allow life. Alter the fine-structure constant a trifle either way and a sun such as ours becomes impossible. Why are we here? Because random factors generated a cosmic structure that allowed us to evolve. An infinity of other universes, not so finely tuned, are living and dying without there being anyone in them capable of observing them.

These "meaningless" universes, meaningless because they contain no participator-observers, do not even "exist" except in the weak sense of being logically possible. Bishop Berkeley said that to exist is to be perceived, and Charles Sanders Peirce maintained that existence is a matter of degree. Taking cues from both philosophers, Wheeler argues that only when a universe develops a kind of self-reference, with the universe and its observers reinforcing one another, does it exist in a strong sense. "All the choir of heaven and furniture of earth have no substance without a mind" was how Berkeley put it.

As far as I can tell, Wheeler does not take Berkeley's final step: the grounding of material reality in God's perception. Indeed, the fact that a tree seems to exist in a strong sense, even when no one is looking at it, is the key to Berkeley's way of proving God's existence. Imagine a god experimenting with billions of cosmic models until he finds one that permits life. Would not these universe be "out there," observed by the deity? There would be no need for flimsy creatures like ourselves, observing and participating, to confer existence on these models.

Wheeler seems anxious to avoid this view. He argues that quantum mechanics requires participator-observers in the universe regardless of whether there is an outside observer or not. In one of his metaphors, a universe without internal observers is like a motor without electricity. The cosmos "runs" only when it is "guaranteed to produce somewhere, and for some little length of time in its history-to-be, life, consciousness and observership." Internal observers and the universe are both essential to the existence of each other, even if the observers exist only in a potential sense. This raises unusual questions. How strongly does a universe exist before the first forms of life evolve? Does it exist in full strength from the moment of big bang, or does its existence get stronger as life gets more complex? And how strong is the existence of a galaxy, far removed from the Milky Way, in which there may be no participator-observers? Does it exist only when it is observed by life in another galaxy? Or is the universe so interconnected that the observation of a minute portion of it supports the existence of all the rest?

There is a famous passage in which William James imagines a thousand beans flung onto a table. They fall randomly, but our eyes trace geometrical figures in the chaos. Existence, wrote James, may be no more than the order which our consciousness singles out of a disordered sea of random possibilities. This seems close to Wheeler's vision. Reality is not something out there, but a process in which our consciousness is an essential part. We are not what we are because the world is what it is, but the other way around. The world is what it is because we are what we are.

When relativity theory first won the day, many scientists and philosophers with a religious turn of mind argued that the new theory supported such a view. The phenomena of nature, said James Jeans, are "determined by us and our experience rather than by a mechanical universe outside us and independent of us." The physical world, wrote Arthur Stanley Eddington, "is entirely abstract and without 'actuality' apart from its linkage to consciousness." Most physicists today would deny that relativity supports this brand of idealism. Einstein himself vigorously opposed it. The fact that measurements of length, time, and mass depend on the observer's frame of reference in no way dilutes the actuality of a space-time structure independent of all observers.

Nor is it diluted by quantum mechanics. What bearing does the statistical nature of quantum laws have on the independent existence of a structure to which those laws apply whenever it is observed? The fact that observations alter state functions of a system of particles does not entail that there is nothing "out there" to be altered. Einstein may have thought that quantum mechanics implies this curious reduction of physics to psychology, but there are not many quantum experts today who agree.

In any case, belief in an external world, independent of human existence but partly knowable by us, is certainly the simplest view and the one held today by the vast majority of scientists and philosophers. As I have suggested, to deny this common-sense attitude adds nothing of value to a theistic or pantheistic faith. Why adopt an eccentric terminology if there is no need for it?

But this is not the place for debating these age-old questions. Let me turn to a strange little book called *Eureka: A Prose Poem*, written by Edgar Allan Poe shortly before his death. Poe was convinced that it was his masterpiece. "What I have propounded will (in good time) revolutionize the world of Physical & Metaphysical Science," he wrote to a friend. "I say this calmly— but I say it." In another letter he wrote, "It is no use to reason with me *now*; I must die. I have no desire to live since I have done *Eureka*. I could accomplish nothing more." (I quote from excellent notes in *The Science Fiction of Edgar Allan Poe*, edited by Harold Beaver, Penguin Books, 1976.)

Poe wanted his publisher, George P. Putnam, to print 50,000 copies. Putnam advanced Poe fourteen dollars for his "pamphlet," and printed 500 copies. Reviews were mostly unfavorable. To this day the book seems to have been taken seriously only in France, where it had been translated by Baudelaire. Now suddenly, in the light of current cosmological speculation, Poe's prose poem is seen to contain a vast vision that is essentially a theist's version of Wheeler's cosmology! As Beaver points out, the "I" in Poe's "Dreamland" has become the universe itself:

> By a route obscure and lonely,
> Haunted by ill angels only,
> Where an Eidolon, named NIGHT,
> On a black throne reigns upright,
> I have reached these lands but newly
> From an ultimate dim Thule—
> From a wild weird clime that lieth, sublime,
>   Out of SPACE—out of TIME.

A universe begins, said Poe, when God creates a "primordial particle" out of nothing. From it matter is "irradiated" spherically in all directions, in the form of an "inexpressibly great yet limited number of unimaginably yet not infinitely minute atoms." As the universe expands, gravity slowly gains the upper hand and the matter condenses to form stars and planets. Eventually gravity halts the expansion and the universe begins to contract until it returns again to nothingness. The final "globe of globes will instantaneously disappear" (how Poe would have exulted in today's black holes!) and the God of our universe will remain "all in all."

In Poe's vision each universe is being observed by its own deity, the way your eye watched the two particles dance in our created world of 1-space. But there are other deities whose eyes watch other universes. These universes are "unspeakably distant" from one another. No communication between them is possible. Each of them, said Poe, has "a new and perhaps totally different series of conditions." By introducing gods Poe implies that these conditions are not randomly selected. The fine-structure constant is what it is in our universe because our deity wanted it that way. In Poe's superspace the cyclical birth and death of an infinity of universes is a process that goes on "for ever, and for ever, and for ever; a novel Universe swelling into existence, and then subsiding into nothingness at every throb of the Heart Divine."

Did Poe mean by "Heart Divine" the God of our universe or a higher deity whose eye watches all the lesser gods from some abode in super-super-space? Behind Brahma the creator, goes Hindu mythology, is Brahman the inscrutable, so transcendent that all we can say about Brahman is *Neti neti* (not that, not that). And is Brahman being observed by a super-super-super-eye? And can we posit a final order of superspace, with its Ultimate Eye, or is that ruled out by the contradiction in standard set theory of the concept of a greatest aleph?

This is the great question asked in the final stanza of the Hymn of Creation in the *Rig Veda*. The "He" of the stanza is the impersonal One who is above all gods:

> *Whether the world was made or was self-made,*
> *He knows with full assurance, He alone,*
> *Who in the highest heaven guards and watches;*
> *He knows indeed, but then, perhaps, He knows not!*

It is here that we seem to touch—or perhaps we are still infinitely far from touching—the hem of Everything. Let C. S. Lewis (I quote from chapter 2 of his *Studies in Words*) make the final comment: " 'Everything' is a subject on which there is not much to be said."

PART VII

RELIGION

I might as well make a clean breast of it. In grade school I considered myself an atheist. In high school I became a convert to Protestant fundamentalism of the most primitive sort, a delusion that lasted through my first two years of college. The University of Chicago quickly demolished these beliefs. For a few years I tried vainly, like John Updike, to preserve Christian faith by way of Karl Barth. I even flirted with G. K. Chesterton's Catholic orthodoxy. Finally I decided that although I could accept the basic theology of what Jesus may have actually taught, as distinct from the bizarre mythology that sprang up around him, it was a dishonest use of language to call myself a Christian.

This agonizing evolution of faith roughly parallels the evolution of the protagonist in my crazy novel The Flight of Peter Fromm. *My present views are in the fideist tradition of Pierre Bayle, Immanuel Kant, Charles Peirce, William James, and above all Miguel de Unamuno. They are defended ad nauseam in my* Whys of a Philosophical Scrivener.

FORTY-FOUR

THE STRANGE CASE OF ROBERT MAYNARD HUTCHINS

Although Hutchins died in 1977, I am convinced that his philosophy of education deserves to be considered seriously today. He believed that the purpose of a university is not to win football and basketball games, or to teach students how to make money. Its purpose is to unsettle student minds, to provide them with a sound liberal education, and to teach them to think about fundamental questions and values. One of his collections of speeches was titled No Friendly Voice. *Our university presidents, faculty members, and trustees would do well to listen to that prophetic voice again.*

I was in my early twenties, newly graduated at the University of Chicago, when I wrote this piece. It appeared in the University of Kansas City's quarterly The University Review *(Winter 1938). For this anthology I have much revised and updated it, mainly with a lengthy postscript about Hutchins and his friend and mentor Mortimer J. Adler.*

"The most striking fact about the higher learning in America," began Robert Hutchins, speaking at Yale University in 1936, "is the confusion that besets it." He then proceeded to add to that confusion by delivering a series of four bewildering lectures that were later reprinted in book form under the title, *The Higher Learning in America*. This small volume soon became one of the most controversial documents in contemporary educational literature.

No one was quite sure what the president of the University of Chicago had intended his words to mean, but nearly everyone was dismayed by the book. Most of the reviews in both popular and scholarly publications were unfavorable. Harvard's distinguished philosopher Alfred North Whitehead wrote an article for the *Atlantic Monthly* (September 1936) that, without mentioning Hutchins by name, took sharp issue with his basic point of view. John Dewey, at Columbia University, in two articles for *Social Frontier* (December 1936, January 1937), intimated that Hutchins was obscurantist, anti-scientific, reactionary, authoritarian, and badly educated. At Hutchins's own university, opposition to his educational theories grew in intensity. Almost every member of the faculty disagreed with him. James Weber Linn of the English department wrote an article for the alumni magazine (December 1936) that chided "Bob" for his immature ideas. Charles E. Clark, dean of the Yale Law School (to whom Hutchins had dedicated his book), arrived at the university in December 1937 to give the annual Moody lecture. He announced his subject to be "The Higher Learning in a Democracy." Hutchins introduced him, then sat courageously on the platform to endure a friendly castigation by one of his former law teachers.

The strongest attack came from Harry D. Gideonse of the economics department, who wrote a book (1937) with the same title as Clark's lecture. Two years later Gideonse became a full professor at Columbia University. "I would certainly not have left the University of Chicago," he told an alumni group in Washington, "because Columbia offered me a higher rank and higher salary. I left because I disagreed with the intellectual and administrative ideas and practices of President Hutchins."

Throughout these attacks (I have mentioned only a few of them), Hutchins maintained that he was seriously misunderstood. To the *Atlantic Monthly* he contributed "A Reply to Professor Whitehead." For the *Social Frontier* he wrote an answer to John Dewey, sarcastic in tone and accusing Dewey of "still fighting nineteenth-century German philosophy."

To see this conflict of ideas in better perspective, it will be worthwhile to glance briefly at some earlier history. After graduating from the Yale Law School at age twenty-seven, Hutchins became a professor of law at Yale and was soon appointed dean of the Law School. In 1929, when he was thirty, the University of Chicago made him president. There were many reasons. He was brilliant, handsome, and articulate. As the youngest college president in America he was great publicity. Above all, he had a reputation as a money-getter.

He was everything the university wanted—and more. Things began to happen fast. The now well known Chicago Plan of undergraduate instruction (four survey courses, noncompulsory class attendance, advance at your own speed, and so on) had been lying about on office desks for years. Hutchins picked it up, believed it to be essentially sound, and after making a few minor changes railroaded it into actuality. When the Big Crash occurred, he was effective in preventing salary cuts. He condensed eighty budgets into twelve. During the thirties he defended the academic freedom of radicals on the faculty who came under fire from conservatives in the city and state governments, aided by conservative Chicago newspapers. And he began to make speeches.

They were strange speeches. For one thing, they contained none of the platitudes and cliches that normally grace the lectures of college presidents. He told a graduating class that they were nearer to truth now than they would ever be again. He told students that the purpose of the university was to unsettle their minds. He told science departments that they were too concerned with fact-finding and not enough concerned with ideas. He maintained that the world was bewildered because it had forgotten how to read and think. He proposed a return to philosophy. He sprinkled his lectures with quotations from Plato and Aristotle and Thomas Aquinas. He had even been reading Gilbert Chesterton.

As Hutchins himself once said, he talked more than any other college president in captivity. But it was invigorating and refreshing talk. It was a new kind of talk. Thornton Wilder, an old schoolmate of Hutchins at Yale (Hutchins brought him to the University of Chicago to teach in the English department), suggested that the president's epitaph should read, "Here lies a college president who never used the word *ideals.*"

At first the campus enjoyed the president's speeches. Then gradually an awful rumor began to take shape and run about "The Grey City on the Midway." The president—yes, it was true—the president had developed an intense interest in Catholic theology! Students and professors rubbed their ears and listened more carefully to what Hutchins was saying. Who could believe it? The little Baptist school that had grown into a great center of unbelief had a president who was studying books by Catholic theologians!

The first intimation the campus had of the president's interest in neo-Thomism—the modern version of the philosophy and theology of Saint Thomas Aquinas—was in 1930 when Hutchins brought Mortimer J. Adler to the university. Adler had been teaching Great Books courses in New York with his friend Scott Buchanan, and he had written a book, *Dialectic*, which (as Hutchins once described it in a speech) "proved there was nothing true, but that there were a great many ways of talking about things, and that you could have a lot of fun seeing how many consistent universes of discourse you could construct to talk about them in. . . . It was this great man whom at this critical juncture in my educational career I had the good fortune to meet."

By the time Adler came to Chicago he had made a 180-degree turn. He had discovered the *Summa Theologica* of Thomas Aquinas. Although Jewish, and unwilling to become a practicing Catholic, Adler had brought himself intellectually to a position in which he was willing to defend the doctrines of Catholicism as God-given truth. Word spread around the country that the University of Chicago was a former Baptist school where Jewish professors were now teaching Catholic theology to atheists.

How the president had become acquainted with Adler, no one knew. They did know that he had placed Adler in the university's department of philosophy without anticipating the furor it would arouse. George Mead, a leading pragmatist, was then head of the department. He objected to Adler's appointment, and when Hutchins turned a deaf ear Mead stomped out of the department in great disgust, never to return. With him went two other philosophers. This historic occasion became known as the great walkout of the philosophers. It left the department in a crippled condition from which it did not recover for years.

When Hutchins realized that he had made an executive blunder, he withdrew Adler from the philosophy department to make him an associate professor of the philosophy of law. It was a title and department created on the spot. Soon he and Adler were teaching an honors course in the intellectual history of western Europe. It was the first of their Great Books seminars, modeled on the courses Adler had been teaching in New York, which in turn had been modeled on courses that had been introduced at Columbia by John Erskine.

Jacques Maritain, one of the world's most respected Catholic Thomists, came from the University of Paris to lecture on the Midway. When his speech was printed as a booklet by the University of Chicago Press, it was observed that Maritain had dedicated it to Hutchins, and Mrs. Hutchins, a talented artist, had drawn a sketch of the author for the frontispiece. Hutchins gave an address somewhere. It sounded so much like a speech by a neo-Thomist that a prominent Catholic journal of philosophy ran an editorial welcoming Hutchins into the ranks.

Hutchins's first book, No Friendly Voice, was enthusiastically reviewed in Catholic journals. The reception on the Midway was not so friendly. The university's International Journal of Ethics carried a vitriolic criticism by its editor, T. V. Smith. When Hutchins's second book, The Higher Learning in America, came off the press, reactions were similar. Catholic universities placed it on required reading lists, but secular philosophers and educators around the nation were profoundly shocked by it.

It is not difficult to understand why. They had heard of Adler and the great walkout of the philosophers. They knew Adler had become a Thomist and that his influence on Hutchins was increasing. It was only natural that when Hutchins set forth a scheme for reforming the higher learning, expressing it in a Thomist vocabulary, they would assume that behind the scheme was a Catholic philosophy that Hutchins for some reason did not want to make explicit.

The modern world, said Hutchins, is "anti-intellectual." Not only is truth "everywhere the same," but there is a "hierarchy of truths." The book proposed that universities revive the medieval trivium of grammar, rhetoric, and logic. It repeated most of the central ideas expressed in Cardinal John Newman's classic work, *The Idea of a University*. Medieval schools and Catholic theology were viewed with what one critic called "a disturbingly fond backward look." For example, consider the following passage:

> Saddest of all is the fate that has overtaken theology itself. Displaced from its position as the queen of the sciences, it now finds itself a feeble imitator of all the rest. In general its students are its students in name only. . . . Its nominal followers, frightened out of their wits by the scientific spirit, have thrown theology overboard and have transferred their affections to those overdressed hoydens, the modern versions of the natural and social sciences.

Statements such as these, in the book and in Hutchins's speeches, gave the impression that behind his cautiously expressed public utterances were unexpressed private convictions hardly in step with the trends of modern thought. To discuss, as Hutchins did, the decline of theological schools implies that before the decline, when the schools were orthodox, they were somehow better than they are now. Hutchins began to emerge as a man who had deep religious convictions but was shy of writing about them. Like Cardinal Newman before him, it seemed as if Hutchins had written a book on education that he hoped would be favorably received by both the faithful and the unbeliever.

The Higher Learning in America falls roughly into two parts. The first section stresses the evils of today's higher learning, especially its confusion as to ends. There is no single, unifying aim. Like a "service station" it reflects every passing need and desire of the populace. The book's second section outlines a new curriculum designed to eliminate this confusion. There must be, said Hutchins, a unifying field of study. In the middle ages, universities were unified by Catholic theology. But theology implies dogma, and dogma implies a church; and our secular age has neither. "To look to theology to unify the modern university is futile and vain." We must turn, therefore, to the next best thing, the discipline that unified the thinking of the ancient Greeks. We must turn to metaphysics.

Perhaps that word *metaphysics*, more than anything else, aroused the ire of Hutchins's critics. It is, of course, a word that has been used with many meanings. But in the absence of a clear understanding of what Hutchins meant by the word, his critics assumed he was using it in a Thomist sense. He had quoted from Aquinas in making statements about metaphysics. As Dewey pointed out, it seemed absurd for Hutchins to refer to Saint Thomas unless he regarded metaphysics in the same way Aquinas did. It seemed that Hutchins was asking modern universities to adopt a final, eternally true metaphysical system that would unify the higher learning in the way Catholic theology had unified medieval schools.

Herbert Spencer, in his influential treatise on education, had maintained that human opinion usually goes through three historical phases: the unanimity of the ignorant, the disagreement of the inquiring, and the unanimity of the wise.

> It is manifest [said Spencer] that the second is parent of the third. They are not sequences in time only; they are sequences in causation. However impatiently, therefore, we may witness the present conflict of educational systems, and however much we may regret its accompanying evils, we must recognize it as a transition stage needful to be passed through and beneficent in its ultimate effects.

Most modern educators, following Spencer, look on contemporary bewilderment in education, deplorable though it may be, as a necessary prelude, something in which we can take a kind of pride. But Hutchins, by his use of the word *metaphysics*, by his disturbingly fond backward look, seemed to view present-day bewilderment as the loss of something splendid.

Hutchins later insisted that he was not using *metaphysics* in the medieval sense. He merely meant to say that a university should be unified by a vigorous search for broad, general truths. The university would be integrated not by an imposed metaphysical system, but by the fact that its faculty and students would be engaged in the cooperative task of seeking a philosophy that might someday provide an intellectual synthesis for the world. Hutchins put it this way in a speech delivered on April 9, 1937:

> We may then hope to have a unified university, not because an official dogma has been imposed upon it, but because teachers and students can know what they are talking about and can have some hope of understanding one another. As I have said before, the ideal of a university is an understood diversity.

The trouble with our chaotic world, Hutchins said, is not that we have wrong ideologies, but that we have no ideology. That is, the average educated man has none. Hutchins had no quarrel, he made clear, with the view that education should be concerned with the reconstruction of society. He agreed with Dewey and with the Marxists that the end of education was "intelligent action." His message was simply that we should put first things first. Intelligent action is impossible without intelligent, well-educated citizens.

Dewey and Hutchins, it seems to me, differ largely not in what they believe to be the end of education, but in the methods they think will best achieve that end. It is mainly a difference of emphasis. Hutchins wants the higher learning to concentrate on the history of ideas. The modern university, he believes, is too preoccupied by empirical science, vocational training, and contemporary writing. It should put more stress on a liberal education, which is best provided by reading the classics. In this stress on the classics Hutchins is close to the American literary humanist movement, whose leading spokesmen were Paul Elmer More and Irving Babbitt. His views are in substantial agreement with those of Norman Foerster, the movement's later voice. Dewey agrees on the virtues of a liberal education, but for him such an education requires an understanding of modern science where reading the classics (books by Galileo, Newton, Harvey, and so on) has little value. The two points of view may not be so far apart as one might suppose.

In any case, Hutchins is certainly far from the Thomism of his friend Adler, although his critics can hardly be blamed for thinking otherwise. His insistence that the university become a "unified diversity," with no imposed metaphysics, seems belied by his repeated expressions of admiration for philosophers who defended vast metaphysical systems and by his constant denigration of anti-metaphysical schools such as pragmatism, empiricism, and positivism.

The history of philosophy from the Renaissance to the present has been one of increasing weariness with the web-spinning of metaphysicians. Because of Hutchins's fascination with the language of Thomism, perhaps because of private religious convictions about which we know nothing, he made the fatal mistake of expressing his views in a terminology that was only too easy to misinterpret. The word *philosophy* would surely have had a less ominous sound than *metaphysics*. Its use might have avoided much of the strident opposition by educators who perhaps would have agreed with Hutchins if they had better understood him. As it was, Hutchins's use of the word *metaphysics* only added to the confusion in educational theory that he was trying to disperse.

It was once a good word, but Hutchins was in the wrong age.

POSTSCRIPT

Aside from some trivial articles in University of Chicago undergraduate publications, in magic magazines, and in a few other obscure periodicals, this was my first published piece of nonfiction.

Hutchins left the University of Chicago in 1951, much to the satisfaction of the faculty, to become an officer of the Ford Foundation. In 1954 he was made president of the foundation's Fund for the Republic, and in 1959 he became the founder and first president of the Center for the Study of Democratic Institutions, in Santa Barbara, California.

By 1975 the center was in shambles. It had run out of funds, associates had been let go or had quit, and those who remained were squabbling furiously. The new president, Malcolm Moos, resigned in opposition to Hutchins's plan to sell the large Santa Barbara estate and move the center to the University of Chicago, where Hutchins would resume leadership. For several years the center had been kept solvent by, of all things, royalties from Dr. Alexander Comfort's best-selling sex manual *The Joy of Sex*.

A former British pediatrician, Comfort had been an associate fellow of the center since 1969. In 1974, after the whopping commercial success of his sex manual, he moved to Santa Barbara as a permanent senior fellow. For tax purposes and other complicated reasons, he assigned 20 percent of his book's royalties to the center, which was supposed to pass the rest along to Comfort in U.S. dollars.

When Hutchins planned to sell the estate and move the center to Chicago, Comfort decided that the center had broken his contract. He sued for $406,000 he claimed was owed him. The center responded with a counter suit of $3.8 million, contending that Dr. Comfort had "intentionally and maliciously" written a second book, *More Joy*, in order to cut down sales of the first one. In 1976 a federal district judge ruled mostly in favor of Comfort's action. The judge called the pact between Comfort and the center a "shabby" one in which the doctor had untruthfully claimed to have written *Joy of Sex* under the center's auspices. The center, said the judge, had "winked at the fraud."

"Hutchins may have set out to study democratic institutions," declared Dr. Comfort, "but he ran this place like a Byzantine harem. . . . The center has no future—it is a fiction and a sham." To outsiders, the imbroglio was high comedy. Here was a distinguished think tank, presided over by a man who believed that an education could be obtained only by reading the Great Books, keeping itself Comfortably alive with royalties from a book that sold mainly because it was filled with erotic drawings.

Hutchins died in 1977. The center, now called the Robert M. Hutchins Center for the Study of Democratic Institutions, has been taken over by the University of California, at Santa Barbara. It continues to publish its *Center Magazine*. For a semi-obit, see Edward Engberg's article "Hutchinsland" in the *New Republic*, July 21, 1979. Engberg likens the center to Charles Dickens's Mudfog Association for the Advancement of Everything.

For a much stronger obit see Joseph Epstein's article, "The Sad Story of the Boy Wonder," in *Commentary* (March 1990). Epstein concludes:

> In the lives of the great, every turn, each unexpected twist, seems in retrospect the exactly right one. Accidents, setbacks, illnesses, unhappiness, family tragedy—all seem to conduce to the production of the masterworks, the grand discoveries, the saving of the nation. In the lives of the almost great who fail, the reverse seems to obtain. Every break, piece of good fortune, natural advantage conduces to the series of sad botches

that end in ultimate failure. It was to Thornton Wilder that Hutchins wrote: "I was right to leave [the University of Chicago]; but I went to the wrong place [the Ford Foundation]." But any other place, one feels on reviewing his life, would have been the wrong place, every turn probably a mistake.

Had Hutchins been a mite less quick, less handsome, less lucky in his early years, might he not, given his natural superiority, have done something genuinely, breathtakingly extraordinary? Perhaps; perhaps not. Poor Hutchins. His life was of a kind to set one to composing apothegms about the sad fate of those whom the gods, with their well-known taste for irony, too heavily favor when young.

As an undergraduate major in philosophy at Chicago during the legendary Hutchins-Adler epoch, and on the staff of the university's public relations office during the years in which Hutchins passionately opposed the nation's entrance into the war against Germany, I have since followed the careers of Hutchins and Adler with more than usual interest. On the whole, I admired Hutchins. He was surely right in deploring the increasing trivialization of America's higher learning, in insisting that a university should provide a liberal education before it allows students to choose courses, and in stressing the importance of philosophy and the Great Books. He may have been naive about communism, but he had the courage to take a strong stand against the crude tactics of Senator Joseph McCarthy and other anti-communists who knew even less about the red menace than he did. Above all, he had an admirable sense of humor. "The faculty doesn't amount to much," he once said about his University of Chicago, "but the president and the students are wonderful." After his divorce and remarriage he told a reporter, "I think I'll try it every year."

What prevented Hutchins from becoming the great educator he had always hoped to be? For one thing, his caustic tongue and arrogant, high-handed ways made endless enemies. For another, he constantly exaggerated. American universities may be in bad shape, but they surely are a bit more than what Hutchins once called "high-class flophouses where parents send their children to keep them off the labor market and out of their own hair." Perhaps more than anything else, he never took the time to learn much about modern science or philosophy. "I have been permitted to glory in the possession of an unmathematical mind," he said in a commencement address at Saint John's College, in Annapolis, the only university that tried to carry out his Great Books program. "My scientific attainments were of the same order." Because Hutchins knew so little about science, his constant sniping at the scientific community for being concerned only with what they could measure, obsessed by facts instead of ideas, could hardly have been persuasive.

In my opinion, Adler might have become a great philosopher if he had not been sidetracked by Aquinas, and Hutchins might have become a great educator if he had not been sidetracked by Adler. Consider, for example, Hutchins's annual Aquinas lecture at Marquette University in 1949. He had been preceded by such distinguished Catholic theologians as Jacques Maritain and Etienne Gilson, and by Adler. Marquette University Press issued the lecture as a small book entitled *St. Thomas and the World State,* and dedicated "To Mortimer Adler for twenty-two years." Hutchins described Aquinas's *Treatise on Law* as "that greatest of all books on the philosophy of law." He urged the Catholic church to assume leadership in working for "a universal church and world state."

Of course this does not mean that Hutchins believed in the doctrines of Rome, or was even close to believing. But just what *did* he believe? I have always agreed with what Chesterton said in his introduction to *Heretics:*

> But there are some people, nevertheless—and I am one of them—who think that the most practical and important thing about a man is still his view of the universe. We think that for a landlady considering a lodger, it is important to know his income, but still more important to know his philosophy. We think that for a general about to fight an enemy, it is important to know the enemy's numbers, but still more important to know the enemy's philosophy. We think the question is not whether the theory of the cosmos affects matters, but whether, in the long run, anything else affects them.

To me the strangest aspect of the strange case of Robert Maynard Hutchins is that he never talked about his own theology except in the haziest way. That he believed in a creator God, transcendent yet personal, there can be no doubt. Indeed, he often sounded like an Old Testament prophet. Civilization, he said in a convocation address at Chicago in 1946, is doomed unless there is a worldwide "moral, intellectual, and spiritual reformation." There is no way, he said, that we can learn to love our neighbors unless we first love God. "The brotherhood of man must rest on the fatherhood of God. If God is denied . . . the basis of community disappears. . . . Unless we believe that every man is the child of God, we cannot love our neighbors. Most cats and most dogs are more attractive than most men. Unless we see men as children of God, they appear to us as rivals, or customers, or foreigners, unrelated to us except as means to our ends."

Hutchins's attack on the very possibility of a naturalistic ethics was unremitting. He admitted that if the world practiced Aristotle's ethics it would be much better off, but he added: "I doubt if any single man, to say nothing of the whole world, can practice Aristotle's ethics without the support and inspiration of religious faith. . . . It is very late; perhaps nothing can save us."

Surely a man who talks so apocalyptically, like Noah warning of the Deluge, owes it to his listeners to let them in on what religious faith he has in mind. Protestants, Catholics, Jews, and Muslims, all believe in the fatherhood of God, yet Protestants and Catholics are now killing each other in Ireland, and Jews and Muslims are killing each other in the Near East. Did Hutchins have a particular faith in mind? Or was he a philosophical theist who did not place any great religious tradition above any other?

In a speech on "Morals, Religion, and Higher Education" (you'll find it in *Freedom, Education, and the Fund*, 1956) Hutchins writes: "By religion I mean belief in and obedience to God. This may not require adherence to a church or creed; but it demands religious faith. Faith is not reason, but it is something more than a vague, sentimental desire to do good and be good." He then cites Saint Augustine as an example of a man whose conversion "followed after tremendous wrestling with the intellectual difficulties of Christianity." Metaphysics and natural theology, he goes on, can throw little light on "the existence and nature of God, the character and destiny of the human soul, and the salvation of man." Naturalistic ethical doctrines "overlook the fallen nature of man and assume that without grace he can reach a terrestrial end to which, almost by definition, no being with such a nature can ever obtain."

The curriculum of an ideal university, Hutchins continues, must include more than a study of morals. "It should include both natural and sacred theology." Scientism, skepticism, and secularism—especially what Hutchins elsewhere called the "anti-philosophies" of pragmatism and positivism—deny that there are objective moral and religious truths. "If higher education is to take morality and religion seriously, it must repudiate these dogmas; for the truths of morality and religion never have been and never can be discovered by experiment or by any allegedly 'scientific' means. Morality and religion cannot be taken seriously unless the possibility of attaining truth by philosophical inquiry and by revelation is admitted."

Revelation? I find it hard to read this 1948 lecture without assuming that Hutchins then believed in the same revelation in which Augustine and Aquinas believed. But wait! There is a curious footnote to the paragraph from which I just quoted. It is a long statement by the vice-chancellor of the University of Punjab declaring education to be "incomplete" unless it is "illuminated" by God's revelation to Islam! Was Hutchins trying to tell us that the Muslim tradition is as true as the Christian? This seems unlikely. Did he believe the Christian revelation to be true and that this ultimately would become clear after, say, a century or two of world dialogue? Did he merely want us to know that even Muslim educators held views similar to his own? Or was he unsure of just what he believed?

This hesitancy to put on the record one's core beliefs was also characteristic of the men with whom Hutchins and Adler were most closely associated. Did Scott Buchanan believe in God? Does Richard McKeon? As for Stringfellow Barr, who died in 1982, we know he was practicing Episcopalian, but today this tells us nothing about a person's doctrinal beliefs. For ten years Barr was president of Saint John's College, with Buchanan as his dean. In a Penguin paperback titled *Christianity Takes a Stand* (1946), edited by Bishop William Scarlett, Barr has an essay on "The Duty of a Christian in the Modern World." His theme is this. The world is moving toward disaster, and this may be God's will. On the other hand, perhaps we can avert it. The only way to do so is by a return to Christ. That the world can solve its problems without seeking first the Kingdom of God strikes him, he says, as harder to believe than the mystery of the Incarnation. He finds very little in modern efforts to build a better world that "is relevant if the Incarnation did indeed take place." The future is, of course, in God's hands. "This fact we must learn to welcome or else we must deny Christ and go it alone. I doubt whether in modern history the choice before us has been clearer."

Note that Barr did not say outright that he personally believed in the Incarnation, but how can you make much sense of his remarks unless he did? With statements like these coming from Hutchins's associates, and from Hutchins himself, it is understandable why American philosophers and educators suspected that behind the Hutchins-Adler rhetoric for the Great Books was an unstated motive. Could it be that the motive, especially in Adler's mind, was not so much to introduce students to the great ideas as it was to introduce them to the great Roman Catholic ideas?

We know that Hutchins's father was an evangelical Presbyterian minister in whose home there were morning prayers and daily Bible readings. We also know that Hutchins early stopped going to church even though, as he said, he often found himself "singing, humming, or moaning third-rate hymns . . . while shaving, while waiting on the platform to make a speech, or in other moments of abstraction or crisis." Milton Mayer, a good friend of Hutchins who often wrote Hutchins's articles for mass-circulation magazines, likes to recall an occasion when Hutchins startled him by saying, "The trouble with you, Mayer, is that you don't believe in God."

But what sort of God? A God who walked the earth as Jesus? I recall a banquet in the University of Chicago's Commons at which Hutchins gave a short speech that was followed by questions from the guests. I asked if he would mind telling us something about his religious beliefs. Yes, Hutchins answered, he would mind. Everybody laughed, and Hutchins went on to the next question.

I did not think this funny. Hutchins, I am persuaded, damaged his career by concealing his religious views. Perhaps someday a biographer will interview those who knew him best and tell us exactly what sort of light he chose to keep hidden under the bushel of his books and speeches.

In the fifth chapter of his first autobiography, *Philosopher at Large* (1977), Adler tells how he became a convert to the theology of St. Thomas Aquinas. It was his friend Richard McKeon, then teaching a course on medieval philosophy at Columbia, who sent Adler to a Catholic bookstore in downtown Manhattan, where he bought the first of twenty-one volumes of an English translation of *Summa Theologica*. Adler describes the effect this book had on him as "cataclysmic."

As for the view he had taken in *Dialectic*, Adler writes: "I cannot now give a wholly satisfactory explanation of why this incorrect view of philosophy should have taken so strong a hold on my mind and dominated it for a number of years." He attributes it in part to the influence of his good friends Arthur Rubin and Scott Buchanan. Buchanan had written a book called *Possibility*, published the same year as Adler's, which took a similar line. (Years later he and Adler had a falling-out over Adler's embracing of Thomism.) Adler says he went through a short period of "intellectual schizophrenia" before completely repudiating his earlier view.

Dialectic is a curious work. Its thesis is that philosophy, rightly viewed, is a dialectical process without end that explores the internal consistency and implications of all points of view without dogmatically affirming that one vision is truer than another. Truth is logical coherence, not correspondence with an external reality. The true philosopher sees his efforts as a game, a comic play of thought, a verbal fencing. Reading his books you can hear the "quiet laughter" of Plato, the supreme dialectician. "The aim of philosophy," wrote Adler, "might almost be described as the attempt to achieve an empty mind, a mind free from any intellectual prepossessions, and unhampered by one belief or another."

Back in 1908, in the section on metaphysics in his book *First and Last Things*, H. G. Wells argued for an approach to philosophy almost indistinguishable from Adler's early vision. Here is how Wells expressed it with a metaphor:

It will perhaps give a clearer idea of what I am seeking to convey if I suggest a concrete image for the whole world of a man's thought and knowledge. Imagine a large clear jelly, in which at all angles and in all states of simplicity or contortion his ideas are imbedded. They are all valid and possible ideas as they lie, none incompatible with any. If you imagine the direction of up or down in this clear jelly being as it were the direction in which one moves by analysis or by synthesis, if you go down for example from matter to atoms and centres of force and up to men and states and countries—if you will imagine the ideas lying in that manner—you will get the beginnings of my intention. But our Instrument, our process of thinking, like a drawing before the discovery of perspective, appears to have difficulties with the third dimension, appears capable only of dealing with or reasoning about ideas by projecting them upon the same plane. It will be obvious that a great multitude of things may very well exist together in a solid jelly, which would be overlapping and incompatible and mutually destructive, when projected together upon one plane. Through the bias in our Instrument to do this, through reasoning between terms not in the same plane, an enormous amount of confusion, perplexity and mental deadlocking occurs.

Some notion of how close Adler came to becoming a Catholic may be gleaned from passages in "Religion in a Modern World," a speech he gave on April 3, 1935. Adler shared the platform with two secular humanists, Max Carl Otto and Albert Eustace Haydon. I have forgotten where this symposium was held, but I have a mimeographed typescript of the speech that was provided later by a Chicago lecture service. Said Adler:

> There is only one true religion because there cannot be opposed truths of faith. There is only one orthodox or right theology because there cannot be two or more opposed correct understandings of those truths. Because of this, religion must be organized by a church and its dogma and ritual must be prescribed by church doctors. It is by the authority of the doctors of the church that infidels are converted. . . . It seems to me that liberal Protestantism and Judaism are heretical. . . . The true religion I wish to expound for you is the Catholic Christianity.

Then comes the most incredible paragraph of all:

> I now want to suggest the possibility of choosing between the religions. As I survey the religions of the Western World, it seems to me that Catholicism is the true religion. The sin of heresy is not the intellectual sin but it is the sin of pride, of egotism. When a church council succeeded in answering a theological question, then a heretic was he who willfully set his opinion against the church. It is this pride that constitutes his error. I am not sure that I would hesitate to say that the church was right in burning heretics.

In hesitating to condemn the Inquisition, Adler was being a faithful Thomist. Saint Augustine had opposed the death penalty for heresy; he thought the church should limit its punishments to flogging, fines, and exile. "To put a heretic to death would be to introduce upon earth an inexpiable crime," declared Saint John Chrysostom. But Saint Thomas thought otherwise. "If false coiners or other felons are justly committed to death without delay by worldly princes," he wrote in his Summa Theologica (II, xi), "much more may heretics, from the moment that they are convicted, be not only excommunicated, but slain justly out of hand." By the end of the sixteenth century hundreds of thousands of poor souls had been savagely tortured and burned alive, or otherwise murdered, for holding opinions contrary to those of the church. Public executions of heretics and witches became festive occasions, like watching the deaths of gladiators.

If it is right to execute those who kill the body, so went the reasoning of devout Christians, how much more right it is to execute those who send souls to eternal punishment. Moreover, killing a heretic does even the heretic a favor. Will it not prevent him from causing greater harm and thereby lighten his torment in hell? Protestants were, of course, just as intolerant. Luther and Calvin followed Aquinas in believing that heretics deserved death; but because the Protestants came later, were fewer in number, and had less political clout, their victims were fewer.

I would guess that Adler is now much ashamed of his 1935 speech, but it helps one to understand why James Farrell, writing in *Partisan Review* in 1940, would call Adler "a provincial Torquemada without an Inquisition." (The article is reprinted in Farrell's *League of Frightened Philistines*, 1945.) "Thanks very much for the chance to see your blast against Mortimer J. Adler," said H. L. Mencken in a letter to Farrell. "You describe him precisely. I hear confidentially that Holy Church is full of hopes that he will submit to baptism anon. If the ceremony is public I'll certainly attend. I invite you herewith to come along in my private plane. I assure you there will be plenty of stimulants aboard" (*Letters of H. L. Mencken*, 1961, p. 451).

In the last chapter of his autobiography Adler struggles manfully to explain why he never became a Catholic. (I have more to say about this in chapter 12 of my *Whys of a Philosophical Scrivener*.) "This whole matter was complicated," Adler writes, ". . . by the conversion to Roman Catholicism of a number of students who had been introduced to the *Summa Theologica* in the Great Books class that Bob Hutchins and I taught, or in the Trivium course I taught with Malcolm Sharp."

Many of Adler's students who converted were Jewish. Although Adler's rhetoric played a role in these conversions, there were others on the campus who were even more influential, such as Adler's close associate William Gorman, an Irish Catholic from birth, and Herbert Schwartz, a Jewish convert to the church who had obtained his doctorate at Columbia under Richard McKeon. Schwartz, whose official position at Chicago was on the faculty of music, had an enormous influence on the Jewish students who converted. Later he became the leader of a Catholic community in New Jersey. He died in 1981, leaving a raft of manuscripts that his disciples published in a periodical called *Filoque* (issued by the Mount Hope Foundation, Middletown, N.Y.). Other Jewish converts included Herbert Ratner, Kenneth Simon, Janet Kalven, Peggy Stern, Paula Myers, and Alice Zucker, all of whom have retained their faith. Ratner, who became a medical doctor, was director of public health, Oak Park, Illinois, and editor of *Child and Family Quarterly*. Simon became Father M. Raphael, at Saint Joseph's Abbey, Spencer, Massachusetts, and a Trappist monk. His book, *The Glory of Thy People* (Macmillan, 1948), tells of his conversion.

Miss Kalven, at age 17, was one of twenty students chosen for the first

Hutchins-Adler Great Books class. After graduation, she taught for five years in the Chicago Great Books program before joining a Catholic lay women's movement called the Grail. She became an administrator in the Grail's educational center at Grailville, in Loveland, Ohio.

Among the dozen or so gentiles who converted after Adler introduced them to Saint Thomas was Winston Ashley, who came to the University of Chicago from a Protestant background in Blackwell, Oklahoma. I admired his poems and published some of them in *Comment*, a campus literary magazine I edited in 1936. Winston joined the Dominican order, became a priest in 1948, and as Father Benedict M. Ashley, a teacher of moral theology at the order's Aquinas Institute, St. Louis University. He was president of the institute from 1962 to 1969. Of his several books, the most important (written with a fellow Dominican) is *Health Care Ethics* (second edition, 1982).

In a letter to me, Father Ashley expressed his debt to Adler, not only "for having awakened in me so early in life to the breadth of our western intellectual tradition," but also for financial support. Ashley and his Catholic friend Leo Shields (who was killed in the Normandy invasion of World War II) had worked for two years as Adler assistants, along with Quentin ("Bud") Ogren, another Catholic convert, who married Paula Myers and became a professor of law at Loyola University of Los Angeles.

Miss Kalven, in response to my query, eloquently summed up her debt to Hutchins and Adler as follows:

> The thirties were a time of extraordinary intellectual ferment at Chicago, in large measure due to Hutchins and Adler. Their stance ran counter to the prevailing campus culture and was propaedeutic so far as Catholicism was concerned. From them I learned to question the received wisdom of the semanticists, psychologists, sociologists, cultural relativists; to respect the intellectual rigor of the Greeks and the medievals; to suspect the reductionism of the physical and biological scientists; to read a text on its own terms, define a concept, and analyze an argument. I cut my intellectual teeth so to speak on all the big questions: the nature of language, knowledge, truth; the nature of man (I was not a feminist then), of society, of justice; the existence of God. . . . The Hutchins-Adler training was a necessary but not sufficient condition for conversion. It made Catholicism intellectually respectable, but it did not make anyone become a Catholic. A much more powerful and intimate witness is necessary, I think, to enable people to act as contrary to our upbringing and education as our little group did.

Several excellent biographies of Hutchins have been written in recent years. None has cleared up the mystery of what were his core theological beliefs.

FORTY-FIVE

THE WANDERING JEW
AND THE SECOND
COMING

The legend of a wandering Jew, unable to die until the Second Coming, is surely the strangest of all myths intended to combat the notion that Jesus was mistaken when he said he would return within the lifetime of someone then living. I have summarized its sad, colorful history in an essay that appeared in Free Inquiry (Summer 1995).

As the year 2000 approaches, it would not surprise me to see a picture of the Wandering Jew on the front page of one of the supermarket tabloids. Some intrepid photographer will spot him trudging a dusty road, with his sturdy walking stick and long white beard, and perhaps obtain an interview about his sufferings over the past two centuries.

For the son of man shall come in the glory of his Father, with his angels; and then he shall reward every man according to his works. Verily I say unto you, There be some standing here, which shall not taste of death, till they see the Son of man coming in his kingdom.
—MATTHEW 16: 27,28

The statement of Jesus quoted above from Matthew, and repeated in similar words by Mark (8:38, 9:1) and Luke (9:26,27), is for Bible fundamentalists one of the most troublesome of all New Testament passages.

It is possible, of course, that Jesus never spoke those sentences, but all scholars agree that the first-century Christians expected the Second Coming in their lifetimes. In Matthew 24, after describing dramatic signs of his imminent return, such as the falling of stars and the darkening of the moon and sun, Jesus added: "Verily I say unto you. This generation shall not pass until all these things be fulfilled."

Until about 1933 Seventh-Day Adventists had a clever way of rationalizing this prophecy. They argued that a spectacular meteor shower of 1833 was the falling of the stars, and that there was a mysterious darkening of sun and moon in the United States in 1870. Jesus meant that a future generation witnessing these celestial events would be the one to experience his Second Coming.

For almost a hundred years Adventist preachers and writers of books assured the world that Jesus would return within the lifetimes of some who had seen the great meteor shower of 1833. After 1933 passed, the church gradually abandoned this interpretation of Christ's words. Few of today's faithful are even aware that their church once trumpeted such a view. Although Adventists still believe Jesus will return very soon, they no longer set conditions for an approximate date.

How do they explain the statements of Jesus quoted in the epigraph? Following the lead of Saint Augustine and other early Christian commentators, they take the promise to refer to Christ's Transfiguration. Ellen White, the prophetess who with her husband founded Seventh-day Adventism, said it this way in her life of Christ, *The Desire of Ages*: "The Savior's promise to the disciples was now fulfilled. Upon the mount the future kingdom of glory was represented in miniature. . . ."

Hundreds of adventist sects since the time of Jesus, starting with the Montanists of the second century, have all interpreted Christ's prophetic statements about his return to refer to *their* generation. Apocalyptic excitement surged as the year 1000 approached. Similar excitement is now gathering momentum as the year 2000 draws near. Expectation of the Second Coming is not confined to adventist sects. Fundamentalists in mainstream Protestant denominations are increasingly stressing the imminence of Jesus' return. Baptist Billy Graham, for example, regularly warns of the approaching battle of Armageddon and the appearance of the Anti-Christ. He likes to emphasize the Bible's assertion that the Second Coming will occur after the gospel is preached to all nations. This could not take place, Graham insists, until the rise of radio and television.

Preacher Jerry Falwell is so convinced that he will soon be raptured—caught up in the air to meet the return of Jesus—that he once said he has no plans for a burial plot. Austin Miles, who once worked for Pat Robertson, reveals in his book *Don't Call Me Brother* (1989) that Pat once seriously considered plans to televise the Lord's appearance in the skies! Today's top native drumbeater for a soon Second Coming is Hal Lindsey. His many books on the topic, starting with *The Late Great Planet Earth*, have sold by the millions.

For the past two thousand years individuals and sects have been setting dates for the Second Coming. When the Lord fails to show, there is often no recognition of total failure. Instead, errors are found in the calculations and new dates set. In New Harmony, Indiana, an adventist sect called the Rappites was established by George Rapp. When he became ill he said that were he not absolutely certain the Lord intended him and his flock to witness the return of Jesus, he would think this was his last hour. So saying, he died.

The Catholic church, following Augustine, long ago moved the Second Coming far into the future at some unspecified date. Liberal Protestants have tended to take the Second Coming as little more than a metaphor for the gradual establishment of peace and justice on earth. Julia Ward Howe, a Unitarian minister, had this interpretation in mind when she began her famous *Battle Hymn of the Republic* with "Mine eyes have seen the glory of the coming of the Lord. . . ." Protestant fundamentalists, on the other hand, believe that Jesus described actual historical events that would precede his literal return to earth to banish Satan and judge the quick and the dead. They also find it unthinkable that the Lord could have blundered about the time of his Second Coming.

The difficulty in interpreting Christ's statement about some of his listeners not tasting of death until he returned is that he described the event in exactly the same phrases he used in Matthew 24. He clearly was not there referring to his transfiguration, or perhaps (as another "out" has it) to the fact that his kingdom would soon be established by the formation of the early church. Assuming that Jesus meant exactly what he said, and that he was not mistaken, how can his promise be unambiguously justified?

During the Middle Ages several wonderful legends arose to preserve the accuracy of Christ's prophecies. Some were based on John 21. When Jesus said to Peter "Follow me," Peter noticed John walking behind him and asked, "Lord, what shall this man do?" The Lord's enigmatic answer was, "If I will that he tarry till I come, what is that to thee?"

We are told that this led to a rumor that John would not die. However, the writer of the fourth gospel adds: "Yet Jesus said not unto him, He shall not die; but if I will that he tarry till I come, what is that to thee?" Theologians in the Middle Ages speculated that perhaps John did not die. He was either wandering about the earth, or perhaps he ascended bodily into heaven. A more popular legend was that John had been buried in a state of suspended animation, his heart faintly throbbing, to remain in an unknown grave until Jesus returns.

These speculations about John rapidly faded as a new and more powerful legend slowly took shape. Perhaps Jesus was not referring to John when he said he could ask someone to tarry, but to someone else. This would also explain the remarks quoted in the epigraph. Someone not mentioned in the gospels, alive in Jesus' day, was somehow cursed to remain alive for centuries until judgment day, wandering over the earth and longing for death.

Who was this Wandering Jew? Some said it was Malchus, whose ear Peter sliced off. Others thought it might be the impenitent thief who was crucified beside Jesus. Maybe it was Pilate, or one of Pilate's servants. The version that became dominant identified the Wandering Jew as a shopkeeper—his name varied—who watched Jesus go by his doorstep, staggering under the weight of the cross he carried. Seeing how slowly and painfully the Lord walked, the man struck Jesus on the back, urging him to go faster. "I go," Jesus replied, "but you will tarry until I return."

As punishment for his rudeness, the shopkeeper's doom is to wander the earth, longing desperately to die but unable to do so. In some versions of the legend, he stays the same age. In others, he repeatedly reaches old age only to be restored over and over again to his youth. The legend seems to have first been recorded in England in the thirteenth century before it rapidly spread throughout Europe. It received an enormous boost in the early seventeenth century when a pamphlet appeared in Germany about a Jewish shoe-maker named Ahasuerus[1] who claimed to be the Wanderer. The pamphlet was endlessly reprinted in Germany and translated into other languages. The result was a mania comparable to today's obsessions with UFOs, Abominable Snowmen, and Elvis Presley. Scores of persons claiming to be the Wandering Jew turned up in cities all over England and Europe during the next two centuries. In the U.S. as late as 1868 a Wandering Jew popped up in Salt Lake City, home of the Mormon adventist sect. It is impossible now to decide in individual cases whether these were rumors, hoaxes by imposters, or cases of self-deceived psychotics.

The Wandering Jew became a favorite topic for hundreds of poems, novels, and plays, especially in Germany where such works continue to proliferate to this day. Even Goethe intended to write an epic about the Wanderer, but only finished a few fragments. It is not hard to understand how anti-Semites in Germany and elsewhere would see the cobbler as representing all of Israel, its people under God's condemnation for having rejected his Son as their Messiah.

Gustave Doré produced twelve remarkable woodcuts depicting episodes in the Wanderer's life. They were first published in Paris in 1856 to accompany a poem by Pierre Dupont. English editions followed with translations of the verse.

By far the best known novel about the Wanderer is Eugene Sue's French work *Le Juif Errant* (The Wandering Jew), first serialized in Paris in 1844–45 and published in ten volumes. George Croly's three-volume *Salathiel* (1827), later retitled *Tarry Thóu Till I Come*, was an enormously popular earlier novel. (In *Don Juan*, Canto 11, Stanza 57, Byron calls the author Reverend Roley-

Poley.) In Lew Wallace's *Prince of India* (1893), the Wanderer is a wealthy Oriental potentate.

George Macdonald's *Thomas Wingfold, Curate* (1876) introduces the Wandering Jew as an Anglican minister. Having witnessed the Crucifixion, and in constant agony over his sin, Wingfold is powerless to overcome a strange compulsion. Whenever he passes a roadside cross, or even a cross on top of a church, he has an irresistible impulse to climb on the cross, wrap his arms and legs around it, and cling there until he drops to the ground unconscious! He falls in love, but realizing that his beloved will age and die while he remains young, he tries to kill himself by walking into an active volcano. His beloved follows, and is incinerated by the molten lava. There is a surprisingly happy ending. Jesus appears, forgives the Wanderer, and leads him off to Paradise to reunite with the woman who died for him. The novel is not among the best of this Scottish writer's many admired fantasies.

My First Two Thousand Years, by George Sylvester Viereck and Paul Eldridge (1928) purports to be the erotic autobiography of the Wandering Jew. The same two authors, in 1930, wrote *Salome, the Wandering Jewess*, an equally erotic novel covering her two thousand years of lovemaking. The most recent novel about the Wanderer is by German ex-Communist Stefan Heym, a pseudonym for Hellmuth Flieg. In his *The Wandering Jew*, published in West Germany in 1981 and in a U.S. edition three years later, the Wanderer is a hunchback who tramps the roads with Lucifer as his companion. The fantasy ends with the Second Coming, Armageddon, and the Wanderer's forgiveness.

Sue's famous novel is worth a quick further comment. The Wanderer is Ahasuerus, a cobbler. His sister Herodias, the wife of King Herod, becomes the Wandering Jewess. The siblings are minor characters in a complex plot. Ahasuerus is tall, with a single black eyebrow stretching over both eyes like a Mark of Cain. Seven nails on the soles of his iron boots produce crosses when he walks across snow. Wherever he goes an outbreak of cholera follows. Eventually the two siblings are pardoned and allowed "the happiness of eternal sleep." Sue was a French socialist. His Wanderer is a symbol of exploited labor, Herodias a symbol of exploited women. Indeed, the novel is an angry blast at Catholicism, capitalism, and greed.

The Wandering Jew appears in several recent science fiction novels, notably Walter Miller's *A Canticle for Leibowitz* (1960), and Wilson Tucker's *The Planet King* (1959) where he becomes the last man alive on earth. At least two movies have dealt with the legend, the most recent a 1948 Italian film starring Vittorio Gassman.

Rafts of poems by British and U.S. authors have retold the legend. The American John Saxe, best known for his verse about the blind men and the elephant, wrote a seventeen-stanza poem about the Wanderer. British poet Caroline Elizabeth Sarah Norton's forgettable "Undying One" runs to more

than a hundred pages. Oliver Herford, an American writer of light verse, in
"Overheard in a Garden" turns the Wanderer into a traveling salesman ped-
dling a book about himself. "The Wandering Jew" (1920) by Edwin Arlington
Robinson, is surely the best of such poems by an American writer.

Charles Timothy Brooks (1813–1883) was a New England Unitarian minister as well as a prolific versifier and translator of Goethe and other German
poets. His "Wandering Jew," based on a German poem whose author I do
not know, was reprinted in dozens of pre-1900 American anthologies.

> The Wandering Jew once said to me,
>> I passed through a city in the cool of the year;
> A man in the garden plucked fruit from a tree.
>> I asked, "How long has the city been here?"
> And he answered me, as he plucked away—
>> "It has always stood where it stands to-day,
> And here it will stand forever and aye."
>> Five hundred years rolled by, and then
>> I traveled the self-same road again.
>
> No trace of the city there I found:
>> A shepherd sat blowing his pipe alone;
> His flock went quietly nibbling round.
>> I asked, "How long has the city been gone?"
> And he answered me, and he piped away—
>> "The new ones bloom and the old decay,
> This is my pasture ground for aye."
>> Five hundred years rolled by, and then
>> I traveled the self-same road again.
>
> And I came to the sea, and the waves did roar,
>> And a fisherman threw his net out clear,
> And when heavy laden he dragged it ashore.
>> I asked, "How long has the sea been here?"
> And he laughed, and he said, and he laughed away—
>> "As long as yon billows have tossed their spray
> They've fished and they've fished in this self-same bay."
>> Five hundred years rolled by, and then
>> I traveled the self-same road again.
>
> And I came to a forest, vast and free,
>> And a woodman stood in the thicket near—
> His axe he laid at the foot of a tree.
>> I asked, "How long have the woods been here?"
> And he answered, "These woods are a covert for aye;
>> My ancestors dwelt here alway,
> And the trees have been here since creation's day."

> Five hundred years rolled by, and then
> I traveled the self-same road again.
>
> And I found there a city, and far and near
> Resounded the hum of toil and glee,
> And I asked, "How long has the city been here?
> And where is the pipe, and the wood, and the sea?"
> And they answered me, as they went their way,
> "Things always have stood as they stand to-day,
> And so they will stand forever and aye."
> I'll wait five hundred years, and then
> I'll travel the self-same road again.

In England, Shelley was the most famous poet to become fascinated by the legend. In his lengthy poem "The Wandering Jew," written or partly written when he was seventeen, the Wanderer is called Paulo. A fiery cross on his forehead is kept concealed under a cloth band. In the third Canto, after sixteen centuries of wandering, Paulo recounts the origin of his suffering to Rosa, a woman he loves:

> How can I paint that dreadful day,
> That time of terror and dismay,
> When, for our sins, a Saviour died,
> And the meek Lamb was crucified!
> As dread that day, when, borne along
> To slaughter by the insulting throng,
> Infuriate for Deicide,
> I mocked our Saviour, and I cried,
> 'Go, go,' 'Ah! I will go,' said he,
> 'Where scenes of endless bliss invite;
> To the blest regions of the light
> I go, but thou shalt here remain—
> Thou diest not till I come again.'—

The Wandering Jew is also featured in Shelley's short poem "The Wandering Jew's Soliloquy," and in two much longer works, "Hellas" and "Queen Mab." In "Queen Mab," as a ghost whose body casts no shadow, Ahasuerus bitterly denounces God as an evil tyrant. In a lengthy note about this Shelley quotes from a fragment of a German work "whose title I have vainly endeavored to discover. I picked it up, dirty and torn, some years ago. . . ."

In this fragment the Wanderer describes his endless efforts to kill himself. He tries vainly to drown. He leaps into an erupting Mount Etna where he suffers intense heat for ten months before the volcano belches him out. Forest fires fail to consume him. He tries to get killed in wars but arrows, spears, clubs, swords, bullets, mines, and trampling elephants have no effect on him.

"The executioner's hand could not strangle me . . . nor would the hungry lion in the circus devour me." Snakes and dragons are powerless to harm him. He calls Nero a "bloodhound" to his face, but the tyrant's tortures cannot kill him.

> Ha! not to be able to die—not to be able to die—not to be permitted to rest after the toils of life—to be doomed to be imprisoned forever in the clay-formed dungeon—to be forever clogged with this worthless body, its load of diseases and infirmities—to be condemned to hold for millenniums that yawning monster Sameness, and Time, that hungry hyena, ever bearing children and ever devouring again her offspring!—Ha! not to be permitted to die! Awful avenger in heaven, hast thou in thine armory of wrath a punishment more dreadful? then let it thunder upon me; command a hurricane to sweep me down to the foot of Carmel that I there may lie extended; may pant, and writhe, and die!

Scholarly histories of the legend have been published in Germany and elsewhere. In English, Moncure Daniel Conway's *The Wandering Jew* (1881) has become a basic reference. See also his article on the Wanderer in *The Encyclopaedia Britannica's* ninth edition. Another valuable account is given by Sabine Baring-Gould in his *Curious Myths of the Middle Ages* (second edition, 1867).

The definitive modern history is George K. Anderson's *The Legend of the Wandering Jew*, published by Brown University Press in 1965. A professor of English at Brown, Anderson made good use of the university's massive collection of literature about the Wanderer. His book's 489 pages contain excellent summaries of European poems, plays, and novels not touched upon here, as well as detailed accounts of the many claimants. The book may tell you more than you care to know about this sad attempt of Christians to avoid admitting that the Galilean carpenter-turned-preacher did indeed believe he would soon return to earth in glory, but, as Albert Schweitzer argues so convincingly in *The Quest of the Historical Jesus*, Jesus was mistaken.

NOTES

1. Three kings named Ahasuerus are mentioned in the Old Testament, notably in the book of Esther. Because this Ahasuerus is portrayed as a villain in Jewish plays presented during Purim, his name may have been assigned to the Wandering Jew.

James Joyce's *Ulysses*, in which Leopold Bloom wanders about Dublin, has several references to the Wandering Jew. (See pages 217 and 506.) On page 338 he is explicitly named: "Ahasuerus I call him. Cursed by God."

FORTY-SIX

PROOFS OF GOD

When I disclosed in my Whys of a Philosophical Scrivener that I was a philosophical theist—one who believes in God but is outside any traditional religion—it profoundly shocked readers who knew me only as a hard-nosed skeptic of psychic phenomena and flying saucers. It was almost as if they assumed that anyone who doubted Uri Geller could bend spoons with his mind had to be an atheist!

The following chapter, taken from my Whys, is a defense of fideism, the view that belief in God rests on an emotional turning of the will, and cannot be supported by logic or science.

> You remind me of the farmer who said to his bishop, after a sermon proving the existence of God, "It is a very fine sermon, but I believe there be a God after all."
>
> —WILLIAM JAMES, in a letter of 1897

If God spoke to us audibly, as Jehovah does so often in Old Testament tales, we might (unless we thought ourselves mad) believe in God's existence for much the same reasons we believe in the existence of other persons. If God demonstrated his power by stupendous miracles, such as turning someone into a pillar of salt, there would be other good empirical grounds for believing. If we could perform experiments that supported, even indirectly, the hypothesis "God exists," we would believe in God for the same reasons we believe in gravity. I do not think God reveals himself, or has ever done so, in such crude ways.

Are there purely logical arguments for God, arguments so convincing that if an intelligent atheist understood them he or she would become a theist? There are no such arguments. In Lecture 18 of his Varieties of Religious Ex-

perience, William James summed up the situation in a few sentences that could have been written last week:

> The arguments for God's existence have stood for hundreds of years with the waves of unbelieving criticism breaking against them, never totally discrediting them in the ears of the faithful, but on the whole slowly and surely washing out the mortar from between their joints. If you have a God already whom you believe in, these arguments confirm you. If you are atheistic, they fail to set you right.

A long line of distinguished thinkers, fully capable of understanding the arguments yet remaining unconvinced, is testimony to the flabbiness of those "proofs." But, you may respond, is there not also a long line of equally distinguished theists who firmly believed God's existence *could* be established by unaided reason?

Yes, and now I must explain why I qualified "logical" by saying there are no "purely" logical arguments. There indeed are partly logical arguments. If you make certain posits, posits unsupported by logic or science, the traditional proofs do make a kind of sense. From my fideist perspective, the posits required to confer validity on the proofs are not rational but emotional. They are made in response to deeply felt needs. Grant these emotive posits and the proofs become compelling, but the posits themselves are from the heart, not the head.

Logical and mathematical systems also require posits, but they are not posits based on passions. We believe in the truth of the Pythagorean theorem, for example, because we can prove it within the formal system of Euclidean geometry and because its truth can be empirically confirmed with physical models. If we could draw a triangle and find that the sum of its interior angles was 90 degrees, our trust in the theorems of Euclidean geometry would be shaken, but of course we cannot draw such a triangle any more than we can produce five pebbles by adding two pebbles to two pebbles. Given the formal system of Euclidean geometry, it follows with iron logic that the angles of every triangle must have a sum of 180 degrees, just as it follows from the formal system of arithmetic that the sum of two and two must be four. Even in the interior of a sun, Bertrand Russell once said, there are three feet in a yard.

The posits that confer plausibility on the traditional proofs of God are of an altogether different sort. Consider the familiar argument from first cause. If every event has a prior cause, we seem to be faced with either believing in a first cause (Aristotle's unmoved mover) that is self-caused or uncaused, or accepting chains of causes that go back forever in time.

Now whenever Thomas Aquinas encountered an infinite regress in one of his proofs of God he simply dismissed it as absurd. But why absurd? This is precisely the spot at which a subliminal emotion stealthily slips into the argument. An endless regress is absurd only to someone who finds it ugly or disturbing. There is nothing *logically* absurd about an infinite regress. We may feel uncomfortable with the infinite set of integers, but who wants to deny that the sequence goes to infinity in both positive and negative directions? Fractions in the sequence ½, ⅓, ¼, ⅕ . . . get smaller and smaller but the sequence never ends with a smallest fraction. The proof by first cause may be emotionally satisfying in its escape from the anxiety generated by an infinite regress, but clearly it is logically flawed.

The same applies to a closely related variant of the argument. We allow the universe to be infinite in time, but insist that the entire sequence of events cannot be uncaused or self-caused. Again, it is emotionally satisfying to many people, perhaps to most people, to hang a beginningless universe on a higher peg, but without this emotion the argument proves nothing. If God, the transcendent peg, is declared to be self-caused or uncaused, we are merely evading the mystery of being, not solving it. Would it not be simpler, as David Hume suggested, to allow the entire universe to be uncaused or self-caused, like one of Saul Steinberg's cartoons that shows a man, pen in hand, drawing himself on the page? For many people it is impossible to think of the universe doing this, but the difficulty springs from an emotion, not from reason. There is nothing irrational about the thought. Every person, Bertrand Russell somewhere says, has a mother. This doesn't entail that the human race had a mother. Every integer has a predecessor. This doesn't entail that the infinite sequence of negative integers had a predecessor.

The teleological argument, or argument from design—that patterns in nature imply a Patternmaker—has been and still is the most popular of all traditional proofs of God. Before Darwin it was constantly invoked with reference to the marvelously adapted parts of living things. We all know how those arguments have been weakened by evolution. It is no longer possible to think of the wondrous structure of a human eye, or even the patterns of such lifeless things as galaxies and solar systems, as having histories analogous to the making of a watch.

This does not, of course, deny that most people, when they contemplate the grandeur of the starry heavens or the humbler patterns of flowers and snow crystals, may experience a strong feeling that behind such marvelous order there must be something like a human intelligence. Even Immanuel Kant, who demolished the logical force of the design argument in his *Critique of Pure Reason*, granted the proof's strong emotional power:

This proof always deserves to be mentioned with respect. It is the oldest, the clearest, and the most accordant with the common reason of mankind. It enlivens the study of nature, just as it itself derives its existence and gains ever new vigour from that source. It suggests ends and purposes, where our observation would not have detected them by itself, and extends our knowledge of nature by means of the guiding-concept of a special unity, the principle of which is outside nature. This knowledge again reacts on its cause, namely, upon the idea which has led to it, and so strengthens the belief in a supreme Author [of nature] that the belief acquires the force of an irresistible conviction.

It would therefore not only be uncomforting but utterly vain to attempt to diminish in any way the authority of this argument. Reason, constantly upheld by this ever-increasing evidence, which, though empirical, is yet so powerful, cannot be so depressed through doubts suggested by subtle and abstruse speculation, that it is not at once aroused from the indecision of all melancholy reflection, as from a dream, by one glance at the wonders of nature and the majesty of the universe—ascending from height to height up to the all-highest, from the conditioned to its conditions, up to the supreme and unconditioned Author [of all conditioned being].

One could easily fill a book with colorful extracts from writers who have testified to the persuasiveness of the proof by design. Here, for instance, are the thoughts of Charlotte Brontë's Jane Eyre, alone on the moor:

Night was come, and her planets were risen: a safe, still night; too serene for the companionship of fear. We know that God is everywhere; but certainly we feel His presence most when His works are on the grandest scale spread before us: and it is in the unclouded night-sky, where His worlds wheel their silent course, that we read clearest His infinitude, His omnipotence, His omnipresence. I had risen to my knees to pray for Mr. Rochester. Looking up, I, with tear-dimmed eyes, saw the mighty Milky-way. Remembering what it was—what countless systems there swept space like a soft trace of light—I felt the might and strength of God. Sure was I of His efficiency to save what He had made: convinced I grew that neither earth should perish, nor one of the souls it treasured. I turned my prayer to thanksgiving: the Source of Life was also the Savior of spirits. Mr. Rochester was safe: he was God's and by God would he be guarded. I again nestled to the breast of the hill; and ere long, in sleep, forgot sorrow.

Listen to Sir Isaac Newton, speaking iambic pentameters in Alfred Noyes's *Watchers of the Sky*:

> Was the eye contrived by blindly moving atoms,
> Or the still-listening ear fulfilled with music
> By forces without knowledge of sweet sounds?
> Are nerves and brain so sensitively fashioned
> That they convey these pictures of the world
> Into the very substance of our life,

While That from which we came, the Power that made us,
Is drowned in blank unconsciousness of all?

Whittaker Chamber's *Witness* provides a final example, one that might have come straight from the pen of the eighteenth-century English theologian William Paley:

> But I date my break [with the Communist Party] from a very casual happening. I was sitting in our apartment on St. Paul Street in Baltimore. It was shortly before we moved to Alger Hiss's apartment in Washington. My daughter was in her high chair. I was watching her eat. She was the most miraculous thing that had ever happened in my life. I liked to watch her even when she smeared porridge on her face or dropped it meditatively on the floor. My eye came to rest on the delicate convolutions of her ear—those intricate, perfect ears. The thought passed through my mind: "No, those ears were not created by any chance coming together of atoms in nature (the Communist view). They could have been created only by immense design." The thought was involuntary and unwanted. I crowded it out of my mind. But I never wholly forgot it or the occasion. I had to crowd it out of my mind. If I had completed it, I should have had to say: Design presupposes God. I did not then know that, at that moment, the finger of God was first laid upon my forehead.

I find nothing in this passage to ridicule. Why should not the ear of a loved child be as good an example of God's design as anything in the universe? The inner ear is no less complex than the eye. Both are far more intricate than the watch Paley used in his famous proof. The argument's emotive force is not in the least diminished by the truth of evolution. In fact it is augmented. Cosmic evolution implies that the elementary particles that came into existence during the first few minutes of the big bang had mathematical properties that would permit them, billions of years later, to form microscopic eggs which would grow to become you and me. I cannot imagine anyone reading *Witness* without being impressed by the authenticity of Chambers's religious experience.

Since the development of organic chemistry, a new version of the argument from the design of living things has been advanced by a number of scientists and thinkers who have no quarrel with biological evolution. The argument focuses instead on the probability that life could arise spontaneously in earth's primeval seas. Presumably life began several billion years ago when carbon-based molecules, shuffling for millions of years in an organic soup, happened to form a self-replicating microorganism. The probability of this occurring by blind chance, so goes the reasoning, is so incredibly low that intervention by a deity is needed to explain how life started.

Pierre Lecomte du Noüy gave this argument in two of his widely read books of the forties. More recently, Sir Fred Hoyle and his associate N. Chandra Wickramasinghe have refined the argument in their book *Evolution from Space*. They estimate the odds against blind chance producing a single self-replicating microorganism to be 10 to the power of 40,000 (1 followed by 40,000 zeros) to 1. Unable to make the leap to a God outside the universe, Hoyle and his friend (who was raised a Buddhist) settle for what they call an "intelligence" within the universe that is constantly fabricating microorganisms in interstellar gas. These tiny life-forms are pushed around the cosmos by the pressure of starlight. Comets carry them to the planets, where they flourish and evolve if conditions are suitable.

Long before the discovery of molecules and atoms, and before the development of evolutionary cosmology, Francis Bacon expressed the same emotion. In the following passage from his essay "On Atheism," Bacon contrasts Democritus's particle theory of matter with the four-elements theory of Aristotle and the Schoolmen:

> For it is a thousand times more credible that four mutable elements and one immutable fifth essence, duly and eternally placed, need no God, than that an army of infinite small portions or seeds, unplaced, should have produced this order and beauty without a divine marshal.

David Hume considered the design argument at such length that it is not easy to say anything about it that Hume did not say. Even evolution enters the argument in Hume's *Dialogues Concerning Natural Religion* when Philo insists that the universe is more like a growing tree than a watch or a knitting-loom. Because a tree knows nothing about the ordering of its parts, why should we assume a universal mind behind what today we call the "tree" of evolution?

Few scientists take Hoyle's new science-fiction theology seriously. Its weakest point is that there are no compelling reasons for assuming that when organic molecules shuffle together, either in organic soups or in outer space, they combine by blind chance alone. Rather they combine by what Isaac Asimov once called "unblind chance"—chance constrained by natural laws about which we as yet know nothing. Because of our vast ignorance, there are no ways to make reasonable probability estimates.

A more subtle recent variant of the design argument centers on the nature of the big bang. Physicists see no reason why this explosion could not have produced a universe in which certain basic constants, such as Planck's constant or the fine-structure constant or the rate of the universe's expansion, would have been other than what they are. But let some of these constants deviate ever so slightly from what they are and we get a possible universe in which not even stars could congeal, let alone planets and microorganisms. Therefore . . .

I find this argument for God as logically fragile as the old design arguments before Darwin. For all we know, as physicist John Wheeler has taught us, billions of big bangs may be constantly taking place in hyperspace and throughout eternity, explosions that manufacture universes in which all possible combinations of constants occur. As the old song goes, "We're here because we're here because we're here because we're here." The argument that God had to fine-tune the fireball to create a cosmos capable of producing intelligent life is compelling only to those who shrink from contemplating an infinity of lifeless universes, who find it more comforting to suppose that a superior intelligence guided our big bang to form just the universe it did.

Note that Wheeler's vision provides the atheist with a way of escaping Hoyle's probability estimate even if we grant that organic molecules combine by blind chance. The odds against life in any one universe may be low, but there is no limit to the number of universes that can live and die if time and space are endless. No matter how low the odds, eventually there will be a universe in which the rare event occurs, and so here we are!

My remarks are not intended to disparage what cosmologists call the "anthropic principle." According to this principle we can "explain" certain properties of the earth, solar system, galaxy, universe, even the original fireball, by asking what sort of conditions are necessary to account for the existence now of cosmologists. Only the name of the principle is new. To chess problemists it is no more than the application to cosmology of "retrograde analysis." Given a position on the chessboard with, say, one piece removed, you can sometimes deduce the nature of the missing piece by reasoning backward through the game.

The principle appeals to physicists with solipsistic urges because it seems to say, though of course it does not, that somehow our consciousness makes the universe what it is. "We have found a strange footprint on the shores of the unknown," wrote Sir Arthur Stanley Eddington in the often-quoted last paragraph of his *Space, Time and Gravitation*. (By "strange footprint" he meant the strange way our universe is put together.) "We have devised profound theories . . . to account for its origin. At last, we have succeeded in reconstructing the creature that made the footprint. And Lo! it is our own."

This may seem profound, but when expressed with less poetry and ambiguity it becomes trivial. "Imagine an ensemble of universes of all sorts," say Robert Dicke and P. J. E. Peebles in their contribution to *General Relativity: An Einstein Centenary Survey*. "It should be no surprise that ours is not an 'average' one, for conditions on the average may well be hostile. We could only be present in a universe that happens to supply our needs."

Dicke and Peebles describe a game of Russian roulette played by thousands of persons. From a large supply of guns each player randomly selects a gun that may or may not be loaded. At the end of the game a statistician

makes a retrograde analysis and concludes "that there is a high probability of
the randomly selected unloaded guns being drawn by the survivors of the
game."

The Russian roulette analogy surely demolishes any effort to invoke the
anthropic principle as an argument for God. Of course you may assume, if
you like, that a Creator carefully selected our particular unloaded-gun universe
in preference to loaded ones, but an assumption is not a proof. Roger Penrose,
in the book cited above, imagines God looking over a large map on which
each point represents the plan for a possible world, then sticking a pin in the
map to cause a universe to explode into reality. Maybe only one such universe
is chosen. Maybe God creates millions of universes by stabbing the map in
many spots, perhaps even stabbing at random, or stabbing simultaneously with
a billion hands. It is a celestial game in which the Creator entertains himself
(and others?) by experimenting with myriads of possible worlds to see how
each works out.

Whatever the scenario, the argument from the fine-tuning of the fireball
to the existence of a Great Tuner seems to me no different in essence from
the early arguments based on design in nature, and which today sound like
Irish bulls. If water did not expand when it freezes, ice would form from the
bottom up in lakes, thus killing all fish. If the earth's axis did not tilt at just
the angle it does, our seasons would be either too mild or too severe for life
(see Dante's *Paradiso*, Canto 10). If the earth's orbit were closer to or farther
from the sun, its surface would be too hot or too cold to support life. Meteors
would destroy our cities if they were not burned out by the earth's atmosphere.
James, in Lecture 20 of *Varieties*, cites dozens of other amusing examples
from theological rhetoric. Even the youthful Kant was not immune to such
reasoning. In his monograph *On the Only Demonstrative Proof of the Existence
of God* (which he later repudiated), Kant extolls the earth's atmosphere for
(among other things) producing twilight, a slow transition to darkness that is
easy on the eyes. Presumably if daylight went out like a snuffed candle we
would have less reason to believe in God.

Such arguments have been interminably caricatured by skeptics. Dr. Pan-
gloss, in Voltaire's *Candide*, observes how carefully the nose is made to support
spectacles. Freud, in his witty book on wit, quotes Jules Michelet: "How beautifully everything is arranged in nature. As soon as the child comes into the
world, it finds a mother who is ready to care for it." How providential that
polar wastes are in regions where nobody lives! How pleasant that Washington
and Lincoln were born on holidays!

The old argument from common consent—that because so many people
have believed in God the belief must be true—obviously is not logically convincing, though it does have a crude kind of merit. The fact that so many
persons, especially persons of towering intellect, have believed in God should
at least give an atheist pause, just as a tone-deaf person might suspect there

is something of value in music because so many admirable people profess to enjoy it. But this, too, is clearly an emotive argument. It does no more than demonstrate what all atheists know, that for large numbers of people a belief in God or gods satisfies deep longings.

It is easy to turn the design proof upside down and argue that the chaos and evil in the world suggest the nonexistence of God—an old argument that C. S. Lewis once called the "argument from undesign." It is particularly forceful when applied to natural evils which beset human life, such as earthquakes and plagues, but it applies to lower forms of life as well. Long before Darwin it was apparent that an anatomical design of great benefit to one species could hardly be called beneficial to the species it preyed upon.

"To the grub under the bark," wrote James in *Pragmatism*, "the exquisite fitness of the woodpecker's organism to extract him would certainly argue a diabolical designer." In 1964 a pair of ants in Johnny Hart's comic strip *B.C.* made the same point. "It's wonderful to be alive, to exist! What magnificent purpose has put me here? Is it to elevate the species? Is it to discover the secret of creation? Am I here to inspire my kind? Am I king? Prince? Prophet?" Says the other ant: "Try anteater food!"

On this score, for now, I will add only the old thought that even if one finds the argument from design valid, it offers no assurance that the Designer had anything more in mind than to design a plaything. Every now and then some whimsical mechanic constructs a large, intricate piece of machinery with thousands of gears, levers, pulleys, chains, shafts, lights, and so on, designed only to run, not to *do* anything. Perhaps the entire universe is just such a joke, a vast cosmic jest fabricated by a god who had no motive except to amuse himself and his friends. It could even be a diabolical joke perpetrated by a demon god. Part of the joke is to place intelligent beings in a universe designed to arouse in them false hopes that they are in the hands of a benevolent God who will reward them with a future life.

The proof of God that I find the least defensible is Saint Anselm's famous ontological argument. C. S. Lewis, in his poem "Abecedarium Philosophicum," summed up Descartes's version this way:

> D for Descartes who said "God couldn't be
> So complete if he weren't. So he is. Q.E.D."

The proof does indeed establish that if we form a concept of God as the most supreme being we can imagine, we cannot avoid adding existence to the concept. Clearly an existing God is superior to one who doesn't exist. But I agree with those critics who fail to see how we are logically compelled to make the ontological leap from a concept of an existing God to the assurance that the concept represents something outside our mind. I am aware that the argument continues to have distinguished advocates who defend it tirelessly and, to my mind, tiresomely: Norman Malcolm, Richard Campbell, my former teacher Charles Hartshorne, and several others. I can only say that I have never found the argument expressed in such a way that I could not find at some juncture a gap crossable only by an emotive jump.

Kant saw the fallacy of the proof quite clearly, but because he expressed it in a terminology easily misunderstood, he has often been unfairly belabored. When Kant said existence is not a predicate, and that a hundred real thalers contain not a thaler more than a hundred possible thalers, he meant only that the *concept* of a hundred thalers is not altered by one's belief, or by the discovery through experience, that thalers actually exist.

Suppose I express my idea of a blue apple by painting a picture of five blue apples. I point to it and say, "This represents five blue apples." If I later learn that blue apples actually exist I can point to the same picture and say, "This represents five real blue apples." Even if I fail to discover that blue apples exist I can point to the picture and say, "This represents five imaginary blue apples." In all three cases the picture remains the same. The concept of five real apples contains not an apple more than the concept of five possible apples. The idea of a unicorn does not acquire additional horns if real unicorns exist. In Kant's terminology you do not add a new property to a concept by expressing your belief that the concept corresponds to an actual object outside your brain.

Of course it is all a matter of words. In other epistemological languages it is quite acceptable to say that existence is a predicate. But to suppose that Kant did not realize it is better to have real money in your pocket than imaginary money is to suppose Kant to have been a moron, which he wasn't. "My financial position," Kant wrote, "is, however, affected very differently by a hundred real thalers than it is by the mere concept of them." When you think you have found a statement by a great philosopher that is obviously absurd, it is a good bet you have not understood the statement. A surprising recent example of such a failure to do homework occurs in Mortimer Adler's *How to Think About God*. Adler chastises Kant severely for falling into a childish blunder:

> Is not a hundred dollars in my pocket better than an imaginary hundred dollars by virtue of its enabling me to buy things with it? Is not a really existent umbrella or raincoat better than an imaginary one so far as protection from the rain is concerned?

As a lifelong champion of the Great Books—his friend Robert Hutchins liked to call him the Great Bookie—Adler above all should not have supposed that Kant was unaware of the value of real money and real umbrellas.

I shall waste no time on trivial variants of the ontological argument that reduce it to such tautologies as that Being must exist, or that if there is a necessarily existing perfect Being, that Being must necessarily exist. Nor do I wish to deny that in thinking through various forms of the ontological argument, a believer in God is led to *feel* that the highest possible Being must exist, but of course the proof claims to be more than that. It claims that the sentence "There is no God" is as self-contradictory as "A triangle has four sides." Not even Aquinas could accept this, and although the argument still mesmerizes a few metaphysicians, I agree with the vast majority of thinkers who see the proof as no more than linguistic sleight-of-hand. There is no existing thing, said Hume, including the entire cosmos, whose nonexistence entails logical contradiction. The thought that everything would be much simpler if nothing existed at all may stab us with anxiety, but there is nothing logically inconsistent in the thought.

Karl Barth wrote a cantankerous and (to me) funny book about Anselm's proof. The book has the following thesis: The ontological argument proves nothing, but it serves to deepen a believer's understanding of God. Some medieval Schoolmen, Bonaventure in particular, said much the same thing, and although I cannot fault this thesis, it certainly is not what Anselm or most later defenders of his proof intended the proof to say. We can rephrase Barth's thesis as follows. For believers in God it is emotionally intolerable that their concept of a perfect God, so sublime and so satisfying, does not include belief in the actual existence of God. Hermann Lotze in his *Microcosmos* (Book 9, chapter 4) put it crisply: "We *feel* the impossibility of God's nonexistence." (Italics mine.)

When Barth's book on Anselm appeared in an English translation in 1962 it was reviewed by John Updike, a great admirer of Barth and a former Barthian. I agree with Updike that Barth wrote more about his own theology than about Anselm's. As you inch your way through Barth's curious monograph, Updike writes, you anticipate "the gigantic leap that lies ahead, from existence as a concept to existence as a fact—from *esse in intellectu* to *esse in re*. Then a strange thing happens. Anselm takes the leap, and Barth does not, yet he goes on talking as if he had never left Anselm's side."

Indeed, Barth ends by accepting the traditional criticisms of the proof, but admiring it nonetheless because it shows, as Updike puts it, "we cannot pray to or believe in a God whom we recognize as a figment of our own imaginations." In Barth's words: "God is the One who manifests himself in the command not to imagine a greater than he." Is this all that Anselm meant? Updike does not think so, nor do I, nor did Étienne Gilson, who criticized Barth's book along similar lines.

I repress the urge to devote more pages to the classic proofs of God, and to their refutations by Hume, Kant, Mill, and many others. Let me capsule my own view: In every proof I find an explicit or implicit emotional leap that springs from a desire or a fear or both, a leap that occurs at some point between the proof's links. As fully rational arguments, instances of what Kant

called pure reason, the proofs are invalid. As partly rational, given certain
emotional posits, they express deeply felt convictions in persuasive, reasonable
ways, and for this reason they continue to flourish. Actually, this view is not
far from that of many Schoolmen who maintained that without special illu-
mination from God, a special grace, it is not possible to find the proofs convincing. Given prior faith, the proofs dramatize the intensity of our hunger
for God. They deepen and strengthen our belief in God.

A curious position held by a few Christian thinkers is that although no
logically flawless demonstration of God's existence has yet been formulated,
one may believe by faith that such a formulation is possible. The scriptural
authority for this, quoted endlessly by medieval theologians, is Saint Paul's
statement: "For the invisible things of him from the creation of the world are
clearly seen, being understood by the things that are made, even his eternal
power and Godhead. . . ." (Romans 1:20) "It may be that there are true demonstrations," wrote Blaise Pascal in his *Pensées*, "but it is not certain. Thus
this proves nothing but that it is not certain that all is uncertain, to the glory
of skepticism." Kant, near the end of his *Critique of Pure Reason*, attributes
the hope for a perfect proof to "certain excellent and thoughtful men," including his Swiss contemporary, the philosopher Johann Georg Sulzer, who
wrote mainly about aesthetics. Kant adds, "I am certain that this will never
happen."

In spite of Pascal's doubts and Kant's certainty, the hope for a valid proof
of God, not yet devised, continues to haunt Mortimer Adler. Back in the
thirties, when Adler was teaching at the University of Chicago, he believed so
firmly in all five of Aquinas's proofs of God that he made strenuous efforts
to persuade his students to accept them. Then he began to have doubts. They
were first expressed in technical detail in an article on "The Demonstration
of God's Existence" in a *Festschrift* issue of *The Thomist* (January 1943) honoring his friend Jacques Maritain. In this paper Adler argued that all five proofs
are seriously flawed. He tried to outline a valid proof that had the form: If
things exist, God exists; things exist, therefore God exists. Kant put it this
way in his *Critique of Pure Reason*: "If anything exists, an absolutely necessary
being must also exist. Now I, at least, exist. Therefore an absolutely necessary
being exists."

Unfortunately, as Adler says in his autobiography *Philosopher at Large*
(1977): "The demonstration, I admitted, left a number of difficulties still to
be resolved. This amounted to saying that although God's existence might be
demonstrated in the future, it had not yet been accomplished. . . ."

Adler's criticism of Aquinas provoked vigorous adverse reactions among
Thomists. "My greatest disappointment," Adler tells us, "occurred when I
learned that I had even failed to make any headway in changing Maritain's
mind on the subject." Indeed, in his book *Approaches to God*, Maritain warns
against Adler's viewpoint.

Adler is still searching for the elusive proof. In *How to Think About God* he repeats the usual objections to the traditional arguments, finding all the arguments invalid. Then in chapter 14 he defends what he calls a "truly cosmological argument" that goes as follows. If the cosmos as a whole needs to be explained, and if it can't be explained by natural causes, then God must have caused it. The second *if* is the troublesome one. In his next chapter Adler argues that the second premise is the same as saying it is impossible for the cosmos to cease to exist and be replaced by nothingness. According to Adler, our cosmos is one of many possible worlds; hence it is possible for it not to exist. Because it does exist, we must assume either that God created it out of nothing (in which case God exists) or that the world has always existed. In the latter case Adler gives his reasons for believing that the continued existence of the cosmos requires God as a "preservative cause." He admits his argument does not furnish certitude that God exists, but he thinks it establishes God's existence either "beyond a reasonable doubt," or at least it shows that there is a "preponderance of reasons" for believing God exists.

The God that Adler thinks he has established as probable is, Adler recognizes, only an impersonal abstraction, not a God to whom one can pray. The argument tells us nothing about whether God cares about us, or will provide us with life after death. These are among those beliefs that demand, Adler says, the leap of faith.

I find it depressing that Adler's long "dogmatic slumber," as Kant described his own earlier thinking about the proofs before Hume awakened him, and his admiration for Étienne Gilson (to whose memory *How to Think About God* is dedicated), still hold Adler back from the simple step to fideism that would dissolve his difficulties. Even among Roman Catholic thinkers, increasing numbers no longer feel obliged to establish God's existence even by probable reasoning, or to hope that some day a flawless proof will come to light.

For Kierkegaard, whose fideism so strongly influenced Barth and Unamuno and Heidegger, the desire to find rational evidence for God betrays a weakness of faith. In his *Concluding Unscientific Postscript*, Kierkegaard draws a parallel with a young woman who is so unsure of her love for a man that she keeps trying to find remarkable traits in him that will revive her fading emotion. Is it not an insult to God, Kierkegaard asks, to try to prove him? Is it not like standing in the presence of a mighty king and demanding irrefutable evidence that he exists?

Atheists will, of course, find all this absurd. But those who make the leap of faith are not only certain of God's existence, they see all Nature as a manifestation of God even though God remains invisible. They "prove" God inwardly, writes Kierkegaard, through worship and prayer and submission to God's will. To all those who demand logical proofs or physical wonders, God "craftily" hides himself. "A poor wretch of an author, whom a later investigator drags out of the obscurity of oblivion may indeed be very glad that the investigator succeeds in proving his existence—but an omnipresent being can only by a thinker's pious blundering be brought to this ridiculous embarrassment." The most interesting references in the bibliography at the back of Adler's book are the books not there. Apparently he has been totally uninfluenced by any of the great Jewish, Christian, or philosophical fideists.

The hope for a valid proof of God strikes me as strangely similar to Bertrand Russell's youthful hope that someday he, or someone else, would discover a logical justification for induction. In his last great book, *Human Knowledge, Its Scope and Limits*, Russell abandoned this hope for the view that induction can be justified only by making certain posits about the structure of the external world. Put simply, induction works because the world is what it is. John Stuart Mill said essentially the same thing. Induction works because nature is orderly. Naturally we learn about the world's order only by induction, but Russell finally concluded that this is not a vicious circle, and he tried to go beyond Mill by specifying a minimum set of posits about nature's structure that would permit induction to work as well as it obviously does.

To my way of thinking, the hope for a logical justification of God's existence is as futile as the hope for a logical justification of induction. With respect to both questions, I believe only pragmatic answers can be given. Is it not the height of human pride and folly to suppose that our finite little brains can construct a proof that the world must be built just the way it is, or a proof that there must be a God who built it?

One way of justifying induction pragmatically was put forth by Hans Reichenbach. If there is any way at all to learn something about the structure of the world, that way is by induction; hence induction is justified. One could similarly argue that if there is a God who has chosen to be indemonstrable by either reason or science, then if we are to know God at all, it can only be through faith.

Please do not suppose from these remarks that I wish to defend an argument, often employed by theists, that a scientist's belief in an ordered world is comparable to a believer's faith in God. The popular American Baptist preacher Harry Emerson Fosdick put it this way in his book *Adventurous Religion* (1926):

> I am sure that the faith by which one thus orders and unifies his spiritual world, although it is more difficult of demonstration, is essentially the same kind of faith as that by which the scientist in his realm is conquering chaos.

The same point has been elaborated by innumerable philosophers. Josiah Royce, for instance, wrote in chapter 9 of *The Religious Aspect of Philosophy* (1885):

To make the parallel a little clearer, we may say that science postulates the truth of the description of the world that, among all the possible descriptions, at once includes the given phenomena and attains the greatest simplicity; while religion assumes the truth of the description of the world that, without falsifying the given facts, arouses the highest moral interest and satisfies the highest moral needs.

All this has often been said, but it has not always been clearly enough joined with the practical suggestion that if one gives up one of these two faiths, he ought consistently to give up the other. If one is weary of the religious postulates, let him by all means throw them aside. But if he does this, why does he not throw aside the scientific postulates, and give up insisting upon it that the world is and must be rational?

In his article on faith in the *Encyclopedia Britannica* (fourteenth edition), the Cambridge philosopher Frederick Robert Tennant draws the same parallel between the faith of a theist and the faith of a scientist. Induction, he writes, rests on "human hope, sanguine expectation, faith in the unseen. . . . Our very rationality of the world, which science would read and expound, is at bottom an idea of faith." Tennant puts it even more preposterously in his masterwork, *Philosophical Theology* (1928): "The electron and God are equally ideal positings of faith-venture, rationally indemonstrable, invisible; and the 'verifications' of the one idea, and of the other, follow lines essentially identical. . . ." Even William James, in his essay on "The Sentiment of Rationality," favors the same inept analogy.

Is not the flaw obvious? There may well be no purely rational demonstration that induction must always work, but the patterns we find in nature are so strongly confirmed that we cannot disregard them without risking our lives. The quickest way to get from a high floor to the street is to jump out a window, but our "faith" in the laws of gravity and the fragility of our bodies make this an irrational act for anyone who cares to stay alive. On the other hand, an atheist gets along quite well, thank you, without believing in God. It only obscures the nature of faith to liken it to the inescapable necessity of believing in causal laws.

We know what it means to say induction works. What does it mean to say that belief in God works? To fideists it can mean only this—that belief in God is so emotionally rewarding, and the contrary belief so desolate, they cannot not believe. Beneath the *credo quia absurdum*, as Unamuno said, is the *credo quia consolans*. I believe because it consoles me. The true water of life, says our Spanish brother, is that which assuages our thirst.

POSTSCRIPT

To me the most fascinating pages in Adler's autobiography *Philosopher at Large* are pages 314 to 317 whereon he struggles to explain why, as a fellow-traveler of Catholicism, he never became a Catholic. In *How to Think About God* he writes: "There have been moments in my life, during my late thirties and early forties and later in my early sixties, when I contemplated becoming a Christian—in the first instance a Roman Catholic, in the second an Episcopalian. Suffice it to say, I have not done so." His autobiography gives the reason:

> I think I now know the answer to that crucial question, though I did not grasp it at the time. It lies in the state of one's will, not in the state of one's mind. The individual who is born a Jew or a Christian, a Catholic or a Protestant, can know himself to be such, however loosely or feebly, without having to live as a truly religious Jew or Christian should live. But the case of the convert to Judaism or Christianity is quite different. The only reason to *adopt* a religion is that one wishes and intends to live henceforth in accordance with its precepts, forswearing conduct and habits that are incompatible. For me to become a Roman Catholic—or, for that matter, an Anglo-Catholic or Episcopalian—would require a radical change in my way of life, a basic alteration in the direction of my day-to-day choices as well as in the ultimate objectives to be sought or hoped for. I have too clear and too detailed an understanding of moral theology to fool myself on that score. The simple truth of the matter is that I did not wish to live up to being a genuinely religious person. I could not bring myself to will what I ought to will for my whole future if I were to resolve my will, at a particular moment, with regard to religious conversion.

Note that Adler not only avoids saying whether he *believes* Christianity to be true—that is, believes with his mind that Jesus was God incarnate—he even evades saying why he evades it. When asked by a reporter, Michiko Kakutani, why he never made the Christian leap of faith, he replied (*The New York Times*, August 15, 1981):

> It's still an open question. I've gotten a great deal of intellectual satisfaction by studying and thinking about theological matters, and I think I understand intellectually what a person of Christian faith affirms. But whatever the reluctance is, I cannot make the affirmation. It may indeed be that if I were less intellectually interested in theology, I might be emotionally more interested in religion. It may be that I'm too intellec-

Proofs of God 549

tual—I don't really know the answer. If I were to confess to any serious fault, it would be the imbalance between my emphasis on the intellectual and my underemphasis on feelings. But you have to take me as I am.

Adler's inability to make the leap with his heart is certainly understandable, but does he believe with his head? Does he half-believe Jesus was the unique Son of God, or does his subjective probability estimate incline more one way than the other? It is a curious blank in Adler's intellectual career. There is something both comic and tragic about a man who has an Aristotelian love of sharp distinctions, who is uncomfortable sitting on things that are neither chairs nor not-chairs, but whose entire life has been a halfway thing. With one foot in Christianity and the other out, he walks around the fringes of the philosophic scene like a man with one foot on the curb and one in the street. Perhaps in this sense he is symbolic of today's Western world.

Hans Küng, Germany's controversial Catholic theologian, is executing a walk that impresses me as equally comic. Although I agree with Küng's approach to the traditional proofs of God as given in his 1978 book *Does God Exist?* (Küng is a fideist in the Kantian tradition, though he seems not to have read Unamuno), I find his unwillingness to walk out of the Roman Church as perplexing as Adler's unwillingness to walk in. And I feel the same way about Karl Rahner, whose "Catholicism" seems to me as bogus as Paul Tillich's "Protestantism."

Back in 1940, Adler gave a speech on "God and the Professors" in which he warned that the "positivistic" philosophy of our teachers was a greater threat to democracy than Hitler. It kicked up an academic ruckus similar to the one kicked up later by William Buckley's *God and Man at Yale.* I sent a tongue-in-cheek letter about it to *The New Republic* which appeared in their December 13, 1940 issue under the heading "The Road to Rome." Now more than forty years later the letter is still timely:

The text of Mortimer Adler's recent paper, "God and the Professors" (to which Sidney Hook replied in the October 28 issue of your magazine), has just been printed in full in the student newspaper of the University of Chicago, and I have just finished reading it.

As a former graduate student in the positivistic-minded philosophy department of the University, and a present resident of the campus community, I would like to make a plea to the readers of *The New Republic*. *Pray for the conversion of Mr. Adler.*

Mr. Adler has stated many times that he intellectually accepts the doctrines of the Roman creed, but that he lacks the divine faith necessary for conversion and entrance into the Church. There is strong traditional precedent for such an attitude. Gilbert Chesterton, for example, wrote his *Orthodoxy*, one of the greatest of modern Catholic apologies, almost fifteen years before he joined the Church.

So let us unite in prayer for Mr. Adler. And on the date that he enters Rome, let academic circles proclaim a day of rejoicing and thanksgiving. For Mr. Adler's brilliant and exasperating rhetoric will at last have found a home; and out of the dialectic fog will emerge a shape definite enough to be recognized, and solid enough to be worthy of honorable combat.

In his book *The Angels and Us* (1982) Adler manages to write an entire monograph on Roman Catholic angelology without revealing whether he believes angels exist or not. Of all Adler's books so far this is the most grotesque. It is almost as funny as Billy Graham's phenomenal best-seller of 1975, *Angels: God's Secret Agents*, though not nearly as funny as Aquinas's several hundred articles on the topic. Of course Adler must be highly selective of the thousands of subtle questions about angels that were debated by top intellects of the Middle Ages. Nowhere, for example, does he consider that fascinating quodlibet: Can angels, when they assume human form, defecate and break wind?

Many distinguished Catholic theologians such as William of Occam (Martin Luther's favorite Scholastic) have been vigorous fideists, but the papacy has usually dealt with them harshly, regardless of how devout their nonrational beliefs in orthodox doctrines were. Occam was imprisoned and excommunicated. His French pupil, Nicolas of Autrecourt, was condemned by Pope Clement VI in 1347, forced to recant, and his books were publicly burned.

The papacy was less harsh on Montaigne's adopted son and disciple, Father Pierre Charron (1541–1603) and Leibniz's Jesuit bishop friend, Pierre Daniel Huet (1630–1721). However, the last of the great French Catholic fideists, Louis Eugene Marie Bautain (1796–1867) was condemned by Pope Gregory XVI and compelled to sign six theses, of which the first stated that reason can prove God's existence with certainty. Similarly condemned by Gregory were the nineteenth-century French traditionalists and fanatical ultramontanists who replaced human reason with a common tradition that began with God's revelation to Adam and Eve, and culminated in the absolute supremacy of the papacy.

It is a measure of the Vatican's increasing tolerance of heresy that a fideist today, like Hans Küng, is in little danger of imprisonment or excommunication. Of course if Adler became an Occamist it would mean turning his back on Thomism, which seems unlikely.

In his second autobiography *A Second Look in the Rear View Mirror* (1992), Adler has a moving account of his final conversion to Christianity. He has joined the Episcopalian Church.

FORTY-SEVEN

SURPRISE

More than any other writer known to me, Gilbert Keith Chesterton emphasized in his fiction, nonfiction, and poetry what he rightly called the chief idea of his life, namely that it is the beginning of wisdom to view the universe, and our miraculous existence, with an ever-present emotion of amazement and gratitude. This is one of many reasons why I can read GK with so much delight.

I am also fond of Chesterton's fiction. I have written an Annotated Innocence of Father Brown, and introductions to a series of Dover reprints of GK's other mystery tales and novels. I think The Man Who Was Thursday is a philosophical masterpiece. I consider Chesterton to be one of the most neglected and unappreciated of modern British poets. I even like his writing style with its paradoxical sentences and frequent alliteration. And who cannot relish his great sense of humor?

It does not bother me in the least to overlook and condemn Chesterton's unconscious anti-Semitism, so little different from what you find in Shakespeare, Dickens, T. S. Eliot, and the novels of Dorothy Sayers and Agatha Christie. I can overlook also his ignorance of science, his conservative Catholic opinions, and his unfortunate momentary admiration for Mussolini.

The essay that follows is a chapter from my Whys of a Philosophical Scrivener.

We glibly talk
of nature's laws
but do things have
a natural cause?

Black earth turned into
yellow crocus
is undiluted
hocus-pocus.

—PIET HEIN

Will science someday discover everything? The question is hopelessly blurry, so let's try to sharpen it. If living organisms are no more than complex arrangements of molecules, it is conceivable that biology and psychology will eventually be reduced to physics. And if waves and particles dissolve into mathematical equations, it is conceivable that physics may eventually become a single deductive system. If this ever occurs, will all the laws of physics, and hence all the laws of the universe, become discoverable in principle?

This notion of physics as a formal system is carried to an ultimate extreme in David Hume's *Dialogues Concerning Natural Religion*. In part IX, Cleanthes is attacking the ontological argument. If God is necessarily existent, he says, may not the universe itself be necessarily existent? "We dare not affirm that we know all the qualities of matter; and for aught we can determine, it may contain some qualities, which, were they known, would make its non-existence appear as great a contradiction as that twice two is five."

In other words, total nothingness is impossible. I have no idea what this could mean. Indeed, if we could know something about matter that would render its nonexistence absurd, that knowledge would solve the superultimate question. I can, however, imagine that, given a small set of axioms (about space, time, matter, logic, and mathematics), all the laws of the universe will follow in the way a theorem follows from the axioms of Euclidean geometry.

Physics seems to me a long long way from this goal, though occasionally an eminent physicist will voice contrary sentiments. In an 1894 speech Albert A. Michelson made the following notorious statement: "The more important fundamental laws and facts of physical science have all been discovered, and these are now so firmly established that the possibility of their ever being supplanted in consequence of new discoveries is exceedingly remote.... Future discoveries must be looked for in the sixth place of decimals."

Other famous physicists have made similar remarks. I find in my files a 1931 assertion by Arthur H. Compton that there are only three basic things in the physical universe: protons, electrons, and photons. That was a year before the neutron was discovered. In 1959, in his *Principles of Modern Physics*, Robert B. Leighton wrote: "With the rapid advances that are being made in particle physics, perhaps it is not too much to expect that in a few more decades *all* physical phenomena will be equally well understood." George Gamow once compared the growth of scientific knowledge with a circle that was rapidly expanding on the surface of a sphere. Beyond a certain point the circle begins to shrink. As late as 1971, Werner Heisenberg was talking about the near approach of the day when there would be no more "surprises" in particle physics.

In 1965, Richard P. Feynman, in *The Character of Physical Laws*, expressed the opinion that ours is an age in which the fundamental laws of nature are being discovered, and that this day, like the discovery of America, "will never come again." Of course there will be other tasks, such as exploring the solar system and investigating the way fundamental laws operate on levels such as biology, but the "perpetual novelty" of finding new structural levels cannot go on "say for a thousand years." To this view he gave the following twist:

> It seems to me that what can happen in the future is either that all the laws become known—that is, if you had enough laws you could compute consequences and they would always agree with experiment, which would be the end of the line—or it may happen that the experiments get harder and harder to make, more and more expensive, so you get 99.9 percent of the phenomena, but there is always some phenomenon which has just been discovered, which is very hard to measure, and which disagrees; and as soon as you have the explanation of that one there is always another one, and it gets slower and slower and more and more uninteresting. That is another way it may end. But I think it has to end in one way or another.

Most physicists, I suspect, hold contrary views. For them nature is infinitely inexhaustible, and there will always be wheels within wheels, and wheels outside wheels. Murray Gell-Mann once compared physics to the task of perpetually cleaning out a cluttered basement. No sooner is the basement's outline seen than somebody finds a cleverly hidden trapdoor leading to a vast subbasement. David Bohm and Stanislaw Ulam were among those who believe that the universe has infinitely many levels of structure in both directions, toward the large and toward the small.

"In the village of World's End," writes Lord Dunsany (in his *Book of Wonder*, 1912),

> at the furthest end of Last Street, there is a hole that you take to be a well, close by the garden wall, but if you lower yourself by your hands over the edge of the hole, and feel about with your feet till they find a ledge, that is the top step of a flight of stairs that takes you down over the edge of the World. "For all that men know, those stairs may have a purpose and even a bottom step," said the arch-idolater, "but discussion about the lower flights is idle." Then the teeth of Pompo chattered, for he feared the darkness, but he that made idols of his own explained that those stairs were always lit by the faint blue gloaming in which the World spins.

"Perhaps the pattern will be summed up," said Philip Morrison in 1970; "perhaps it will become lost in an endless regress of intricacy. I do not know.

But I would bet right now that matter, like logic, is destined to remain forever in part within, and in part without, the reach of any closed form."

In an admirable essay on "The Art of Teaching Science," Lewis Thomas proposes that the best way to interest young people in science is to teach not only what is known, but also what is unknown. There should be "courses dealing systematically with ignorance," with "informed bewilderment." To see science as a great adventure, young minds should be told that "every important scientific advance that has come in looking like an answer has turned, sooner or later—usually sooner—into a question. And the game is just beginning."

> On any Tuesday morning, if asked, a good working scientist will tell you with some self-satisfaction that the affairs of his field are nicely in order, that things are finally looking clear and making sense, and all is well. But come back again on another Tuesday, and the roof may have just fallen in on his life's work. All the old ideas—last week's ideas in some cases—are no longer good ideas. The hard facts have softened, melted away and vanished under the pressure of new hard facts. Something strange has happened. And it is this very strangeness of nature that makes science engrossing, that keeps bright people at it, and that ought to be at the center of science teaching.

Suppose for argument's sake that someday physics will indeed reach the closed form of an axiomatic system. There will still be severe limitations on what science can tell us. For one thing, we could never be absolutely sure that the axioms are permanent. We do not know if they were the same in the far distant past, especially before the big bang, if indeed there was a "before." We do not know if they will be the same in the far future, or if they hold in parallel universes, if there are parallel universes. It may be, as John Wheeler and other physicists have suggested, that many of our basic laws are the result of pure chance events that occurred during the first few seconds of the primeval explosion; that if those events had been slightly different, as they might well have been, some of the fundamental constants of nature would have been different.

For another thing, in a formal system such as Euclidean geometry there is an infinity of theorems to discover, even though they are, in a sense, given by the system's finite axioms and rules. If physics is ever formalized, an infinity of laws could follow, many of which—perhaps an infinity of which—will be beyond the reach of the human species, even though in principle they may be discoverable on the unlikely assumption that the human race has an endless future. The decimal expansion of pi, to give a simple analog, follows inexorably from the axioms of number theory, but no one will ever calculate pi to the last decimal digit because pi *has* no last digit.

Since the discoveries of Kurt Gödel, the situation has become even more hopeless. If physics turns out to be a formal system, or at least describable by one, there will be undecidable laws that can be expressed in the system's language but established only by adopting a new system with new axioms. Physicists may find themselves burdened with an infinite hierarchy of formal systems similar to the infinite hierarchy of such systems in logic and mathematics.

It is hard for me to imagine how any mathematician could be distressed by Gödel's incompleteness theorem. In his marvelous book, *Infinity and the Mind*, Rudy Rucker speaks of how an understanding of Gödel's theorem can hit one like a religious conversion, bringing with it a great feeling of liberation from anxiety. Rucker describes Gödel's laughter as frequent, rhythmic, and hypnotic. I sometimes fancy that God invaded Gödel's mind (note the "God" in his name) for the purpose of letting us mortals in on one of Heaven's transcendent jokes; that even in elementary number theory there are truths we will never know with certainty to be true.

A still deeper limitation of science is built into the nature of all formal systems. At any stage of the game one may ask: Why this particular system? Obviously there is no way to answer if the question is asked about the ultimate system. The only way science can explain a law is to subsume it under a more general law. Suppose that physicists eventually discover one monstrous equation that describes how space-time gets itself tied into all those fantastic little knots called particles. We could then ask: Why *that* equation? Clearly physics, regardless of how close it gets to bedrock axioms, has to accept the ultimate structure of the universe as something given. It is the nature of the scientific enterprise that it cannot in principle ever answer the superultimate question of why there is something rather than nothing, or even the lesser question of why the something that is our universe has the basic structure it has. The statement that science can in principle discover everything is defensible only when reduced to the trivial tautology that science can discover everything science is capable of discovering.

Anyone who has read this far surely realizes that I believe there are truths totally beyond the reach of science and reason, even assuming an infinite time for the human mind to evolve. I do not mean anything so trivial as whether the cosmos will stop expanding, or whether there are black holes, or if gravity and electromagnetism can be unified, or if there are intelligent creatures on other planets, or whether the Riemann hypothesis and Goldbach's conjecture are true. I mean questions that are in principle beyond the capacity of any mind (other than God's) to formulate; truths that lie beyond the farthest rim science is capable of reaching.

Georg Cantor was criticized by some of his unworthy opponents for implying that God did not exist, because in Cantor's transfinite set theory, one can prove there is no highest transfinite number. Cantor not only did not imply this, he did not even believe it. He was a deeply religious man who placed God in a region that transcends all finite and infinite sets. It is because I, too, believe in this "wholly other" realm, a realm in which our universe is an infinitesimal island, that I can call myself a mystic in the Platonic sense.

I am, of course, not arguing a case but only expressing an emotion. It has no agreed-upon name. There is no way you can talk someone into feeling it, any more than you can talk someone into falling in love or liking a piece of music or a type of cheese. Rudolf Otto, the German Protestant theologian, coined the word *numinous* (from the Latin *numen*, meaning divine power) to express this emotion. (The word should not be confused with Immanuel Kant's *noumena*, which refers to the unknowable realities behind the *phenomena* of our experience.) For Otto, the essence of the emotion is an awareness of what he called the *mysterium tremendum*, the tremendous mystery of the wholly other. Otto did not invent the phrase "wholly other." It is a translation of what Saint Augustine called the *aliud valde*. Two thousand years earlier, the Hindus called it the *anyad eva*, applying it to Brahman, their ultimate God.

For Otto, the sense of the numinous is compounded of feelings expressed by such words as awe, terror, dread, mystery, fascination, astonishment, wonder. If one is a theist, the emotion combines with strong feelings of humility, of the littleness of one's self, of holiness, of gratitude for the privilege of existing. I believe that the degree to which a person feels such emotions is roughly proportional to the strength of that person's faith in God. I know of no great theologians, in or out of any organized religion, who did not have a profound sense of the numinous. It is the secret of the book of Job. It is the emotion that engenders and sustains all the religious faiths of history.

Pantheists vary widely in the degree to which they are moved by the numinous. The emotion is understandably weak among those for whom all existence is no more than a dreary repetition of the fields we know. It is strong among pantheists who see the universe as a shadow of some vaster realm, as a world of illusion, the maya of the Hindus. It is strong in Taoism, for the Tao is as far beyond our comprehension as Brahman. It is strong in Spinoza, who, although he had no personal God to whom he could pray, thought of Being as having an infinite number of attributes that transcend human comprehension. The emotion was strong in Albert Einstein, who considered himself a Spinozist.

"The most beautiful experience we can have is the mysterious," Einstein wrote in a passage that is often quoted.

It is the fundamental emotion which stands at the cradle of true art and true science. Whoever does not know it and can no longer wonder, no longer marvel, is as good as dead, and his eyes are dimmed. It was the experience of mystery—even if mixed with fear—that engendered religion. A knowledge of the existence of something we cannot penetrate, our perceptions of the profoundest reason and the most radiant beauty, which only in their most primitive forms are accessible to our minds—it is this knowledge and this emotion that constitute true religiosity; in this sense, and in this alone. I am a deeply religious man.

The last sentence could almost have been lifted out of Otto's best known work, *The Idea of the Holy.*

We all know the statement by Sir Isaac Newton, about how he thought of himself as a boy playing on the seashore and diverting himself by now and then finding "a smoother pebble or a prettier shell than ordinary, whilst the great ocean of truth lay all undiscovered before me." Using a less familiar metaphor, Einstein once said to an interviewer:

> We are in the position of a little child, entering a huge library whose walls are covered to the ceiling with books in many different tongues. The child knows that someone must have written those books. It does not know who or how. It does not understand the languages in which they are written. The child notes a definite plan in the arrangement of the books, a mysterious order, which it does not comprehend, but only dimly suspects. That, it seems to me, is the attitude of the human mind, even the greatest and most cultured, toward God.

"Madam," said Dr. Lao, "the role of skeptic becomes you not; there are things in the world not even the experience of a whole life spent in Abalone, Arizona, could conceive of." "Human knowledge," Jean-Henri Fabre somewhere wrote, "will be erased from the world's archives before we possess the last word that a gnat has to say to us." Substitute *stone* for *gnat* and I think the statement is still true. Jorge Luis Borges recalls an old Buddhist text that says: "If there were as many Ganges Rivers as there are grains of sand in the Ganges and again as many Ganges Rivers as grains of sand in those new Ganges Rivers, the number of grains of sand would be smaller than the number of things *not known* by the Buddha."

One of Hamlet's familiar remarks is that "there are more things in heaven and earth, Horatio, than are dreamt of in your philosophy." It is quoted less often these days than a similar remark by J.B.S. Haldane in his 1928 book *Possible Worlds.* "Now, my own suspicion is that the universe is not only queerer than we suppose, but queerer than we *can* suppose." Change *we* to *you* and Haldane's statement is a good summary of what God shouts to Job out of the whirlwind.

Herbert Spencer, more than any other British philosopher who called himself an agnostic or atheist, stressed the mystery of the wholly other. Spencer called it the Unknowable—not the Unknown. It contains all the transcendent truths of Kant's noumena as well as the infinity of other truths totally beyond our grasp. Theodore Dreiser was so taken by the concept of the Unknowable that he closes his novel *The Genius* by reproducing a long passage in which Spencer writes about the mystery of space and the Sartrean "nausea" it arouses in him:

> Beyond the reach of our intelligence as are the mysteries of the objects known by our senses, those presented in this universal matrix are, if we may say so, still further beyond the reach of our intelligence, for whereas, those of the one kind may be, and are, thought of by many as explicable on the hypothesis of creation, and by the rest on the hypothesis of evolution, those of the other kind cannot by either be regarded as thus explicable. Theist and Agnostic must agree in recognizing the properties of Space as inherent, eternal, uncreated—as anteceding all creation, if creation has taken place. Hence, could we penetrate the mysteries of existence, there would still remain more transcendent mysteries. That which can be thought of as neither made nor evolved presents us with facts the origin of which is even more remote from conceivability than is the origin of the facts presented by visible and tangible things. . . . The thought of this blank form of existence which, explored in all directions as far as eye can reach, has, beyond that, an unexplored region compared with which the part imagination has traversed is but infinitesimal—the thought of a space, compared with which our immeasurable sidereal system dwindles to a point, is a thought too overwhelming to be dwelt upon. Of late years the consciousness that without origin or cause, infinite space has ever existed and must ever exist produces in me a feeling from which I shrink.

Here is atheist Bertrand Russell in one of his rare numinous moods: "I want to stand at the rim of the world and peer into the darkness beyond, and see a little more than others have seen of the strange shapes of mystery that inhabit that unknown night. . . ." That was from a letter Russell wrote when he was in prison during the First World War. Later, in *Some Problems of Philosophy* (1927), he wrote: "But if there be a world which is not physical, or not in space-time, it may have a structure which we can never hope to express or to know." Russell hastens to add that he has now "lapsed into mystical speculation," and will say no more because by the very nature of the case there is nothing more he can *say*.

George Santayana, another honest atheist, admired Spencer's concept of the Unknowable, and occasionally allowed himself to report on this region. "A really naked spirit," he wrote in *Obiter Scripta* (1936), "cannot assume that the world is thoroughly intelligible. There may be surds, there may be hard facts, there may be dark abysses before which intelligence must be silent for fear of going mad." Do you not sense, behind that casual remark, Santayana's awareness of the *mysterium tremendum*?

H. G. Wells, another atheist (aside from his momentary flirtation with a finite God), also had occasional glimpses of the tremendous mystery. His most numinous writing is a section on "Ultimate Truth" in *The Work, Wealth and Happiness of Mankind* (1931):

> It may be that we exist and cease to exist in alternations, like the minute dots in some forms of toned printing or the succession of pictures on a cinema film. It may be that consciousness is an illusion of movement in an eternal, static, multidimensional universe. We may be only a story written on a ground of inconceivable realities, the pattern of a carpet beneath the feet of the incomprehensible. We may be, as Sir James Jeans seems to suggest, part of a vast idea in the meditation of a divine circumambient mathematician. It is wonderful exercise for the mind to peer at such possibilities. It brings us to the realization of the entirely limited nature of our intelligence, such as it is, and of existence as we know it. It leads plainly towards the belief that with minds such as ours the ultimate truth of things is forever inconceivable and unknowable. . . .
>
> It is impossible to dismiss mystery from life. Being is altogether mysterious. Mystery is all about us and in us, the Inconceivable permeates us, it is "closer than breathing and nearer than hands and feet." For all we know, that which we are may rise at death from living, as an intent player wakes up from his absorption when a game comes to an end, or as a spectator turns his eyes from the stage as the curtain falls, to look at the auditorium he has for a time forgotten. These are pretty metaphors, that have nothing to do with the game or the drama of space and time. Ultimately the mystery may be the only thing that matters, but *within the rules and limits of the game of life*, when you are catching trains or paying bills or earning a living, the mystery does not matter at all.

Commenting on these pages in his 1934 autobiography, Wells summarizes:

> I realize that Being is surrounded east, south, north and west, above and below, by wonder. Within that frame, like a little house in strange, cold, vast and beautiful scenery, is life upon this planet, of which life I am a temporary speck and impression. There is interest beyond measure within that house; use for my utmost. Nevertheless at times one finds an urgency to go out and gaze at those enigmatical immensities. But for such a thing as I am, there is nothing conceivable to be done out there. Ultimately those remote metaphysical appearances may mean everything, but so far as my present will and activities go they mean nothing.

Nothing? Observe how quickly Wells, like Russell, dismisses the *mysterium tremendum* as unworthy of worship or prolonged contemplation.

Among more recent philosophers John Dewey seems to me the outstanding example of an atheist for whom a sense of the numinous was minimal. I have been unable to find a single passage in all of Dewey's writings that strikes me as a memorable expression of wonder about the mystery of being. Nothing seems ever to have mystified Dewey. Never, so far as I can recall, did he see anything tragic or comic or absurd about the human condition. We are all organisms interacting with our environment, and that's that. I suggest it is this almost total absence of a sense of mystery in Dewey, and a sense of the comic, that makes his writing so incredibly dull. Who can read him anymore?

I find in my files a reference to a letter in *The New Leader* in which someone complains of Dewey's lack of a sense of wonder. I have saved only the published reply, a letter from Corliss Lamont. On the contrary, says Lamont, Dewey had a "keen awareness of the awesome and grand totality of the cosmos." To prove it, Lamont quotes the following passage from Dewey's *A Common Faith* (1934):

> The community of causes and consequences in which we, together with those not born, are enmeshed is the widest and deepest symbol of the mysterious totality of being the imagination calls the universe. It is the embodiment for sense and thought of that encompassing scope of existence the intellect cannot grasp. It is the matrix within which our ideal aspirations are born and bred. It is the source of the values that the moral imagination projects as directive criteria and as shaping purposes.

I rest my case. If this is the most numinous statement Lamont can find in Dewey's books (and I have not found a better one), it testifies to Dewey's remarkable uninterest in the wholly other. Indeed, as Lamont recognizes, the purpose of *A Common Faith* was to redefine *religion* and *faith* so that all feeling for the supernatural would be eliminated. In this respect Dewey is a type of the practical down-to-earth person who finds metaphysical speculation a waste of time. I do not mean someone who recognizes there are no rational or empirical ways to solve metaphysical puzzles, but one who seems never to be troubled by the puzzles. Greatly as I admire Rudolf Carnap for his contributions to the philosophy of science, I find him akin to Dewey in this respect. Both men recognized the mystery that envelops all scientific knowledge, yes, but emotionally they were low in metaphysical awe. In Richard Burgin's *Conversations with Jorge Luis Borges* (1969), Borges recalls a highly intelligent woman he once knew who was incapable of getting anything out of the books by Bishop Berkeley and William James that he gave her:

> She didn't see why people should be poring over things that seemed very simple to her. So I said, "Yes, but are you sure that time is simple, are you sure that space is simple, are you sure that consciousness is simple?" "Yes," she said. "Well, but could you define them?" She said, "No, I don't think I could, but I don't feel puzzled by them."

Unlike most atheists and agnostics, Borges is perpetually astonished by the world, even though he is not sure there is a God, even though he professes no desire to live again. The majority of men and women, and especially women, he told Burgin (I do not go along with Borges in distinguishing between the sexes here), take the universe for granted:

> They never wonder at anything, no? They don't think it's strange that they should be living. I remember the first time I felt that was when my father said to me, "What a queer thing," he said, "that I should be living, as they say, behind my eyes, inside my head, I wonder if that makes sense?" And then, it was the first time I felt that, and then instantly I pounced upon that because I knew what he was saying. But many people can hardly understand that. And they say, "Well, but where else could you live?"

No modern writer lived with a more pervasive sense of ontological wonder, of surprise to find himself alive, than Gilbert Chesterton. Surely it is one reason why Borges was so fond of GK's poetry and fiction. In his autobiography Chesterton accurately calls it "the chief idea of my life" and defines it as not taking the world for granted, but taking it with humility and gratitude. It is to see everything, even the most common thing, as something both unexpected and undeserved. "The only way to enjoy a weed is to feel unworthy even of a weed." All the evils of the world are a small price to pay for the privilege of existing.

One could assemble a large volume of excerpts from GK's books in which he plays beautiful and amusing variations on this theme of enjoying the world the way a happy child enjoys it, as something miraculous. It would include Chesterton's preface to an edition of Job. It would include that refreshing rhapsody to order in the opening chapter of *The Man Who Was Thursday*. An anarchist poet maintains that order is dull, that disorder is the soul of poetry. Why do the riders on the London subway look so sad and tired? "It is because they know that the train is going right. . . . It is because after they have passed Sloane Square they know that the next station must be Victoria, and nothing but Victoria. Oh, their wild rapture! oh, their eyes like stars and their souls again in Eden, if the next station were unaccountably Baker Street!"

Nonsense, replies Gabriel Syme. "The rare, strange thing is to hit the mark; the gross, obvious thing is to miss it. We feel it is epical when man with one wild arrow strikes a distant bird. Is it not also epical when man with one wild engine strikes a distant station? Chaos is dull; because in chaos the train might indeed go anywhere, to Baker Street or to Bagdad. But man is a magician, and his whole magic is in this, that he does say Victoria, and lo! it is Victoria."

My anthology would include many of Chesterton's short stories, such as

"The Unthinkable Theory of Professor Green" in which an astronomer, stricken suddenly by a sense of awe toward ordinary things, delivers a solemn lecture on his discovery of a new planet. As he talks on, it slowly dawns on his learned listeners that he is talking about the earth.

My anthology would include at least two of GK's poems. One of them, "The Sword of Surprise," is short enough to quote in full:

> Sunder me from my bones, O sword of God,
> Till they stand stark and strange as do the trees;
> That I whose heart goes up with the soaring woods
> May marvel as much at these.
>
> Sunder me from my blood that in the dark
> I hear that red ancestral river run,
> Like branching buried floods that find the sea
> But never see the sun.
>
> Give me miraculous eyes to see my eyes,
> Those rolling mirrors made alive in me,
> Terrible crystal more incredible
> Than all the things they see.
>
> Sunder me from my soul, that I may see
> The sins like streaming wounds, the life's brave beat;
> Till I shall save myself, as I would save
> A stranger in the street.

The other poem, "A Second Childhood," is so much longer that I shall quote only the first two stanzas. If you don't know this poem, I urge you to look it up in *The Collected Poems of G. K. Chesterton*. I think it is one of the greatest religious lyrics ever written:

> When all my days are ending
> And I have no song to sing,
> I think I shall not be too old
> To stare at everything;
> As I stared once at a nursery door
> Or a tall tree and a swing.
>
> Wherein God's ponderous mercy hangs
> On all my sins and me,
> Because He does not take away
> The terror from the tree
> And stones still shine along the road
> That are and cannot be.

My book of Chestertonian wonder would include many essays and passages in which GK praised the glory and mystery of ordinary things—*Tremendous Trifles*, as he calls them in the title of one of his best books. And there are those passages in which he combines awe with a sense of absurdity, seeing the pelican as one of God's jokes, seeing men and women as four-footed animals balancing precariously on their hind legs. I find in my GK files a clipping (dated 1945) of the comic strip "Blondie." Dagwood has made one of his giant sandwiches, and while eating it he startles Blondie by reflecting aloud: "Eating is a silly thing. In order to get food into your stomach you've got to push it through your face." The sentiment is pure Chesterton. In *The Napoleon of Notting Hill*, GK describes eating as the stuffing of alien substances through a hole in the head, and somewhere else he sees drinking as pouring liquid through an opening the way one fills a bottle. If he hadn't thought it bad taste he could have written hilarious descriptions of the sex act. A great admirer of Edward Lear and Lewis Carroll, GK often called attention to the role of nonsense in arousing an emotion of spiritual wonder toward the world.

My anthology would be incomplete without the chapter on "The Ethics of Elfland" from *Orthodoxy*. In the spirit of Hume, though Hume is never mentioned, Chesterton argues that all natural laws should be looked upon as magic because there is no logical connection between any cause and its effect. Fairy tales, said GK, remind us that the laws of nature have an arbitrary quality in that they could, for all we know, be quite other than what they are. Maybe the regularities of nature, its weird repetitions, as Chesterton called them, are not logically necessary but exist because God, like a small child, is

> strong enough to exult in monotony. It is possible that God says every morning "Do it again" to the sun; and every evening, "Do it again" to the moon. It may not be automatic necessity that makes all daisies alike; it may be that God makes every daisy separately, but has never got tired of making them. It may be that He has the eternal appetite of infancy; for we have sinned and grown old, and our Father is younger than we. The repetition in Nature may not be a mere recurrence; it may be a theatrical *encore*. Heaven may *encore* the bird who laid an egg.

This way of viewing Nature as sheer magic, which of course implies a Magician, is surely part of the fascination of watching a great conjuror. The art of prestidigitation has been one of the loves of my life, and like Chesterton I find it intimately connected with a love of fantasy fiction. Science reminds us of the reason behind things. Magic and fantasy remind us of the unreason behind things. The British poet Ralph Hodgson put it this way:

> *Reason has moons, but moons not hers*
> *Lie mirror'd on her sea,*

Confounding her astronomers,
But, O! delighting me.

Conjuring, wrote Max Beerbohm in his novel about a beautiful lady magician, *Zuleika Dobson,* is "an art which, more potently perhaps than any other, touched in mankind the sense of mystery and stirred the faculty of wonder; the most truly romantic of all the arts. . . ." We enjoy seeing a conjuror perform because his counterfeit miracles make us realize that natural laws could easily permit women to float in the air and elephants to disappear. A spectator with a sense of the numinous leaves the theater with heightened surprise that objects fall when dropped, that stars vanish in the daytime only to reappear mysteriously at night.

You can be sure that Chesterton, like Charles Dickens (who actually performed magic on the stage) and Lewis Carroll, enjoyed seeing magic shows. In fact, GK wrote an unusual play called *Magic,* in which a professional conjuror is the main character. I can easily imagine Wells and Einstein and Santayana sitting entranced through a magic show. It is hard to imagine Dewey or Carnap watching a magician without being bored. Both men, although no doubt they would have agreed that natural laws could be other than they are, saw little value in speculating about such nonsense possibilities. They were like the man from Cadiz in an anonymous limerick:

> *There was a young man of Cadiz*
> *Who inferred that life is what it is,*
> *For he early had learnt,*
> *If it were what it weren't,*
> *It could not be that which it is.*

To the atheist and positivist the world is what it is. How could it be otherwise? Where else could we live? There is no point in speculating on why it is what it is, because there is no way reason or science can get a handle on the question. Accept the only universe we know. Find out what you can about its structure. Try to be as happy as possible before you vanish back into the Black Hat from which you popped into existence.

Just as knowing how a magic trick is done spoils all its wonder, so let us be grateful that wherever science and reason turn they plunge finally into stygian darkness. I am not in the least annoyed because I do not understand time and space, or consciousness, or free will, or evil, or why the universe is made the way it is. I am relieved beyond measure that I do not need to comprehend more than dimly the nature of God or an afterlife. I do not want to be blinded by truths beyond the capacity of my eyes and brain and heart. I am as contented as a Carnap with the absence of rational methods for penetrating ultimate mysteries.

Must we conclude, then, that all metaphysical speculation is futile? A metaphysician asks this question in one of Raymond Smullyan's wry dialogs, in his book *The Tao Is Silent* (1977). A mystic answers as follows:

> Oh, not at all! It is sometimes absolutely necessary to bat one's head against a stone wall trying to use objective methods which cannot possibly work before one sees for oneself the necessity of direct introspective methods. Metaphysics is essentially one giant koan, not for an individual, but for the human race as a whole—a koan whose purpose is to force the realization of the impossibility of metaphysical methods being pushed any further. Stated otherwise, metaphysics is the necessary ripening process of the human race to prepare it for mysticism.

I agree with Smullyan—for the mystic's voice is his. There *are* no metaphysical methods. There is no rational way to approach God—or, as Smullyan would prefer to say, the Tao—except inwardly. As for the heart's leap that leads to theism, I confess again that I do not know why some people are compelled to make it and others find it impossible. I do not even know if a sense of the numinous is essential for such a leap.

In the second Oz book, when Tip brings a wooden sawhorse to life with Mombi's magic powder, the creature is more surprised than Tip. "He rolled his knotty eyes from side to side, taking a first wondering view of the world in which he had now so important an existence." Have none of the quotations in this chapter aroused in you, patient reader, a similar sense of surprise and wonder? Have you never felt amazed to find yourself not only living in an Ozzy world but, more incredibly, aware of the fact that you are alive? Are you capable of identifying with the Sawhorse when he says, in the third Oz book, "A creature like me has no business to live"?

If you are looking puzzled and shaking your head, that small cavelike region in which you are so mysteriously hiding for a time—and for so brief a time!—then *The Night Is Large* is not for you. After all, where else could you hide?

INDEX

Page numbers in *italics* refer to figures.

Index